Frommer's®

AUSTRALIA

20th Edition

By Lee Mylne

FrommerMedia LLC

Published by:
Frommer Media LLC

Frommer's Complete Guide to Australia 2020, 20th Edition
ISBN 978-1-62887-452-5 (paper), 978-1-62887-453-2 (e-book)

Editorial Director: Pauline Frommer
Editor: Alexis Lipsitz Flippin
Production Editor: Lindsay Conner
Cartographer: Roberta Stockwell
Photo Editor: Meghan Lamb
Assistant Photo Editor: Phil Vinke

For information on our other products or services, see www.frommers.com.

Frommer Media LLC also publishes its books in a variety of electronic formats. Some content that appears in print may not be available in electronic formats.

Manufactured in China

5 4 3 2 1

HOW TO CONTACT US

In researching this book, we discovered many wonderful places—hotels, restaurants, shops, and more. We're sure you'll find others. Please tell us about them, so we can share the information with your fellow travelers in upcoming editions. If you were disappointed with a recommendation, we'd love to know that, too. Please write to: Support@FrommerMedia.com.

FROMMER'S STAR RATINGS SYSTEM

Every hotel, restaurant and attraction listed in this guide has been ranked for quality and value. Here's what the stars mean:

★ Recommended
★★ Highly Recommended
★★★ A must! Don't miss!

AN IMPORTANT NOTE

The world is a dynamic place. Hotels change ownership, restaurants hike their prices, museums alter their opening hours, and buses and trains change their routings. And all of this can occur in the several months after our authors have visited, inspected, and written about these hotels, restaurants, museums, and transportation services. Though we have made valiant efforts to keep all our information fresh and up-to-date, some few changes can inevitably occur in the periods before a revised edition of this guidebook is published. So please bear with us if a tiny number of the details in this book have changed. Please also note that we have no responsibility or liability for any inaccuracy or errors or omissions, or for inconvenience, loss, damage, or expenses suffered by anyone as a result of assertions in this guide.

CONTENTS

LIST OF MAPS

ABOUT THE AUTHOR

Lee Mylne is an award-winning travel journalist who has visited nearly every corner of Australia and is still enthralled by what she sees. She has written several *Frommer's* guidebooks and her work appears regularly in a wide range of Australian consumer and travel trade publications. She is a former president and *Life Member of the Australian Society of Travel Writers*. Lee lives in Brisbane, Australia.

ABOUT THE FROMMER TRAVEL GUIDES

For most of the past 50 years, Frommer's has been the leading series of travel guides in North America, accounting for as many as 24% of all guidebooks sold. I think I know why.

Though we hope our books are entertaining, we nevertheless deal with travel in a serious fashion. Our guidebooks have never looked on such journeys as a mere recreation, but as a far more important human function, a time of learning and introspec- tion, an essential part of a civilized life. We stress the culture, lifestyle, history, and beliefs of the destinations we cover, and urge our readers to seek out people and new ideas as the chief rewards of travel.

We have never shied from controversy. We have, from the beginning, encouraged our authors to be intensely judgmental, critical—both pro and con—in their comments, and wholly indepen- dent. Our only clients are our readers, and we have triggered the ire of countless prominent sorts, from a tourist newspaper we called "practically worthless" (it unsuccessfully sued us) to the many rip-offs we've condemned.

And because we believe that travel should be available to everyone regardless of their incomes, we have always been cost-conscious at every level of expenditure. Though we have broadened our recommendations beyond the budget category, we insist that every lodging we include be sensibly priced. We use every form of media to assist our readers, and are particularly proud of our feisty daily website, the award-winning Frommers.com.

I have high hopes for the future of Frommer's. May these guidebooks, in all the years ahead, continue to reflect the joy of travel and the freedom that travel represents. May they always pursue a cost-conscious path, so that people of all incomes can enjoy the rewards of travel. And may they create, for both the traveler and the persons among whom we travel, a community of friends, where all human beings live in harmony and peace.

Arthur Frommer

WHAT'S GREAT ABOUT AUSTRALIA

Australia is like nowhere else you've been. It has truly unique wildlife, some of the world's best natural scenery, the most brilliant scuba diving and snorkeling, the best beaches, the oldest rainforest (110 million years and counting), the oldest human civilization (some archaeologists say 40,000 years, others 120,000), the best wines, the best weather, and the most innovative East-meets-West-meets-someplace-else cuisine—all bathed in sunlight that brings everything up in living Technicolor. Prepare yourself for a lifetime of memories.

Scarcely a visitor lands on these shores without having the **Great Barrier Reef** at the top of their to-do list. And so they should. While parts of the reef are in dire straits from coral bleaching caused by rising water temperatures, those that aren't affected show what a glorious natural masterpiece it is—don't wait until it's too late to see it! Also high on most lists is **Uluru,** a sacred monolith that (rightly) attracts hundreds of thousands of tourists (including celebrities and royalty, such as Britain's Prince William and his wife, Catherine, the Duchess of Cambridge). And it's not just "The Rock" you should see; the vast Australian desert all around it is equally unmissable.

The third attraction on most visitors' lists? **Sydney,** Australia's glittering harborside city.

Of course, there is much more to Australia than just its highlights. For those who have more time, the Australian Capital Territory, South Australia, Western Australia, vast tracts of inland Queensland, and many Outback areas have much to offer, too. But I know you can't do everything or go everywhere, so in this book, I'll introduce you to those three iconic attractions and the places that are their gateways—Brisbane, Cairns, the Reef-adjacent coastal cities of Queensland, and Darwin and Alice Springs in the Northern Territory. I'll also cover Australia's other state and territory capital cities: Melbourne, Adelaide, Perth, Hobart, and the

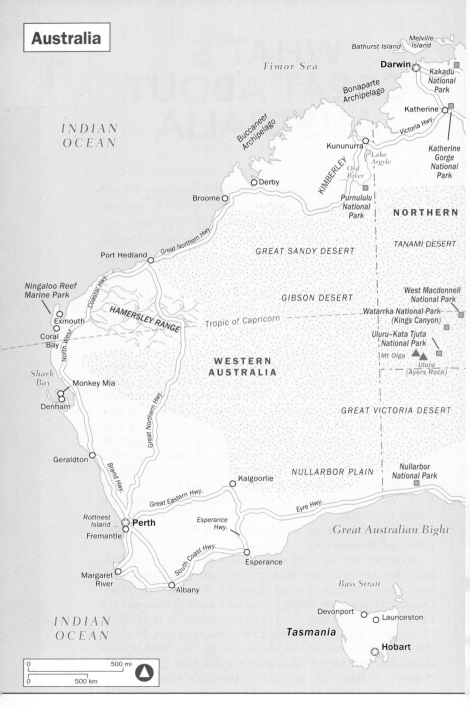

Australia

Timor Sea

Melville Island

Bathurst Island

Darwin

Kakadu National Park

INDIAN OCEAN

Bonaparte Archipelago

Katherine

Victoria Hwy.

Buccaneer Archipelago

Kununurra

Lake Argyle

Ord River

KIMBERLEY

Katherine Gorge National Park

○ Derby

Broome ○

Purnululu National Park

NORTHERN

Great Northern Hwy.

GREAT SANDY DESERT

TANAMI DESERT

Port Hedland ○

Coastal Hwy.

Ningaloo Reef Marine Park

GIBSON DESERT

West Macdonnell National Park

HAMERSLEY RANGE

Watarrka National Park (Kings Canyon)

○ Exmouth

North West

Tropic of Capricorn

Uluru-Kata Tjuta National Park

Coral Bay

Mt Olga ▲▲

Uluru (Ayers Rock)

Shark Bay

WESTERN AUSTRALIA

Monkey Mia ○

Denham

Great Northern Hwy.

GREAT VICTORIA DESERT

Geraldton ○

Brand Hwy.

NULLARBOR PLAIN

Nullarbor National Park

Kalgoorlie ○

Rottnest Island

Great Eastern Hwy.

Perth

Esperance Hwy.

Eyre Hwy.

Great Australian Bight

Fremantle

South Coast Hwy.

Esperance ○

Margaret River

Bass Strait

Albany ○

Devonport ○

○ Launceston

INDIAN OCEAN

Tasmania

Hobart

0 ———— 500 mi

0 ———— 500 km

2

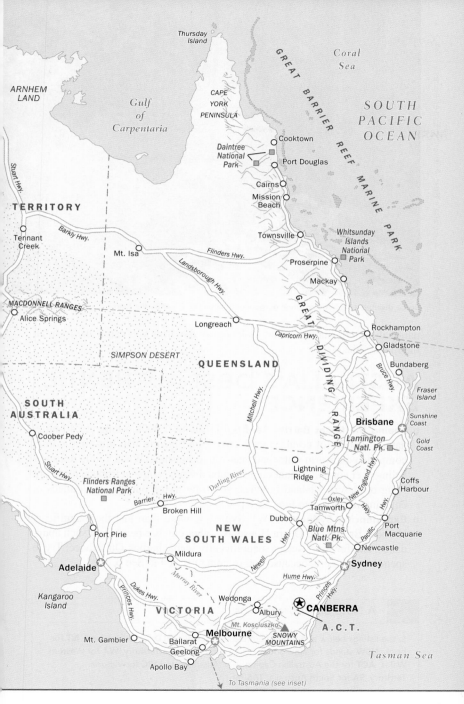

Thursday Island

Coral Sea

GREAT BARRIER REEF MARINE PARK

ARNHEM LAND

Gulf of Carpentaria

CAPE YORK PENINSULA

SOUTH PACIFIC OCEAN

Cooktown

Daintree National Park

Port Douglas

Cairns

Mission Beach

Stuart Hwy.

TERRITORY

Barkly Hwy.

Tennant Creek

Mt. Isa

Flinders Hwy.

Townsville

Whitsunday Islands National Park

Landsborough Hwy.

Proserpine

Mackay

MACDONNELL RANGES

Alice Springs

Longreach

Capricorn Hwy.

GREAT DIVIDING RANGE

Rockhampton

Gladstone

SIMPSON DESERT

QUEENSLAND

Bundaberg

Bruce Hwy.

Fraser Island

SOUTH AUSTRALIA

Mitchell Hwy.

Brisbane

Lamington Natl. Pk.

Sunshine Coast

Gold Coast

Coober Pedy

Stuart Hwy.

Flinders Ranges National Park

Darling River

Lightning Ridge

New England Hwy.

Coffs Harbour

Barrier Hwy.

Broken Hill

Dubbo

Oxley Hwy.

Tamworth

Port Macquarie

Port Pirie

NEW SOUTH WALES

Blue Mtns. Natl. Pk.

Pacific Hwy.

Newcastle

Adelaide

Mildura

Murray River

Sydney

Kangaroo Island

Dukes Hwy.

Princes Hwy.

VICTORIA

Wodonga

Newell Hwy.

Hume Hwy.

CANBERRA

A.C.T.

Mt. Gambier

Ballarat

Geelong

Albury

Mt. Kosciuszko

SNOWY MOUNTAINS

Princes Hwy.

Melbourne

Apollo Bay

Tasman Sea

To Tasmania (see inset)

Scuba diver viewing large common gorgonian coral on the Great Barrier Reef.

national capital, Canberra, and look at easy day trips you can make from all the major cities.

AUSTRALIA'S best AUTHENTIC EXPERIENCES

o **Seeing the Great Barrier Reef** (QLD): It's a 2,000km-long (1,240-mile) natural wonder of coral, vibrant colors, and bizarre fish life—and comes complete with warm water and year-round sunshine. When you're not snorkeling over coral and giant clams, scuba diving, calling at tropical towns, or lying on deserted island beaches, you'll be trying out the sun lounges or enjoying the first-rate food. See p. 217.

o **Experiencing Sydney** (NSW): Sydney is more than just the magnificent Harbour Bridge and Opera House. No other city has beaches in such abundance, and few have such a magnificently scenic harbor. Our advice: Try to spend a week here, because you're going to need it. See p. 55.

A Note on Abbreviations

In the listings below and throughout the book, **NSW** stands for New South Wales, **ACT** for the Australian Capital Territory, **SA** for South Australia, **TAS** for Tasmania, **QLD** for Queensland, **NT** for the Northern Territory, **WA** for Western Australia, and **VIC** for Victoria.

- **Exploring the Wet Tropics Rainforest** (QLD): Folks who come from sky-scraper cities such as New York City and London can't get over the moisture-dripping ferns, the neon-blue butterflies, and the primeval peace of this World Heritage rainforest stretching north, south, and west from Cairns. Hike it, four-wheel-drive it, or glide over the treetops in a Skyrail Rainforest Cableway gondola. See p. 224.
- **Bareboat Sailing** (QLD): "Bareboat" means unskippered—that's right, even if you think port is an after-dinner drink, you can charter a yacht, pay for a day's instruction from a skipper, and then take the helm yourself and explore the 74 island gems of the Whitsundays. It's easy. Anchor in deserted bays, snorkel over dazzling reefs, fish for coral trout, and feel the wind in your sails. See p. 267.
- **Exploring Kata Tjuta (the Olgas) & Uluru** (NT): This sacred, mysterious, and utterly unforgettable landscape may well be the highlight of your time in Australia. Uluru and Kata Tjuta demand at least 3 days to see everything there is to offer. See p. 321.
- **Taking an Aboriginal Culture Tour:** Seeing the landscape through the eyes of Australia's indigenous people, hearing the creation stories of their ancestors, and learning more about Aboriginal culture will give you a different perspective on Australia, no matter which part of it you are in. See p. 295.

The Skyrail Rainforest Cableway near Cairns glides above the canopy of the Wet Tropics Rainforest.

THE best OF THE OUTDOORS

- **Blue Mountains** (NSW): Many bushwalks in the Blue Mountains National Park offer awesome views of valleys, waterfalls, cliffs, and forest. All are easy to reach from Sydney. See p. 109.

- **Four Mile Beach** (QLD): The sea is turquoise, the sun is warm, the palms sway—and even the low-rise hotels lining this country beach in Port Douglas can't spoil the feeling that you're a million miles from anywhere. But isn't there always a serpent in paradise? In this case, the "serpents" are north Queensland's seasonal and potentially deadly marine stingers. Come from June through September to avoid them; confine your swimming to the stinger-net enclosures the rest of the year. See p. 247.

- **Larapinta Trail** (NT): Starting from Alice Springs in the Red Centre, this 250km (155-mile) semi-desert trail winds through the stark crimson McDonnell Ranges. You don't have to walk the entire length—plenty of day-length and multi-day sections are possible. This one's for the cooler months only (Apr–Oct). See p. 317.

- **The MacDonnell Ranges** (NT): Aboriginal people say these red-rock hills were formed by the "Caterpillar Dreaming" that wriggled from the earth here. To the east and west of Alice Springs are dramatic gorges, idyllic (and icy cold) water holes, cute wallabies, and ancient Aboriginal rock carvings. See p. 306.

The entire continent of Australia is ringed with legendary surfing spots. FACING PAGE: Enjoying the views of Blue Mountain National Park.

Whitehaven Beach, on uninhabited Whitsunday Island.

o **Surfing:** No visit to Oz could really be considered complete without checking out one of the iconic Aussie activities: surfing. It's not just the rush of the waves that pulls people in, it's the ethos and everything that goes with surfing. Every state has its special spots where the surf can be especially challenging—and in Sydney, those spots are right in the suburbs (see p. 103)!

o **Uluru–Kata Tjuta National Park** (NT): Don't go home until you've felt the powerful heartbeat of the desert. Uluru will enthrall you with its eerie beauty. Nearby Kata Tjuta is equally interesting, so make the time to wander through the Valley of the Winds. Hike or cycle around Uluru's base, burn around it on a Harley-Davidson, or saunter up to it on a camel. See p. 321.

o **Whitehaven Beach** (QLD): It's not a surf beach, but this 6km (3¾-mile) stretch of white silica sand on uninhabited Whitsunday Island is pristine and peaceful. Bring a book, curl up under the rainforest lining its edge, and fantasize that the cruise ship is going to leave without you. See p. 268.

AUSTRALIA'S best RESTAURANTS

o **Bennelong** (Sydney, NSW): With an unbeatable location inside the Sydney Opera House, with views of the Sydney Harbour Bridge, this is one of Australia's best restaurants. And it's just perfect for a pre- or post-theater supper. See p. 78.

- **Donovans** (Melbourne, VIC): What better way to end the day than with a glass in hand, watching the sun go down over St Kilda Beach, while you're perched on the veranda at this beachy restaurant in a former 1920s bathing pavilion? See p. 158.
- **e'cco bistro** (Brisbane, QLD): Simple food elegantly prepared and accompanied by an extensive wine list has won this stylish bistro a stack of awards. Booking ahead is essential. See p. 203.
- **Flower Drum** (Melbourne, VIC): Praise pours in for this upscale eatery serving exquisite Cantonese food. Service is impeccable. See p. 155.
- **Hanuman** (Darwin, NT): A fusion of Chinese and Malaysian cuisine amply demonstrates Darwin's connection to Asia, in a stylish setting with excellent service. See p. 288. There's also a branch in Alice Springs (see p. 312).
- **Icebergs Dining Room and Bar** (Sydney, NSW): Come here for exquisite food and one of the best ocean views in the Southern Hemisphere. Not surprisingly, seafood features highly on the menu. It's our top pick for lunch in Sydney. See p. 85.
- **MoVida** (Melbourne, VIC): Like a little corner of Spain, this spot is relaxed and fun, with seriously good food and good wine. Melburnians flock here for the tapas and *raciones*. If it's full, try one of the two sister restaurants, **MoVida Next Door** and **MoVida Aqui.** See p. 156.

St. Kilda Beach, Melbourne.

- **Salsa Bar & Grill** (Port Douglas, QLD): The animated atmosphere and attractive surroundings set the scene for an excellent dining experience. Appetizers and main courses run the gamut from simple fare to sophisticated tropical creations; desserts are fantastic. Book as far ahead as possible. See p. 247.
- **Tetsuya's** (Sydney, NSW): Chef Tetsuya Wakuda is arguably Sydney's most famous chef, and his imaginative nouveau Japanese creations guarantee that this hip eatery is not only a constant number one in Australia, but also ranks among the top restaurants in the world. See p. 79.

AUSTRALIA'S best HOTELS

- **Sir Stamford at Circular Quay** (Sydney, NSW): Plush and luxurious, with a clubby feel that's relaxed rather than stuffy, Sir Stamford is also perfectly located, a short walk from Circular Quay and the Opera House, and just across the road from the Royal Botanic Gardens. See p. 67.
- **Sofitel Sydney Darling Harbour** (Sydney, NSW): Exceptional views of Darling Harbour, spacious rooms, and touches of French style combine to make this one of Sydney's most beautiful hotels, all just a short walk from the city center. See p. 74.

Longitude 131°, a luxury safari camp in the Outback.

- **The Reef House** (Palm Cove, QLD): Airy rooms look onto tropical gardens, waterfalls cascade into pools, mosquito nets drape over the beds, and you could swear pith-helmeted colonial officers will be back any minute to finish their gin-and-tonics in the Brigadier Bar. Idyllic Palm Cove Beach is just across the road. See p. 228.

- **qualia** (Hamilton Island, Whitsundays, QLD): This is one of Australia's most glamorous island resorts, an exclusive adults-only enclave away from the hurly-burly of the main island lodgings. Each private pavilion has its own plunge pool, and there's a decadent day spa. See p. 263.

- **Longitude 131°** (Uluru, Red Centre, NT): The luxury option at the Ayers Rock resort scene, Longitude 131° is an African-style safari camp set in the dunes, with great views of Uluru. It's very exclusive and very expensive, but you'll experience the Outback in style. See p. 326.

- **The Russell** (The Rocks, Sydney, NSW): This B&B, wonderfully positioned in the city's old quarter, is the coziest place to stay in Sydney. It has creaky floorboards, a ramshackle feel, brightly painted corridors, and rooms with immense character. See p. 70.

- **The MONA Pavilions** (Hobart, TAS): Eight luxury state-of-the-art pavilions dedicated to Australia's most famous artists and architects are set on the banks of the Derwent River, as part of the Museum of Old and New Art (MONA) complex. See p. 410.

- **The Louise** (Barossa Valley, SA): Fine attention to details and sweeping views over the neighboring vineyard combine to make these 15 contemporary suites the perfect getaway from Adelaide. See p. 398.

- **The Olsen** (Melbourne, VIC): With a giant mural by one of Australia's greatest living artists, John Olsen, and a stunning suspended swimming pool, this flagship of the Art Series Hotels is worth the splurge. Or try one of its sister hotels in Melbourne: **The Cullen, The Blackman,** or **The Larwill Studio.** See p. 150.

- **Como The Treasury** (Perth, WA): Perth's grand 19th-century State Buildings now house the city's top hotel, offering luxuries large and small, including some of the largest hotel rooms in Australia, Italian crafted furniture, crisp linens, and heated bathroom floors. See p. 341.

THE best PLACES TO VIEW WILDLIFE

- **Lone Pine Koala Sanctuary** (QLD): Cuddle a koala (and have your photo taken doing it) at this park in Brisbane, the world's first and largest koala sanctuary. Apart from some 130 koalas, lots of other Aussie wildlife—including wombats, Tasmanian devils, 'roos (which you can hand-feed), and colorful parakeets—are on show. See p. 207.

o **Hartley's Crocodile Adventures** (QLD): Cruise a beautiful lagoon surrounded by paperbark trees to spot crocodiles in their natural setting, and then watch the daily "croc attack" show. This family-run wildlife park just north of Cairns is home to other animals as well, including snakes, koalas, and cassowaries. See p. 235.

o **Australian Butterfly Sanctuary** (QLD): Walk through the biggest butterfly "aviary" in Australia, in Kuranda, near Cairns, and you'll spot some of the most gorgeous butterflies on the continent, including the electric-blue Ulysses. See many species of butterfly feed, lay eggs, and mate; and inspect caterpillars and pupae. Wearing pink, red, or white encourages the butterflies to land on you. See p. 242.

o **Heron Island** (QLD): Any time of year, you'll spot wonderful wildlife on this "jewel in the reef" off Gladstone, but the best time to visit is November to March, when the life cycle of giant green loggerhead and hawksbill turtles is in full swing. From November to January, the turtles come ashore to lay their eggs. From late January to March, the hatchlings emerge and head for the water. You can see it all by strolling down to the beach, or join a university researcher to get the full story. See p. 269. **Mon Repos Regional Park,** near Bundaberg in Queensland (p. 273), is another good turtle-watching site.

o **Moonlit Sanctuary** (VIC): For the chance to see many of Australia's nocturnal animals, including some that are now extinct in the wild (the eastern quoll, the red-bellied pademelon, the southern bettong), take a guided night tour at this sanctuary on the Mornington Peninsula. See p. 182

o **Rottnest Island** (WA): Meet the quokkas—more than 10,000 of them—on one of Western Australia's favorite holiday islands. These cute little marsupials roam the island freely, almost the only place in Australia that you will find them. See p. 365.

Get up close with the colorful residents of the Australian Butterfly Sanctuary in Kuranda.

THE best DIVING & SNORKELING

o **Port Douglas** (QLD): Among the fabulous dive sites off Port Douglas, north of Cairns, are Split-Bommie, with its delicate fan corals and schools of fusiliers; Barracuda Pass, with its coral gardens and giant clams; and the swim-through coral spires of the Cathedrals. Snorkelers can glide over the coral and reef fish life of Agincourt Reef. See p. 249.

o **Cairns** (QLD): Moore, Norman, Hardy, Saxon, and Arlington reefs and Michaelmas and Upolu cays—all about 90 minutes off Cairns—offer great snorkeling and endless dive sites. Explore on a day trip from Cairns, or join a live-aboard adventure. See p. 239.

o **The Whitsunday Islands** (QLD): These 74 breathtaking islands offer countless dive sites both among the islands and on the Outer Great Barrier Reef, 90 minutes away. Bait Reef on the Outer Reef is popular for its drop-offs. Snorkelers can explore not just the Outer Reef but also patch reefs among the islands and rarely visited fringing reefs. See p. 267.

o **Heron Island** (QLD): Easily the number-one snorkel and dive site in Australia—if you stayed in the water for a week, you couldn't snorkel all the acres of coral stretching from shore. Take your pick of 22 dive sites: the Coral Cascades, with football trout and anemones; the Blue Pools, favored by octopus, turtles, and sharks; Heron Bommie, with its rays, eels, and Spanish dancers; and more. Absolute magic. See p. 270.

o **Lady Elliot Island** (QLD): Gorgeous coral lagoons, perfect for snorkeling, line this coral cay island off the town of Bundaberg. Boats take you farther out to snorkel above manta rays, plate coral, and big fish. Divers can swim through a blowhole, 16m (52 ft.) down, and see gorgonian fans, soft and hard corals, sharks, barracudas, and reef fish. See p. 275.

o **Rottnest Island** (WA): Just 19km (12 miles) off Perth, this popular holiday spot has excellent snorkeling and more than 100 dive sites. Wrecks, limestone overhangs, and myriad fish will keep divers happy. On this car-free island, snorkelers can rent a bike and snorkel gear and simply head off to find their own private underwater garden. The sunken grotto at Fishhook Bay is a top spot. See p. 364.

AUSTRALIA IN CONTEXT

When most people think of Australia, they conjure up images of bounding kangaroos, dusty red deserts, and golden sandy beaches. The Sydney Opera House is right up there, too. They imagine drawling accents and slouch hats, suntanned lifeguards, and men who wrestle crocodiles for the fun of it. Well, it's all that—and more (apart from the crocodile wrestling)! This huge continent is truly remarkable, offering everything from rolling green hills, dense ancient rainforests, and historic towns to vast areas of sparsely inhabited ochre-red Outback and giant coral reefs, deserted beaches, unique animals and plants, cosmopolitan modern cities, and intriguing Aboriginal culture.

Most people visiting Australia for the first time head straight to Sydney or Melbourne. They explore the Red Centre and the giant rock Uluru; or they take to the warm waters of the Great Barrier Reef to dive or snorkel. But it's also often the places that come to visitors by chance, or through deeper research, that remain locked in their memories forever. Who could forget holding a koala in your arms or feeding a kangaroo from the palm of your hand? Or traveling red-dirt tracks accompanied by emus running alongside your 4WD? This book concentrates on the areas that are the most traveled (and on every visitor's wish list), but it also takes you to some of the lesser-known treasures of each city and some of our personal favorite places and experiences. Of course, no travel experience is complete without a little background information, which is where this chapter comes in.

AUSTRALIA TODAY

Perhaps it's to do with the weather, or the wide-open spaces, or the quality of the light, but Australians are generally an optimistic, positive lot—and to me, that's a big part of the country's appeal. Phrases like "It's a lucky country, mate," and "She'll be right" (meaning everything will be okay) may be clichés, but they sum up the attitude held by most Australians. The food is good and there's plenty of it; the education system is mostly good (and mostly free, unless you choose to pay for a private school or you happen to be saddled with student loans to cover university fees); gun ownership is heavily restricted; the public health-care system is universal and largely free or inexpensive; and the government (whichever persuasion it is) is generally stable. It's a great place to live—even though it can sometimes feel a long, long way from everywhere else.

Of course, nothing is totally clear-cut. The country has plenty of socially disadvantaged areas, and many of Australia's indigenous people in particular are struggling on the fringes of mainstream society.

As a nation, Australia is also facing tough challenges in balancing the benefits of industry with caring for the environment. Australia makes a massive amount of revenue from mining, supplying China with a significant proportion of its iron and other metals, as well as importing everything from uranium and coal to natural gas to the rest of the world. This inevitably means the ruin of some once-pristine landscapes. Australia also has one of the world's highest per capita levels of greenhouse gas emissions (nearly twice the OECD average and more than four times the world average) and suffers from severe droughts and dramatic weather events that most experts believe are the result of human-induced climate change.

Australia is also one of the world's fastest-growing industrialized nations. In 2019, the population hit the 25-million mark, a figure driven in recent years

Aboriginal rock art at Nourlangie, Kakadu National Park, Northern Territory.

by immigration, with around 28% (or 7 million people) of Australian residents born overseas.

One thing Australia realized early on was the importance of tourism to its economy. Around 9.2 million people visited in 2018. You'll find Australians helpful and friendly, and services, tours, and food and drink to rival any in the world. Factor in the landscape, the indigenous culture, the sunshine, the unique wildlife, and some of the world's best cities, and, all in all, you've got a fascinating, accessible destination of amazing diversity and variety.

LOOKING BACK AT AUSTRALIA

The Beginning

In the beginning, there was the Dreamtime. Australia's indigenous people have lived on this land for 60,000 years or more. Their "Dreamtime" stories explain how they see the creation story and what followed. In scientific terms, a supercontinent split into two, and over millions of years continental drift carried the great landmasses apart. Australia was part of what we call Gondwanaland, which also divided into South America, Africa, India, Papua New Guinea, and Antarctica. Giant marsupials evolved to roam the continent of Australia. The last of these creatures are believed to have died out around 20,000 years ago, possibly helped toward extinction by drought, or by Aboriginal hunters, who lived alongside them for thousands of years.

Early European Explorers

The existence of a great southern land had been on the minds of Europeans since the Greek astronomer Ptolemy drew a map of the world in A.D. 150 showing a large landmass in the south, which he believed existed to balance out the land in the Northern Hemisphere. He called it Terra Australia Incognita—the "Unknown Southland."

Portuguese ships reached Australia as early as 1536 and charted part of its coastline. In 1606, William Jansz was sent by the Dutch East India Company to open up a new route to the Spice Islands and to find New Guinea. He landed on the north coast of Queensland instead and fought with local Aborigines. Between 1616 and 1640, many more Dutch ships made contact with Australia as they hugged the west coast of what they called "New Holland," after sailing with the westerly winds from the Cape of Good Hope.

In 1642, the Dutch East India Company, through the governor general of the Indies, Anthony Van Diemen, sent Abel Tasman to search for and map the great Southland. During two voyages, Tasman charted the northern Australian coastline and discovered Tasmania, which he named Van Diemen's Land.

The Arrival of the British

In 1766, the Royal Society hired James Cook to travel to the Pacific Ocean to observe and record the transit of Venus across the sun. In 1770, Cook charted the east coast of Australia in his ship the HMS *Endeavour*. He claimed the

THE ancient art OF AUSTRALIA

A history of the Aboriginal people lies partly in the **rock paintings** they have left behind all over Australia. In the tropical north, for example, a wide-ranging body of prehistoric art decorates sandstone gorges near the tiny township of Laura on the rugged Cape York Peninsula. Depictions on rock-shelter sites range from spirit figures of men and women to eels, fish, wide-winged brolga birds, crocodiles, kangaroos, snakes, and stenciled hands. One wall, the "Magnificent Gallery," stretches more than 40m (131 ft.) and is adorned with hundreds of Quinkan figures—Quinkans being the Aboriginal spirits associated with this region.

Much Aboriginal rock art is preserved in national parks. Some of the best are Nourlangie Rock and Ubirr Rock in the Northern Territory's Kakadu National Park (p. 296). Nourlangie features "X-ray"-style paintings of animals, and from there you can also walk to see more paintings at Nanguluwur. There are also ancient paintings near Uluru in the Red Centre (p. 277). Other rock art sites readily accessible on day trips from major Australian cities include Ku-Ring-Gai Chase National Park, and the Royal National Park near Sydney; the Grampians National Park west of Melbourne; and the fabulous hand stencils at Mutawintji National Park near Broken Hill in New South Wales. In Queensland, Carnarvon National Park (about 400km/249 miles west of Brisbane) offers a breathtaking display of early indigenous paintings.

land for Britain and named it New South Wales. On April 29, Captain Cook landed at Botany Bay, which he named after the discovery of scores of plants hitherto unknown to science. Turning northward, he passed an entrance to a possible harbor that appeared to offer safe anchorage and named it Port Jackson, after the secretary of the admiralty, George Jackson. Back in Britain, King George III viewed Australia as a potential colony and repository of Britain's overflowing prison population, which could no longer be transported to the United States of America following the War of Independence.

The First Fleet left England in May 1787, made up of 11 store and transport ships (none of them bigger than the passenger ferries that ply modern-day Sydney Harbour from Circular Quay to Manly) led by Arthur Phillip. Aboard were 1,480 people, including 759 convicts. Phillip's flagship, the *Supply,* reached Botany Bay in January 1788, but Phillip decided the soil was poor and the surroundings too swampy. On January 26, now celebrated as Australia Day, he settled for Port Jackson (Sydney Harbour) instead.

The convicts were immediately put to work clearing land, planting crops, and constructing buildings. Phillip decided to give some convicts pardons for good behavior and service, and even granted small land parcels to those who were especially industrious.

When gold was discovered in Victoria in 1852 and in Western Australia 12 years later, hundreds of thousands of immigrants from Europe, America, and China flooded the country in search of fortune. By 1860, more than a million non-Aboriginal people were living in Australia.

The final 10,000 convicts were transported to Western Australia between 1850 and 1868, bringing the total shipped to Australia to 168,000. Some early colonial architecture, built and designed by those convicts, still remains in Sydney, Tasmania, and to a lesser extent in Brisbane. Be on the lookout for buildings designed by the colonial architect Francis Greenway. Between 1816 and 1818, while still a prisoner, Greenway was responsible for the Macquarie Lighthouse on South Head, at the entrance to Sydney Harbour, and also Hyde Park Barracks and St. James Church in the city center.

Federation & the Great Wars

On January 1, 1901, the six states that made up Australia proclaimed themselves to be part of one nation, and the Commonwealth of Australia was formed. In the same ceremony, the first governor-general was sworn in as the representative of the Queen, who remained head of state.

In 1914, Australia joined Britain in World War I. In April of 1915, the Australian and New Zealand Army Corps (ANZAC) formed a beachhead on the peninsula of Gallipoli in Turkey. The Turkish troops had been warned, and 8 months of fighting ended with 8,587 Australian dead and more than 19,000 wounded. That day, April 25, is commemorated each year as Anzac Day.

Australians fought in World War II in North Africa, Greece, and the Middle East. In March 1942, Japanese aircraft bombed Broome in Western Australia

The Macquarie Lighthouse on South Head, Sydney Harbour.

In 1964, a group of 20 nomadic women and children became the last Aboriginal people to make "first contact" with Europeans. They were living in the Great Sandy Desert, south of Broome, in Western Australia. When they first saw two officers from the Weapons Research Establishment, who were checking land destined for a series of rocket tests, the Aborigines presumed the white-skinned creatures were ghosts.

and Darwin in the Northern Territory. In May 1942, Japanese midget submarines entered Sydney Harbour and torpedoed a ferry before ultimately being destroyed. Later that year, Australian volunteers fought an incredibly brave retreat through the jungles of Papua New Guinea on the Kokoda Track against superior Japanese forces.

Recent Times

In 1986, an act of both British and Australian Parliament once and for all severed any remaining ties to the United Kingdom. Australia had begun the march to complete independence. Today, Australia is a member of the British Commonwealth and Queen Elizabeth II is the head of state, but a democratically elected Parliament is headed by a Prime Minister who is leader of the majority or coalition ruling party. As well as the Commonwealth (federal) Government, each state also has its own "local" government.

Waves of immigration have brought in millions of people since the end of World War II. It was not until 1974 that the left-of-center Whitlam Labor government put an end to the White Australia policy, which had largely restricted black and Asian immigration from 1901 on. ("White" Australia—a term always used to distinguish the Anglo-Saxon population from that of the indigenous people of Australia—widened its scope in the 1850s due to conflict between European settlers and Chinese immigrants in the gold fields.) Today, Australia has one of the most multicultural populations in the world; migrants have come from the U.K., New Zealand, Europe, and Asia, and more recently from countries such as Iraq, Sudan, and Somalia. So what's the typical Australian like? Well, he's hardly Crocodile Dundee.

AUSTRALIA IN POPULAR CULTURE

Movies

Australia has produced its fair share of movies, good and bad. Some of the better ones are listed here.

o **Walkabout (1971):** Hauntingly beautiful and disturbing, this movie set in the Australian desert stars Jenny Agutter and the Aboriginal actor David

THE ABORIGINAL "stolen generations"

When Captain James Cook landed at Botany Bay in 1770 determined to claim the land for the British Empire, at least 300,000 **Aborigines** were living on the continent. Despite varying estimates of how long Aboriginal people have inhabited Australia (some believe it to be since the beginning of time), there is scientific evidence that people were walking the continent at least 60,000 years ago.

At the time of the arrival of Europeans, there were at least 600 different tribal communities, each linked to their ancestral land by **"sacred sites"** (certain features of the land, such as hills or rock formations). They were hunter-gatherers, spending about 20 hours a week harvesting the resources of the land, the rivers, and the ocean. The rest of their time was taken up by complex social and belief systems, as well as by life's practicalities such as making utensils and weapons.

The basis of Aboriginal spirituality rests in the **Dreamtime** stories, which recount how ancient spirits created the universe—earth, stars, moon, sun, water, animals, and humans. Much Aboriginal art is related to their land and the sacred sites that are home to the Dreamtime spirits. Some Aboriginal groups believe these spirits came in giant human form, while others believe they were animals or huge snakes. According to Aboriginal custom, individuals can draw on the power of the Dreamtime spirits by reenacting various stories and practicing certain ceremonies.

When the British came, bringing their unfamiliar diseases along with them, entire coastal communities were virtually wiped out by the onset of smallpox. Even as late as the 1950s, large numbers of Aborigines in remote regions of South Australia and the Northern Territory succumbed to deadly outbreaks of influenza and measles.

Although relationships between the settlers and Aborigines were initially peaceful, conflicts over land and food led to skirmishes in which Aborigines were massacred and settlers and convicts attacked. Within a few years, some 10,000 Aborigines and 1,000 Europeans had been killed in Queensland alone, while in Tasmania, a campaign to rid the island entirely of local Aborigines was

Gulpilul. A white girl and her brother get hopelessly lost and survive with help from a doomed Aboriginal hero.

o **Picnic at Hanging Rock (1974):** This mesmerizing Peter Weir movie is about a group of schoolgirls and a teacher who go missing at an eerie rock formation north of Melbourne. It's set at the beginning of the 20th century, when bonnets and teapots were the norm.

o **Mad Max (1979):** Mel Gibson fights to the death in the Outback, which presents the ideal setting for a post-apocalyptic world. The movie was so popular it spawned three sequels: *The Road Warrior* (1981), *Mad Max: Beyond Thunderdome* (1985), and *Mad Max: Fury Road* (2015).

o **Gallipoli (1981):** Peter Weir brilliantly captures the World War I military disaster that saw Australian and New Zealand troops fighting against overwhelming odds on the Turkish coastline.

o **The Man from Snowy River (1982):** Kirk Douglas, Tom Burlinson, and Sigrid Thornton star in this startling Australian movie that showcases the mountainous wilderness of Australia, where wild horses roam.

ultimately successful, with the last full-blooded Tasmanian Aborigine dying in 1876. By the start of the 20th century, the Aboriginal people were considered a dying race. Most of those who remained lived in government-owned reserves or church-controlled missions.

Massacres of Aborigines continued to go largely or wholly unpunished into the 1920s, by which time it was official government policy to remove light-skinned Aboriginal children from their families. Many children of these "stolen generations" were brought up in white foster homes or church mission stations and never reunited with their biological families. Many children with living parents were told that their parents were dead. This continued into the 1970s.

Today, there are some 798,400 people living in Australia who claim Aboriginal and Torres Strait Islander descent—3.3% of the population. About 60% of indigenous people live in New South Wales and Queensland, but the Northern Territory has the greatest proportion of Aboriginal residents, at around 30%. In general, a great divide still exists between them and the rest of the population. Aboriginal life expectancy is 10 to 12 years lower than that of other Australians, with overall death rates around two times higher. Aborigines make up the highest percentage of the country's prison population, and reports continue to emerge about Aborigines dying while incarcerated.

It was not until 1962 that Aboriginal people were given the right to hold citizenship or vote in Australia, and only in 1992 did the High Court of Australia expunge the concept of *terra nullius* and acknowledge the pre-existing rights of indigenous Australians. Aboriginal people are still not recognized in the Australian Constitution.

In 2007, then-Prime Minister Kevin Rudd made an official apology on behalf of his Labor Government to the "stolen generations." National Sorry Day is held on May 26 each year, when Australians of all backgrounds march in parades and hold other events around the country to honor the Stolen Generations. It is followed by National Reconciliation Week (May 27–June 3).

- **Crocodile Dundee (1986):** Paul Hogan shot to worldwide fame as a "typical" crocodile-wrestling Outback hero. He wears the same hat and a few more wrinkles in *Crocodile Dundee II* (1988) and *Crocodile Dundee in L.A.* (2001).
- **Shine (1991):** This portrayal of the real-life classical pianist David Helfgott, who rose to international prominence in the 1950s and '60s before having a nervous breakdown, is remarkable. Oscar-winner Geoffrey Rush gives a powerful performance as Helfgott; Sir John Gielgud plays Helfgott's teacher.
- **Strictly Ballroom (1992):** A boy, played by Paul Mercurio, becomes a champion ballroom dancer in this whimsical, playful movie.
- **Muriel's Wedding (1994):** This classic Australian comedy tells the tale of Muriel Heslop (Toni Collette), a young woman who dreams of getting married and moving far away from her boring life in Porpoise Spit. Fabulous characters, great catchphrases, and ABBA music abound.
- **The Adventures of Priscilla, Queen of the Desert (1994):** A trans woman takes to traveling through the desert in a big pink bus with two drag queens. They sing ABBA classics and dress the part, kind of. Where else but Australia . . .?

- **The Dish (2000):** This comedy about Australia's role in the Apollo 11 mission in 1969 was set around a group of characters operating the Parkes/Canberra radio telescope.
- **Rabbit-Proof Fence (2002):** This fictionalized tale addresses the real-life experience of Aboriginal children plucked from their homes in order to put them in white foster families, or—as is the case in this true story of three girls—to train them to work as domestic servants.
- **Australia (2008):** An English aristocrat in the 1930s, played by Nicole Kidman, arrives in northern Australia. After an epic journey across the country with a rough-hewn cattle drover played by Hugh Jackman, she is caught in the bombing of Darwin during World War II. Mixed reviews for this one—make up your own mind, if you're inclined!
- **Samson and Delilah (2009):** This challenging movie depicts two indigenous Australian 14-year-olds living in a remote Aboriginal community who steal a car and escape their difficult lives by heading off to Alice Springs.
- **Animal Kingdom (2010):** Jacki Weaver's role as a crime family matriarch in this gripping drama set in Melbourne won her multiple awards, and an Oscar nomination for Best Supporting Actress.
- **Red Dog (2011):** A tearjerker family flick about a kelpie looking for his master in a Western Australian Outback mining town, this film was adapted from the novel by Louis de Bernières and based on a true story. A prequel, *Red Dog: True Blue*, was released in 2016.
- **Last Cab to Darwin (2014):** A taxi driver from outback Broken Hill discovers he has terminal cancer and decides to drive to Darwin to take advantage of new euthanasia laws. The film is uplifting rather than morbid, with a great performance by Michael Caton in the lead role.
- **Lion (2016):** Based on the true story of Saroo Brierley (played by Dev Patel), an Indian orphan adopted by an Australian couple (played by Nicole Kidman and David Wenham), Lion traces Saroo's search for his birth family. Shot in Tasmania and India, it garnered a slew of awards including six Oscar nominations (including one for Best Picture).
- **Breath (2018):** The film adaptation of Tim Winton's bestselling novel of the same name (p. 25) is worth seeing if only for its spectacular Western Australia scenery and surf scenes. Then there's the star and director, Simon Baker, of *The Mentalist*.

Music

Aboriginal music has been around for tens of thousands of years. Best known is the sound of the **didgeridoo,** made from a hollowed-out tree limb. Listen carefully and you might hear animal sounds, including the flapping of wings and the thumping of feet on the ground. You might hear the sounds of wind, or of thunder, or trees creaking, or water running. It just goes to show how connected the Aboriginal people were, and still are in many cases, to the

FACING PAGE: The haunting tones of the musical instrument known as the didgeridoo include animal sounds and the flapping of wings.

landscape they lived in. For contemporary fusions of indigenous and Western music, look for music by Yothu Yindi, Christine Anu, and the late Geoffrey Gurrumul Yunupingu (who sings only in his own language).

As far as Australian rock 'n' roll goes, you might know a few of the following names. The big star in the 1950s was Johnny O'Keefe, but he soon gave way to the likes of the Easybeats. Running into the 1970s, you find the Bee Gees, AC/DC, Sherbet, John-Paul Young, and the Little River Band. Others who made a name for themselves included the solo stars Helen Reddy, Olivia Newton-John, and Peter Allen. The 1980s saw Men at Work, Crowded House, The Go-Betweens, Hunters and Collectors, Kylie Minogue, and Midnight Oil. INXS, Silverchair, and Savage Garden took us into the 1990s, which Kylie managed to stitch up, too. Jet, Tame Impala, and the Vines were Australian rock groups that saw considerable international success in the 21st century, along with, you guessed it, Kylie Minogue. For songs with a contemporary Australian voice, go no further than Paul Kelly. In recent years, the best-known Australian singer in the U.S. has probably been Gotye, who won three Grammy awards in 2013.

Australia's Literature

Australian literature has come a long way since the days when the bush poets A. B. "Banjo" Paterson and Henry Lawson penned odes to a way of life now largely lost. The best known of these is Paterson's epic *The Man from Snowy River,* which first hit the bestseller list in 1895 and was made into a film. But the Australian literary scene has always been lively, with a wealth of classics, many of them with the Outback at their heart.

Miles Franklin wrote *My Brilliant Career,* the story of a young woman faced with the dilemma of choosing between marriage and a career, in 1901 (made into a film starring Judy Davis in 1979). *We of the Never Never* (1902), by Mrs. Aeneas Gunn, tells the story of a young woman who leaves the comfort of her Melbourne home to live on a cattle station in the Northern Territory. *Walkabout* (1959), by James V. Marshall, explores the relationship between an Aborigine and two lost children in the bush (made into a powerful film by Peter Weir in 1971). Colleen McCullough's romantic epic *The Thorn Birds* (1977) is about forbidden love between a Catholic priest and a young woman (made into a TV miniseries in 1983).

A good historical account of Australia's early days is Geoffrey Blainey's *The Tyranny of Distance,* first published in 1966. Robert Hughes's classic *The Fatal Shore: The Epic of Australia's Founding* (1987) is a best-selling nonfiction study of the country's European history.

For a contemporary, if somewhat dark, take on the settlement and development of Sydney, delve into John Birmingham's *Leviathan* (1999). From an Aboriginal perspective, *Follow the Rabbit-Proof Fence* (1997), by Doris Pilkington, tells the true story of three young girls from the "Stolen Generation" who ran away from a mission school to return to their families. (A movie version was released in 2002; see p. 22.)

Modern novelists include David Malouf, Elizabeth Jolley, Helen Garner, Sue Woolfe, and Peter Carey, whose *True History of the Kelly Gang* (2001), a fictionalized autobiography of the outlaw Ned Kelly, won the Booker Prize in 2001. West Australian Tim Winton evokes his part of the continent in stunning prose; his 2008 novel *Breath* was turned into a movie in 2018 (p. 22). Matthew Condon's *The Trout Opera* (2007) remains one of my all-time favorite Australian novels, covering a century through one man's life. The multi-award-winning *The Light Between Oceans,* by Australian novelist M. L. Stedman, is set in a Western Australian lighthouse. And don't pass up Richard Flanagan's masterpiece *The Narrow Road to the Deep North,* which won the Booker Prize in 2014.

Outsiders who have tackled Australia include Jan Morris and Bill Bryson. Morris's *Sydney* was published in 1992, and Bryson's *In a Sunburned Country* (2001), while not always a favorite with Australians, may appeal to American readers.

THE ANCIENT ART OF AUSTRALIA

A history of the Aboriginal people lies partly in the rock paintings they have left behind all over Australia. In the tropical north, for example, a wide-ranging body of prehistoric art decorates sandstone gorges near the tiny township of Laura on the rugged Cape York Peninsula. Depictions on rock-shelter sites range from spirit figures of men and women to eels, fish, wide-winged brolga birds, crocodiles, kangaroos, snakes, and stenciled hands. One wall, the "Magnificent Gallery," stretches more than 40 m (131 ft.) and is adorned with hundreds of Quinkan figures—Quinkans being the Aboriginal spirits associated with this region.

Much Aboriginal rock art is preserved in national parks. Examples readily accessible on day trips from major Australian cities include Ku-Ring-Gai Chase National Park, and the Royal National Park near Sydney. Then there's the Grampians National Park west of Melbourne and the fabulous hand stencils at Mutawintji National park near Broken Hill in New South Wales. There are also ancient paintings near Uluru in Australia's Red Centre.

In Queensland, Carnarvon National Park (about 400 km/249 miles west of Brisbane) offers a breathtaking display of early indigenous paintings.

EATING & DRINKING IN AUSTRALIA

For a long time, the typical Aussie home-cooked meal consisted of the English-style "meat and three veg" and a Sunday roast. Spaghetti was something foreigners ate, and zucchini and eggplant (aubergine) were considered exotic. Then came mass immigration and all sorts of food that people once only read about in *National Geographic.*

The first big wave of Italian immigrants in the 1950s caused a national scandal. The great Aussie dream was to have a quarter-acre block of land with a hills hoist (a circular revolving clothesline) in the backyard. When Italians started hanging freshly made pasta out to dry on this Aussie icon, it caused an uproar, and some clamored for the new arrivals to be shipped back to their homeland. As Australia matured, southern European cuisine became increasingly popular, until olive oil was sizzling in frying pans the way only lard had previously done.

In the 1980s (following the repeal of the White Australia policy in 1973), waves of Asian immigrants hit Australia's shores. Suddenly, everyone was cooking with woks. These days, a fusion of spices from the East and ingredients and styles from the Mediterranean make up what's become known as Modern Australian cuisine.

Still, some of the old ways remain. Everyone knows that Aussies like a barbecue, usually referred to as a "barbie." Most Aussies aren't really that adventurous when it comes to throwing things on the hot plate and are usually content with some cheap sausages and a steak washed down by a few beers. While you might see kangaroo, crocodile, and emu on the menu at some restaurants, Australians tend not to indulge in their local wildlife that much, preferring to stick to introduced species instead.

Bush tucker, hunter-gatherer foods indigenous to Australia, are increasingly popular on restaurant menus.

Seafood is popular, as you would expect, and a typical Christmas Day meal usually includes prawns and/or fish.

In the big cities, you'll find every kind of cuisine, including Thai, Vietnamese, Italian, Spanish, Middle Eastern, and Indian. Even the smallest town usually has a Chinese restaurant (of varying quality). Melbourne is proud of its coffee culture, but American readers should note that the bottomless cup of coffee is rare.

Note: Many Australian restaurants are flexible on hours, generally staying open until the last diners leave. In the listings in this book, a restaurant is often said to be open until "late." In practice, midnight would probably be the latest for a restaurant to stay open—if the diners were still spending!

Another note: Many restaurants allow you to bring your own wine (referred to simply as BYO), but some charge a corkage fee of a few dollars, even when there's a screw-cap and no cork.

Beer & Wine

If you order a beer in a pub or bar, you should be aware that the standard glass size differs from state to state. Thus, in Sydney you can order a schooner or a smaller midi. In trendy places, you might be offered an English pint or a half-pint. In Melbourne and Brisbane, a midi is called a pot, while in Darwin it's called a handle, and in Hobart a ten. It can be confusing! You can get smaller glasses, too, though thankfully they're becoming rare. These could either be called a pony, a seven, a butcher, a six, or a bobbie, depending on which city you're in. If in doubt, just mime a big one or a small one, and you'll get your meaning across.

As far as wine goes, Australia has come a long way since the first grape vines arrived on the First Fleet in 1788. Today, more than 550 major companies and small winemakers produce wine commercially in Australia. Among the dozens of recognized wine-growing regions, the most well-known include the Hunter Valley in New South Wales; the Barossa Valley, McClaren Vale, Coonawarra, Adelaide Hills, and the Clare Valley in South Australia; the Yarra Valley in Victoria; and Margaret River in Western Australia.

Aboriginal Foods

In the past couple of decades, many Australian chefs have woken to the variety and tastes of "bush tucker," as native Aussie food is tagged. Now it's all the rage in the most fashionable restaurants, where wattleseed, lemon myrtle, and other native tastes have a place in one or two dishes on the menu. Below are some of the Aboriginal foods you may encounter.

- **Bunya nut:** Crunchy nut of the bunya pine, about the size of a macadamia.

- **Bush tomato:** Dry, small, darkish fruit; more like a raisin in look and taste.

- **Native cranberry:** Small berry that tastes a bit like an apple.

- **Illawarra plum:** Dark berry with a strong, rich, tangy taste.

o **Kangaroo:** A strong meat with a gamey flavor. Tender when correctly prepared, tough when not. Excellent smoked.

o **Lemon aspen:** Citrusy, light-yellow fruit with a sharp, tangy flavor.

o **Lemon myrtle:** Gum leaves with a fresh lemon tang; often used to flavor white meat.

o **Lillipilli:** Delicious juicy, sweet pink berry.

o **Quandong:** A tart, tangy native peach.

o **Rosella:** Spiky petals of a red flower with a rich berry flavor.

o **Wattleseed:** Roasted ground acacia seeds that taste a little like bitter coffee. Sometimes used in cakes.

o **Wild lime:** Smaller and more sour than regular lime.

One ingredient you will not see on menus is **witchetty grubs;** most people are too squeamish to eat these fat, juicy, slimy white creatures. They live in the soil or in dead tree trunks and are a common source of protein for some Aborigines. You eat them alive, not cooked. If you are offered one in the Outback, you can either freak out (as most locals would do)—or enjoy its pleasantly nutty taste as a reward for your bravery.

THE LAY OF THE LAND

People who have never visited Australia wonder why such a huge country has a population of just 24.5 million. The truth is, much of Australia is uninhabitable, and about 90% of the population lives on only 2.6% of the continent, mainly clustered around the coast, where the only relatively decent rainfall occurs. Compounding that is the fact that Australia falls victim to long droughts. Most of Australia is harsh Outback, characterized by saltbush plains, arid brown crags, shifting sand deserts, and salt-lake country. People survive where they can in this arid land because of one thing—the Great Artesian Basin. This saucer-shaped geological formation comprises about a fifth of Australia's landmass, stretching over much of inland New South Wales, Queensland, South Australia, and the Northern Territory. Beneath it are massive underground water supplies stored during Jurassic and Cretaceous times (some 66–208 million years ago), when the area was much like the Amazon basin is today. Bore holes bring water to the surface and allow sheep, cattle, and humans a respite from the dryness.

As for the climate, as you might expect with a continent the size of Australia, it can differ immensely. The average rainfall in central Australia ranges between just 200 to 250mm (8–10 inches) a year. Summer daytime temperatures range from 90° to 104°F (32°–40°C). In winter, temperatures range from around 64° to 75°F (18°–24°C). Summer in the Southern Hemisphere roughly stretches from early November to the end of February, though it can be hot for a couple of months on either side of these dates, depending where you are.

Parts of the Northern Territory and far northern Queensland are classified as tropical, and as such suffer from very wet summers—often referred to simply as "the Wet." Flooding can be a real fact of life up here. The rest of the year is called "the Dry," for obvious reasons.

Most of Queensland and northern New South Wales are subtropical. This means warm summers and cool winters. Sydney falls into the "temperate" zone, with generally moderate temperatures and no prolonged periods of extreme hot or cold conditions. Parts of central Victoria can get snow in winter, while the Australian Alps, which run through southern central NSW and northeastern Victoria, have good snow cover in winter.

The Queensland coast is blessed with one of the greatest natural attractions in the world. The **Great Barrier Reef** (see chapter 8) stretches 2,000km (1,240 miles) from off Gladstone in Queensland to the Gulf of Papua, near Papua New Guinea. It's relatively new, not more than 8,000 years old, although many fear that rising seawater, caused by global warming, will cause its demise. As it is, significant damage has already been caused by the invasive crown-of-thorns starfish and a bleaching process believed to be the result of excessive nutrients flowing into the sea from Australia's farming land.

Australia's other great natural formation is, of course, **Uluru**—which is sometimes (but not commonly) still called by the name Europeans gave it, Ayers Rock (p. 321).

Australia's Wildlife

Australia's isolation from the rest of the world over millions of years has led to the evolution of forms of life found nowhere else. Probably the strangest of all is the **platypus.** This monotreme, or egg-laying marsupial, has webbed feet, a ducklike bill, and a tail like a beaver's. It lays eggs, and the young suckle from their mother. When a specimen was first brought back to Europe, skeptical scientists insisted it was a fake—a concoction of several different animals sewn together. It is unlikely you will see this shy, nocturnal creature in the wild, but several wildlife parks have them.

Australia is also famous for **kangaroos** and **koalas.** There are 45 kinds of kangaroos and **wallabies,** ranging in scale from small rat-size kangaroos to the man-size red kangaroos. The koala is a fluffy marsupial (not a bear!) that eats gum (eucalyptus) leaves and sleeps about 20 hours a day. There's just one koala species, although those found in Victoria are much larger than those in more northern climes.

The animal you're most likely to come across in your trip is the **possum,** named by Captain James Cook after the North American opossum, which he thought they resembled. (In fact, they are from entirely different families of the animal kingdom.) The brush-tailed possum is commonly found in suburban gardens, including those in Sydney.

Then there's the **wombat.** There are four species of this bulky burrower in Australia, but the common wombat is, well, most common.

The **dingo** is a wild dog, varying in color from yellow to a russet red, mainly seen in the Outback. Because dingoes can breed with escaped "pet" dogs, full-blooded dingoes are becoming increasingly rare.

Commonly seen birds in Australia include the fairy penguin or **Little Penguin** along the coast, **black swans, parrots, cockatoos,** and **honeyeaters.**

DANGEROUS NATIVES

Snakes are common in Australia, but you will rarely see one. The most dangerous land snake is the taipan, which hides in the grasslands in northern Australia—one bite contains enough venom to kill up to 200 sheep. If by the remotest chance you are bitten, immediately demobilize the limb, wrapping it tightly (but not tight enough to restrict the blood flow) with a cloth or bandage, and call ℂ **000** for an ambulance. Antivenin should be available at the nearest hospital.

Hand-feeding kangaroos at Brisbane's Lone Pine Koala Sanctuary.

One creature that scares the living daylights out of anyone who visits coastal Australia is the **shark,** particularly the Great White (though these marauders of the sea are mostly only found in colder waters, such as those off South Australia). Unprovoked shark attacks are relatively rare, particularly when you consider how many people go swimming. The Australian Shark Attack File kept at Sydney's Taronga Zoo recorded 17 unprovoked attacks in 2016, and two deaths. To put this in perspective, 53 unprovoked attacks (and no fatalities) occurred in U.S. waters (including 10 in Hawaii) that year—the most worldwide—according to the International Shark Attack File maintained by the Florida Museum of Natural History. (More than 60% of these occurred off the coast of Florida.) You are more likely to get hit by a car on your way to the beach than to get taken by a shark. Certainly, more people drown in Australian waters than are victims of shark attack.

There are two types of **crocodile** in Australia: the relatively harmless freshwater croc, which grows to 3m (10 ft.) long, and the dangerous estuarine (or saltwater) crocodile, which reaches 5 to 7m (16–23 ft.). Freshwater crocs eat fish; estuarine crocs aren't so picky. Never swim in or stand on the bank of any river, swamp, or beach in northern Australia unless you know with certainty that it's croc-free.

Spiders are common all over Australia, with the funnel web spider and the red-back spider being the most aggressive. Funnel webs live in holes in the ground (they spin their webs around a hole's entrance) and stand on their back legs when they're about to attack. Red-backs have a habit of resting under toilet seats and in car trunks, generally outside the main cities. Caution is a good policy.

If you go bushwalking, check your body carefully. **Ticks** are common, especially in eastern Australia, and can cause severe itching and fever. If you find one on you, pull it out with tweezers, taking care not to leave the head behind.

Fish to avoid are **stingrays** (Australian television star Steve Irwin was killed by a stingray barb through the heart), as well as **porcupine fish, stonefish,** and **lionfish.** Never touch a **cone shell,** or an **octopus** if it has blue rings on it, and be wary of the painful and sometimes deadly tentacles of the **box jellyfish** along the northern Queensland coast in summer. This jellyfish is responsible for more deaths in Australia than snakes, sharks, and saltwater crocodiles. Closely related to the box jellyfish is the **Irukandji,** which also inhabits northern Australian waters. This deadly jellyfish is only 2.5 centimeters (1 in.) in diameter, which makes it very hard to spot in the water. If you brush past a jellyfish, or think you have, pour vinegar over the affected site immediately—authorities leave bottles of vinegar on beaches for this purpose. Vinegar deactivates the stinging cells that haven't already affected you, but doesn't affect the venom that has already been injected. If you are in the tropics and you believe you may have been stung by a box jellyfish or an Irukandji, seek medical attention immediately.

In Sydney and north Queensland, you might come across **"stingers,"** also called "blue bottles." These long-tentacled blue jellyfish can inflict a nasty stinging burn that can last for hours. Sometimes you'll see warning signs on patrolled beaches. The best remedy if you are severely stung is to wash the affected area with fresh water and have a very hot bath or shower (preferably with someone else, just for the sympathy).

Threats to the Landscape

Australia is suffering from climate change, water shortages, and serious threats to wildlife and ecosystems. The country is one of the highest per capita polluters in the world, thanks largely to its reliance on mining and coal-fired power generation.

Meanwhile, the Great Barrier Reef is being damaged by coral bleaching, which occurs when water temperatures rise. Corals can recover, but if the heat persists, or if bleaching happens too frequently, they can die. Nutrient-rich sediment washed out to sea from farmland doesn't help matters much, as nutrient-loving algae colonize the already hard-hit corals. The runoff can also contain pesticides and herbicides, which damage the reef further and make it more vulnerable to the introduced crown-of-thorns starfish, which likes snacking on coral.

As for Australia's native animals and birds—well, history hasn't been too kind to them. At least 22 species of birds, 4 frog species, and 27 mammal species have become extinct since European settlement in Australia. Habitat destruction and introduced species have been the main causes of extinctions. Classified as "critically endangered" or "endangered" today are 24 species of fish, 19 species of frogs, 28 species of reptiles, 65 species of birds, 44 species of mammals, 49 other animals, and 683 species of plants. Many more are classified as vulnerable.

RESPONSIBLE TRAVEL

Sustainable travel—and its close cousin, responsible travel—are important issues in Australia, and you'll find plenty of places that claim to be eco-friendly. So how do you find the places that will truly help you make as little impact as possible on our fragile environment? When planning your trip, look for Australian tourism operators who are accredited under **Ecotourism Australia's** Eco Certification Program (www.ecotourism.org.au). The **Eco Certification** logo is carried by tours, attractions, cruises, or accommodations that have been recognized as environmentally, socially, and economically sustainable. Ecotourism Australia's online **Green Travel Guide** carries a list of its accredited businesses.

Australians are increasingly aware of their environmental responsibilities. Recycling is common, with local government areas providing bins for general household refuse, paper, and glass. All states of Australia—except New South Wales—have now banned single-use plastic bags; bring along a reusable bag to carry your shopping in. There is also a growing national campaign to ban plastic straws because of their impact on marine life; at least 30 tour operators, including some island resorts, on the Great Barrier Reef have agreed to ban them.

Because of frequent and prolonged droughts, Australians have become more aware of where their water supply is coming from. You might be surprised at how water-conscious the average Australian is these days. That said, what we gain on one hand we often lose on the other. Gas-guzzling four-wheel-drives are popular, four-wheelers zip around the Outback and on some beaches, and air travel within Australia is generally necessary. If you are keen to offset the large carbon footprint created by your flight to Australia, use public transport where you can, turn electronic gadgets off at the wall when you aren't using them, and recycle batteries if possible. Don't throw cigarette butts on the ground—you risk a possible hefty fine, and your butt might end up polluting Australia's waterways.

Choose a **hotel** designed to reduce its environmental impact with its use of non-toxic cleaners and renewable energy sources. Hotels may be reducing their emissions further by utilizing local food, energy-efficient lighting, and eco-friendly forms of transport. Most hotels now offer you the choice of using

RESOURCES FOR responsible TRAVEL

In addition to the resources for Australia listed above and below, the following websites provide valuable wide-ranging information on sustainable travel.

o **Sustainable Travel International** (www.sustainabletravel.org) promotes ethical tourism practices.

o **Carbonfund** (www.carbonfund.org) and **Cool Climate Network** (www.coolclimate.berkeley.edu) provide info on "carbon offsetting," or offsetting the greenhouse gas emitted during flights.

For general info on volunteer travel, visit www.goabroad.com/volunteer-abroad and www.idealist.org.

the same towels for more than 1 night—and of course, you should, because laundry makes up around 40% of an average hotel's energy use. Some accommodations offer the same option regarding bed linens if you're staying more than 1 night.

Choose **tours** that are eco-friendly, environmentally sustainable, and preferably employ local guides. Opt for a sailing boat rather than a giant motor cruiser to discover the Barrier Reef or the Whitsunday Islands in Queensland, for example, or an Aboriginal guided walking tour over a large coach excursion.

If you are looking for a way of giving something back on your holiday, several organizations offer the opportunity to do **volunteer work** in Australia, such as helping to save endangered wildlife. Often there is a fee involved to cover transportation, accommodations, meals, and so on.

o **Conservation Volunteers Australia** (www.conservationvolunteers.com.au; ℭ **1800/032 501** in Australia, or 03/5330 0200) offers a range of projects across Australia, including tree planting, wildlife surveys, heritage restoration, and more.

o **Real Gap Experience** (www.realgap.com.au) offers several volunteer options in Australia, including in a wildlife sanctuary on Kangaroo Island in South Australia.

o **Willing Workers on Organic Farms** (WWOOF) offers the chance for volunteers to do 4 to 6 hours of work a day in exchange for meals and accommodations, usually in the farmers' family home. WWOOFers (as they are known) have the pick of more than 1,500 host farms around the country. Check out the website for more information (www.wwoof.com.au) or call ℭ **03/5155 0218.**

o The state tourism website for **Victoria** (www.visitvictoria.com/information/volunteer) also recommends volunteering opportunities in that state. Another useful resource is the government website, **www.volunteer.vic.gov.au.**

WHEN TO GO

When it is winter in the Northern Hemisphere, Australia is basking in the Southern Hemisphere's summer, and vice versa. Midwinter in Australia is July and August, and the hottest months are November through March. Remember, unlike in the Northern Hemisphere, the farther south you go in Australia, the colder it gets.

The Travel Seasons

Airfares to Australia are lowest from mid-April to late August—the best time to visit the Red Centre and the Great Barrier Reef.

HIGH SEASON   The peak travel season in the most popular parts of Australia is the Aussie winter. In much of the country—particularly the northern half—the most pleasant time to travel is April through September, when daytime temperatures are 66°F to 88°F (19°C–31°C) and it rarely rains. June, July, and August are the busiest months in these parts; you'll need to book hotels and tours well in advance, and you will pay higher rates then, too.

On the other hand, Australia's summer is a nice time to visit the southern states, and even in winter temperatures rarely dip below freezing.

Generally, the best months to visit Australia are September and October, when it's often still warm enough to hit the beach in the southern states, it's cool enough to tour Uluru, and the humidity and rains have not come to Cairns (although it will be very hot by Oct).

> **Steer Clear of the Vacation Rush**
>
> Try to avoid Australia from Boxing Day (December 26) to the end of January, when Aussies take their summer vacations. In popular seaside holiday spots, hotel rooms and airline seats get as scarce as hen's teeth, and it's a rare airline or hotel that will discount full rates by even a dollar.

LOW SEASON   October through March (summer) is just too hot, too humid, or too wet—or all three—to tour the Red Centre. North Queensland, including Cairns, suffers an intensely hot, humid wet season from November or December through March or April. This is known as "the Wet" and affects most of northern Australia ("the Dry" is from May to October). So if you decide to travel at this time—and lots of people do—be prepared to take the heat, the inconvenience of potential flooding, and the slight chance of encountering cyclones.

Australian National Public Holidays

On national public holidays, services such as banking, postal needs, and purchase of alcohol might be limited or unavailable. There may also be additional holidays as declared by individual states and territories, such as Melbourne

Cup Day (first Tuesday in November), based on the country's most famous thoroughbred horse race—"the race that stops the nation."

o **New Year's Day,** January 1. Expect the usual fireworks and festivities to begin the night of December 31 to ring in the New Year.

o **Australia Day,** January 26. This national day recognizes the First Fleet's arrival in 1788, when 11 ships made their way from England to establish a colony in Australia.

o **Good Friday,** the Friday before Easter, observed the first Friday after the full moon (on or after March 21).

o **Easter Monday,** day after Easter Sunday.

o **Anzac Day,** April 25. ANZAC (Australian and New Zealand Army Corps) Day recognizes those who have served the nation in times of war.

o **Christmas Day,** December 25. *Note:* If Christmas is on a weekend day, the next Monday is termed a public holiday.

o **Boxing Day,** December 26. Originally a British tradition involving gift-giving, Boxing Day is now an Australian holiday, and some sports kick off their seasons on this date. If Boxing Day falls on a Saturday, the next Monday is deemed a public holiday. If it falls on a Sunday, the next Tuesday is the holiday.

New Year's fireworks over Sydney Harbour Bridge.

Australia Calendar of Events

For an exhaustive list of events beyond those listed here, check www.frommers.com, where you'll find a searchable, up-to-the-minute roster of what's happening in cities all over the world.

JANUARY

Sydney Festival. Highlights of Sydney's visual and performing-arts festival include 75 free events at indoor and outdoor venues—including the Sydney Opera House, Royal Botanic Garden, and Barangaroo Reserve—across the city. The festival involves about 154 events featuring 1,330 artists. Call ✆ **02/8248 6500** or go to www.sydneyfestival.org.au. 3 weeks from early January.

The Australian Open. The Asia/Pacific Grand Slam is played every year at the Melbourne Park National Tennis Centre. Tickets go on sale in October via Ticketek (www.ticketek.com.au; ✆ **1300/888 104** in Australia, or 03/9039 9407). For more info, check out www.ausopen.com. January 20 to February 2, 2020.

Australia Day. This national public holiday marks the landing of the First Fleet of convicts at Sydney Cove in 1788. Every town puts on some kind of celebration; in Sydney, there are ferry races and tall ships on the harbor, food and wine stalls in Hyde Park, open days at museums, and evening fireworks. www.australiaday.com.au. January 26.

FEBRUARY

Sydney Gay & Lesbian Mardi Gras. Two weeks of events, culminating in a spectacular parade of costumed dancers and decorated floats, watched by several hundred thousand onlookers. Contact Sydney Gay & Lesbian Mardi Gras (www.mardigras.org.au; ✆ **02/9383 0900**). Late February/early March.

Perth Festival. This 3-week-long festival covers everything from theater and music to film, visual arts, street art, literature, and free community events, and attracts around 300,000 patrons. It also incorporates the Perth Writers Festival. For more details, contact the festival info center (www.perthfestival.com.au; ✆ **08/6488 5555**). February 7 to March 1, 2020.

MARCH

Adelaide Festival. Australia's largest performing arts festival offering an outstanding array of internationally acclaimed theater, music, dance, and visual arts, and incorporates Adelaide Writers Week, Australia's largest free literary festival, with some of the world's biggest names in attendance. For tickets, call ✆ **131 246** in Australia, or book online at www.adelaidefestival.com.au. First 3 weeks of March.

Formula 1 Australian Grand Prix, Melbourne. The first Grand Prix of the year, on the international FIA Formula 1 World Championship circuit, is battled out on one of its fastest circuits. For tickets, call ✆ **1800/100 030** in Australia, or order online at www.grandprix.com.au. 4 days in second week of March.

Melbourne International Comedy Festival. Venues all over the city participate in this festival of laughs, which attracts top Australian and international talent. For ticketing, go to www.comedyfestival.com.au. Late March/mid-April.

Enlighten Festival. Venues all over Canberra light up with fabulous illuminations, and national attractions open their doors after dark. The festival also includes the **Canberra Balloon Spectacular,** when the morning skies are filled with colorful hot-air balloons. Contact the Canberra Region Visitors Centre (✆ **1300/852 780**) or check out www.enlightencanberra.com. First 3 weeks of March.

APRIL

Anzac Day, nationwide. This is Australia's national day of mourning and remembrance for servicemen and -women who have died in wars and conflicts. Commemorative services are held in even the smallest towns; major cities hold parades for servicemen and -women. Visit www.anzacportal.dva.gov.au for details of services throughout Australia. April 25.

The Sydney-to-Hobart Yacht Race takes place every December.

MAY

Vivid. Sydney's spectacular light festival illuminates some of the city's top locations, including the Sydney Opera House, Sydney Harbour Bridge, Darling Harbour, and Sydney Town Hall, along with other venues around the city. And it's all free. Contact Vivid Sydney (www.vividsydney.com; ℂ **02/9931 1111**). 3 weeks in late May–mid-June.

JUNE

Sydney Film Festival. Premieres of Aussie and international movies take place in the State Theatre and other venues. Contact the Sydney Film Festival (www.sff.org.au; ℂ **02/8220 6600**). 2 weeks in June.

AUGUST

Henley-on-Todd Regatta, Alice Springs. Sounds sophisticated, doesn't it? It's actually a harum-scarum race down the dry bed of the Todd River in homemade "boats," made from anything you care to name—an old 4WD chassis, say, or beer cans lashed together. The only rule is the vessel has to look *vaguely* like a boat. Contact the organizers at ℂ **0417/864 085** (mobile phone) or visit www.henleyontodd.com.au. Third Saturday in August.

Melbourne International Film Festival. About 350 films—new releases, shorts, and avant-garde movies—from 50 countries play at venues around the city (www.miff.com.au; ℂ **03/8660 4888**). 3 weeks in August.

SEPTEMBER

AFL Grand Final. This hugely popular Australian Football League (AFL) rules match in the Melbourne Cricket Ground (MCG) is the country's biggest sporting event—Grand Final Day is so popular, in fact, that it has been declared a public holiday. It's accompanied by a big parade where AFL team players ride Utes (trucks) down the street to much fanfare. For more information, go to www.afl.com.au. Final Saturday in September.

Floriade. A million tulips, daffodils, hyacinths, and other blooms carpet the banks of Canberra's Lake Burley Griffin in stunning themed flower-bed designs, while the city is also alive with entertainment and arts (www.floriadeaustralia.com; ℂ **1300/852 780** in Australia). Mid-September to mid-October.

Melbourne Fringe. The city's streets, pubs, theaters, and restaurants play host to everyone from jugglers and fire-eaters to musicians and indie productions covering all art forms at this festival celebrating independent art. Get the full lineup at https://melbournefringe.com.au or call ✆ **03/9660 9666.** 3 weeks in September.

Brisbane Festival. A highlight of this arts festival is **Riverfire,** a spectacular pyrotechnics display best seen from the riverbank. Attracting some 1 million people annually, the festival program includes music, theater, dance, comedy, opera, circus, and more. For information and tickets, check www.brisbanefestival.com.au. 3 weeks in September.

NOVEMBER

Melbourne Cup. They say the entire nation stops to watch this A$3.5-million horse race. If you're not actually at the track at Flemington in Melbourne, you're glued to the TV—or, well, you're probably not an Australian. It's a public holiday in Melbourne, but all over the country women wear race-day hats to the office and work is abandoned for a late chicken and champagne lunch while the race is run at 3pm. For tickets, contact Ticketek (www.ticketek.com.au; ✆ **132 849** in Australia); for information, visit www.flemington.com.au. First Tuesday in November.

DECEMBER

Woodford Folk Festival. Music and cultural festival that attracts 125,000 people every year to see the weird and the wonderful, hear top musicians and speakers, and revel in the color and splendor of life. It's got a terrific, fun, hippie vibe, in a rural setting about 72km north of Brisbane. Expect more than 2,000 performers in 438 acts at 35 venues. For details and the latest lineup of musicians and more, check out www.woodfordfolkfestival.com or call ✆ **07/5496 1066.** December 27 to January 1.

Sydney Hobart Yacht Race. Find a cliff-top spot near the Heads to watch the glorious show of spinnakers, as 100 or so yachts leave Sydney Harbour for this grueling world-class race to Hobart, Tasmania. The organizer is the Sydney-based Cruising Yacht Club of Australia (www.cyca.com.au; ✆ **02/8292 7800**). Starts December 26.

New Year's Eve, Sydney. Watching the Sydney Harbour Bridge light up with fireworks is a treat. The main show is at 9pm, not midnight, so that young kids don't miss out. Pack a picnic and snag a harborside spot by 4pm, or even earlier at the best vantage point—Mrs. Macquarie's Chair in the Royal Botanic Garden. Go to www.sydneynewyearseve.com for all the details. December 31.

SUGGESTED ITINERARIES

Australia's size and its distance from Northern Hemisphere destinations are the two most daunting things about planning a visit here. A week or two is just enough time to scrape the surface of this vast, complex, and fascinating place. It's a long way to come for just a week, but if that's all you can spare, you still want to see as much as possible. While my inclination is to immerse myself in one spot, I know that not everyone can do that. Seeing as much as possible is often a priority, so here are some ideas on how to do just that.

If you're a first-time visitor, with just 1 or 2 weeks, consider **"Australia in 1 Week"** or **"Australia in 2 Weeks."** These itineraries can be adapted to suit your needs; for example, you could replace the Cairns section of "Australia in 1 Week" with the Uluru/Red Centre suggestions in "Australia in 2 Weeks," flying from Sydney to Uluru.

If you're traveling as a family, the **"Australia for Families"** itinerary is designed to give you some ideas on keeping the young ones occupied (while still being interesting for parents!).

Getting around this continent, where major attractions are thousands of miles apart, can be challenging and time-consuming. Flying is the only way to cover long distances efficiently, but it can also be expensive. Remember to build flying time into your itineraries, and don't try to pack in too much on the days you fly—even domestic flights can be draining, some clocking in at around 3 hours. See "Arriving" and "Getting Around," in chapter 13, for information on air passes and getting the best rates on Australia's domestic carriers.

My best advice: If the pace gets too hectic, just chill out and re-order your sightseeing priorities. Take time to meet the locals and ask their advice on what you should see as well.

Cable Beach, featuring the famous Broome camel ride.

AUSTRALIA IN 1 WEEK

Australia is so vast that in 1 week you'll only be able to get to a small corner of it—perhaps one city or a few of its natural wonders. It will be memorable, nevertheless, and careful planning will maximize your time and allow you to see some of the major sights.

Use the following itinerary to make the most of your week in Australia, but make sure you don't exhaust yourself trying to cram everything in. Australians are a laid-back lot, generally, and in some places the pace is relaxed. And that's just the way to enjoy it. One week provides barely enough time to see the best of Sydney, which for most people is the entry point to Australia.

If you have 1 week and want to head farther afield, there are two main choices, depending on your interests. The **Great Barrier Reef** is a must for divers, but you have to allow time on either side of your reef trip for flying. There are no such problems with Australia's other icon, **Uluru,** in the heart of the **Red Centre.** This triangle of highlights is something of a cliché, but it still gives you a complete Australian experience. Realistically, you will have to choose between the Reef and the Rock, or forego scuba diving while you are in Queensland.

Day 1: Arrive in Sydney ★★★

Check into your hotel and spend whatever time you have upon arrival recovering from the almost-guaranteed jet lag. If you arrive in the morning and have a full day ahead of you, try to stay up. Hit the nearest cafe for a shot of caffeine to keep you going. Head to **Circular Quay,** and from there get a fantastic view of **Sydney Harbour Bridge** ★★★ (p. 90) before strolling to the **Sydney Opera House** ★★★ (p. 92) and soaking up some history at **The Rocks** ★★★. If you have time, take the ferry from Circular Quay to Manly Beach and round off a fairly easy day with fish and chips. Then head to bed for some much-needed sleep.

Day 2: Explore Sydney

Start with a ride to the top of the **Sydney Tower** ★ (p. 97) which stands 309m (984 ft.) above the city. From this vantage point you can experience Sydney's best views and see all its landmarks, including the Sydney Harbour Bridge, the Sydney Opera House, the harbor, and even the Blue Mountains beyond. For an introduction to Australia's wildlife, head to **Taronga Zoo** ★★★ (p. 98) or the **Sydney Aquarium** ★ (p. 95). If you have time to spare, another great choice is **Featherdale Wildlife Park** ★★★ (p. 98), but keep in mind it's about an hour and a half from the city center. If you enjoy museums, put the **Australian Museum** ★★ (p. 96), the **Australian National Maritime Museum** ★★ (p. 94) at Darling Harbour, and the **Museum of Sydney** ★ (p. 96) on your list for the day. For insight into Sydney's beginnings as a convict settlement, visit the **Hyde Park Barracks Museum** ★★ (p. 96), a convict-built prison. Finish off your day with a twilight (or later on weekends) **Bridge-Climb** ★★★ (p. 90) up the Sydney Harbour Bridge.

Sydney's Circular Quay.

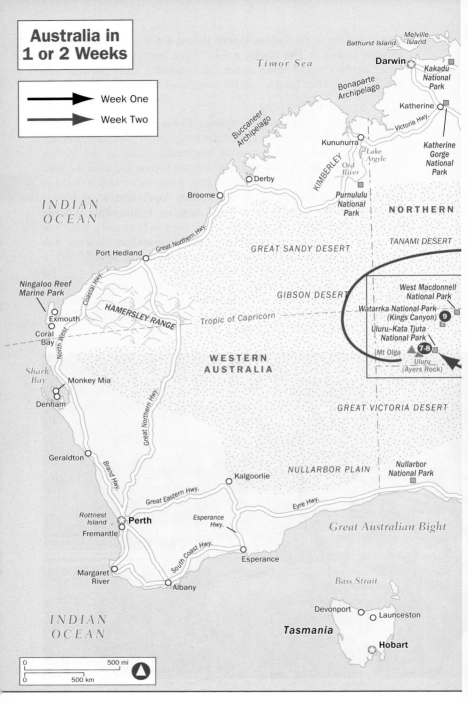

Australia in 1 or 2 Weeks

Week One
Week Two

Timor Sea

Melville Island
Bathurst Island
Darwin
Kakadu National Park
Katherine
Victoria Hwy.
Katherine Gorge National Park

Bonaparte Archipelago

Kununurra
Lake Argyle
Ord River

Buccaneer Archipelago

KIMBERLEY

Derby
Purnululu National Park

Broome

NORTHERN

INDIAN OCEAN

Great Northern Hwy.

Port Hedland

GREAT SANDY DESERT

TANAMI DESERT

Ningaloo Reef Marine Park

Coastal Hwy.

HAMERSLEY RANGE

GIBSON DESERT

West Macdonnell National Park

Watarrka National Park (Kings Canyon) ⑨

Uluru-Kata Tjuta National Park ⑦-⑧

Exmouth
Coral Bay
North West Hwy.

Tropic of Capricorn

WESTERN AUSTRALIA

Mt Olga
Uluru (Ayers Rock)

Shark Bay

Monkey Mia
Denham

Great Northern Hwy.

GREAT VICTORIA DESERT

Geraldton

Brand Hwy.

Kalgoorlie

NULLARBOR PLAIN

Nullarbor National Park

Rottnest Island
Perth
Fremantle

Great Eastern Hwy.

Esperance Hwy.

Eyre Hwy.

Great Australian Bight

Margaret River

South Coast Hwy.

Esperance

Albany

Bass Strait

Tasmania

Devonport
Launceston

Hobart

INDIAN OCEAN

0   500 mi
0   500 km

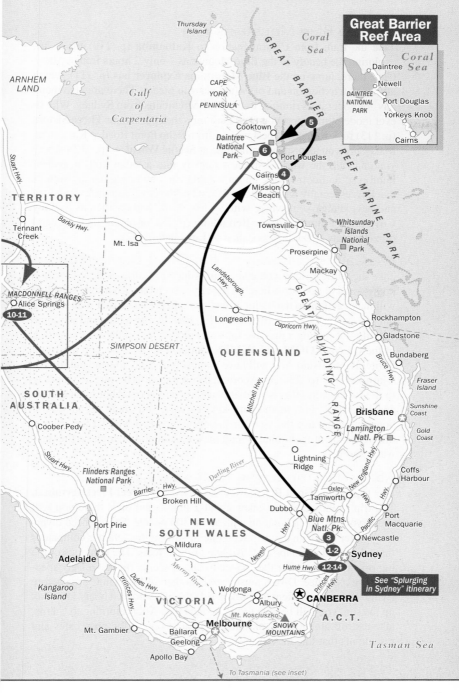

Great Barrier
Reef Area

Coral
Sea

Daintree

Newell

DAINTREE
NATIONAL
PARK

Port Douglas

Yorkeys Knob

Cairns

Thursday
Island

Coral
Sea

GREAT BARRIER

ARNHEM
LAND

Gulf
of
Carpentaria

CAPE
YORK
PENINSULA

Cooktown

Daintree
National
Park

6

Port Douglas

Cairns **4**

Mission
Beach

5

REEF MARINE PARK

TERRITORY

Tennant
Creek

Barkly Hwy.

Mt. Isa

Townsville

Whitsunday
Islands
National
Park

Proserpine

Mackay

Stuart Hwy.

MACDONNELL RANGES

Alice Springs

10-11

SIMPSON DESERT

Longreach

Landsborough Hwy.

Capricorn Hwy.

QUEENSLAND

GREAT DIVIDING RANGE

Rockhampton

Gladstone

Bundaberg

Bruce Hwy.

Fraser
Island

SOUTH
AUSTRALIA

Coober Pedy

Flinders Ranges
National Park

Stuart Hwy.

Barrier Hwy.

Broken Hill

Darling River

Mitchell Hwy.

Lightning
Ridge

Dubbo

Tamworth

Oxley Hwy.

Brisbane

Lamington
Natl. Pk.

Sunshine
Coast

Gold
Coast

New England Hwy.

Coffs
Harbour

Pacific Hwy.

Port
Macquarie

Port Pirie

Adelaide

Mildura

NEW
SOUTH WALES

Murray River

Newell Hwy.

Blue Mtns.
Natl. Pk.

3

1-2

Sydney

Newcastle

Kangaroo
Island

Dukes Hwy.

Princes Hwy.

VICTORIA

Wodonga

Albury

Hume Hwy.

12-14

Mt. Gambier

Ballarat

Geelong

Melbourne

Mt. Kosciuszko

SNOWY
MOUNTAINS

Princes Hwy.

CANBERRA

A.C.T.

See "Splurging
in Sydney" itinerary

Apollo Bay

Tasman Sea

To Tasmania (see inset)

43

Day 3: The Blue Mountains ★★★

Take the train from Central Station to **Katoomba** (p. 110) for a day, exploring the beauty of the Blue Mountains—only 2 hours from Sydney. Once there, jump on the **Blue Mountains Explorer** bus (p. 111), which allows you to hop on and off wherever you please. There are also many day-tour operators running to the Blue Mountains from Sydney. Whichever mode of transport you use, don't miss the spectacular **Three Sisters** (p. 113) rock formation, best viewed from Echo Point Road at Katoomba. Make sure you also spend some time at **Scenic World ★** (p. 112), where you can ride the world's steepest railway into a valley full of ancient rainforest, and come back up on a cable car—among other adventures that kids especially will enjoy. At the end of the day, head back to Sydney and have dinner somewhere with a view of the harbor, such as **Sydney Cove Oyster Bar** (p. 79) or **Bennelong** (p. 78), or one of the new band of restaurants at Barangaroo, such as **Love.fish** (p. 82).

Day 4: Cairns, Gateway to the Great Barrier Reef

Take the earliest flight you can from Sydney to Cairns—flight time is 3 hours—and check into a hotel in the city, which on such a tight schedule will make getting to the major attractions quicker and easier than staying out of town on the northern beaches. Explore the city a little and see some wildlife—including a massive saltwater crocodile—in the bizarre setting of the **Cairns ZOOM and Wildlife Dome ★★** (p. 233), atop the Hotel Sofitel Reef Casino. You will have the rest of the day to head out to visit **Tjapukai ★★** (p. 234), an Aboriginal cultural park. If you are not going to the Red Centre, this is a great place to learn about Aboriginal culture and life, albeit in a theme-park kind of way. You could spend several hours here, or save the visit for the evening, when **Night Fire** offers a different look at traditional ceremonies, including dinner and a fire-and-water show.

Day 5: A Day Trip to the Reef ★★★

Day trips to the Great Barrier Reef leave from the **Reef Fleet Terminal.** The trip to the outer reef takes about 2 hours, and once there you will spend your day on a pontoon with about 300 people. Experienced divers may prefer to take a day trip with one of several dive charter companies that take smaller groups and visit two or three reefs. The pontoons of the big operators also offer the chance to take a scenic flight—a truly spectacular experience. Divers must spend another 24 hours in Cairns before flying. If you are content to snorkel, ride the glass-bottom boats, and soak up the sun, you will be able to fly the next day. After returning to Cairns, take a stroll along the **Esplanade** and eat at one of the busy cafes and restaurants that line the strip.

FACING PAGE: Crawling koala at Featherdale Wildlife Park in the Blue Mountains.

Tjapukai offers enthralling Aboriginal experiences.

Day 6: Kuranda, a Rainforest Village ★★

Waiting out the day after diving (you can't fly for 24 hours after you've been on a dive) gives you a chance to discover another aspect of Australia— its rainforests. Take a trip to the mountain village of **Kuranda** aboard the steam train along the **Kuranda Scenic Railway** ★★★ (p. 241), past water-falls and gorges. In Kuranda, explore the markets and the nature parks and maybe take a **Kuranda Riverboat Tour** ★★ (p. 243), which runs about 45 minutes. Return on the **Skyrail** ★★★ cableway (p. 233), which carries you over the rainforest (you can get to ground level at a couple of stations on the way) to the edge of Cairns. The views are sensational. This is a big day out!

Day 7: Cairns to Sydney

In the morning, head to the airport for your flight to Sydney. Unless you are lucky enough to have an international flight directly out of Cairns, you will spend most of your last day in Australia returning to Sydney. With the time you have left in Sydney, treat yourself to dinner at a res-taurant overlooking the harbor, with its bridge and the Opera House illuminated. It's a sight you'll carry home with you.

AUSTRALIA IN 2 WEEKS

With 2 weeks, your visit to Australia will be much more relaxed and you'll get a greater sense of the diversity of Australia's landscape, wildlife, and people. You will be able to explore the country's trio of icons—Sydney, the Great

Barrier Reef, and Uluru—in more depth, and maybe even have time to go outside those areas, especially if you limit your icons to two instead of three.

Days 1–6: Sydney to Cairns

Follow the itinerary as outlined in "Australia in 1 Week," above.

Day 7: Cairns to Uluru

Leave Cairns as early as you can. Your flight to Ayers Rock Airport will take around 3 hours. Make sure you book a direct flight, not one that goes via Sydney! Try to get a window seat for the spectacular views as you fly over the Outback. If you take the early flight, you can be in **Uluru** by around 10am, which gives you the entire day to soak in the enormity of this fabulous monolith. Take the shuttle from **Ayers Rock Resort** (the only place to stay, albeit one with many accommodation choices; p. 325) to the Rock. Spend some time in the impressive and interesting **Uluru–Kata Tjuta Cultural Centre** (p. 321), near the base of Uluru, and explore the area on one of the many walking trails or tours. End the day by watching the sun set over Uluru—an unforgettable sight. After doing all that in a day, you'll be ready for a quiet dinner at whatever hotel you've chosen.

Taking a walk around Uluru-Kata Tjuta National Park.

Day 8: Exploring Uluru ★★★

Sunrise is one of those magical times at Uluru, so make the effort to get up early. This is also a great time to do the 10.6km (6½-mile) **Base Walk** circumnavigating Uluru (p. 330), which takes 2 to 3 hours. There are many ways to experience Uluru, including camel rides, Harley-Davidson tours, and helicopter joy flights, but walking up close to the Rock beats them all.

You will also have time today to head to **Kata Tjuta** (also called "The Olgas"; p. 332), where you'll see there's much more to the Red Centre than just one rock. Kata Tjuta is about 48km (30 miles) west of Uluru, but plenty of tour operators go there if you don't have your own wheels.

End your day in the desert with the **Sounds of Silence** dinner or the slightly more upmarket, more intimate **Tali Wiru** ★★★ dinner (p. 328), run by Ayers Rock Resort. Sip champagne as the sun sets over Uluru to the eerie music of the didgeridoo, and then tuck into kangaroo, barramundi, and other native foods. But it's not the food you're here for—it's the silence and the stars. Package it with a visit to the incredible **Field of Light,** to walk through an amazing art installation of 50,000 stems of light.

Day 9: Uluru to Kings Canyon

Hire a four-wheel-drive vehicle and tackle the long Outback drive from Uluru to Alice Springs, stopping for a night at **Kings Canyon Resort** (www.kingscanyonresort.com.au). It is 306km (190 miles) from Uluru to Kings Canyon (also known as **Watarrka National Park**), which offers another unbeatable look at Outback Australia. You can spend the afternoon walking up the side of the canyon and around the rim. Parts of it are very steep, and the whole hike will take you around 4 hours, but the trip is well worth the effort. A gentler walk is the short and shady canyon floor walk.

Day 10: Kings Canyon to Alice Springs

Get an early start for Alice Springs, and take the unpaved but interesting **Mereenie Loop Road,** which threads through the **Glen Helen Gorge** or the historic **Hermannsburg** mission settlement (p. 319). Whichever road you take, the scenery is like nowhere else. You will probably spend most of the day driving to Alice, making a few stops along the way.

On arrival, check into a hotel and head out to one of the local restaurants, several of which offer sophisticated versions of "bush tucker," including kangaroo, emu, and crocodile dishes.

Day 11: Alice Springs

If you can stand another early start, take a **dawn balloon flight** over the desert (p. 316), usually followed by a champagne breakfast. If you don't head back to bed immediately for a few hours of catch-up sleep, there are plenty of attractions to discover, including the **Alice Springs Desert Park** ★★★ (p. 313) for a look at some unusual Australian creatures;

Hiking in Kings Canyon/Watarrka National Park.

the **School of the Air** ★★ (p. 315); and the **Royal Flying Doctor Service** ★★ base (p. 315). In the afternoon, drop into the **Mbantua Fine Art Gallery and Cultural Museum** (p. 317) to see some of the best Aboriginal art from the outlying communities in the desert region called Utopia, famed for its paintings. Alternatively, visit the **Alice Springs Telegraph Station Historical Reserve** ★★ (p. 314), set in an oasis just outside town, for a look at early settler life. Finish the day with a **sunset camel ride** (p. 331) down the dry Todd River bed, and have dinner at the camel farm.

Day 12: Alice Springs to Sydney

Direct flights from Alice Springs to Sydney leave in the early afternoon, so you'll have all morning to explore more of the town and perhaps buy some Aboriginal art. (This is one of the best places to get it.)

On arrival in Sydney, after an almost 3-hour flight, check into your hotel and spend the evening discovering the city's nightlife.

Day 13: A Day at Bondi Beach

For sands of a different hue from those you've experienced in recent days, take the bus to Sydney's most famous beach, **Bondi** (p. 55), and spend the day lazing on the sand or—in summer, at least—taking a dip in the surf. Get there via public bus or the Bondi Explorer from Circular Quay, which gives you a choice of harborside bays and coastal beaches. The scenic cliff-top walk to **Bronte Beach** is recommended, or you can continue farther to **Coogee.**

Day 14: Sydney

Your final day in Australia can be spent on last-minute shopping and seeing those Sydney sights that you haven't yet had time for. Cap it all off with a seafood dinner somewhere with a fantastic view of the Harbour Bridge.

AUSTRALIA FOR FAMILIES

Australia is a wonderful destination for kids—and not just because of the kangaroos and koalas. Our suggestion is to explore Sydney for 2 days with family in tow, then head up to the beautiful Blue Mountains on a day trip to ride the cable car and the world's steepest railway. The climax comes with a few days of exploring the Barrier Reef and the rainforest around Port Douglas.

Days 1 & 2: Sydney

First off, head to Circular Quay to see the **Sydney Opera House** ★★★. A tour inside might be a bit much for younger kids, but you can walk around a fair bit of it and take the obligatory photos of Australia's most famous landmark. To stretch your legs, head from here into the **Royal Botanic Garden** (p. 105) to spot long-beaked ibises wandering around

Sharks at SEA LIFE Sydney Aquarium.

The Scenic World Railway descends through a forest of ancient tree ferns in the Blue Mountains.

the grass and hundreds of fruit bats squabbling among the treetops. Walk back past the Opera House and the ferries to **The Rocks,** where you can take a quick stroll through the historic streets, stopping for a look at some of the trendy shops or the market on Saturdays.

There are plenty of places to eat lunch at Circular Quay, where you can sit outside and watch the world go by. After lunch, take a ferry to **Taronga Zoo ★★★**, where a cable car zips you up the hill to the main entrance. All the kids' favorite animals are here, from kangaroos and koalas to platypuses, located in a nocturnal house. A farmyard section edges onto a playground, with lots of water features to give your kids a cool sprinkle on a hot day.

On **Day 2,** head to the city center for an elevator ride up to the top of **Sydney Tower ★** (p. 97), where you can look right across Sydney as far as the Blue Mountains in the distance. Entry includes admission to the 4-D Cinema Experience. It's a short walk from here to Darling Harbour, where you can cap off the morning with a visit to **SEA LIFE Sydney Aquarium ★**. The sharks that swim right above your head are huge, but the penguins are hard to beat for cuteness.

Eat lunch at one of the many cheap eateries at Darling Harbour before taking the ferry from near the Aquarium back to Circular Quay.

If it's a hot day, or you simply want to hit the beach, you have two choices: From Circular Quay, you can take a half-hour ferry ride or a 15-minute high-speed JetCat trip to **Manly** (p. 102). Here you can laze the afternoon away and even rent a surfboard or bodyboard. Or hop a bus to **Bondi Beach** (p. 76), where you can reward your efforts with gelato or a late-afternoon pizza from **Pompei's** (p. 85).

Day 3: The Blue Mountains

You could easily spend a couple more days with the kids having fun in Sydney, but you shouldn't miss a trip to the mountains. If you go, prepare for a long day; pack plenty of snacks and a few favorite toys. Several companies run tour buses to the area, stopping off at an animal park along the way. The best one to visit is **Featherdale Wildlife Park ★★★** (p. 98), where you can get up close to more kangaroos, koalas, and Tasmanian devils. The tour also stops at **Scenic World ★** (p. 112), where you can take the short ride on the Scenic Railway. It's very steep, so hold on tight. At the bottom, you'll find yourselves among an ancient tree fern forest—it's truly remarkable. A short walk takes you to the **Skyway,** a cable car that travels 300m (984 ft.) above the Jamison Valley.

Elsewhere in the mountains, there are fabulous views across craggy bluffs and deep bowls of gum trees. See chapter 4 for details.

Days 4, 5 & 6: The Reef & the Rainforest

Now it's time to head north to the Tropics. You'll need to fly, of course; otherwise it would take you several days to drive up the coast. The flight from Sydney to Cairns takes 3 hours. As a family, you might prefer to

Swimming hole at Mossman Gorge.

Yirrganydji Aboriginal men play traditional music on didgeridoo during Aboriginal culture show in Queensland.

base yourselves in **Port Douglas** (p. 244) rather than Cairns—the Port Douglas beach is huge and uncrowded, and some of the best Barrier Reef trips originate from here. "Port," as the locals call it, is about an hour's drive from Cairns, so your first day will be largely taken with getting there.

After all that traveling, take the rest of the day to relax on beautiful **Four Mile Beach,** but remember to swim inside the nets off the sand; the "stingers" (box jellyfish) around here can cause life-threatening stings, especially where kids are concerned.

On **Day 5,** it's time to visit the **Reef.** Thankfully, the dangerous jelly-fish are very uncommon on the Reef itself. Cruise boats take around 90 minutes to get from Port Douglas to the outer reef; but once there, you are in for some amazing snorkeling. Expect to see numerous species of corals and fish, and even an occasional turtle. A good seafood lunch is generally served on board, so you won't go hungry!

Day 6 will be another nature experience, this time meeting some of the giants of the north. In the morning, head out to **Mossman Gorge** ★★★ (p. 248), a 15- to 20-minute drive from Port Douglas, for some Aboriginal culture in the rainforest with **Ngadiku Dreamtime Walks,** guided by a member of the local Kuku-Yalanji tribe. On your way back to Cairns, stop off at **Hartley's Crocodile Adventures** ★★★ (p. 235) to see crocs in their natural habitat. After the 3pm "croc attack" show, you'll have time for a leisurely drive back to Cairns to get ready for your departure. See chapter 8 for detailed information on these attractions.

The Palais Theatre and famed Luna Park.

Day 7: Fly Back to Sydney

If you have time to kill before you leave Sydney, take the kids by ferry to **Luna Park** ★, just across from Circular Quay, or walk there across the Harbour Bridge. Although this fun park is small, with few rides suitable for younger kids, it does boast a magnificent view across to the Harbour Bridge and Opera House, which look glorious after the sun's gone down.

SYDNEY

Warm-natured, sun-kissed, and naturally good-looking, Sydney is rather like its lucky residents. Situated on one of the world's most striking harbors, where the twin icons of the Sydney Opera House and Harbour Bridge steal the limelight, relaxed Sydney is surprisingly close to nature. Within minutes you can be riding the waves on Bondi Beach, bushwalking in Manly, or gazing out across Botany Bay, where the first salt-encrusted Europeans arrived in the 18th century. You can understand why they never wanted to leave.

4

For that "I'm in Sydney!" feeling, nothing beats the first glimpse of the white-sailed Opera House and the iconic Harbour Bridge, which you can climb for a bird's-eye view of the sparkling harbor. Move on to the Royal Botanical Garden's tropical greenery and the Museum of Contemporary Art's cutting-edge exhibitions. With 70 beaches close by—from the fizzing surf of famous Bondi Beach to Manly's coastal walks and pine-flanked bays—it's no wonder Sydneysiders look so bronzed and relaxed.

Don't let the knockout views of Sydney Harbour distract you from your shopping in The Rocks' specialty shops and galleries, or under the soaring glass arches of the Queen Victoria Building. You can also dine on a different cuisine every night in multicultural Sydney—whether late-night noodles in Chinatown, tasty tapas in the Spanish Quarter, or authentic Thai curries on bohemian King Street. BYO restaurants and sensible prices make eating out affordable in all but the very top places—French-Japanese Tetsuya's, for instance. Head to Circular Quay's sleek waterfront restaurants for the Opera House view and Australia's distinctive modern cuisine—a fusion of Australian, Mediterranean, and spicy Asian flavors.

There's so much to do in Sydney that you could easily spend a week here and still not see it all.

ESSENTIALS

Arriving

BY PLANE

Sydney International Airport (SYD; www.sydneyairport.com. au) is Australia's largest and busiest airport, used by more than 40 international airlines. Free shuttle buses and the Airport Link train link the international and domestic terminals. The train costs A$6.40 one-way. The bus journey takes up to 10 minutes, the train 2 minutes. Buses run every 30 minutes from 6am to 9pm (more often in the morning peak period); the train is more frequent, and runs from 5am to midnight. Bus stops are on arrivals levels at both terminals. **Qantas** and **Virgin Australia** offer seamless transfer services.

In both terminals, you'll find luggage carts, wheelchairs, a post office (daily 6:15am–8pm), mailboxes, currency exchange, duty-free shops, restaurants, bars, stores, showers, luggage lockers, a baggage-hold service for larger items, ATMs, and tourist-information desks. You can rent mobile phones in the international terminal. **Smarte Carte** (at the southern end of the arrivals level) has luggage storage for A$14 a day for a small bag and A$17 for a suitcase or backpack. Luggage trolleys are free to use in the international arrival terminal but cost A$4 outside departure terminals (you'll need coins).

Between the Airport and the City Center
The airport is 8km (5 miles) from the city center. **Airport Link** (www.airport link.com.au) trains connect both terminals to the city stations of Central, Museum, St. James, Circular Quay, Wynyard, and Town Hall. You'll need to change trains for other Sydney stations. Unfortunately, the line has no dedicated luggage areas, and because it's also a commuter train to the city from

The iconic Sydney Opera House.

Taxi Savvy

Taxi queues can be long, and drivers may try to cash in by insisting you share a cab with other passengers in line at the airport. Here's the scam: After dropping off the other passengers, the cab driver will attempt to charge you the full price of the journey, despite the fact that the other passengers paid for their sections. You certainly won't save any money sharing a cab if this happens, and your journey will be a long one. If you are first in line in the taxi stand, the law states that you can refuse to share the cab. Taxi drivers appreciate a tip, but there is no compulsion to do so. If you've had good service, a 10% tip is enough.

A taxi from the airport to the city center costs about A$55. An expressway, the Eastern Distributor, is the fastest way to reach the city from the airport. There's an A$8 toll (the taxi driver pays the toll and adds the cost to your fare), but there is no toll on the road heading back to the airport. A 10% credit-card charge applies, and the Sydney airport charges a A$4.25 fee to catch a taxi from there. An **Uber** ride is a better deal, costing around A$43 from the international terminal to the city center.

the suburbs, it gets very crowded during rush hours (around 7–9am and 4–6:30pm). If you have lots of luggage, it's probably best to take a taxi. The train takes 10 minutes to reach the Central Railway Station. Trains leave every 10 minutes and cost A$19 one-way for adults and A$15 for children from the international terminal. Round-trip tickets are available only if you want to return to the airport on the same day.

KST Airporter coaches (www.kst.com.au; ☎ **02/9666 9988**) travel to the city center from bus stops outside the terminals every 15 minutes. This service will drop you off (and pick you up) at hotels in the city, Kings Cross, and Darling Harbour. Pickups from hotels require at least 3 hours' advance notice; you can book online. One-way tickets cost A$18 adults and A$12 children 4–10; round-trip tickets cost A$32 adults and A$20 children.

BY TRAIN

Central Station (☎ **131 500** for Sydney Trains, or 132 232 for NSW Train-Link interstate trains) is the main city and interstate train station. It's at the top of George Street in downtown Sydney. All interstate trains arrive here, and it's a major Sydney Trains hub. Many city buses leave from neighboring Railway Square for such places as Town Hall and Circular Quay.

BY BUS

Greyhound coaches (☎ **02/9212 9505**) operate from the Central Station Coach Terminal at the Western Forecourt of the station (Bays 5 and 6, up the escalators from Eddy Ave.).

BY CRUISE SHIP

Ships dock at the **Overseas Passenger Terminal** in The Rocks, opposite the Sydney Opera House, or the **White Bay Cruise Terminal** in the suburb of Rozelle, about 5km (3 miles) from the city center.

BY CAR

Drivers enter Sydney from the north on the Pacific Highway, from the south on the M5 and Princes Highway, and from the west on the Great Western Highway.

Visitor Information

The Sydney Visitor Centre, corner of Argyle and Playfair streets, The Rocks (www.australianvisitorcentres.com.au; © **02/8273 0000**), is a good place to pick up maps, brochures, Youth Hostel Association (YHA) cards, and general tourist information. It is open from 9:30am to 5:30pm daily (closed Good Friday and Christmas Day). In Manly, find the **Hello Manly Booking and Information Centre** (www.hellomanly.com.au; © **02/9976 1430**) at Manly Wharf (where the ferries come in). It's open Monday to Friday from 9am to 5pm; on weekends and public holidays, it's open 10am to 4pm. It's closed Christmas Day and Good Friday.

City of Sydney information kiosks are at four locations, providing maps, brochures, and advice. The main one is at Customs House, 31 Alfred St. (Mon–Fri 9am–8pm, Sat 10am–5pm, and Sun 11am–5pm). Others are at Haymarket, corner of Goulburn and Dixon sts. (daily 11am–7pm) and Kings Cross, corner of Darlinghurst Rd. and Springfield Ave. (daily 9am–5pm). A kiosk at Circular Quay (corner of Loftus and Alfred sts.) is open on Saturday 9 to 10am and Sunday 9 to 11am. All kiosks are closed Christmas Day.

A good website for events, entertainment, dining, and shopping is **www.sydney.com**.

City Layout

Sydney is one of the largest cities in the world, covering more than 1,730 sq. km (675 sq. miles) from the sea to the foothills of the Blue Mountains. Thankfully, the city center, or Central Business District (CBD), is compact. The jewel in Sydney's crown is its magnificent harbor, which empties into the South Pacific Ocean through headlands known as North Head and South Head. On the southern side of the harbor are the high-rises of the city center; the Sydney Opera House; a string of beaches, including Bondi; and the inner suburbs. Next to Circular Quay and across Sydney Cove from the Opera House is The Rocks, a cluster of small streets that was once part of a historic slum—it's now a tourist attraction. The Sydney Harbour Bridge and a tunnel connect the city center to the high-rises of the North Sydney business district and the affluent suburbs and beaches beyond.

MAIN ARTERIES & STREETS

The city's main thoroughfare, George Street, runs up from **Circular Quay,** past Wynyard train station and Town Hall, to Central Station. From Circular Quay to The Rocks, it's a 5- to 10-minute stroll; to Wynyard a 10-minute walk; and to Town Hall a 20-minute stroll. At the time of this writing, George Street was undergoing construction work as a new light-rail system, due to be completed in mid-2020, is being built. Other main streets running parallel to

George include Pitt, Elizabeth, and Macquarie streets. **Macquarie Street** runs up from the Sydney Opera House, past the Royal Botanic Garden and Hyde Park. **Martin Place** is a pedestrian thoroughfare between Macquarie and George streets, about halfway between Circular Quay and Town Hall—in the heart of the city center. The easy-to-spot Sydney Tower, facing onto pedestrian-only **Pitt Street Mall** on Pitt Street, is the main city-center landmark. Roads meet at **Town Hall** from Kings Cross to the east and Darling Harbour to the west. From Town Hall to the near side of Darling Harbour it's about a 10-minute walk.

Sydney Neighborhoods in Brief

SOUTH OF SYDNEY HARBOUR

Circular Quay Tucked between the Harbour Bridge and the Sydney Opera House, this transport hub for ferries, buses, and trains is a good spot for a stroll, with outdoor restaurants and street performers. The Rocks, the Royal Botanic Garden, the Contemporary Art Museum, and the main shopping area (centered on Pitt and George sts.) are a short walk from here.

The Rocks This small historic area, a short stroll west of Circular Quay, is packed with colonial stone buildings, intriguing back streets, boutiques, pubs, tourist shops, restaurants, and hotels. It's the most exclusive place to stay in the city, with stores geared toward Sydney's yuppies and wealthy tourists. On weekends, a portion of George Street becomes The Rocks Market, selling souvenirs and crafts. There's a food market on Fridays. Check out www.therocks.com for event info.

Town Hall In the heart of the city, this area is home to the main department stores and two Sydney landmarks, the Town Hall and the Queen Victoria Building (QVB) shopping arcade. Nearby are Sydney Tower and the stores of Pitt Street Mall. Farther up George Street you'll find Sydney's Spanish district (enter at Liverpool St.) and Chinatown.

Darling Harbour Designed as a tourist precinct, Darling Harbour features Sydney's main convention, exhibition, and entertainment centers; a waterfront promenade; the Sydney Aquarium; an IMAX theater; the Australian Maritime Museum; the Powerhouse Museum; The Star casino; a food court; and plenty of shops. Nearby are the restaurants of Cockle Bay and King Street Wharf. To reach Darling Harbour, take a ferry from Circular Quay (Wharf 5) or the light rail from Central Station. Check out www.darlingharbour.com.

Kings Cross & the Suburbs Beyond "The Cross" is the city's red-light district—and also home to some of Sydney's best-known nightclubs and restaurants, along with backpacker hostels and some upscale hotels. The colorful main drag, Darlinghurst Road, is crammed with strip joints, prostitutes, and drunks—there's a heavy police presence and usually plenty of "ordinary" people around, but do take care. Beyond the Cross lie the waterfront neighborhoods of Elizabeth Bay, Double Bay, and Rose Bay (take train to the Edgecliff stop).

Paddington/Oxford Street This central-city neighborhood, centered on trendy Oxford Street, is known for its terrace houses, off-the-wall boutiques and bookshops, restaurants, pubs, and nightclubs. It's also the heart of Sydney's large gay community and has lots of gay bars and dance spots. Take bus nos. 333, 380, or 397 from Circular Quay; no. 440 from Central Station; or nos. 333, 378, or 380 from Bondi Junction; or the train to Museum Station.

Darlinghurst Between grungy Kings Cross and upscale Oxford Street, this grimy, terraced area is home to some of Sydney's best cafes—though it's probably not wise to wander around here at night alone. Take the train to Kings Cross and head right from the exit.

Central The congested, polluted streets around Central Station have little to attract visitors beyond train and bus connections. The Sydney Central YHA (youth hostel) is here.

Glebe Young professionals and students come to this central-city neighborhood for the cafes, restaurants, pubs, and shops along the main thoroughfare, Glebe Point Road. It's a good place for budget-conscious travelers, only 15 minutes from the city. Take the light rail from Central Station or Darling Harbour.

Bondi & the Southern Beaches Some of Sydney's most glamorous surf beaches—Bondi, Bronte, and Coogee—lie along the South Pacific coast, southeast of the city center. Bondi has a wide sweep of beach (crowded in summer), some interesting restaurants and bars, and plenty of attitude—but no train station. It's a 40-minute bus ride (bus no. 333) from Circular Quay. (Buy tickets in advance at a newsstand or 7-Eleven store.) Bus no. 440 goes to Bronte from Railway Square; bus no. 373 travels to Coogee from Circular Quay.

Watsons Bay Known for a section of dramatic sea cliffs called The Gap, Watsons Bay has several good restaurants and a nice beer

garden. It's a terrific spot to spend a sunny afternoon. Take bus no. 324 from Circular Quay, or a ferry from Wharf 4.

NORTH OF SYDNEY HARBOUR

North Sydney You can see the giant clown face of Luna Park from Circular Quay, but North Sydney—across the Harbour Bridge—has little in the way of tourist attractions. It's mostly a business area. Chatswood (take train from Central or Wynyard station) has some good suburban-type shopping.

The North Shore Across the Harbour Bridge, gorgeous Balmoral Beach, Taronga Zoo, and upscale boutiques are the attractions in Mosman. Take a ferry from Circular Quay (Wharf 2) to Taronga Zoo (10 min.) and a bus to Balmoral Beach (another 10 min.).

Manly Half an hour from Circular Quay by ferry, Manly is famous for its ocean beach and scores of cheap food outlets.

WEST OF THE CITY CENTER

Balmain Once Sydney's main shipbuilding area, in the last few decades Balmain has become trendy and expensive, with lots of restaurants and pubs. There's a popular Saturday market at the local church. Take bus nos. 441 or 442 from Town Hall or a ferry from Circular Quay.

Getting Around Sydney

State Transit operates the city's buses and ferry network; **Sydney Trains** runs the urban and suburban trains; and **Sydney Ferries** runs the public passenger ferries. Some private bus lines operate buses in the outer suburbs. In addition, a light-rail line runs between Central Station and Wentworth Park in Pyrmont; an expansion is in the works and slated for completion in mid-2020.

Infoline (www.transportnsw.info; © **131 500**) is a one-stop search engine for bus, train, light rail, and ferry timetables. Public transit fares are subject to change, so the prices below should act only as a guide.

BY PUBLIC BUS

Buses are frequent and reliable and cover a wide area of metropolitan Sydney. For regular public buses, the minimum fare (which covers most short hops in the city) is A$2.80 for a 3km (1.8-mile) "section." The farther you go, the cheaper each section. For example, the 44km (27-mile) trip to Palm Beach, way past Manly, costs A$5.80. Sections are marked on bus-stand signs, but if you're confused or in doubt, ask the bus driver.

SYDNEY

Sydney Neighborhoods in Brief

4

Most buses bound for the northern suburbs, including night buses to Manly and the bus to Taronga Zoo, leave from Wynyard Park on Carrington Street, behind the Wynyard train station on George Street. Buses to the southern beaches, such as Bondi and Bronte, and the western and eastern suburbs leave from Circular Quay. Buses to Balmain leave from behind the QVB.

Buses run from 4:30am to around midnight during the week, less frequently on weekends and holidays. Some night buses to outer suburbs run throughout the night. You can buy single tickets onboard from the driver, if you don't have an Opal Card (see below).

BY SIGHTSEEING BUS

Bright red open-top **Big Bus Sydney** buses (www.theaustralianexplorer.com. au; ℂ **02/9567 8400**) operate daily on two routes, around Sydney city and around Bondi Beach. The city circuit takes in 23 places of interest, including the Sydney Opera House, the Royal Botanic Garden, the State Library, Mrs. Macquarie's Chair, the Art Gallery of New South Wales, Kings Cross, Elizabeth Bay House, the QVB, Sydney Tower, the Australian Museum, Chinatown, Darling Harbour, and The Rocks. Bus stops are identified by a distinctive red sign. The interval between services is about 15 to 20 minutes, and you can board the bus at any stop on the route. The first departure from Alfred Street (near the corner of Pitt St.) at Circular Quay is at 8:30am, and the last service returns you to Circular Quay at 7:30pm.

An open-top Sydney Explorer sightseeing bus on George Street, the city's main drag.

The Bondi route travels a 30km (19-mile) circuit around the eastern harbor-side bays and coastal beaches. The 10 stops along the way include Chinatown, Sydney Tower, Double Bay, Rose Bay, Bondi Beach, North Bondi, and Paddington's Oxford Street. The interval between the hop-on, hop-off services is around 30 minutes. The first departure is from Central Station (Stop A on Pitt St., bus bay 18) at 9:30am. Tickets, which allow you to do both the Sydney and Bondi tours, cost A$58 for adults, A$40 for children 5 to 16, and A$156 for a family of four for 24 hours; or A$75 adults, A$50 children, and A$200 families for 48 hours. If you stay on the bus, the full circuit of each tour will take around 90 minutes. When planning your itinerary, remember that some attractions, such as museums, close at 5pm. Buy tickets on board the bus.

BY FERRY

The best way to get a taste of a city that revolves around its harbor is to jump aboard a ferry. The main ferry terminal is at Circular Quay. For ferry information, call *C* **131 500,** check out **www.transportnsw.info**, or visit the ferry information office opposite Wharf 4. One-way trips within the inner harbor (virtually everywhere except Manly) cost A$7.40 for adults and A$3.50 for children ages 4 to 15. Kids 3 and under travel free.

The ferry to Manly takes 30 minutes, and one-way tickets cost A$9.20 for adults and A$4.60 for children. It leaves from Wharf 3. Ferries run from 6am to midnight. You can also use your Opal Card on the privately run **Manly Fast Ferry** (www.manlyfastferry.com.au; *C* **02/9583 1199**) which departs from Wharf 2 at Circular Quay. Tickets cost around A$19 adults and A$11 kids, round-trip, depending on the time of day. Ferries operate regularly between around 6am and 9pm, depending on the day of the week, and the journey takes around 20 minutes. Fast Ferry also offers sightseeing tours including a Harbour Beaches ferry (Sat and Sun only) that goes from Manly to Watsons Bay and Rose Bay, for A$15 adults, A$10 children 4 to 15.

BY TRAIN

Sydney's publicly owned train system is a good news/bad news way to get around. The good news is that it can be a cheap and relatively efficient way to see the city; the bad news is that the system is limited. Many tourist

Travel with an Opal Card

An electronic ticketing system, the **Opal Card** (www.opal.com.au, *C* **02/136 725**) is used for trains, buses, ferries, and light rail. While you can buy single tickets, these still use an electronic Opal Card. It is much cheaper to travel with an Opal Card. Buy your card at train stations, or from convenience stores, newsagents, and other shops (listed online).

There is no charge for the card, but you must pay a minimum value of A$10 for an adult card (or A$5 for a child's card). Then you top up the payment as needed at authorized retailers, train stations, online, by phone, or via the Opal app. On Sundays your card allows all-day travel for a maximum of A$2.70.

The best—and cheapest—way to see Sydney Harbour is from the deck of a passenger ferry.

areas—including Manly, Bondi Beach, and Darling Harbour—are not connected to the network. Though trains tend to run regularly, the timetable is unreliable. And many carriages aren't air-conditioned, so it can be really hot in summer.

Single tickets within the city center cost A$4.40 adults and A$2.20 children. Round-trip tickets cost twice as much. Weekly tickets are also available. Information is available from **Infoline** (www.transportnsw.info; or © **131 500** in Australia).

BY METRO LIGHT RAIL

A system of trams runs on a 3.6km (2¼-mile) route between Central Station and Wentworth Park in Pyrmont. The route is currently being extended to a 12km (7½-mile) network that will have 19 stops, running from Circular Quay along George Street to Central Station, through Surry Hills to Moore Park, then to Kensington and Kingsford and Randwick. The new services are expected to start running in mid-2020; see www.sydneylightrail.transport. nsw.gov.au for updates. The current light-rail line provides good access to Chinatown, Paddy's Markets, Darling Harbour, The Star casino and entertainment complex, and the Sydney Fish Markets; and from Pyrmont to inner-west suburbs such as Glebe and Leichhardt. Trams run every 10 minutes. The one-way fare is A$2.80 to A$4.40 for adults and A$1.40 to A$2.20 for kids 4 to 15, depending on the distance. You will need to buy an Opal Card (p. 62), even for a single trip. Round-trip tickets are available. Call © **131 500** or check out www.transportnsw.info for details.

BY TAXI

Several taxi companies serve the city center and suburbs. All journeys are metered. If you cross either way on the Harbour Bridge or through the Harbour Tunnel, it will cost a few extra dollars (depending on the time of day). An extra 10% will be added if you pay by credit card.

In the city, taxis line up at stands such as those opposite Circular Quay and Central Station. They are also frequently found in front of hotels. A yellow light on top of the cab means it's vacant. Cabs can be hard to come by on Friday and Saturday nights and between 2 and 3pm every day, when cabbies are changing shifts after 12 hours on the road. Passengers must wear seatbelts in the front and back seats. Taxis are licensed to carry up to four people. The **Taxi Complaints Hotline** (℅ **1800/648 478** in Australia) deals with problem taxi drivers.

The main taxi companies are **Taxis Combined Services** (www.taxiscombined.com.au; ℅ **133 300**), **Silver Service Fleet** (www.silverservice.com.au; ℅ **133 100**), **RSL Cabs** (www.rslcabs.com.au; ℅ **02/9581 1111**), **Legion Cabs** (www.legioncabs.com.au; ℅ **131 451**), **Premier Cabs** (www.premiercabs.com.au; ℅ **131 017**), and **St. George Cabs** (www.stgeorgecabs.com.au; ℅ **132 166**). **Uber** also operates in Sydney.

BY WATER TAXI

Water taxis operate 24 hours a day and are a quick, convenient way to get to waterfront restaurants, harbor attractions, and some suburbs. They can also be chartered for private cruises. Fares for a direct transfer are based on an initial flag-fall for the hire of the vessel and then a charge per person traveling. A 60-minute jaunt on Sydney Harbour costs A$25 adults, A$20 children 15 and under. On most transfers, the more people traveling, the lower the fare per person. The main operators are **Yellow Water Taxis** (www.yellowwatertaxis.com.au; ℅ **1800/326 822** in Australia) and **Water Taxis Combined** (www.watertaxis.com.au; ℅ **02/9555 8888**).

BY CAR

Traffic restrictions, parking, and congestion can make getting around by car frustrating, but if you plan to visit some of the outer suburbs or take excursions elsewhere in New South Wales, renting a car will give you more flexibility. The **National Roads and Motorists' Association (NRMA)** is the New South Wales auto club; for emergency breakdown service call ℅ **131 111.**

Tolls apply for some roads, including the Cross City Tunnel and Sydney Harbour Bridge; increasingly you must go through automatic toll booths using a prepaid electronic tag called an **E-Tag.** If you are renting a car, you may be provided with an E-Tag, but make sure to ask about how you pay. Drivers without E-Tags have 2 days to pay; call the **Roads and Traffic Authority** at ℅ **131 865** within 2 days for details on your payment options.

Car-rental agencies in Sydney include **Avis** (www.avis.com.au) and **Budget** (www.budget.com.au)—both at 395 Pitt St. and sharing the same phone number (℅ **02/8255 1616**); **Europcar,** 818 George St. (www.europcar.com.au;

02/8255 9050); **Hertz,** corner of William and Riley streets, Kings Cross (www.hertz.com.au; © **02/9360 6621**); and **Thrifty,** 9A York St. (www.thrifty.com.au; © **02/9276 7330**). All agencies also have desks at the airport. One of the best-value operations is **Bayswater Car Rental,** trading as **No Birds,** 180 William St., Kings Cross (www.bayswatercarrental.com.au; © **02/9360 3622**), which has small cars from around A$40 a day, sometimes less, and offers a direct shuttle transfer from the airport to its office for A$5 per person.

[FastFACTS] SYDNEY

ATMs/Banks Banking hours are Monday to Friday 9am to 5pm. Many banks, especially in the city center, also open Saturday 9:30am to 12:30pm. ATMs are easy to find in the city center, and most are available 24 hrs.

Business Hours General office hours are Monday to Friday 9am to 5pm. Shopping hours are usually 8:30am to 5:30pm daily (9am–5pm Sat). Most stores stay open until 9pm on Thursday. Most city-center stores are open 10am to 4pm on Sunday.

Dentists **CBD Dental Practice,** Level 2, 74 Castlereagh St. (www.cbd dental.com.au; © **02/9221 2453**), offers same-day emergency treatment. It's open by appointment Mon–Fri 8am–6pm. The **Sydney Dental Hospital** is on 2 Chalmers St., Surry Hills (© **02/9293 3333**).

Doctors & Hospitals **St. Vincent's Hospital** is at Victoria and Burton sts. in Darlinghurst, near Kings Cross (© **02/8382 1111**). In the city center, the **V Health Plus** medical center (© **02/ 8188 2299**), 40 Park St.

(corner of Pitt St.), is open Monday to Friday 8am to 5pm, and the **Travellers' Medical & Vaccination Centre,** Level 16, 60 Margaret St. (www.traveldoctor. com.au; © **02/9221 7133**), administers travel-related vaccinations and medications Monday to Friday 9am to 5pm. Appointments essential.

Embassies & Consulates All foreign embassies are based in Canberra. The following consulates are in Sydney: **United States,** Level 10, MLC Centre, Martin Place (© **1300 139 399** in Australia or 02/9373 9200); **Canada,** Level 5, 111 Harrington St. (© **02/9364 3000**); **Britain,** Level 16, 1 Macquarie Place (© **02/ 9247 7521**).

Emergencies Dial © **000** to call the police, the fire service, or an ambulance. Call the **NRMA** for car breakdowns (© **131 111**). Other emergency lines include the **NSW Poisons Information Centre** (© **131 126**), the **Rape Crisis Centre** (© **1800/424 017** in Australia), and the 24-hr. **Lifeline** counseling service (© **131 114**).

Mail & Postage The **General Post Office (GPO)** is at 1 Martin Place (© **02/ 9244 3711**). It's open Monday to Friday 8:15am to 5:30pm and Saturday 10am to 2pm. For the nearest post office, call © **131 318** or find it online at www.auspost.com.au.

Newspapers & Magazines The **Sydney Morning Herald** is available throughout metropolitan Sydney. The daily **The Australian** is available nationwide. The metropolitan **Daily Telegraph** is a more casual read. A newcomer to the market is **The Saturday Paper,** an independent weekend newspaper. The **International Herald Tribune** and other U.S. and U.K. newspapers can be found at Circular Quay newspaper stands and most news dealers. The quarterly **Time Out Sydney** is a free guide to everything that's on in and around the city (find the online version at www.time out.com/Sydney). It's handed out at major train stations, hotels, cafes, shops, and entertainment venues.

Pharmacies Most suburbs have pharmacies that are open late. For after-hours referral, contact the **Chemist Emergency Prescription Referral Service** (☏ **02/9467 7100**).

Police In an emergency, dial ☏ **000**. Make nonemergency police inquiries through the **City Central** police station (☏ **02/9265 6499**).

Safety Sydney is generally a safe city, but as anywhere else, it's good to keep your wits about you and your wallet hidden. Be wary in the evenings in Kings Cross, Redfern, around Central Station, and on the cinema strip on George Street near Town Hall station—the latter is a hangout for local gangs. Other places of concern are the back lanes of Darlinghurst, around the naval base at Woolloomooloo, and along the Bondi restaurant strip when sunburned drunken tourists spill out after midnight. If traveling by train at night, ride in the carriages next to the guard's van, marked with a blue light on the outside.

Wi-Fi Sydney has a widespread network of free Wi-Fi hot spots around the city center and even onboard Sydney Ferries.

WHERE TO STAY IN SYDNEY

The best location for lodging in Sydney is in The Rocks and around Circular Quay—a short stroll from the Sydney Opera House, the Harbour Bridge, the Royal Botanic Garden, and the ferry terminals.

Hotels around Darling Harbour offer good access to museums, the Sydney Aquarium, and The Star casino. Most Darling Harbour hotels are a 10- to 15-minute walk, or a short light-rail trip, from Town Hall and the central shopping district.

More hotels are grouped around Kings Cross, Sydney's red-light district. Some of the city's best hotels are here; you'll also find a range of cheaper lodgings and hostels. Kings Cross can sometimes be unnerving (and noisy), especially on Friday and Saturday nights when the strip joints and nightclubs are jumping, but it's close to excellent restaurants and cafes around Kings Cross, Darlinghurst, and Oxford Street.

If you want to stay near the beach, check out the options in Manly and Bondi, though you should consider their distance from the city center and the lack of trains to these areas. A taxi to Manly from the city will cost around A$55 and to Bondi around A$35.

Almost all hotels offer nonsmoking rooms. Most moderately priced to expensive rooms will have tea- and coffee-making facilities and an iron and ironing board. Coffeemakers are rare in Australian hotels, which instead offer tea bags, instant coffee, small plastic milk cartons, and a kettle. Some smarter hotels have an in-room espresso machine.

MAKING A DEAL The prices given below for expensive hotels are mostly the **rack rates,** the recommended retail price, which guests often pay at the busiest periods if they book at short notice or walk in off the street. Check out **www.lastminute.com.au, www.wotif.com,** or a hotel's own website, for discounted rates. **Apartment hotels** may be worth considering, because you can save a bundle by cooking at least some of your own meals, and many also have free laundry facilities.

Most Australian hostels go beyond dorm-type accommodations and also offer private double rooms (some with en-suite bathrooms) and a limited number of family rooms (sleeping four or five), making hostels a viable option for families and older travelers. Check **www.yha.com.au** for a full list of its eight Sydney hostels (some are listed in this section).

Around The Rocks & Circular Quay
EXPENSIVE

The Langham ★★★ Many think this turn-of-the-20th-century beauty is the best hotel in town. This exclusive property, a 10-minute walk uphill from The Rocks and 15 minutes from Circular Quay (or a stroll down to Wynyard train station), is renowned for its personalized service and contemporary style, with a grand marble lobby and quiet guest rooms with huge bathrooms. Some rooms have city views; others look out over the harbor. The pool here is one of the best in Sydney (note the Southern Hemisphere constellations on the roof). The Langham's day spa is one of the most exclusive in the city.

89–113 Kent St. www.langhamhotels.com. (✆ **02/9256 2222.** 98 units. A$368–A$478 double; A$800–A$2,600 suite. Breakfast A$35. Parking A$60. Bus: nos. 339, 431, or 433. **Amenities:** Restaurant; bar; concierge; health club; chemical-free heated indoor pool; 24-hr. room service; sauna; lighted tennis court; free Wi-Fi.

Pier One Sydney Harbour ★★ Tucked just around the corner from Circular Quay, almost under the Harbour Bridge, Pier One is right on the waterfront (you can even arrive by boat at the private pontoon, if you wish). Some rooms offer harbor views, in both directions. Rooms are updated and contemporary but come with interesting features, such as old timbers from the original Pier One Wharf, built in 1912. It's just far enough from the bustle of the city center to be in a world of its own but with all the benefits of being 5 minutes away.

11 Hickson Rd. www.pieronesydneyharbour.com.au. (✆ **02/8298 9999.** 189 units. A$263–A$343 double; A$423–A$1,280 suite. Valet parking A$60. Train, bus, or ferry: Circular Quay. **Amenities:** Restaurant; bar; babysitting; concierge; exercise room; room service; free Wi-Fi.

Sir Stamford at Circular Quay ★★★ This is one of my favorite Sydney hotels. It's plush and luxurious, with gorgeous antique furniture and a clubby European feel, but like all the really great hotels, its staff is warm and welcoming and its atmosphere relaxed, not stuffy. There's even a large mascot wombat (of the toy variety) called Morris who pops up in the most unexpected places (and can be with you for company, on request). The location is perfect, a short walk from Circular Quay and the Opera House, and just across the road from the Royal Botanic Garden. Rooms are large and luxurious, with good-size marble bathrooms. Most rooms have a small balcony. The rooms on the east side of the hotel have the best views across the Botanic Garden. Most rooms are accessible to wheelchairs.

93 Macquarie St. www.stamford.com.au/sscq. (✆ **02/9252 4600.** 120 units. A$359–A$409 double; A$659–A$1,500 suite. Parking A$40, valet parking A$69. Train, bus, or ferry: Circular Quay. **Amenities:** Restaurant; bar; babysitting; concierge; exercise room; outdoor heated pool; room service; sauna; free Wi-Fi.

4

SYDNEY | Where to Stay in Sydney

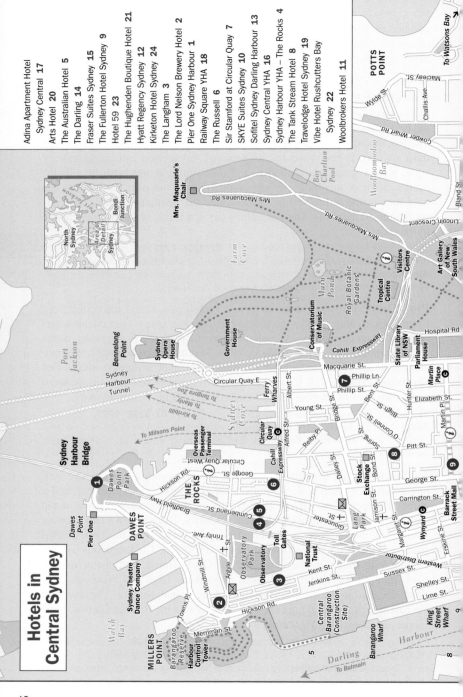

Hotels in Central Sydney

Adina Apartment Hotel Sydney Central **17**
Arts Hotel **20**
The Australian Hotel **5**
The Darling **14**
Fraser Suites Sydney **15**
The Fullerton Hotel Sydney **9**
Hotel 59 **23**
The Hughenden Boutique Hotel **21**
Hyatt Regency Sydney **12**
Kirketon Hotel Sydney **24**
The Langham **3**
The Lord Nelson Brewery Hotel **2**
Pier One Sydney Harbour **1**
Railway Square YHA **18**
The Russell **6**
Sir Stamford at Circular Quay **7**
SKYE Suites Sydney **10**
Sofitel Sydney Darling Harbour **13**
Sydney Central YHA **16**
Sydney Harbour YHA – The Rocks **4**
The Tank Stream Hotel **8**
Travelodge Hotel Sydney **19**
Vibe Hotel Rushcutters Bay Sydney **22**
Woolbrokers Hotel **11**

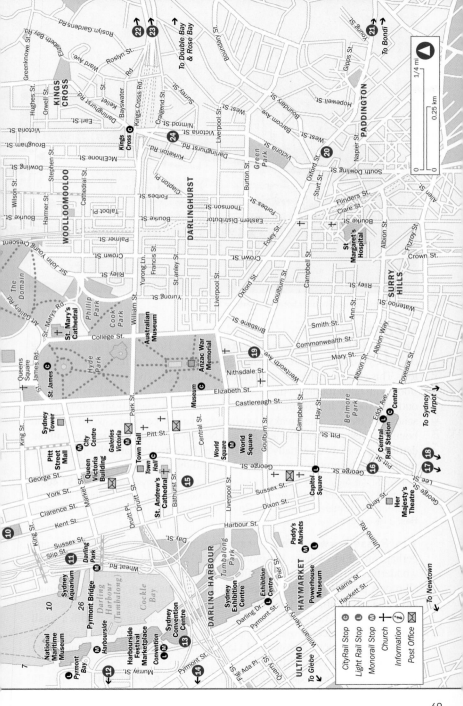

The Pier One Sydney Harbour hotel and Harbour Bridge.

MODERATE

The Lord Nelson Brewery Hotel ★★★   Book a room upstairs in one of Sydney's oldest pubs (established in 1841) to be part of the city's living history. This attractive, three-story sandstone building is a busy pub on the ground floor, with hotel rooms on the second and third floors. The simple but stylishly outfitted rooms are compact, and some have walls made from convict-hewn sandstone blocks. The creaky floorboards, narrow corridors, wood fire, and boutique brewery in the bar add to Lord Nelson's colonial atmosphere without detracting from its essentially modern style. The smallest (and cheapest) of the rooms has a bathroom across the corridor; all the others are en suites.

19 Kent St. (at Argyle St.), The Rocks. www.lordnelsonbrewery.com. © **02/9251 4044.** 8 units. A$210 double with external bathroom; A$250 double with en suite bathroom. Rates include continental breakfast. No parking. Train or ferry: Circular Quay. **Amenities:** 2 restaurants; bar; free Wi-Fi.

The Russell ★★★   This is the coziest place to stay in The Rocks and perhaps in all of Sydney. It's more than 120 years old, and it shows its age wonderfully in the creaks of the floorboards. There are no harbor views, but all rooms provide immense character and are furnished in period style. Some have shared bathrooms (and all rooms have bathrobes). Single rooms are available for solo travelers. Guests have access to a sitting room with a small library and a balcony overlooking Circular Quay. The rooftop garden is another perfect spot for wonderful views of the harbor, with tables and chairs and sun umbrellas. A real find.

143A George St., The Rocks. www.therussell.com.au. © **02/9241 3543.** 29 units, 19 with bathroom. A$130–A$155 double with shared bathroom; A$183–A$319 double with bathroom. Rates include continental breakfast. Parking nearby (A$25 for 24 hr. single entry). Train or ferry: Circular Quay. **Amenities:** Restaurant; bar; free Wi-Fi.

INEXPENSIVE

The Australian Hotel ★   Rooms here are above one of Sydney's most historic pubs, but despite that, they're not noisy. Carry your bags up the narrow stairs and you'll find a charming—if somewhat frayed around the edges—little haven overlooking the action on the street. Each room has a double or queen bed, or twin beds, and the nine rooms share five bathrooms. The guest lounge, overlooking the street, has a TV, books and magazines, and nice little touches like free tea and coffee available all day, bowls of fruit, and a decanter of port. A second, quieter lounge is down another hallway. The Australian is clean, comfortable, and a bargain.

100 Cumberland St. (entry off Gloucester St.), The Rocks. www.australianheritagehotel. com. ✆ **02/9247 2229.** 9 units. A$149–A$159 double; A$299 family suite. Rates include continental breakfast. Train or ferry: Circular Quay. No parking. **Amenities:** Restaurant; bar; free Wi-Fi.

Sydney Harbour YHA—The Rocks ★★   The Sydney Harbour YHA offers basic, clean rooms at a very reasonable price for this sought-after part of the city. Some rooms have harbor views (if you crane your neck). All are air-conditioned, and even the dorms have private bathrooms. There are also some thoughtful design features, including an electric socket in each of the lockers, so you can securely charge your iPod/laptop/camera. It has a very large common area, and the roof terrace is an excellent place to hang out, particularly because of the fabulous views of the Opera House and the Sydney Harbour Bridge. *Note:* You do have to lug your luggage up a lot of steps to get to the building. There are also a couple of other YHA hostels worth considering (p. 73).

110 Cumberland St., The Rocks. www.yha.com.au. ✆ **02/8272 0900.** A$41–A$62 dorm; A$149–A$222 double; A$179–A$259 family room (sleeps 5). Train or ferry: Circular Quay. **Amenities:** Self-catering kitchen and dining area; Internet cafe; coffee bar; lounge; convenience store; free Wi-Fi.

In the City Center

EXPENSIVE

Adina Apartment Hotel Sydney Central ★★   Built in 1821, and once the parcels post office for Central Station next door, this Heritage-listed property now offers elegant and roomy studios and apartments. My pick is the one-bedroom Premier apartments, which are on the higher levels of the hotel; some are corner rooms, which have wonderful round windows with views of the Central Station clock tower. There's no restaurant, but the hotel is surrounded by plenty of cafes and restaurants, and also offers an online restaurant delivery service.

2 Lee St., Haymarket. www.tfehotels.com. ✆ **02/8396 9800.** 98 units. A$249–A$279 studio; A$309–A$319 1-bedroom apt; A$429–A$489 2-bedroom apt. Parking A$39. Train: Central. **Amenities:** Gym; Jacuzzi; outdoor heated pool; free Wi-Fi.

Fraser Suites Sydney ★★★   One of Sydney's most luxurious apartment hotels, Fraser Suites is just a few minutes' walk from the Queen Victoria Building and Darling Harbour. Choose from studios, one- and two-bedroom suites, or two- and three-bedroom penthouse suites. There are only seven apartments on each floor, and the views are to die for. Studios offer kitchenettes, while larger apartments have separate bedrooms, lounges, and full kitchen and laundry facilities. All rooms have Nespresso coffee machines, iPod docking stations, and a small study area. A buffet breakfast (A$32; A$14 kids) is available daily on the mezzanine floor, and room service is available for breakfast (6:30–10:30am) and dinner (6–11pm).

488 Kent St. www.sydney.frasershospitality.com. ✆ **02/8823 8888.** 201 units. A$225 studio; A$280 1-bedroom suite; A$505 2-bedroom suite; A$999 penthouse. Self-parking A$42; valet parking A$52. Train: Town Hall. **Amenities:** Concierge; indoor heated pool, Jacuzzi; sauna; health club; free Wi-Fi.

The Fullerton Hotel Sydney ★★★   One of Sydney's most celebrated five-star hotels, the Fullerton (until late 2019, the Westin Sydney) is located in the center of the city, in the Martin Place pedestrian mall. Integrated into Sydney's original 19th-century General Post Office, this hotel has a charm that's modern and classic all at once. The large rooms have wonderfully comfortable beds and floor-to-ceiling windows. The hotel is home to several bars, restaurants, and clothing shops. Just steps from the central shopping streets and the Queen Victoria Building, and a 10- to 15-minute walk from both the Sydney Opera House and Darling Harbour, the hotel features an impressive seven-story atrium, a fabulous two-level health club, and an exclusive day spa.

1 Martin Place. www.the-fullerton-hotel-sydney.com. ✆ **02/8223 1111.** 416 units. A$416–A$586 double; A$626–A$666 suite. Parking A$68. Train: Martin Place. **Amenities:** Cafe; bar; babysitting; health club; day spa; free Wi-Fi.

Hyatt Regency Sydney ★★★   Opened in early 2017 after a A$250-million redevelopment, this super-swanky hotel is positioned between the city heart and Darling Harbour, across the street from the Sydney Aquarium and a short walk from Cockle Bay. It's one of the largest five-star properties in Australia, and has added 222 new rooms, including suites and club rooms. Some have views of Darling Harbour, and some have balconies. A highlight is the rooftop bar with harbor views.

161 Sussex St. www.sydney.regency.hyatt.com. ✆ **02/8099 1234.** 892 units. A$297–A$450 double; A$585–A$612 suite. Parking A$70. Bus: no. 441. Train: Town Hall. **Amenities:** Restaurant; bar; concierge; 24-hr. gym; free Wi-Fi.

MODERATE

SKYE Suites Sydney ★   A lobby themed to look like an ice cave, with a knockout swimming pool just off it, makes an instant impact upon arriving guests at this apartment hotel, which opened in November 2018. Upstairs, the studios and one- and two-bedroom suites are generously proportioned, with full kitchens and laundries. All have queen-sized beds, with bathrobes, slippers, and quality toiletries. Some two-bedroom suites also have two bathrooms. Blackout blinds keep out the city lights, if not all the sound (a bonus: windows that open). There are plenty of restaurants in the surrounding streets, and it's a short walk to Darling Harbour or Barangaroo.

300 Kent St. www.skyehotels.com.au. ☏ **02/9052 7588.** 73 units. A$250–A$270 double studio; A$290 double 1-bedroom apt; A$400–A$450 double 2-bedroom apt. Valet parking A$65. Train: Wynyard. **Amenities:** Gymnasium; indoor pool; free Wi-Fi.

The Tank Stream Hotel ★★   One of Sydney's newest hotels is situated on one of its most historic sites. Just a few minutes' walk from Circular Quay, the Sydney Opera House, Hyde Park, and Barangaroo, this modest but stylish hotel tells a terrific Sydney story. The Tank Stream is built over the freshwater stream that was the water source for Australia's first European colony in 1788. Rooms are simply furnished and some are compact, but they are all you need and the location is hard to beat. The complimentary (nonalcoholic) minibar is a nice touch. Ask about underground tours of the original tank stream.

97–99 Pitt St. www.tankstreamhotel.com. ☏ **02/8222 1200.** 280 units. A$249–A$274 double. Parking A$25. Train: Wynyard. **Amenities:** Restaurant; bar; free Wi-Fi.

INEXPENSIVE

Sydney Central YHA ★★   This multiple-award-winning hostel is one of the biggest and busiest in the world, so book as far ahead as possible. The rooms are clean and basic, and come dorm-style for four, six, or eight people or as doubles (with private bathrooms). Family rooms (for up to 4 people) are also available. In the basement is a bar with pool tables and occasional entertainment. There's also an entertainment room with more pool tables and e-mail facilities, TV rooms on every floor, and a cinema. The YHA is accessible to travelers with disabilities.

There's also the **Railway Square YHA** at the corner of Upper Carriage Lane and Lee Street, or enter via the Henry Dean Plaza (☏ **02/9281 9666**). The historic 1904 building adjoining "Platform Zero" at Central Railway Station has 64 beds in four- to eight-bed dorm rooms and 10 double rooms. Some dorm rooms are in old railway carriages. The facility has a sauna, pool, Internet cafe, tour desk, indoor and outdoor communal areas, and a self-catering kitchen.

11 Rawson Place (at Pitt St., outside Central Station). www.yha.com.au. ☏ **02/9281 9000.** 150 units. A$32–A$42 dorm bed; A$115–A$165 double/twin per room; A$160–A$168 family room (sleeps 4). Parking A$30. Train: Central. **Amenities:** Restaurant; bar; small heated outdoor pool; sauna; free Wi-Fi.

Travelodge Hotel Sydney ★   This business-oriented hotel is cheap for Sydney, comfortable, and reasonably well located, making it a good option for travelers who just want to unpack and explore. The lobby and public areas underwent a much-needed upgrade in 2019 to create a more welcoming look. The IKEA-style rooms include a kitchenette with a microwave and a queen bed or two twin-size beds. From here it's a short walk to Oxford Street, Town Hall, and Hyde Park.

27–33 Wentworth Ave. www.tfehotels.com. © **1300/886 886** in Australia, or 02/8267 1700. 406 units. A$135–A$167 double. Parking (around corner) A$25. Train: Museum. **Amenities:** Restaurant; babysitting; health club; free Wi-Fi.

In Darling Harbour
EXPENSIVE

The Darling ★★★   Part of The Star casino complex, this chic hotel stands out from the crowd with splashes of color—purple sheets, even!—and luxurious amenities. All rooms have floor-to-ceiling windows; some boast views of the Sydney Harbour Bridge. The marble bathrooms have rain showers, bathtubs, and gorgeous Molton Brown products. Touch controls from the bedside allow you to operate the window blinds, air-conditioning, and television (although sometimes these prove challenging!). It's an easy walk to anywhere in Darling Harbour, or across the Pyrmont Bridge to the city center.

80 Pyrmont St., Pyrmont. www.thedarling.com.au. © **1800/800 830** in Australia, or 02/9777 9888. 171 units. A$328–A$458 double; A$518–A$1,778 suite. Valet parking A$45–A$55. Bus: no. 389. Light rail: The Star. **Amenities:** 5 restaurants; 3 bars; outdoor heated pool; gym; spa; free Wi-Fi.

Sofitel Sydney Darling Harbour ★★★   The "wow" factor is strong from the moment you arrive at this beautiful hotel, one of Sydney's newest. All rooms are spacious, but for something special book a corner room, where the bathtub has one of the best views of Darling Harbour. Rooms are decorated in subtle colors without the blandness that besets so many contemporary hotels, and the beds are supremely comfortable. The **Champagne Bar** has stellar views of the city skyline. And of course, befitting the Paris-based Sofitel, it all has a French flavor. The hotel is next door to the Sydney International Convention Centre and just a short walk across the Pyrmont Bridge to the city center.

12 Darling Dr., Pyrmont. www.sofitelsydneydarlingharbour.com.au. © **02/8388 8888.** 590 units. A$394–A$659 double; A$819–A$1,069 suite. Valet parking A$79. Bus: no. 389. Light rail: Convention Centre. **Amenities:** 1 restaurant; 3 bars; babysitting; outdoor pool; gym; spa; free Wi-Fi.

INEXPENSIVE

Woolbrokers Hotel ★   You'll find this friendly, circa-1886 Heritage building on the far side of Darling Harbour, next to the prominent Novotel hotel and hidden behind a monstrous parking garage. It's on a noisy road, so unless you're unfazed by traffic sounds, avoid the rooms at the front. Rooms are simply furnished and come with a fridge and TV. Room no. 3 is one of the nicer choices. Family rooms are outfitted with a king-size bed and a pair of bunk beds. The hotel has 19 shared bathrooms, though some rooms have private bathrooms. Check the website for discounts. This is a good budget option, but note that the hotel has no elevator or air-conditioning.

22 Allen St., Pyrmont. www.woolbrokershotel.com.au. © **02/9552 4773.** 27 units. A$95 double with shared bathroom; A$130 double with bathroom; A$170 family room

(sleeps up to 8). Continental breakfast A$7.50. Parking A$16 (across the street). Bus: no. 501. Light rail: Convention Centre. **Amenities:** Guest laundry; free Wi-Fi.

In Kings Cross & Suburbs Nearby

INEXPENSIVE

Hotel 59 ★   This popular, well-priced, friendly B&B is well worth considering if you want to be near the Kings Cross action but just far enough away to get some peace and quiet. It has two rooms for single travelers and three family rooms that sleep two adults and two children. Rooms are well-kept and comfortable, with private bathrooms and TVs. *Note:* A flight of stairs (and no elevator) might make Hotel 59 unsuitable for travelers with disabilities.

59 Bayswater Rd., Kings Cross. www.hotel59.com.au. ✆ **02/9360 5900.** 9 units. A$140–A$150 double. Rates include breakfast. No parking. Train: Kings Cross. **Amenities:** Cafe; TV lounge; free Wi-Fi.

Kirketon Hotel Sydney ★   Popular among hip, fashionable types, this slightly offbeat boutique hotel in Darlinghurst offers rooms with modernist furniture and custom-made fittings, including mirrored headboards and sleek bathrooms hidden away behind mirrored doors. Standard rooms are quite compact and come with a double bed. Premium rooms have a queen-size bed. Superior and Executive rooms are quite large, with a king-size bed, and some have a small balcony overlooking the main road. For a quiet sleep, ask for a room away from the main road.

229 Darlinghurst Rd., Darlinghurst. www.kirketon.com.au. ✆ **02/9332 2011.** 40 rooms. A$129–A$179 double. Parking A$25. **Amenities:** Restaurant; bar; gym; free Wi-Fi.

Vibe Hotel Rushcutters Bay Sydney ★★   Compared with other hotels in its price bracket, this flagship Vibe Hotel on the far side of Kings Cross really is a bargain, especially when you book online. Standard rooms are a reasonable size, and I love the brightly accented and colorful—well, yes—vibe. All rooms have king-size beds (which split into twins if necessary), and families can get connecting rooms. The whole place underwent a major refurbishment in 2016, including the heated rooftop swimming pool and gym. The hotel has a good cafe, called **Curve.**

100 Bayswater Rd., Rushcutters Bay. www.vibehotels.com/hotel/rushcutters-by-sydney. ✆ **02/8353 8988.** 258 units. A$189–A$219 double; A$319–A$589 suite. Parking A$25. Train: Kings Cross. **Amenities:** Restaurant; bar; concierge; gym; heated outdoor pool; free Wi-Fi.

Around Oxford Street & Darlinghurst

MODERATE

The Hughenden Boutique Hotel ★★   I love this hotel, part of which is set in an 1870s mansion and full of antique furnishings. It's warm and comfortable with lots of sitting areas. A full refurbishment by new owners in 2018 included the addition of a speakeasy-style bar and private upper-floor terrace. Wander through to enjoy the artwork and architecture, including lovely black-marble fireplaces. You might run into cricket buffs, given the proximity to the

Sydney Cricket Ground. The location is great, at the top end of Oxford Street and just across the road from Centennial Park. Another eight suites are situated in a house across the street.

14 Queen St., Woollahra. www.thehughendenhotel.com.au. © **02/9363 4863.** 32 units. A$191–A$304 double; A$359 suite; A$359 family room (sleeps up to 5). Rates include breakfast. Limited secured parking (A$33 per night). Bus: no. 440. **Amenities:** Restaurant; bar; guest lounge; free Wi-Fi.

INEXPENSIVE

Arts Hotel ★ This family-run hotel is right in the heart of the action in one of Sydney's most popular shopping, entertainment, restaurant, and gay pub and club areas. About half of the hotel's guests come from overseas, and it's popular with Americans during Mardi Gras. Rooms are simple, compact, and motel-like, but fine for a few nights. Standard rooms and garden rooms (which are quieter) have two single beds or a queen-size bed. Art rooms are more up-market, with rainfall showerheads, hypoallergenic bedding, art on the walls, and other little luxury touches—and are offered as upgrades for bookings of 4 nights or more.

21 Oxford St., Paddington. www.artshotel.com.au. © **02/9361 0211.** 64 units. A$130–A$168 double. Limited free parking. Bus: no. 378 from Central Station or no. 380 from Circular Quay. **Amenities:** Breakfast cafe; bikes; gym; small heated outdoor pool; free Wi-Fi.

In Bondi

If you want to be close to the surf and sand, Bondi Beach has a couple of recommended backpacker hostels that are good for budget-conscious travelers: **Surfside Backpackers,** 35a Hall St. (www.surfsidebackpackers.com.au; © **02/9365 4900**), offers four- to eight-person dorm rooms from A$25 to A$40, depending on the time of year. Single, double, and family rooms are in a separate building (at higher rates). **Noah's Bondi,** 2 Campbell Parade (www.noahsbondibeach.com; © **02/9365 7544**), has a great ambience and modern four- to eight-person dorm rooms for A$25 to A$31 (doubles are A$65–A$75). Rates are higher in the summer peak season (Dec–Jan). Ask about weekly rates.

EXPENSIVE

Hotel Ravesis ★★ Right on Australia's most famous golden sands, this boutique property offers chic and modern minimalist rooms with white marble bathrooms and Juliet balconies. All rooms were renovated in 2017. Side View doubles are spacious and modern, but the Beach Front king rooms have the best ocean views. Four split-level suites have a bathroom downstairs and a bedroom, lounge area, and private outdoor terrace on the second level. The hotel has a lively bar downstairs (which can mean noise until late, especially on weekends) and a good restaurant.

Corner of Hall St. and Campbell Parade. www.hotelravesis.com. © **02/9365 4422.** 12 units. A$285–A$379 double; A$335–A$525 suite. Valet parking A$20. Bus: no. 333. **Amenities:** Restaurant; bar; room service; free Wi-Fi.

In Manly

If you decide to stay in Manly for a few days, consider buying a multiple-ride ferry ticket, which will save you a bit of money. But be warned that ferries from Sydney stop running at midnight. If you get stranded, you'll be facing an expensive taxi ride back.

Manly has several backpacker hostels that are worth checking out; the best of the bunch is **Manly Backpackers Beachside,** 28 Raglan St. (www.manly backpackers.com.au; ℂ **1800/662 500** in Australia, or 02/9977 3411), which offers dorm beds from A$39 to A$50 and doubles from A$90 to A$159, depending on the time of year (pricier during peak summer period).

MODERATE

Manly Paradise Beachfront Motel and Apartments ★   The refurbished motel rooms are spacious, and some offer glimpses of the sea. The traffic can make it a little noisy in your room during the day, but you'll probably be on the beach anyway. Rooms come with queen, double, or twin beds, and the magnificent roomy apartments have everything you need, including a full kitchen with dishwasher, a washing machine and dryer, and two bathrooms (one with a tub). Sea views from the main front balcony are heart-stopping, and there's a pool on the rooftop.

54 N. Steyne, Manly. www.manlyparadise.com.au. ℂ **1800/815 789** in Australia, or 02/9977 5799. 40 units. A$175–A$300 double (motel); A$395–A$515 2-bedroom apt; A$495–A$610 3-bedroom apt. Parking A$25 for motel; free for apts. Ferry: Manly. **Amenities:** Outdoor rooftop pool; free Wi-Fi.

At the Airport

MODERATE

Stamford Plaza Sydney Airport ★★   This elegant and comfortable airport hotel is within walking distance of the terminals, or you can take the short trip via the Airport Shuttle (A$7). The Stamford Plaza has large rooms, each with a king or two double beds, access to airport information, and a good-size bathroom with tub. Suites and deluxe rooms have airport views, but all windows have been reinforced to keep out the aircraft noise!

Corner of O'Riordan and Robey sts., Mascot. www.stamford.com.au/ssa. ℂ **02/9317 2200.** 315 units. A$249–A$299 double; A$399–A$849 suite. Parking A$30. **Amenities:** 2 restaurants; bar; babysitting; concierge; gym; Jacuzzi; outdoor rooftop pool; room service; sauna; free Wi-Fi.

INEXPENSIVE

Ibis Budget Sydney Airport ★   If all you want is a clean place to crash before an early flight, this no-frills hotel will do the job. This Ibis has almost no facilities, but it's next to a couple of fast-food joints and has an all-you-can-eat breakfast. You can have dinner at its sister hotel, Mantra, next door. Rooms are air-conditioned and have TVs. You can reach the airport via the Airport Shuttle, which costs A$7 (or walk there in 10 min.).

5 Ross Smith Ave., Mascot. www.accorhotels.com. ℂ **02/8339 1840.** 200 units. A$139–A$179 double. Rates include breakfast. Parking A$35 per day. **Amenities:** Breakfast room; free Wi-Fi.

WHERE TO EAT IN SYDNEY

Sydney is a gourmet paradise, boasting some of the world's best chefs. Asian and Mediterranean cooking have had a major influence on Australian cuisine, with spices and herbs finding their way into most dishes. Immigration has brought with it almost every type of cuisine, from African to Tibetan, Russian to Vietnamese.

Sydney is a great place to try the Australian style of contemporary cuisine, which emphasizes fresh ingredients and a creative blend of European styles with Asian influences. And because a really great meal will stay in your mind long after your visit to Australia is over, I've included some of Australia's very top restaurants here. The prices may be high but are almost always well worth it, especially if you are looking for an experience rather than just a meal.

Breakfast is big in Australia, a favorite time of day to meet friends and linger over a hearty repast (albeit often a late one). As for coffee, Australians favor a range of Italian-style creations. Ask for a latte if you just want coffee with milk.

And remember that in Australia, the first course is called the entree and the second course the main.

Circular Quay, City Center & The Rocks
EXPENSIVE

Aria ★★★ CONTEMPORARY   With front-row views of the Harbour Bridge and the Sydney Opera House, Aria stands in one of the most enviable spots in the city. The windows overlooking the water are huge, the atmosphere is elegant and buzzy, and many of the intimate tables have a stunning view. The food, created by one of Australia's great chefs, Matt Moran, is imaginative and mouthwatering. Some examples: duck with red wine, cauliflower and salted grapes; or snapper with leek, kohlrabi, sea greens, and finger lime. For lunch on weekdays, a set menu offers two or three courses (A$90 or A$120). Pre- and post-theater menus are available for the same prices from 5:30 to 7pm and after 10pm respectively. Reservations are essential.

1 Macquarie St. www.ariasydney.com.au. ⓒ **02/9240 2255.** A$145 for 3 courses, A$170 for 4 courses. Seasonal 6-course tasting menu A$205, or A$450 with wine pairings. Mon–Fri noon–2:15pm and 5:30–10:30pm; Sat noon–1:30pm and 5–11pm; Sun noon–1:45pm and 5:30–10:30pm. Train, bus, or ferry: Circular Quay.

Bennelong ★★★ CONTEMPORARY   This is one of Australia's best restaurants, coupled with one of the world's best locations, inside the Sydney Opera House. Executive chef Peter Gilmore and his team are creative but down-to-earth, and that's reflected in the menu. You can dine in one of several different areas, from the casual Cured & Cultured in the beautiful Circle dining room (with views of the Harbour Bridge) to the more formal lower level restaurant. Selections from the three-course dinner menu might include roasted lamb loin with smoked harissa, green olives, barletta onion, and herbs; or a ravioli of mushrooms, chestnut, and ricotta with smoked hazelnuts,

WHAT TO KNOW ABOUT dining IN SYDNEY

Most moderate and inexpensive restaurants in Sydney are **BYO,** as in "bring your own" bottle (wine only), though many also have extensive wine and beer lists. Some of these restaurants are also introducing **corkage fees,** which mean you pay anywhere from A$2 to A$10 per person for the privilege of having the waiter open your bottle of wine. Very expensive restaurants are usually fully licensed and don't allow you to BYO.

Sydney's **cheap eats** congregate in center-city areas such as Crown Street in Darlinghurst, and Glebe Point Road in Glebe. There are also inexpensive joints scattered among the more upscale restaurants in Kings Cross and along trendy Oxford Street.

Some restaurants add a **surcharge** on public holidays and Sundays, usually around 5% or 10% per person. Restaurants argue that it's difficult to get staff to work on these days, so they need to provide a cash incentive. In Australia, waiters rely on wages rather than tips.

Smoking is banned in all Sydney restaurants, except at some with sidewalk tables or courtyards. Always ask before lighting up.

raisins, and black garlic. Pre- and post-theater sittings are offered (check website for details). Reservations are essential.

Sydney Opera House, Bennelong Point. www.bennelong.com.au. ℂ **02/9240 8000.** Lunch: 2 courses A$110, 3 courses A$145. Dinner: 3-course menu A$145. Cured & Cultured bar tasting menu with 6 tasting plates A$70. Fri–Sun noon–2:15pm; Sun–Thurs 5:30–9pm and Fri–Sat 5pm–9pm. Train, bus, or ferry: Circular Quay.

Sydney Cove Oyster Bar ★★ SEAFOOD   Just before you reach the Sydney Opera House, you'll notice a couple of small shedlike buildings with tables and chairs set up to take in the stunning views of the harbor and bridge. This is where you'll find some of the best oysters in town. Oysters are A$54 for a dozen (A$27 for a half-dozen), but reliable mains, such as charcoal-roasted barramundi, tiger prawn linguini, or the signature seafood hotpot with swimmer crab, tiger prawns, squid, mussels, and fish, are also on the menu. Share a dozen oysters and follow up with more shellfish or tapas-style bites plus a bottle of crisp white wine or sparkling champagne. It's a perfect lunchtime spot on a sunny day.

Eastern Esplanade, Circular Quay East. www.sydneycoveoysterbar.com. ℂ **02/9247 2937.** Main courses A$36–A$59. Daily 11am–late. Train, bus, or ferry: Circular Quay.

Tetsuya's ★★★ JAPANESE/FRENCH FUSION   This is one of the world's best restaurants—it's that simple. To have a chance of getting a table, you need to book as early as possible, and you may be asked to reconfirm a few days before. Request a table next to the floor-to-ceiling windows with intimate views across a Japanese-inspired courtyard of maples and waterfalls. The service is impeccable and the food truly inspired—many diners consider this a once-in-a-lifetime experience. Chef Tetsuya Wakuda's signature dish is

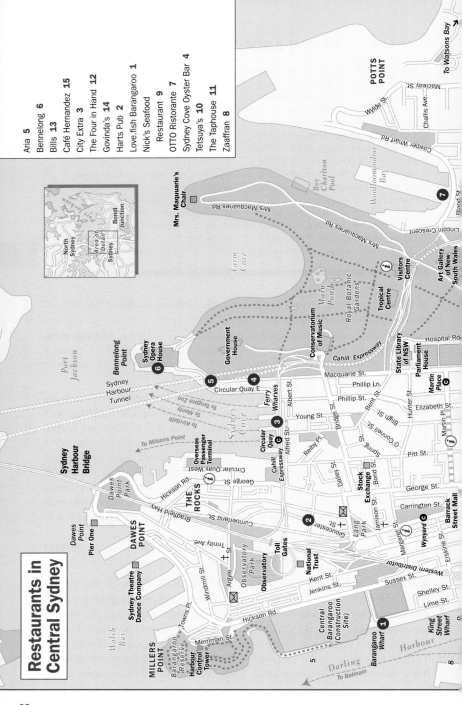

Restaurants in Central Sydney

Aria **5**
Bennelong **6**
Bills **13**
Café Hernandez **15**
City Extra **3**
The Four in Hand **12**
Govinda's **14**
Harts Pub **2**
Love.fish Barangaroo **1**
Nick's Seafood Restaurant **9**
OTTO Ristorante **7**
Sydney Cove Oyster Bar **4**
Tetsuya's **10**
The Taphouse **11**
Zaaffran **8**

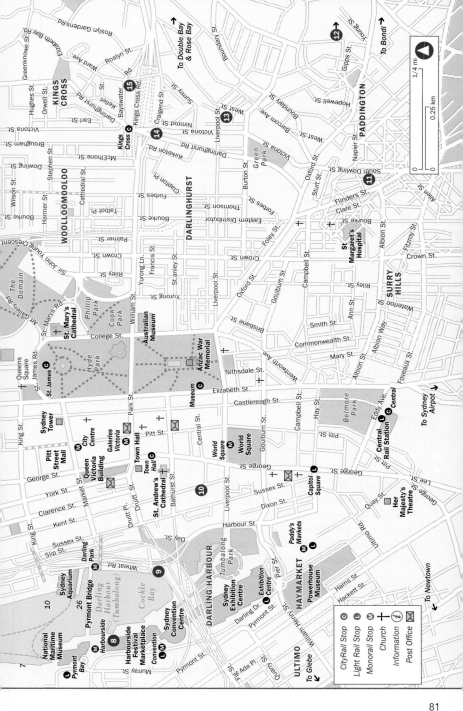

Best Pub Grub

You can get some really good food with a glass of wine or a schooner of beer on the side in several city pubs. Among the best is **The Four in Hand,** 105 Sutherland St., Paddington (www.fourinhand. com.au; *C* **02/7200 5577**), which has a great restaurant and also does good bar meals, including hearty sandwiches and grilled steaks, with most main courses under A$30. **Harts Pub,** corner of Essex and Gloucester streets, The Rocks (www.hartspub.com; *C* **02/9251 6030**), has a great range of craft beers, with gourmet and pub-grub offerings for A$20 to A$34. In Darlinghurst (Kings Cross), delve into the massive beer list at **The Taphouse,** 122 Flinders St. (www. taphousedarlo.com.au; *C* **02/9360 0088**), and graze from the extensive menu; on Sundays, a roast dinner's on offer from noon on.

a confit of ocean trout served with a salad of celery, endive, apple, and ocean-trout roe.

529 Kent St. www.tetsuyas.com. *C* **02/9267 2900.** 9-course tasting menu A$240 per person. Tues–Fri 5:30–10pm; Sat noon–3pm and 6:30–10pm. Train: Town Hall.

MODERATE

City Extra ★ ITALIAN/AUSTRALIAN   Because this place stays open around the clock, it's convenient if you get hungry at a ridiculous hour. It's also nicely situated, right next to the ferry terminals. The food varies in quality; if in doubt, stick to the burgers. It's always busy, and service can be a mixed bag too, but the plastic chairs and outdoor tables make it a pleasant enough spot for a quick bite any time of the day or night. It has a kids' menu and free Wi-Fi.

Shop E4, Circular Quay. www.cityextra.com.au. *C* **02/9241 1422.** Main courses A$20–A$36. Open 24 hrs. Train, bus, or ferry: Circular Quay.

Love.fish Barangaroo ★★★ SEAFOOD   One of the exciting dining options in Sydney's new Streets of Barangaroo precinct (p. 105), this indoor/outdoor waterside eatery combines great cocktails with delicious food (and a focus on sustainable seafood) and a helpful staff that can get you in and out quickly for a pre-theater meal. With seating for 160, it's a bustling place offering beautifully presented dishes—anything from oysters and champagne to an impressive seafood platter (A$165) to share.

Wulugul Walk, 23 Barangaroo Ave., Barangaroo. www.lovefishbarangaroo.com.au. *C* **02/8077 3700.** Main courses A$18–A$42. Mon–Fri noon–3pm and 5–11pm; Sat–Sun noon–11pm.

Darling Harbour
MODERATE

Nick's Seafood Restaurant ★ SEAFOOD   This nice indoor and alfresco eatery overlooking the water on the same side as Darling Harbour (to the left of Sydney Aquarium if you're looking at the boats) offers good

4

SYDNEY | Where to Eat in Sydney

cocktails and plenty of seafood. The best seats are outside in the sunshine, where you can watch the world go by over a bottle of wine. A seafood platter for two (A$185) arrives piled with crab, prawns, mussels, fish, oysters, and lobster. A kids' menu for under 12s offers pasta, chicken, calamari, or fish with French fries and a soft drink, followed by ice cream for A$16. Nick's has another equally pleasant eatery on the other side of the Aquarium called **Nick's Bar & Grill.** A sister establishment, **I'm Angus Steakhouse**—also at Cockle Bay Wharf—does good steaks, a great Guinness pie, and some seafood. The food and prices at all three places are similar, and they share the same phone number for bookings.

The Promenade, Cockle Bay Wharf (on the city side of Darling Harbour). www.nicks group.com.au/venue/nicks-seafood-restaurant. ℂ **1300/989 989.** Main courses A$32–A$68. Mon–Sat 11:30am–3pm and 5:30–10pm (11pm on Sat); Sun 11:30am–10pm. Ferry: Darling Harbour.

Zaaffran ★★ INDIAN Forget the dark interiors and exotic murals you often find in an Indian restaurant; here are white surfaces, a glass-fronted wine cellar, and magnificent views of the water and the Sydney skyline from the far side of Darling Harbour. An outdoor terrace provides the best views. Chef Vikrant Kapoor, formerly the chef de cuisine at Raffles in Singapore, has revolutionized classic Indian cuisine on the menu here. Expect such delights as chicken *biryani,* baked in a pastry case and served with mint yogurt, or tiger prawns in coconut cream and turmeric broth, not to mention many interesting vegetarian options.

Level 2, Harbourside Centre, 10 Darling Dr. www.zaaffran.com. ℂ **02/9211 8900.** Main courses A$20–A$30. Daily noon–2:30pm; Mon–Thurs 6–9:30pm; Fri–Sat 5:30–10:15pm; Sun 5:30–9:30pm. Ferry: Darling Harbour.

Woolloomooloo Wharf
EXPENSIVE
OTTO Ristorante ★★ ITALIAN Recognized as one of Sydney's premier restaurants, Otto is all lush designer appointments and dim lighting, making it popular with local celebrities and socialites. Hence the price of the food, perhaps. Outside it's light and breezy, with nice views of a boardwalk and some harbor water. Menu possibilities include hand-rolled pici, with Berkshire pork and fennel ragu; or an eye filet steak with Jerusalem artichokes and green peppercorn sauce.

6 Cowper Wharf Rd. www.ottoristorante.com.au/sydney. ℂ **02/9368 7488.** Main courses A$39–A$69. Daily noon–10pm. Bus: no. 311 from Circular Quay (or take a water taxi).

Kings Cross & Darlinghurst
INEXPENSIVE
Bills ★★★ CAFE Strewn with flowers and magazines, this bright and airy place serves nouveau cafe–style food. It's so popular you might have trouble finding a seat. The signature breakfast dishes—including ricotta hotcakes with honeycomb butter and banana, and sweet corn fritters with roasted tomatoes,

Vic's Rosé Veal T-Bone Salad at OTTO.

spinach, and bacon—are the stuff of legend. In fact, some of my friends think Bills serves the best breakfast in Sydney. Find other Bills cafes in Surry Hills (359 Crown St.; ℂ **02/9360 4762**) and Bondi Beach (79 Hall St.; ℂ **02/8412 0700**).

433 Liverpool St., Darlinghurst. www.bills.com.au. ℂ **02/9360 9631.** Main courses A$16–A$26. Mon–Sat 7:30am–3pm; Sun and public holidays 8am–3pm. Reservations Mon–Fri only. Train: Kings Cross.

Café Hernandez ★★ CAFE   The walls of this tiny, cluttered cafe are crammed with eccentric fake masterpieces, and the aroma of 20 types of coffee roasted and ground on the premises permeates the air. It's almost a religious experience for discerning central-city coffee addicts—and even better, it never closes! The Spanish espresso is a treat. Light meals are served: sandwiches, wraps, focaccias, and tortillas, as well as some sweet treats such as churros, Portuguese custard tarts, and Spanish rice pudding.

60 Kings Cross Rd., Potts Point. www.cafehernandez.com.au. ℂ **02/9331 2343.** Main courses A$5–A$10. Open 24 hr. Train: Kings Cross.

Govinda's ★★ VEGETARIAN   Simple vegetarian food—usually curries of some kind—coupled with a happy vibe and very cheap prices make this place a winner. Based in the Hare Krishna center, Govinda's serves buffet-style meals in a basic room of black-lacquer tables. The menu changes nightly but always includes a delicious Indian dahl soup, vegetable curry, penne pasta, lentil pie or potato au gratin, cauliflower pakoras, potato wedges, rice, papadums, and salads. It's BYO, doctrine-free, and very bohemian. After the meal,

Govinda's hosts a recent-release movie (on a different floor), which you watch prostrate on large futon-style chairs. It's hugely popular, so book ahead.

112 Darlinghurst Rd., Darlinghurst. www.govindas.com.au. ℂ **0425 333 086** mobile phone. Dinner A$25 adults or A$14 children 3–14. Movie A$14 (if dining) or A$19. Wed–Sun 5:30–11pm. Train: Kings Cross.

In Bondi Beach

EXPENSIVE

Icebergs Dining Room & Bar ★★★ MEDITERRANEAN   Overlooking Bondi Beach and the sea baths at the Bondi Icebergs Club (famed for its year-round swimming), this is a truly fabulous place to dine. From its corner position on the cliffs, the Icebergs Bar looks directly across the beach and water, with floor-to-roof windows offering what is probably the best view in Sydney. The bar features lots of cushions and has a casual bar menu. The dining-room menu is Italian, with seafood featuring as well, and the service is faultless. Go for brunch on Sunday; you won't be disappointed. A seven-course tasting menu (A$145 per person) will have you swooning.

1 Notts Ave. www.idrb.com. ℂ **02/9365 9000.** Reservations essential. Main courses A$42–A$52. Daily noon–3pm and 6:30pm–midnight; Sun brunch 10am–noon. Bus: no. 333.

INEXPENSIVE

Pompei's ★ ITALIAN   The formula is simple: Use good ingredients, like an organic tomato sauce, and you'll get good pizzas. In fact, some people think these are the best pizzas in Sydney. The pizzas have a huge range of interesting toppings, but Pompei's also offers a variety of other fare, including salads, antipasto, focaccia, and steaks. Don't miss the homemade gelato, the best in Sydney by far—try chocolate, tiramisu, or pistachio. The water views and outside tables are another plus. When it's busy, it can get cramped inside, and service can vary.

126–130 Roscoe St., at Gould St. www.pompeis.com.au. ℂ **02/9365 1233.** Pizza A$21–A$25. Main courses A$24–A$34. Mon–Fri noon–11pm; Sat–Sun 11:30am–11pm. Bus: nos. 380 or 333 from the city.

EXPLORING SYDNEY

The only problem with visiting Sydney is fitting in everything you want to do and see. Of course, you won't want to miss the iconic attractions: the **Opera House** and the **Harbour Bridge.**

You should also check out the native wildlife in **Taronga Zoo,** stroll around the tourist precinct of **Darling Harbour,** and get a dose of Down Under culture at the **Australian Museum.** If it's hot, take your "cozzie" (swimsuit) and towel to **Bondi Beach** or **Manly.**

Sydney Harbour & The Rocks

Officially called Port Jackson, **Sydney Harbour** is the focal point of Sydney and one of the features—along with the beaches and easy access to

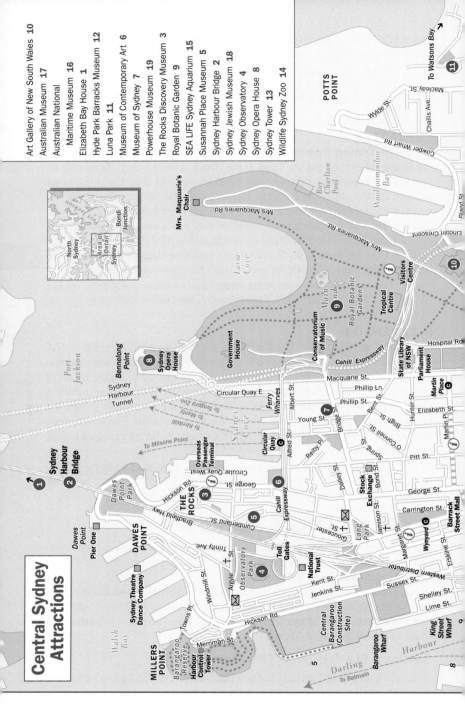

Central Sydney Attractions

Art Gallery of New South Wales **10**
Australian Museum **17**
Australian National Maritime Museum **16**
Elizabeth Bay House **1**
Hyde Park Barracks Museum **12**
Luna Park **11**
Museum of Contemporary Art **7**
Museum of Sydney **7**
Powerhouse Museum **19**
The Rocks Discovery Museum **3**
Royal Botanic Garden **9**
SEA LIFE Sydney Aquarium **15**
Susannah Place Museum **5**
Sydney Harbour Bridge **2**
Sydney Jewish Museum **18**
Sydney Observatory **4**
Sydney Opera House **8**
Sydney Tower **13**
Wildlife Sydney Zoo **14**

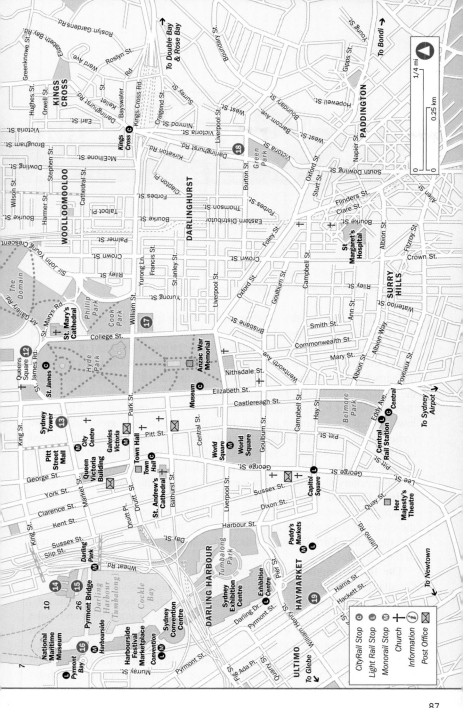

A classic view of Sydney with the Opera House and the Harbour Bridge.

surrounding national parks—that make this city so special. It's entered through the **Heads,** two bush-topped outcrops (you'll see them if you take a ferry to Manly), beyond which the harbor laps at some 240km (149 miles) of shoreline before stretching out into the Parramatta River. Visitors are often awestruck by the harbor's beauty, especially at night, when the sails of the Opera House and the girders of the Harbour Bridge are lit up, and the waters are swirling with the reflection of lights from the abutting high-rises—reds, greens, blues, yellows, and oranges. During the day, the harbor buzzes with green-and-yellow ferries pulling in and out of busy Circular Quay, sleek tourist craft, fully rigged tall ships, giant container vessels making their way to and from the wharves of Darling Harbour, and hundreds of white-sailed yachts.

The greenery along the harbor's edges is a surprising feature, thanks to the **Sydney Harbour National Park,** a haven for native trees and plants, and a feeding and breeding ground for lorikeets and other nectar-eating bird life. In the center of the harbor is a series of islands; the most impressive is the tiny isle supporting **Fort Denison,** which once housed convicts and acted as part of the city's defense.

The Rocks neighborhood is compact and close to the ferry terminals at Circular Quay. Sydney's historic district is hilly and crosscut with alleyways. Some of Australia's oldest pubs are here, as well as boutique restaurants, stores, and hotels. Pick up a walking map from the visitor center and make sure to get off the main streets to see the original working-class houses that survived development. Today, there are 96 heritage buildings in The Rocks. The oldest house is Cadmans Cottage, built in 1815, while the Dawes Point Battery, built in 1791, is the oldest remaining European structure. On Observatory Hill, you'll find the three remaining walls of Fort Phillip, built in 1804.

Museum of Contemporary Art (MCA) ★★★ MUSEUM This imposing sandstone museum, set back from the water on The Rocks side of Circular Quay, features the works of more than 150 Australian artists in two MCA Collection Galleries (Level 2 and Level 1 South). Founded in 1989, the museum also offers a changing program of exhibitions by Australian and international artists and is worth at least an hour (probably more!) of your time. Free guided tours are conducted daily at various times, including in the evenings, and feature different aspects of the museum; check the website for details. There's also a program of free talks. The **MCA Café** has good views of the harbor and Opera House (but does not take bookings).

140 George St., The Rocks. www.mca.com.au. ✆ **02/9245 2400.** Free. Daily 10am–5pm (until 9pm on Wed). Closed Christmas Day. Train, bus, or ferry: Circular Quay.

The Rocks Discovery Museum ★★ MUSEUM   Housed in a restored 1850s sandstone warehouse, this small but compelling museum is dedicated to telling the story of The Rocks from pre-European days to the present. Learn about the area's traditional landowners; the establishment of the English colony; the sailors, whalers, and traders who called the area home; and the 1970s union-led protests that preserved this unique part of Sydney.

Kendall Lane (off Argyle St.), The Rocks. www.therocks.com/things-to-do/the-rocks-discovery-museum. ✆ **02/9240 8680.** Free. Daily 10am–5pm. Closed Good Friday and Dec 25. Train: Circular Quay or Wynyard.

The Museum of Contemporary Art during the Vivid Sydney Light, Music & Ideas Festival.

Susannah Place Museum ★★ MUSEUM Entry to this small museum is by guided tour only, but don't let that put you off—it may enhance your visit. Contained in a terrace of four houses built in 1844, this museum is a real highlight of The Rocks area. It provides visitors with the opportunity to explore domestic working-class life from 1844 to 1990. The modest interiors and rear yards illustrate the restrictions of 19th-century inner-city life. The layers of paint, wallpapers, and floor coverings that have survived provide a valuable insight into the tastes of the working class. There's also a delightful little shop selling cordials, postcards, old-fashioned candies, and knickknacks.

58–64 Gloucester St., The Rocks. www.sydneylivingmuseums.com.au. ✆ **02/9241 1893.** Entry by guided tour only, A\$12 adults, A\$8 children, A\$30 family of 4. Daily 2–5pm (last tour at 4pm). Closed Good Friday and Dec 25. Bus, ferry, or train: Circular Quay.

Sydney Harbour Bridge ★★★ ICON One thing few tourists do—which is a shame—is to walk across the Harbour Bridge. The bridge, completed in 1932, is 1,150 meters (3,772 feet) long and spans 503 meters (1,650 feet) from the south shore to the north. It has pedestrian walkways, two railway lines, and an eight-lane road. The 30-minute walk from one end to the other offers excellent harbor views. From the other side, you can take a train from Milsons Point back to the city.

As you walk across, stop off at the **Pylon Lookout** (www.pylonlookout. com.au; ✆ **02/9240 1100**) at the southeastern pylon. Admission is A\$15 for adults, A\$8.50 for children ages 5 to 12. There are four levels inside the pylon, with displays about the bridge's history. Level two has observation balconies on both sides, and when you reach the top, 89m (292 ft.) above the water, you get panoramic views of Sydney Harbour, the ferry terminals of Circular Quay, and beyond. The Pylon Lookout is open daily from 10am to 5pm (closed Christmas Day).

Another very popular way of enjoying the wonderful views from the Bridge is to climb to the top. The Sydney **BridgeClimb,** 3 Cumberland St., The Rocks (www.bridgeclimb.com; ✆ **02/8274 7777**), is an exhilarating achievement, and one you won't forget. Of the three climbs you can choose to do,

---

Sydney Harbour on the Cheap

The best way to see Sydney Harbour is from the water. Several companies operate tourist craft (see "Harbor Cruises," p. 99), but it's easy enough just to hop on a regular passenger ferry (see "Getting Around," p. 60). The best ferry excursions are to the beachside suburb of **Manly** (return after dusk to see the lights ablaze around The Rocks and Circular Quay); to **Watsons Bay,** where you can have lunch and wander along the cliffs; to **Darling Harbour,** traveling right under the Harbour Bridge; and to **Mosman Bay,** to see the grand houses that overlook exclusive harbor inlets.

The Sydney BridgeClimb takes you along catwalks and ladders to the top of the bridge.

BridgeClimb takes you along the outer arch of the bridge on catwalks and ladders all the way to the summit. The **Bridgeclimb Express** takes climbers into the heart of the bridge. You traverse the suspension arch and then wind your way through a tangle of hatchways and girders suspended above the traffic. You also climb between the arches to the summit. Both experiences take 3½ hours from check-in to completion. For those with limited time, the **BridgeClimb Sampler** (A$174 adults, A$148 children) delivers you to the halfway point of the climb, and takes only 90 minutes. Climbers wear "Bridge Suits" and are harnessed to a safety line; everyone must pass an alcohol breathalyzer test. Daytime climbs cost A$308 for adults and A$208 for children ages 10 to 15. Dawn climbs cost A$388 adults, A$278 kids; twilight climbs cost A$374 adults, A$264 kids; night climbs cost A$268 adults, A$188 kids (bundle up, it can be cold up there!). You're not allowed to carry anything, even cameras, with you on the climb, but the guides will take plenty of photos of you along the way, which you can buy at the end. Children 7 and under are not allowed to climb. The **Visitor Centre,** where you set out from, has good displays featuring Sydney's famous icon and two short films about the bridge.

Sydney Observatory ★★ OBSERVATORY The city's only major observatory offers visitors a chance to see the southern skies through modern and historic telescopes. The best time to visit is during the night on a guided tour, when you can take a close-up look at the stars and planets. Two-hour night tours start at 6:30 and 8:30pm and must be booked in advance. There are also tours at 7pm and 9pm on Friday and Saturday. On weekends and school holidays, 30-minute guided tours run every hour from 10:15am, including a planetarium show and a telescope viewing. Schedules are subject to change, so check the times when you book. The planetarium and hands-on exhibits are also interesting. Daytime admission to the gardens and the exhibitions is free, but doesn't include the telescope towers, telescope viewings, and 3-D theater. For A$330 you can also name a star after yourself or someone you love!

Observatory Hill, 1003 Upper Fort St., Millers Point. www.maas.museum/sydney-observatory. (✆ **02/9217 0111.** Daytime tours A$10 adults, A$8 children 4–16, A$26 family of 4. Guided night tours (reservations required) A$27 adults, A$20 children, A$80 families. Daily 10am–5pm. Closed Dec 25–26 and Dec 31. Train, bus, or ferry: Circular Quay.

Sydney Opera House ★★★ ICON/PERFORMING ARTS VENUE Only a handful of buildings around the world are as architecturally and culturally significant as the Sydney Opera House, a white-sailed construction caught mid-billow over the waters of Sydney Cove. But what sets it apart from many other famous architectural icons is that this is a working building, housing a full-scale performing-arts complex with four major performance spaces. The biggest and grandest is the 2,690-seat **Concert Hall.** Come here to experience chamber music, symphonies, dance, choral performances, and even rock 'n' roll. The **Joan Sutherland Theatre** is smaller, seats 1,547, and books opera, ballet, and dance. The **Drama Theatre,** seating 544, and the **Playhouse,** seating 398, specialize in plays and smaller-scale performances.

The history of the building is as intriguing as the design. The New South Wales Government raised the construction money with a lottery, and Danish architect Jørn Utzon won an international competition to design it. Following a disagreement, however, Utzon returned home without ever seeing his finished project. Budgeted at A$7 million, by its completion in 1973 the project

---

Fast Action on Sydney Harbour

For a thrill ride, you can board a 420-horsepower jet boat, which zooms about on three high-speed waterway tours at speeds of up to 40 knots (about 80kmph/50 mph), with huge 240-degree turns and instant stops. **Harbour Jet** (www.harbourjet.com; (✆ **1300/887 373** in Australia) offers a 35-minute Jet Blast ride costing A$60 adults, A$30 kids 14 and under, and A$175 for a family. It leaves at 11am, noon, 2pm, and 3pm Thursday through Sunday. Rides are fast and furious and pump with rock music. The boat leaves from the King Street Jetty 9 (near the Sydney SEA LIFE Aquarium) at Darling Harbour.

Another option is **Oz Jet Boat** (www.ozjetboating.com; (✆ **02/9808 3700**), with departures every hour from the Eastern Pontoon at Circular Quay (on the walkway to the Opera House). These large red boats are a bit more powerful than the blue Harbour Jet ones, but you might not notice the difference. This company offers a 30-minute Shark Attack Thrill Ride for A$85 adults, A$49 kids 15 and under, and A$219 for a family of four (cheaper if you book online). Rides leaves regularly from 11am to 4pm daily (5pm in summer). Kids must be at least 1.2m (3 ft., 11 in.) tall.

SEEING SYDNEY HARBOUR THROUGH
aboriginal EYES

Every visitor to Sydney should get out on the harbor with descendants of the original inhabitants of this most famous waterway. The **Tribal Warrior Association** is an Aboriginal-operated nonprofit organization that provides maritime training programs for Aboriginal youths, and also offers an Aboriginal perspective of Sydney Harbour in 2-hour **Aboriginal Cultural Cruises ★★★** (www.tribalwarrior.org; ℂ **02/9699 3491**). Aboard the ketch *Mari Nawi* you will sail past the Royal Botanic Garden as your indigenous guide tells stories of the early Europeans and their hopeless farms, and the smallpox epidemic of 1789. You'll hear tales of the first Aboriginal tour guides, who took early settlers inland from the harbor, and much more. The cruise stops at Clark Island, where visitors will see cave shelters with roofs stained black from ancient fireplaces, convict engravings, and a natural fish trap. Two Aboriginal guides, their bodies plastered in ghostly white ochre, beat a rhythm with hardwood sticks and growl through a didgeridoo as they beckon tourists to the Welcoming Ceremony. Then comes a repertoire of haunting songs, music, and dance. Cruises cost A$66 adults, A$44 children 4 to 14, and A$198 for a family of four. Bookings are essential; tours run subject to minimum numbers and availability. Times vary each day, so check the website for details.

cost a staggering A$102 million, most raised through a series of lotteries. After a A$152-million upgrade in recent years, the Opera House has never looked better.

Guided tours of the Opera House last about an hour and are conducted daily from 9am to 5pm, except on Good Friday and Christmas Day. You may not get to see everything, because there's almost always some performance, practice, or setting up going on. Tour sizes are limited—reservations are essential—but it is worth planning for, as the tour is fascinating. Two-and-a-half-hour backstage tours, which include breakfast in the Green Room, require climbing up to 300 stairs (no children 9 and under).

The Tourism Services Department at the Sydney Opera House can book **combination packages,** including dinner and a show; a tour, dinner, and a show; or a champagne-interval performance. Prices vary depending on shows and dining venues. Visitors from overseas can buy tickets by credit card and pick them up at the box office on arrival. Advance purchases are a good idea, because performances are very popular.

The Opera House is where you will see performances by the Melbourne-based **Australian Ballet** during its Sydney season (www.australianballet.com.au). **Opera Australia** (www.opera.org.au; ℂ **02/9318 8200** for bookings) performs at the Joan Sutherland Theatre. The **Sydney Symphony Orchestra** (www.sydneysymphony.com; ℂ **02/8215 4600** box office) performs throughout the year in the Concert Hall. The main symphony season runs March through November, and there's a summer season in February.

Free performances take place outside on the Opera House boardwalks on Sunday afternoons and during festival times. The artists range from musicians and performance artists to school groups.

Bennelong Point. www.sydneyoperahouse.com. (C) **02/9250 7250** for guided tours and information, or 02/9250 7777 box office. Box office Mon–Sat 9am–8:30pm; Sun 10am–6pm. Tours A$42 adults, A$22 kids, A$106 family of 4. Book online for discounts. Tours daily 9am–5pm (every 30 min.). Backstage tour A$175 starts daily at 7am, for 2½ hr., with breakfast. Train, bus, or ferry: Circular Quay.

Darling Harbour

Many tourists head to Darling Harbour for the cheap eateries and a few interesting shops, but Sydney's dedicated tourist precinct has much more to offer. See **www.darlingharbour.com** for current events.

Australian National Maritime Museum ★★ MUSEUM   Australia owes almost everything to the sea, so it's not surprising that it has a museum dedicated to seafarers and ships, from Aboriginal vessels to submarines. In fact, it now calls itself the "mu-sea-um." The museum's outdoor Welcome Wall, which celebrates the arrival of waves of migrants as part of Australia's maritime history, is inscribed with more than 29,000 names from more than 200 countries. The museum's "Big Ticket" gives access to everything—the Australian navy destroyer *Vampire,* an Oberon Class submarine, the tall ship *James Craig,* and a replica of the *Endeavour,* the ship Captain James Cook commanded when he laid claim to Australia—as well as galleries, exhibitions, the Cape Bowling Green lighthouse, and the Kids on Deck program (Sun and school holidays). You'll find ships' logs and things to pull and tug at and clamber over—kids love it! Allow 2 hours.

2 Murray St., Darling Harbour. www.sea.museum. (C) **02/9298 3777.** Free admission to permanent galleries; "Big Ticket" admission to galleries, exhibitions, ships, and Kids on Deck A$32 adults, A$20 children 4–15, A$79 families of 5. Additional fees for special exhibitions. Daily 9:30am–5pm (until 6pm Jan). Closed Dec 25. Ferry: Darling Harbour. Bus: 389. Light Rail: L1 from Central Station to Pyrmont Bay.

Powerhouse Museum ★★★ MUSEUM   Sydney's most interactive museum is expected to relocate to Parramatta, in the city's far western suburbs, with a scheduled opening date of 2023. The current museum will close sometime in 2020, and the building will be redeveloped as a creative arts center, including a **design and fashion museum.** Meanwhile, if you arrive early enough in 2020, you'll find displays, sound effects, and gadgets relating to the sciences, transportation, human achievement, decorative art, fashion, and social history, much of it with relevance or connections to Sydney and Australian exploration. You could easily spend 2 or 3 hours discovering everything here. There's plenty to keep kids interested as well.

500 Harris St., Ultimo (near Darling Harbour). www.maas.museum/powerhouse-museum. (C) **02/9217 0111.** A$15 adults, free for children 16 and under. Daily 10am–5pm. Closed Dec 25. Ferry: Darling Harbour. Bus: 501. Light Rail: Exhibition Centre.

SEA LIFE Sydney Aquarium ★ AQUARIUM Sharks, crocodiles, penguins, *dugongs* (sea cows), and platypuses are just some of the marine life you will encounter at this aquarium. The main attractions are the underwater walkways through two enormous tanks—one full of giant rays and gray nurse sharks and the other where you can see the seals. At Penguin Island, you can raft though a sub-Antarctic environment populated with King and Gentoo penguins. Other exhibits include a section on the Great Barrier Reef, where thousands of colorful fish school around coral outcrops. A touch pool allows you to stroke baby sharks. Among many experiences and animal encounters, you can take a 20-minute behind-the-scenes tour of the Great Barrier Reef oceanarium in a glass-bottom boat (every 30 min. noon–4pm; A$66 adults, A$46 kids 3–15; no children under 3). Tour prices include general admission. Try to visit during the week, when it's less crowded. Allow around 2 hours.

Aquarium Pier, Darling Harbour. www.sydneyaquarium.com.au. © **02/8251 7800.** A$46 adults, A$33 children 3–15; cheaper if booked online. Daily 10am–6pm (last entry 5pm). Train: Town Hall. Ferry: Darling Harbour.

Other Top Attractions

Art Gallery of New South Wales ★★★ MUSEUM This beautiful gallery, established in 1871, has a fine collection of international and Australian art that you should take time to see. Contemporary works are displayed in light-filled galleries with views of Sydney and the harbor, while colonial and 19th-century Australian art and European Old Masters are housed in the Grand Courts. There are also dedicated galleries for Asian and Aboriginal and Torres Strait Islander art. The gallery hosts more than 30 temporary exhibitions each year, including the annual Archibald Prize for portraiture (late Mar–early June), in which you'll see plenty of famous Australian faces. Enter

---

Deals on Sightseeing

Several major Sydney attractions offer discounts if you buy passes to more than one of them. If you plan to visit the Sydney Eye Tower, SEA LIFE Sydney Aquarium, or Sydney Wildlife Zoo, check their websites for information on **Sydney Big Ticket** passes, which can be used for two, three, or four of the listed attractions. Once you visit your first attraction, you've got 30 days to visit the others on the pass. Prices start from A$50 adults and A$35 children 4 to 15 for two attractions and go up to A$99 adults and A$70 children for four attractions (that's less than A$25 per attrac-

tion for adults—compare that to the hefty A$46 you'd pay for the aquarium, for example). Buy tickets online. There's also the **Sydney Museums Pass** (www. sydneylivingmuseums.com.au), which provides access to 12 museums and historic houses for A$24 adults, A$16 children 5 to 15, or A$50 for a family of four. Many of these museums cost A$12 adults—visit more than two and you're ahead! Buy online or at any of the attractions, which include the Museum of Sydney, Susannah Place Museum, Elizabeth Bay House, and others listed in this book.

from the Domain parklands (across the road from the Royal Botanic Garden) onto the third floor (ground level) of the museum. Allow at least 1 hour, more if you are interested in any of the many free tours on offer.

Art Gallery Rd., The Domain. www.artgallery.nsw.gov.au. ℂ **1800/679 278** in Australia, or 02/9225 1744. Free admission; prices vary for special exhibitions. Sun–Tues and Thurs–Sat 10am–5pm; Wed 10am–10pm. Closed Good Friday and Dec 25. Tours of collection highlights daily 11am. Tours of Aboriginal galleries daily 10:30am. Bus: no. 441. Train: St. James.

Australian Museum ★★ MUSEUM

This is Sydney's premier natural history museum. Displays are presented thematically; the Aboriginal section, with traditional clothing, weapons, and everyday implements, is among the best. There are plenty of stuffed Australian mammals and birds, an insect display, and a mineral collection. Children are well catered to, with plenty of dinosaurs, mummies, and other wonderful things to observe.

1 William St. www.australianmuseum.net.au. ℂ **02/9320 6000.** A$15 adults, free for children 15 and under, A$30 families of 4. Special exhibits extra. Daily 9:30am–5pm. Closed Dec 25. Train: Museum, St. James, or Town Hall.

Elizabeth Bay House ★ HISTORIC HOME

Perched on a headland with some of the best harbor views in Sydney, this mansion was built in 1835 and was considered "the finest house in the colony." You can tour the house and get a feel for the history of that fledgling settlement.

7 Onslow Ave., Elizabeth Bay. www.sydneylivingmuseums.com.au. ℂ **02/9356 3022.** A$12 adults, A$8 children, A$30 families. Fri–Sun 10am–4pm. Closed Good Friday and Dec 25. Bus: no. 311 from Circular Quay. Train: Kings Cross.

Hyde Park Barracks Museum ★★ MUSEUM

This fascinating museum, dedicated to telling the stories of some of the 50,000 convicts who passed through the Hyde Park Barracks between 1819 and 1848, was closed for almost the whole of 2019 for a A$18 million upgrade. At the time of writing, it was expected to reopen by late 2019, in time to commemorate 200 years since the first 600 convicts arrived at the barracks in 1819. The Georgian-style barracks, designed by the convict Francis Greenway (an architect), were built by convicts and inhabited by others. The barracks are among 11 convict sites in Australia that are on the World Heritage Site list. The new-look museum will display more than 4,000 original objects from its collection. If you are interested in Sydney's early beginnings, I highly recommend a visit.

Queens Sq., 10 Macquarie St. www.sydneylivingmuseums.com.au/hyde-park-barracks-museum. ℂ **02/8239 2311.** Check the website for details of hours and entry prices. Train: St. James or Martin Place.

Museum of Sydney ★ MUSEUM

In a postmodern building near Circular Quay, encompassing the remnants of Sydney's first Government House, the museum is certainly not what you might expect. No conventional showcase of history, it houses a collection of first-settler and Aboriginal objects, with multimedia displays that invite you to discover Sydney's past. Some of it is underfoot, in the archaeological digs exposed through "windows" in the paths. A forest of poles filled with hair, oyster shells, and crab claws in the courtyard, called *Edge of Trees*, represents first contact between Aborigines and the British. Modern…yes. And very interesting. There are plenty of reasons to linger, for a game of outdoor chess, perhaps, or just to lounge on the grass.

37 Phillip St. (at Bridge St.). www.sydneylivingmuseums.com.au. *C* **02/9251 5988.** A\$15 adults, A\$12 children 14 and under, A\$38 families of 4. Daily 10am–5pm. Closed Good Friday and Dec 25. Train, bus, or ferry: Circular Quay.

Sydney Jewish Museum ★★★ MUSEUM   A major permanent exhibition developed in consultation with Holocaust survivors, many of whom are volunteer guides at the museum, gives voice to their history. One of the most moving aspects of any visit to this museum has always been the chance to talk to Holocaust survivors. Another permanent exhibition here is *Serving Australia*, which showcases the contribution that Jewish servicemen and women have made to the Australian armed forces. The museum also has a shop, a resource center, a small theater, and a kosher cafe. Allow 1 to 2 hours. Plan to visit in the afternoon to avoid large school groups.

148 Darlinghurst Rd. (at Burton St.), Darlinghurst. www.sydneyjewishmuseum.com.au. *C* **02/8294 1448.** A\$15 adults, A\$9 children, free for kids 9 and under, A\$40 families of 4. Free 1-hr. guided tours Mon–Fri 2pm, Sun noon and 2pm. Mon–Thurs 10am–4:30pm; Fri 10am–3:30pm; Sun 10am–4pm. Closed Sat, public holidays, and Jewish holidays. Train: Kings Cross.

Sydney Tower ★ OBSERVATION TOWER   The Sydney Tower is hard to miss—it resembles a giant steel pole skewering a golden marshmallow. Standing 309m (984 ft.) tall, the tower offers stupendous 360-degree views across Sydney and as far as the Blue Mountains. At the top is a revolving restaurant and bar, and an indoor viewing platform called the Sydney Tower Eye. (Don't be too concerned if you feel the building tremble slightly, especially in a strong wind—it's built to do that.) The ticket price includes admission to a 4-D cinema, where you can watch a film about Sydney with footage of the harbor, coastline, famous landmarks, and events.

Sydney Tower is the city's largest structure and an easy-to-spot landmark.

Westfield Shopping Centre, 100 Market St. (another entrance on Pitt St. Mall). www.sydney towereye.com.au. *C* **1800/258 693** in Australia, or 02/9333 9222. A\$29 adults, A\$20 children 4–15. Daily 9am–9pm (last entry 8pm); Christmas Day 10am–6pm (last entry 5pm); New Year's Eve 9am–7pm (last entry 6pm). Train: St. James or Town Hall.

Kangaroos, Koalas & Other Aussie Wildlife

See p. 95 for SEA LIFE Sydney Aquarium.

Featherdale Wildlife Park ★★★ WILDLIFE VIEWING   If you have time to visit only one wildlife park in Sydney, make it this one. The selection of Australian animals is excellent, and, most important, the animals are very well cared for. You could easily spend a couple of hours here, despite the park's compact size. You'll have the chance to hand-feed friendly kangaroos and wallabies and get a photo taken next to a koala, or have breakfast with one for an extra A$43 (weekends only). If you're visiting between September and April, there's a free crocodile feeding session daily. The **Reptilian Pavilion** houses 30 native species of reptiles in 26 realistic exhibits. If you are heading to the Blue Mountains (p. 109) on a bus tour, choose one that stops off here. Allow 1½ hours to get here by public transport or 45 minutes by car from the city center.

217 Kildare Rd., Doonside. www.featherdale.com.au. (C) **02/9622 1644.** A$32 adults, A$19 children 3–15, A$58–A$88 families. Daily 8am–5pm. Closed Dec 25. Train: Blacktown station; then bus no. 729.

Koala Park Sanctuary ★ NATURE CENTER   In all, around 55 koalas roam within the park's leafy boundaries (it's set in 4 hectares/10 acres of rainforest). Free koala feeding sessions take place at 10:20 and 11:45am, and 2 and 3pm daily (and you can have your photo taken with them too!). There are wombats, dingoes, kangaroos, wallabies, emus, and native birds here as well. Live sheep shearing takes place at 10:30am and 2:30pm daily. Allow 1½ hours to get here by public transport from the city center or about 30 minutes to drive.

84 Castle Hill Rd., West Pennant Hills. www.koalapark-sanctuary.com.au. (C) **02/9484 3141.** A$28 adults, A$15 children 4–14, A$77 family of 4. Daily 9am–4:30pm (to 5pm Apr–Sept). Closed Dec 25. Train: Pennant Hills station via North Strathfield (45 min.). Cross over railway line and join Glenorie Bus routes 651 to 655. The bus takes about 10 min. to Koala Park.

Taronga Zoo ★★★ ZOO   Taronga has the best views of any zoo in the world. Set on a hill, it looks out over Sydney Harbour, the Opera House, and the Harbour Bridge. It's easiest on the legs to explore the zoo from the top down (admission includes a trip on the cable car from the ferry pier to the main entrance). The big attractions are the fabulous chimpanzee exhibit, the gorilla enclosure, and the Nocturnal Houses, where you can see some of Australia's unique marsupials, including the platypus and the cute bilby. There's an interesting reptile display, a couple of impressive Komodo dragons, a scattering of indigenous beasties—including a few koalas, echidnas, kangaroos, dingoes, and wombats—and lots more. Animals are fed at various times during the day, and there's a chance to have close encounters with koalas, giraffes, penguins, and birds of prey. Despite the steep entry price, the zoo can get crowded on weekends, so it's a good idea to plan your visit for a weekday or go early in the morning on weekends. Allow around 3 hours.

Bradley's Head Rd., Mosman. www.taronga.org.au/taronga-zoo. ✆ **02/9969 2777.** A$47 adults, A$27 children 4–15. Daily 9:30am–5pm. Ferry: Taronga Zoo. Lower zoo entrance is at ferry terminal. Bus: M30 or 238.

Wildlife Sydney Zoo ★★ ZOO   Not to be confused with Taronga Zoo (Sydney's premier outdoor zoo; see above), this inner-city attraction has a big collection of Australian creatures, including kangaroos, a cassowary, snakes, wallabies, Tasmanian devils, birds, butterflies, and a large saltwater crocodile. You'll find koalas lazing around in the rooftop garden. Take a walk through six themed Australian habitats including the Daintree Rainforest and Kakadu Gorge. No elephants or giraffes here, but it might not matter! Behind-the-scenes tours (A$99 per person) run daily at 10am and 2pm. You can also get up close with a koala (photos are A$35 for up to 4 people).

Aquarium Pier, Darling Harbour. www.wildlifesydney.com.au. No phone. A$44 adults, A$31 kids 3–15. Daily 10am–5pm (last entry 4pm). Ferry: Darling Harbour. Train: Wynyard or Town Hall.

ORGANIZED TOURS

For details on the **Big Bus Sydney** sightseeing buses, see "Getting Around," p. 61.

Harbor Cruises

The best thing about Sydney is the harbor, and you shouldn't leave without taking a cruise. **Captain Cook Cruises,** departing Wharf 6, Circular Quay (www.captaincook.com.au; ✆ **02/9206 1111**), offers several harbor excursions on its sleek vessels, with commentary along the way. One-hour afternoon "High Tea Cruises" cost A$59, and there's a range of dining cruises as well. The popular 1-hour, 15-minute "Harbour Highlights Cruise" costs A$39 adults and A$25 children 4 to 15 and runs daily at 2:30pm from Circular Quay. Whale-watching cruises run from mid-May to early November, some incorporating a morning at Taronga Zoo (p. 98), costing A$109 adults and A$75 children. Check the website for special deals. Captain Cook Cruises has ticket booths at Wharf 6, Circular Quay (daily 8:30am–7pm), at King Street Wharf 1 (Mon–Fri 9am–7:30pm, Sat–Sun 4–7:30pm) and at Pier 26, Darling Harbour (daily 8:30am–5pm).

   Yellow Water Taxis (www.yellowwatertaxis.com; ✆ **1800/326 822** in Australia) offers a 60-minute tour by small water taxi from its bases at King Street Wharf in Darling Harbour and Circular Quay Jetty 1. These "snapshot" tours are good for a quick look at Sydney's famous harbor and a great way to travel to or from Darling Harbour and Circular Quay. Tours cost A$20 adults, A$15 children 4 to 12, and A$55 for a family of four. A 45-minute sunset cruise starts from either Circular Quay or Cockle Bay about 15 to 30 minutes before sunset. This tour costs A$45 adults, A$30 kids, and A$135 for a family of four.

Check websites or pop into a ticket office at Darling Harbour or Circular Quay, because cruise options, departure times, and prices change frequently.

Walking Tours

If you want to learn more about Sydney's early history, book an excellent guided tour with **The Rocks Walking Tours,** based at Clocktower Square, corner of Argyle and Harrington streets (www.rockswalkingtours.com.au; ✆ **02/9247 6678**). Walks leave daily at 10:30am and 1:30pm. The 1½-hour tour costs A$32 adults, A$15 children 5 to 16, and A$79 for families of four.

Culture Scouts (www.culturescouts.com.au; ✆ **02/9016 5531**) runs interesting walking tours that focus on art, food, and conversation (think galleries, cafes, bars, street art, and boutiques) in the inner suburbs of Chippendale, Redfern, Darlinghurst, Surry Hills, Ultimo, and Newtown. Tours last 2 to 3 hours, go at a gentle pace, and can be customized if you wish. Tours cost A$65 to A$99 per person; they're not recommended for kids 14 and under. Two-hour street art tours (A$65 per person) run every second Saturday morning.

Motorcycle Tours

Wild Ride Australia (www.wildride.com.au; ✆ **1300/738 338** in Australia or 02/9623 8338) runs Harley-Davidson tours of Sydney, the Blue Mountains, and beyond. A 1-hour ride (you sit on the back of the bike) around the city or Bondi costs A$130. A 1½-hour ride through the city and out to Bondi costs A$160. A 3-hour trip to the northern beaches costs A$250. Full-day trips cover the Blue Mountains and the Hawkesbury region. If you love motorcycles and want to rent one for a self-guided or guided tour, contact **Bikescape** (www.bikescape.com.au; ✆ **1300/736 869** in Australia, or 02/8123 0917).

ESPECIALLY FOR KIDS

Sydney is a great city to visit with kids. It's got a load of zoos and wildlife viewing experiences (p. 98), and several engaging attractions with hands-on and interactive displays, including the Australian National Maritime Museum (p. 94), SEA LIFE Sydney Aquarium (p. 95), and the Australian Museum (p. 96). There are many different options for getting out onto the waters of famous Sydney Harbor, from short water-taxi rides (p. 99) to high-speed jet boats (p. 92). Older kids may love the thrill of a BridgeClimb (p. 90). Add in a day at the beach and you've got a vacation they'll long remember.

Luna Park ★ AMUSEMENT PARK   The huge smiling clown face and the fairground attractions, which are visible from Circular Quay, make up one of Australia's most iconic attractions. It's fun for kids, with traditional theme-park amusements rather than high-tech rides. Luna Park has a carousel, bumper cars, a Ferris wheel, and the like. Many rides are suitable for small children, too. You buy tickets at booths inside the park. The best way to get here is either to walk over the Sydney Harbour Bridge from The Rocks or to catch a train from the city center to Milsons Point. Leave some time for a walk along the foreshore of Sydney Harbour, right beneath the bridge. Hours vary, so check online before setting out.

1 Olympic Dr., Milsons Point. www.lunaparksydney.com.au. © **02/9922 6644.** Free admission. Ride passes based on height: unlimited ride pass A$25 small child, A$47 big kids, A$57 adults. Other prices and deals available. Expect higher prices during school holidays, but better rates if booked online. Mon 11am–4pm; Fri–Sat 11am–11pm; Sun 10am–6pm. During school holidays: Sun–Thurs 10am–6pm; Fri–Sat 10am–10pm. Ferry or train: Milsons Point.

OUTDOOR ACTIVITIES

Hitting the Beach

One of the big bonuses of visiting Sydney in the summer (Dec–Feb) is that you get to experience the beaches in their full glory. Most major city beaches, such as Manly and Bondi, have lifeguards on patrol, especially during the summer. They check the water conditions and are on the lookout for **"rips"**—strong currents that can pull a swimmer far out. Always swim in the area between the red and yellow flags that mark the patrolled area. Fiberglass surfboards must be used outside the flags. (Expect a warning from the loudspeakers and a fine if you fail to do this.)

SOUTH OF SYDNEY HARBOUR

Sydney's most famous beach is **Bondi ★★★**. The beach, sadly, is cut off from the cafe and restaurant strip that caters to beachgoers by a busy road that pedestrians must cross to reach the sand. On summer weekend evenings, it's popular with young men driving souped-up cars and strutting their stuff. To reach Bondi Beach, take the train to Bondi Junction, and then transfer to bus no. 380 or 333 (a 15-min. bus journey). The no. 333 bus takes about 40 minutes from Circular Quay.

Escaping a Rip

Plenty of tourists get into real trouble on Sydney's beaches each year by being caught in a riptide—a fast current that moves away from the shore (but will not pull you under the water). If this happens, the most important thing to do is not to panic. If you can't stand up and are being pulled out to sea, try to attract attention by raising a hand in the air. Whatever you do, don't try to battle it out with the rip by swimming against it back to shore. You will quickly become exhausted; this is how people drown. Keep calm, and swim parallel to the beach. If you run out of energy, float on your back. If you swim parallel to the beach you will be pulled a little farther out to sea—it won't take you far out—but before long you should be out of the rip and able to swim back to the beach. Never swim outside of the area marked by yellow and red flags on a beach patrolled by lifeguards. If there are no lifeguards around, it's safest not to swim.

Bronte Beach.

If you're facing the water at Bondi, to your right is a scenic cliff-top trail that takes you to **Bronte Beach ★★★** (a 20-min. walk) via gorgeous little **Tamarama ★★★**, nicknamed "Glamourama" for its trendy sun worshippers. Bronte has better swimming; Tamarama is known for its dangerous rips and is often closed to swimming. To go straight to Bronte, catch bus no. 378 from Circular Quay or pick up the bus at the Bondi Junction train station.

Clovelly Beach ★★★, farther along the coast, is blessed with a large rock pool carved into a rock platform that's sheltered from the force of the Tasman Sea. This beach is accessible for visitors in wheelchairs on a series of ramps. To reach Clovelly, take bus no. 339 from Circular Quay.

The cliff walk from Bondi will eventually bring you to **Coogee ★★**, which has a pleasant strip of sand with a couple of hostels and hotels nearby. To reach Coogee, take bus no. 373 or 374 from Circular Quay.

NORTH OF SYDNEY HARBOUR

On the North Shore you'll find **Manly ★★★**, a long curve of golden sand edged with Norfolk Island pines. The best way to reach Manly is on a ferry from Circular Quay. Follow the crowds through the pedestrian Corso to the main ocean beach, ignoring the two small beaches on either side of the ferry terminal.

Facing the ocean, head to your right along the beachfront and follow the coastal path to small and sheltered **Shelly Beach ★★★**, a nice area for snorkeling and swimming. This is one of Sydney's most pleasant walks. Follow the path up the hill to the car park. Here, a track cuts up into the bush and leads toward a firewall, which marks the entrance to the Sydney Harbour National Park and offers spectacular ocean views across to Manly and the northern beaches.

The best harbor beach is at **Balmoral ★★★**, a wealthy suburb with some good cafes and restaurants. Reach Balmoral on the ferry to Taronga Zoo and then a 10-minute ride on a connecting bus from the ferry wharf, or catch the bus from the stop outside the zoo's top entrance.

Surfing

Bondi Beach and **Tamarama** are the best surf beaches on the south side of Sydney Harbour. **Manly, Narrabeen, Bilgola, Collaroy, Long Reef,** and **Palm** beaches are the most popular on the north side. Most beach suburbs have surf shops where you can rent a board.

At Bondi Beach, **Lets Go Surfing,** 128 Ramsgate Ave. (www.letsgosurfing.com.au; ✆ **02/9365 1800**), offers 2-hour surfing lessons in a small group for A$85 per person.

In Manly, **Manly Surf Guide** (www.manlysurfguide.com; ✆ **0412/417 431** mobile) rents (and delivers) surfboards for A$40 a day. **Manly Surf School** (http://manlysurfschool.com; ✆ **02/9932 7000**) offers 2-hour small-group surf classes for A$70 adults and A$60 children. The more lessons you take, the cheaper it is. For A$120 you get a full day's outing that includes pickup from the city, lessons, and surfing at various places on the northern beaches.

If you're already proficient, consider a 1-day trip to the Royal National Park with **Waves Surf School** (www.wavessurfschool.com.au; ✆ **1800/616 667** in Australia, or 02/9641 2358). Trips cost A$119 weekdays and A$139 weekends, including lunch. Waves also offers a 2-day surfing trip to Seal Rocks, north of Sydney, for A$349 per person.

4

SYDNEYSYDNEY | Outdoor Activities

Sharks & Other Nasties

One of the first things visitors ask before they hit the water in Australia is: "Are there sharks?" The answer is yes, but fortunately they are rarely spotted inshore—you are far more likely to spy a migrating whale. In reality, the chance of a shark attack is very small. Some beaches—such as the small beach next to the Manly ferry wharf—have permanent shark nets, while others rely on portable nets that are moved from beach to beach. Shark attacks are most likely in early morning and at dusk—avoid swimming during these times.

More common off Sydney's beaches are **"blue bottles"**—small blue jellyfish, often called "stingers" in Australia (and Portuguese man-o'-war elsewhere). You'll often find these creatures (which are not the same as the stingers in north Queensland) washed up on the beach. Be on the lookout for warning signs erected on the shoreline. Minute stinging cells that touch your skin can cause minor itching. You might be hit by the full force of a blue bottle if it wraps its tentacles around you, which causes a severe burning sensation almost immediately. Wearing a T-shirt in the water reduces the risk somewhat. If you are stung, rinse the area liberally with seawater or fresh water to remove any tentacles stuck in your skin. To combat intense pain, take a hot shower. In the unlikely event that you experience breathing difficulties or disorientation, seek medical attention immediately.

Parks & Gardens

If you have time to spend in one of Sydney's green spaces, make it the **Royal Botanic Garden ★★★** (www.rbgsyd.nsw.gov.au; ℂ **02/9231 8111**), next to the Sydney Opera House. Open daily (7am–dusk), these lovely informal gardens were laid out in 1816 on the site of a farm that supplied food for the colony. The gardens have a scattering of duck ponds and open spaces, with several areas dedicated to particular plant species. These include the rose garden, the cacti and succulent display, and the central palm and rainforest groves. Try to spot the thousands of large fruit bats, which chatter and bicker among the rainforest trees. Free 90-minute guided walks are run daily at 10:30am and also at 1pm Monday to Friday (except Good Friday, Christmas Day, and December 26). **Aboriginal Heritage Tours** (A$41 adults; children 7 and under free) run at 10am Wednesday, Friday, and Saturday (except public holidays). **Mrs. Macquarie's Chair ★★**, along the coast path, offers superb views of the Opera House and the Harbour Bridge. The "chair" bears the name of Elizabeth Macquarie (1788–1835), the wife of Governor Lachlan Macquarie. The sandstone building dominating the gardens nearest the Opera House is **Government House.** The gardens are open most days from 10am to 4pm, and the house is usually open Friday through Sunday and on public holidays, except Good Friday and Christmas Day (ℂ **02/9228 4111** to check times and closures). Entrance is free, but you'll need a ticket from the gatehouse (bring photo ID) to tour the house. Tours run every 30 minutes from 10:30am to 3pm and take about 45 minutes. Note that the house is sometimes closed for official functions.

In the center of the city is **Hyde Park ★**, a favorite with lunching businesspeople. Here you will find the **Anzac Memorial** to Australian and New Zealand troops killed in action, and the **Archibald Fountain,** complete with spitting turtles and sculptures of Diana and Apollo.

Another Sydney favorite is the giant **Centennial Park ★★★** (www.centennialparklands.com.au; ℂ **02/9339 6699**). The park has five main entrances, but the easiest one from the city is at the top of Oxford Street. Opened in 1888 to celebrate the centenary of European settlement, today the park encompasses huge lawns, several lakes, picnic areas with barbecues, cycling and running paths, and a cafe. It's open from sunrise to sunset. The visitor information desk is open 9am to 4pm weekdays, 9am to 2pm weekends.

Opened in 2015 and still a work in progress, the harborside **Barangaroo Reserve ★★★** (www.barangaroo.com; ℂ **1300/966 480** in Australia, or 02/9255 1700) is a spectacular 6-hectare (15-acre) parkland on the headland opposite Luna Park. Half of the Barangaroo precinct is public space with a 2km (1¼-mile) waterfront walkway lined with restaurants and cafes; the rest of the 22-hectare (54-acre) space comprises retail and apartment development. The parkland is planted with 74,000 native plants and landscaped with sandstone blocks, forming a natural amphitheater to be used for concerts and other

FACING PAGE: **Surfing on Bondi Beach.**

events. Barangaroo was a key figure in local Aboriginal culture in early colonial times (and the wife of Bennelong, for whom Bennelong Point, site of the Sydney Opera House, is named). **Aboriginal Cultural Tours** of the site run at 10:30am Monday to Saturday for about 90 minutes and cost A$36 adults, A$17 children 17 and under. Barangaroo is an easy walk from Circular Quay, either along the harborfront or along Argyle Street. The closest train station is Wynyard, and there's a ferry terminal at Barangaroo South.

Biking

The best place to cycle in Sydney is Centennial Park. Rent bikes from **Centennial Park Cycles,** 50 Clovelly Rd., Randwick (www.cyclehire.com.au; ℗ **02/9398 5027**), which is 200m (656 ft.) from the Musgrave Avenue entrance. Bikes cost A$15 for the first hour, A$20 for 2 hours, A$30 for 4 hours, and A$50 for a full day. Extra days cost just A$15 each.

 Bonza Bike Tours (www.bonzabiketours.com; ℗ **02/9247 8800**), at 30 Harrington St., The Rocks, runs guided bike tours of the city. A half-day city tour costs A$129 adults, A$99 kids, or A$369 families of 4 (extra riders A$79 each), including a bike and helmet. They also offer a tour of Manly and another that goes across Sydney Harbour Bridge. You can rent bikes from them for A$15 an hour, A$30 a half-day, or A$40 a day.

Kayaking

Paddle out in Sydney Harbour with **Natural Wanders** (www.naturalwanders. com.au; ℗ **0427/225 072** mobile), the only kayaking company that takes you under Sydney Harbour Bridge. Tours start from Lavender Bay, near Luna Park. Group tours run on weekends only, but if you'd like a private tour, owner Patrick Dibben will take you during the week too. A 3½-hour paddle costs A$120 and takes you from Lavender Bay west, across the Harbour and south to explore Balmain, then north to land at Berry Island before returning to Lavender Bay (about 10–12km/6–7 miles). Private tours cost A$190 for one person or A$160 each for two or more people. These tours usually go under Sydney Harbour Bridge and past the Opera House and stop on a beautiful beach in a bushland setting before returning. Check the website for tour options. You must be 15 years or older, have a good level of fitness, and be able to swim.

Swimming

With all that ocean, why bother with a pool? Well, Sydney has some great pools you might want to try just for their settings. The **Bondi Icebergs Club,** 1 Notts Ave. (www.icebergs.com.au; ℗ **02/9130 4804**), at Bondi Beach, has an Olympic-size ocean tidal pool built into the rocks with the ocean lapping into it. It also has a children's pool. Entrance costs A$8 adults, A$5.50 kids, or A$24 for a family of five. Towel hire is A$4. The pool is open from 6am (6:30am Sat–Sun) until 6:30pm Friday through Wednesday (closed Thurs for cleaning). *Be warned:* This is a true ocean pool, so the water is sometimes very cold (hence the name of the club!).

The Bondi Icebergs Club is an ocean-fed public pool.

There are fabulous views across Sydney Harbour from the outdoor **Andrew (Boy) Charlton Swimming Pool,** the Domain, Mrs. Macquaries Road, near the Royal Botanical Garden (www.abcpool.org; ℂ **02/9358 6686**). It also has a learner's pool and a toddler's pool. Entry is A$6.50 adults, A$4.90 kids, A$18 for a family of four. It's open 6am to 7pm daily.

Yachting

Sydney by Sail (www.sydneybysail.com.au; ℂ **02/9280 1110**), based at Darling Harbour and run by former Olympic yachtsman Matt Hayes, offers day sails on Sydney Harbour. A skippered, 3-hour afternoon sail leaving at 1pm costs A$175 adults, A$80 kids 13 and under, and A$475 for a family of four. Two-hour twilight sails run on the first Friday of each month, departing at 5:30pm and costing A$100 adults and A$50 kids. You can help sail, or just relax.

SYDNEY SHOPPING

You'll find plenty of places to keep your credit cards in action in Sydney. Most shops of interest to the visitor are in **The Rocks** and along **George and Pitt streets** (including the shops below the Sydney Tower and along Pitt Street Mall). Other precincts worth checking out are **Mosman,** on the North Shore; **Double Bay,** in the eastern suburbs, for boutique shopping; **Chatswood,** for its shopping centers; and various **weekend markets** (see box p. 108). For really trendy clothing, walk up Oxford Street to **Paddington** or head to **Surry Hills,** and for alternative clothes, go to **Newtown.** If you are looking for

SYDNEY'S street markets

Sydney has many good markets worth a look for quirky gifts or souvenirs and to soak up the local vibe, especially on weekends.

Closest to the city is **The Rocks Market** (www.therocks.com), held every Saturday and Sunday (with a smaller "foodies" market on Fri). This touristy market has more than 100 vendors selling everything from crafts, housewares, and posters to jewelry and curios. George Street in The Rocks is closed to traffic from 10am to 5pm to make it easier to stroll around.

Paddy's Markets (www.paddys markets.com.au) are a Sydney institution, with hundreds of stalls selling everything from cheap clothes and plants to chickens. It's open Wednesday to Sunday 10am to 6pm. Above Paddy's Markets is **Market City** (www.market city.com.au), which has three floors of fashion stalls, food courts, and specialty shops, and a huge Asian-European supermarket. Paddy's is at the corner of Thomas and Hay streets, Haymarket, near Chinatown.

Balmain Market (www.balmainmarket. com.au), held from 9am to 3pm on the second and fourth Saturday of each month, has about 140 vendors selling crafts, jewelry, and knickknacks. Take the ferry to Balmain (Darling St.); the market is a 10-minute walk up Darling Street, on the grounds of St. Andrew's Church.

Bondi Markets (www.bondimarkets. com.au) is a nice place to stroll around on Sunday and discover upcoming young Australian designers. This market specializes in clothing and jewelry, new, secondhand, and retro. It's open Sunday from 9am to 4pm at the Bondi Beach Public School, Campbell Parade.

Paddington Markets (www.paddington markets.com.au) is a Saturday-only market where you'll find 150 stalls offering everything from essential oils and designer clothes to New Age jewelry and Mexican hammocks. Expect things to be busy from 10am to 4pm. Take bus no. 380 or 333 from Circular Quay and follow the crowds. It's held in the grounds of St. John's Church, Oxford Street, on the corner of Newcombe Street.

trendy surf- and swimwear, the main drags at **Bondi Beach** and **Manly Beach** offer plenty of choices.

Don't miss the **Queen Victoria Building (QVB;** qvb.com.au), on the corner of Market and George streets. This ornate Victorian shopping arcade, built 1893–1898, has around 200 boutiques—mostly men's and women's fashion—on four levels. Here you'll find fashion-statement stores featuring the best of Australian design, including SABA, Country Road, and Leona Edmiston. The arcade is open 24 hours, but the shops do business Monday through Saturday from 9am to 6pm (Thurs to 9pm) and Sunday from 11am to 5pm.

The **Strand Arcade** (between Pitt Street Mall and George St.), built in 1892, has small boutiques, food stores, and cafes. Labels to look for include Manning Cartell, Scanlan Theodore, and Ginger & Smart. Nearby on **Pitt Street Mall** you'll find a few shops and a Westfield Shopping Centre full of fashion boutiques.

Oxford Street runs from the city to Bondi Junction through Paddington and Darlinghurst and is home to countless stylish clothing stores. You could spend anywhere from 2 hours to an entire day making your way from one end to the other. Detour down **William Street,** once you get to Paddington, to visit trendy boutiques including the luxury recycled goods of Di Nuovo.

The two big department store names in Sydney are **David Jones** (www.davidjones.com) and **Myer** (www.myer.com.au; ✆ **1800/811 611** in Australia). David Jones is the city's largest department store, selling everything from fashion to designer furniture. You'll find the women's section on the corner of Elizabeth and Market streets, and the men's section on the corner of Castlereagh and Market streets. The food section offers expensive delicacies. Myer is similar, but the building is newer and flashier. It's on the corner of George and Market streets.

Nearer to Circular Quay is **Chifley Plaza** (at Hunter and Elizabeth sts.), home to a selection of the world's most famous and stylish international brands.

A DAY TRIP TO THE BLUE MOUNTAINS ★★★

Katoomba: 114km (71 miles) W of Sydney; Leura: 107km (66 miles) W of Sydney; Blackheath: 114km (71 miles) W of Sydney; Wentworth Falls: 103km (64 miles) W of Sydney.

The **Blue Mountains** offer breathtaking views, rugged tablelands, sheer cliffs, deep, inaccessible valleys, enormous chasms, colorful parrots, cascading waterfalls, historic villages, and stupendous walking trails. In 2000, UNESCO classified it as a World Heritage Site.

Although the Blue Mountains are where Sydneysiders now go to escape the humidity and crowds of the city, in the early days of the colony the mountains kept at bay those who wanted to explore the interior. In 1813, three explorers—Gregory Blaxland, William Charles Wentworth, and William Lawson—managed to conquer the cliffs, valleys, and dense forests and cross the mountains to the plains beyond. There they found land the colony urgently needed for grazing and farming. The **Great Western Highway** and **Bells Line of Road** are the access roads through the region today—winding and steep in places, they are surrounded by the Blue Mountains and Wollemi national parks.

This area is known for its spectacular scenery, particularly the cliff-top views into valleys of gum trees and across to craggy outcrops that tower from the valley floor. It's colder up here than in the city, and clouds can sweep in and fill the canyons with mist in minutes, while waterfalls cascade down sheer drops, spraying the dripping ferns that cling to the gullies. A day tour may only scratch the surface but should give you a glimpse into why Sydneysiders love it. The Blue Mountains are also one of Australia's best-known adventure playgrounds, where rock climbing, caving, abseiling (rappelling), bushwalking, mountain biking, horseback riding, and canoeing are practiced year-round.

There are four main towns in the Blue Mountains. **Katoomba** (population 11,200) is the largest and the focal point of the Blue Mountains National Park. It's an easy 1½- to 2-hour trip from Sydney by train, bus, or car.

Leura (3km/2 miles west of Katoomba) is known for its gardens, its attractive old buildings (many holiday homes for Sydneysiders), and its cafes and restaurants. Just outside Leura is the **Sublime Point Lookout,** which has spectacular views of the **Three Sisters** (p. 112–113) in Katoomba. From the southern end of Leura Mall, a cliff drive takes you all the way back to **Echo Point** in Katoomba; along the way you'll enjoy stunning views across the Jamison Valley.

The pretty town of **Wentworth Falls** (7km/4½ miles east of Katoomba) has numerous crafts and antiques shops, but the area is principally known for its 281m (922-ft.) waterfall, situated in **Falls Reserve.** On the far side of the falls is the **National Pass Walk**—one of the best in the Blue Mountains. It's cut into a cliff face with overhanging rock faces on one side and sheer drops on the other. The views over the Jamison Valley are spectacular. The track takes you down to the base of the falls to the **Valley of the Waters.** Climbing up out of the valley is quite a bit more difficult, but just as rewarding.

Blackheath (14km/8½ miles northwest of Katoomba) is the highest town in the Blue Mountains at 1,049m (3,441 ft.). Take the Cliff Walk from **Evans Lookout** to **Govetts Leap** for magnificent views over the **Grose Valley** and **Bridal Veil Falls.** The 1½-hour trek passes through banksia, gum, and wattle forests, with wonderful views of mountain peaks and valleys.

Essentials

ARRIVING   By car from central Sydney, take Parramatta Road and turn off onto the M4 motorway (around 2 hr. to Katoomba). Another route is via the Harbour Bridge to North Sydney, along the Warringah Freeway (following signs to the M2). Then take the M2 to the end and follow signs to the M4 and the Blue Mountains. This takes around 1½ hours.

Frequent rail service connects Sydney to Katoomba and Blackheath from Central Station; contact **Sydney Trains** (www.transportnsw.info; *©* **131 500**) for details. The trip takes around 2 hours. Trains leave almost hourly. An adult round-trip ticket costs around A$15 (less during off-peak hours).

VISITOR INFORMATION   You can pick up maps, walking guides, and other information and book accommodations at **Blue Mountains Tourism,** Echo Point Road, Katoomba (www.visitbluemountains.com.au; *©* **1300/653 408** in Australia). The information center is an attraction itself, with glass windows overlooking a gum forest, and cockatoos and lorikeets feeding on seed dispensers. It's open 9am to 5pm daily (closed Christmas Day).

The **Blue Mountains Heritage Centre,** end of Govetts Leap Road, Blackheath (www.nationalparks.nsw.gov.au; ℂ **02/4787 8877**), run by the National Parks and Wildlife Service, offers detailed information about the Blue Mountains National Park. It's open daily from 9am to 4:30pm (closed Christmas Day).

Another good website is **www.bluemts.com.au**.

GETTING AROUND   The best way to get around the Blue Mountains without a car is the **Blue Mountains Explorer** bus (www.explorerbus.com. au; ℂ **1300/300 915** in Australia). The double-decker hop-on, hop-off bus leaves from outside the Katoomba train station about every 30 minutes between 9:15am and 4:15pm and stops at 29 attractions, resorts, galleries, and tearooms in and around Katoomba and Leura. Tickets cost A\$55 adults, A\$28 children, and A\$138 for a family; other passes include entry to Scenic World and rides on the Scenic Railway and the Skyway (see "Exploring the Blue Mountains," below).

Tours

Many private bus operators offer day trips from Sydney, but it's important to shop around. Some offer a guided coach tour, during which you just stretch your legs occasionally, while others let you get your circulation going with a couple of longish bushwalks. Remember, this will be a long day, leaving at 7 or 8am and returning to the city about 6pm.

Sydney Tours-R-Us (www.sydneytoursrus.com.au; ℂ **02/9498 4084**) runs minicoaches to the Blue Mountains, stopping off at Sydney Olympic Park on the way. Then you see all the major sights in the mountains and come home via ferry from Parramatta to Circular Quay. The trip costs A\$145 for adults and A\$110 for kids ages 4 to 12 (lunch is A\$15 extra). The tour includes a stop at Featherdale Wildlife Park (p. 98).

Blue Mountains Walkabout (www.bluemountainswalkabout.com; ℂ **0408/443 822** mobile) is owned and operated by Evan Yanna Muru, an Aboriginal. This guided walk follows a traditional walkabout song line for about 3.5km (2 miles), exploring part of the Blue Mountains wilderness for a full day (about 2 hr. walking and 4 hr. of relaxation and activities). You'll see ancient art, ceremonial sites, and artifacts, and hear Dreamtime stories. Also included is ochre-bark and body painting, bush-tucker tastings, wildlife viewing, sandstone cave exploring, and bathing in a crystal-clear billabong (pool) below a waterfall. You should be reasonably fit. Bring wet-weather gear, good boots or walking shoes, lots of water, and lunch. The trek costs A\$95 per person (no kids 6 and under). The walk begins in the Blue Mountains on Faulconbridge Railway Station platform at 10:50am. Take the train from

---

4

> ### Timing Is Everything: When to Visit
>
> If you can, try to visit the Blue Mountains on **weekdays,** when most Sydney-siders are at work and prices are lower. Note that the colder winter months (June–Aug) are the busiest season.

Central Station in Sydney (see "Arriving," p. 55). You can get the 4:30pm train back to the city.

Exploring the Blue Mountains

Almost every other activity in the Blue Mountains costs money, but bushwalking (hiking) is the exception. There are some 50 walking trails, ranging from routes you can cover in 15 minutes to the 3-day **Six Foot Track.** The staff at the national park and tourist offices will be happy to point you in the right direction.

The most visited and photographed attraction in the Blue Mountains is the rock formation known as the **Three Sisters.** For the best vantage point, head to **Echo Point Road,** across from the Blue Mountains Tourism office. Or try Four attractions in one are offered at **Scenic World** (www.scenicworld.com. au; © **1300/759 929** in Australia, or 02/4780 0200). The **Scenic Railway,** the world's steepest, consists of a carriage on rails that is lowered 415m (1,361 ft.) into the Jamison Valley at a maximum incline of 52 degrees. It's *very* steep and quite a thrill. The trip takes only a few minutes; at the bottom is the 2.4km (1½-mile) **Scenic Walkway,** a boardwalk through forests of ancient tree ferns. Another way to get down is on the **Scenic Cableway,** not to be confused with the **Scenic Skyway,** a different form of cable car that travels 270m (885 ft.)

The famous Three Sisters rock formation in the Blue Mountains National Park.

The Legend of the Three Sisters

The Aboriginal Dreamtime legend has it that three sisters (Meehni, Wimlah, and Gunnedoo) lived in the Jamison Valley as members of the Katoomba tribe. These beautiful young women had fallen in love with three brothers from the Nepean tribe, yet tribal law forbade them to marry. The brothers were not happy with this law and so decided to capture the three sisters, which caused a major tribal battle. As the lives of the three sisters were in danger, a witch doctor from the Katoomba tribe took it upon himself to turn the three sisters into stone to protect them from any harm. He had intended to reverse the spell later, but was killed in the battle, and the sisters were doomed to remain in their magnificent rock formation forever.

above—and across—the Jamison Valley, between two cliffs. A ticket that includes all four attractions costs A$44 adults, A$24 children 4 to 13, and A$112 for families of up to seven (you can't buy separate tickets for any of the attractions). Prices are slightly higher on weekends. Scenic World is open 9am to 5pm daily. You'll find it on Violet Street (corner of Cliff Dr.), Katoomba.

If you are driving back to Sydney, take the Bells Line of Road through Bilpin and stop off at the wonderful **Blue Mountains Botanic Garden** (www.bluemountainsbotanicgarden.com.au; ℂ **02/4567 3000**) at Mount Tomah. (Look for a large sign on your right about 10 min. before you get to Bilpin.) An adjunct of Sydney's Royal Botanic Garden, it is well worth a stop.

Where to Eat in the Blue Mountains

Katoomba Street has many ethnic dining choices, whether you're hungry for Greek, Chinese, or Thai. Restaurants in the Blue Mountains are generally more expensive than equivalent places in Sydney.

Conservation Hut Cafe ★ CAFE   This pleasant mudbrick cafe is in the national park on top of a cliff overlooking the Jamison Valley. It's a good place for a bit of lunch on the balcony after the Valley of the Waters walk, which leaves from outside, or a Devonshire tea. In addition to lighter meals like soup or a steak sandwich, dishes may include homemade pies (try the lamb and rosemary) or burgers. It can get busy on weekends, and service can be slow. There's a nice log fire inside in winter. Children are welcome.

Fletcher St., Wentworth Falls. ℂ **02/4757 3827.** Main courses A$15–A$31. Daily 9am–4pm (from 10am public holidays; closed Dec 25).

Elephant Bean ★★ CAFE   This groovy little cafe is a good stop for a light breakfast, lunch, or just a coffee. The menu changes often, but you might find dishes like Italian vegetable and cannellini bean soup alongside sandwiches on organic sourdough, with interesting fillings (including veggie options).

159 Katoomba Rd., Katoomba. www.elephantbeancafe.com. ℂ **02/4782 4620.** Main courses A$11–A$14. Daily 7am–4pm (3pm on Sun).

CANBERRA

Unlike most other Australian cities that grew up organically around pioneer settlements, there is nothing haphazard about Canberra (pronounced *Can*-berra, with the accent on "can"). Australia's national capital is all about symbolism, architecture, planning, and symmetry.

In 1911, an international competition to design the new city was held. More than 130 entries were received from around the world, and the winning entry was that of Chicago architects Walter Burley Griffin and his wife, Marion Mahony Griffin, with a design based on a series of geometrically precise circles and axes. The Australian Capital Territory (ACT) was declared on January 1, 1911. It became a self-governing territory in 1989.

Fast-forward more than a century, and the city remains true to the Griffins' original "garden city" vision, with tree-lined streets and buildings set in expanses of grassed parkland. The streets radiate out in a wheel-and-spoke design from Capital Hill, rather than following a traditional grid. But unless you're a local, the circular roads can be confusing, and almost everyone who has been to Canberra will tell you how easy it is to get lost there.

Most of the 452,500 people who live here are civil servants. And most visitors come simply to see Canberra's amazing range of museums, including the National Museum of Australia, the Questacon science museum, and the National Gallery of Australia. Dig a little deeper, however, and you'll find many other intriguing aspects to Canberra, including a thriving festival and arts scene and an emerging food and wine culture, with around 30 of the country's best cool-climate wineries just an easy day trip from the city.

ESSENTIALS

Arriving
BY PLANE
Canberra Airport (CBR) (www.canberraairport.com.au; ☏ **02/6275 2222**) is 10 minutes from the city center. It has car-rental desks, a currency exchange, a bar, a bistro, and a mailbox for cards and letters (but no post office). The newsdealer sells stamps. There are no lockers or showers.

Qantas (www.qantas.com.au; ☏ **13 13 13** in Australia) runs frequent daily service to Canberra from Sydney, Melbourne, Brisbane, and Perth. **Virgin Australia** (www.virginaustralia.com.au; ☏ **13 67**

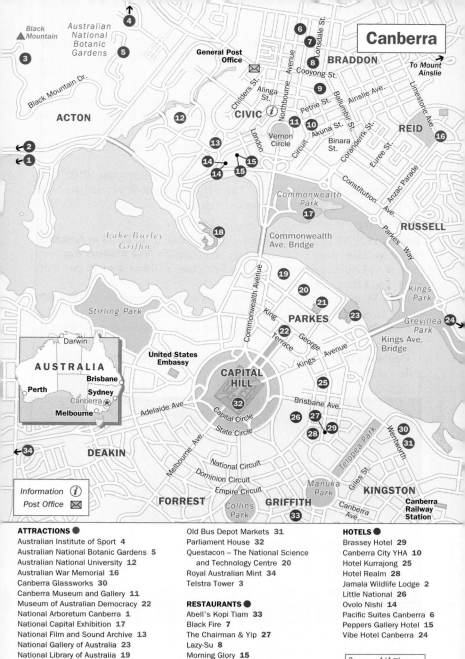

Canberra

Black Mountain

Australian National Botanic Gardens

General Post Office

To Mount Ainslie

BRADDON

Cooyong St.

Lonsdale St.

CIVIC

Alinga St.

Childers St.

Petrie St.

Northbourne Avenue

Ballumbir St.

Ainslie Ave.

Limestone Ave.

REID

ACTON

London

Vernon Circle

Akuna St.

Binara St.

Circuit

Coranderrk St.

Euree St.

Anzac Parade

Commonwealth Park

Constitution Ave.

RUSSELL

Lake Burley Griffin

Commonwealth Ave. Bridge

Parkes Way

Kings Park

Stirling Park

Commonwealth Avenue

King

Terrace

George

Kings Avenue

PARKES

Grevillea Park

Kings Ave. Bridge

AUSTRALIA

Darwin

Brisbane

Perth

Sydney

Canberra

Melbourne

United States Embassy

CAPITAL HILL

Capital Circle

State Circle

Adelaide Ave.

Brisbane Ave.

Kings Park

Melbourne Ave.

National Circuit

Dominion Circuit

Empire Circuit

Collins Park

Telopea Park

Giles St.

Wentworth

Manuka Park

KINGSTON

FORREST

DEAKIN

GRIFFITH

Canberra Ave.

Canberra Railway Station

Information ⓘ
Post Office ✉

ATTRACTIONS ●

Australian Institute of Sport **4**
Australian National Botanic Gardens **5**
Australian National University **12**
Australian War Memorial **16**
Canberra Glassworks **30**
Canberra Museum and Gallery **11**
Museum of Australian Democracy **22**
National Arboretum Canberra **1**
National Capital Exhibition **17**
National Film and Sound Archive **13**
National Gallery of Australia **23**
National Library of Australia **19**
National Museum of Australia **18**
National Portrait Gallery **21**
National Zoo & Aquarium **1**

Old Bus Depot Markets **31**
Parliament House **32**
Questacon – The National Science
   and Technology Centre **20**
Royal Australian Mint **34**
Telstra Tower **3**

RESTAURANTS ●

Abell's Kopi Tiam **33**
Black Fire **7**
The Chairman & Yip **27**
Lazy-Su **8**
Morning Glory **15**
Monster Kitchen & Bar **14**
Sammy's Kitchen **9**

HOTELS ●

Brassey Hotel **29**
Canberra City YHA **10**
Hotel Kurrajong **25**
Hotel Realm **28**
Jamala Wildlife Lodge **2**
Little National **26**
Ovolo Nishi **14**
Pacific Suites Canberra **6**
Peppers Gallery Hotel **15**
Vibe Hotel Canberra **24**

0   1/4 mi
0   0.25 km

89 in Australia) offers direct flights to Canberra from Melbourne, Brisbane, the Gold Coast, Adelaide, Perth, and Sydney. **Tigerair Australia** (www.tiger air.com.au; ✆ **07/3295 2104**) also has daily flights from Melbourne and Brisbane.

Public **buses** 11 and 11A service the airport from the city bus station daily. The cash fare is A$4.80 adults. **CBD Transport** (www.cbdtransport.com.au; ✆ **02/6297 9899**) operates private door-to-door transfers between the airport and city, with prices starting from A$55 for one to three passengers. A **taxi** to the city will cost around A$25 to A$30.

Avis (✆ 02/6219 3033), **Budget** (✆ 02/6219 3040), **Europcar** (✆ 02/6213 0300), **Hertz** (✆ 02/6249 6211), **Thrifty** (✆ 02/6248 9081) and **Redspot** (✆ 02/6248 9966) all have desks at the airport.

BY TRAIN

Transport NSW (www.transportnsw.info/regional; ✆ **13 22 32** in Australia) runs three trains daily between Sydney and Canberra. The 4¼-hour trip costs around A$37 in economy or A$52 in first class; children 4 to 15 pay half-price, and a round-trip costs double.

From Melbourne, the trip with **V/Line** (www.vline.com.au; ✆ **1800 800 007** in Australia or 03/9662 2505) involves a 3¾-hour train ride and a 6½-hour bus trip. It costs A$67 for adults (free for up to two children ages 5–18 traveling with a full-paying adult).

Canberra Railway Station is on Burke Crescent Kingston, about 5km (3 miles) southeast of the city center.

Fireworks over Canberra City.

BY BUS

Greyhound (www.greyhound.com.au; ☏ **1300/473 946** in Australia) does several runs a day from Sydney to Canberra; the trip takes around 3½ hours. Tickets cost A$45 for adults, and around half-price for children 3 to 14. From Melbourne, tickets to Canberra cost around A$85 for adults. Book online for special deals.

Murrays Australia (www.murrays.com.au; ☏ **13 22 51** in Australia) runs from Sydney to Canberra every hour from 7am to 7pm (with a 5am and 10pm service as well), with fares from A$39 to A$46. Interstate buses arrive at **Jolimont Tourist Centre,** at the corner of Northbourne Avenue and Alinga Street, Canberra City.

BY CAR

The ACT is surrounded by New South Wales. Sydney is 280km (174 miles) northeast, and Melbourne is 651km (404 miles) southwest of Canberra. From Sydney, you can use an extension to the M5 motorway that links with the Eastern Distributor highway near Sydney Airport. The drive takes between 3 and 3½ hours. From Melbourne, take the Hume Highway to Yass and switch to the Barton Highway; the trip will take about 8 hours.

Visitor Information

The new **Canberra and Region Visitors Centre,** Regatta Point, Barrine Dr. (off Commonwealth Ave.), Parkes (www.visitcanberra.com.au; ☏ **1300/554 114** in Australia or 02/6205 0044), dispenses information and books accommodations and tours. You can also rent folding Brompton bikes here on a first come, first served basis (A$20 adults, A$15 children 2 hrs.; A$45 adults and A$30 children for the entire day); helmets, saddlebags, locks, and maps are included. It's open Monday through Friday from 9am to 5pm and Saturday and Sunday and public holidays from 9am to 4pm (closed Christmas Day).

City Layout

Canberra's focal point is **Lake Burley Griffin,** an artificial lake with the **Captain Cook Memorial Jet** (a fountain that reaches 147m/482 ft. into the air) at its center. Most of the country's more culturally and politically significant buildings—**Parliament House,** the much smaller (in comparison) **Old Parliament House,** the **National Archives,** the **National Library,** the **National Gallery** and **National Portrait Gallery,** the **High Court of Australia,** and **Questacon, the National Science and Technology Centre**—are clustered around it, making it easy for visitors to go from one attraction to the next. Officially, the area is called Parkes (after Sir Henry Parkes, the "father of Federation"), but it is more commonly referred to as the **Parliamentary Triangle,** which is bounded by Commonwealth, Kings, and Constitution avenues. Capital Hill is at the apex of the triangle, while City Hall, in the city center, and the headquarters of the Australian Defence Force, in the suburb of Russell, are at the other two points.

Visitors in the House of Representatives chamber at the Old Parliament House in the Canberra Parliamentary Zone.

Canberra's main shopping district is on the other side of the lake, centered on Northbourne Avenue, one of the city's main thoroughfares. Compared with that of other capital cities, Canberra's Central Business District (CBD) is quite small. Among the hotspots are the **New Acton** precinct, for its modern architecture and buzzing cafes and restaurants, and **Kingston,** where the foreshore development has created an arts precinct that keeps locals and visitors coming back.

Getting Around Canberra

Transport Canberra (www.transport.act.gov.au; ✆ **13 17 10** in Australia, or 02/6207 7611) coordinates Canberra's public transport system. The cheapest way to travel is using an electronic MyWay card, which you can buy from newsdealers or post offices (check the website for details). The central **bus** terminal is on Alinga Street, in Civic. Single cash fares, purchased on the bus, cost A$5 for adults and A$2.50 for children 5 to 15. Daily tickets cost A$9.60 adults and A$4.80 kids; MyWay fares are A$2.55 single during off-peak times and A$3.22 in peak times, but you will never pay more than A$9.60 per day. The **light rail** runs from the City to Gungahlin, along Northbourne Avenue and Flemington Road, and uses the same ticketing and fare system as the buses.

The free **Culture Loop** shuttle bus stops at nine points of interest, including Parliament House and other attractions listed in this book. It runs daily, leaving every hour from 9am to 4pm from the Canberra Museum and Gallery. Pick up a timetable from the Visitor Information Centre or hotels.

Canberra has an extensive system of cycle tracks—some 120km (74 miles) of them—which makes sightseeing on two wheels a pleasure. You can hire a bike at the **Canberra and Region Visitors Centre** (see p. 117). **ShareABike** (www.shareabike.com.au; ℂ **1300/588 533**) allows you to rent a bike for A$12 for an hour, falling to A$1.50 an hour if you hire it for 24 hours. Bike stations are at seven hotels around the city (see the ShareABike website for details). **CycleLifeHQ** (www.cyclelifehq.com/canberra) is a great resource for finding everything you need for biking in the city, including hire locations, maps and guides.

For a taxi, call **ACT Cabs** (ℂ **02/6280 0077**) or **Silver Service** (ℂ **13 31 00**).

[FastFACTS] CANBERRA

ATMs/Banks Banks are open Monday to Thursday 9:30am to 4pm (until 5pm Fri). ATMs are easy to find in the city center and are open 24 hours.

Business Hours Canberra shops and offices are open Monday to Friday 9am to 5:30pm. Many shops, particularly in the large malls, are open on weekends and until 9pm on Fridays.

Dentists **Northside Family Dental,** 33 Hibberson St., Gungahlin (www.northsidefamilydental.com.au; ℂ **02/6242 7777**) offers an after-hours emergency dental service.

Doctors & Hospitals For medical attention, go to the **Canberra Hospital,** Yamba Drive, Garran (ℂ **02/5124 0000**). The **Canberra Afterhours Locum Medical Service** (CALMS); (ww.calms.net.au; ℂ **1300/422 567**) runs a call center from 6pm to 8:30am and has clinics at the Canberra Hospital, or will send a doctor to you. Appointments are essential. The **Travellers' Medical &**

Vaccination Centre, Lena Carmel Lodge, 1 Childers St., Acton (www.traveldoctor.com.au; ℂ **02/6222 2300**), offers vaccinations and travel medicine and is open weekdays from 8:30am to 5pm. The **Poison Information Centre** is at ((ℂ **13 11 26**).

Embassies & Consulates The **U.S. Embassy** is at Moonah Place, Yarralumla (ℂ **02/6214 5600**); the **British High Commission** (consular section; ℂ **02/6270 6666**) and the **Canadian High Commission** (ℂ **02/6270 4000**) are on Commonwealth Avenue, Yarralumla; the **New Zealand High Commission** ((ℂ **02/6270 4211**) is at 65 Canberra Avenue.

Emergencies Dial ℂ **000** for fire, ambulance, or police help in an emergency. This is a free call from a private or public telephone. **Lifeline** (ℂ **131 114**) is a 24-hour emotional crisis counseling service.

Mail & Postage The **Canberra General Post Office,** 53–73 Alinga St., Civic, is open Monday through Friday from 8:30am

to 5:30pm, Saturday 9:30am to 1pm.

Newspapers & Magazines The **Canberra Times** (www.canberratimes.com.au), is the capital's local newspaper, published daily.

Pharmacies (Chemist Shops) The **Chemist on Northbourne,** 65 Northbourne Ave (ℂ **02/6162 1133**) is open daily 8am to 11pm.

Police Dial ℂ **000** in an emergency, or ℂ **131 444** for police headquarters. The **Canberra City Police Station** is at 16-18 London Circuit (ℂ **02/6256 7777**).

Safety Canberra is relatively crime-free, but as in any large city, stay aware of your personal safety, especially when you're out at night.

Wi-Fi Canberra has plenty of free public Wi-Fi, with hotspots throughout the city center and suburbs. The **National Library of Australia,** Parkes Place, Parkes (www.nla.gov.au; ℂ **02/6262 1111**), offers free access to computers and the Internet.

WHERE TO STAY IN CANBERRA

Expensive

Hotel Realm ★★   From the vast lobby, with its mirror-image entrances, twin fireplaces, and plush sofas, to the soaring atrium, it's clear that this five-star hotel makes a stylish first impression. Located a stone's throw away from Parliament House and within walking distance of a good range of restaurants and bars, all rooms are light, bright, and airy, with a muted decor and art photographs of Canberra on the walls. Goose-down bed toppers ensure a fabulous night's sleep. Suites have spacious balconies and kitchens. The restaurant is French, and **Mudd the Spa** has a range of pampering treatments.

18 National Circuit, Barton. www.hotelrealm.com.au. ✆ **02/6163 1800.** 163 units. A$254–A$274 double; A$449–A$675 suite. Valet parking A$20. Bus: 5. **Amenities:** Restaurant; bar; health club; spa; heated pool; sauna; free Wi-Fi.

Ovolo Nishi ★★★   It's all about texture at this ultra-cool hotel in the New Acton precinct. If the outside of the building isn't enough, the interiors pack a real punch. Most people arrive at the front door, but the stairs from the back entrance (on Phillip Law St.), lined with tiers of recycled timber, give a hint of what's to come. Seventeen new rooms were added in 2019, each as interesting as the next. Start small with a "cozy" room or spread out in a "meandering" room. All have great views, electronic blinds, and lots of industrial chic (think ribbed walls and concrete bathtubs). Book direct for the "freebies" that Ovolo includes. There are 260 pieces of original art throughout the hotel, which is also known for its **Monster Kitchen & Bar** restaurant (see p. 123).

25 Edinburgh Ave., New Acton. www.ovolohotels.com.au/ovolonishi. ✆ **02/6287 6287.** 85 units. A$425–A$645 double. Parking A$35 (public carpark next door). Bus: 53. **Amenities:** Restaurant; bar; room service; gymnasium; free Wi-Fi.

Moderate

Brassey Hotel ★   Rooms in this 1927 heritage-listed building, formerly a boardinghouse for visiting government officials, are large, quiet, and somewhat plush. All rooms are different sizes and shapes, but share a genteel feel about them. There is no restaurant, but the guest lounge has snacks and mini-bar items as well as tea- and coffee-making facilities; charge-back facilities are available at other hotels and restaurants in the Realm Precinct, a short walk away, including the Little National (p. 121) and Hotel Realm (p. 120) and the Chairman & Yip restaurant (p. 123). Other good points include its proximity to Parliament House and other major attractions. There's also no elevator, but the hotel is only three levels.

Belmore Gardens (at Macquarie St.), Barton. www.brasseyhotel.com.au. ✆ **02/6273 3766.** 80 units. A$189–A$249 double. Free parking. Bus: 4, 5, 80, 938, or 980. **Amenities:** Bar; spa; sauna; free Wi-Fi.

Hotel Kurrajong ★★★   One of Canberra's most historic lodgings, this hotel combines old-world charm with modern conveniences (USB charging ports; LCD TVs with Wi-Fi connectivity). Famed as the place where Australia's 16th Prime Minister, Ben Chifley, lived (and died), it has a welcoming aura from the moment you step into the lobby, with its comfy leather sofas, fireplace, and beautiful timber paneling. Rooms are large and comfortable, with coffee machines, bathtubs, and full-length mirrors. The **Chifley Bar & Grill** opens out onto a gorgeous rose garden, perfect for summer. It's also a short walk to Parliament House and Old Parliament House; you'll pass a wonderful statue of Ben Chifley on the way.

8 National Circuit, Barton. www.hotelkurrajong.com.au. © **02/6234 4444.** 147 units. A$179–A$269 double; A$255–A$369 suite. Parking A$15. **Amenities:** Restaurant; bar; 24-hr. gym; room service; free Wi-Fi.

Little National ★★ From the outside, this smart hotel is an intriguing black box, suggesting there's more to be discovered inside. And there is: a trestle-table reception desk, for starters. Design and sustainability are the watchwords here, with much attention to detail. Built in 2015, these hotel rooms are all identical (prices vary midweek and weekends), but size is a factor. Ideal for single travelers, I'd find them too much of a squeeze for a couple, with one side of the bed against the wall. That said, there's much to recommend this smart hotel, from the terrific guest lounge and work center to thoughtful touches like non-fog mirrors in the bathrooms.

21 National Circuit, Barton. www.littlenationalhotel.com.au. © **02/6188 3200.** 120 units. A$129–A$299 double. Parking A$12 (free Fri–Sun). Bus: 5. **Amenities:** Restaurant; bar; gymnasium (off-site); free Wi-Fi.

Pacific Suites Canberra ★ You'll appreciate the generous size of these one- and two-bedroom apartments, which outweighs their slight lack of soul. All of the apartments have private balconies, fully equipped kitchens, and laundry facilities, and two-bedroom apartments also have two bathrooms (one with a tub). It's a popular hotel for families and business travelers. The former restaurant has been converted into a huge playroom for children, with mini-pool and other games; the lack of restaurant is compensated by its location, a 10-minute walk from at least 35 restaurants (some even deliver to the hotel).

100 Northbourne Ave., Braddon. www.pacificsuitescanberra.com.au. © **02/6262 6266.** 153 units. A$169–A$350 1-bedroom apt; A$199–A$400 2-bedroom apt. Free parking if booked direct, or A$15. **Amenities:** Restaurant; gymnasium; 25m (82-ft.) pool; free Wi-Fi.

Peppers Gallery Hotel ★★ This luxury boutique hotel, with its eclectic art collection and dark, moody color schemes, has more personality than most of Canberra's businesslike hotels. Built in 1926 but with a modern extension, it has quirky touches such as a herringbone carpet, color-coded doors on each floor, and a cozy library bar (ask the staff about the underground whiskey bar). Bathrooms are generous, but only some have tubs. For more space than a standard room offers, opt for a deluxe or premier room or a one-, two- or

A ROOM WITH A ZOO

Tigers, cheetahs, lions, and bears prowl outside the glass walls of your room at the fabulous **Jamala Wildlife Lodge** (www.jamalawildlifelodge.com.au; ✆ **02/6287 8444**), one of Australia's most interesting places to stay. Built inside the National Zoo & Aquarium (p. 132), rooms here are "shared" with the wildlife. The lodge has 18 suites; seven are in the main building, with views of meerkats, lemurs, hyenas, or the impressive aquarium; five are bungalows inside enclosures for the big cats and bears; and six are treehouses overlooking the home of a curious giraffe who's likely to poke his head over the balcony.

An overnight stay at Jamala includes a welcome afternoon tea, breakfast, two free guided walking tours, and a sumptuous all-inclusive dinner in an underground "cave," with windows looking into the "bedrooms" of two white lions and the hyenas. It's all somewhat surreal, but unlike anywhere else you will stay. Like the whole lodge, rooms are African-themed, filled with animal prints, carvings, and artworks collected by the owners on their travels. Four-poster beds and plush furnishings complete the romantic picture. Book well ahead; this is a very popular experience despite the price.

Double rooms start from A$1,195 in the main lodge, A$1,475 for the giraffe tree houses, and A$2,125 for the jungle bungalows (higher for Fri and Sat nights; an additional A$150/A$350 respectively). Jamala does not accommodate children under 6, and some rooms are only allocated to families with children 14 or older, depending on the animals you will be "bunking" with. Children are not allowed in the jungle bungalows in the lion enclosure. Ask about **family nights,** held once a month and tailored for families with children as young as 4.

three-bedroom apartment, just across the street. It's in a good location close to Lake Burley Griffin and a 5-minute walk from the city.

15 Edinburgh Ave., New Acton. www.peppers.com.au/gallery. ✆ **1300/987 600** in Australia or 02/6175 2222. 91 units. A$150–A$210 double; A$260 suite; A$218 1-bedroom apt; A$318 2-bedroom apt; A$418 3-bedroom apt. Parking A$15. Bus: 53. **Amenities:** Restaurant; bar; gymnasium; room service; free Wi-Fi.

Vibe Hotel Canberra ★★★ Airport hotels are often dull, but there's nothing ordinary about this one! Brimming with style—I'd almost go so far as to say glamour—this hotel really lives up to its name. Rooms are large, with gorgeous bathrooms outfitted with bathtubs as well as dual showerheads, double sinks, and funky circular mirrors. Double-glazed windows keep out any noise. For those who want more space, the Vibe has nine one- and two-bedroom apartments. Reception is open 24 hours, and there's a bar/lounge area off the lobby below a circular light-filled atrium. It's a 2-minute walk to the airport terminal.

1 Rogan St., Canberra Airport. www.tfehotels.com/vibe. ✆ **02/6201 1500.** 191 units. A$229–A$269 double; A$309 1-bedroom apt; A$200–A$432 2-bedroom apt. Parking A$14. Bus: 11, 11A. **Amenities:** Restaurant; bar; gymnasium; room service; free Wi-Fi.

Inexpensive

Canberra City YHA ★ The location is good, close to the intercity bus terminal and with a bus stop for the Culture Loop shuttle right outside. This hostel has 265 beds across a range of rooms including double rooms with en suites, renovated in 2019. There's a self-catering kitchen, sauna, and a small swimming pool, as well as a rooftop with pool tables, barbecue, and hammocks for hanging out, where Friday night movies are screened in summer.

7 Akuna St. www.yha.org.au/hostels/nsw/canberra. ℭ **02/6248 9155.** 65 units. A$104–A$122 double; A$32–A$44 dorms; A$157–A$192 family room (sleeps 4). Parking (off-site) A$12. **Amenities:** Restaurant; bar; pool; sauna; laundry; free Wi-Fi.

WHERE TO EAT IN CANBERRA

Expensive

Black Fire ★★ MEDITERRANEAN Rustic style with an emphasis on local and organic produce is what you'll find at this restaurant. Carnivores will love it, but there's also a swag of pasta dishes and always a fish of the day. But the main event is steak, lamb, or suckling pig, grilled, open-fire-roasted, or wood-fired, along with mustards and sauces and a range of excellent side dishes such as organic carrots and charcoal pumpkin with basil pesto, or rosemary- and thyme-infused roasted potatoes.

45/38 Mort St., Braddon. www.blackfirecanberra.com.au. ℭ **02/6230 5921.** Main courses A$26–A$39. Daily noon–2:30pm and 6pm–late; Sat and Sun 10am–11:45am.

The Chairman & Yip ★★★ MODERN CANTONESE Dramatic black and red decor sets the tone for one of Canberra's best restaurants. The entrance is lined with floor-to-ceiling books and wine, with stone pillars and old wooden floorboards providing texture. Then there's the food: roast duck and shiitake pancakes and peppered beef and scallop hot-pot, and thoughtful touches like a banquet menu for one (A$50), testament, perhaps, to Canberra's business clientele. Upbeat and popular with political bigwigs, it has a reputation of being the place to see and be seen. Chinese classics are given an East-meets-West twist, and the result is delicious.

1 Burbury Close, Barton. www.chairmangroup.com.au/chairmanyip. ℭ **02/6162 1220.** Main courses A$26–A$40. Banquet menu (for 2–8 people) A$88. Tues–Fri noon–2:30pm; Mon–Sat 6–10:30pm.

Monster Kitchen & Bar ★★★ MODERN AUSTRALIAN A large circular fireplace is the centerpiece of this hip restaurant. Then there's the chandelier and the giant artworks. Monster's menu is designed for sharing, and uses local and seasonal produce wherever possible. Try a feast of small plates: choose from beef tartare, oysters, spiced lamb ribs, fried spatchcock, and more. For something heartier, the shared plates include twice-cooked duck breast, pulled lamb shoulder with pistachio yoghurt, Szechuan pepper tofu, and buffalo mozzarella—the list is long and tempting. At lunch, a smaller menu might include soups or pasta as well as a Rueben sandwich. I recommend the Spring Bay mussels with jamon and white wine, with sourdough bread to sop it all up.

25 Edinburgh Ave., New Acton (in the Ovolo Nishi hotel). www.monsterkitchen.com.au. ℰ **02/6287 6287.** Small plates A$9–A$23; main courses A$20–A$34. Daily 6:30am–11pm (until midnight Fri & Sat).

Moderate

Abell's Kopi Tiam ★★ ASIAN Bright, cheap, and cheerful—what this little place lacks in decor it makes up for in flavor. The menu is a mix of Southeast Asian cooking, with a strong Nonya (fusion of Malay and Chinese) influence. It gets busy, but service is brisk and the food is always good. Expect dishes like Mongolian lamb or Malayan beef rendang.

7 Furneaux St., Manuka. www.abellskopitiam.com.au. ℰ **02/6239 4199.** Main courses A$20–A$33. Tues–Sun 11:30am–2:30pm and 5:30–10pm (9pm on Sun).

Lazy-Su ★ ASIAN There's a happy buzz beyond the pink lanterns that hang in the front window. Bigger inside than it first appears, this is a great restaurant for a quick lunch—perhaps a "salaryman" poke bowl brimming with rice, shaved cabbage, edamame, shiitake, pickles, cucumber, and kim chi mayo, or some gyoza dumplings or slow-cooked beef cheeks. The offerings are varied and cover a range of cuisines from Korean to Japanese, but all is tasty and comes in varying sizes.

9 Lonsdale St., Braddon. www.lazy-su.com.au. ℰ **02/5150 3812.** Main courses A$15–A$32. Mon 5–11pm; Tues–Thurs & Sun noon–11pm; Fri–Sat noon–1am.

Inexpensive

Morning Glory ★★ MODERN AUSTRALIAN With an interesting all-day menu that goes beyond the usual breakfast choices—but offers some of those as well—this is a popular place for lunch. Quick and friendly service and some very good food tick the boxes. You can go for eggs Benedict, but the burgers are more tempting, with interesting fillings. For my money, the Hainanese chicken, with scallion salsa, avocado, and spicy chili relish served on roti, is deservedly one of the most popular dishes on the menu.

15 Edinburgh St., New Acton. www.morning-glory.com.au. ℰ **02/6257 6464.** Main courses A$14–A$27. Daily 7am–3pm.

Sammy's Kitchen ★ CHINESE/MALAYSIAN Sammy's is a bit of Canberra institution, with a perennially buzzing atmosphere. It's always busy, even though it has room for 100 diners. Food is great, but the brisk service can be a bit hit and miss at times. It's the place to go for the best *laksa* in Canberra, but the sizzling king prawns are also worth ordering.

North Quarter, Canberra Centre, Bunda St. www.sammyskitchen.com.au. ℰ **02/6247 1464.** Main courses A$13–A$28. Daily 11:30am–2:30pm; Mon–Thurs 5–10:30pm; Fri–Sat 5–11pm; Sun 5–10pm.

5

Where to Eat in Canberra | **CANBERRA**

EXPLORING CANBERRA

Australian Institute of Sport (AIS) ★★ MUSEUM   Sports nuts and champions in the making love the AIS, where Australian sporting superstars are made. Go behind the scenes on a 90-minute guided tour and learn the secrets of what it takes win a gold medal, watch gymnasts in action, or see the country's top swimmers doing their laps. The indoor heated pool is open to the public at certain times during the day (check the website for schedules). Adults pay A$6.80 to swim, children A$5.20.

Leverrier Cres., Bruce (about 7km/4 miles from the city center). www.experienceais. com. (✆ **02/6214 1010.** Admission and tour A$20 adults, A$12 children 5–17, A$55 family (2 adults and up to 3 children). Tours depart daily at 10, 11:30am, 1, and 2:30pm. Bus: 4, 9, or 980.

Australian War Memorial ★★★ MONUMENT/MUSEUM   The Commemorative Courtyard, with its eternal flame and reflection pool, leads to the main focus of the memorial, the Hall of Memory, where the body of an unknown soldier brought back from a World War I battlefield lies entombed among beautiful mosaics and stained-glass windows. More than just a monument to Australian troops who gave their lives for their country, the relics, artifacts, and displays tell the story of Australia's conflicts abroad but do not glorify war. The "Conflicts 1945 to Today" gallery looks at Asian conflicts

Poppies decorate the Wall of Fallen Soldiers at the Australian War Memorial.

Canberra celebrates many major events scattered throughout the year. Here are the most popular. Check exact dates at **www.visitcanberra.com.au**.

o A host of free events—from concerts to competitions—is part of the annual **Canberra National Multicultural Festival** held over 10 days each February.

o The city celebrates its founding with the monthlong **Canberra Festival** throughout March, including lots of free events on Canberra Day, which is a local public holiday, on the second Monday in March.

o Famous buildings are illuminated on various nights in March during the **Enlighten Festival**, the biggest of which is the annual free spring flower show **Floriade,** when Commonwealth Park erupts in a blaze of color with more than 1.5 million bulbs and annuals in bloom.

o The **Summernats** street machine car festival in January, the Easter **National Folk Festival,** and the **Australian Science Festival** in August also draw big crowds.

and peacekeeping operations since 1947. Children will gravitate toward the Discovery Zone, where you can dodge sniper fire in a WWI trench, take control of an Iroquois helicopter, and peer through the periscope of a Cold War submarine. Free guided 30-, 60-, and 90-minute tours are run by volunteers throughout the day. A visit here is a moving experience; allow at least 2 hours.

Anzac Parade on Limestone Ave., or Treloar Crescent. www.awm.gov.au. © **02/6243 4211.** Free. Daily 10am–5pm (when the Last Post is played). Closed Dec 25. Bus: 10 on weekdays, 910 on weekends.

Canberra Museum and Gallery ★ MUSEUM
The highlight of this small museum and art gallery—which focuses only on the Canberra district—is the Sir Sidney Nolan collection, which includes some of his famous Ned Kelly series of paintings. It's a good place to visit on a rainy day, but not at the expense of the National Gallery, Portrait Gallery, or National Museum of Australia.

Corner London Circuit and Civic Square, Canberra City. www.cmag.com.au. © **02/6207 3968.** Free. Mon–Sat 10am–5pm. Closed public holidays. Bus: Culture Loop.

Lake Burley Griffin ★ NATURAL ATTRACTION
Named for the architect of Canberra, this huge lake is the focal point of the city, around which its major attractions are ranged. It has three basins and three designated swimming beaches. The lake is 9km (5 miles) long, with a 40.5km (25-mile) shore length, but you can walk a 5km (3-mile) loop using the Commonwealth Avenue and Kings Avenue bridges. Being out on the lake is a great way to get a new perspective on the city. You can hire an electric-powered "picnic boat" from **GoBoat** (www.goboatcanberra.com.au; book online) to explore the lake. The cost is A$99 for 1 hour, up to A$249 for 3 hours. Boats hold up to eight

people, and no license is required to drive the boat; lifejackets and instructions are given and off you go. From September to May, **Lake Burley Griffin Cruises** (www.lakecruises.com.au; ℂ **0419 418 846** cellphone), runs 1-hour cruises daily at 10:30am, 1:30pm, and 3pm. The cost is A$20 adults and A$9 children 6 to 12. On Sundays, there's also a 2-hour morning tea cruise, which takes in the view of Government House, costing A$30 adults and $12 children.

Barrine Dr., Acton. www.nca.gov.au/attractions-and-memorials/lake-burley-griffin. Free.

Museum of Australian Democracy at Old Parliament House

★★★ MUSEUM   Old Parliament House was the seat of government from 1927 to 1988. If you need a refresher course on how democracy is meant to work, or if you're just a political junkie, free guided tours bring the history of the house alive and are highly recommended. All the offices, including the Prime Minister's, have been pretty much left exactly as they were when the politicians moved out to the new Parliament House on the hill. And don't miss the offices of the Parliamentary Press Gallery, upstairs. Opposite the main entrance is the Aboriginal Tent Embassy, set up in 1972 in a bid to highlight the land ownership claims of Aboriginal and Torres Strait Islander people. It was the first place the red, black, and yellow Aboriginal flag was flown. Take time for a walk in the **Old Parliament House Gardens** next door.

Tulips blossom at the Floriade Festival, the country's biggest celebration of spring and an iconic Canberra event.

The National Multicultural Festival is celebrated with colorful dances, food, and more in Australia's national capital.

18 King George Terrace, Parkes. www.moadoph.gov.au. ℂ **02/6270 8222.** Admission A\$2 adults, A\$1 children, A\$5 families. Daily 9am–5pm (closed Dec 25). Bus: Culture Loop.

National Arboretum Canberra ★★ PARKS & GARDENS   Just 6km (3 miles) from the city center, the Arboretum is made up of 94 forests of rare, endangered, and symbolic trees from Australia and around the globe. The distinctive dome-like Village Centre, which incorporates the National Bonsai Collection and the Pod Playground (kids will love this), is at the heart of it and a good place to start your exploration. Free guided forest walks run every Wednesday, Saturday, and Sunday.

Forest Dr. (off Tuggeranong Parkway), Weston Creek. www.nationalarboretum.act.gov. au. ℂ **02/6207 8484.** Free. Daily 7am–5:30pm (extended hours during summer). Parking A\$2.10 per hour. Bus: 81 weekdays and 981 weekends.

Market Mania

Every Sunday, the best place to be is the **Old Bus Depot Markets,** 21 Wentworth Ave., Kingston (www.obdm.com. au; ℂ **02/6295 3331;** Sun 10am–4pm), where you can pick up some great handmade souvenirs—arts, crafts, clothes, soaps, jewelry—from more than 200 stalls. The quality is generally excellent, and it's also a great place to stock up on fresh fruit, cheeses, and produce if planning a picnic. A range of food stalls serves inexpensive lunches and good coffee, and there's always a mix of buskers to entertain the crowd.

National Capital Exhibition ★ EXHIBITION   Dedicated to the story of how Canberra came into existence, this display is a great way to understand the original vision of Walter Burley Griffin and Marion Mahony Griffin, the American architects behind the city's unique design, and its evolution since then. You may have to dodge school groups, but it's worth it.

Regatta Point, Barrine Dr. (in the same building as the Visitor Information Centre). www. nca.gov.au. ✆ **02/6272 2902.** Free. Mon–Fri 9am–5pm; Sat–Sun 10am–4pm. Closed public holidays except Australia Day (Jan 26) and Canberra Day (second Mon in Mar). Free parking. Bus: Culture Loop.

National Film and Sound Archive ★ MUSEUM   Changing exhibitions related to some of Australia's most popular and important movies, and the chance to see regular movie screenings, are the best reasons to visit the NFSA. The National Film and Sound Archive holds 100 years of Australian film, radio, and television history in a gorgeous Art Deco building that used to be the Institute of Anatomy (and is reputedly the most haunted building in Canberra). Check out the website for the latest programs.

McCoy Circuit, Acton. www.nfsa.gov.au. ✆ **1800/067 274** in Australia or 02/6248 2000. Free (movies and some exhibitions cost extra). Daily 10am–4pm. Closed Jan 1 and Dec 25. Bus: 3, 7, 81 on weekdays, 934 on weekends, or Culture Loop.

Gardener trimming Japanese-style bonsai trees at the National Arboretum Canberra.

Aboriginal Memorial in the National Gallery of Australia in Canberra. This beautiful work of contemporary indigenous Australian art comprises 200 decorated hollow log coffins.

National Gallery of Australia ★★★ ART GALLERY   Home to more than 100,000 works of art, the National Gallery has the largest, and best, collection of Australian indigenous art in the world. Beyond the 11 indigenous galleries, the permanent and temporary displays showcase Australian and international art and traveling blockbuster exhibitions from international collections. Collections focus on historical culture and art as well as contemporary indigenous works. The Aboriginal Memorial, work of 43 Ramingining artists, is a hauntingly beautiful reminder of the Aboriginal lives lost during Britain's occupation of the country from 1788 to 1988. The free 1-hour guided tours are brilliant and depart daily at regular intervals; see the website for times and topics.

Parkes Place. www.nga.gov.au ℂ **02/6240 6501.** Free admission (except for major touring exhibitions). Daily 10am–5pm. Closed Dec 25. Bus: 2, 3, 6, 934, or 935.

National Library of Australia ★★ LIBRARY   In addition to its vast collection of books, the National Library is worth visiting for its changing exhibitions. The Treasures Gallery is home to some of Australia's most important documents, beautifully displayed. Free tours of the gallery run daily at 11:30am and take around 30 minutes. Rotating exhibitions of works drawn from the library's collections are also held, often with accompanying talks. Naturally, the library has a very good bookshop. Free behind-the-scenes tours run on Thursdays at 2pm, and a free library tour is offered on Saturdays at 2pm. Both take around 45 minutes.

Parkes Place. www.nla.gov.au ℂ **02/6262 1111.** Free. Daily 9am–5pm; reading rooms open until 8pm some days. Bus: 1, 2, 3, 4, 6, 80, 81 on weekdays or 934, 935, and 981 on weekends, or Culture Loop.

GLASS act

Canberra Glassworks, 11 Wentworth Ave., Kingston (www.canberraglassworks.com; ✆ **02/6260 7005**), one of the city's best contemporary glass art galleries and studio spaces, is a great place to see artists at work, and even try your own hand. The gallery offers creative sessions of 20 to 40 minutes, in which you can make your own paperweight, glass bird, or small vase or glass. No experience is necessary, but you must make a booking. Your finished artwork can be mailed home to you after it has been fired or cooled. Admission is free; classes are A$80 to A$120. It's open Wednesday to Sunday 10am to 4pm; classes on weekends only.

National Museum of Australia ★ MUSEUM   With state-of-the-art technology and hands-on exhibits that use images, soundscapes, and personal stories rather than objects, this large museum profiles 50,000 years of indigenous heritage, settlement since 1788, and other key events in Australia's history. The collection has everything from a carcass of the extinct Tasmanian tiger to Australia's largest collection of bark paintings, racehorse Phar Lap's heart, and the No. 1 Holden Prototype car. Guided tours (daily 10am and 1pm; First Australians tour focusing on Aboriginal and Torres Strait Islander history and culture daily at 3pm) are well worth taking to get the most out of a visit.

Lawson Crescent, Acton Peninsula (about 5km/3 miles from the city center). www.nma.gov.au. ✆ **1800/026 132** in Australia or 02/6208 5000. Free (fees for special exhibitions). Guided tours A$15 adults, A$10 children, A$40 family of 4. Daily 9am–5pm. Closed Dec 25. Bus: 53 or Culture Loop.

A projection on the National Library of Australia during the 2018 Enlighten festival in Canberra.

National Portrait Gallery ★★★ ART GALLERY   The faces of Australia—or at least the famous ones—are all here in this important and interesting gallery. Don't come expecting to see lots of gilt-framed figures in suits and robes; the National Portrait Gallery focuses instead on more modern figures. It's all about the people who have shaped Australia, here displayed in a range of styles, from traditional paintings to sculpture, textiles, photography, digital media, and even cartoons. It's well worth a look.

King Edward Terrace, Parkes. www.portrait.gov.au. ⓒ **02/6102 7000.** Free (except for special exhibitions). Daily 10am–5pm (closed Dec 25). Bus: 1, 2, 3, and 80 on weekdays or 935 on weekends and public holidays.

National Zoo & Aquarium ★★★ ZOO   Privately owned and funded, Canberra's zoo has a strong focus on conservation efforts and breeding programs. Here you'll see all the exotic animals—including brother-and-sister white lions, giraffes, Bengal tigers, zebras, red pandas, white rhinos, and more—as well as some Australian creatures. The zoo has a full program of free daily keeper talks and animal encounters (for which you'll pay more). The ZooVenture Tour allows you to hand-feed a tiger or lion, pat a rhino, and stroke a snake. It runs daily at 3:15pm and costs A$125 per person (including entry to the zoo) on weekdays and A$155 on weekends. You can choose from a number of other "close encounters," from A$55 per person, with big cats,

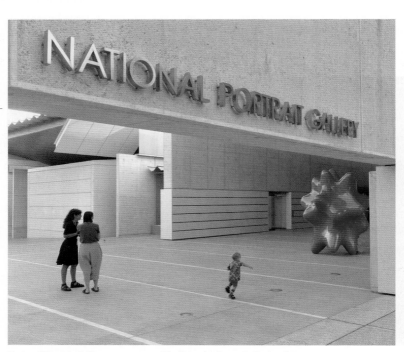

National Portrait Gallery. FACING PAGE: Giraffe at the Australia National Zoo.

THE bush CAPITAL

Canberra is called "the bush capital" with good reason. Designed to fit in with the landscape, the city has plenty of places where you can get back to nature. The **Australian National Botanic Gardens,** Clunies Ross St., Acton (www.anbg.gov.au/gardens; ✆ **02/6250 9540**), is a must-see for anyone with a passing interest in Australian native plants. The 51-hectare (126-acre) gardens on the lower slopes of Black Mountain contain more than 600 species of eucalyptus, a rainforest, a Tasmanian alpine garden, and walking trails. Free guided tours depart from the visitor center at 11am and 2pm each day. The gardens are open daily from 8:30am to 5pm (extended in Jan to 6pm weekdays and 8pm weekends). The visitor center is open daily from 9am to 4:30pm.

A great place to see Australian wildlife is at the **Tidbinbilla Nature Reserve** (www.tidbinbilla.act.gov.au; ✆ **02/6205 1233**), a 40-minute drive from the city center. It has 23 walking trails, ranger-guided activities, picnic facilities, and prolific wildlife, including koalas and the endangered brush-tailed rock wallaby. The surrounding mountains are of huge cultural significance to Aboriginal people; Tidbinbilla is derived from the Aboriginal word *jedbinbilla*, a place where "boys became men." There are lots of Aboriginal sites in the reserve, including the 21,000-year-old **Birrigai Rock Shelter.** The elevated boardwalk across the terrain protects the wetlands and is well worth taking, especially if you like bird-watching. Admission is A$13 per car, and the reserve is open daily from 7:30am to 6pm (will 8pm in summer; closed Christmas Day). An information center at the park entrance operates 9am to 5pm daily.

Namadgi is the Aboriginal word for the rugged mountains southwest of Canberra, and **Namadgi National Park,** at 105,900 hectares (261,684 acres), makes up more than half of the Australian Capital Territory. **Bimberi Peak** (1,911m/6,270 ft.) is the park's highest feature and is only 318m (1,043 ft.) lower than Mount Kosciuszko, Australia's highest mountain. A network of public roads inside the park passes through the majestic mountain country, but the unsealed roads are narrow and can be slippery when wet or frosty. (Watch out for kangaroos, too.) Much of Namadgi's beauty, however, lies beyond its main roads and picnic areas. The park has some 170km (106 miles) of marked walking trails, but you need to be well prepared if you plan to walk into the more remote areas. Before you depart, make sure you sign one of the bushwalking registers located at the visitor center and elsewhere in the park. The **Namadgi Visitors Centre,** on the Nass/Boboyan Road, 3km (1¾ miles) south of the township of Tharwa (✆ **02/6207 2900**), has maps and details on walking trails.

pandas, giraffes, and other animals. You can also stay overnight at the zoo's **Jamala Wildlife Lodge** (p. 122), an amazing (but expensive) experience.

Lady Denman Dr. https://nationalzoo.com.au. ✆ **02/6287 8400.** A$47 adults, A$26 children 3–15, A$130 family of 5. Daily 9:30am–5pm (closed Dec 25). Bus: 81 or 981.

Parliament House ★★★ LANDMARK Such an imposing building could be intimidating, but Parliament House exudes a welcoming atmosphere, enhanced by the numbers of ordinary people wandering through it daily. Conceived by American architect Walter Burley Griffin in 1912, but not built until

1988, Canberra's focal point was designed to blend organically into its setting at the top of Capital Hill; only a national flag supported by a giant four-footed flagpole rises above the peak of the hill. Inside are more than 3,000 works of Australian art, and extensive areas of the building are open to the public. Just outside the main entrance, look for a mosaic by Michael Tjakamarra Nelson, *Meeting Place,* which represents a gathering of Aboriginal tribes. Make time to look at the portraits of Australia's prime ministers and visit the rooftop for terrific views. Parliament is usually in session Monday through Thursday between mid-February and late June and from mid-August to mid-December (check the website for scheduled sittings). Both the Lower House (the House of Representatives, where the prime minister sits) and the Upper House (the Senate) have public viewing galleries. The best time to see the action is during Question Time, which starts at 2pm. Make reservations for gallery tickets through the **sergeant-at-arms** (© **02/6277 4889**) at least before 12:30pm on the day of your visit (bookings are not necessary for the Senate). Free 40-minute tours of the building run at 9:30am, 11am, 1pm, 2pm, and 3:30pm daily. **Behind-the-scenes tours** run daily at 10am, noon, and 3pm, take around an hour, and cost A$15 per person (you'll need photo ID for this tour).

Capital Hill. www.aph.gov.au. © **02/6277 5399**. Free. Daily 9am–5pm. Closed Dec 25. Bus: 57, 58, or Culture Loop.

The National Science and Technology Centre has more than 200 interactive exhibits on science and technology.

Questacon – The National Science and Technology Centre

★★★ MUSEUM   A museum that makes science fun, Questacon has more than 200 hands-on exhibits that will keep you (and your kids) entertained for hours. Exhibits cluster in seven galleries, each representing a different aspect of science. The full-motion roller-coaster simulator and artificial earthquake are usually big hits.

King Edward Terrace, Parkes. ℭ **02/6270 2800.** www.questacon.edu.au. Admission A$23 adults, A$18 children, A$70 families. Daily 9am–5pm. Closed Dec 25. Bus: 3, 934, 935, or Culture Loop.

Royal Australian Mint

Royal Australian Mint ★★ FACTORY   Take a free 30-minute tour, view rare coins, learn about the history of Australia's currency, and be mesmerized by the cascading coins being made on the factory floor. If you're interested in making money, you'll love the Mint. You can even make your very own A$1 coin—but it will cost you A$3 to do so! Free guided tours run at 10am, 11am, and 2pm Monday to Friday and 11am, 1pm, and 2pm weekends and public holidays.

Denison St., Deakin. www.ramint.gov.au. ℭ **02/6202 6999.** Free. Mon–Fri 8:30am–5pm; weekends and public holidays 10am–4pm. Closed Good Friday and Dec 25. Free parking. Bus: 1 and 2 weekdays or 932 weekends.

The Royal Australian Mint is the sole producer of all of Australia's circulating coins.

WEIRD canberra

If you're looking for something really different—and a little bit spooky—take an evening tour with "cryptonaturalist" **Tim the Yowie Man** (yes, that's his real name; he changed it after spotting an unidentified big black hairy creature in Canberra's Brindabella Mountains in 1994). Four tours are offered, depending on the day you are visiting. The 3-hour **Weird Canberra Ghost and History Tour ★★** costs A$99 and visits around 10 weird and/or spooky sites, including a funeral parlor that was once a hotbed of espionage activity, a haunted pioneer's house, a hotel haunted by one of Australia's former prime ministers, and a very spooky air-disaster memorial. Other tours take in the top-secret aspects of Old Parliament House (A$59), and the National Film and Sound Archive (A$70)—home to the former Institute of Anatomy. All tours are very popular, so book as far in advance as you can. To check dates, visit www.yowieman.com.au.

Telstra Tower ★ OBSERVATION TOWER   The 195m (640-ft.) tower on the summit of Black Mountain is both landmark and must-see attraction for every first-time visitor to Canberra. The open-air and enclosed viewing galleries—at 54m (177-ft.) and 66m (216-ft.), respectively—offer magnificent 360-degree views over the city and the surrounding countryside, and there's a café too. The tower provides telecommunications facilities for the city.

Black Mountain Dr. www.telstratower.com.au. ⓒ **1800/806 718** in Australia or 02/6230 0907. A$7.50 adults, A$3 children, A$17 family of 4. Daily 9am–10pm. Bus 81 or 981.

5

CANBERRA | Exploring Canberra

MELBOURNE

It's rare to find anyone who lives in Melbourne who doesn't adore it. I've lived there, and I love it too, and I hope this chapter illustrates the many reasons why. Victoria's capital, Melbourne (pronounced *Mel*-bun) is a cultural melting pot. For a start, more people of Greek descent live here than in any other city except Athens, Greece. Multitudes of Chinese, Italian, Vietnamese, and Lebanese immigrants have all left their mark. Almost a third of Melburnians were born overseas or have parents who were born overseas. With such a diverse population—and with trams rattling through the streets and stately European-style architecture surrounding you—it is sometimes easy to think you are somewhere else.

Melbourne's roots can be traced back to the 1850s, when gold was discovered in the surrounding hills. British settlers took up residence here and prided themselves on coming freely to their city, rather than having been forced here in convict chains. The city grew wealthy and remained a conservative bastion until World War II, when another wave of immigration, mainly from southern Europe, made it a more relaxed place.

With elegant tree-lined boulevards and a lively cafe culture, Victoria's capital maintains a distinctly European feel. Expect wonderful architecture, both old and new, and green spaces like the Royal Botanic Gardens. Wander down atmospheric laneways, often adorned with street art. This cosmopolitan city is also Australia's culture capital, with vibrant dining, shopping, and nightlife.

In fact, Melbourne, which has a population of around 4.9 million, is at the head of the pack when it comes to shopping, restaurants, fashion, music, and nightlife. It frequently beats other state capitals in bids for major concerts, plays, exhibitions, and sporting events. Oh, and everyone wears black.

ESSENTIALS

Arriving
BY PLANE
The international and domestic terminals at **Melbourne Airport (MEL)** (www.melbourneairport.com.au) are at Tullamarine, 22km

Melbourne skyline looking towards Flinders Street Station.

(14 miles) northwest of the city center (which is why the airport is often referred to as Tullamarine). It has four passenger terminals. The international terminal (T2) and Qantas (T1) and Virgin Australia (T3) terminals are all under one roof. A separate domestic terminal (T4) is home to Jetstar, Tigerair, and Regional Express (REX). The **travelers' information service desk,** on the ground floor of the international arrivals hall (T2), is open from 7am until midnight daily. The international terminal has snack bars, a restaurant, currency-exchange facilities, duty-free shops, and showers (on the first floor). ATMs are available at both terminals. Baggage carts are free in the international baggage claim hall but cost A$4 in the parking lot, departure lounge, or domestic terminal; baggage storage, available in the international terminal, costs A$10 to A$18 per day, depending on the size of your bag (daily 5am–12:30am; photo ID required).

The airport has five hotels. **Parkroyal Melbourne Airport** (www.pan pacific.com; ℂ **03/8347 2000**), **Holiday Inn Melbourne Airport** (www.holi dayinnmelbourneairport.com.au; ℂ **03/9933 5111**), and **Ibis Budget Melbourne Airport** (www.accorhotels.com; ℂ **03/8336 1811**) are all within a 5-minutes walk of the terminals. A 5-minute drive away are the **Quest Melbourne Airport** (www.questmelbourneairport.com.au; ℂ **03/8340 8400**), an apartment hotel in the Melbourne Airport Business Park, and **Mantra Tullamarine** (www.mantrahotels.com/mantra-tullamarine-hotel; ℂ **03/9093 6500**), which runs a free shuttle.

Qantas (www.qantas.com.au; ℂ **131 313** in Australia) and **Virgin Australia** (www.virginaustralia.com.au; ℂ **136 789** in Australia) both fly to Melbourne from all state capitals and some regional centers. Qantas's discount arm, **Jetstar** (www.jetstar.com.au; ✆ **131 538** in Australia) flies to and from Townsville, Hamilton Island in the Whitsundays, Uluru, and various other cities around the country. Jetstar also flies between Avalon Airport, about a 50-minute drive outside Melbourne's city center, and Sydney. Low-cost carrier **Tigerair** (www.tigerair.com.au; ✆ **1300/174 266** in Australia, or 07/3295 2104 in Australia) has its hub in Melbourne, and from there flies to Sydney, Adelaide, Canberra, Perth, Hobart, Cairns, and Brisbane, as well as several other cities.

Between the Airport and the City

The distinctive red **Skybus** (www.skybus.com.au; ✆ **03/9600 1711**) runs between the airport and Melbourne's Southern Cross station in Spencer Street every 10 minutes, 24 hours a day, every day. Buy tickets from Skybus desks outside the baggage claim areas or at the information desk in the international terminal. Returning to the airport, a free Skybus hotel shuttle will pick you up at your hotel to connect with the larger airport-bound bus at Southern Cross railway station in the city center; you must book this in advance. It operates from 6am to 10:30pm weekdays and 7am to 7pm Saturday and Sunday, except Christmas Day. Skybus also operates from the airport to Southbank Docklands on the city fringe, and to the suburb of St Kilda, 6:30am to 7pm daily, every 30 minutes weekdays and every hour Saturday and Sunday. One-way **tickets** cost A$20 for adults to either the city or Southbank/Docklands, and A$38 round-trip. Tickets for children ages 4 to 16 cost A$10 one-way or A$20 round-trip, but if you buy online, up to four children travel free on your adult ticket. The trip takes about 30 minutes from the airport to Southern Cross station and about an hour to St Kilda, but allow extra time (at least 15 minutes) for your return journey.

Skybus also operates the **Avalon City Express** transfer service to Avalon Airport for Jetstar flights. One-way fares from Avalon Airport are A$24 for adults and A$11 for children 4 to 16 to Southern Cross station, more to other central business district (CBD) locations and other suburbs.

A **taxi** to the city center takes about 30 minutes and costs around A$65.

Car-rental desks at the airport include **Avis** (www.avis.com.au; ✆ **03/8855 5333**), **Budget** (www.budget.com.au; ✆ **03/9241 6366**), **Europcar** (www.europcar.com.au; ✆ **03/9241 6800**), **Hertz** (www.hertz.com.au; ✆ **03/9338**

Take a Swim Between Flights

For travelers with extra time between flights, the **Parkroyal Melbourne Airport** hotel (see above) offers a A$25 "lounge/swim" package (available 6am–11pm), giving access to its pool, gym, spa, and sauna (plus showering facilities) for 3 hours, plus free Wi-Fi and discounts in the bar. Transiting passengers can also book rooms for 3, 5, or 8 hours (7am–7pm only) for A$89, A$109, or A$130 per room, with access to all facilities. The hotel is a 5-minute walk from the airport terminals.

Making Waves at the Airport

Australia's first **urban surf park** will be open near Melbourne Airport by the time you visit. At press time, construction was underway on the huge lagoon that will pump out waves of up to 2m (6.5 ft.) for eager surfers. It puts a whole new meaning on waving goodbye! The park will also have food outlets and bars, a surf pro shop, gymnasium, and skate ramps. Go to www.urbnsurf.com for details.

4044), **Thrifty** (www.thrifty.com.au; ℗ **03/9241 6100**), and **Redspot** (www. redspot.com.au; ℗ **03/9335 1177**). The Tullamarine freeway to and from the airport joins with the CityLink, an electronic tollway system. Drivers will need a CityLink pass; check with your car-rental company.

BY TRAIN

Interstate trains arrive at **Southern Cross Railway Station,** Spencer and Little Collins streets (5 blocks from Swanston St., in the city center). Locals often refer to it as Spencer Street Station. Taxis and buses are available here.

The **Sydney–Melbourne** *XPT* travels between Australia's two largest cities daily; trip time is 11 hours. For details, contact **NSW Trainlink** (www.trans portnsw.info; ℗ **132 232** in Australia, or 02/4907 7501). **V/Line** services (www.vline.com.au; ℗ **1800/800 007** in Australia, or 03/9662 2505) also connect Melbourne with destinations around Victoria and other capital cities.

BY BUS

Several bus companies connect Melbourne with other capitals and regional areas of Victoria. Among the biggest are **Greyhound Australia** (www.grey hound.com.au; ℗ **1300/473 946** in Australia, or 03/8667 8701). Coaches serve Melbourne's **Transit Centre,** 58 Franklin St., two blocks north of the Southern Cross Railway station on Spencer Street. Trams and taxis serve the station; **V/Line buses** (www.vline.com.au; ℗ **1800/800 007** in Australia), which travel all over Victoria, depart from the Spencer Street Coach Terminal.

BY CAR

You can drive from Sydney to Melbourne along the Hume Highway (a straight trip of about 9½ hr.). Another route is along the coastal Princes Highway, for which you will need a minimum of 2 days, with stops. For information on all aspects of road travel in Victoria, contact the **Royal Automotive Club of Victoria** (www.racv.com.au; ℗ **137 228** in Australia, or 03/8832 7980).

Visitor Information

The first stop on any visitor's itinerary should be the **Melbourne Visitor Hub,** Melbourne Town Hall, corner of Swanston and Little Collins streets (www. whatson.melbourne.vic.gov.au; ℗ **03/9658 9658**). The center serves as a one-stop shop for tourism information, maps, and public transport details, and has

Cheap Tix

Buy tickets for entertainment events, including opera, dance, and drama, on the day of the performance from **Half-Tix** in the Melbourne Town Hall administration building on Swanston Street (right next to the Town Hall). The booth is open Monday from 10am to 2pm, Tuesday through Thursday 11am to 6pm, Friday 11am to 6:30pm, and Saturday 10am to 4pm (also selling for Sun shows). Tickets must be purchased in person and in cash. Available shows are displayed on the booth door and on the website, www.halftixmelbourne.com. The Arts Centre (p. 160) offers **tixatsix** every day from 6pm for A$30 each (limit of 2 per person), where you can take a chance on what you see. Available shows are announced at 5pm at the box office, depending on availability across that night's performances, anything from classical music to circus. Be spontaneous!

free Wi-Fi. The center is open daily from 9am to 6pm (10am–5pm Good Friday; closed Christmas Day). It is also home to the **Melbourne Greeter Service,** which connects visitors to enthusiastic local volunteers who offer free 2- to 4-hour orientation tours of the city at 9:30am daily. Book at least 24 hours in advance (*©* **03/9658 9658** Mon–Fri, 03/9658 9942 Sat–Sun, or online). The Melbourne Visitor Hub also operates a staffed information booth in **Bourke Street Mall,** between Swanston and Elizabeth streets, open daily 9am to 5pm (closed Good Friday and Christmas Day). In the central city area (mainly along Swanston Street, at Federation Square, or near the Arts Centre on St Kilda Rd.), also look for Melbourne's **City Ambassadors**—volunteers who give tourist information and directions. They'll be wearing bright red shirts.

Good websites about the city include the official tourism site, **www.visitmel bourne.com**, and the locally run **www.onlymelbourne.com.au**. Also worth a look is the official City of Melbourne site, **www.melbourne.vic.gov.au**.

Melbourne City Layout

Melbourne is on the Yarra River and stretches inland from Port Phillip Bay, which lies to its south. On a map, you'll see a distinct central oblong area surrounded by Flinders Street to the south, Latrobe Street to the north, Spring Street to the east, and Spencer Street to the west. Cutting north to south through its center are the two main shopping thoroughfares, Swanston Street and Elizabeth Street. Cross streets between these major thoroughfares include Bourke Street Mall, a pedestrian-only shopping promenade. If you continue south along Swanston Street and over the river, it turns into St Kilda Road, which runs to the coast. Melbourne's various urban "villages," including South Yarra, Richmond, Carlton, and Fitzroy, surround the city center. The seaside suburb of St Kilda is known for its diverse restaurants.

Melbourne Neighborhoods in Brief

At more than 7,695 sq. km (2,971 sq. miles), Melbourne is one of the biggest cities in the world by area, with a population of about 4.9 million. Below are the neighborhoods of most interest to visitors.

City Center　Made up of a grid of streets north of the Yarra River, the city center—bounded by Flinders, Latrobe, Spring, and Spencer streets—offers good shopping and a charming cafe scene; in recent years an active nightlife has sprung up with the opening of a swath of funky bars and restaurants playing live and recorded music to suit all ages. The gateway to the city is the Flinders Street Station, with its dome and clock tower, flanked by the Federation Square precinct (p. 162).

Chinatown　Centering on Little Bourke Street, between Swanston and Exhibition streets, Australia's oldest permanent Chinese settlement dates from the 1850s, when a few boardinghouses catered to Chinese prospectors lured by gold rushes. Plenty of cheap restaurants crowd its alleyways.

Southgate & Southbank　This flashy entertainment district on the banks of the Yarra River opposite Flinders Street station (linked by pedestrian bridges) is home to the huge Crown Casino (p. 160), as well as myriad restaurants, bars, cafes, nightclubs, cinemas, and designer shops. On the city side of the river is the SEA LIFE Melbourne Aquarium (p. 169). All are a 10-minute stroll from Flinders Street Station. Tram: 8 from Swanston Street.

The River District　Southeast of the center, the muddy-looking Yarra River runs past the Birrarung Marr parkland and Royal Botanic Gardens (p. 174); nearby are the Arts Centre, the National Gallery of Victoria, and the Melbourne Cricket Ground. It is accessible by the free City Circle Tram.

Docklands　Near the city center, at the rear of the Spencer Street station, this industrial area has become the biggest new development in Melbourne. NewQuay on the waterfront has a diverse range of restaurants, shops, and cinemas, along with the 52,000-seat Etihad Stadium, where Melbourne dominates Australian Rules football. Docklands is accessible by the free City Circle Tram.

Carlton　North of the center, this rambling suburb is known for Italian restaurants along Lygon Street, with varying food quality but lots of outdoor seating. Melbourne University is in Carlton, so there's a healthy student scene. From Bourke Street Mall, it's a 15-minute walk to Lygon Street. Tram: 1 or 22 from Swanston Street.

Fitzroy　A ruggedly bohemian place 2km (1¼ miles) north of the city center, Fitzroy is filled with students and artists; it's popular for people-watching and amazing street art. Its hub is Brunswick Street, lined with cheap restaurants, busy cafes, late-night bookshops, art galleries, and pubs. Around the corner on Johnston Street, a growing Spanish quarter has tapas bars, flamenco restaurants, and Spanish clubs. Tram: 11 from Collins Street.

Richmond　One of Melbourne's earliest settlements, noted for its historic streets and back lanes, Richmond today is a multicultural quarter lying east of the city center. Victoria Street is reminiscent of Ho Chi Minh City, with Vietnamese sights, sounds, aromas, and restaurants. Bridge Road is a discount-fashion precinct. Tram: 48 or 75 from Flinders Street; 70 from Princes Bridge; 109 from Bourke Street.

St Kilda　Once Melbourne's red-light district, this shabby-chic bayside suburb (6km/3¾ miles south of the city center) now has the city's highest concentration of restaurants, from glitzy to cheap, as well as superb cake shops and delis. The Esplanade hugs a beach with a vintage pier and a lively Sunday arts-and-crafts market. Check out Luna Park, one of the world's oldest fun parks, built in 1912. Tram: 10 or 12 from Collins Street; 15 or 16 from Swanston Street; 96 from Bourke Street.

South Yarra/Prahran　This posh part of town abounds with boutiques, cinemas, nightclubs, and galleries. Chapel Street has upscale eateries and designer fashions;

Commercial Road is popular with the LGBTQ community. Off Chapel Street in Prahran, Greville Street is full of boutiques and music outlets. Tram: 8 or 72 from Swanston Street.

South Melbourne One of the city's oldest working-class districts, South Melbourne is known for its historic buildings, old-fashioned pubs and hotels, and markets. Tram: 12 from Collins Street; 1 from Swanston Street.

Williamstown Bypassed by developers, this waterfront suburb preserves a rich architectural heritage. Parts of Ferguson Street and Nelson Place look just like English High Streets, and along The Strand is a line of seaside bistros and a World War II warship museum. Ferry: From Southgate, or St Kilda Pier.

Getting Around Melbourne
BY PUBLIC TRANSPORTATION

Trams are the major form of transport in the city; you will probably only use a train or bus if you are going into the suburbs. Melbourne's transport system uses an electronic ticketing system called **myki,** a reusable smart card to pay for your travel. The card costs A$6, then you put money on it for travel. You "touch on" and "touch off" at an electronic machine on board the tram or bus, or as you enter the train station. When your myki balance gets low, just top up your card. A 2-hour trip in Zones 1 and 2, which will allow you to travel on all trams and trains within the city and close surrounding suburbs from 5:30am to midnight (when transportation stops), costs A$4.40; the daily fare of A$8.80 allows unlimited travel. On weekends and public holidays, pay the off-peak rate of A$6.40 per day. A **7-day myki pass** will cost A$44 to travel in Zones 1 and 2. You can get cards at Flinders Street or Southern Cross stations, at the MetShop, or at most 7-Eleven convenience stores, and top them up through the **Public Transport Victoria** website (www.ptv.vic.gov.au) or at the call center (☎ **1800/800 007**); you can also top up as little as A$1 at myki machines in train stations and at selected tram platforms and bus interchanges.

You can pick up a free route map from the Melbourne Visitor Centre, Federation Square, or from the **PTV Hub** at Southern Cross station (www.ptv.vic.gov.au; ☎ **1800/800 007** in Australia), open Monday through Friday from 7am to 7pm, and weekends and public holidays (except Christmas Day) 9am to 6pm. There's another hub at 750 Collins St., Docklands, open from 8am to 6pm weekdays only (closed Sat–Sun and public holidays).

Money-Saving Transit Passes

Visitors to Victoria can buy a **myki Explorer** card, which gives 1 day's unlimited travel as well as discounts on entry to 16 major attractions around the city and region. Buy this at Southern Cross station or the Skybus terminal at Melbourne Airport. It costs A$15 adults or A$7.50 children, and you can top it up for another day.

BY TRAM

Melbourne has the oldest tram network in the world. Trams are an essential part of the city, a major cultural icon, and a great non-smoggy way of getting around. Several hundred trams run over 325km (202 miles) of track.

Trams stop at numbered tram-stop signs, sometimes in the middle of the road (so beware of oncoming traffic!). To get off the tram, press the button near the handrails or pull the cord above your head.

A **free tram zone** operates in the inner city center, bounded by Spring, Flinders, and La Trobe streets, running along Victoria, William, and Elizabeth streets (around the Victoria Market) and to Docklands. Drivers announce when you are leaving the free zone. If you are staying in the free zone, you don't need to "touch on" with your myki, but if you are beginning or ending your trip outside the free zone, you must do so.

A free **City Circle Tram** (tram no. 35) travels a circular route between all the major central attractions and past shopping malls and arcades. The trams run in both directions every 12 minutes between 10am and 6pm (and until 9pm Thurs–Sat), except on Good Friday and Christmas Day, and run along all the major corridors including Flinders and Spencer streets.

BY BUS

Melbourne's bus services generally only serve the far-flung suburbs where trams don't reach. If you're looking for a bus tour, see **City Sightseeing Melbourne** (p. 172).

BY TAXI

Cabs are plentiful in the city, but it may be difficult to hail one in the city center late on Friday and Saturday nights. Major taxi ranks can be found in Queen Street (between Little Collins and Bourke streets), outside Flinders Street station, at Bourke Street (near Russell St.) and on King Street (near Flinders St.). Otherwise, order one by phone: Taxi companies include **Silver Top** (*℗* **131 008** in Australia) and **13CABS** (Yellow) (*℗* **132 227** in Australia). Note that from 10pm to 5am, anywhere in Victoria, you must prepay your fare. The driver estimates the fare at the start of the journey, gives you a receipt, and then adjusts it according to the meter reading (plus any fees such as road tolls) at the end of your trip.

A Quirky Melbourne Road Rule

One rule to remember about turning right from the left lane at certain major intersections in the downtown center and in South Melbourne: In order to leave the left lane free for trams and through traffic, you must pull into the left lane opposite the street you are turning into, and make the turn when the traffic light in the street you are turning into becomes green. Luckily, these intersections are signposted.

Uber also operates in Melbourne, and at press time announced that Melbourne would be one of its test cities for "flying taxis"—piloted electric flying vehicles, still under development but set to launch by 2023.

BY CAR

Driving in Melbourne can be challenging. Roads can be confusing, there are trams everywhere (you must *always* stop behind a tram if it stops, because passengers usually step directly into the road). Plus, there's a general lack of parking, and hotel valet parking is expensive. It's better to avoid driving and hop on a tram instead.

If you must drive, keep in mind that seatbelts and child restraints are required. For a full rundown of road rules, go to www.vicroads.vic.gov.au and click on "Safety & Road Rules," or pick up a copy of the **Victorian Road Traffic** handbook from bookshops or from a **Vic Roads** office (✆ **131 171** in Australia for the nearest office).

If you plan to travel beyond Melbourne, wait to pick up your rental car until the day you're leaving the city. (See p. 140 for car rental companies.) Most car-rental offices in the city center are on Franklin Street.

[FastFACTS] MELBOURNE

ATMs/Banks Banks are open Monday through Thursday from 9:30am to 4pm, and Friday from 9:30am to 5pm. Most ATMs operate 24 hours and are found throughout the CBD.

Business Hours In general, stores are open daily from 9am to 5:30pm; many stay open until 9pm on Fridays, and on Saturdays and Sundays hours are often 10am to 4pm. Shops are generally not open on Good Friday and Christmas Day.

Dentists The **Royal Dental Hospital of Melbourne** (✆ **1800/833 039** in Australia, or 03/9341 1000), at 720 Swanston St., Carlton, offers emergency services Monday to Friday 8:15am to 9:15pm and weekends and public holidays 8:45am to 9:15pm.

Doctors & Hospitals The emergency department at the **Royal Melbourne Hospital,** 300 Grattan St., Parkville (✆ **03/9342 7000**), is open 24 hours. The **Traveller's Medical & Vaccination Centre,** Second Floor, 393 Little Bourke St. (www. traveldoctor.com.au; ✆ **03/9935 8100**), offers full vaccination and travel medical services. It is open Monday to Friday 9am to 5pm (until 7:30pm Thurs) and Saturday 9am to 1pm.

Embassies & Consulates The following English-speaking countries have consulates in Melbourne: **United States,** Level 6, 553 St Kilda Rd. (✆ **03/9526 5900**); **United Kingdom,** Level 17, 90 Collins St. (✆ **03/9652 1600**); and **New Zealand,** Level 4, 45 William St. (✆ **03/9678 0201**).

Emergencies In an emergency, call ✆ **000** for police, ambulance, or the fire department.

Mail & Postage The **General Post Office (GPO)** at 260 Elizabeth St. (✆ **131 318** in Australia) is open Monday to Friday 8:30am to 5:30pm, Saturday 9am to 5pm.

Newspapers & Magazines Melbourne's daily newspapers are **The Age** and the **Herald Sun.** Both have Sunday versions as well.

Pharmacies (Chemist Shops) The **Mulqueeny Pharmacy,** 99 Swanston St. (✆ **03/9654 8569**), is open Monday to Friday 8am to 8pm, Saturday 9am to 6pm, Sunday 11am to 6pm. The **Mulqueeny Midnight Pharmacy,** 416 High St., Windsor (✆ **03/9510 3977**), is open daily 9am to midnight.

Safety St Kilda might be coming up in the world, but walking there alone at night still isn't wise. Parks and gardens can also be risky after dark, as can the area around the King Street nightclubs in the city center.

Wi-Fi The **State Library of Victoria**, 328 Swanston St. (www.slv.vic.gov.au; *C* **03/8864 7000**), has free Wi-Fi in all areas of the library and powering stations in all reading rooms. It is open Monday to Thursday 10am to 9pm and Friday to Sunday 10am to 6pm. Free public Wi-Fi is available in the Melbourne CBD at train stations and the Bourke Street Mall, Queen Victoria Market, and South Wharf Promenade at the Melbourne Convention and Exhibition Centre.

WHERE TO STAY IN MELBOURNE

Getting a room is easy enough on weekends, when business travelers are back home. You need to book well in advance, however, during the city's hallmark events (say, the weekend before the Melbourne Cup, and during the Grand Prix and the Australian Open). Hostels in the St Kilda area tend to fill up quickly in December and January.

You'll feel right in the heart of the action if you stay in the city center, which seems to buzz all day (and night). Otherwise, the inner-city suburbs are all exciting satellites, with good street life, restaurants, and pubs—and just a quick tram ride from the city center. Transportation from the airport to the suburbs is a little more expensive and complicated than to the city center, however.

In the City Center
EXPENSIVE

Hotel Lindrum ★★ This gorgeous hotel has always felt quite "clubby" to me; perhaps the billiard room has something to do with it. That said, the rooms are stylish and contemporary. Studios have queen-size beds or two singles, plenty of hardwood, soft lighting, and neutral tones with red accents. Superior rooms have king-size beds and lovely polished-wood floorboards, and deluxe rooms have wonderful views across to the Botanic Gardens through large bay windows. The hotel also boasts a worthy restaurant and a bar with an open fire.

26 Flinders St. www.hotellindrum.com.au. *C* **03/9668 1111.** 59 units. A$330–A$450 double; A$450 suite. Public parking next door (discounted for guests). Train: Flinders St. **Amenities:** Restaurant; bar; nearby health club; room service; free Wi-Fi.

The Hotel Windsor ★★ One of Australia's grandest and most historic hotels, the Windsor has over the past few years, after a long debate over planning issues, undergone a controversial A$330-million redevelopment and restoration, expected to be completed in 2020. But it's still business as usual, as guests settle in to the opulent rooms and sit down to high tea each afternoon, as has been the custom for 130 years. The Windsor opened in 1883, an upper-crust establishment that oozed sophistication, and has hosted the rich, famous, and glamorous ever since. The hotel holds a special place in Australia's history as the setting for the drafting of the country's Constitution in 1898. The redevelopment adds a 26-story tower (and 152 guest rooms) behind the heritage building. Many guest rooms have striking views of Parliament House and the Treasury Gardens. I'd suggest you stay here as soon as you can!

103 Spring St. www.thehotelwindsor.com.au. © **03/9633 6000.** 180 units. A$269–A$359 double; A$409–A$1,350 suite. Valet parking A$35. Train: Parliament. **Amenities:** Restaurant; 2 bars; babysitting; concierge; health club; room service; free Wi-Fi.

Quest Grand Hotel Melbourne ★★ This majestic, Heritage-listed six-story building—originally home to the Victorian railway administration—is striking for its remarkable scale and imposing Italianate facade. Building started in 1887, and it became a hotel in 1997. Studios have plush carpets and full kitchens with dishwashers; one-bedroom loft suites have European-style espresso machines and a second TV in the bedroom, and some have great views over the new Docklands area beyond—though rooms are whisper-quiet. All vary in size; some have balconies (mostly on the 6th floor). Many of the suites are split-level, with bedrooms on the second floor.

33 Spencer St. www.grandhotelmelbourne.com.au. © **03/9611 4567.** 95 units. A$209–A$239 studio; A$249–A$339 apt. Parking A$45. Tram: 48 or 75 from Flinders St. **Amenities:** Restaurant; bar; babysitting; concierge; golf course nearby; exercise room; Jacuzzi; heated indoor swimming pool (with retractable roof); room service; sauna; free Wi-Fi.

Treasury on Collins ★★★ The giant bell on the reception desk is a sign that here, you'll get attention whenever you need it. Ding! Just ring that bell (or call from your room). It's one of the personal and quirky touches that make this a top choice. And then there's the inner-city location right on bustling Collins Street, the spacious suites and apartments, each with a fully equipped kitchen, and lots of personal touches such as games, magazines, and ceramic ducks in the bathroom. Feather toppers on the beds ensure a comfortable sleep, and some suites have balconies. Built in 1876 as the Bank of Australasia, the building is classical Renaissance Revival style and has lots of gorgeous features. A brochure in your room outlines a self-guided tour of some of the hotel's historical elements. All in all, it's a treasure.

394 Collins St. (at Queen St.). www.treasuryoncollins.com.au. © **03/8535 8535.** 115 units. A$208–A$358 double; A$304–A$457 apt. Valet parking A$38. Train: Flinders St. **Amenities:** Restaurant; bar; gym; room service; free Wi-Fi.

MODERATE

Ibis Melbourne Hotel and Apartments ★ The Ibis Melbourne is a good deal, next door to a tram stop, close to the bus station, *and* a short walk from the central shopping areas and Queen Victoria Market. Standard rooms and apartments in this midrange hotel are spacious, immaculate, and bright (if somewhat bland and colorless), but for something different pay a little more for a MyRoom, where a feature wall is painted brightly with a local

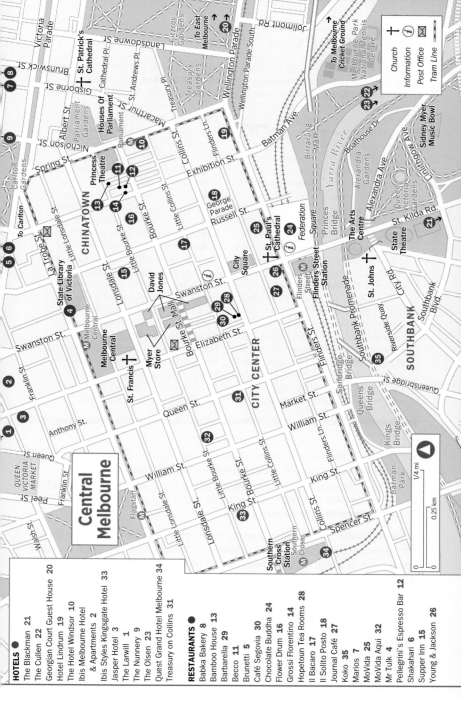

Central Melbourne

HOTELS ●
The Blackman **21**
The Cullen **22**
Georgian Court Guest House **20**
Hotel Lindrum **19**
The Hotel Windsor **10**
Ibis Melbourne Hotel & Apartments **2**
Ibis Styles Kingsgate Hotel **33**
Jasper Hotel **3**
The Larwill **1**
The Nunnery **9**
The Olsen **23**
Quest Grand Hotel Melbourne **34**
Treasury on Collins **31**

RESTAURANTS ●
Babka Bakery **8**
Bamboo House **13**
Barbarella **29**
Becco **11**
Brunetti **5**
Café Segovia **30**
Chocolate Buddha **24**
Flower Drum **16**
Grossi Florentino **14**
Hopetoun Tea Rooms **28**
Il Bacaro **17**
Il Solito Posto **18**
Journal Café **27**
Koko **35**
Marios **7**
MoVida **25**
MoVida Aqui **32**
Mr Tulk **4**
Pellegrini's Espresso Bar **12**
Shakahari **6**
Supper Inn **15**
Young & Jackson **26**

Some of Melbourne's most interesting boutique hotels belong to the **Art Series Hotel Group** (www.artseries hotels.com.au), which themes its hotels to well-known Australian artists. The flagship is **The Olsen ★★★**, at Chapel Street and Toorak Road, South Yarra (**℃ 03/9040 1222**), named for John Olsen, regarded as Australia's greatest living painter. It has 224 spacious rooms and claims to have the world's largest glass-bottom swimming pool, suspended over the street. Rates start from A$249 to A$309 double per night for a studio suite. It's a little bit out of the city center, but a tram delivers you almost on the doorstep, and I vote it one of my favorite hotels. **The Cullen ★★**, a 115-room boutique hotel at 164 Commercial Rd., Prahran (**℃ 03/9098 1555**), is named for the controversial artist Adam Cullen and has a rooftop cocktail bar and two restaurants. Room rates range from A$229 to A$259 double. **The Blackman ★★**, named for Sydney artist John Blackman and housed within the Heritage-listed Airlie House (backed by a modern

high-rise annex), is at 452 St Kilda Rd. (**℃ 03/9039 1444**) and has 209 rooms, with rates ranging from A$259 to A$319 double. North of Melbourne's city center, **The Larwill ★★**, 48 Flemington Rd., Parkville (**℃ 03/9032 9111**), is dedicated to artist David Larwill, and has rooms from A$199 to A$259.

Each hotel features a major artwork commissioned especially for the hotel foyer by the naming artist: The Cullen has one from Adam Cullen's *Ned Kelly* series, and the Olsen's spectacular glass lobby features John Olsen's 6m (19-ft.) mural *The Yellow Sun and Yarra*. Prints and a photographic history of each artist's life adorn guest-room walls and public spaces; the architecture, interior design, linens, and stationery also reflect the artist's style. If you like the concept, there are Art Series hotels in other Australian cities: **The Schaller** in Bendigo, **The Johnson** and **The Fantauzzo** in Brisbane, and **The Watson** in Adelaide. At press time, another had been announced for Perth. Visit the Art Series website for links to all properties.

scene—street art, the zoo, or a scene from the Queen Victoria Market. All apartments come equipped with kitchenettes and bathtubs.

15–21 Therry St. www.ibis.com. **℃ 03/9666 0000.** 250 units. A$153 double; A$173 1-bedroom apt; A$233 2-bedroom apt; A$183–A$253 MyRoom. Parking A$25. Tram: 19, 57, 59. **Amenities:** Restaurant; bar; free Wi-Fi.

Jasper Hotel ★★   Smart-looking and welcoming, this is a good choice for an inner-city boutique hotel. There are 16 suites on the hotel's second level, some of which open out onto a guest courtyard with walled gardens and artificial grass. Levels 2 and 3 also have small executive lounges with free refreshments (and check out the hallways' star-spangled ceilings). Some rooms have balconies overlooking Elizabeth Street. The **Jasper Kitchen** restaurant sources most of its produce from the Queen Victoria Market, just outside the back door. Hotel guests get free entry to the nearby Melbourne City Baths swimming pool.

489 Elizabeth St. www.jasperhotel.com.au. **℃ 03/8327 2777.** 90 units. A$109–A$259 double; A$274 suite. Parking nearby (around A$35 per day). Tram: 19, 57, 59. Train: Melbourne Central. **Amenities:** 2 restaurants; bar; gym; room service; free Wi-Fi.

INEXPENSIVE

Ibis Styles Kingsgate Hotel ★ A 10-minute walk from the city, this interesting hotel resembles a terrace building from the outside, but inside it's a maze of corridors and rooms. At the time of writing the hotel was undergoing renovations of its guest rooms, due for completion in mid-2020, which means there may be some daytime noise issues from time to time. The least expensive economy rooms have double beds (no twins); these rooms are small but a good value if you just want somewhere to sleep. Standard rooms have double or twin beds. The 21 family rooms have double beds and two singles. There's a 24-hour reception desk, free luggage-storage facilities, a guest laundry, and free use of safety deposit boxes. Check the hotel's website for excellent deals.

131 King St. www.kingsgatehotel.com.au. © **03/9629 4171**. 171 units. A$104–A$164 double; A$169 family room. Parking at nearby Southern Cross Station, A$25 per day. Tram: 19, 57, 59. **Amenities:** Restaurant (breakfast only); bar; gym; free Wi-Fi.

In East Melbourne

INEXPENSIVE

Georgian Court Guest House ★ The appearance of the comfortable Georgian Court, set on a beautiful tree-lined street, hasn't changed much since it was built in 1910. The sitting and dining rooms have high ceilings and offer old-world atmosphere. The guest rooms are simply furnished, and some are in need of a refurbishment; others have already been refreshed. Some have en-suite bathrooms; others have private bathrooms in the hallway. One room comes with a queen-size bed and Jacuzzi. The Georgian Court is a 15-minute stroll through the Fitzroy and Treasury Gardens from the city center and is also close to the fashion shops of Bridge Road.

21 George St., East Melbourne. www.georgiancourt.com.au. © **03/9415 8225.** 31 units. A$90–A$129 double; A$129–A$159 family room. Rates include breakfast. Free parking. Tram: 75 from Flinders St., or 48 from Spencer St. **Amenities:** Free Wi-Fi.

In Fitzroy

MODERATE/INEXPENSIVE

The Nunnery ★★ This former convent offers smart budget accommodations—and something a little more upmarket—a short tram ride from the city center, close to the restaurants and nightlife of Brunswick and Lygon streets in nearby Carlton. The informal, welcoming 1860s main building has high ceilings, handmade light fittings, polished floorboards, marble fireplaces, and a hand-turned staircase. There's also a clever and rather irreverent play on its past in the decor. It's well-suited to couples and families. The Guesthouse next door, built in the early 1900s, is also comfy, stylish, and decorated with tasteful furnishings and artwork; its seven rooms share three bathrooms. The Nunnery, former home of the Daughters of Charity, also offers dorm rooms with 4, 8, or 12 beds. *Note:* There are no elevators.

116 Nicholson St., Fitzroy. www.nunnery.com.au. © **1800/032 635** in Australia, or 03/9419 8637. 30 units, all with shared bathroom. A$132 family room; A$28–A$40 per-person bunk rooms. Guesthouse: A$155–A$225 double or family room. Rates include breakfast. Free parking (reservation required). Tram: 96. **Amenities:** Kitchen; free Wi-Fi.

In St Kilda

EXPENSIVE

Novotel Melbourne St Kilda ★   Ask for a room with a view at this sleek contemporary seaside hotel; the best of them overlook St Kilda beach, the pier, and Port Phillip Bay. Standard rooms have a queen or king bed, a small desk, and minibar; some have a Jacuzzi. This well-located property is a 2-minute walk to the beach, Luna Park, and Acland Street shopping—and on Sundays you're right across the street from the St Kilda arts-and-crafts markets lining the Esplanade.

16 The Esplanade. www.novotelstkilda.com.au. ✆ **03/9525 5522.** 211 units. A$160–A$240 double; A$310 1-bedroom penthouse; A$207 family room (sleeps 4). Parking A$25. Tram: 16, 96. **Amenities:** Restaurant; bar; outdoor heated pool; fitness center; free Wi-Fi.

MODERATE

Tolarno Hotel ★★   Quirky Tolarno is in the middle of St Kilda's cafe and restaurant strip and just a short stroll from the beach. Set in the former private residence and gallery of artist Mirka Mora, the rooms and corridors of this modern, colorful property are adorned with 150 contemporary works by Melbourne artists, many of them by Mora, for whom the hotel's restaurant is named. Rooms vary, but the deluxe doubles in the front of the building, with balconies overlooking the main street, are the most popular. These are larger than the standard rooms, but if you are a light sleeper you might prefer something away from the noise of the trams running by. Superior doubles come with microwaves, and two have Japanese baths. Suites have a separate kitchen and lounge, but no balcony. The hotel restaurant is a pasta bar, open for lunch and dinner, serving "traditional Italian with a twist." If that's not to your taste, there are plenty of other options right on Fitzroy Street, the heart of St Kilda's restaurant strip.

42 Fitzroy St. www.tolarnohotel.com.au. ✆ **03/9537 0200.** 37 units. A$89–A$119 double; A$129–A$200 suite. Free street parking or A$10 in the building opposite. Tram: 16 from Swanston St., 12 from Collins St., or 96 from Flinders St. **Amenities:** Restaurant; bar; babysitting; bikes; concierge; room service; free Wi-Fi.

WHERE TO EAT IN MELBOURNE

Melbourne's ethnically diverse population ensures a healthy selection of international cuisines. Chinatown, in the city center, is a fabulous hunting ground for Chinese, Malaysian, Thai, Indonesian, Japanese, and Vietnamese fare, often at bargain prices. Carlton has plenty of Italian restaurants, but some of the outdoor eateries on Lygon Street target unsuspecting tourists with overpriced and disappointing fare; avoid them. Richmond is crammed with Greek and Vietnamese restaurants, and Fitzroy has cheap Asian, Turkish, Mediterranean, and vegetarian food. To see and be seen, head to Chapel Street or Toorak Road in South Yarra, or travel to St Kilda, where you can join the throng of Melburnians dining out along Fitzroy and Acland streets.

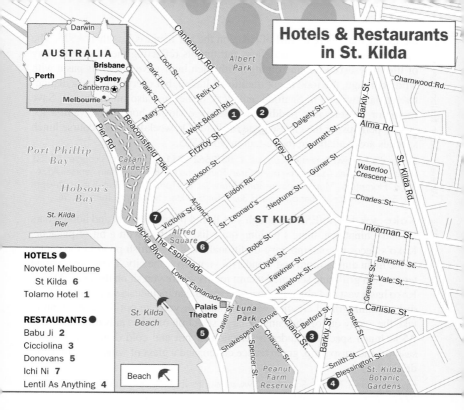

Most of the cheaper places in Melbourne are strictly BYO (bring your own wine or beer). Smoking is banned in Melbourne cafes and restaurants, so don't even think about lighting up.

For restaurant locations, see map on p. 149.

In the City Center
EXPENSIVE

Becco ★★ ITALIAN   Tucked away on a quiet lane, this favorite of Melburnians consistently lives up to its many accolades. The simplicity of the surroundings—terrazzo floors, white tablecloths, views of the lane—belie the sophistication of this stylish restaurant. The cuisine mixes Italian flavors with Australian flair. Try the veal saltimbocca, one of the tasty pasta dishes, or the specials, which your waiter will fill you in on. If you prefer something lighter, a bar menu offers equally tempting dishes.

11–25 Crossley St., near Bourke St. www.becco.com.au. ✆ **03/9663 3000.** Main courses A$29–A$70. Mon–Fri noon–3pm; Mon–Sat 6–11pm.

Grossi Florentino ★★★ ITALIAN   Under the management of the Grossi family, this is probably the best Italian restaurant in Melbourne, with three dining options. The casual bistro, the Grill, is downstairs, right next to the Cellar Bar where a bowl of pasta on the bar menu is less than A$26. The upstairs, outfitted with chandeliers and murals reflecting the Florentine way of life, is reserved for fine dining. With such innovative dishes as pasta with wild boar ragu, the food is not traditional Italian, but everything has a distinctive Italian twist to it. Seafood and steak dishes are also on the menu. Save room for dessert: rice pudding with orange flower honey and vanilla ice cream, perhaps, or the cheese plate to share? On weekdays, two-course lunch specials are available in the restaurant for A$65.

80 Bourke St. www.florentino.com.au. ℰ **03/9662 1811.** Florentino: 3 courses A$150, additional courses A$25; or 6-course Gran Tour menu A$180. Grill: main courses A$26–A$58. Florentino: Mon–Fri noon–3pm; Mon–Sat 6–11pm. Grill: Mon–Sat noon–3pm and 5:30–11pm (cellar bar opens at 7:30am for breakfast Mon–Sat). Tram: 86, 96.

Koko ★★ JAPANESE   Though you'll find plenty of sushi and noodle bars around Chinatown, there's nothing quite like raw fish with a bit of panache. Koko's decor is contemporary-traditional, with a goldfish pond in the center of the main dining room and wonderful views over the city. There are separate teppanyaki grills and screened tatami rooms where you sit on the matted floor. Koko has a vast and changing seasonal menu that includes a variety of seafood dishes (think grilled crayfish with soy salt), or you can opt for a set menu to take the agony out of choosing. A large selection of sakes aids digestion. The A$50 lunch special includes a selection of hot and cold dishes, as well as sashimi and miso soup, green tea ice cream, and a glass of wine, beer, or a soft drink.

Level 3, Crown Towers, Southbank. www.crownmelbourne.com.au/koko. ℰ **03/9292 5777.** Main courses A$40–A$115. Daily noon–2:30pm; Sun–Thurs 6–10pm; Fri–Sat 6–10:30pm.

MODERATE

Bamboo House ★★ CHINESE/CANTONESE   Esteemed by both the Chinese community and local business big shots, this restaurant is worth writing home about. Service here is a pleasure; the waiters will help you construct a feast from the myriad Cantonese and northern Chinese dishes. Order ahead to get a taste of the signature dish, Szechuan tea-smoked duck. Other popular dishes include pan-fried beef dumplings and spring-onion pancakes.

47 Little Bourke St. www.bamboohouse.com.au. ℰ **03/9662 1565.** Main courses A$26–A$39. Mon–Fri noon–3pm (except public holidays); Mon–Sat 5:30–11pm; Sun 5:30–10pm. Tram: 35, 86, 96.

Chocolate Buddha ★★ JAPANESE   This place offers mostly organic produce, including some organic wines. Based on Japanese-inspired noodle, ramen, and soba dishes to which the kitchen adds meat, chicken, or seafood, it's casual yet satisfying dining. The best way to eat here is to order dishes to share. The food is creative, and the view across the square to the Yarra River and Southbank is a delight at dusk. It can get very crowded, so book ahead.

Federation Sq., corner of Flinders and Swanson sts. www.chocolatebuddha.com.au. ℰ **03/9070 6251.** Main courses A$15–A$24. Daily 11:30am–9:30pm. Train: Flinders St.

Since the first pour from one of Australia's earliest espresso machines at **Pellegrini's Espresso Bar** in 1954, Melbourne has been hooked on good coffee. Cafe culture is huge here, and there are plenty of places to get your caffeine hit. Pellegrini's, at 66 Bourke St. (✆ **03/9662 1885**), is still buzzing, and also offers authentic Italian food. Another of my favorites is **Journal Café** at 253 Flinders Lane (✆ **03/9650 4399**), next to the City Library and themed to fit. Not far away in Block Place, a lane off Collins Street, are the French-style **Café Segovia** (✆ **03/9650 2373**), which spills out into the lane and has an international/seafood menu, and **Barbarella** (www.barbarella.melbourne; ✆ **03/9663 2214**), which has a reputation for some of the best coffee in Melbourne. At the other end of the city center, **Mr Tulk** (www.mrtulk.com.au; ✆ **03/8660 5700**) is a light, airy, and spacious cafe in the State Library on Swanston St., popular with university students.

Flower Drum ★★★ CANTONESE   Praise pours in from all quarters for this upscale restaurant just off Little Bourke Street, Chinatown's main drag. Take a slow elevator up to the restaurant, which has widely spaced tables (perfect for politicians and businesspeople to clinch their deals). Take note of the specials—the chefs are extremely creative and use the best ingredients they find in the markets each day. A smart idea is to put your menu selections into the hands of the waiter. The signature dish is Peking duck, and the seafood dumplings in soup is a great starter. Or, you can order more unusual dishes, such as abalone (at a price: A$1,700 per kg) or pearl meat. The atmosphere is clubby and a bit old-fashioned; the service is impeccable. But be prepared to pay for the privilege.

17 Market Lane. www.flowerdrum.melbourne. ✆ **03/9662 3655.** Main courses A$20–A$45. Mon–Sat noon–3pm and 6–11pm; Sun 6–10:30pm. Tram: 86, 96.

Il Bacaro ★★ ITALIAN   Walk into Il Bacaro and you'll experience a little piece of Venice. Dominated by a horseshoe-shaped bar, it's jam-packed with small tables and weaving waiters carrying interesting dishes such as tagliatelle with rabbit ragu or duck breast with red grapes and liver parfait. The pasta dishes and the risotto of the day always go down well, as do the side salads. It's often crowded at lunch with business folk digging into the excellent wine list.

168–170 Little Collins St. www.ilbacaro.com.au. ✆ **03/9654 6778.** Main courses A$38–A$49. Mon–Sat noon–3pm; Mon–Thurs 6–10:30pm; Fri–Sat 6–11pm. Tram: 11, 12, 48, 86, 96, 109.

Il Solito Posto ★★ ITALIAN   This below-ground restaurant consists of two parts. The casual bistro or *caffeteria* has a blackboard menu offering good pastas, soups, and salads. Then there's the sharper and more upmarket trattoria, with an a la carte menu of northern Italian dishes offering the likes of slow-braised lamb in white wine, chili, garlic, herbs, fresh peas, and tomato, as well as steak, fish, and veal dishes. It's open for breakfast, lunch, and dinner. You'll find the coffee excellent, too.

113 Collins St., basement (enter through George Parade). www.ilsolitoposto.com.au. ☎ **03/9654 4466.** Main courses A$28–A$34 in bistro, A$34–A$46 in trattoria. Mon–Fri 7:30am–1am; Sat 9am–1am. Tram: 11, 12, 48, 109.

MoVida ★★★ SPANISH   Barcelona-born chef and co-owner Frank Camorra has made MoVida one of the most talked-about restaurants in Melbourne. His relaxed and fun restaurant reflects the spirit of Spain, with seriously good food and good wine. Melburnians flock here, and it's truly one of those places I was tempted to keep a secret (if that's possible, considering that everyone talks about how great it is). MoVida offers a choice of tapas (small individual dishes) or *raciones* (plates to share among two or more people, or a larger dish for one). Specials are available every night to keep the regulars happy. So successful was the first MoVida that there's also now **Next Door,** which is…you guessed it, next door. And if you have a group (up to six people) or want to dine outdoors, there is **MoVida Aqui,** at level 1, 500 Bourke St. (entry off Little Bourke St.), which has a huge casual dining area and a terrace and serves the same great food. Be sure to book ahead.

1 Hosier Lane. www.movida.com.au. ☎ **03/9663 3038** (for all restaurants). Tapas A$4–A$9.50; *raciones* (main courses) A$10–A$39. Daily noon–10pm (till 10:30pm Fri–Sat). Train: Flinders St.

Young & Jackson ★★ PUB   Melbourne's oldest and most famous pub is a great place to stop in for a drink at the bar or a meal in the stylish upstairs restaurant or bistro areas. It has fairly standard pub food (burgers, schnitzel, ribs, and so on) in the cafe downstairs and at the rooftop bar, but offerings are more refined in the restaurant. It's a landmark on the corner opposite Federation Square and Flinders Street Station. Head upstairs to see the nude *Chloe,* the famous painting brought to Melbourne from Paris for the Great Exhibition in 1880, which has a special place in the hearts of customers and Melburnians. The pub, which was built in 1853 and started selling beer in 1861, has a few years on *Chloe,* which was painted in Paris in 1875.

At the corner of Flinders and Swanston sts. www.youngandjacksons.com.au. ☎ **03/9650 3884.** Main courses A$29–A$40. Bar meals available 10am–late. Restaurant: daily noon–2:30pm; Sun–Thurs 5:30–9pm; Fri–Sat 5:30–10pm. Train: Flinders St.

INEXPENSIVE

Hopetoun Tea Rooms ★ CAFE   The first cup of tea served in this Melbourne institution left the pot in 1892. With its green-and-cream Regency wallpaper and marble tables, the Tea Rooms cater to a loyal clientele of little old ladies and students, with the odd tourist or businessperson thrown into the mix. At times, there are long queues waiting for a table, but most people think it's worth it. There's a full lunch menu, but really you should come for tea or coffee and the very good cakes. Try the chocolate strawberry Swiss roll. Scones, croissants, pasta, and grilled food are also available. Traditional "High Tea" at A$65 per person can be taken between 10am and 2:30pm.

Block Arcade, 280–282 Collins St. www.hopetountearooms.com.au. © **03/9650 2777.**
Main courses A$17–A$27; sandwiches A$13–A$19. Mon–Sat 8am–5pm; Sun 9am–5pm.
Tram: 11, 12, 48, 109.

Supper Inn ★★ CANTONESE   Head here if you get the Chinese-food
munchies late at night. It's a friendly place with a mixed crowd of locals and
tourists chowing down on such dishes as steaming bowls of *congee* (rice-
based porridge), dumplings, barbecued suckling pig, mud crab, pepper squid,
and stuffed scallops. Everything here is the real thing.

15 Celestial Ave. © **03/9663 4759.** Main courses A$11–A$40. Daily 5:30pm–2:30am.
Train: Melbourne Central.

In Carlton
INEXPENSIVE

Brunetti ★★ ITALIAN   Don't be daunted by the crowds around the cake
counters—and there *will* be crowds! This is a real Italian/Melbourne experience. If you can get past the mouthwatering array of excellent cakes, the cafe
menu offers authentic Italian cuisine, done very well. The open kitchen allows
you to watch the chefs in action; there's a wood-fired pizza oven (imported
from Italy) and a traditional *gelatieri* (ice-cream maker) at work. Or pop in for
breakfast. If you can't get to Carlton, there's another Brunetti store at 250
Flinders Lane in the city, and another on level three of the Myer department
store (p. 176). And you can check out their cafe at Terminal 4 at Melbourne
Airport before you leave town!

380 Lygon St. www.brunetti.com.au. © **03/9347 2801.** Main courses A$16–A$23.
Sun–Thurs 6am–11pm; Fri–Sat 6am–midnight. Tram: 1, 15, 21, or 22 going north on
Swanston St.

Shakahari ★ VEGETARIAN/VEGAN   Good vegetarian or vegan food
isn't just a meal without meat; it's a creation in its own right. At Shakahari
you're assured a creative meal that's not at all bland. The large restaurant is
quite low-key, and there's a lovely courtyard out the back. The signature
satay—skewered, lightly fried vegetables and tofu in a mildly spicy peanut
sauce—is a perennial favorite. Also available are curries, croquettes, green
papaya salad, a pasta dish, and a fragrant laksa. A second restaurant, **Shakahari Too,** is located in South Melbourne (© **03/9682 2207**).

201–203 Faraday St. www.shakahari.com.au. © **03/9347 3848.** Main courses A$22–
A$24. Mon–Sat noon–3pm; Mon–Fri 6–9:30pm; Sat–Sun 6–10:30pm. Tram: 1, 8, 16, or
96 (or any traveling north along Swanston St.).

In Fitzroy
MODERATE

Marios ★★★ ITALIAN   Opened in 1986 by two Italian-Australian
friends, both named Mario, this place has ambience, groovy retro decor, and
impeccable service. And after more than 30 years in business, there's little
here you can fault, including the food. Offerings include a range of cakes and
pastas (like fettuccine with eggplant, tomato, chili, garlic, feta, and mint), and

breakfast is served all day. The coffee is excellent, and the art on the walls, all by local artists, is always interesting—and for sale. You can also buy a jar of Marios's strawberry jam to take home for A$8.

303 Brunswick St. www.marioscafe.com.au. © **03/9417 3343.** Main courses A$18–A$33. Mon–Sat 7am–10pm (till 10:30pm Thurs–Sat); Sun & public holidays 8am–10pm. Tram: 112 from Collins St.

In St Kilda
EXPENSIVE

Cicciolina ★★★ CONTEMPORARY   It's difficult enough to get a table at this wonderful but understated place without encouraging more people to line up, but I'd be depriving you of a terrific night out if I kept quiet. Cicciolina is intimate, crowded, and well run and serves simple but superb food. Although you cannot book for dinner (there's a waitlist after 6pm), you may have to wait an hour or so for a table. Have a drink in the **Back Bar,** and they'll call you when your table is ready; I assure you it will be worth it for delights such as a blue swimmer crab soufflé with shallot and lemon thyme and a champagne and chive veloute, or a simple linguini with Tasmanian salmon, braised leek, baby spinach, lemon, and olive oil (my eternal favorite). If you're not into the wait, Cicciolina does take reservations for lunch.

130 Acland St. www.cicciolinastkilda.com.au. © **03/9525 3333.** Main courses A$32–A$48. Mon–Sat noon–11pm; Sun noon–10pm. Reservations for lunch only. Tram: 16 from Swanston St., or 94 or 96 from Bourke St.

MODERATE/EXPENSIVE

Donovans ★★ CONTEMPORARY   Watching the sun go down over St Kilda Beach from the veranda at Donovans (with glass in hand) is a perfect way to end the day. The welcome by owners Gail and Kevin Donovan into their much-loved restaurant—housed in a 1920s bathing pavilion—feels like being invited into their home (or at least their beach house). Lots of comfy cushions, a log fire, coffee-table books, and the sound of jazz and breakers on the beach create a wonderful atmosphere. The menu includes a mind-boggling array of dishes, many big enough for two. Try the seafood linguine or perhaps an old-fashioned chicken pie with mushrooms and vegetables. The bombe Alaska for two is legendary. There's also a children's menu.

40 Jacka Blvd. www.donovanshouse.com.au. © **03/9534 8221.** Main courses A$36–A$68. Daily noon–10:30pm. Tram: 16, 94, or 96.

The Staff of Life

The aroma of fresh bread will draw you to **Babka Bakery,** a Russian-style cafe-bakery that's nearly always packed. Come for breakfast or a light lunch of eggs on fresh sourdough, or any of the bakery's quiches, tarts, and brioches. Or perhaps try the homemade borscht. It's at 358 Brunswick St., in Fitzroy (© **03/9416 0091**), and is open Tuesday to Sunday 7am to 7pm.

Pay What You Think

With a novel approach that not surprisingly has become a hit, the vegetarian restaurant **Lentil as Anything** (www.lentilasanything.com) has a menu without prices. Here you eat—then pay "as you feel" (or for some people, what they can afford) for the meal and service. The food is organic, with lots of noodles and veggies, plus tofu, curries, and stir-fry. Before you leave, you put your money in a box. The original restaurant is at 41 Blessington St., St Kilda (© **0424/345 368** mobile; daily noon–9pm). A second outlet at the Abbotsford Convent, 1 St. Heliers St., Abbotsford (© **03/9419 6444**), is open daily from 9 to 11:30am, noon to 4pm, and 5:30 to 9pm. To avoid long waits, you can now book a table at Abbotsford (for a fee of A$15 per person). Cash only.

INEXPENSIVE

Babu Ji ★★ INDIAN   This very popular Indian eatery is fun and noisy and focuses on good food and good service. The menu offers curries of all kinds and Indian street food. Sundays features a A$28 "thali" all-you-can-eat meal (cash only), and there are tasting menus daily for A$49 (four courses) and A$69 (six courses) per person. Tuesday nights are vegan, with a A$25 all-you-can-eat menu featuring three curries and rice. Pair your meal with a craft beer (grab your own from the good selection in the fridge; everything is A$9) or glass of wine—BYO with A$10 per bottle corkage fee, or buy it there. Takeout service available.

The George Building, 4–6 Grey St. www.babuji.com.au. © **03/9534 2447**. Reservations for parties of 4 or more only (for a set menu). Main courses A$16–A$26. Sat–Sun 11:30am–2:30pm; daily 5:30–9:30pm. Closed Jan 1, Dec 25, Dec 31. Tram: 16 from Swanston St. or 96 from Bourke St.

Ichi Ni ★★ JAPANESE   Join Melbourne's beautiful people at one of the city's most popular *izakaya* (Japanese gastropub), a great place for a casual meal with a view of Port Phillip Bay. Take a booth inside, or a table on the deck (heated in winter), for the full experience—sharing is best—of yakitori, sashimi, sushi, and Japanese-style tapas. The prices are great, the atmosphere lively, and the service good—a fine combination that keeps me coming back.

12 The Esplanade. www.ichini.com.au. © **03/9534 1212**. Main courses A$15–A$40. Daily noon–10:30pm. Tram: 16, 94, or 96.

EXPLORING MELBOURNE

Visitors to Melbourne come to experience the contrasts of old-world architecture and the exciting feel of a truly multicultural city. This is a wonderfully compact city, with all the major attractions within easy reach of the city heart. Most visitors also venture to the bayside suburb of St Kilda, an easy tram ride away.

The Arts Centre ★★ PERFORMING ARTS CENTER   The spectacular 162m-high (531½-ft.) spire that glitters atop the Theatres Building of the Arts Centre, on the banks of the Yarra River, crowns the city's leading performing arts complex. Beneath it, the **State Theatre,** the **Playhouse,** and the **Fairfax Studio** present performances that are the focal point of culture in Melbourne. The Arts Centre has been the hub of Melbourne's cultural world for more than 30 years, and you can see some of that history in the changing themed exhibitions of costumes, photographs, and memorabilia. The State Theatre, seating 2,085 on three levels, can accommodate elaborate stagings of opera, ballet, musicals, and more. The Playhouse is a smaller venue that often books the Melbourne Theatre Company. The Fairfax is more intimate still and is often used for experimental theater or cabaret. Adjacent to the Theatres Building is **Hamer Hall,** home of the Melbourne Symphony Orchestra and often host to visiting orchestras. Many international stars have graced this stage, known for its excellent acoustics. Make sure you book ahead, as Melburnians love this place, and performances are often sold out. If you love music, check out the new **Australian Music Vault** exhibition, a free showcase of Australian music history and the stories of today's music scene.

You can do a guided "Theatres and Exhibition Tour" daily (except Sun) at 11am. The tour takes an hour, and costs A$20 adults and A$15 children 17 and under; it includes morning tea. On Sunday at 11am, the "Backstage Tour" takes about 90 minutes and costs A$25 per person (not suitable for children 11 and under).

100 St Kilda Rd. www.artscentremelbourne.com.au. ℭ **1300/182 183** for tickets. Ticket prices vary depending on the event. Box office (in the Theatres Bldg.): Mon–Sat 9am–8:30pm; Sun 10am–5pm. Train: Flinders St. Tram: 1, 3, 3a, 5, 6, 16, 64, 67, 72.

Cooks' Cottage ★ HISTORIC HOME   Built in 1755 by the parents of explorer Captain James Cook, this golden-brick cottage was moved to Melbourne from Great Ayton, in Yorkshire, England, in 1934 to mark Victoria's centenary. Inside, it's spartan and cramped, not unlike a ship's cabin. Displays provide the opportunity to learn about Cook's voyages of discovery around the world.

Fitzroy Gardens, off Wellington Parade. www.melbourne.vic.gov.au/cookscottage. ℭ **03/9658 9658.** A$6.70 adults, A$3.60 children 5–15, A$19 family of 4. Daily 9am–5pm (last entry 4:45pm). Closed Dec 25. Tram: 48, 75, 35 (City Circle).

Crown Casino ★ CASINO   Australia's largest casino is a plush affair that's open 24 hours. You'll find all the usual roulette and blackjack tables, as well as an array of gaming machines. This is also a major venue for international headline acts, and some 25 restaurants and 11 bars are on the premises, with more in the extended Southgate complex.

8 Whiteman St. (at Clarendon St.), Southbank. www.crownmelbourne.com.au/casino. ℭ **03/9292 8888.** Daily 24 hr., except on Dec 25, Good Friday, and Apr 25 when it is closed 4am–noon. Tram: 12, 96, 109.

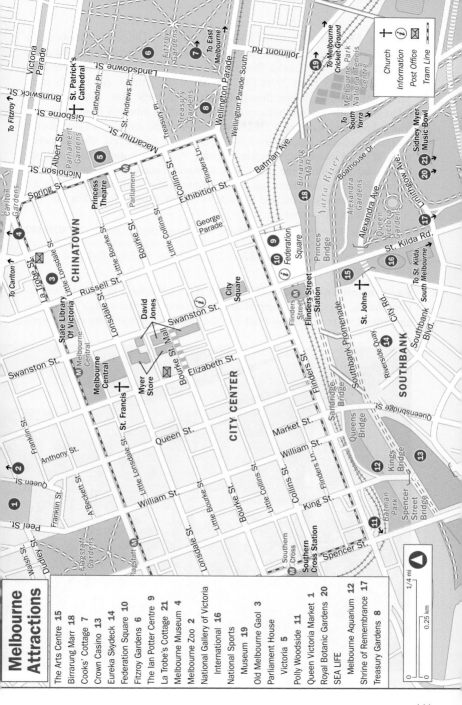

Melbourne Attractions

The Arts Centre **15**
Birrarung Marr **18**
Cooks' Cottage **7**
Crown Casino **13**
Eureka Skydeck **14**
Federation Square **10**
Fitzroy Gardens **6**
The Ian Potter Centre **9**
La Trobe's Cottage **21**
Melbourne Museum **4**
Melbourne Zoo **2**
National Gallery of Victoria International **16**
National Sports Museum **19**
Old Melbourne Gaol **3**
Parliament House Victoria **5**
Polly Woodside **11**
Queen Victoria Market **1**
Royal Botanic Gardens **20**
SEA LIFE Melbourne Aquarium **12**
Shrine of Remembrance **17**
Treasury Gardens **8**

Eureka Skydeck ★ OBSERVATION DECK The vertigo-challenging Skydeck is the highest public vantage point in the Southern Hemisphere. On the 88th floor of the Eureka Tower, a viewing deck gives a 360-degree panorama of the city from 297m (935 ft.) above the ground. But there's more adrenaline-pumping action than just the view: A huge glass cube called the Edge is actually a 6-ton horizontal elevator, which emerges from inside the walls of Skydeck carrying 12 passengers out over the tower's east side. As the opaque glass cube reaches its full extension, the reinforced, 45-millimeter-thick (1¾-in.) glass becomes clear, giving passengers uninterrupted views below, above, and to three sides. All this is accompanied by recorded sounds of creaking chains and breaking glass—just to further scare you! Actually, it's not as scary as it sounds, and the ride is only 4 minutes long. For an extra A$15 you can buy a photo.

Eureka Tower, Riverside Quay, Southbank. www.eurekaskydeck.com.au. ✆ **03/9693 8888.** A$23 adults, A$15 children 4–16, A$48–A$67 families (extra child A$12); additional A$12 adults, A$8 children, A$20–A$29 families for the Edge. Daily 10am–10pm (last entry 9:30pm). Tram: 58.

Federation Square ★★ PUBLIC PLAZA You have to get into Federation Square, physically, to appreciate it. The controversial design (Melburnians either love it or hate it—I fall into the former category) is the city center's

Visitors at the Eureka Tower Observation deck, Eureka Skydeck 88, the highest public vantage point in a building in the Southern Hemisphere.

major gathering place, and you only have to visit on the weekends to see that it works. A conglomerate of attractions is centered on a large open piazza-style area cobbled with misshapen paving. Here you'll find the **Ian Potter Centre** (see below) and the **Australian Centre for the Moving Image (ACMI),** which will reopen in mid-2020 after a A\$40-million redevelopment. One corner of Fed Square, opposite St Paul's Cathedral, is undergoing major construction work until 2022 to create a new Metro train station entrance. It's worth visiting "Fed Square" just to see the architecture, made up of strange geometrical designs, and the glass Atrium. There are many cafes and coffee shops throughout the precinct. Lots of events happen in the square's 450-seat amphitheater, including theatrical performances and free concerts. Other events take place on the plaza and along the banks of the Yarra River. There's free Wi-Fi anywhere in the square. Free 50-minute guided tours are run Monday through Saturday at 11am (except public holidays).

Flinders St. (at St Kilda Rd.). www.fedsquare.com.au. © **03/9655 1900.** Free; charges for some special events and exhibitions. Outdoor spaces open 24 hr. Tram: City Circle.

The Ian Potter Centre ★★★ GALLERY   This fascinating gallery, featuring 20 rooms dedicated to Australian art, is in the heart of Federation Square. Part of the National Gallery of Victoria (NGV), it contains the country's largest collection of Australian art, including works by Sidney Nolan, Russell Drysdale, and Tom Roberts, as well as Aborigines and Torres Strait Islanders. Some 20,000 objects are stored here, although only about 800 are on display at any one time. Aboriginal art and colonial art collections are the centerpieces of the gallery, but you will find modern paintings here, too. Temporary exhibitions include anything from ceramics to shoes. Free tours are run daily.

Federation Sq. (corner of Flinders St. and St Kilda Rd.). www.ngv.vic.gov.au. © **03/8620 2222.** Free. Daily 10am–5pm. Closed Dec 25, and until 1pm on Anzac Day (Apr 25). Tram: City Circle. Bus: City Explorer.

Melbourne Museum ★★★ MUSEUM   This museum is Australia's largest and one of its most interesting. For me, the highlight is **Bunjilaka,** the Aboriginal Cultural Centre, which gives an insight into the Victorian Koori people. Other highlights include a genuine blue-whale skeleton, an indoor rainforest, and a brilliant insect and butterfly collection with lots of real-life exhibits, including revolting cockroaches, ant colonies, and huge spiders (kids love these creepy-crawlies). Apart from that, there are interactive exhibits and science displays and social history, including a stuffed racehorse called Phar Lap. Check out the brightly colored **Children's Gallery,** which will bring hours of enjoyment to the little ones with hands-on fun like a dinosaur dig. Allow 2 hours, more if you would like to tour the adjacent **Royal Exhibition Building,** a magnificent piece of 19th-century architecture, with soaring domed ceilings and colonnaded galleries. Tours of the building, built in 1879 and used as the venue for the first Commonwealth Parliament of Australia in

1901, run at 2pm daily and cost A$10 adults and A$7 children. Worth every cent.

11 Nicholson St., Carlton. www.museumsvictoria.com.au/melbournemuseum. ⓒ **131 102** in Victoria, or 03/8341 7777. A$15 adults, free for children 15 and under. Daily 10am–5pm. Closed Good Friday and Dec 25. Tram: 86, 96, or 35 (City Circle).

Melbourne Zoo ★★ ZOO   Built in 1862, this is one of the oldest zoos in the world and makes a great day out for the family. Some 3,000 animals reside here, including kangaroos, wallabies, echidnas, koalas, wombats, and platypuses. Rather than being locked in cages, most animals live in almost natural surroundings or well-tended gardens. Don't miss the butterfly house, with its thousands of colorful occupants flitting around; the free-flight aviary; the lowland gorilla exhibit; and the treetop orangutan exhibit. Allow at least 90 minutes if you just want to see the Australian natives, and around 4 hours for the entire zoo.

Elliott Ave., Parkville. www.zoo.org.au. ⓒ **1300/966 784.** A$37 adults, A$19 children 4–15. Entry free for children Sat–Sun, public holidays, and school holidays. Daily 9am–5pm. Tram: 55 north on William St. to stop 25; 19 from Elizabeth St. to stop 16 (then a short walk to your left, following signposts). Train: Royal Park Station.

National Gallery of Victoria International ★★ GALLERY   The NGV International is a showcase for Australia's finest collections of

Feeding kangaroos at the Melbourne Zoo.

international art. On display are Gainsboroughs and Constables, as well as paintings by Bonnard, Delacroix, Van Dyck, El Greco, Monet, Manet, Magritte, and Rembrandt. Architecturally, the building itself is a masterpiece, with high ceilings, fabulous lighting, and great open spaces. Free tours are run daily; check the website for the current tour schedule.

180 St Kilda Rd. www.ngv.vic.gov.au. ⓒ **03/8620 2222.** Free; fees for some temporary exhibitions. Daily 10am–5pm. Closed Dec 25, and until 1pm on Anzac Day (Apr 25). Tram: Any tram from Swanston St. to Victorian Arts Centre.

National Sports Museum ★★★ MUSEUM   In a nation that's quite frankly sports-mad, you really can't miss this outstanding and interesting museum, located within the Melbourne Cricket Ground (MCG). It tells Australia's sporting story from its early beginnings to the present, celebrating memorable moments and achievements in just about every sport you can think of, from basketball and boxing to hockey, rugby, tennis, and everything in between. It also includes the **Australian Cricket Hall of Fame, the Sport Australia Hall of Fame,** and the **Champions Racing Gallery.** The huge collection includes Australia's first-ever Olympic gold medal, Ian Thorpe's swimsuit, and the Malvern Star bicycle that Hubert Opperman rode in his record-breaking 24-hour cycling marathon in Sydney in 1940. Recognition has been given to Australia's first Paralympic gold medalist and first female Paralympian in the Paralympic display. There's lots of interactive areas, and even room for kids to bowl a ball or two. Allow 1 hour (more if you are a real sports fanatic).

During MCG major event days, including the AFL Grand Final, Day 1 of the Boxing Day Test, and Anzac Day football, access to the museum (at half-price) is restricted to patrons holding an event ticket. Opening hours vary when events are being held within the MCG arena, so check the website.

Tours of the MCG run daily from 10am to 3pm and take about 75 minutes. Tickets include admission to the museum. Tours leave from Gate 3 in the Olympic Stand on non-event days only.

Gate 3, Melbourne Cricket Ground, Yarra Park, East Melbourne. www.nsm.org.au. ⓒ **03/9657 8879.** Museum only: A$25 adults, A$14 children 5–15, A$60 families of 4; museum and MCG tour: A$35 adults, A$18 children, A$76 families. Daily 10am–5pm (last admission 4:30pm). Closed Good Friday and Dec 25. Bus: Melbourne City Tourist Shuttle. Tram: 75 or 70 from the city center. Train: Jolimont.

Old Melbourne Gaol ★★★ HISTORIC SITE   This is number one on my list of favorite Melbourne attractions. Roaming the Old Melbourne Gaol complex is a fascinating way to spend a few hours. Start off at the spooky old prison, with its stone walls, tiny cells, and bizarre collection of death masks and artifacts of 19th-century prison life. Among the 135 hangings that took place here was that of notorious bushranger Ned Kelly, in 1880. The scaffold where he was hanged still stands, and his gun, as well as a replica suit of homemade armor (similar to those used by his gang), is on display. Profiles of former prisoners give a fascinating insight into what it was like to be imprisoned here, before the jail finally closed in 1924.

Melbourne's street art is some of the best in the world. Often tucked away in alleyways or where you'd least expect them, these massive colorful murals—often covering whole walls and multi-story buildings—are among the city's most popular attractions and worth seeking out. Some of the best known in the city center are in **Hosier Lane** (off Flinders St.), **Union Lane** (off the Bourke Street Mall), **Centre Place** (off Degraves St.), and **Croft Alley**—but these spots have been outshone lately by others in the suburb of **Fitzroy,** north of the city. Head there by tram to take a walk around Johnston, Gertrude, and Brunswick streets, remembering to head into the alleys as well. You'll also find some good street art in **St Kilda.** To see the best street art, and possibly even meet some of the artists and see them at work, take a 3½-hour walking tour from **Melbourne Street Art Tours** (www.melbournestreettours.com; ✆ **03/9328 5556**), run by street artists. Tours cost A$69 (half-price for kids 15 and under).

After exploring the jail, move next door for a guided interactive tour of the former City Watch House. The lockup, which operated from 1908 to 1994, is just across the road from the scene of one of Melbourne's most notorious crimes, the 1986 bombing of the Russell Street police station. There's role-playing involved for everyone, but it can be quite challenging for children. During holiday times, you can also visit the adjacent former Magistrate's Court and take part in a reenactment of Ned Kelly's trial.

Three tours give the brave a chance to explore the gaol by night, and they are not for the fainthearted. Ghost tours and equally chilling "hangman" tours run by candlelight and last for an hour. Check the website for session days and times. "A Night in the Watch House" tours, set in the cellblock, run for 1 hour, are conducted in the dark, and are not for anyone under 16 years old. Tickets for all night tours cost A$38 per person. Ghost and hangman's tours are not recommended for children 11 and under.

377 Russell St. www.oldmelbournegaol.com.au. ✆ **03/9663 7228.** A$28 adults, A$15 children 5–15, A$48–A$65 families. Daily 9:30am–5pm. Closed Good Friday and Dec 25. Tram: 30 or 35 (City Circle) to corner of Russell and Latrobe sts.

Parliament House Victoria ★ HISTORIC SITE Now the home of Victoria's Parliament, this monument to Victorian (as in Queen Victoria) pride and power was built in 1856, a neoclassical statement of empire with ranks of fluted columns and a grand sweep of sandstone steps. During the Australian Federation (1900–27), it was used as the national parliament. When the state government is in session—generally on Tuesday afternoon and all day Wednesday and Thursday March through July, and again from August through November (there's a break between sessions)—you can view the proceedings from the public gallery. Call ahead or check the website, as sitting times do vary. During non-sitting times, both the opulent Upper House

FACING PAGE: Old Melbourne Gaol, where bushranger Ned Kelly was hanged.

and the less ornate Lower House chambers are open to the public by guided tour. In addition to regular tours, free architecture tours are held at 2pm on the last Friday of the month. Free tours of the gardens are also run twice a month, usually on Tuesday and Thursday at 10:30am, and of the Parliament's extensive art collection, usually only once a month (check the website for dates). Finally, there's a guided tour that finishes with High Tea in the Strangers Corridor, offered weekdays from 2:30 to 4pm. The cost is A$50 per person.

Spring St. www.parliament.vic.gov.au. © **03/9651 8568.** Free. Mon–Fri 8:30am–5:30pm. Free 1-hr. guided tours Mon–Fri at 9:30, 10:30, 11:30am, 1:30, 2:30, and 3:30pm when Parliament is not in session; 20-min. "Express Tours" Mon–Fri at 1 and 4pm. Reservations required for 1-hr. tours for groups of 6 or more and for all specialized tours. Train: Parliament.

Polly Woodside ★★ VINTAGE SHIP Floating beside the original Dockside sheds, the historic tall ship *Polly Woodside* is beloved by generations of Melburnians for its many fun diversions and hands-on activities for kids. The exhibit includes six zones with interactive displays about life at sea, the crew, navigation, maritime language, and Melbourne's docks (you can even try your hand at loading coal onto a robot ship!). Launched in 1885 in Ireland, the ship sailed to all corners of the globe between 1885 and 1904, rounding the infamous Cape Horn 16 times. After World War II, it was towed back to Melbourne and worked as a coal supply ship for the next 20 years.

Tall Ship Polly Woodside, sailing ship and maritime museum on the Yarra River, Southbank.

Queen Victoria Market.

Tours are offered throughout the day, and the first Sunday of the month is "Pirate Day" for kids.

21 South Wharf Promenade, South Wharf. www.pollywoodside.com.au. ℰ **03/9656 9889.** A$16 adults, A$9.50 children, A$30–A$43 families. Sat–Sun 10am–4pm (last entry 3:15pm); daily during Victorian school holidays. Closed Jan 1, Easter Day, and Dec 25–26. Tram: 96, 109, or 12.

Queen Victoria Market ★ MARKET   This Melbourne institution—the "Vic Market"—covers several blocks. Ignore the hundreds of stalls selling everything from live rabbits to bargain clothes. There's a lot of junk here, and the crowds can be awful. The indoor food section, particularly the interesting delicatessen area, is the best part of the markets. The 90-minute **Queen Vic Market Ultimate Foodie Tour** explores the market's food and heritage and is well worth doing. It departs Tuesday, Thursday, and Saturday at 11am, and costs A$69 adults and A$49 children 5 to 14; the tour includes generous tastings and a A$5 shopping voucher. Bookings (online) are essential. **Night markets** are held every Wednesday from 5 to 10pm in winter (June–Aug) and 5:30 to 10pm in summer (Nov–late Feb, except the last week of Dec).

Btw. Peel, Victoria, Elizabeth, and Therry sts. on the northern edge of the city center. www.qvm.com.au. ℰ **03/9320 5822.** Tues and Thurs 6am–2pm; Fri 6am–5pm; Sat 6am–3pm; Sun 9am–4pm. Closed Mon, Wed, and public holidays. Tram: 35 (City Circle) or 19, 57, 58, or 59.

SEA LIFE Melbourne Aquarium ★ AQUARIUM   The prize exhibit in the Melbourne Aquarium is an Antarctica display featuring King and Gentoo penguins playing in the pool (with underwater viewing) and sliding across the

Fit for a King—Or a Governor

Northwest of the city center, the sprawling parklands called **King's Domain** surround **Government House,** residence of Victoria's governor. Free tours of the Government House gardens run on the third Thursday of every month at 11am. Online registration is essential (www.governor.vic.gov.au/government-house/tours/monthly-garden-tours). To see inside the house, you'll need to take a National Trust tour, which also includes nearby **La Trobe's Cottage,** Victoria's first Government House. It was built in England and transported to Australia brick by brick in 1836. The tour starts at Government House, taking in the ballroom, state dining room, and several other parts of the house, and ends at La Trobe's Cottage. It costs A$18 adults and A$10 children, and runs Monday and Thursday from 10am to 12:15pm. You need to book at least 2 weeks ahead (www.nationaltrust.org.au; ℂ **03/9656 9889**). If you want to visit La Trobe's Cottage on your own, it is open on Sunday from 2 to 4pm, October through April. Admission is A$5 adults, A$4 children, A$12 families. Across Birdwood Avenue, stop by the **Shrine of Remembrance,** a memorial to servicemen lost in Australia's wars. It's designed so that at 11am on Remembrance Day (Nov 11), a beam of sunlight hits the Stone of Remembrance in the Inner Shrine. Note the eternal flame in the forecourt.

snow-covered ice. These beguiling birds are Australia's only collection of sub-Antarctic penguins. The aquarium also features a reef exhibit, a crocodile exhibit, jellyfish displays, and a 2.2-million-liter (581,000-gal.) oceanarium walk-through tank with larger fish, sharks, and rays. You can arrange to dive with the sharks (A$299 per person; must be 15 years or older). Bookings are required; call ℂ **03/9923 5911.** A behind-the-scenes tour, including entry ticket and a ride in a glass-bottom boat, costs A$62 adults and A$50 children.

Corner of Flinders and Kings sts. www.melbourneaquarium.com.au. ℂ **03/9923 5999.** A$42 adults, A$28 children 4–15, A$89–A$116 families (cheaper if booked online). Mon–Fri 10am–5:30pm (last admission 4:30pm); Sat–Sun and public holidays 9:30am–6pm (last admission 5pm). Tram: 35 (City Circle).

Outlying Attractions

Healesville Sanctuary ★★★ NATURE PRESERVE   Opened in 1921 to preserve endangered species and educate the public, this sanctuary out in Healesville (70km/43 miles northwest of the city) is a prime spot for seeing native animals in almost-natural surroundings. Walk through the peppermint-scented gum forest, which rings with the chiming of bellbirds, and see wedge-tailed eagles, dingoes, koalas, wombats, reptiles, and more. The daily platypus show at 11:15am (and again at 1:30pm Sat–Sun) is a great chance to get up close to these elusive creatures. The sanctuary played a major role in saving and rehabilitating the hundreds of animals injured or displaced by the bush-fires that devastated parts of Victoria in 2009; you can visit the **Wildlife**

Health Centre to see veterinarians caring for injured or orphaned wildlife. The sanctuary has a gift shop, a cafe, and picnic grounds.

Badger Creek Rd., Healesville. www.zoo.org.au. ℂ **1300/966 784** in Australia or 03/5957 2800. A$37 adults, A$19 children 4–15. Children free Sat–Sun, public holidays, and Victorian school holidays. Daily 9am–5pm (closed Dec 25). Train from Flinders St. station to Lilydale; then bus no. 685 to Healesville and bus no. 686 toward Badger Creek, which will stop at the sanctuary.

Puffing Billy Railway ★★★ VINTAGE TRAIN   Generations of Australians have clambered aboard the Puffing Billy steam train to chug over a 13km (8-mile) track from Belgrave to Emerald and Lakeside. Passengers ride on open carriages and enjoy lovely views as the train passes through forests and fern gullies and over a National Trust–classified wooden trestle bridge. Trips take around an hour each way, and there's time to walk around the lake before the return journey. Special "Steam and Cuisine" fares are available daily: choose from a cheese platter and dessert for A$90 adults or A$80 children, or a three-course lunch (and perhaps a glass of wine) in a "first class" enclosed carriage with white tablecloths for A$115 adults, A$105 children (excluding drinks). Dinner trains also run, usually only once a month, with three courses for A$115 per person (no children 4 and under). Other special trains—jazz

Puffing Billy Railway, a popular steam-train ride.

nights, murder themes, and so on—also run; check the website for details. Trains do not run on days of total fire ban.

Belgrave Station, Belgrave. www.puffingbilly.com.au. ☎ **03/9757 0700.** Round-trip fares A$59–A$78 adults, A$31–A$39 children 4–16, A$118–A$155 families of 6 (depending on how far you travel). Closed Dec 25. Train from Flinders St. station in Melbourne to Belgrave (1 hr. 10 min.); Puffing Billy station is a 2-min. walk away.

Werribee Mansion ★★★ HOUSE MUSEUM   I never tire of visiting this stately 60-room Italianate mansion, just a 30-minute drive along the Princes Freeway from Melbourne, at Werribee Park. Dubbed "the palace in the paddock," it was built in 1877 and is surrounded by 132 hectares (326 acres) of magnificent formal gardens and bushland. Be sure to meander through the interesting and extensive contemporary sculpture garden. There's a cafe on-site. The **Werribee Park Shuttle** (www.werribeeparkshuttle.com. au; ☎ **03/9748 5094**) provides private shuttle service from city hotels, starting from A$180 for up to 5 people (reservations essential).

K Rd., Werribee. www.parkweb.vic.gov.au/explore/parks/werribee-park. ☎ **131 963.** A$10 adults, A$7.60 children 4–15, A$33 families of 4. Oct–mid-Apr daily 10am–5pm; mid-Apr–Sept Mon–Fri 10am–4pm, Sat–Sun and public holidays 10am–5pm. Closed Dec 25. Train from Flinders St. station to Werribee (45 min.); then bus no. 439.

Werribee Open Range Zoo ★ ZOO   Part of Zoos Victoria, which runs the Melbourne Zoo, this Werribee facility also has a collection of Aussie animals, but the main focus is on its open-range section, where you will see giraffes, hippos, rhinoceros, lions, zebras, and more. The zoo also has one of the largest gorilla exhibits in the world, home to the silverback Motaba and his two sons. Access to the zoo's open-range area is strictly by a 40-minute guided tour on a safari bus. On busy days, it might pay to spend the extra money to take a small group tour in an open-sided jeep, as you'll get a better view and better photo opportunities. The zoo also has a walk-through section featuring African cats, including cheetahs, and monkeys. If you've been to Africa, you may find little to excite you, but kids love it, and it's crowded with families. The **Werribee Park Shuttle** (www.werribeeparkshuttle.com.au; ☎ **03/9748 5094**) provides private transfers from the city for A$180 for up to 5 people (bookings essential).

K Rd., Werribee. www.zoo.org.au/werribee. ☎ **1300/966 784** in Australia, or 03/9731 9600. A$37 adults, A$19 children 4–15 (Mon–Fri only). Children free Sat–Sun, public holidays, and school holidays. Daily 9am–5pm. Safari tours run regularly all day. Take train from Flinders St. station to Werribee, then bus no. 439.

Organized Tours

City Sightseeing Melbourne (www.citysightseeing.melbourne; ☎ **03/8353 2578**) offers a range of tours on open-top double-decker buses. It's a hop-on, hop-off service to 27 stops around the city center and St Kilda, with an audio commentary. A 24-hour pass costs A$35 adults, A$15 kids age 4 to 14, or A$70 families of 6. A 48-hour pass costs A$45 adults, A$25 children, or A$90 family.

Melbourne River Cruises (www.melbcruises.com.au; *℃* **03/8610 2600**) offers boat trips up and down the Yarra River, lasting 1 to 2 hours. It's a great way to get a feel for the city, and the tours include commentaries. One-hour tours, either up-river or down-river, cost A\$27 adults, A\$14 children 3 to 12, or A\$75 for a family of four. A 2-hour Melbourne Highlights tour, which combines both tours, costs A\$39 adults, A\$20 kids 3 to 12, or A\$95 families of four. Cruises run two or three times a day, but call ahead to confirm departure times, because they can change. Cruises depart from Berth 2, on the South Bank Promenade.

Real Melbourne Bike Tours (www.rentabike.net.au/bike-tours.htm; *℃* **0417/339 203** mobile) can help you find your bearings and discover some of hidden Melbourne—back streets and bluestone lanes, markets, cafes, arcades, and bike paths. Run by former journalist Murray Johnson, the tours are fun and interesting. The cost is A\$120 adults and A\$79 children 12 to 18, or A\$333 for a family of four, and includes bike hire, helmet, and guided tour, plus coffee, cake, and lunch along the way. Tours leave at 10am (or other times by arrangement) from Rentabike at Federation Square and return around 2pm. Tours can be customized to suit your needs and interests. Bookings are essential.

Sports Lovers Tours (www.melbournesportstours.com.au; *℃* **03/8802 4547**) are designed for passionate sports fans or those who just want to get

Melbourne River Cruises offers scenic boat tours on the Yarra River.

Melbourne is a terrific family-friendly city, with lots to do that will keep kids of all ages amused and entertained. In the city center, the **Melbourne Museum** (p. 163) has a special children's section, and the historic ship **Polly Woodside** (p. 168) has lots of interactive fun for kids. Hop on a bike from **Melbourne Bike Share** (p. 175) and ride along the riverfront paths or through the **Royal Botanic Gardens** (p. 174). Animal lovers will love **Melbourne Zoo** (p. 164), hand-feeding the wildlife at **Healesville** Sanctuary (p. 170), the touch tanks at **SEA LIFE Melbourne Aquarium** (p. 169), or seeing the waddling little penguins on **Phillip Island** (p. 177). Older kids will like the **National Sports Museum** (p. 165) and the spooky **Old Melbourne Gaol** (p. 165), as well as the sky-high thrill of the **Eureka Skydeck** (p. 162). For a big day out, take the train to Ballarat to step back in time at **Sovereign Hill** (p. 188) and discover what life was like in the gold rush days.

into the spirit of some local sporting action. Half- and full-day tours cater to all tastes and include visits to the National Sports Museum (p. 165), Flemington Racecourse, the Albert Park Formula 1 track, and behind the scenes at the Melbourne Cricket Ground or Rod Laver Arena. Other options include attending an Aussie Rules football game with a local host who can explain the rules, or a horse-racing themed tour for fans of the Melbourne Cup. Tour prices range from A$119 per person for a 5-hour tour to A$159 for a full day.

Outdoor Activities

Birrarung Marr, along the Yarra River east of Federation Square on Batman Avenue (www.melbourne.vic.gov.au/parks; © **03/9658 9658**), is Melbourne's newest major parkland. *Birrarung* means "river of mists" in the Woiwurrung language of the Wurundjeri people who originally inhabited the area; *marr* relates to the side of the river. The wide-open spaces and large, sculptured terraces were designed to host some of Melbourne's top events and festivals throughout the year, and the terraces provide views of the city, Southbank, King's Domain, and the Yarra River.

The **Royal Botanic Gardens,** 2km (1¼ miles) south of the city on Birdwood Avenue, off St Kilda Road (www.rbg.vic.gov.au; © **03/9252 2300**), are the best gardens in Australia and well worth a few hours of wandering. More than 40 hectares (99 acres) are lush and blooming with some 12,000 plant species from all over the world. Don't miss a visit to the oldest part of the garden, the Tennyson Lawn, with its 120-year-old English elm trees. Other special corners include a fern gully, camellia gardens, an herb garden, rainforests packed with fruit bats, and ponds full of ducks and black swans. Free guided walks run daily from the Visitor Centre, leaving at 10:30am. A hop-on, hop-off "Garden Explorer" tour operates year-round from 10am to 3pm daily, offering a golf-buggy-style transport (with commentary) and stops around the gardens. It costs A$10 adults, A$8 children 5 to 17. Buy tickets at the visitor center or from the driver, or book online. Aboriginal Heritage Walks, in which you learn about traditional uses of plants for food, tools, and medicine, are run Sunday to Friday at 11am, and are well worth doing. The tour takes about 90 minutes and costs A$35 adults, A$12 children. The gardens are open daily from 7:30am to sunset. Admission is free. To get there, catch the no. 8 tram and get off at stop 21. Allow at least 2 hours.

Extensive bicycle paths wind through the city and suburbs. **Melbourne Bike Share,** Melbourne's public bike hire (www.melbournebikeshare.com. au; ✆ **1300/711 590**), has 50 bike stations and 600 bikes at locations around the city. You can't miss the racks of bright blue bikes. You can pay for a bike with Visa or MasterCard (limit of two bikes per credit card). Your card swipe will also take a A$10 security deposit, which will be refunded after return of the bikes. You pay a daily rate of A$3 (or A$8 for a week) and the first 45 minutes of usage are free; then you pay A$2 for 15 minutes (up to your first hour) and A$7 for 90 minutes, then A$10 for every half-hour after that. The daily rate makes the bike-share system one of the cheapest transport options in town, but only if you have the bike for less than about 2 hours. If you need a bike for longer than that, it's probably cheaper to rent a bike elsewhere. Bike helmets are compulsory by law, and come free when you hire a bike. You must be 16 years or older to use the bike-share system. Melbourne Bike Share has a range of suggested bike tours that you can download from the website.

MELBOURNE SHOPPING

Ask almost any Melburnian to help you plan your time in the city, and he or she will advise you to shop until you drop. All of Australia regards Melbourne as a shopping capital—it has everything from fashion houses to major department stores and unusual souvenir shops. So even if you're also visiting Sydney, save your money until you get to Melbourne, and then indulge!

Start at the magnificent city arcades, such as the **Block Arcade** (between Collins and Little Collins sts), which has more than 30 shops, including the

---

Shop 'til You Drop

For an easy way to shop—with local guidance—take a tour with Jessica Lothian, either to Melbourne's outlet stores or to hunt out designer styles. **Melbourne Shopping Experiences** (www.melbourneshoppingexperiences. com.au; ✆ **03/8822 4568**) offers small group tours for some retail therapy. Jess will help you explore back-street warehouses, pop-up sales, and discount shopping streets such as Swan Street and Bridge Road. Tours operate Monday to Saturday, 9am to 5pm, with half-day tours for A$75, including one focused on vintage clothing. Full-day tours cost A$94 adults, A$71 children 13 and under (not recommended for under-10s). The tour includes lunch and a glass of bubbles, and is adapted to fit the interests of the group. Pickups from city hotels on request.

The Highpoint Shopping Centre in Maribyrnong, Melbourne, has some 500 stores.

historic **Hopetoun Tea Rooms** (p. 156); and the **Royal Arcade** (stretching from Little Collins St. to the Bourke Street Mall). Then hit the courts and lanes around **Swanston Street** and the huge **Melbourne Central shopping complex** between Latrobe and Lonsdale streets.

Department store giants **David Jones** (www.davidjones.com.au; ✆ **03/9643 2222**)—or DJs, as it's affectionately known—and **Myer** (www.myer.com.au; ✆ **03/9661 1111**) both have stores in the city center (and in Highpoint Shopping Centre, a 500-store mall in Maribyrnong, Melbourne). DJs spans 2 blocks separated into men's and women's stores and has a vast and tantalizing food hall. Myer, the grande dame of Melbourne's department stores, is in hot competition with David Jones. It has household goods, perfume, jewelry, and fashions, as well as a food section. Both stores are on the Bourke Street Mall.

High-fashion boutiques line the eastern stretch of **Collins Street,** between the Grand Hyatt and the Hotel Sofitel. Collins Street features most international labels, as well as shoe heaven **Miss Louise,** 205 Collins St. (www.misslouise.com.au; ✆ **03/9654 7730**). For fabulous bags and other accessories, head to Level 2 at 14 Collins St., for **Christine** (christineaccessories.com; ✆ **03/9654 2011**), where women have reputedly fainted over the goodies in stock. **Little Collins Street** is another fashion hot spot with lots of local labels.

Next, fan out across the city, taking in **Chapel Street** in South Yarra for its Australian fashions and the **Jam Factory** (500 Chapel St., South Yarra), a series of buildings with a range of shops and food outlets as well as 16 cinema screens. Get there on tram no. 8 or 72 from Swanston Street.

There's also **Toorak Road** in Toorak, for Gucci and other high-priced, high-fashion names; **Bridge Road** in Richmond, for budget and outlet fashion stores; **Lygon Street** in Carlton, for Italian fashion, footwear, and accessories; and **Brunswick Street** in Fitzroy, for a more alternative scene.

DAY TRIPS FROM MELBOURNE
Phillip Island: Penguins on Parade ★★★
139km (86 miles) S of Melbourne

Phillip Island's **penguin parade,** which happens every evening at dusk, is one of Australia's most popular animal attractions. There are other, less crowded places in Australia where watching homecoming penguins feels less staged, but at least the guides and boardwalks protect the little ones and their nesting holes from the throngs. Nevertheless, the commercialism of the penguin parade puts a lot of people off—busloads of tourists squashed into a sort of amphitheater hardly feels like being one with nature. But Phillip Island also offers nice beaches, good bushwalking, fishing, and Seal Rocks.

ESSENTIALS
ARRIVING   Most visitors come to Phillip Island on a day trip from Melbourne and arrive in time for the penguin parade and dinner. Several tour companies run day trips. Among them are **Gray Line** (www.grayline.com.au;

Phillip Island penguins.

C **1300/858 687** in Australia), which operates a number of different tours, including daily "penguin express" trips for those who are short of time. The express tour departs Melbourne at 4:30pm and returns around 11:30pm. Tours cost A$145 for adults and A$73 for children, and can be booked online. Upgrades to premium seating at the penguin parade and various other options are available.

If you're driving yourself, Phillip Island is an easy 2-hour trip from Melbourne along the South Gippsland Highway and then the Bass Highway. A bridge connects the island to the mainland.

V/Line (www.vline.com.au; *C* **136 196** in Australia) runs a bus from Melbourne to Cowes, but does not take you to any of the attractions on Phillip Island. Once on the island, you need to hire a car, take a tour, or rent a bicycle to get around. The parade is 15km (9½ miles) from the center of Cowes.

VISITOR INFORMATION   The island has two information centers. The **Phillip Island Information Centre**, at 895 Phillip Island Rd., Newhaven, just a few kilometers onto the island, is open daily from 9am to 5pm (6pm Dec–Jan) and closed Christmas Day. The **Cowes Visitor Information Centre,** at Thompson Avenue (corner of Church St.), Cowes, is open daily 9am to 5pm (except Christmas Day). The centers share both a toll-free number *C* **1300/366 422** in Australia, and the website **www.visitphillipisland.com**.

DISCOUNT PASSES   A **4 Parks Pass** gives discounted entry to Phillip Island's top attractions: the **Koala Conservation Centre,** the **Penguin Parade, Churchill Island Heritage Farm,** and the **Antarctic Journey** (all covered below). The pass costs A$59 adults, A$29 children ages 4 to 15; it can be purchased online (www.penguins.org.au) or at any of the attractions. A variety of other passes are also available; see the website for details.

EXPLORING PHILLIP ISLAND

Visitors approach the island from the east, passing through the town of **Newhaven.** The main town on the island, **Cowes** (pop. 4,000), is on the north coast. The penguin parade and other nature attractions are on the far southwest coast, on Phillip Island's Summerland Peninsula. The peninsula ends in an interesting rock formation called the **Nobbies,** a strange-looking outcropping that can be reached at low tide by a basalt causeway. You'll get some spectacular views of the coastline and two offshore islands from here. On the farthest of these islands is a population of up to **12,000 Australian fur seals,** the largest colony in Australia. This area is also home to thousands of nesting silver gulls. Bring your binoculars, or, for a closer view, take a 1-hour speedboat ride with **EcoBoat Adventure Tours** (www.penguins.org.au; *C* **03/5951 2800**) to the seal colony for A$85 adults, A$65 children, or A$235 for a family of 4 (or combine with a 4 Parks Pass, Penguin Parade ticket, or other attractions). Boats leave from the Cowes jetty, on The Esplanade. The modern Nobbies Centre provides boardwalks and a cafe, as well as the **Antarctic Journey** attraction (p. 179).

On the north coast of the island, you can explore **Rhyll Inlet,** an intertidal mangrove wetland inhabited by wading birds such as spoonbills, oystercatchers, herons, egrets, cormorants, and the rare bar-tailed godwit and whimbrel. Birders will also love **Swan Lake,** another breeding habitat for wetland birds.

Elsewhere, walking trails lead through heath and pink granite to **Cape Woolamai,** the island's highest point, where there are fabulous coastal views. From September through April, the cape is home to thousands of short-tailed shearwaters (also known as mutton birds).

PHILLIP ISLAND ATTRACTIONS

Antarctic Journey ★ NATURAL HISTORY MUSEUM   Covering three levels, this high-tech attraction at the Nobbies Centre showcases the natural world of Phillip Island and the Antarctic landscape and wildlife to its far south—whales, sharks, penguins, and the like. Expect lots of multimedia displays, immersive virtual reality experiences, sensory learning activities, and hands-on interactive stations.

Nobbies Centre, Phillip Island. www.penguins.org.au. ℂ **03/5951 2800.** A$18 adults, A$9 children 4–15, A$45 family of 4; also included in 4 Parks Pass (p. 178). Daily 10am–2 hrs. before sunset. 20-min. guided tours at 11am, 1, and 3pm daily.

Churchill Island Heritage Farm ★ OUTDOOR MUSEUM/FARM   On adjacent Churchill Island, connected by causeway to Phillip Island, visitors can roam this tranquil working farm, a re-creation of Victoria's oldest agricultural settlement, worked continuously since the 1850s. Daily farming demonstrations include cow milking and sheep shearing; the dog-herding demonstrations are particularly fun.

246 Samuel Arness Dr., Churchill Island, Newhaven. www.penguins.org.au. ℂ **03/5951 2800.** A$13 adults, A$6.60 children, A$33 family of 4; also included in 4 Parks Pass (p. 178). Daily 10am–5pm (opens 2pm on Dec 25).

Koala Conservation Centre ★★ NATURE CENTER   Koalas were introduced to Phillip Island in the 1880s, and at first they thrived in the predator-free environment. However, overpopulation, the introduction of foxes and dogs, and the clearing of land for farmland and roads have taken their toll. Though you can still see a few koalas in the wild, the best place to find them is at this sanctuary, set up for research and breeding purposes. Visitors can get quite close to them, especially on the elevated boardwalk, which lets you peek into their treetop homes. Around 4pm, the ordinarily sleepy koalas are on the move—but this is also the time when tour buses converge on the place, so it can get crowded.

Fiveways, Phillip Island Tourist Rd., Phillip Island. www.penguins.org.au. ℂ **03/5951 2800.** A$13 adults, A$6.60 children 4–15, A$33 families of 4; also included in 4 Parks Pass (p. 178). Daily 10am–5pm, slightly later in summer (2–5:30pm on Dec 25).

National Vietnam Veterans Museum ★★ MUSEUM   Phillip Island may seem an unusual place to find a national museum, but it's definitely worth a stop. Dedicated to the Australian veterans of the Vietnam War, the collection includes about 6,000 artifacts, including marbles used in Australia's conscription lottery, uniforms, vehicles, and weapons. Four galleries tell the story of Australia's involvement in the war: a Remembrance Gallery and separate Air, Ground, and Naval Operations galleries. There is also a large exhibit telling the Vietnamese story, and by the time you visit there may be a new life-size diorama showing a Viet Cong tunnel system. The big-ticket item is a Bell AH-IG HueyCobra helicopter gunship, one of only three in Australia, and the museum is also restoring a Canberra bomber, the only surviving example of its kind in the world. There's a moving audiovisual on Australia's involvement in the war from 1962 to 1972. You can have a coffee in the **Nui Dat Café** or buy books and memorabilia from the shop.

25 Veterans Dr., Newhaven. www.vietnamvetsmuseum.org. © **03/5956 6400.** A$15 adults, A$12 veterans, A$10 children 5–15, A$40 families of 5. Daily 10am–5pm. Closed Good Friday, from noon on Dec 24, Dec 25–26 and Jan 1.

Phillip Island Penguin Reserve ★★ NATURE ATTRACTION The penguin parade takes place every night at dusk, when hundreds of Little Penguins appear at the water's edge, gather in the shallows, and waddle up the beach toward their burrows in the dunes. They're the smallest of the world's 17 species of penguins, standing just 33 centimeters (13 in.) high, and the only penguins that breed on the Australian mainland. **Photography is banned,** because it scares the penguins; both smoking and touching the penguins are prohibited. Wear a sweater or jacket, because it gets chilly after the sun goes down. A kiosk selling food opens an hour before the penguins turn up. Reservations for the parade are essential during busy holiday periods such as Easter and in summer.

For a better experience, exclusive small-group tours give you a closer view of the penguins. **Penguins Plus** allows you to watch the parade from a boardwalk in the company of rangers, while an **Underground Viewing** option allows you to watch up-close from indoors. The **Ultimate Adventure Tour** for groups of only 10 people (no children 15 and under) takes you to a secluded beach away from the main viewing area to watch penguins coming ashore. Other options include ranger-guided tours a few hours before the penguins appear, or a behind-the-scenes tour with researchers, ending with front-row seats on the viewing platform. In school holidays, 30-minute tours run specially for families, at a very affordable A$12 adults, A$6 children, and A$30 families.

Summerland Beach, Phillip Island Tourist Rd., Ventnor. www.penguins.org.au. © **03/5951 2830.** A$27 adults, A$13 children 4–15, A$66 families of 4; also included in 4 Parks Pass (p. 178). Penguins Plus A$55 adult, A$28 children, A$138 families; Underground Viewing A$70 adults, A$35 children, A$175 families of 4; VIP Tour (no children 11 and under) and Guided Ranger Tour (no children 11 and under) A$85; Ultimate Adventure Tour A$95. Visitor center opens daily at 10am (2pm on Dec 25).

The Mornington Peninsula ★★

80km (50 miles) S of Melbourne

The Mornington Peninsula, a scenic 40km (25-mile) stretch of windswept coastline and hinterland, is one of Melbourne's favorite day-trip and weekend-getaway destinations—and not just because it's a popular wine-producing region. The peninsula's fertile soil, temperate climate, and rolling hills produce excellent wine, particularly pinot noir, shiraz, and chardonnay. Many wineries offer cellar-door tastings; others have excellent restaurants.

ESSENTIALS

ARRIVING   From Melbourne, you can drive to the Mornington Peninsula in about an hour. There are two toll roads, but taking the toll-free Neapean Highway, and then the Point Nepean Road, is just as easy. Getting there by public transport is a time-consuming process, and does not solve the problem of how to get around once you are there.

VISITOR INFORMATION   The **Mornington Peninsula Visitor Information Centre,** 359 Point Nepean Rd., Dromana (www.visitmornington peninsula.org; ✆ **03/5950 1579**), has plenty of maps and information on the area and can also help book accommodations. It's open daily from 10am to 4pm (except Christmas Day and Good Friday), and from 1 to 5pm on Anzac Day (Apr 25).

EXPLORING THE MORNINGTON PENINSULA

As you're driving south from Melbourne, stop in the gateway city of Mornington to check out the **Mornington Peninsula Regional Gallery,** 350 Dunns Rd. (www.mprg.mornpen.vic.gov.au; ✆ **03/5950 1580**), which exhibits the work of well-known Australian artists. Free guided tours are run at 3pm Saturday and Sunday. It's open every day except Monday, from 10am to 5pm; closed Christmas Day, Boxing Day (Dec 26), New Year's Day, Good Friday and Anzac Day (Apr 25). Admission is A$4 adults, A$2 children. A little farther down the coast, just past Dromana, drive up to the summit at **Arthurs Seat State Park** for glorious views of the coastline. Continue on B110 toward Point Nepean, stopping off at the town of **Sorrento** to spot pelicans on the jetty or visit the town's many galleries.

There are lovely beaches all around the peninsula, but some of the best face onto the Bass Strait, along the southwest coast from Portsea to Cape Schank. Take the timbered boardwalk and stairs to the beach at **Cape Schanck,** keeping an eye out for gray kangaroos, southern brown bandicoots, echidnas, native rats, mice, reptiles, bats, and many forest and ocean birds. The Cape Schanck lighthouse has a small museum, and numerous interconnecting walking tracks provide access to remote beaches. You can get more information on this and all the other Victorian national parks from www.parkweb.vic.gov.au or by calling ✆ **131 963.**

East of Cape Schank, there are also some fine beaches around Point Leo and Shoreham. Kids in particular should enjoy a stop at Australia's oldest maze, **Ashcombe Maze & Lavender Gardens,** 15 Shoreham Rd., Shoreham (www.ashcombemaze.com.au; ✆ **03/5989 8387**). In addition to the big hedge maze, there is also a rose maze comprised of 1,200 rose bushes, and the gardens are huge. It has a pleasant cafe with indoor and outdoor dining. The park is open daily from 9am to 5pm, except Christmas Day; admission is A$19 adults, A$10 children 4 to 15, and A$52 to A$66 families.

For fabulous wildlife viewing, take a night tour of **Moonlit Sanctuary,** 550 Tyabb-Tooradin Rd., Pearcedale (www.moonlitsanctuary.com.au; © **03/5978 7935**), at the northern end of the peninsula. The sanctuary is open daily from 10am to 5pm (except Christmas Day), but the best way to see Australia's nocturnal animals is on a guided evening tour. These bushland tours enable you to see animals such as the eastern quoll, the red-bellied pademelon, and the southern bettong, all of which are extinct in the wild on Australia's mainland. Night tours must be booked in advance (at least by 3pm on the day of your visit). I highly recommend it—it's a wonderful way to see and interact with animals and birds you'd never see during daylight hours. Day admission is A$24 adults, A$12 children 4 to 17, and A$64 families of four (extra children A$8). Nighttime admission and guided tour is A$50 adults, A$30 children, A$19 children 3 and under, or A$150 families of four (extra children A$25). Night tours begin at dusk, with times varying throughout the year; call ahead for current times.

WHERE TO EAT ON THE MORNINGTON PENINSULA

The Portsea Hotel ★★ BISTRO/BEER GARDEN   The large restaurant at this Tudor-style pub on the seafront is very popular, and the outdoor beer garden overlooking the sea is hard to beat on a sunny day. This lovely sprawling old hotel, completely renovated in 2018, has a large terrace area at the back so you can enjoy the sea views from a sheltered spot. The bistro menu features plenty of choices: pizza, steaks, burgers, fish-and-chips, and small plates for sharing. Daily A$25 specials include a glass of wine. There's also a kids' menu. After dining, it's an easy walk down the stairs through the sand dunes to the beach below (keep your eye out for dolphins).

3746 Point Nepean Rd., Portsea. www.portseahotel.com.au. © **03/5984 2213.** Main courses A$24–A$38. Mon–Fri noon–3pm and 5–9:30pm, Sat–Sun noon–9:30pm.

The Macedon Ranges ★★

Some of Victoria's finest gardens dot the hills and valleys of the Macedon Ranges, just an hour northwest from Melbourne. In bygone times, the wealthy swapped the city's summer heat for the cooler climes of Macedon. Their legacy of "hill station" private gardens and impressive mansions, along with the region's 40 cool-climate wineries and gourmet foods, are enough reason to visit. The best times to visit the Macedon Ranges for the gardens are April (autumn) and November (spring).

ESSENTIALS

ARRIVING & GETTING AROUND   The Macedon Ranges are less than an hour's drive from Melbourne along the Calder Freeway, a continuation of the Tullamarine Freeway. Follow the signs toward Bendigo until you reach Gisborne, and then move off the freeway. **V/Line** (www.vline.com.au; © **136 196** in Australia) trains from Melbourne to Bendigo pass through the Macedon Ranges, stopping at stations including Macedon, Woodend, Kyneton, and Malmsbury.

VISITOR INFORMATION   The region has two visitor information centers: the **Woodend Visitor Centre,** 711 High St., Woodend (✆ **03/5427 2033**), and the **Kyneton Visitor Information Centre,** 127 High St., Kyneton (✆ **03/5422 6110**). Both share the same telephone information line (✆ **1800/244 711**) and are open daily 9am to 5pm (except Christmas Day and Good Friday). The website **www.visitmacedonranges.com** is a good source of information.

ORGANIZED TOURS   With more than 40 vineyards and 20 cellar doors in the region, wine buffs who want to sample the product should consider a tour. **Wine Tours Victoria** (www.winetours.com.au; ✆ **1800/946 386** in Australia, or 03/5428 8500) runs small-group (minimum 2 people) day tours from Melbourne, visiting four or five wineries. Pickup in Melbourne is at 9am, returning by about 5:30pm. The A$180 cost per person includes morning tea and lunch.

EXPLORING THE MACEDON RANGES

Swinging northward through the region, the Calder Freeway passes the main towns of Macedon, Woodend, Kyneton, and Malmsbury. Some private homestead gardens are open to the public, including two in **Mount Macedon: Duneira** (www.duneira.com.au; ✆ **03/5426 1490**) and **Tieve Tara** (www.gardensoftievetara.com.au; ✆ **0418/337 813** mobile). It pays to call ahead to check times and access (the gardens are often closed in winter). Entry fees apply.

After the gold rush of the 1850s, **Woodend** became a resort town with guesthouses, gardens, a racecourse, a golf club, and hotels. Reminders of those days are found in the historical buildings and clock tower on High Street. Cafes, boutiques, and galleries abound. Stop in for a beer at the family-run **Holgate Brewhouse,** in the historic Keatings Hotel on High Street (www.holgatebrewhouse.com; ✆ **03/5427 2510**). The brewery produces a range of draught beers; you can buy "tastings" until you decide on your favorite. The beer is brewed using just four ingredients—malt, hops, yeast, and pure Macedon Ranges water. It's open daily noon 'til late (except Christmas Day).

For many visitors, however, Woodend's chief draw is the **Hanging Rock Recreation Reserve,** South Rock Road, Woodend (✆ **1800/244 711** in Australia, or 0418/373 032 [mobile] for the ranger), where the ghost of Miranda—the fictional schoolgirl who vanished at Hanging Rock in author Joan Lindsay's evocative 1967 novel *Picnic at Hanging Rock*—is never far away. Peter Weir's 1975 film of the novel cemented its fame, but the natural beauty of the area overshadows its slightly spooky reputation. You can climb the rock, walk the tracks, and explore caves like the Black Hole of Calcutta and the Cathedral. You can also take a guided tour (night tours are offered in summer). The **Hanging Rock Discovery Centre** explains the geology and history of the area and revisits the book and movie. The reserve is also home to lots of wildlife including koalas, kangaroos, sugar gliders, echidnas, and wallabies. It's open daily 9am to 5pm (except Christmas Day). Admission is A$10 per car or A$4 per pedestrian.

A 15- or 20-minute drive north of Woodend brings you to **Kyneton,** where you can stroll along Piper Street for antiques, homewares, cafes, a heritage pub, and more. The **Kyneton Farmers' Market** is held at Saint Paul's Park in Piper Street on the second Saturday of the month from 8am to 1pm. Near Kyneton, **Bringalbit** (www.bringalbit.com.au; © **03/5423 7223**) is another private homestead garden worth checking out.

The hamlet of **Malmsbury** may be small but it offers some compelling reasons to drive this far north. First is the **Malmsbury Botanic Gardens,** next to the Town Hall, designed to take advantage of the Coliban River valley and a billabong that was transformed into a group of ornamental lakes. The 5-hectare (12-acre) gardens have a superb collection of mature trees; it's also a popular spot for barbecues, and at Apple Hole you'll find kids leaping into the river from a rope swing. At quiet times, you may even spot a platypus. But Malmsbury's most famous landmark may be the **bluestone railway viaduct** built by 4,000 men in 1859. At 25m (82 ft.) high, with five 18m (59-ft.) spans, it is one of Australia's longest stone bridges and is best viewed from the gardens. I also like to pop in to **Tin Shed Arts** (75 Mollison St. East, © **03/5423 2144**), a spacious gallery near the Town Hall that displays contemporary and traditional art from both local artists and well-known names from around Australia. It always has something interesting and unexpected—paintings, mixed media, sculpture, and craftwork. It's open Friday to Monday 10am to 5pm. The gallery is next door to the **Malmsbury Bakery** (© **03/5423 2369**), a local institution selling plenty of tempting hot pies, bread, and pastries.

WHERE TO EAT IN THE MACEDON RANGES

Royal George Hotel ★★ PUB GRUB An adventurous bar menu of snacks or a full-blown meal in the lovely old dining room: The choice is yours at this 1860s pub, long part of the Kyneton village dining scene. Whichever you choose, it will come with a distinctly Eastern European tang: Siberian *pelmeni* dumplings—filled with beef and pork and served with sour cream and paprika—or Ukrainian *vareniki* filled with potato and quark. Those are just the small plates; more mainstream are the tarragon chicken braise and the fish pie, or a good old mac and cheese.

22 Piper St., Kyneton. www.royalgeorge.com.au. © **03/5417 2345.** Main courses A$28–A$29. Thurs–Sun 6pm–late; Sat–Sun noon–3pm.

Daylesford ★★★

108km (67 miles) NW of Melbourne

Daylesford can be a terrific day trip from Melbourne or easily combined with a trip to the Macedon Ranges (see above). Part of "spa country," this village is a bit of a trendy getaway for Melburnians. Along the main street, you'll find small galleries, homewares shops, and some smart foodie outlets.

ESSENTIALS

ARRIVING From Melbourne, take the CityLink toll road (the M2) north toward Melbourne Airport. Take the Calder Highway turnoff toward Bendigo

(M79) and continue until you see the turnoff to Daylesford (C792); then follow the signs. The road will take you through Woodend, Tylden, and Trentham. At Trentham take the C317 to Daylesford. When you arrive in Daylesford, turn right at the roundabout as signposted to get to Hepburn Springs.

VISITOR INFORMATION   The **Daylesford Visitor Information Centre,** 98 Vincent St. (www.visithepburnshire.com.au; ℭ **1800/454 891** in Australia, or 03/5321 6123), features an interpretive display about the area's mineral waters. It's open daily from 9am to 5pm, except Christmas Day.

EXPLORING DAYLESFORD

Australians have been heading to Hepburn Springs, on the edge of Daylesford, to "take the waters" since 1895, and the region now has about a dozen or so day spas. The original, and most famous, is **Hepburn Bathhouse & Spa** (www.hepburnbathhouse.com; ℭ **03/5321 6000**). Not everyone likes the slick, modern, and rather cold new extension that has replaced the elegant old wooden building, but sink into the hot pools and it's easy to forget about the exterior. Enjoy traditional communal bathing in the Bathhouse and the Sanctuary, or book one of the usual range of therapies and treatments in the Spa (in the original bathhouse building; reservations essential). The complex includes an aroma steam room, salt therapy pool, relaxation pool, and "spa couches" submerged in mineral water (which I didn't find very comfortable). The complex is on Mineral Springs Reserve Road and is open Monday to Thursday 9am to 6:30pm, Friday 9am to 9pm, Saturday 8am to 9pm, and Sunday 8am to 6:30pm. Closed Christmas Day. Tuesday to Thursday Bathhouse entry for 2 hours costs A$42 adults, A$24 children 2 to 16, and A$125 for a family of four; Friday to Monday and on public holidays it's A$52 adults, A$27 children, and A$158 families. Towel rental is A$5 (and they even sell swimwear if you've left yours at home). Entry to the Bathhouse and Sanctuary is A$89 Tuesday to Thursday (or arrive before 8:30am weekends) and A$99 Friday to Monday and public holidays, including towel and robe rental. A 30-minute private mineral bath at the Spa costs from A$99 to A$109 depending on the day of the week.

On the hill behind Daylesford's main street is **The Convent** (www.convent gallery.com.au; ℭ **03/5348 3211**), a historic 19th-century mansion, complete with twisting staircases. The Convent comprises a restaurant, a gallery, gardens, a chapel, and shops, as well as a small museum that speaks to its origins as a private home, which later became the Holy Cross Convent and Boarding School for Girls. After years of dereliction, it reopened as a gallery in 1991, but the nuns' infirmary and one of the "cells," or bedrooms, were left unrestored. You'll find it on the corner of Hill and Daly streets. It's open daily 10am to 4pm (3pm on New Year's Eve), closed Good Friday, Easter Monday, Christmas Day, Boxing Day (Dec 26), and New Year's Day. Admission is A$5 per person. Take time to wander through the lovely gardens, with their sculptures and bench seats.

Just outside Daylesford is **Lavandula** (www.lavandula.com.au; ☎ **03/5476 4393**), a Swiss-Italian lavender farm with a rustic trattoria-style cafe and a cobblestone courtyard with a cluster of farmhouse buildings. Swiss immigrants ran a dairy farm here in the 1860s; today you can see the process of lavender farming and buy lavender products. Free tours of the restored stone farmhouse run daily at noon, 2, and 4pm. The lavender is in full bloom in December, with harvesting in January. Lavandula is at 350 Hepburn-Newstead Rd., Shepherds Flat, about 10 minutes' drive north of Daylesford. From September to May (except Dec 23–26) it is open Friday to Tuesday from 10:30am to 5:30pm; from June through August it is open only on Saturday, Sunday, public holidays, and school holidays. Admission is A$4 adults, A$1 school-age children.

WHERE TO EAT IN DAYLESFORD

The Lake House ★★★ CONTEMPORARY   Treat yourself to one of Australia's best restaurants while you're in Daylesford. Set on the edge of Lake Daylesford, on 2.4 hectares (6 acres) of beautiful gardens, the Lake House is the creation of Alla and Allan Wolf-Tasker. Alla is the executive chef, and Allan's vibrant artworks adorn the walls of the light-filled restaurant overlooking the lake (with adjoining accommodation, if you can't tear yourself away). The restaurant is renowned for its commitment to local and seasonal produce, and the menu changes daily. If—like me—you are tempted by tastes not often on offer at city restaurants, you will relish the lunch menu, with items like chestnut gnocchi with a ragout of forest mushrooms, sage, and truffled pecorino; or John Dory (fish) with mussels, tomato jam, and greens from the restaurant farm. Walk it off on the track around the lake!

King St., Daylesford, VIC 3460. www.lakehouse.com.au. ☎ **03/5348 3329.** Lunch and dinner A$105–A$155 for 2 to 4 courses; 8-course tasting menu A$165. Daily noon–2:30pm and 6–9pm.

Ballarat ★★★

113km (70 miles) W of Melbourne

History buffs will love Ballarat. Victoria's largest inland city (pop. 100,000) is synonymous with two major events in Australia's past: the gold rush of the 1850s and the birth of Australian democracy in the early 20th century. It all started with gold; in 1851 two prospectors found gold nuggets scattered on the ground at a place known as, ironically, Poverty Point. Within a year, 20,000 people had drifted into the area, and Australia's El Dorado gold rush had begun.

In 1858, the second-largest chunk of gold discovered in Australia (the Welcome Nugget) was found, but by the early 1860s, most of the easy diggings were gone. Larger operators continued digging until 1918, but by then Ballarat had developed enough industry to survive without mining. Today, you can still see the gold rush's effects in the impressive buildings, built from the miners' fortunes, lining Ballarat's streets.

ESSENTIALS

ARRIVING From Melbourne, Ballarat is a 1½-hour drive on the Great Western Highway. **V/Line** (www.vline.com.au; ℂ **136 196** in Victoria, or 03/8608 5011) runs trains between the cities every day; the trip takes about 90 minutes.

Several companies offer day trips from Melbourne, one of which is **AAT Kings** (www.aatkings.com; ℂ **1300/228 546** in Australia). A full-day tour costs A$175 for adults and A$88 for children ages 2 to 15.

VISITOR INFORMATION The **Ballarat Visitor Information Centre** is at 225 Sturt St., in the Ballarat Town Hall (www.visitballarat.com.au; ℂ **1800/446 633** in Australia, or 03/5337 4337). It is open daily from 9am to 5pm (except Christmas Day).

EXPLORING BALLARAT

Art Gallery of Ballarat ★★★ GALLERY Founded in 1884, this is Australia's oldest regional gallery and houses a fine collection of Australian art, including paintings from the Heidelberg School and a stunning collection of 20th-century modernists. It also hosts interesting contemporary exhibitions on popular themes (that usually require a fee). Free guided tours are at 11:30am daily.

40 Lydiard St. N. www.artgalleryofballarat.com.au. ℂ **03/5320 5858.** Free. Daily 10am–5pm. Closed Christmas Day and Boxing Day (Dec 26).

Ballarat Botanical Gardens ★★★ GARDEN The gold-rich citizens of Ballarat bestowed magnificent gifts on these delightful gardens from its early days, including the collection of 12 marble statues that now stand in the conservatory, the elegant Statuary Pavilion and its contents—including the wonderful *Flight from Pompeii*—and a statue of William Wallace near the gardens' entrance. Other highlights include Prime Ministers Avenue, lined with bronze busts of Australia's 29 former PMs, and the striking Australian Ex-Prisoners of War Memorial at the southwestern end of the gardens. One of the greatest attractions is an avenue of 70 giant redwoods, planted about 130 years ago. Free guided tours run every Sunday at 11am and on request by advance booking. The gardens' cafe overlooks Lake Wendouree.

Wendouree Parade. www.ballaratbotanicalgardens.com.au. ℂ **03/5320 5135.** Free. Daily 7:30am–9pm (Oct–Apr) and 7:30am–6pm (May–Sept). Conservatory daily 9am–4:30pm. Bus: 16.

The Eureka Centre ★★ MUSEUM A highlight of a visit to Ballarat—especially after you've learned the story of the Eureka Uprising (see "A Eureka Moment," p. 188)—is the sight of the large, beautiful, and now fragile blue-and-white flag made from petticoat fabric by the women of the uprising and enshrined here. The small museum on the site of the 1854 Eureka Stockade also has a cafe and gardens in which you can see the site of the stockade, marked by a plaque and cannons.

102 Stawell St. S. (at Eureka St.). ℂ **03/5333 0333.** A$6 adults, A$4 children 6–15, A$18 families. Daily 10am–5pm. Closed Christmas Day.

A eureka **MOMENT**

The story that is central to Ballarat's history, and many of its attractions, is that of the **Eureka Uprising** in 1854. The story goes like this: After gold was discovered, the government introduced gold licenses, charging miners even if they came up empty-handed. The miners had to buy a license every month, and corrupt goldfield police (many of them former convicts) instituted a vicious campaign to extract the money. When license checks intensified in 1854, resentment flared. Prospectors began demanding political reforms, such as the right to vote, parliamentary elections, and secret ballots. The situation exploded when the Eureka Hotel's owner murdered a miner but was set free by the government. The hotel was burned down in revenge, and more than 20,000 prospectors joined together, burned their licenses in a huge bonfire, and built a stockade over which they raised a flag. Troops arrived at the "Eureka Stockade" the next month, but only 150 miners remained. The stockade was attacked at dawn, with 24 miners killed and 30 wounded. The uprising forced the government to act: The licenses were replaced with "miners' rights" and cheaper fees, and the vote was introduced to Victoria. It was a definitive moment in Australia's history, and the Eureka flag (p. 187) is still a potent (and often controversial) symbol of nationalism.

The Gold Museum ★ MUSEUM   A 4.4kg (nearly 10-lb.) gold nugget—known as "Goldasaurus"—is the latest highlight in this surprisingly interesting small museum. Found by a local prospector, it is one of many curious objects you will discover here, as well as a large collection of gold nuggets unearthed at Ballarat, displays of alluvial deposits, gold ornaments, coins, and the history of gold mining in the area.

Bradshaw St. (opposite Sovereign Hill). ☎ **03/5337 1107.** A$14 adults, A$7.40 children 5–15, A$37 family of 6. Free with entry to Sovereign Hill (see below). Daily 9:30am–5:30pm. Closed Christmas Day.

Sovereign Hill ★★★ MUSEUM   Ballarat's history comes to life at Sovereign Hill, long described as Australia's best outdoor museum, which transports you back to the 1850s and the heady days of the gold rush. Living in the gold-rush times wasn't all beer and skittles, as Sovereign Hill's latest multi-million-dollar underground exhibit—the multisensory experience "Trapped"—conveys, depicting an 1882 mining disaster as a tale of bravery, love, and loss. More than 40 reproduction buildings, including shops and businesses on Main Street, sit on the 25-hectare (62-acre) former gold-mining site. There are also tent camps around the diggings on what would have been the outskirts of town. Sovereign Hill has a lot to see and do, so expect to spend at least 4 hours here. The township bustles with actors in period costumes going about their daily business. You can pan for real gold, ride in horse-drawn carriages, and watch potters, blacksmiths, and tanners make their wares. Don't miss the gold pour at the smelting works, or the redcoats as they parade through the streets. On top of Sovereign Hill are the mineshafts and pithead equipment. The guided tour of a typical underground gold mine takes around 45 minutes and costs A$7.50 for adults, A$4 for children, and A$20 for a family of six. A restaurant and several cafes and souvenir stores are scattered around the site. In the evening, you can see the sound-and-light show **AURA,** which tells the story of the gold rush. Tickets are A$64 adults, A$34 children 5 to 15, or A$145 to A$195 families. Dinner-and-show packages are also available.

Bradshaw St. www.sovereignhill.com.au. *Ⓒ* **03/5337 1199.** A$59 adults, A$26 children 5–15, A$106–A$148 families. Daily 10am–5pm. Closed Christmas Day. A free bus meets the 9:16am train (the "Goldrush Special" from Melbourne's Southern Cross railway station) when it arrives at Ballarat Station and takes visitors direct to Sovereign Hill. Return service connects with the 3:52pm (4:13pm on Sat–Sun) train back to Melbourne.

WHERE TO EAT IN BALLARAT

Eclectic Tastes Café & Pantry ★★ CAFE This unusual cafe, spread out over five rooms, serves up all-day breakfast, lunch, coffee, and snacks. Menu offerings may include a simple croque monsieur, a Vietnamese-style calamari salad, or Eclectic's own take on *yum cha* (similar to dim sum), with pork dumplings, chicken gyozas, and prawn toast. Or grab a fresh filled baguette from the fridge. You'll find this smart little cafe opposite the Ballarat Cemetery near the shores of Lake Wendouree (a bit off the beaten track but worth the effort). There's a kids' menu too.

2 Burnbank St. www.eclectictastes.com.au. *Ⓒ* **03/5339 3391.** Main courses A$17–A$29. Mon–Fri 7am–4pm; Sat–Sun 8am–4pm.

Panning for gold on Sovereign Hill, a reconstructed gold-digger village and tourist attraction in Ballarat.

Oscar's ★ CONTEMPORARY   This cafe and bar inside one of Ballarat's historic old pubs is in the heart of the town, walking distance from shopping, the art gallery, and many other attractions. The former gold rush–era hotel has an appealing open-plan restaurant, with a courtyard and bar. It's open for breakfast, lunch, and dinner, and you can get snacks all day. Meals include Italian favorites (pizzas, lasagna, risotto, pasta), as well as steaks, a Thai green curry, salads, and gluten-free dishes—something for everyone (including kids).

18 Doveton St. S. www.oscarshotel.com.au. *©* **03/5331 1451.** Main courses A$17–A$30. Daily 7am–10pm.

BRISBANE

Brisbane is one of those cities that seems always to be changing, without ever losing its essential heart and character. It's that most Australian of cities—big-hearted, blue-skied, and with a down-to-earth attitude that quickly rubs off on you. Brisbane will most likely be your first port of call in Queensland, and you can even reach the south-ernmost part of the Great Barrier Reef on a day trip from here.

Brisbane (pronounced *Briz*-bun), "Brizzie" to locals, functions on a very human scale. It's a place where you can cuddle koalas, join bronzed urbanites on the beaches on the weekend, and sunbathe by the Brisbane River while gazing up at gleaming skyscrapers. Beyond landmarks such as the 1920s City Hall and the Treasury Building's graceful colonnades, Brisbane's most iconic experiences seem to all take place out of doors—strolling through the Brisbane City Gardens, adventure-climbing on Story Bridge, taking in the city skyline from the gently revolving Wheel of Brisbane, cuddling koalas at the Lone Pine Koala Sanctuary. Even its top arts and entertainment complexes—the Queensland Cultural Centre and South Bank Parklands—are built as open-air malls with lots of plazas and alfresco gathering places.

The city center and surrounding suburbs represent fusion cuisine at its finest, particularly nightlife hotspot Fortitude Valley, which serves the world on a plate—everything from Spanish tapas to Thai—in chic lounge-style restaurants.

On the city riverbank, opposite South Bank and adjacent to the Treasury Casino and Hotel, a major redevelopment to be called **Queen's Wharf** will transform the city over the next 4 years. It will include five new hotels, three residential towers, around 50 new restaurants, cafes, and bars, and a riverfront outdoor cinema. A pedestrian bridge will link the precinct to South Bank.

ESSENTIALS

Arriving

BY PLANE   Brisbane International Airport (BNE) (www.bne. com.au) is 16km (10 miles) from the city, and the domestic terminal is 2km (1¼ miles) farther away. There is a free interterminal bus, or

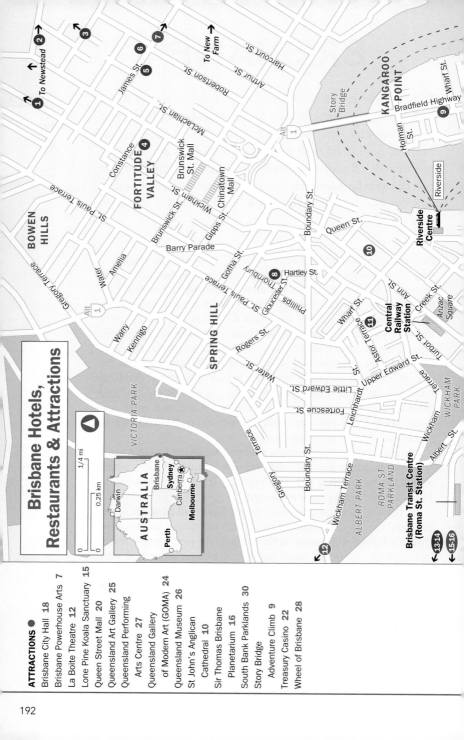

Brisbane Hotels, Restaurants & Attractions

ATTRACTIONS ●

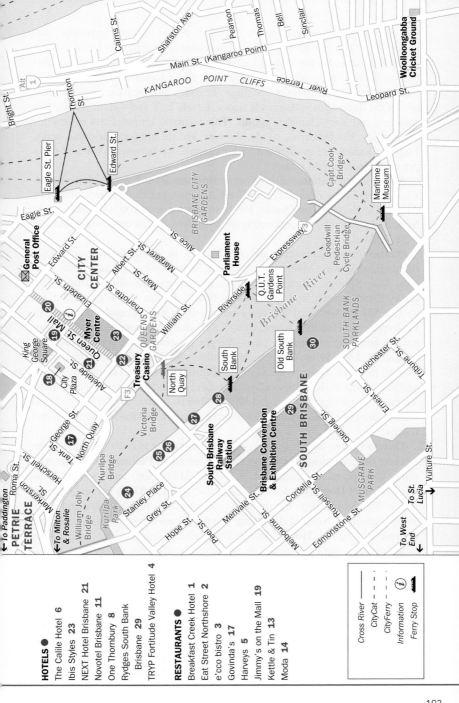

HOTELS ●

The Calile Hotel **6**
Ibis Styles **23**
NEXT Hotel Brisbane **21**
Novotel Brisbane **11**
One Thornbury **8**
Rydges South Bank
 Brisbane **29**
TRYP Fortitude Valley Hotel **4**

RESTAURANTS ●

Breakfast Creek Hotel **1**
Eat Street Northshore **2**
e'cco bistro **3**
Govinda's **17**
Harveys **5**
Jimmy's on the Mall **19**
Kettle & Tin **13**
Moda **14**

Cross River
CityCat
CityFerry
Information *i*
Ferry Stop

you can catch the train (see below) for A$5. A taxi between terminals costs about A$15. The arrivals floor of the international terminal, on Level 2, has a check-in counter for passengers transferring to domestic flights and an information desk to meet all flights, help with flight inquiries, dispense tourist information, and make hotel bookings. **Travelex** currency-exchange bureaus are on the departures and arrivals floors. Levels 2, 3, and 4 have ATMs, free showers, and baby-changing rooms. The domestic terminal has a Travelex currency-exchange bureau, ATMs, showers, and the big four car-rental desks. Luggage lockers are available at both terminals, for between A$10 and A$14 per day, depending on size.

About 30 international airlines serve Brisbane from Europe, North America, Asia, and New Zealand. From North America, you can fly direct from Los Angeles to Brisbane on Qantas, but from other places you will likely fly to Sydney first, then take a connecting flight to Brisbane, or come via Auckland, New Zealand.

Qantas (www.qantas.com.au; ✆ **131 313** in Australia) operates daily flights from Sydney, Melbourne, Adelaide, Perth, Canberra, Launceston, Darwin, Alice Springs, Cairns, Townsville, Bundaberg, Hamilton Island, Gladstone, Rockhampton, and several other towns. **Jetstar** (www.jetstar.com.au; ✆ **131 538** in Australia) has daily service from the Queensland centers of Proserpine and Hamilton Island, as well as Sydney, Melbourne, Hobart, Launceston, and other Australian cities. **Virgin Australia** (www.virginaustralia.com.au; ✆ **136 789** in Australia) offers direct services from all capital cities as well as Alice Springs, Launceston, Cairns, Townsville, Hamilton Island, and Proserpine in the Whitsundays, Bundaberg, Gladstone, and other centers. **Tigerair** (www.tigerair.com; ✆ **1300/174 266** in Australia, or 07/3295 2104) flies to Brisbane from Sydney, Melbourne, Darwin, Adelaide, Canberra, and Cairns.

There are three airport hotels, two at the domestic terminal and one at the Skygate precinct close to the international terminal. **Pullman Brisbane Airport** (www.pullman.accorhotels.com; ✆ **07/3188 7300**) and the **Ibis Brisbane Airport Hotel** (www.ibisba.com.au; ✆ **07/3139 8100**) are on Dryandra Rd., a 3-minute walk to the domestic terminal. The hotels adjoin and share some facilities. **Novotel Brisbane Airport** (www.novotelbrisbaneairport.com.au; ✆ **07/3175 3100**) is in the Skygate shopping precinct, with shuttle buses running from the terminals. All three hotels offer a **day rate** (9am–5pm), which includes a room, free Wi-Fi, and use of the pool and other facilities. At the Ibis, the rate is A$85, at the Novotel it's A$145, and at the Pullman A$155.

Between the Airport and the City

Con-x-ion (www.con-x-ion.com; ✆ **1300/910 943** in Australia) runs a shuttle between the airport and city hotels and the Brisbane Transit Centre every 30 minutes from 5am to 11pm. The one-way cost is A$20 adults, A$11 children 12 and under. The trip takes about 40 minutes. No public buses serve the airport.

Airtrain (www.airtrain.com.au; ℰ **1800/119 091** in Australia, or 07/3216 3308), a rail link between the city and Brisbane's domestic and international airport terminals, runs every 15 minutes from around 5am (6am Sat–Sun) to 10pm daily. Fares from the airport to city stations are A$18 per adult one-way, A$34 round-trip; children ages 14 and under travel free. The trip takes about 20 minutes.

A **taxi** to the city costs around A$55, plus a A$3.90 airport fee for departing taxis. **Uber** can also pick you up at the airport; follow the Ride Booking signs from the terminal to the pickup area.

Car-rental companies are located on Level 2 in the airport, including **Avis** (www.avis.com.au; ℰ **07/3633 8666**), **Budget** (www.budget.com.au; ℰ **07/3000 1030**), **Europcar** (www.europcar.com.au; ℰ **07/3874 8150**), **Hertz** (www.hertz.com.au; ℰ **07/3860 4522**), **Thrifty** (www.thrifty.com.au; ℰ **07/3000 8600**), and local company **Enterprise** (www.enterpriserentacar. com.au; ℰ **07/3860 5766**).

BY TRAIN Queensland Rail (www.queenslandrailtravel.com.au; ℰ **1300/131 722** in Australia, or 07/3606 6630) operates long-distance trains north from Brisbane along the coast. The swish Spirit of Queensland takes about 24 hours between Brisbane and Cairns and costs A$390 for an airline-style "rail bed" seat, including meals. The high-speed Tilt Train takes about 4½ hours from Brisbane to Bundaberg or 7½ hours to Rockhampton. **NSW Trainlink** (www.transportnsw.info; ℰ **131 500** in Australia) runs daily train services to Brisbane from Sydney. The trip takes around 14½ hours, with the final 3½ hours (from the town of Casino, south of the Queensland border) by bus. Fares vary but cost around A$91 for an adult economy seat or A$130 for a first-class seat. A sleeper costs around A$216.

All intercity and interstate trains pull into the city center's **Brisbane Transit Centre** at Roma Street. In 2020 (and onward), this area will be undergoing a major redevelopment with the creation of an underground railway station, so expect some disruption, but most city and Spring Hill hotels are still only a few blocks' walk or a quick cab ride away.

Queensland Rail CityTrain (ℰ **131 230** in Queensland) provides daily train service from the Sunshine Coast and plentiful service from the Gold Coast.

BY BUS All intercity and interstate coaches pull into the **Brisbane Coach Terminal** at the Roma Street train station (see "By Train," above), adjacent to Roma Street Parkland. **Greyhound Australia** (www.greyhound.com.au; ℰ **1300/473 946** in Australia, or 07/3736 2601) serves the city several times daily. A one-way Cairns-Brisbane ticket costs around A$359; the trip takes nearly 30 hours. The Sydney-Brisbane trip takes about 17 hours and costs around A$211 one-way.

BY CAR The Bruce Highway from Cairns enters the city from the north. The Pacific Highway enters Brisbane from the south.

Letter-making Brisbane sign in South Bank Parklands.

Visitor Information

The **Brisbane Visitor Information Centre** (www.visitbrisbane.com.au;
℡ **07/3006 6290**) is in the Regent Theatre building in the Queen Street Mall,
between Edward and Albert streets. It's open Monday through Thursday from
9am to 5:30pm, Friday 9am to 7pm, Saturday 9am to 5pm, Sunday 10am to
5pm. It's closed Christmas Day, Anzac Day (Apr 25), and Good Friday. There
are also visitor information centers at the airport and at South Bank Parklands
(p. 211).

City Layout

The **city center**'s office towers shimmer in the sun on the north bank of a
curve of the Brisbane River; across the river lie the **South Bank Parklands**
and the **Queensland Cultural Centre,** known as South Bank. At the tip of the
river's curve lie the lush **Brisbane City Gardens** (sometimes called the City
Botanic Gardens); across from them, on the eastern side of the south bank,
rise the 30m (98-ft.) sandstone cliffs of **Kangaroo Point.** Two pedestrian
bridges link South Bank with the city: **Kurilpa Bridge** links Tank Street, in
the city center, with the Gallery of Modern Art at South Bank, and the **Good-
will Bridge** links South Bank with the City Gardens. To the west 5km (3
miles), Mount **Coot-tha** (pronounced *Coo*-tha) looms out of the flat plain.

MAIN ARTERIES & STREETS It's easy to find your way around central
Brisbane once you know that the east-west streets are named after female
British royalty, and the north-south streets are named after their male counter-
parts. The northernmost is Ann, followed by Adelaide, Queen, Elizabeth,
Charlotte, Mary, Margaret, and Alice. From east to west, the streets are

Edward, Albert, George, and William, which becomes North Quay, flanking the river's northeast bank.

Queen Street, the main thoroughfare, becomes a pedestrian mall between Edward and George streets. **Roma Street** exits the city diagonally to the northwest. **Ann Street** leads all the way east into Fortitude Valley. The main street in Fortitude Valley is **Brunswick Street**, which runs into New Farm.

Brisbane Neighborhoods in Brief

City Center This is where Brisbane residents eat, shop, and socialize. Queen Street Mall, in the heart of town, is popular with shoppers and moviegoers, especially on weekends and Friday night (when stores stay open until 9pm); at its other end is pleasant Post Office Square, with food and shopping options and grassy areas to rest your feet. The Eagle Street financial and legal precinct has restaurants with great views of the river and Story Bridge. Much of the city's surviving colonial architecture is here, too. Strollers, bike riders, and in-line skaters shake the summer heat in the green haven of the Brisbane City Gardens at the business district's southern end.

Fortitude Valley "The Valley," as locals call it, was once one of the sleazier parts of town. Today, it is a stamping ground for street-smart young folk who meet in restored pubs and eat in cool cafes. The lanterns, food stores, and shopping mall of **Chinatown** are here, too. On weekends, you'll find Brisbane's only alternative market, Valley Markets in the Brunswick Street and Chinatown malls (take Turbot St. from the city center). Venture a little farther to the trendy boutiques and cafes of James Street.

New Farm Always an appealing suburb, New Farm is an in-spot for cafe-hopping.

Merthyr Street is where the action is, especially on Friday and Saturday nights. From the intersection of Wickham and Brunswick streets, follow Brunswick southeast for 13 blocks to Merthyr.

Paddington This hilltop suburb, a couple of miles northwest of the city, is one of Brisbane's most attractive. Brightly painted Queenslander cottages line the main street, Latrobe Terrace, as it winds west along a ridge top. Many of the houses have been turned into shops and cafes, where you can browse, enjoy coffee and cake, or just admire the charming architecture.

Milton & Rosalie Park Road, in Milton, is not quite a little bit of Europe, but it tries hard—right down to a replica Eiffel Tower above the cafes and shops. Italian restaurants line the street, buzzing with office workers who down espressos at alfresco restaurants, scout interior-design stores for a new objet d'art, and stock up on European designer rags.

West End This small inner-city enclave is alive with ethnic restaurants, cafes, and a few interesting housewares or fashion stores. Most action centers on the intersection of Vulture and Boundary streets, where Asian grocers and delis abound.

Getting Around Brisbane
BY PUBLIC TRANSPORTATION

TransLink operates a single network of buses, trains, and ferries. For timetables and route inquiries, call **TransInfo** (www.translink.com.au; ✆ **131 230**). It uses an integrated ticket system, and the easiest place to buy your tickets is on the buses and ferries or at the train stations. You can also buy tickets and pick up maps and timetables at the Queen Street bus station information center (in the Myer Centre, off Queen Street Mall) and the Brisbane

Post Office Square, a shopping and leisure area in downtown Brisbane.

Visitor Information Centre in the Queen Street Mall. Tickets and electronic **go cards** (see below) are also sold at some inner-city newsdealers and convenience stores.

A trip in a single sector or zone on the bus, train, or ferry costs A$4.80. A single ticket is good for up to 2 hours on a one-way journey on any combination of bus, train, or ferry. When traveling with a parent, kids 4 and under travel free, and kids 5 to 14 and students pay half fare. If you plan on using public transport a lot, it is worth investing in a **go card,** which gives discounted rates (you can also buy it online and just top up the card balance as you need it). This reduces the price of a one-zone one-way trip to A$3.31 or less, depending on the time of day. You will probably not need to travel farther than four zones on the transport system. This will cost you less than A$12. You might also like to buy a **seeQ card,** specially designed for visitors, which offers 3 or 5 consecutive days' travel on all public transport services (including to the Gold Coast), and includes two Airtrain trips. SeeQ cards cost A$79 adults and A$40 children for 3 days or A$129 adults and A$65 children for 5 days.

BY PUBLIC BUS

Buses operate from around 5am to 11pm Monday through Friday, with less service on weekends. On Sunday, many routes stop around 5pm. Most buses depart from City Hall at King George Square, Adelaide, or Ann Street. The **Loop** is a free bus service that circles the city center, with distinctive red buses running on two routes, stopping at convenient places including Central Station, Queen Street Mall, Brisbane City Gardens, Riverside Centre, and King

George Square. Look for the red bus stops. Loop buses run every 10 minutes Monday through Friday 7am to 6pm.

BY FERRY

The fast **CityCat** ferries (www.transdevbrisbane.com.au) run to many places of interest, including South Bank and the Queensland Cultural Centre; the restaurants and Sunday markets at the Riverside Centre; and New Farm Park, not far from the cafes of Merthyr Street. CityCat ferries run every half-hour between the University of Queensland to the south of the city center, and Hamilton to the north (a route of around 20km/12 miles). Two hours on the CityCat takes you the entire length of the run (and there's free Wi-Fi on board!). The slower but more frequent CityFerry service (the **Inner City** and **Cross River** ferries) has stops at points including the south end of South Bank Parklands, Kangaroo Point, and Edward Street right outside the Brisbane City Gardens. Ferries run from around 6am to 10:30pm daily.

BY TRAIN

Brisbane's suburban rail network is fast, quiet, safe, and clean. Trains run from around 5am to midnight (until about 11pm on Sun). All trains leave Central Station, between Turbot and Ann streets at Edward Street.

BY BICYCLE

CityCycle (www.citycycle.com.au; ✆ **1300/229 253**) has 150 bike parking stations across central Brisbane, with bright yellow bikes and helmets

One of Brisbane's speedy CityCat ferries.

(compulsory by law) to rent. You can hire a bike between 5am and 10pm daily and return it to the station at any time. You can buy a casual subscription for A$2 a day, and the first 30 minutes on a bike is free. After that, usage charges start from A$2 for 30 minutes and then A$5 for every 30 minutes—so unless you are only planning a short ride, it's cheaper to hire a bike elsewhere.

BY CAR OR TAXI

Brisbane's grid of one-way streets can be confusing, so plan your route before setting out. Apart from that, it's easy to get around, and a car is useful here (Brisbane's a sprawling place and quite hilly too). Brisbane's biggest parking lot is at the Myer Centre (66 Elizabeth St.), open 24 hours (℃ **07/3229 1699**). Most hotels and motels have parking for guests. Most car rental companies (see p. 195 for contact information) have outlets in the city center.

For a taxi, call **Yellow Cabs** (℃ **131 924** in Australia) or **Black and White Taxis** (℃ **133 222** in Australia). There are taxi stands at each end of Queen Street Mall, on Edward Street and on George Street (outside the Treasury Casino). **Uber** also operates in Brisbane.

[FastFACTS] BRISBANE

ATMs/Banks Banks are open Monday to Thursday 9:30am to 4pm, until 5pm Fri. ATMs are easy to find in the city center and are open 24 hrs.

Business Hours Brisbane shops are open Monday to Thursday 9am to 6pm, Friday 9am to 9pm (except in Paddington, where shops are open until 9pm Thurs), Saturday 9am to 5:30pm, and Sun 10am to 6pm. Some restaurants close Monday night, Tuesday night, or both; bars are generally open from 10 or 11am until midnight.

Dentists Maven Dental, 171 Moray St., New Farm (℃ **07/3358 1333**), is open 8am to 7pm Monday to Thursday, and 9am to 5pm Friday to Saturday. For after-hours emergencies, call for recorded info on whom to contact.

Doctors & Hospitals The **Royal Brisbane Hospital** is about a 15-minute drive from the city at Herston Road, Herston (℃ **07/3636 8111**). The **Travel Doctor** (www.thetravel doctor.com.au; ℃ **07/3221 9066**) is on Level 5, 247 Adelaide St., between Creek and Edward streets. It's open Monday to Friday 8am to 4:30pm (Wed 10am–6:30pm) and Saturday 8:30am to 12:30pm.

Embassies & Consulates The United States, Canada, and New Zealand have no representation in Brisbane; see chapter 4, "Sydney," for those countries' nearest offices. The **British Consulate** is at Level 9, 100 Eagle St. (℃ **07/3223 3200**); it's open Monday to Friday 9am to 5pm.

Emergencies Dial ℃ **000** for fire, ambulance, or police help in an emergency. This is a free call from a private or public telephone. **Lifeline** (℃ **131 114**) is a 24-hour emotional crisis counseling service.

Mail & Postage The **General Post Office** is at 261 Queen St., opposite Post Office Square. It's open Monday to Friday 7am to 6pm and Saturday 9am to 12:30pm.

Newspapers & Magazines The *Courier-Mail* (Mon–Sat) and the *Sunday Mail* are Brisbane's daily newspapers. Another good news source is the online newspaper *Brisbane Times* (www.brisbanetimes. com.au). The free weekly *Brisbane News* magazine is a good guide to dining, entertainment, and shopping.

Pharmacies (Chemist Shops) The **Queen Street Pharmacy,** 141 Queen St. (on the mall)

(☎ **07/3221 4585**), is open Monday to Thursday 7am to 9pm, Friday 7am to 9:30pm, Saturday 8am to 9pm, Sunday 8:30am to 7pm, and public holidays 9am to 7:30pm.

Police Dial ☎ **000** in an emergency, or ☎ **131 444** for police headquarters.

Police are stationed 24 hours a day at 67 Adelaide St. (☎ **07/3224 4444**).

Safety Brisbane is relatively crime-free, but as in any large city, be aware of your personal safety, especially when you're out at night. Stick to well-lit streets and busy precincts.

Wi-Fi Brisbane has plenty of public Wi-Fi, with hotspots throughout the city center and suburbs. If you need access to a computer, try the **State Library of Queensland,** Stanley Place, South Bank (www.slq.qld. gov.au; ☎ **07/3840 7666**).

WHERE TO STAY IN BRISBANE

Brisbane has undergone a hotel boom in the past couple of years, particularly in the four- and five-star market, with potential guests now spoiled for choice.

Expensive

The Calile Hotel ★★★ Positioned in the fashionable James Street precinct, this is one of Brisbane's newest hotels, oozing urban cool and retro style. The unusual name—it's pronounced Kal-*isle*—is a tip to the owners' Lebanese family heritage and a hint that the personal is important. Service standards are high, the pool is dazzling, and the rooms are discreetly color-coded in muted pastel tones. Ask for a pink one, with a balcony overlooking the pool deck.

48 James St., Fortitude Valley. www.thecalilehotel.com. ☎ **07/3607 5888.** 175 units. A$235–A$359 double; A$429–A$1,279 suite. Parking A$25; valet parking A$45. Bus: 470. **Amenities:** Restaurant; bar; gymnasium; outdoor pool; room service; spa; free Wi-Fi.

Rydges South Bank Brisbane ★★★ Right in the heart of the South Bank cultural precinct, this is a perfect spot for theater- or museum-goers. After a A$30-million refurbishment in 2017, this hotel practically sparkles. All rooms have new beds and a selection of pillows, and those above the sixth floor have views of the city skyline, the river (one block away), Mount Coottha, and the Wheel of Brisbane. Some rooms have balconies. The main action is in the **Soleil Pool Bar,** where Brisbane's beautiful people gather at cocktail hour; look up for changing images on the ceiling. **Bacchus Restaurant** is fine dining at its best, and puts on a lavish breakfast buffet.

9 Glenelg St. www.rydges.com. ☎ **07/3364 0800.** 304 units. A$309–A$359 double; A$379–A$539 suite. Valet parking A$35 per day. Train: South Brisbane. **Amenities:** Restaurant; bar; concierge; gymnasium; outdoor heated pool; room service; sauna; free Wi-Fi.

Moderate

NEXT Hotel Brisbane ★★★ This is one of my favorite Brisbane hotels. Not just for the location—up an escalator at the top of the Queen Street Mall—and fabulous city and river views, but for service that is casual, friendly, and efficient. NEXT opened in 2015 after a major redevelopment transformed one of the city's old hotels into one of its smartest. And I don't just mean the sleek contemporary look of it: This is Australia's first hotel to use smart technology that lets guests control just about everything. You can even use your smartphone as your room "key." Don't have a smartphone? That's okay, there's one in the room for you to use. Add to this an outdoor terrace bar overlooking the 20m (65-ft.) lap pool, and "sleep pods" if you're in transit. Don't forget to take advantage of the four free items each day from the minibar. Seems they've thought of everything.

72 Queen St. www.silverneedlehotels.com/next. © **1800/303 186** in Australia, or 07/3222 3222. 304 units. A$229–A$259 double. Valet parking A$45. Train: Central. **Amenities:** Restaurant; bar; babysitting; concierge; gym; outdoor pool; room service; free Wi-Fi.

TRYP Fortitude Valley Hotel ★★   Brisbane's first street art hotel is as colorful inside as it is outside, with huge artworks painted onto almost every wall. Some of the world's top street artists were commissioned for this hotel, where each of the five room types is designed for two. Some rooms have balconies, others have private courtyards, and all bathrooms have very cool glass washbasins (more art!). Located on a side street just off one of the main roads, it's also close to the James Street restaurants, cinemas, and boutiques, and buses run regularly from almost outside the door.

14-20 Constance St., Fortitude Valley. www.trypbrisbane.com. © **07/3319 7888.** 65 units. A$149–A$209 double. Parking A$25. Train: Brunswick St. **Amenities:** Restaurant; bar; gymnasium; free access to nearby pool; room service; free Wi-Fi.

Inexpensive

Ibis Styles ★★   This bright and breezy inner-city hotel is a great budget choice, appealing to travelers of all ages. Opened in 2016, it is one of the most colorful hotels I've stayed in; each floor is painted in vivid pink, green, purple, or blue (easy to remember which floor you are staying on!). Standard rooms are small, but the beds are comfortable and all rooms have city, river, or South Bank views. If you don't plan to spend too much time in your room, it's a great choice. The Queen Street Mall is just around the corner.

40 Elizabeth St. www.ibisstylesbrisbaneelizabeth.com.au. © **07/3337 900**. 386 units. A$127–A$187 double. Parking (at the Myer Centre next door) A$20–A$38. Train: Central. Bus: Downtown Loop. **Amenities:** Restaurant; bar; babysitting; small exercise room; free Wi-Fi.

One Thornbury ★★   In the lovely inner-city suburb of Spring Hill, this heritage cottage is a stylish boutique bed-and-breakfast where you will feel right at home. A courtyard garden, a rescue greyhound named Rosie, and rooms with espresso machines and bathrobes all add up to a great feeling of comfort. Owner Geof Harland is on hand to cook breakfast and help with directions or anything you need. A two-bedroom suite is on the top floor (no elevator); the rest are roomy doubles. It's about 5 minutes' walk to Chinatown and 15 minutes to the city center.

1 Thornbury St., Spring Hill. www.onethornbury.com. © **07/3839 5334.** 6 units. A$119–A$179 double; A$199 suite. Rates include breakfast. Limited parking. Bus: 196. **Amenities:** Bar; free Wi-Fi.

WHERE TO EAT IN BRISBANE

Brisbane has a sophisticated dining scene. Stylish bistros and cafes line the riverfront at South Bank; cute cafes are plentiful in Paddington; Asian eateries are a good choice in West End; and in Fortitude Valley, you'll find Chinatown. A street lined with upscale but laid-back restaurants, many with a Mediterranean flavor, sits under the kitschy replica Eiffel Tower on Park Road in Milton, and in the city center you'll find slick waterfront restaurants at Eagle Street Pier and Riverside. The intersection of Albert and Charlotte streets buzzes with inexpensive, good-quality cafes.

Expensive

e'cco bistro ★★★ CONTEMPORARY *E'cco* means "here it is" in Italian, and that's the philosophy behind the food at this award-winning bistro, considered one of Australia's best. It serves simple food, done exceptionally well and with passion. A move to new premises has enabled different styles of dining (although the food remains at the high standard regulars expect), with the inclusion of an outdoor bar and dining area serving a more casual menu. Dishes include such delights as crispy pork belly with parsnip, gala apple, and black pudding crumble; or risotto with Moreton bay bugs (seafood), fennel, and chili. The bistro is enormously popular, so reservations are advisable (although less imperative at lunch).

63 Skyring Terrace, Newstead. www.eccobistro.com.au. ✆ **07/3831 8344.** Main courses A$38–A$89. 5-course chef's menu A$89 (A$149 with wine pairings). Tues–Sat noon–3pm and 5:30–10pm. Bus: 60.

Moda ★★★ CONTEMPORARY A change of premises in 2019 has taken this popular Spanish-flavored restaurant out of the city center into a more atmospheric space, in Heritage-listed brick stables that are a fitting setting for the rustic food served up. Owner-chef Javier Codina has combined his Catalan, French, and Italian influences with fresh (often organic) Queensland produce to make marvelous dishes. Steaks come off the grill served with Mediterranean vegetables and Rioja sauce, and the smattering of fish dishes includes a seafood *parrillada* (grill). Plates meant to be shared among two to four diners are a good choice for A$55, as is Javier's three-course "table experience" for A$95 per person. *Fair warning:* The wines are expensive (buy by the glass).

The Barracks, 61 Petrie Terrace. www.modarestaurant.com.au. ✆ **07/3221 7655.** Main courses A$25–A$59. Tues 3pm–late; Wed–Sun 11:30am–late. Train: Roma St.

Moderate

Breakfast Creek Hotel ★★ STEAKHOUSE Built in 1889 and listed by the National Trust, this Renaissance-style pub is a Brisbane icon. Fondly known as the Brekky Creek—or simply the Creek—the quintessentially Queensland establishment is famed for its gigantic steaks (choose your own), served with baked potato (or chips), coleslaw, salad, and a choice of

Eat Street

Brisbane foodies love **Eat Street North-shore** (www.eatstreetmarkets.com.au; (C) **0428 485 242** mobile phone), a vibrant outdoor market designed to emulate the street food stalls of Asia. Eat Street unleashes the aromas of exotic foods every Friday and Saturday from 4 to 10pm and Sunday noon to 8pm, at Hamilton Wharf on Brisbane's North Shore. Around 180 shipping containers have been transformed into kitchens and cafes, and it's all very industrial-chic. There's also live music and other entertainment and design galleries. Bars serve craft beers, cocktails, and other cool drinks, and practically every type of cuisine is represented here, from Thai to Turkish, noodles and dumplings to tacos, seafood, and salads, and even a good old Aussie (gourmet) pie. You'll find it by heading to Macarthur Avenue, Hamilton, where there's parking for 1,200 cars, but a better way to get here is by CityCat ferry to North Shore Hamilton, or take bus no. 305 from George Street, in the city, or bus no. 300 from Adelaide Street, outside City Hall. There's an entry fee of A$3 per person 12 and older.

mushroom, pepper, or chili sauce. It's also famed for serving beer "off the wood" (from the keg). The pub's **Spanish Garden Steakhouse** and the **Staghorn beer garden** are always popular, and an outdoor dining area overlooks Breakfast Creek. The **Substation No. 41** bar, created in the shell of a derelict electricity substation next to the hotel, makes the most of its exposed brick walls and soaring ceilings. The 4.5m-long (15-ft.) wooden bar is just the place to sip the latest cocktail.

2 Kingsford Smith Dr. (at Breakfast Creek Rd.), Albion. www.breakfastcreekhotel.com. (C) **07/3262 5988.** Main courses A$26–A$48. Daily 10am–late. (Substation No. 41 daily noon–late.) Bus: 300 or 322. Wickham St. becomes Breakfast Creek Rd.; the hotel is just off the route to the airport.

Harveys ★★ CONTEMPORARY Take a table in this modern, light-filled restaurant in the heart of trendy James Street and prepare for something wonderful. Chef/owner PJ McMillan has a strong local following for his deceptively simple dishes. Personally, I can never get past the Asian chicken salad, with coriander, mint, peanuts, coconut, and tamarind dressing—and it always seems that half the other patrons are having it, too. Service is friendly and attentive, and the coffee's good, too!

31 James St., Fortitude Valley (next to the Centro Cinemas). www.harveys.net.au. (C) **07/3852 3700.** Main courses A$30–A$44. Mon–Fri 7am–3pm; Sat–Sun 7:30am–3pm; Tues–Sat 5:30pm–late. Closed public holidays. Train: Brunswick St.

Jimmy's on the Mall ★★ INTERNATIONAL/CAFE FARE Jimmy's is a Brisbane institution, at the heart of the city's shopping precinct and open around the clock. The food here is consistently good, which is why the place is always busy and takes no reservations. On the lower level, the vertical gardens that decorate the eatery walls open up to the passing shopping trade, while upstairs you can take a bar-style table overlooking the mall, or grab a booth. The downstairs menu focuses on Asian fusion and includes wok dishes such as pad Thai noodles or satay chicken; the upstairs menu adds pizza—try the gambero, with prawns, prosciutto, tomato, and olives. An open kitchen adds to the lively atmosphere.

Queen Street Mall, at Albert St. www.jimmysonthemall.com.au. ℭ **07/3077 7126.** Main courses A$22–A$45. Daily 24 hrs. Train: Central.

Inexpensive

Govinda's ★★ VEGETARIAN   Tasty, cheap vegetarian food is served up at this Hare Krishna restaurant. That means a buffet of vegetable curry, *dahl* (lentil) soup, papadums, koftas, and other tasty stuff with a north Indian influence. And it's a stimulant-free zone, so don't come expecting alcohol, tea, or coffee—you're likely to get something like homemade ginger-and-mint lemonade instead. Check the website for details about Govinda's other locations, in Fortitude Valley and the inner suburb of West End.

358 George St. www.brisbanegovindas.com.au. ℭ **07/3210 0255.** A$13 all-you-can-eat; A$10 students. No credit cards. Mon–Fri 7am–8pm; Sat 11am–8pm. Bus: 360, 470, 475, 476.

Kettle & Tin ★★ CAFE   I've been a fan of this cute cafe, with its picket fence outside, since my daughter took me here for lunch. In the Paddington cafe strip, it's a converted cottage, opened up for tables on the veranda or

Eat Street, an outdoor dining market in repurposed shipping containers by the Brisbane riverfront.

Sup at the Summit

A teahouse of some kind has been on top of Mount Coot-tha for more than a century. Part 19th-century Queenslander house and part modern extension, the **Summit** restaurant (www.brisbane lookout.com; ⓒ **07/3369 9922**) has wraparound covered decks with views of the city and Moreton Bay. A changing menu features local produce and wines. The sunset dinner menu—A$46 for three courses if you finish by 7pm—is available starting at 5pm. After your meal, enjoy the observation deck—the city lights provide a glittering panorama. On Sundays, high tea is served from 10am to noon and 3 to 5pm (A$40 per person or A$50 with a glass of champagne). Reservations are recommended for Friday, Saturday, and Sunday evenings. The Summit is open daily 11:30am to 2:30pm and 5 to 9pm. For breakfast (starting at 8am Mon–Fri and 7am Sat–Sun) or lighter fare (served from 11am daily), there's also the casual **Kuta Café** (no bookings taken). To get to the summit, take bus no. 471 from Adelaide Street, in the city; if you're driving, take Upper Roma Street from the city center, then Milton Road 3.5km (2¼ miles) west to the Western Freeway roundabout at Toowong Cemetery. Veer right onto Sir Samuel Griffith Drive, and follow the road about 3km (2 miles) up the mountain. A taxi from the city will cost about A$30.

tucked away in its few rooms. My favorite time to come—along with lots of locals—is for weekend brunch. I love the Vietnamese crepe with pork and prawns, but it also serves more traditional fare if you prefer. At night, shared plates are on offer—and if you go on Thursday night you might get involved in the trivia quiz. There's live music every Sunday from 3pm.

215 Given Terrace, Paddington. www.kettleandtin.com.au. ⓒ **07/3369 3778.** Main courses A$15–A$30. Mon–Tues 7am–3pm; Wed–Sat 7am–10pm; Sun 7am–7pm. Bus: 377.

EXPLORING BRISBANE

Many of Brisbane's attractions are outdoors or nature-based, and many are free, making it a popular destination for families. The riverfront provides its own attractions, with much of the city turned toward it, with bikeway and walking paths providing terrific views.

Brisbane City Hall ★★★ HISTORIC ARCHITECTURE   The imposing Brisbane City Hall, built in the 1920s in Italian Renaissance style, was once the city's tallest building, standing at the heart of the city center. Free 45-minute guided tours are offered daily at 10:30 and 11:30am and 1:30 and 2:30pm. Tours are hugely popular and numbers are limited, so it's essential to book your spot. This is still a working civic building, so at times some of the rooms and features are not open. Separate free tours are run to the top of the **Clock Tower** every 15 minutes daily from 10:15am to 4:45pm. You cannot book ahead for these tours, and it pays to arrive early, because the vintage elevator only holds seven passengers. You'll need to get a ticket from the **Museum of Brisbane** reception counter on Level 3, and then wait your turn. After Dark tours of the clock tower allow a look at the city lights from on high; these run from 5 to 7pm on Friday only. The museum is also well worth spending time in; it provides an insight into the history and essence of Brisbane. Changing exhibitions relate the stories, events, and ideas that have shaped the city. Free guided tours of the current exhibitions run at 12:30pm daily. This is a beautiful building—don't miss it!

City Hall, King George Sq. www.museumofbrisbane.com.au. © **07/3339 0845**. Free. Sat–Thurs 10am–5pm; Fri 10am–7pm. Closed Jan 1, Good Friday, Dec 25–26, and until 1pm Anzac Day (Apr 25). Train: Roma St. or Central. Bus: The Loop.

Brisbane Powerhouse Arts ★★ ARTS CENTER   A former electricity powerhouse, this massive brick factory is now a dynamic space for exhibitions, contemporary performance, and live art. The building retains its character, an industrial mix of metal, glass, and stark surfaces etched with 20 years of graffiti. It's a short walk from the New Farm ferry terminal along the riverfront through New Farm Park. **Farmer's markets** operate every Saturday morning, and a restaurant/cafe/bar overlooks the river. Check the website for the latest events.

119 Lamington St., New Farm. www.brisbanepowerhouse.org. © **07/3358 8600**. Daily 9am until the last show finishes. CityCat to New Farm Park.

La Boite Theatre ★★ THEATER   This well-established, innovative company performs contemporary Australian plays and some classics in the 400-seat Roundhouse Theatre, ensuring an intimate theater experience. Tickets typically cost A$30 to A$60. Located in the Queensland University of Technology precinct, it offers an affordable night out and some cutting-edge productions.

6 Musk Ave., Kelvin Grove. www.laboite.com.au. © **07/3007 8600**. Take bus no. 390 from the city to Kelvin Grove Rd., and get off at stop 12.

Lone Pine Koala Sanctuary ★★ WILDLIFE VIEWING   This is the best place in Australia to cuddle a koala—and one of the few places where koala cuddling is still allowed. Banned in New South Wales and Victoria, holding a koala is legal in Queensland under strict conditions: Each animal is handled for less than 30 minutes a day—and gets every third day off! When it opened in 1927, Lone Pine had just two koalas, Jack and Jill; it is now home to more than 130. You can have a photo taken holding one (for an extra A$25); once you've paid, you can have some photos taken using your own camera, too. Lone Pine isn't just koalas—you can also hand-feed kangaroos and wallabies and get up close with emus, snakes, baby crocs, parrots, wombats, Tasmanian devils, skinks, lace monitors, frogs, bats, turtles, possums, and other native wildlife. There is a currency exchange, a gift shop, a restaurant, and a cafe. Picnic and barbecue facilities are also available.

The nicest way to get to Lone Pine is a cruise down the Brisbane River aboard the **MV** *Mirimar* (www.mirimarcruises.com.au; © **0412/749 426**), which leaves the Cultural Centre pontoon at South Bank Parklands at 10am.

A shepherd prepares for a sheepdog trial in Lone Pine Sanctuary.

The 19km (12-mile) trip to Lone Pine takes 75 minutes and includes commentary. You have 3 hours to explore before returning, arriving in the city at 3:30pm. Return cruises leave Lone Pine at 1pm and 2pm. The round-trip fare is A$80 for adults, A$48 for children ages 3 to 13, and A$220 for families of five, and includes entry to Lone Pine. A shorter, faster "express" cruise also runs daily at 9am and 11am, allowing half an hour less at Lone Pine and costing A$90 adults, A$50 children, and A$240 families each way (including entry). Cruises run daily except Anzac Day (Apr 25) and Christmas Day.

708 Jesmond Rd., Fig Tree Pocket. www.koala.net. ✆ **07/3378 1366.** A$38 adults, A$22 children 3–13, A$60–A$85 families. Daily 9am–5pm; Anzac Day (Apr 25) 1:30–5pm. By car (20 min. from city center), take Milton Rd. to the roundabout at Toowong Cemetery, and then Western Fwy. toward Ipswich. Signs point to Fig Tree Pocket and Lone Pine. Bus: nos. 430 or 445 from the city center. A taxi from the city center will cost about A$40.

Queen Street Mall ★ SHOPPING DISTRICT   Brisbane's inner-city shopping centers around **Queen Street Mall,** which has around 500 stores. Fronting the mall at 171–209 Queen Street, the three-level **Wintergarden** shopping complex (www.wgarden.com.au; ✆ **07/3229 9755**) houses upscale jewelers and Aussie fashion designers. Farther up the mall at 91 Queen Street (at Albert St.) is the **Myer Centre** (www.themyercentre.com.au; ✆ **07/3223 6900**), which holds Brisbane's biggest department store and five levels of moderately priced stores, mostly fashion. The gorgeous **Brisbane Arcade,** 160 Queen St. (www.brisbanearcade.com.au; ✆ **07/3231 9777**), runs through to Adelaide Street and abounds with jewelers and the boutiques of local Queensland designers. Across from the Edward Street end of the mall, at 255

Queen St., is a smart fashion and lifestyle shopping precinct, **MacArthur Central** (www.macarthurcentral.com.au; ✆ **07/3007 2300**), right next door to the General Post Office on the block between Queen and Elizabeth streets. This is where you'll find top designer labels, Swiss watches, galleries, and accessory shops. You'll find more chic shopping at **QueensPlaza** (www.queensplaza.com.au; ✆ **07/3234 3900**), at Edward and Adelaide streets. Weekly **farmer's markets** are held in the Queen Street Mall (at the Victoria Bridge/George Street end) on Wednesday from 8am to 6pm.

Queen St. www.queenstreetmall.com.au.

Queensland Cultural Centre ★★★ ARTS CENTER

This modern complex stretching along the south bank of the Brisbane River houses many of the city's performing-arts venues as well as the state art galleries, museum, and library. With plenty of open plazas and fountains, it is a pleasing place to wander or just sit and watch the river and the city skyline. It's a 7-minute walk from town, across the Victoria Bridge from the Queen Street Mall.

The **Queensland Performing Arts Centre** (www.qpac.com.au; ✆ **136 246** for bookings Mon–Sat 9am–8:30pm) houses the 2,000-seat Lyric Theatre for musicals, ballet, and opera; the 1,800-seat Concert Hall for orchestral performances; the 850-seat Playhouse theater for plays; and the 315-seat Cremorne Theatre for theater-in-the-round, cabaret, and experimental works. The complex has a restaurant and a cafe. Resident companies include the **Queensland Theatre** (www.queenslandtheatre.com.au), which offers eight or nine productions a year, from the classics to new Australian works; **Opera Queensland** (www.oq.com.au), which performs a lively repertoire of traditional as well as modern works, musicals, and choral concerts; and the **Queensland Symphony Orchestra** (www.qso.com.au), which provides classical-music lovers with a diverse mix of orchestral and chamber music, plus the odd foray into fun material, such as movie themes, pop, and gospel music. It schedules about 30 concerts a year.

The **Queensland Art Gallery** ★★★ (www.qagoma.qld.gov.au; ✆ **07/3840 7303**) is one of Australia's most attractive galleries, with vast light-filled spaces and interesting water features inside and out. It is a major player in the Australian art world, attracting blockbuster exhibitions of works by the likes of Renoir, Picasso, and van Gogh, and showcasing diverse modern Australian painters, sculptors, and other artists. It also has an impressive collection of Aboriginal art. The adjacent **Queensland Gallery of Modern Art (GOMA)** ★★★ houses collections of modern and contemporary Australian, Indigenous Australian, Asian, and Pacific art, and also gives a stunning sense of light and space. Admission is free to both galleries, and both run regular free tours that take around 30 to 40 minutes. Tours of each gallery's collection highlights are held daily at 11am and 1pm. The galleries are open daily 10am to 5pm; closed Good Friday, Christmas Day, Boxing Day (Dec 26), and until noon on Anzac Day (Apr 25).

Stanley Place, South Brisbane.

Queensland Museum ★★★ MUSEUM   Fossils 50 million years old—including a frog, snail, crocodile, and fish—are just some of the many fascinating "lost creatures" on show at this interesting and eclectic museum. Displays range from natural history specimens to insects, dinosaurs—including Queensland's own *Muttaburrasaurus*—and more. Children will love the blue whale model that greets you at the entrance. The museum also has a cafe and gift shop. Admission is free, except for special exhibitions and the new **SparkLab** Sciencentre, which opened in 2019. Targeting kids ages 6 to 13, with 40 interactive STEM exhibits designed to spark their creativity, this gallery is on level 1 of the museum. Admission is timed-entry, which means you should book ahead; entry times start at 9:40am, then every half-hour from 10:30am until 3:30pm.

Grey St. (at Melbourne St.), next to the Queensland Art Gallery. www.qm.qld.gov.au. 🕾 **07/3840 7555.** Daily 9:30am–5pm; closed Good Friday, Dec 25–26, and until 1:30pm on Anzac Day (Apr 25). Free. SparkLab: A$16 adults, A$13 children 5–15, A$46 families of 4. Ferry: South Bank (CityCat) or Old South Bank (Inner City Ferry). Bus: Numerous buses from Adelaide St. (near Albert St.). Train: South Brisbane.

St John's Anglican Cathedral ★★ CHURCH   Brisbane's stunning neo-Gothic Anglican cathedral took more than a century to complete, but the result has been worth the wait. Plagued by lack of funding throughout its

Life-size skeleton of a Muttaburrasaurus langdoni dinosaur, a large, plant-eating ornithopod, in the Queensland Museum.

The manmade beach at South Bank Parklands.

history, the building was finally completed in 2009, making it one of the last Gothic-style cathedrals to be completed anywhere in the world, with stonemasons using traditional medieval building techniques. Volunteer guides are on hand to point out some of the details that make this cathedral uniquely Queensland—such as the carved possums on the organ screen and the hand-stitched cushions.

373 Ann St. (btw. Wharf and Queen sts.). www.stjohnscathedral.com.au. ℂ **07/3835 2222.** Daily 9:30am–4:30pm. Closed to visitors, except for services, Anzac Day (Apr 25), Dec 25, and some other public holidays. Train: Central Station.

Sir Thomas Brisbane Planetarium & Cosmic Skydome ★★

PLANETARIUM   Digital multimedia systems that present real-time digital star shows and computer-generated images in the Cosmic Skydome theater are a popular feature here for all ages. The fascinating 40-minute astronomical show includes a re-creation of the Brisbane night sky using a Zeiss star projector. Show times vary, and there are also special shows designed for kids ages 6 and under. Check the website for details.

Brisbane Botanic Gardens, Mt. Coot-tha Rd., Toowong. www.brisbane.qld.gov.au/planetarium. ℂ **07/3403 2578.** A$16 adults, A$9.80 children 3–14, A$44 families of 4. Tues–Thurs 10am–4pm; Fri 10am–7:30pm; Sat 10:45am–7:30pm; Sun 10:45am–4pm. Closed Mon (except school holidays) and public holidays. Bus: nos. 471, 598, or 599.

South Bank Parklands ★★★ PARKLAND   Follow the locals' lead and

spend some time at this delightful 16-hectare (40-acre) complex of parks, restaurants, cafes, playgrounds, street theater, and weekend markets. There's a manmade beach lined with palm trees, with waves and sand, where you can swim, stroll, and cycle the meandering pathways. From the parklands it's an easy walk to the museum, art gallery, and other parts of the adjacent **Queensland Cultural Centre** (p. 209). Hop on the **Wheel of Brisbane** (www.thewheelofbrisbane.com.au; ℂ **07/3844 3464**) for a 13-minute ride in an enclosed air-conditioned gondola, where you get a 360-degree bird's-eye view of Brisbane from 60m (197 ft.) up; it costs A$22 adults, A$15 children 4 to 11, and A$64 families of four. The buzzing outdoor **Collective Markets** (www.collectivemarkets.com.au) is illuminated by fairy lights at night; it's open Friday 5 to 9pm, Saturday 10am to 9pm, and Sunday 9am to 4pm. The South Bank Parklands are a 7-minute walk from the city center.

South Bank. www.visitbrisbane.com.au/South-Bank. ℂ **07/3156 6366** for Visitor Centre. Free. Park daily 24 hr.; Visitor Centre daily 9am–5pm (closed Good Friday and Dec 25, open from 1pm on Anzac Day [Apr 25]). Train: South Brisbane. Ferry: South Bank (CityCat or Cross River Ferry). Bus: Numerous routes from Adelaide St. (near Albert St.), including nos. 100, 111, 115, and 120, stop at the Queensland Cultural Centre; walk through the Centre to South Bank Parklands.

Story Bridge Adventure Climb ★★★ ACTIVITY Brisbane seems to have a fascination with building bridges across its wide river. There were 15 at last count, but the most interesting is the Story Bridge, built in 1940. If you are over 10 years old, at least 130 centimeters (just over 4 ft., 3 in.) tall, and accompanied by an adult (if you are under 16), you can "climb" this overgrown Meccano set. The Story Bridge Adventure Climb peaks at a viewing platform on top of the bridge, 44m (143 ft.) above the roadway and 80m (262 ft.) above the Brisbane River. On Sunday mornings, you can also rappel down to the park below from the top of the bridge. You'll be rewarded with magnificent 360-degree views of the city, river, and Moreton Bay and its islands, not to mention interesting stories from your guide. Don't be scared—you'll love it!

170 Main St. (at Wharf St.), Kangaroo Point. www.storybridgeadventureclimb.com.au. ℂ **07/3188 9070.** Day climbs A$129 adults, A$110 children; night climbs A$139 adults, A$118 children; dawn climbs, twilight climbs, and abseil climbs (Sat only) A$159 adults, A$135 children. Ferry: Holman St.

Treasury Casino ★ CASINO This lovely heritage building—built in 1886 as, ironically enough, the state's Treasury offices—houses a modern casino. Three levels of 100 gaming tables offer roulette, blackjack, baccarat, craps, sic bo, and traditional Aussie two-up. Open 24 hours, the casino has more than 1,600 gaming machines, six restaurants, and five bars. DJs bring music to **LiveWire Bar** on Friday, Saturday and Sunday nights, or you can relax in the clubby atmosphere of **Ryan's on the Park.** A massive 10-block redevelopment of the George Street precinct around the casino is currently taking place, but once you're inside you'd never know it.

159 William St. (corner of Queen St.). www.treasurybrisbane.com.au. ℂ **07/3306 8888.** Must be 18 years old to enter; neat, casual attire required (no beachwear or flip-flops). Closed Dec 25, from 3am Good Friday, and from 3am until 1pm Anzac Day (Apr 25). Train: Central or South Brisbane, and then walk across the Victoria Bridge.

FACING PAGE: Fireworks over Story Bridge in Brisbane.

ORGANIZED TOURS

RIVER CRUISES   The best way to cruise the river, in my view, is aboard the fast **CityCat ferries** ★★★. Board at Riverside and head downstream under the Story Bridge to New Farm Park, past Newstead House to the restaurant row at Brett's Wharf, or cruise upriver past the city and South Bank for only a few dollars. For more information, see "Getting Around," earlier in this chapter.

Kookaburra Showboat Cruises (www.kookaburrariverqueens.com; ℂ 07/3221 1300) run a range of river cruises on the **Kookaburra Queen** paddlewheelers, including 2-hour sightseeing cruises Thursday through Sunday afternoons. The cost is A$40 adults, A$20 children 4 to 12. For those who'd like to dine as they cruise, 90-minute lunch cruises run on weekdays, costing A$49 adults and A$20 kids, and dinner cruises run on Thursday, Friday, and Saturday for A$79 to A$99 adults and A$20 to A$40 children. The boat departs from the Eagle Street Pier at 7pm. High Tea cruises on Saturday or Sunday at 1pm cost A$55 to A$59 adults and A$20 children (ages 4–12).

WALKING TOURS   The best walking tours in town are run by the **Brisbane Greeters** (www.visitbrisbane.com.au/brisbane-greeters)—and even

The Kookaburra River Queen paddlewheeler.

Whale-Watching in Moreton Bay

Gasps of delight and wonder are the norm aboard Captain Kerry Lopez's whale-watching boat, and Australia's only female whale-watching captain never tires of hearing them. Lopez's purpose-built vessel, the MV *Eye-Spy*, carries up to 320 passengers out into Moreton Bay between June and November for one of the most awesome sights you may ever see. On my trip out, we witnessed the antics of 17 humpback whales as they breached and displayed in the waters around the boat. It was an amazing, unforgettable experience. **Brisbane Whale Watching ★★★** (www.brisbanewhalewatching.com.au; ✆ **07/3880 0477**) will organize your 30-minute transfers from city hotels to the departure point in the northern suburb of Redcliffe. If you choose to drive yourself, there's free all-day parking near the jetty. Tours depart daily at 10am, returning around 2:30 to 3pm. The trip onto the bay features excellent educational commentary about the whales while Kerry and her crew keep a lookout for these gentle giants of the deep. Prices are A$135 adults, A$125 seniors and students, A$95 children 4 to 14, or A$365 for families of four, including lunch and morning and afternoon tea. Transfers from Brisbane hotels are an extra A$30 per person.

The best part? There's a guarantee you'll see a whale—or you can take another cruise for free.

better, they're free. You get your own personal tour guide (or you can join a group), often a local with a particular area of expertise or interest in some aspect of the city. You can choose from tours that look at architecture, arts and culture, history, and more, or at a particular neighborhood or precinct. Guides are volunteers with a passion and enthusiasm for the city, and you'll learn a lot along the way. But really, it's up to you to decide what to do and how long the walk will be. You'll likely see the Greeters in their bright red shirts out and about in the city. Tours start from the Visitor Information Centre in the Queen Street Mall, and last anywhere from 1 to 4 hours. Try to book at least 48 hours ahead. Book online or at the Visitor Information Centre.

Free guided walks of the **City Botanic Gardens** at Alice Street leave from the rotunda at the Albert Street entrance Monday through Saturday at 11am and 1pm (except public holidays and mid-Dec to mid-Jan). The walks take about 1 hour. Bookings are not necessary.

Prepare for shivers up your spine when you take one of local "horror historian" Jack Sim's **Ghost Tours ★** (www.brisbaneghosttours.com.au; ✆ **0401/666 441** mobile), which relive Brisbane's gruesome past. Sim's 90-minute "Haunted Brisbane" walking tours depart from the Queen Street Mall at 7:30pm Thursday and Sunday (A$26 adults, A$15 kids 5–17, or A$65 families of four). On Friday and Saturday nights, you can take a 2-hour tour of the historic and haunted Toowong cemetery (A$45 adults, A$25 children 10–17). Or choose from a range of other spooky tours. Reservations are essential; some tours are not suitable for children 11 and under.

A DAY TRIP TO THE GREAT BARRIER REEF ★★★

Brisbane is south of the most southern parts of the Great Barrier Reef (see chapter 7), but it is still possible to experience the Reef in a day trip to **Lady Elliot Island,** off the coast near Bundaberg (384km/238 miles north of Brisbane). If you are pressed for time before heading south or to Central Australia and Uluru, this is an excellent option.

Lady Elliot (www.ladyelliot.com.au; ✆ **1800/072 200** in Australia) is a small coral cay ringed by a lagoon filled with coral and marine life. Reef walking, snorkeling, and diving are the main reasons people come to this coral cay, but you can snorkel and reef walk only for the 2 to 3 hours before and after high tide, so your day-trip activities will be reliant on nature to some extent.

Keep in mind that you will not be able to dive and fly on the same day. But the snorkeling on Lady Elliot is a wonderful experience (and the island has accommodations if you wish to stay longer or do some diving; see p. 275). You will see beautiful corals, brightly colored fish, clams, sponges, urchins, and anemones, and with luck, green and loggerhead turtles (which nest on the beach Nov–Mar), and manta rays. Whales migrate through these waters from June through September.

Be aware that Lady Elliot is a sparse, grassy island rookery, not a sandy tropical paradise. Some find it too spartan; others relish chilling out in a beautiful, peaceful spot with reef all around. Just be prepared for the smell and constant noise of the birds.

Lady Elliot's own airline, **Seair,** offers a day-trip package from Brisbane for A$959 adults and A$599 children ages 3 to 12. In addition to the flights, the price includes snorkel gear, a glass-bottom-boat ride, lunch, and guided activities (and the Reef tax).

Your day trip begins with an early pickup (around 6:30am) from your Brisbane hotel to drive to the northern Brisbane suburb of Redcliffe for the coastal scenic flight. The flight takes about 80 minutes. Seair operates a fleet of 9- and 13-seat aircraft. All you need to bring is a daypack with swimwear, camera, sunscreen, and footwear suitable for getting wet (no more than 10kg [22 lb.] in luggage). Take some cash too, in case you decide to buy an underwater camera or a small souvenir from the resort gift shop.

You'll have around 5 hours to explore the island and Reef. You can take an island orientation tour, a guided reef walk at low tide (if possible), a snorkeling lesson in the resort pool (if you need it), and a glass-bottom-boat or guided snorkel tour, and even feed the fish in the lagoon fish pool.

All snorkel equipment (mask, snorkel, fins, and wetsuit) is provided, along with towels and reef-walking shoes. Storage lockers are available, as are resort shower facilities. A hot and cold buffet lunch includes fresh prawns, champagne, wine, beer, and soft drinks.

You'll be boarding your light plane for the return trip at 2:30pm, arriving back at your Brisbane hotel at around 4:45pm—but you'll feel like you've been gone much longer. Such is the magic of a day on the Great Barrier Reef!

CAIRNS & THE GREAT BARRIER REEF

Fish out your flippers and prepare to dive! Or snorkel. Beneath the aqua blue waters off Queensland's northern coast lie the jewels of the deep—gardens of coral, inhabited by colorful reef fish. Welcome to Australia's most famous natural attraction, the Great Barrier Reef. And while the Reef is by no means the only thing worth seeing in a state that's two and a half times the size of Texas, it is the main focus of this chapter. There are many gateways to the Reef along the Queensland coast, but Cairns is the major center; most commercial boat tours depart from here.

White sandy beaches grace nearly every inch of coastline in Queensland, and a string of islands and coral reefs dangles just offshore. Cairns, set between rainforest hills, sugarcane fields, and the Coral Sea, still has few options for direct arrivals; for most people, Brisbane or Sydney will be the first stop before heading to the far north of Australia's east coast. In Cairns, a harbor full of boats awaits to take you to the Reef. An hour north, the village of **Port Douglas** provides another point of departure for the Reef.

Farther south, **Townsville** boasts 320 days of sunshine a year and is home to the Great Barrier Reef Marine Park Authority. It is a hotspot for divers, with one of Australia's best wreck dives, and also marks the start of the Great Green Way—an area of lush natural beauty on the way to Cairns—for those who choose to drive.

Departing from Airlie Beach on the Whitsunday Coast, you'll be tempted by one tropical island after another; a cluster of 74 makes up the **Whitsunday** and **Cumberland** groups. These idyllic islands are laced by coral reefs rising out of calm, blue waters teeming with colorful fish—warm enough for swimming year-round.

The most southern part of the Great Barrier Reef is where you'll find turtle breeding grounds on **Heron Island** and on the mainland near **Bundaberg**. Snorkelers and divers will revel in the reefs around Heron Island, **Lady Musgrave Island,** and **Lady Elliot Island.**

Aerial view of Cairns.

ESSENTIALS
Visitor Information

The **Tourism & Events Queensland** website at **www.queensland.com** is a great resource on traveling and touring the state, including the Great Barrier Reef, and on this site you can select information specifically designed for travelers from your country. In Australia, call **Go Queensland** (www.goqueensland.com.au; ✆ **1300/730 039** in Australia) to book online or speak to a Queensland travel specialist.

When to Go

Winter (June–Aug) is high season in Queensland; the water can be chilly—at least to Australians—but its temperature rarely drops below 72°F (22°C). April through November is the best time to visit the Great Barrier Reef, because although southeast tradewinds can sometimes make it a tad choppy at sea, this is peak visibility time for divers. December through March can be uncomfortably hot and humid, particularly as far north as the Whitsundays, Cairns, and Port Douglas.

Getting Around
BY PLANE

This is the fastest way to cover the most ground in such a big state. **Qantas** (www.qantas.com.au; ✆ **131 313** in Australia) and its subsidiaries **Qantas-Link** and **Jetstar** (www.jetstar.com.au; ✆ **131 538** in Australia) serve most coastal towns from Brisbane, and a few from Cairns. **Virgin Australia** (www.

virginaustralia.com; ℂ **136 789** in Australia) serves Brisbane, Cairns, Townsville, Gladstone, Bundaberg, and Proserpine and Hamilton Island in the Whitsundays, as well as other centers.

BY TRAIN

Queensland Rail (www.queenslandrailtravel.com.au; ℂ **1300/131 722** in Australia) operates two long-distance trains along the coast north from Brisbane, a 24-hour trip aboard the *Spirit of Queensland* to Cairns or about 5 hours less on the **Tilt Train** to Bundaberg and Rockhampton. See the "Getting Around" section in chapter 13 for more details.

BY CAR

The Bruce Highway travels along the coast from Brisbane to Cairns. It is mostly a narrow, two-lane highway, with the scenery varying from eucalyptus bushland to sugarcane fields.

Tourism & Events Queensland (see "Visitor Information," p. 218) publishes regional motoring guides, but all you are likely to need is a state map from the **Royal Automobile Club of Queensland (RACQ)** (www.racq.com.au; ℂ **131 905** in Australia). A large range of touring maps is available online, and the website is brimming with advice about driving in Australia. For recorded road-condition reports, call ℂ **131 940.** Brisbane-based online specialist map shop **World Wide Maps & Guides** (www.worldwidemaps.com.au) offers a wide range of Australia maps, atlases, and street directories.

Exploring the Great Barrier Reef

First, a few facts: The Great Barrier Reef is the only living thing on earth that's visible from the moon; at 348,700 sq. km (135,993 sq. miles), it's bigger than the United Kingdom and more than 2,000km (1,240 miles) long, stretching from Lady Elliot Island off Bundaberg to Papua New Guinea. It's home to 1,500 kinds of fish, 400 species of corals, 4,000 kinds of clams and snails, and who knows how many sponges, starfish, and sea urchins; the Great Barrier Reef region is listed as a World Heritage Site and contains the biggest marine park in the world.

See It Now

In recent years, parts of the Great Barrier Reef have been affected by changing environmental factors that cause coral to degrade and, in some cases, die. One of the major problems on the reef is coral bleaching, caused by heat stress resulting from rising sea temperatures. Other stressors can also cause bleaching, including freshwater inundation (low salinity) and poor water quality from sediment or pollutant run-off from agriculture, mining, and other coastal development. Tour operators are well aware of the best places to see healthy coral, so you can still have the experience you expect—but of course, things can change in a relatively short time. Get there while you can still see some of the glory of the Reef.

There are three kinds of reef on the Great Barrier Reef—*fringing, ribbon,* and *platform.* **Fringing reef** is the stuff you see just off the shore of islands and along the mainland. **Ribbon reefs** create "streamers" of long, thin reef along the outer edge of the continental

shelf and are only found north of Cairns. **Platform** or **patch reefs** can be up to 16 sq. km (10 sq. miles) of coral emerging off the continental shelf all the way along the Reef's length. Platform reefs, the most common kind, are what most people think of when they refer to the Great Barrier Reef. Island resorts in the Great Barrier Reef Marine Park are either "continental," meaning part of the Australian landmass, or "cays," crushed dead coral and sand amassed on the reef tops over time by water action.

The rich colors of the coral can be seen best with lots of light, so the nearer the surface, the brighter and richer the marine life. That means snorkelers are in a prime position to see it at its best. Snorkeling the Reef can be a wondrous experience. Green and purple clams, pink sponges, red starfish, purple sea urchins, and fish from electric blue to neon yellow to lime green are truly magical sights.

Apart from the impressive fish life around the corals, the Reef is home to large numbers of green and loggerhead turtles, one of the biggest dugong (relative of the manatee) populations in the world, sharks, giant manta rays, and sea snakes. In winter (June–Aug), humpback whales gather in the warm waters south of the Reef around Hervey Bay and as far north as Cairns to give birth to calves. This is what you've come to see!

For most people, the Great Barrier Reef means the Outer Reef, the network of reefs that are an average of 65km (40 miles) off the coast (about 60–90 min. by boat from the mainland). You can snorkel the Reef, dive, ride a semisubmersible, or fly over it.

If your Reef cruise offers a guided **snorkel tour** or "snorkel safari," take it. Some include it as part of the price, but even if you have to pay extra it is worth it. Most safaris are suitable for beginners and advanced snorkelers and

	The Reef Tax
	Every passenger over 4 years old must pay an **Environmental Management Charge (EMC),** commonly called the "reef tax," of A$7 per person per day, or A$3.50 per person for trips of less than 3 hours, every time they visit the Great Barrier Reef. This money goes toward the management and conservation of the Reef. Your tour operator will collect it from you when you pay for your trip (or it may be included in the tour price).

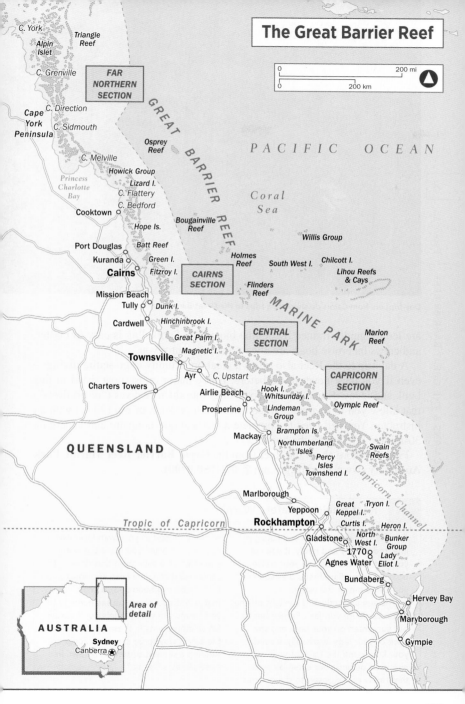

The Great Barrier Reef

C. York
Alpin Islet
Triangle Reef
C. Grenville

FAR NORTHERN SECTION

C. Direction
Cape York Peninsula
C. Sidmouth

Osprey Reef

PACIFIC OCEAN

C. Melville
Howick Group
Princess Charlotte Bay
Lizard I.
C. Flattery
C. Bedford
Cooktown
Hope Is.

GREAT BARRIER REEF

Coral Sea

Bougainville Reef
Willis Group

Port Douglas
Batt Reef
Kuranda
Green I.
Fitzroy I.
Cairns

Holmes Reef
South West I.
Chilcott I.
Lihou Reefs & Cays

CAIRNS SECTION

Flinders Reef

Mission Beach
Tully
Dunk I.
Cardwell
Hinchinbrook I.
Great Palm I.
Magnetic I.

CENTRAL SECTION

Marion Reef

MARINE PARK

Townsville
Ayr
C. Upstart

Charters Towers

Airlie Beach
Prosperine

Hook I.
Whitsunday I.
Lindeman Group

CAPRICORN SECTION

Olympic Reef

Mackay
Brampton Is.
Northumberland Isles
Percy Isles
Townshend I.

Swain Reefs

QUEENSLAND

Capricorn Channel

Marlborough
Yeppoon
Rockhampton
Great Keppel I.
Tryon I.
Curtis I.
Heron I.

Tropic of Capricorn

Gladstone
North West I.
Bunker Group
1770
Lady Eliot I.
Agnes Water

Bundaberg
Hervey Bay
Maryborough
Gympie

0 — 200 mi
0 — 200 km

AUSTRALIA
Area of detail
Sydney
Canberra

Day-trippers from Cairns do snorkeling trips to the Great Barrier Reef.

are led by guides trained by marine biologists. Snorkeling is easy to master, and crews on cruise boats are always happy to tutor you.

A day trip to the Reef also offers a great opportunity to go **scuba diving**—even if you have never dived before. Every major cruise boat listed in this book and many dedicated dive boats offer introductory dives ("resort dives") that allow you to dive without certification to a depth of 6m (20 ft.) with an instructor. You will need to complete a medical questionnaire and undergo a 30-minute briefing on the boat.

Find out more about the Reef from the **Great Barrier Reef Marine Park Authority** (www.gbrmpa.gov.au; ☎ **07/4750 0700**).

Reef Health & Safety Warnings

Coral is very sharp, and coral cuts get infected quickly and badly. If you cut yourself, ask the staff on your cruise boat for immediate first aid as soon as you come out of the water.

The sun and reflected sunlight off the water can burn you fast. Remember to put sunscreen on your back and the back of your legs, especially around your knees and the back of your neck, and even behind your ears—all places that rarely get exposed to the sun but will be exposed as you swim facedown. Apply more when you leave the water. If you can, use a sunscreen that does not contain Oxybenzone (also known as BP-3 or Benzophenone-3), a chemical that scientists believe causes damage to coral reefs. However, labels don't always list all ingredients in these products so the safest way to be sure is to cover up wearing a wetsuit or sunsuit (known in Australia as a "rashie").

DIVING the reef

Divers have a lot to choose from: dive boats that make 1-day runs to the Outer Reef, boats that offer overnight stays, live-aboard dive boats that make excursions that last up to a week, or staying on an island. As a general rule, on a typical 5-hour day trip to the Reef, you will fit in about two dives. The companies listed in this book give you an idea of the kinds of trips available and how much they cost. Prices quoted include full gear rental; knock off about A$20 if you have your own gear. It is recommended that you only dive with members of **Dive Queensland.** The website, **www.dive-queensland.com.au,** has more information on diving in Queensland.

Many dive companies in Queensland offer instruction, from initial open-water certification all the way to dive-master level, rescue-diver, and instructor level. To take a course, you will need to have a medical exam done by a Queensland doctor. (Your dive school will arrange it; it usually costs between A$45 and A$70.) You can find out more about dive medicals on **www.divemedicals.com.au**. You will also need two passport photos for your certificate, and you must be able to

swim! Courses usually begin every day or every week. Some courses take as little as 3 days, but 5 days is regarded as the best. Open-water certification usually requires 2 days of theory in a pool, followed by 2 or 3 days on the Reef, where you make four to nine dives. Prices vary but are generally around A$700 for a 4-day open-water certification course, or A$800 for the same course as a live-aboard.

Deep Sea Divers Den (www.divers den.com.au; © **07/4046 7333**) has been in operation since 1974 and claims to have certified more than 55,000 divers. Courses range from 4-day open-water courses (from A$715 per person) to 6-day courses on a live-aboard boat, which cost from A$1,405 per person, and include all meals on the boat, all gear, a wetsuit, and transfers from your city hotel. Prices include reef tax, port and administration charges, and fuel levy. New courses begin every day of the week.

Virtually every Great Barrier Reef dive operator offers dive courses. Most island resorts offer them, too. You will find dive schools in Cairns, Port Douglas, Townsville, and the Whitsundays.

Choosing a Gateway to the Reef

Think carefully about where to base yourself. The main gateways, north to south, are **Port Douglas, Cairns, Townsville,** the **Whitsunday Islands, Gladstone** (for Heron Island), and **Bundaberg** (for Lady Elliot Island). The Reef is generally about 90 minutes away by high-speed catamaran from any of these towns, except **Townsville,** which is about 2½ hours away. The quality of the coral is equally good anywhere along the coast.

The major launching points for day trips to the Reef are Port Douglas, Cairns, Townsville, and the Whitsundays. Day-trip options for each are outlined in their dedicated sections of this chapter.

Many people stay in Cairns simply because of its easy international airport access. The Whitsundays, however, have the added attractions of dazzling islands to sail among; beautiful island resorts offering a wealth of watersports and other activities; and a large array of diving, fishing, and day cruises. You can snorkel every day off your island or join a sailing or cruise day trip to a number of magnificent fringing or inner shelf reefs much nearer than the main Outer Reef.

If you are a nonswimmer, choose a Reef cruise that visits a coral cay, because a cay slopes gradually into shallow water and the surrounding coral. The **Low Isles** at Port Douglas; **Green Island, Michaelmas Cay,** or **Upolu Cay** off Cairns; and **Heron Island,** off Gladstone, are all good locations. Swimmer supports are available so nonswimmers can snorkel, too.

CAIRNS ★★

346km (215 miles) N of Townsville; 1,807km (1,120 miles) N of Brisbane

Cairns is the only place on earth where two World Heritage–listed sites—the Wet Tropics Rainforest and Great Barrier Reef—are side by side. Explore the reef and offshore islands and slip into the distinctive pace, heat, and style of a truly tropical city.

This is the departure point for the large-scale Reef boats that take hundreds of people out every day. Many smaller operators offer a more intimate experience, some on sailing boats. Offshore, **Michaelmas Cay** and **Upolu Cay** are two pretty coral sand blips in the ocean, 30km (19 miles) and 25km (16 miles) off Cairns, surrounded by reefs. Michaelmas is vegetated and is home to 27,000 seabirds; you may spot dugongs (cousins of manatees) off Upolu. Michaelmas and Upolu are great for snorkelers and introductory divers.

Cairns Esplanade offers top-to-bottom-dollar shopping plus an array of food halls, but its sparkling jewel is the manmade **lagoon** on the Esplanade, where you can cool off from the heat. There's plenty to do on days when the Reef's not on your radar.

Essentials

ARRIVING

BY PLANE **Cairns Airport (CNS)** (www.cairnsairport.com.au; ✆ **07/4080 6703**) is 8km (5 miles) north of downtown. A 5-minute walk along a covered walkway connects the international terminal with the domestic terminal.

Qantas (www.qantas.com.au; ✆ **131 313** in Australia) has direct flights to Cairns from Sydney, Brisbane, Townsville, Hamilton Island, Melbourne, Darwin, Uluru, and Alice Springs. **Virgin Australia** (www.virginaustralia.com.au; ✆ **136 789** in Australia) flies to Cairns direct from Brisbane, Sydney, and Melbourne. **Jetstar** (www.jetstar.com.au; ✆ **131 538** in Australia) flies from Perth and Adelaide. **Tigerair** (www.tigerair.com.au; ✆ **1300/174 266** in Australia, or 07/3295 2104) flies to Cairns from Brisbane, Melbourne, and

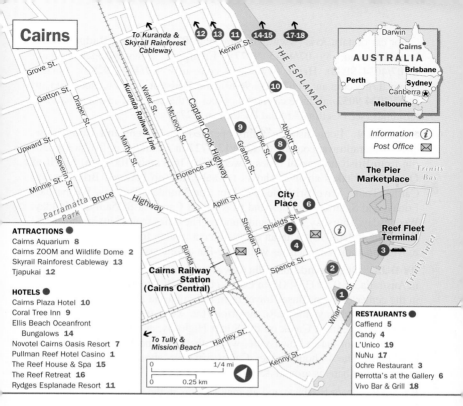

Cairs

To Kuranda & Skyrail Rainforest Cableway

ATTRACTIONS ●
Cairns Aquarium **8**
Cairns ZOOM and Wildlife Dome **2**
Skyrail Rainforest Cableway **13**
Tjapukai **12**

HOTELS ●
Cairns Plaza Hotel **10**
Coral Tree Inn **9**
Ellis Beach Oceanfront
    Bungalows **14**
Novotel Cairns Oasis Resort **7**
Pullman Reef Hotel Casino **1**
The Reef House & Spa **15**
The Reef Retreat **16**
Rydges Esplanade Resort **11**

RESTAURANTS ●
Caffiend **5**
Candy **4**
L'Unico **19**
NuNu **17**
Ochre Restaurant **3**
Perrotta's at the Gallery **6**
Vivo Bar & Grill **18**

Cairns Railway Station (Cairns Central)

To Tully & Mission Beach

The Pier Marketplace

Reef Fleet Terminal

City Place

Information (i)
Post Office ✉

Sydney. **Regional Express**, also known as Rex (www.rex.com.au; ℭ **131 713** in Australia, or 02/6393 5550) flies between Cairns and Townsville. Some international carriers serve Cairns from various Asian cities and New Zealand.

Between the Airport and the City Center

Sun Palm Transport (www.sunpalmtransport.com.au; ℭ **07/4099 1191**) provides transfers from the airport to the city center. The one-way fare is A$16 adults and A$8 children under 12 to Cairns. Sun Palm also offers the **Airport Connect** bus service from the airport to connect you to the Sunbus public transport network on Sheridan Street in the city center. This costs A$6 per person one-way or A$8 round-trip. From there, you can jump on a Sun Bus service to the northern beaches for just a couple of dollars. To catch Airport Connect back to the airport, wait at the C9 bus stop on Sheridan Street (opposite the Tobruk Pool) and hail the driver of the Sun Palm Transport bus. Prebookings can be made online.

A **taxi** from the airport costs around A$30 to the city, A$55 to Trinity Beach, A$75 to Palm Cove, and A$200 to Port Douglas. Call **Cairns Taxis** (ℭ **131 008** in Australia). An airport fee of A$4.40 is added to all pickups at the domestic and international terminals.

For car rentals, **Avis** (www.avis.com.au; ℂ **07/4033 9555**), **Budget** (www.budget.com.au; ℂ **07/4033 9777**), **Europcar** (www.europcar.com.au; ℂ **07/4034 9088**), **Hertz** (www.hertz.com.au; ℂ **07/4035 9299**), **Thrifty** (www.thrifty.com.au; ℂ **07/4033 9800**), and **Redspot** (www.redspot.com.au; ℂ **07/4034 9052**) all have car-rental offices at the domestic and international terminals (see "Getting Around By Car," p. 227).

BY TRAIN Long-distance trains operated by **Queensland Rail** (www.queenslandrailtravel.com.au; ℂ **1300/131 722** in Australia, or 07/3606 6630) run from Brisbane several times a week. The 160kmph (100-mph) **Spirit of Queensland** takes about 24 hours to make the trip between Brisbane and Cairns. Trains leave Brisbane at 3:45pm on Monday, Tuesday, Wednesday, Friday, and Saturday; southbound runs depart Cairns at 8:35am on Monday, Wednesday, Thursday, Friday, and Sunday. The trains feature luxury business-class seating (A$390), with an entertainment system for each seat, including movie and audio channels, as well as lie-flat airline-style "railbeds" (A$519).

BY BUS **Greyhound Australia** (www.greyhound.com.au; ℂ **1300/473 946** in Australia, or 07/4033 4811 in Cairns) buses pull into Trinity Wharf Centre in the center of town. Buses travel from the south via all towns and cities on the Bruce Highway; they also run from the west, from Alice Springs and Darwin, via Tennant Creek on the Stuart Highway, and the Outback mining town of Mount Isa to Townsville, where they join the Bruce Highway and head north. The 48-hour Sydney-Cairns trip costs about A$510; the 29-hour trip from Brisbane is around A$340.

BY CAR From Brisbane and all major towns in the south, you'll approach Cairns on the Bruce Highway. To reach the northern beaches or Port Douglas, take Sheridan Street in the city center, which becomes the Captain Cook Highway.

VISITOR INFORMATION

Cairns has no street-front visitor information center, but **Tourism Tropical North Queensland** has a useful website (www.tropicalnorthqueensland.org.au) that is packed with information for visi-

Croc Alert!

Dangerous crocodiles inhabit Cairns' waterways. Do not swim in or stand on the bank of any river or stream.

tors. Another good source for information on tours and to make bookings is the **Cairns Visitor Centre** (www.cairnsvisitorcentre.com.au; ℂ **07/4036 3341**)—but there is no physical office to drop in to.

CITY LAYOUT

The focal point of the city is the **Esplanade,** which has a 4,000-sq.-m (43,000-sq.-ft.) manmade saltwater swimming lagoon, with a wide, sandy beach and surrounding parkland with public artworks and picnic areas. Suspended over the mud flats and providing a platform for birding, a boardwalk runs 600m (1,968 ft.) along the waterfront and is lit at night. A walkway links the Esplanade to the **Reef Fleet Terminal,** the departure point for Great Barrier Reef boats.

Downtown Cairns is on a grid 5 blocks deep, bounded in the east by the Esplanade and in the west by **McLeod Street,** where the train station and the Cairns Central shopping mall are situated.

Heading 15 minutes north from the city along the Captain Cook Highway, you come to the **northern beaches:** Holloway's Beach, Yorkey's Knob, Trinity Beach, Kewarra Beach, Clifton Beach, Palm Cove, and Ellis Beach.

GETTING AROUND

BY BUS Sunbus (www.sunbus.com.au; ☎ **07/4057 7411**) buses depart Cairns City Mall at the intersection of Lake and Shields streets. Buy all tickets and passes on board, and try to have correct change. The standard fare is A$2.30, or you can travel all day in one zone for A$4.60. Bus no. 110 travels to Palm Cove and no. 111 will take you to Trinity Beach. Routes and timetables change, so check with the driver. Most buses run from around 7am until almost midnight.

BY CAR As well as the car-rental desks in the airport, listed on p. 226, **Avis** (www.avis.com.au; ☎ **07/4048 0522**), **Budget** (www.budget.com.au; ☎ **07/4048 8166**), **Europcar** (www.europcar.com.au; ☎ **07/4033 4800**), and **Thrifty** (www.thrifty.com.au; ☎ **07/4051 8099**) have offices in Cairns city as well. One long-established local outfit, **Sugarland Car Rentals** (www.sugarlandcarrental.com.au; ☎ **07/4052 1300**), has reasonable rates. **Britz Campervan Rentals** (www.britz.com; ☎ **1300/738 087** in Australia, or 07/4032 2611) and **Maui Rentals** (www.maui-rentals.com; ☎ **1800/827 821** in Australia) rent motorhomes.

BY TAXI Call Cairns Taxis (☎ **131 008**).

Where to Stay in Cairns & the Northern Beaches

High season in Cairns includes 2 weeks at Easter, the period from early July to early October, and the Christmas holiday through January. Book ahead in those periods. In low season (Nov–June), many hotels offer discounts or negotiate fees. Cairns has a good supply of affordable accommodations, both in the heart of the city and along the northern beaches. You don't have to stay in Cairns city if you don't have a car—most tour and cruise operators provide transfers.

EXPENSIVE

Pullman Reef Hotel Casino ★★ This stylish seven-story hotel is a block from the water, with Trinity Inlet views from some rooms, and city/hinterland outlooks from others. All the rooms have lots of natural light, high-quality amenities, robes, and small balconies with smart timber furniture. The **Cairns Wildlife Dome** (p. 233) and **Reef Casino** are attached to the hotel. Be aware that there are two Pullman hotels in Cairns (the other is on the next street), which can be confusing even to your taxi driver! The **Tamarind** restaurant is one of Cairns' best dining spots (open daily for dinner).

35–41 Wharf St. www.pullmanhotels.com/2901. ℂ **07/4030 8888.** 128 units. A$284–A$309 double; A$324–A$784 suite. Rates include breakfast. Valet parking A$15. **Amenities:** 5 restaurants; 3 bars; babysitting; concierge; health club; Jacuzzi; small outdoor rooftop pool; room service; sauna; free Wi-Fi.

The Reef House & Spa – M Gallery by Sofitel ★★★

The old colonial-style Reef House has a romantic feel about it—the white walls are swathed in bougainvillea, some rooms have love-seat swings on the veranda, and all are decorated in earthy tones with gold accents. The Verandah spa rooms have a Jacuzzi on the balcony and overlook the pool, waterfalls, and lush gardens. They also come with extra touches, such as bathrobes and balconies within earshot of the ocean. One-, two-, and four-bedroom apartments are also available. Every night at sunset, all the candles throughout the resort are lit, and Brigadier's Punch is served to guests in an old tradition. The beachfront restaurant, on a covered wooden deck beneath towering paperbark trees, is a favorite for locals and tourists alike for its ocean views and gentle breezes.

99 Williams Esplanade, Palm Cove. www.reefhouse.com.au. ℂ **07/4080 2600.** 69 units. A$457–A$672 double; A$597–A$721 1-bedroom apt; A$1,091 2-bedroom apt; A$1,451 4-bedroom apt. Limited free parking; ample street parking. Bus: no. 110. **Amenities:** 2 restaurants; bar; babysitting; concierge; 3 small heated outdoor pools; room service; spa; free Wi-Fi.

MODERATE

Cairns Plaza Hotel ★★

The harbor views at this five-story complex are better than those at most of the more luxurious hotels in Cairns. Two blocks from town, the accommodations are a good size, with fresh, appealing furnishings and modern bathrooms. Suites and studios have kitchenettes. If your balcony does not have a water vista, you overlook a nice aspect of the city or mountains instead. This is a great place for families—most rooms sleep three or four, and if you need more space and privacy, you can book a connecting suite and standard room. A children's playground is located just across the street.

145 The Esplanade (at Minnie St.). www.cairnsplaza.com.au. ℂ **07/4051 4688.** 60 units. A$180–A$210 double; A$280 suite. Limited free parking. **Amenities:** Restaurant (breakfast only); bar; babysitting; Jacuzzi; small outdoor pool; room service; free Wi-Fi (restaurant/lobby and 6th floor only).

Novotel Cairns Oasis Resort ★

The large pool, complete with swim-up bar and a little sandy beach, is the focus of this attractive six-story resort. All the contemporary-style rooms have balconies with views over the tropical gardens, the mountains, or the pool. The suites, with a large Jacuzzi bathtub, could well be the best-value suites in town, and the whole resort was given a makeover in 2019.

122 Lake St. www.novotelcairnsresort.com.au. ℂ **07/4080 1888.** 314 units. A$215–A$295 double; A$375 suite. Parking A$9. **Amenities:** Restaurant; 2 bars; babysitting; concierge; gym; lagoon pool; kids' pool; room service; spa; Wi-Fi (A$12/hr.; A$25/24 hr.).

The Reef Retreat ★★   Tucked back one row of buildings from the beach is this little gem—a collection of contemporary studios and suites built around a swimming pool in a grove of palms and silver paperbark trees. All the rooms have cool tile floors and smart teak and cane furniture. The studios are a terrific value and much larger than the average hotel room. Some suites have two rooms; others have a Jacuzzi and a kitchenette outside on the balcony. Rooms also have iPod docks. There's a barbecue and a Jacuzzi on the grounds, but no elevator.

10–14 Harpa St., Palm Cove. www.reefretreat.com.au. ② **07/4059 1744.** 36 units. A$174–A$190 double; A$190–A$379 suite. Free parking. Bus: no. 110. **Amenities:** Jacuzzi; heated saltwater pool; free Wi-Fi.

Rydges Esplanade Cairns Resort ★★   Despite its lack of glitz, this 14-story hotel has been the lodging of choice for a number of movie stars on location in Cairns. A 20-minute waterfront walk from downtown, the resort offers a range of units, from hotel rooms to penthouse apartments. The one- and two-bedroom apartments face the sea; hotel rooms have sea or mountain views. Kitchenettes are in studios and apartments only. Rooms are spacious, but bathrooms are not. Out back are cheaper studios and apartments, with upgraded furnishings; in front is a pool and sun deck. Family rooms include a queen bed and separate "kids zone" with bunk beds, each featuring a personal 15-inch TV linked to an Xbox. On-site are a masseuse and a tour desk.

209 Abbott St. (at Kerwin St.). www.rydges.com. ② **07/4044 9000.** 240 units. A$197–A$345 double; A$278 family room; A$482–A$500 2-bedroom apt. Free covered parking. Bus stop about 100m (328 ft.) from the hotel. **Amenities:** 2 restaurants; 3 bars; airport transfers; babysitting; bikes; concierge; health club; Jacuzzi; 3 outdoor pools; room service; sauna; 2 lighted tennis courts; free Wi-Fi.

INEXPENSIVE

Coral Tree Inn ★   The focal point of this airy, modern resort-style motel—a 5-minute walk from the city center—is the friendly communal kitchen that overlooks the palm-lined saltwater pool and paved sun deck. It's a great spot to cook a steak or reef fish on the free barbecue and join other guests at the big shared tables. The smallish, basic-but-neat motel rooms have painted brick walls, terra-cotta tile or carpeted floors, and new bathrooms with marble-look laminate countertops. In contrast, the eight suites, which have kitchenettes, are huge and stylish—and some of the best-value rooms in town. All rooms have a balcony or patio; some overlook the commercial buildings next door, but most face the pool. Ask about packages that include cruises and other tours.

166–172 Grafton St. www.coraltreeinn.com.au. ② **07/4031 3744.** 58 units. A$222–A$242 double; A$231 family room; A$214 suite. Limited free parking; ample street parking. **Amenities:** Restaurant; bar; airport shuttle; babysitting; bike rental; outdoor saltwater pool; free Wi-Fi.

Ellis Beach Oceanfront Bungalows ★★   Set on what is arguably the loveliest of the northern beaches, about 30 minutes from Cairns, these

The **Spirit of Freedom** (www.spiritof
freedom.com.au; ℂ **07/4047 9150**) in
Cairns offers a chance to "sleep on the
Reef" aboard the 36m (120-ft.) *Spirit of
Freedom,* a sleek, modern motor yacht
with electronic stabilizers, a widescreen
TV with DVD player, comfortable
lounge areas, sun decks, and 11 luxury
double or quad shared cabins, each
with an en-suite bathroom. You will visit
the popular Cod Hole and Ribbon Reef
and on longer trips venture into the
Coral Sea. A 3-day, 3-night trip will cost
A$1,850 to A$2,700 depending on your
choice of cabin and ends with a 193km
(120-mile) one-way, 1-hour, low-level
flight from Lizard Island back to Cairns.
You can fit in up to 11 dives. Prices
include meals and pickup from your
Cairns accommodations. Allow A$130
extra for equipment rental. Additional
4- and 7-day cruises are offered, the
latter a combination of both shorter
trips.

bungalows and cabins sit under palm trees between the Coral Sea and a backdrop of mountainous rainforest. Lifeguards patrol the beach, and there are
stinger nets in season as well as a shady pool and a toddlers' wading pool.
You'll have plenty of privacy, and rooms are basic but pleasant. As you sit on
your veranda and gaze at the ocean, keep an eye out for dolphins. Each bungalow and cabin sleeps two or four and has kitchen facilities (with microwave,
fridge, and freezer), but cabins have no en-suite bathrooms (they have use of
the communal facilities at the campground in the same complex). Beachfront
bungalows are the priciest; those behind them are slightly cheaper. The property has a laundry, coin-operated barbecues, and a public phone you can use
(but no phone in your room—and no Wi-Fi).

Captain Cook Hwy., Ellis Beach. www.ellisbeach.com. ℂ **1800/637 036** in Australia, or
07/4055 3538. 15 units. A$95–A$115 double cabin; A$150–A$210 double bungalow or
studio. 2-night minimum stay; 3-night minimum June–Sept. Free parking. **Amenities:**
Restaurant; bar; laundry; 2 outdoor pools; no Wi-Fi.

Where to Eat in Cairns

For cheap eats, head to the Esplanade along the seafront; it's lined with cafes,
pizzerias, fish-and-chips shops, food courts, and ice-cream parlors. The northern beaches—particularly Palm Cove—also have some great restaurants
(sometimes with prices to match!).

EXPENSIVE

NuNu ★★★ CONTEMPORARY With an absolute-beachfront location
under the palm trees, this Palm Cove favorite offers the kind of food that
makes you drag your eyes from the view to your plate. Dining fare includes
some bold choices, such as pork belly in a pineapple and turmeric curry, cin-
namon-roasted lamb, or the pricey (A$125) Queensland mud crab with a
tamarind and ginger broth. The menu changes seasonally, and you can always
count on some surprises. To savor a bit of everything, NuNu offers four- and

seven-course tasting menus (A$89 and A$129 per person respectively). You could easily settle in here for hours.

1 Veivers Rd., Palm Cove (in the Alamanda Resort). www.nunu.com.au. ℭ **07/4059 1880.** Main courses A$45–A$125. Daily 7am–4pm and 5pm–late. Bus: no. 110.

MODERATE

L'Unico ★★ ITALIAN   Ask for a table on the veranda, overlooking Trinity Beach's esplanade and the sea. This smart but relaxed Italian eatery has a great vibe and terrific staff. A wood-fired oven produces pizzas with unexpected toppings (such as lamb with caramelized onion, tomato, and spinach), and the kitchen makes good use of local ingredients in all dishes (the angel-hair pasta with Moreton Bay bugs—that would be seafood—with chili, garlic, and white wine is one of my favorite dishes here). The cocktail bar offers a bar menu throughout the day, and there's a kids' menu, too.

75 Vasey Esplanade, Trinity Beach. www.lunico.com.au. ℭ **07/4057 8855.** Main courses A$24–A$46. Sat–Mon 8–11am; daily noon–3:30pm and 5:30–9:30pm. Bus: no. 110.

Ochre Restaurant ★★ GOURMET BUSH TUCKER   With a fabulous waterfront location, this Cairns institution is the place to visit if you want a taste of crocodile or kangaroo. You could accuse this restaurant/bar of using weird and wonderful Aussie ingredients as a gimmick, but the diners who have flocked to Ochre for more than a decade know good food when they taste it. Daily specials are big on fresh local seafood, and the regular menu changes often. There may be ingredients you've never heard of—but this is a place to be adventurous! Try salt-and-native-pepper crocodile and prawns with Vietnamese pickles and lemon aspen sambal; chargrilled kangaroo sirloin with a quandong chili glaze, sweet potato mash, and bok choy; or wallaby filet with puffed amaranth, chimichurri, green tomato, and salt bush. It can be very busy, and you may have to wait for a table, but the food is very good.

1 Marlin Parade, Cairns. www.ochrerestaurant.com.au. ℭ **07/4051 0100.** Main courses A$18–A$46. Australian game platter A$54 per person; seafood platter A$76 per person; 4-course set menu A$70 per person (minimum 2 people). Daily 11:30am–9:30pm.

Vivo Bar and Grill ★★★ CONTEMPORARY   Done in a white-painted colonial style, complete with wooden shutters and a wide veranda, this is an inviting choice, looking through the palm trees to the water. There's a touch of the exotic about Vivo's beautifully presented food: at breakfast, a Vietnamese crepe with tiger prawns, or an Indonesian-style nasi goreng; at lunch, a duck crepe made with coconut and coriander, or soft-shell crab with Asian slaw and soba noodles. At dinner choose from the tempting pasta dishes (such as spanner crab linguine) or something heavier like a Wagyu eye filet steak. Vivo also serves a tapas menu of tasty bites, from duck dumplings and barramundi spring rolls to spiced baby calamari.

49 Williams Esplanade, Palm Cove. www.vivo.com.au. ℭ **07/4059 0944.** Main courses A$33–A$54. Daily 7am–10pm. Bus: nos. 110 or 111.

INEXPENSIVE

Caffiend ★★ CAFE   Tucked away between an alley full of street art and an arcade, this atmospheric little cafe is easy to miss. I first found it after being tipped off by a friend, and headed here for what I'd been told was the best coffee in Cairns (it's roasted in house). The menu was so appealing I ended up staying for lunch! A Katz-inspired Reuben sandwich, sushi bowl with brown rice, baked tofu, and avocado, and chili poached eggs, among other delicious eats, are on a menu that changes monthly—but don't forget to check the specials board. The breakfast menu offers some unusual dishes, such as miso-infused scrambled eggs, and pan-fried mushrooms with buffalo feta. The café hosts regular art exhibitions.

Shop 5, 78 Grafton St., Cairns. www.caffiend.com.au. ℂ **07/4051 5522.** Main courses A$16–A$24. Daily 7am–3pm.

Candy ★★ CAFE   Huge murals and dangling chandeliers give this quirky little cafe/bar an offbeat but sophisticated feel. A tip from a local—and yes, the coffee here is good—led me to this standout on the Grafton Street cafe strip. Candy is a popular breakfast spot, offering the usual range of eggs, avocado on toast with feta cheese, sweet corn fritters, and pancakes. For lunch, you might go for something like a burger or a healthy salmon and avocado salad.

70 Grafton St., Cairns. www.facebook.com/candycairns. ℂ **07/4031 8816.** Main courses A$10–A$20. Mon–Fri 6am–4pm; Sat 6am–3pm; Sun 7am–2pm.

Perrotta's at the Gallery ★★ CONTEMPORARY   Locals flock here for brunch and lunch, particularly on weekends, and you can team a meal here with a visit to the Cairns Regional Art Gallery next door. Breakfast differs from the usual, offering delights such as strawberry ricotta pancakes with pistachios and lemon syrup. The all-day menu includes bruschetta, burgers, pizza, salads, and pasta, or mains such as fish tacos (Spanish mackerel with avocado and Italian-style coleslaw), or spaghetti with prawns—and perhaps a vanilla-bean panna cotta with mango for dessert.

Abbott and Shields sts., Cairns. www.perrottasatg.com. ℂ **07/4031 5899.** Breakfast A$5–A$23; main courses A$19–A$28. Daily 6:30am–10pm.

Exploring Cairns

Many of the Cairns region's attractions lie outside the city center. Apart from the Reef, there is a string of white sandy beaches just 15 minutes north of the city center. **Trinity Beach,** 15 minutes from the airport or 25 minutes from the city center, is secluded, elegant, and scenic. The most upscale is **Palm Cove,** 20 minutes from the airport or 30 minutes from the city. If you're staying in Cairns, also check out activities in and around Port Douglas (p. 244). Many tour operators in Port Douglas offer transfers from Cairns. Ask about packages that include discounted entry when you visit several of Cairns' attractions, such as Tjapukai Aboriginal Cultural Park, Cairns Tropical Zoo, Skyrail, and Kuranda Scenic Rail.

Cairns Aquarium ★★ AQUARIUM   This world-class aquarium, one of Cairns' newest attractions, is dedicated to the animals and habitats found only in Australia's Wet Tropics and the Great Barrier Reef. Over three levels, the 16m-high (52-ft.) building houses 15,000 animals from 10 different ecosystems and 71 habitats in Tropical North Queensland. A program of talks is offered every half-hour from 9:30am to 4pm, where you can also touch some of the creatures on display. You can ride a submarine simulator through an animated underwater world or take a behind-the-scenes tour that includes a visit to the **Cairns Turtle Rehabilitation Centre.** The aquarium restaurant (accessible from Abbott St.) has its own 70,000-liter shark tank to keep you mesmerized while eating.

5 Florence St. www.cairnsaquarium.com.au. © **07/4044 7300.** A$42 adults, A$28 children 3–14, A$88–A$126 families. Daily 9am–5pm (last entry 4pm).

Cairns ZOOM and Wildlife Dome ★★ WILDLIFE VIEWING/ ATTRACTION   Here, 200 animals—including a large saltwater crocodile named Goliath—are housed in a 20m-high (66-ft.) glass dome on the rooftop of the Pullman Reef Hotel Casino (p. 227). Birds soar overhead, and you can get up close with koalas, lizards, frogs, pademelons, turtles, and snakes. There are wildlife presentations and free, guided tours throughout the day. For A$28 (pay when you buy your entry ticket), you can have a photo taken with a koala, snake, or baby croc. Thrill-seekers can zipline through the dome, "climb" around its exterior, or do other adrenaline-charged activities (for an extra cost).

35–41 Wharf St. www.cairnszoom.com.au. © **07/4031 7250.** A$25 adults, A$13 children 4–14, A$63 family. Tickets are valid for reentry for up to 4 days. Daily 9am–6:15pm (last entry 5pm). Closed Dec 25.

Skyrail Rainforest Cableway ★★★ ATTRACTION/RIDE   This magnificent feat of engineering is one of Australia's top tourist attractions. Six-person gondolas leave every few seconds from Cairns for the 7.5km (4½-mile) journey to the rainforest village of Kuranda (p. 240). The view of the coast as you ascend is so breathtaking that even those afraid of heights should find it worthwhile. As you rise over the foothills of the coastal range, watch the lush green of the rainforest take over beneath you. Looking back, you have spectacular views over Cairns and north toward Trinity Bay. On a clear day, you can see…if not forever, then at least to Green Island. Take a Diamond View gondola for even better views—looking down, between your feet through the glass floor. This slightly more expensive option (A$20 extra per adult, A$10 per child one-way) also gives you a dedicated boarding queue—and shorter wait—at all stations. If you're really fearless, the **Canopy Glider** is an open-air option, where for A$110 extra per person (one-way) four passengers and a ranger guide travel in an open gondola.

There are two stops during the 90-minute trip, at Red Peak and Barron Falls. After about 10 minutes, you reach Red Peak. You are now 545m (1,788 ft.) above sea level, and massive kauri pines dominate the view. You must change gondolas at each station, so take the time to stroll around the boardwalks for the ground view of the rainforest. Free, guided walks run regularly throughout the day. On board again, you continue on to Barron Falls station, built on the site of an old construction camp for workers on the first hydroelectric power station on the Barron River in the 1930s. A rainforest information center is here, as well as boardwalks to the lookouts for wonderful views of the Barron Gorge and Falls. From Barron Falls station, the gondola travels over the thick rainforest of the range. As you reach the end of the trip, the gondola passes over the Barron River and across the Kuranda railway line into the station. Don't worry if it rains on the day you go—one of the best trips of several I've made on Skyrail was in a misty rain, which added a new dimension to the rainforest.

Tip: For a wonderful day trip from Cairns I strongly recommend that you combine Skyrail with a trip on the **Kuranda Scenic Rail** (p. 241). The best way is to take the train from Cairns in the morning and return on Skyrail in the afternoon—for the views going down the range.

Cairns Western Arterial Rd. and Captain Cook Hwy., Smithfield. www.skyrail.com.au. © **07/4038 5555.** Round-trip ticket A$105 adults, A$53 children, A$263 families, including transfers from Cairns or northern beaches hotels. Daily 9am–5:15pm. Closed Dec 25. You must make a reservation to travel within a 15-min. time frame. Last boardings at 2:45pm for a round-trip or 3:30pm for a one-way journey. Bus: no. 123.

Tjapukai ★★ INTERACTIVE ENTERTAINMENT Tjapukai (pronounced Jab-oo-*guy*) offers indigenous experiences in an all-weather venue. This Aboriginal cultural park uses cutting-edge theater technology and an open-plan glass design to showcase the park's rainforest. Two state-of-the-art theater spaces—History and Hero's Walk—and a restaurant and outdoor bar complement the interactive cultural village, where you can try your hand at fire-making, didgeridoo playing, and boomerang and spear throwing, and learn about bush foods, medicines, and hunting techniques. In addition to Aboriginal culture, the Torres Strait Islander dance is part of the Tjapukai experience. Allow 2 to 3 hours to see everything (although you could spend longer here). Start in the **Creation Theatre,** where performers use the latest in illusion, theatrics, and technology to tell the story of the creation of the world according to the spiritual beliefs of Tjapukai people. Move on through the **Magic Space** museum and gallery section of the complex to the **History Theatre,** where a 20-minute film relates the history of the Tjapukai people since the arrival of white settlers 120 years ago.

Art of My People is a performance that explains the varying styles of Australian Indigenous art, including the role of totems, body-painting traditions, and differing types of artistic expression used to identify tribes, languages, dialects, and geographical landscapes. A gallery stocks the work of Aboriginal artists and crafts workers.

Night Fire by Tjapukai tours include interactive time in the Magic Space museum, a Creation Show performance, and an outdoor Serpent Circle—a show featuring tap sticks for each guest to use, a join-in *corroboree* (an

Kuranda Scenic Rail train.

Aboriginal nighttime dance), and a ceremony involving fire and water. A buffet dinner and dance show follow, where you get the chance to meet the dancers.

4 Skyrail Dr., Caravonica (beside the Skyrail terminal). www.tjapukai.com.au. © **07/4042 9999.** A$62 adults, A$42 children 5–14, A$166 families. Daily 9am–4:30pm. Night Fire tours (daily 7–9:30pm) A$150 adults, A$90 children, A$390 families including transfers to/from Cairns. Ask about packages with other attractions. Closed Dec 25. Bus: no. 123. Tjapukai shuttle: A$28 adults, A$18 children, and A$91 families round-trip.

Outlying Attractions

Hartley's Crocodile Adventures ★★★ ENTERTAINMENT   Hartley's is the original Australian croc show and quite possibly the best. Its fantastic natural setting is a 2-hectare (5-acre) lagoon surrounded by melaleuca (paperbark) and bloodwood trees that is home to 23 estuarine crocs. The best time to visit is for the 3pm "croc attack" show, when you can witness the saltwater crocodile "death roll" during the 45-minute performance. At 11am you can see these monsters being hand-fed or hear an eye-opening talk on the less-aggressive freshwater crocs.

You can also have a **"Big Croc Experience,"** where you get to pole-feed a large crocodile yourself—and believe me, this is the way to feel the sheer power of these creatures as they tug the chicken off the pole. Available twice a day at 10:30am and 1pm (bookings essential), you'll be one of four adults (16 and over) to take part in each group (but your friends and family can come along to watch). The cost is A$135 per person. From October to April, the whole family can take part in "freshie feeding" of the smaller freshwater crocs, after the 11am croc feeding, for A$15 per person. There are tours of the

235

Wildlife Passes

Wildlife enthusiasts who plan to visit several of the attractions in the Cairns region can save a few dollars by buying a **Four Park Pass,** which gives entry to the Cairns ZOOM and Wildlife Dome, the Wildlife Habitat at Port Douglas, and two Kuranda attractions (see "Day Trip to Kuranda," p. 240): the Rainforestation Nature Park and the Australian Butterfly Sanctuary (all owned by the same local family). The discounted price of A$95 adults, A$48 children, and A$238 for a family of four is a savings of A$38 per adult or A$96 per family. Buy it at any of the participating parks. A **Kuranda Wildlife Experience pass** offers discounted admission to Birdworld, the Kuranda Koala Gardens, and the Australian Butterfly Sanctuary (p. 242). It can be bought at any of the three sanctuaries for A$51 adults, A$26 for children 4 to 15.

croc farm at 10am and 1:30pm; at 2pm there is a snake show; 4:30pm is koala-feeding time. Cassowaries are fed at 9:30am and 4:15pm. There are also croc- and snake-handling opportunities and heaps of other interesting things to see and do.

Captain Cook Hwy. (40km/24 miles north of Cairns; about 100m [109 yds.] off the high-way). www.crocodileadventures.com. © **07/4055 3576.** A$41 adults, A$21 children 4–15, A$103 families of 4 (admission good for 3 days). Daily 8:30am–5pm. Closed Dec 25.

Day Trips from Cairns to the Reef ★★★

For an introduction to the Great Barrier Reef, most visitors take one of the large-scale tour boats. These motorized catamarans can carry up to 300 passengers each and tie up at their own private, permanent pontoons anchored to a platform reef. The boats are air-conditioned and have a bar, videos, and educational material, as well as a marine biologist who gives a talk on the Reef's ecology en route. The pontoons have glass-bottom boats for passengers who don't want to get wet, dry underwater viewing chambers, sun decks, shaded seats, and often showers. But be aware that you will be in a crowded environment. And if you are prone to seasickness, make sure you take preventive measures before you set out!

An alternative is to go on one of the many smaller boats. These typically visit two or three Reef sites rather than just one. There are usually no more than 20 passengers on board, so you get more personal attention. Another advantage is that you will have the coral pretty much all to yourself. The drawbacks of a small boat are that you have only the cramped deck to sit on when you get out of the water, and your traveling time to the Reef may be longer. If you're a nervous snorkeler, you may feel safer on a boat where you will be swimming with 300 other people.

Most day-trip fares include snorkel gear—fins, mask, and snorkel (plus wetsuits in winter, if you want one)—free use of the underwater viewing chambers and glass-bottom-boat rides, a plentiful buffet or barbecue lunch, and morning and afternoon refreshments. Diving is an optional activity for which you pay extra. The big boats post snorkeling scouts to keep a lookout for anyone in trouble and count heads periodically. If you wear glasses, ask whether your boat offers prescription masks—this will make a big difference to the quality of your experience. Don't forget that you can travel as a snorkel-only passenger on most dive boats, too.

Great Adventures ★ (www.greatadventures.com.au; © **07/4044 9944**) does daily cruises from Cairns on fast, air-conditioned catamarans that take you to a three-level pontoon on the Outer Reef. The pontoon has a kids' swimming area, a semisubmersible, and an underwater observatory. The cost for the day is A$250 for adults, A$136 for children 4 to 14, and A$643 for families. You spend at least 3 hours on the Reef. Hotel transfers are available from Cairns, the northern beaches, and Port Douglas for an extra cost. The boat departs the Reef Fleet Terminal at 10:30am.

You can also depart Cairns with Great Adventures at 8:30am and spend 2 hours on Green Island en route. This gives you time to walk nature trails, rent snorkel gear and watersports equipment, or laze on the beach before continuing to the Outer Reef. This cruise costs an extra A$20 per person, or A$50 per family.

Ocean Freedom ★★★ (www.oceanfreedom.com.au; © **07/4052 1111**) offers a more intimate experience, giving you the option of a motor cruise or a sailing tour—in both cases with limited numbers to ensure you don't feel crowded. *Ocean Freedom* is a high-speed launch that gives you 6 hours on the reef with no more than 75 passengers and takes you to two Reef sites including Upolu Cay. The day starts at 7:30am at the Reef Fleet Terminal, returning about 4:30pm. The cost is A$220 adults, A$135 children, and A$647 for a family of four and includes glass-bottom-boat rides, all snorkeling gear, and lunch. You can do an introductory dive for A$105 (and a second one for A$50); if you are certified you can dive for A$70 (and a second one for A$35). This is a great way to see the Reef. On the sailing trip aboard *Ocean Free* (www.oceanfree.com.au) you'll be one of only 25 passengers. *Ocean Free* sails at 7:30am, bound for Pinnacle Reef, an exclusive mooring on the eastern lee of Green Island. Prices are the same as *Ocean Freedom.*

Packaging Your Day Trip

Several options exist for a 1-day Cairns adventure. A package combining one-way travel on Skyrail (p. 241) and a trip back on the Kuranda Scenic Railway (p. 241) is A$128 for adults, A$64 for children 4 to 14, and A$320 for families of four with round-trip transfers from Cairns or the northern beaches. A package including the Skyrail, the Scenic Railway, and entry to the Tjapukai Aboriginal cultural park (p. 234) is A$179 for adults, A$100 for kids, and A$457 for families of four. An option including the Skyrail, Scenic Railway, and Rainforestation Nature Park (p. 243) is A$180 for adults, A$90 for kids, and A$450 for families of four. In most cases, these packages represent convenience rather than savings. Book them through Skyrail, Queensland Rail, or Tjapukai.

Ocean Spirit Cruises ★★ (www.oceanspirit.com.au; *©* **07/4044 9944**) operates a 32m (105-ft.) luxury sailing catamaran that takes no more than 150 passengers to Michaelmas Cay, a lovely white-sand cay on the Outer Reef surrounded by rich reefs. This trip includes a 2-hour sail to the cay, snorkeling gear, and a guided beach walk—plus the usual reef ecology talks, semisubmersible rides, lunch, and morning and afternoon tea. You get about 4 hours on the Reef and spend your out-of-water time on a beautiful beach, not on a boat. The cost is A$219 adults, A$115 children 4 to 14, and A$570 for families of four. If you'd like a guided snorkeling safari rather than going it alone, add A$66 adults, A$34 children, or A$166 family. Introductory dives cost A$132 with all gear included. The trip departs Reef Fleet Terminal at 8:30am daily and returns around 5pm. Transfers from Cairns hotels are A$29 adults and A$19 kids; from the northern beaches it's A$26 adults, A$20 kids.

Sunlover Reef Cruises ★ (www.sunlover.com.au; *©* **07/4050 1333**) motors large, fast catamarans to Moore Reef on the Outer Reef. The trip costs A$234 for adults, A$139 for children 4 to 15, and A$607 for families of four, including 4 hours on the Reef, a glass-bottom-boat ride, and semisubmersible viewing. Moore Reef's pontoon includes a special children's swimming area and an 8m (26-ft.) waterslide. Introductory dives cost A$149; certified divers pay A$99, including all gear. The cruise includes lunch and leaves from the Reef Fleet Terminal in Cairns at 10am daily. Sunlover also operates an

Helicopter ride over Moore Reef.

Diving Made Easy

Can't swim? Don't want to get your hair wet? Don't worry—you can still get underwater and see the wonders of the Reef. Several companies offer travelers the chance to don a dive helmet and "walk" underwater. Similar to old-style diving helmets, which allow you to breathe underwater, the helmet has air pumped into it by a hose. You walk into the water to a depth of about 4m (13 ft.), accompanied by instructors, and the Reef is right before you. **Quicksilver Cruises** (p. 249) calls it "Ocean Walker"; with **Sunlover Reef Cruises** (p. 238) and at **Green Island Resort** (p. 240) it's called "Sea Walker." You must be at least 12 years old to walk (A$159–A$177/20 min.).

overnight "sleep on the reef" where you can stay on its Moore Reef pontoon, have a barbecue dinner, watch the sunset, and star-gaze before sleeping in a swag (a kind of sleeping bag) on the deck. It costs A$549 per person (no children under 12), with a minimum of four bookings needed.

You can also take a coach transfer from Cairns or Palm Cove to Port Douglas to join the **Quicksilver *Wavepiercer*** (www.quicksilver-cruises.com; ✆ **07/4087 2100**) for a day trip to the Outer Reef; see p. 249 for more details. Transfers from Cairns to Port Douglas cost A$33 per adult or A$17 per child, A$83 for families of four.

Great Adventures, Quicksilver, and Sunlover all offer helicopter flights over the Reef from their pontoons—a spectacular experience! There are fly-and-cruise trips as well.

FOR DIVERS

Tusa Dive ★★ (www.tusadive.com; ✆ **07/4047 9100**) runs a custom-built 24m (72-ft.) dive boat daily to two dive sites from a choice of 15 locations on the Outer Reef. The day costs A$270 for certified divers, or A$300 for two dives and A$320 for three dives. Introductory divers pay A$290 for one dive or A$345 for two. Snorkelers pay A$220 adults and A$145 children age 4 to 14, with wetsuits, guided snorkel tours, and lunch provided. Transfers from your Cairns or northern beaches hotel cost A$18 or A$25 per person, respectively. The boat takes a maximum of 60 people, with a staff-to-passenger ratio of one to five, so you get a good level of personal attention.

Day Trips from Cairns to the Islands

Cairns has several coral cays and reef-fringed islands within the **Great Barrier Reef Marine Park.** Less than an hour from the city wharf, **Fitzroy Island** is a rainforest-covered national park, with a coral beach and great snorkeling right off the shore. **Green Island** is a coral cay with snorkeling equal to that of most other places on the Great Barrier Reef. It is also a popular diving spot. You can visit it in half a day if time is short.

Fitzroy Island ★★★ This scenic island is 45 minutes from Cairns by boat. The island has a small resort, and day-trippers visit for snorkeling and diving, glass-bottom-boat rides, watersports, rainforest walks, or hikes to the lighthouse at the top of the hill. The **Fitzroy Island Fast Cat** ferry to the island leaves Cairns' Marlin Marina at 8am, 11am, and 1:30pm daily, leaving Fitzroy Island for the return trip at 12:15pm and 5pm. The fare is A$78 adults, A$39 for kids 4 to 13, or A$205 for a family round-trip; for a little extra you can add glass-bottom-boat rides or snorkel gear to the package. A kiosk on the beach rents out snorkeling gear, coral viewing boards, paddle skis, and stand-up paddling boards, or you can book a glass-bottom-boat tour. The **Cairns Turtle Rehabilitation Centre (CTRC)** on the island is also worth visiting.

Raging Thunder Adventures (www.ragingthunder.com.au; © **07/4030 7990**) runs activities including snorkeling, paddle-boarding, a glass bottom boat, and an ocean trampoline. Prices include lunch and the Raging Thunder ferry to the island, and start from A$120 adults, A$80 children 4 to 14, or A$343 for a family of four.

www.fitzroyislandcairns.com.

Green Island ★★ This 15-hectare (37-acre) coral cay is just 27km (17 miles) east of Cairns. You can rent snorkel gear, windsurfers, and paddle skis; take glass-bottom-boat trips; go parasailing; take an introductory or certified dive; walk vine-forest trails; or laze on the beach. The beach is coral sand, so it's a little rough underfoot. Day visitors have access to one of the **Green Island Resort** (www.greenislandresort.com.au) pools, its main bar, casual or upscale restaurants, and lockers and showers. Ask the beach staff to recommend the best snorkeling spots. The island is home to **Marineland Crocodile Park** (www.greenislandcrocs.com.au; © **07/4051 4032**), where you can see old nautical artifacts, a Melanesian artifacts collection, a turtle and reef aquarium, and live crocodiles, including Cassius, who—at almost 5.5m (18 ft.) in length—is listed by Guinness World Records as the largest croc in captivity in the world. Admission is A$20 adults, A$9.50 kids 5 to 14. Crocodile Park is open daily 9:30am to 4pm; croc shows are at 10:30am and 1:30pm.

Great Adventures (www.greatadventures.com.au; © **07/4044 9944**) and **Big Cat Green Island Reef Cruises** (www.greenisland.com.au; © **07/4051 0444**) run to Green Island from Cairns. Both offer a range of half-day and full-day trips with lots of options. Half-day trips with snorkel gear or a glass-bottom-boat cruise cost around A$99 adults, A$52 children 4 to 14, or A$250 for a family of four. Both tours offer pickup from hotels in Cairns, the northern beaches, and Port Douglas for a fee.

www.greenislandcairns.com.

Day Trip from Cairns to Kuranda ★★

34km (21 miles) NW of Cairns

Few travelers visit Cairns without making a trip to the mountain village of **Kuranda,** near the Barron Gorge National Park. Although it's undeniably touristy, the cool mountain air and mist-wrapped rainforest refuse to be

Kuranda mountain village is known for its local crafts market.

spoiled, no matter how many tourists clutter the streets. The shopping in Kuranda—for leather goods, Australian-wool sweaters, opals, crafts, and more—is more unusual than in Cairns and the handful of cafes and restaurants much more atmospheric. The town is easy to negotiate on foot; pick up a visitors' guide and map at the Skyrail gondola station or train station. Aside from the village, you can explore the rainforest, the river esplanade, or Barron Falls along a number of easy walking trails.

ESSENTIALS
Getting There
Getting to Kuranda is part of the fun. Some people drive up the winding 25km (16-mile) mountain road, but the most popular approaches are to chuff up the mountainside in a scenic train or to glide silently over the rainforest canopy in the world's longest gondola cableway, the **Skyrail Rainforest Cableway**. The most popular round-trip is one-way on the Skyrail and the return on the train. Mornings are best for photography on Skyrail, but the view is spectacular coming down in the afternoon. Make up your own mind; both are wonderful!

BY SKYRAIL   The **Skyrail Rainforest Cableway** (p. 233) takes you up the Kuranda Range in a six-person gondola suspended over the rainforest.

BY TRAIN   The 34km (21-mile) **Kuranda Scenic Railway** (www.ksr.com. au; ℂ **1800/577 245** in Australia, or 07/4036 9333) is one of the most scenic rail journeys in the world. The train snakes through the magnificent vistas of the Barron Gorge National Park, past gorges and waterfalls on the 90-minute trip from Cairns to Kuranda. It rises 328m (1,076 ft.) and goes through 15 tunnels before emerging at the pretty Kuranda station, which is smothered in ferns. Built by hand over 5 years in the late 1880s, the railway track is today a monument to the 1,500 men who toiled to link the two towns. The train departs Cairns Central at 8:30 and 9:30am daily (except Christmas Day) and leaves Kuranda at 2 and 3:30pm. The one-way fare is A$50 for adults, A$25 for children 4 to 14, and A$125 for families of four. An upgrade to "Gold Class" (A$99 adults, A$74 children, A$321 for a family) adds snacks, drinks, and waiter service.

BY BUS   **Trans North Bus & Coach Service** (www.transnorthbus.com; *©* **07/4095 8644**) operates a bus to Kuranda from Cairns five times a day. The fare is A$6.70 one-way. *Tip:* Buying a return ticket will give you priority if the bus is full at the end of the day. Catch it at Orchid Plaza shopping center (79 Abbott St.), at the railway station, or at the Cairns Central train station.

Visitor Information

The **Kuranda Visitor Information Centre** (www.kuranda.org; *©* **07/4093 9311**) is in Centenary Park, at the top end of Coondoo Street. It is open 10am to 4pm daily, except Christmas Day.

EXPLORING KURANDA

Kuranda is known for its markets. The **Kuranda Original Rainforest Markets,** at 7 Therwine St. (enter through the Kuranda Market Mall; (www.kurandaoriginalrainforestmarket.com.au; *©* **07/4093 9440;** daily 9:30am–3pm), are devoted exclusively to local artisans who vend fashion, jewelry, leather work, and indigenous art, as well local produce including honey, coffee, fruit, sugarcane juice, coconuts, and macadamias.

The 90-stall **Kuranda Heritage Markets** (www.kurandamarkets.com.au; *©* **07/4093 8060**) is open daily from 9:30am to 3:30pm on Rob Veivers Drive, with a range of souvenirs, food, produce, and crafts.

A group of about 50 local artisans sell their work in the **Kuranda Co-Operative** gallery on Coondoo Street, opposite the church (www.kurandaartscoop.com; *©* **07/4093 9026**). It's open from 10am to 4pm daily. The gallery sells furniture crafted from recycled Australian hardwoods, jewelry, photography, glasswork, and more.

Australian Butterfly Sanctuary ★★ NATURE CENTER   The fluttering array of 1,500 colorful tropical butterflies—including the electric-blue Ulysses and Australia's largest species, the Cairns bird wing—occupies a lush walk-through enclosure here. They may keep you entranced for hours (I was!). Take the free 30-minute guided tour and learn about the butterfly's fascinating life cycle. The butterflies will land on you if you wear pink, red, and other bright colors.

8 Rob Veivers Dr. www.australianbutterflies.com. *©* **07/4093 7575.** A$20 adults, A$10 children 4–15, A$50 families of 4. Daily 9:45am–4pm. Closed Dec 25.

Birdworld ★ NATURE CENTER   Behind the markets off Rob Veivers Drive, Birdworld has eye-catching macaws, a pair of cassowaries, and

Australia's largest collection of free-flying birds—about 500 of them, representing 75 worldwide species. Two lakes are home to water birds including stilts, herons, and Australia's black swan.

Rob Veivers Dr. www.birdworldkuranda.com. © **07/4093 9188.** A$19 adults, A$9.50 children 4–15. Daily 9am–4pm. Closed Dec 25.

Kuranda Koala Gardens ★ WILDLIFE VIEWING   You can cuddle a koala and have your photo taken at this small wildlife park next to the Heritage Markets. Other animals include freshwater crocodiles, wombats, lizards, and wallabies. Or take a stroll through the walk-through snake enclosure while they slither at your feet—not for the fainthearted.

Rob Veivers Dr. www.koalagardens.com. © **07/4093 9953.** A$19 adults, A$9.50 kids 4–15. Daily 9am–4pm. Closed Dec 25.

Kuranda Riverboat Tours ★★ BOAT RIDE   If you want to learn about the rainforest, take one of these informative 45-minute river cruises. Cruises depart five times a day from 10:45am from the riverside landing across the footbridge, near the train station, and are the only ones with rights to operate on the Barron River. A team of local naturalists will answer your questions and point out some of the rainforest secrets. Buy your tickets online or pay onboard (cash only). The last cruise of the day returns in time for the 3:30pm train to Cairns.

Rob Veivers Dr. www.kurandariverboat.com.au. A$20 adults, A$10 children 5–15, A$50 family of 4.

Rainforestation Nature Park ★★ NATURE CENTER/TOUR   At this 40-hectare (99-acre) nature and cultural complex, you can take a 45-minute ride into the rainforest in a World War II amphibious Army Duck. You'll hear commentary on orchids and other rainforest wildlife along the way. You can also see a performance by Aboriginal dancers; learn about Aboriginal legends and throw a boomerang on the Dreamtime Walk; or have your photo taken cuddling a koala or holding a small freshwater crocodile in the wildlife park (photos extra, from A$22). The Army Duck runs on the hour, beginning at 10am; the Aboriginal dancers perform at 10:30am, noon, and 2pm; and the 30-minute Dreamtime Walk leaves at 10, 11, and 11:30am, and 12:30, 1:30, and 2:30pm.

Kennedy Hwy., a 5-min. drive from the center of Kuranda. www.rainforest.com.au. © **07/4085 5008.** A$51 adults, A$26 kids 4–14, A$128 families of 4. Daily 9am–4pm. Closed Dec 25. Shuttle from the Butterfly Sanctuary, Rob Veivers Dr., every 30 min. 10:45am–2:45pm for A$13 adults, A$6 children, or A$31 family, round-trip.

WHERE TO EAT IN KURANDA

Frogs Restaurant ★★ CAFE   This is a good place to stop for lunch, tucked into the wildlife attractions and Heritage Markets just off the main street. Simple offerings like wraps, pizzas, and salads dominate, but you can also get a hearty steak, seafood, or a bush-tasting platter (kangaroo, emu, crocodile). Or try the Curry of the Day, which might be something like a Sri

Lankan–style crocodile and green apple curry, a bargain at only A$9.50. Be on the lookout for the water dragons (they're harmless) on the deck overlooking the rainforest. It also has free Wi-Fi.

2/4 Rob Veivers Dr. www.frogsrestaurant.com.au. *©* **07/4093 8952.** Main courses A$9.50–A$38. Daily 9am–3:30pm. Closed Dec 25.

PORT DOUGLAS ★★★

Port Douglas: 67km (42 miles) N of Cairns; Mossman: 19km (12 miles) N of Port Douglas

The fishing village of Port Douglas is where the rainforest meets the Reef. Just over an hour's drive from Cairns, through rainforest and along a winding (sometimes treacherously so) road beside the sea, Port Douglas may be small, but stylish shops and seriously trendy restaurants line the main street, and beautiful **Four Mile Beach** is not to be missed. This is a favorite spot with celebrities big and small. Travelers often base themselves in "Port," as the locals call it, because they like the rural surroundings, the uncrowded beach, and the absence of tacky development (so far, anyway). Many Reef tours originate in Port, and many of the tours in the Cairns section (earlier in this chapter) pick up participants here as well.

The waters off Port Douglas boast just as many wonderful reefs and marine life forms as those around Cairns; the reefs are equally close to shore and equally colorful and varied. The closest Reef site off Port Douglas, the **Low Isles,** is only 15km (9 miles) northeast. Coral sand and 22 hectares (55 acres) of coral surround these two cays; the smaller is a sand cay covered in rich vegetation, and the larger is a shingle/rubble cay covered in mangroves, home to thousands of nesting Torresian Imperial pigeons. (If you visit the Low Isles, wear shoes that you can get wet, because the coral sand can be rough underfoot.) The coral is not quite as dazzling as the Outer Reef's—which is where you should head if you have only 1 day to spend on the Great Barrier Reef—but the fish life here is rich, and you may spot sea turtles. Because you can wade out to the coral right from the beach, the Low Isles are a good choice for nervous snorkelers. A half-day or day trip to the Low Isles makes for a more relaxing day than a visit to Outer Reef sites, because in addition to exploring the coral, you can sunbathe on the sand or laze under palm-thatched beach umbrellas.

Essentials

ARRIVING

There is no train to Port Douglas, and no scheduled air service. A small airport handles light aircraft and helicopter charters.

BY CAR Port Douglas is a scenic 65-minute drive from Cairns, in part along a narrow winding road that skirts the coast. Take Sheridan Street north out of the city as it becomes the Captain Cook Highway; follow the signs to Mossman and Mareeba until you reach the Port Douglas turnoff on your right. A **taxi** fare from Cairns to Port Douglas will set you back around A$200; call **Cairns Taxis** (*©* **131 008** in Cairns).

BY BUS A one-way ticket with **Sun Palm Transport** (www.sunpalmtrans port.com.au; © **07/4099 1191**) to Port Douglas hotels from Cairns airport is A$44 for adults, half price for children.

VISITOR INFORMATION

The biggest and most central information center in town is the privately run **Port Douglas Tourist Information Centre,** 23 Macrossan St. (www.info portdouglas.com.au; © **07/4099 5599**), open from 8:30am to 5:30pm daily. There is no official visitor information office in Port Douglas, but the websites **www.visitportdouglasdaintree.com** and **www.tourismportdouglas.com.au** are both good sources.

GETTING AROUND

Avis (© 07/4099 4331), **Budget** (© 07/4099 5702), and **Thrifty** (© 07/4099 5555) have offices in Port Douglas. All rent regular vehicles as well as four-wheel-drives, which you'll need if you plan to drive to Cape Tribulation. For a taxi, call **Port Douglas Taxis** (© **131 008**).

There is no bus service in Port Douglas, but several companies operate shuttles between the town center and major resorts. Ask your hotel or resort which one services them.

A good way to get around the town's flat streets is by bike. **Port Douglas Bicycle Centre,** 3 Warner St. (www.portdouglasbikehire.com; © **07/4099 5799**), rents bikes from A$20 for 4 hours, A$24 for a full day (or A$18/day for multi-day rental).

Where to Stay in Port Douglas

Port Douglas Accommodation Holiday Rentals (www.portdouglasaccom. com.au; © 07/4099 1340) rents a wide range of apartments and homes.

EXPENSIVE

By the Sea ★ You won't find a friendlier or more convenient place to stay in Port Douglas than these apartments, 10 seconds from the beach and less than a 10-minute walk from town. It offers heaps of "extras" such as bikes, iPads, laptops, beach towels, and water sports equipment on loan. Some of the apartments are on the small side (most suit only three people), but all are well cared for and were renovated in 2017. You can opt for a tiny Garden apartment with a patio; Balcony and Seaview apartments are a bit larger and have private balconies. Seaview apartments are quite roomy and have side views of Four Mile Beach. Towels are changed daily and linen weekly, and rooms are serviced every 4 days (or you can pay A$15 per day extra for daily service). It has no elevator and no porter, so be prepared to carry your luggage upstairs.

72 Macrossan St. www.bytheseaportdouglas.com.au. © **07/4099 5387.** 21 units. A$259–A$359 double studio; A$455–A$695 2-bedroom apt. or villa. Free parking. **Amenities:** Jacuzzi; outdoor heated pool; bikes; free Wi-Fi.

Thala Beach Nature Reserve ★★ Open to the elements—and the odd curious wallaby—the reception area of this stunning rainforest hideaway makes a striking first impression. From the restaurant upstairs, the impact is even greater, with sweeping views of the coastline and rainforest. Thala (pronounced *Ta*-la) Beach is 16km (10 miles) outside Port Douglas, set on a 58-hectare (145-acre) private peninsula, bordered on three sides by private beaches and coves. Owners Rob and Oonagh Prettejohn took their inspiration from the flora and fauna of the World Heritage area that surrounds it to create secluded treehouse bungalows. I've stayed here twice, and all the rooms are spacious and comfortable, with timber-paneled walls and king-size or twin beds. The Coral Sea bungalows overlook the ocean; the rest have forest and mountain views. Some of the bungalows are a bit of a hike from the public areas, but it's a small price to pay for the privacy and the rainforest setting (and you can call for a golf-buggy pickup).

Private Rd., Oaks Beach. www.thalabeach.com.au. ℂ **07/4098 5700.** 85 units. A$415–A$829 double; A$1,009 suite. Free parking. Hotel shuttle to Port Douglas. **Amenities:** Restaurant; bar; 2 outdoor pools; spa; free Wi-Fi (in main lodge only).

INEXPENSIVE

Coral Beach Lodge ★★ This modest lodge, popular with backpackers, families, and budget travelers, is on a suburban street that's just a 10-minute walk from town. All rooms were renovated in 2016, building on the lodge's reputation as an award-wining hostel-style accommodation. You can swap stories with other guests as you cook and eat in the communal kitchen and dining room. The rooms have small patios and are air-conditioned at night (you can pay an extra A$10 per day for 24-hr. air-conditioning). Dorm-style rooms (male and female) for 4 to 6 people have shared bathrooms, although deluxe private rooms (sleeping 1–5 people) have private bathrooms. Facilities also include an outdoor cinema and a kiosk selling essentials.

7 Craven Close. www.coralbeachlodge.com. ℂ **07/4099 5422.** 28 units. A$121 double; A$136 quad; 4- or 5-share rooms A$30–A$36 per person. Free parking. Bus: no. 110 (stop at front door). **Amenities:** Outdoor pool; free Wi-Fi.

Port Douglas Retreat ★ This well-kept two-story studio apartment complex on a quiet street, featuring white-battened balconies in the Queenslander architectural style, is a good value. Even some of the ritzier places in town can't boast its lagoonlike saltwater pool, surrounded by dense jungle and wrapped by an ample, shady sun deck that cries out to be lounged on with a good book and a cool drink. The apartments are not enormous, but they're fashionably furnished with terra-cotta tile floors, wrought-iron beds, cane seating, and colorful bedcovers. All have large furnished balconies or patios looking onto tropical gardens; some on the ground floor open onto the common-area boardwalk, so you might want to ask for a first-floor (second-story) unit. The town and beach are a 5-minute walk away.

31–33 Mowbray St., at Mudlo St. www.portdouglasretreat.com.au. ℂ **07/4099 5053.** 36 units. A$114–A$190 double. Minimum 2 or 3-night stay (depending on time of year). Secure covered parking. **Amenities:** Free airport transfers; outdoor saltwater pool; free Wi-Fi.

Where to Eat in Port Douglas

EXPENSIVE

Sassi Cucina e Bar ★★ ITALIAN   Presided over by gregarious Italian owner/chef Tony Sassi—who's something of a local celebrity—this traditional Italian *cucina* offers fresh seasonal flavors done simply and well. Start with some *spuntini,* small plates of delicacies such as crispy fried small local prawns with garlic and chili. Then move on to a pasta or risotto. There are always specials, depending on what's fresh…but make sure you try Tony's special meatballs, or chili mud crab if it's on offer. Sit inside in the air-conditioning, on the pavement outside, or in the garden out the back. Prices are lower at lunch.

4 Macrossan St. (at Wharf St.), Port Douglas. www.sassi.com.au. ✆ **07/4099 6744.** Main courses A$34–A$54. Daily 11am–9:30pm.

MODERATE

Salsa Bar & Grill ★★★ CONTEMPORARY   This trendy restaurant, in a timber Queenslander with wraparound verandas, has seriously good food, great prices, and lively, fun service. Little wonder you need to book well ahead—sometimes up to 2 weeks in advance—and it's the restaurant of choice for everyone from presidents to pop stars. Choose simple fare such as gnocchi or Caesar salad or such mouthwatering delights as a seafood *moqueca* with Portuguese rice, white fish, prawns, squid, crab, and mussels; or kangaroo filet, dusted with mountain pepper and served with beetroot, quinoa, horseradish, and goat's curd. Save room for dessert: a chocolate and Cointreau soufflé with double choc ice cream, perhaps? There's a kids' menu too.

26 Wharf St. (at Warner St.), Port Douglas. www.salsaportdouglas.com.au. ✆ **07/4099 4922.** Main courses A$34–A$45. Daily noon–2:30pm and 5:30–9pm.

Zinc Restaurant & Bar ★★ CONTEMPORARY   If you're like me, you may find yourself coming back more than once to this casual but very smart restaurant during your Port Douglas stay. The food is simple but very good, with plenty of choices, from seafood (local tiger prawns grilled with pineapple, chile, and mint salsa) to steak and both vegetarian and vegan options. Zinc opens at 2pm for a light late lunch from the bar menu and at 5pm for dinner. Be sure to check out the restrooms, which have floor-to-ceiling aquariums.

Macrossan St. (at Davidson St.), Port Douglas. www.zincportdouglas.com. ✆ **07/4099 6260.** Main courses A$29–A$45. Daily 2pm–late.

Exploring Port Douglas

Some companies in Cairns that offer outdoor activities will pick up from Port Douglas hotels. The best outdoor activity in Port Douglas, however, is to do absolutely nothing on spectacular **Four Mile Beach** ★★★. From May through

---

The Secret of the Seasons

High season in Port Douglas is roughly June 1 through October 31. Low-season holiday periods run from approximately November to May (excluding Christmas and New Year's).

September, the water is stinger-free. From October through April, swim within the stinger safety net.

Every Sunday from 8am to 2pm, a colorful **handicrafts and food market** is held on the lawn under the mango trees by Dickson Inlet, at the end of Macrossan Street. Stalls offer everything from foot massages to fresh coconut milk.

Kuku Yalanji Cultural Habitat Tours ★★★ TOUR/CULTURAL ACTIVITY   Brothers Linc and Brandon Walker will take you on the walk of a lifetime, on the beach opposite their parents' house. This is the traditional fishing ground of the Kubirri Warra people, when the mudflats and mangroves are exposed at low tide; you will spend 2½ hours here learning to throw a spear, hunt and stalk, and use coastal resources wisely. If you are lucky, you may spear a crab (not so lucky for the crab!), and when enough has been foraged to make a small meal, you'll take it back to the house where Linc and Brandon's mother will cook it up for you to eat on the veranda. It's an authentic and unforgettable experience. Don't forget to take insect repellent (just in case), and wear shoes you don't mind getting wet (though bare feet are best). Night fishing tours, either by boat or foot, are run on request. Bookings are essential for all tours.

Bougainvillea St., Cooya Beach (north of Port Douglas; take Bonnie Doon Rd., off the Captain Cook Hwy.). www.kycht.com.au. ✆ **07/4098 3437** or 0403 403527 mobile phone. A$90 adults, A$75 kids 4–12; A$150 per person night tours. Daily at 9:30am and 1:30pm; night tours 7:30pm.

Mossman Gorge Centre ★★★ NATURE CENTER/TOUR   This is the gateway to wonderful Mossman Gorge, where the gushing Mossman River tumbles over massive boulders through the rainforest. You can visit the gorge on your own and take the short boardwalks along the river, but I highly recommend joining one of the guided **Ngadiku Dreamtime Walks,** with a member of the local Kuku Yalanji tribe. You will learn about Aboriginal bush medicines and food, Dreamtime legends, and the sacred sites tribal families have called home for thousands of years. Five tours are offered daily (10am, 11am, noon, 1pm, and 3pm) and cost A$78 adults, A$39 children 5 to 15, or A$195 for a family of four. The center has a gift shop, art gallery, and cafe. You can only access the gorge by taking the shuttle bus, which leaves the visitor center every 15 minutes between 8am and 5:30pm daily. The cost is A$12 adults, A$5.90 children, or A$30 for a family of four. Most tour companies from Cairns and Port Douglas will get you here.

Mossman Gorge Rd., Mossman (20km/12 miles north of Port Douglas). www.mossman gorge.com.au. ✆ **07/4099 7000.** Daily 8am–6pm. Closed Dec 25.

Wildlife Habitat ★★★ WILDLIFE VIEWING   This is a great place to see animals that are too shy to be spotted in the wild, with 180 animal species from the Wet Tropics all in one place for you to observe up close. You can watch saltwater and freshwater crocodiles, hand-feed kangaroos, and have

The Black Mountains are steeped in myths and legends and hold special cultural importance for the native Kuku Yalanji people.

your photo taken with a koala. The highlight is the walk-through aviary, housing more than 100 Wet Tropics bird species, including cassowaries. Between 9 and 10:30am, the park serves "breakfast with the birds," and between noon and 2pm "lunch with the lorikeets." Breakfast costs A$60 adults, A$30 kids, and A$150 families, and includes Habitat admission; lunch costs a few dollars more. Don't miss one of the excellent, free guided tours that run regularly from 9:30am to 4pm. You can also do a "wildnight" tour for A$43 adults, A$32 children, or A$118 families, to see some of Australia's amazing nocturnal creatures. Allow at least 2 hours here.

Port Douglas Rd. (corner Captain Cook Hwy.). www.wildlifehabitat.com.au. ℂ **07/4099 3235.** A$37 adults, A$19 kids 4–14, A$93 families of 4. Daily 8am–5pm. Closed Dec 25.

Day Trips from Port Douglas to the Reef

The waters off Port Douglas are home to dramatic coral spires and swim-throughs at the Cathedrals; giant clams at Barracuda Pass; a village of parrot fish, anemone fish, unicorn fish, and two moray eels at the pinnacle of Nursery Bommie; fan corals at Split-Bommie; and many other wonderful sites.

Without a doubt, the most popular large vessels visiting the Outer Reef are the **Quicksilver Wavepiercers** (www.quicksilver-cruises.com; ℂ **07/4087 2100**), based out of Port Douglas. These ultrasleek, high-speed, air-conditioned 37m (121-ft.) and 46m (151-ft.) catamarans carry 300 or 440 passengers to Agincourt Reef, a ribbon reef 39 nautical miles (72km/45 miles) from shore on the outer edge of the Reef. After the 90-minute trip to the Reef, you tie up at a two-story pontoon, where you spend 3½ hours.

Quicksilver departs Marina Mirage at 10am daily except on December 25. The cost for the day is A$264 adults, A$136 kids 4 to 14, and A$671 families of four. Guided snorkel safaris cost A$66 adults, A$34 kids, A$165 families; introductory dives cost A$177 per person. Qualified divers can take a dive-tender boat to make one dive for A$128 or two dives for A$180 per person, all gear included. Booking in advance is a good idea.

The dive boat *Poseidon* (www.poseidon-cruises.com.au; © **07/4087 2100**) also welcomes snorkelers. It presents a Reef ecology talk and takes you on a guided snorkel safari. The *Poseidon* is a fast 24m (79-ft.) vessel that visits three Outer Reef sites. The day-trip price (A$254 adults, A$182 kids 4–14) includes snorkel gear, a marine-biology talk, snorkel safaris, lunch, and pick-ups from Port Douglas hotels. You can try an introductory dive for A$71 for one dive or A$138 for two. Certified divers pay an extra A$55 for one dive, A$80 for two dives, or A$100 for three, including all gear. Guides will accompany you, free of charge, to show you great locations. The boat departs the Reef Marina daily at 8:30am, taking about 2 hours to get to the first of three reef sites you will visit during the day at Agincourt Reef. Among the 25-plus dive sites visited by Poseidon's cruises are **Turtle Bay,** where you may meet a friendly Maori wrasse; the **Cathedrals,** a collection of coral pinnacles and swim-throughs; and **Barracuda Pass,** home to coral gardens, giant clams, and schooling barracuda.

The snorkeling specialist boat *Wavelength* (www.wavelength.com.au; © **07/4099 5031**) does a full-day trip to the Outer Reef for A$240 adults, A$200 children 8 to 12. *Note:* This trip is not suitable for children age 7 and under. The trip visits three different snorkel sites each day and incorporates a guided snorkel tour and a reef presentation by a marine biologist. It carries only 30 passengers and includes snorkel gear, sunsuits, lunch, and transfers from your Port Douglas hotel. Both beginners and experienced snorkelers will like this trip, which departs daily at 8:30am.

THE LOW ISLES

Another way to spend a pleasant day—closer to shore—on the Great Barrier Reef is to visit the **Low Isles,** 15km (9½ miles) northeast of Port Douglas. The isles are 1.5-hectare (3¾-acre) coral-cay specks of lush vegetation surrounded by white sand and 22 hectares (54 acres) of coral—which is what makes them so appealing. The coral is not quite as good as the Outer Reef's, but the fish life is rich, and the proximity makes for a relaxing day.

The trip aboard the 30m (98-ft.) luxury sailing catamaran *Wavedancer,* operated by Quicksilver (www.wavedancerlowisles.com; © **07/4087 2100**), is A$210 adults, A$109 kids 4 to 14, and A$536 for families of 4. You'll leave Port Douglas at 10am, and once there, you can snorkel, take a glass-bottom-boat ride, or do a guided beach walk with a marine biologist. Coach transfers are available through Quicksilver from your Port Douglas accommodations for A$17 adults, A$8 kids, or A$42 for a family.

TOWNSVILLE & MAGNETIC ISLAND ★★

346km (215 miles) S of Cairns; 1,371km (850 miles) N of Brisbane

Australia's largest tropical city (population 140,000), with an economy based on mining, manufacturing, and education as well as tourism, Townsville is sometimes—rather unjustly, I think—overlooked as a holiday destination. The people are friendly, the city is pleasant, and there's plenty to do. The town nestles by the sea below the pink face of Castle Rock, which looms 300m (about 1,000 ft.) directly above. Townsville's popular waterfront parkland, **The Strand** (p. 254), is complemented by the **Jezzine Barracks,** a A$40-million redevelopment of unused land that now offers a stunning collection of outdoor sculptures and memorials honoring the city's wartime history (with more than a passing nod to the American forces who served here in World War II). It is a wonderful parkland that's well worth exploring.

Cruises depart from Townsville harbor for the Great Barrier Reef, about 2½ hours away, and just 8km (5 miles) offshore is **Magnetic Island**—"Maggie" to the locals—a popular place for watersports, hiking, and spotting koalas in the wild.

Townsville's waters boast hundreds of large patch reefs, some miles long, with excellent coral and marine life, including mantas, rays, turtles, and sharks, and sometimes canyons and swim-throughs in generally good visibility. One of the best reef complexes is **Flinders Reef,** which is actually in the Coral Sea, beyond the Great Barrier Reef Marine Park boundaries. At 240km (149 miles) offshore, it has 30m (100-ft.) visibility, plenty of coral, and big walls and pinnacles with big fish to match, such as whaler shark and barracuda.

What draws most divers to Townsville, though, is one of Australia's best wreck dives, the **SS *Yongala,*** which went down here in 1911 during a tropical cyclone. Still largely intact, the sunken remains of this steamer lie in 15m to 30m (50–98 ft.) of water, with visibility of 9m to 18m (approximately 30–60 ft.). Diving the *Yongala* is not for beginners—most dive companies require that customers have advanced certification or have logged a minimum of 15 dives with open-water certification. The boat is usually visited on a live-aboard trip of at least 2 days, but some companies run day trips.

Although Townsville can be hot and humid in the summer—and sometimes in the path of cyclones—it is generally spared the worst of the wet-season rains and boasts 300 days of sunshine a year.

Essentials

ARRIVING

BY PLANE **Qantas** (www.qantas.com.au; ℭ **131 313** in Australia) flies direct from Brisbane, Cairns, and Darwin. **Jetstar** (www.jetstar.com.au; ℭ **131 538** in Australia) flies direct into **Townsville Airport (TSV)** (www.townsvilleairport.com.au) from Sydney and Melbourne's Tullamarine airport.

Virgin Australia (www.virginaustralia.com.au; *C* **136 789** in Australia) flies direct from Brisbane, Melbourne, and Sydney daily. **Regional Express** (www.rex.com.au; *C* **131 713** in Australia, or 02/6393 5550) flies from Cairns.

Townsville Shuttle Services (www.shuttletsv.com.au; *C* **0478/160 036** mobile) operates an airport shuttle service to the city for A$10 adults, A$15 for two or three passengers, and A$20 for a group of four. Bookings are essential. A **taxi** from the airport to most central hotels costs about A$25.

BY TRAIN Queensland Rail (www.queenslandrailtravel.com.au; *C* **1300/131 722** in Queensland, or 07/3606 6630) long-distance trains stop at Townsville on the Brisbane-Cairns route. The 17-hour *Spirit of Queensland* journey from Brisbane costs A$315 for a premium economy seat.

BY BUS Greyhound Australia (www.greyhound.com.au; *C* **1300/473 946** in Australia, or 07/4799 3715 in Townsville) coaches stop at Townsville several times a day on their Cairns-Brisbane-Cairns routes. The fare from Cairns is A$72; trip time is around 5 to 6 hours. The fare from Brisbane is A$307; trip time is 24 hours (sometimes longer).

BY CAR Townsville is on the Bruce Highway, a 3-hour drive north of Airlie Beach and 4½ hours south of Cairns. The Bruce Highway breaks temporarily in the city. From the south, take Bruce Highway Alt. 1 route into the city. From the north, the highway leads into the city. The drive from Cairns to Townsville through sugarcane fields, cloud-topped hills, and lush bushland is a pretty one—one of the most picturesque stretches in Queensland.

VISITOR INFORMATION

The town has two official information centers. The **Townsville Bulletin Square Information Centre** is in the heart of the city on Townsville Bulletin Square, just off Flinders Street (www.townsvillenorthqueensland.com.au; *C* **07/4721 3660**); it's open Monday through Friday 9am to 5pm and weekends from 9am to 1pm. It is closed Good Friday, Christmas Day, and until 1pm on Anzac Day (Apr 25). The **Bruce Highway Visitor Information Centre** (*C* **07/4780 4397**) is at Billabong Sanctuary (p. 255); it's open Monday to Saturday 9am to 4pm and Sunday 10am to 2pm.

GETTING AROUND TOWNSVILLE

Local **Sunbus** (www.sunbus.com.au; *C* **07/4771 9800**) buses depart from Flinders Street. Car-rental chains include **Avis** (*C* **07/4799 2022**), **Budget** (*C* **07/4762 7433**), **Europcar** (*C* **07/4760 1380**), **Hertz** (*C* **07/4728 9530**), and **Thrifty** (*C* **07/4725 4600**).

For a taxi, call *C* **131 008**.

Where to Stay in Townsville

EXPENSIVE/MODERATE

Grand Hotel and Apartments ★★ Just off the bustle of the Palmer Street restaurant strip, all the rooms at this smart hotel, opened in 2014, have private balconies. There's no restaurant—but no need of one. The hotel offers a charge-back service from six nearby restaurants (and room service for breakfast as well). In addition to standard hotel rooms, you have the choice of one- or two-bedroom apartments, each of which has an open-plan kitchen and living space, separate bedroom(s) and bathroom, and a washing machine and dryer.

8–10 Palmer St. www.grandhoteltownsville.com.au. © **07/4753 2800.** 230 units. A$170–A$204 double; A$219–A$241 1-bedroom apt; A$378–A$438 2-bedroom apt. Free parking. **Amenities:** Gym; Jacuzzi; outdoor pool; room service; Wi-Fi (A$5.50/1 hr.; A$24/24 hr.), free if you book direct.

MODERATE

Hotel Grand Chancellor Townsville ★   Just a stroll from all the city's major attractions and the Magnetic Island ferries, this 20-story hotel is fairly standard but a good choice for its heart-of-the-city location. The locals call it the "Sugar Shaker" because of its distinctive circular shape (which gives every room a view of the city, the bay, or Castle Hill). Suites have kitchenettes, and one-bedroom apartments give extra space. The star attractions are the rooftop pool and sun deck with barbecues. Parking is in a separate building, which can be inconvenient at times.

334 Flinders St. www.grandchancellorhotels.com. © **1800/753 379** in Australia, or 07/4729 2000. 200 units. A$137–A$156 double; A$183–A$213 suite; A$160–A$223 apt. Parking A$13 per day. **Amenities:** Restaurant; 2 bars; babysitting; bikes; concierge; gym; rooftop pool; room service; free Wi-Fi.

Mercure Townsville ★★   Set in tropical gardens on the shores of a large lake, this resort-style hotel is a pleasant surprise. It's a bit out of town (on the main road north), right next to a big shopping center, but once you're there you may not want to travel far. The free-form swimming pool is Townsville's largest (it also has a Jacuzzi); take a dip or go for a stroll around the lake and watch the birds. Rooms are a good size, and family suites sleep four and have kitchenettes.

Woolcock and Attlee sts. www.mercuretownsville.com.au. © **07/4759 4900.** 162 units. A$137–A$179 double; A$199 family room. Free parking. **Amenities:** Restaurant; bar; babysitting; pool; room service; 2 lighted tennis courts; free Wi-Fi.

INEXPENSIVE

Seagulls Seafront Resort ★★   This popular, low-key resort, a 5-minute drive from the city, is built around an inviting freeform saltwater pool in 1.2 hectares (3 acres) of tropical gardens. Despite the Esplanade location, the motel-style rooms do not boast waterfront views, but they are comfortable and a good size. The larger deluxe rooms have painted brick walls, sofas, dining furniture, and kitchen sinks. Studios and family rooms have kitchenettes. Apartments have a main bedroom and a bunk bedroom (sleeps three), a kitchenette, dining area, and a roomy balcony. The resort is wheelchair-accessible, with some ground-floor rooms specially adapted for guests with disabilities. The accommodations wings surround the pool and its pretty open-sided

restaurant, which is popular with locals. It's a 10-minute walk to the Strand, and most tour companies pick up at the door.

74 The Esplanade, Belgian Gardens. www.seagulls.com.au. ✆ **07/4721 3111.** 70 units. A$99–A$149 double; A$169 family rooms; A$189 2-bedroom apt. Free parking. Bus: no. 7. **Amenities:** Restaurant; bar; children's playground; 2 large outdoor saltwater pools and children's wading pool; room service; small tennis court; free Wi-Fi.

Where to Eat in Townsville

There are many restaurants and cafes on **Palmer Street,** an easy stroll across the river from Flinders Street, and on the Strand.

C Bar ★★ CONTEMPORARY   Right on the waterfront, C Bar is a great place for casual seaside dining any time of day, offering good, healthy choices for breakfast and an interesting all-day menu (from 11:30am). It's a lovely spot for sundowners or dinner, too. At lunch or dinner, try a prawn and chicken coconut *laksa* with rice noodles and Asian greens, a simple fish 'n' chips, or maybe a roasted sweet potato and haloumi salad. A loaded seafood platter for two, served with a warm potato salad, costs A$96. There's also a kids' menu, with all meals A$16. For my money, the view is one of the best in town.

Gregory Street Headland, The Strand. www.cbar.com.au. ✆ **07/4724 0333.** Main courses A$18–A$47. Daily 6am–10pm.

JAM Restaurant ★★★ CONTEMPORARY   Dishes that will make you groan with pleasure, with flavors designed to delight…that's what you will find at this smart, friendly restaurant. It's so good that when visiting Townsville, I usually eat here more than once! At breakfast, try the Asian chicken omelet with snow peas, bean shoots, fried shallots, and chili jam (or the most popular item on the menu, the Queensland avocado on whole-grain sourdough with whipped Danish feta and poached eggs). For dinner, you might find dishes like duck breast and confit leg with beet and feta ravioli; or for steak lovers, a rib filet with creamy mashed potato, black garlic, and seeded mustard butter. The menu changes regularly, but you can be assured that the quality won't. Really, don't miss this restaurant. It's no wonder the awards keep rolling in.

1 Palmer St. www.jamcorner.com.au. ✆ **07/4721 4900.** Main courses A$29–A$38; 6-course tasting menu A$75 (or A$120 with matched wines). Tues–Fri 6:30am–2pm and 5:30pm–late; Sat 7am–2pm and 5:30pm–late; Sun 7:30am–11am.

Exploring Townsville

Don't miss the views of the city, Cleveland Bay, and Magnetic Island from **Castle Hill;** it's a 2.5km (1½-mile) drive or a shorter, steep walk up from town (make sure to do it in the cool part of the day). To drive to the top, follow Stanley Street west from Flinders Street to Castle Hill Drive; the walking trails up are posted en route.

The Strand is a 2.5km (1½-mile) strip with safe swimming beaches, a fitness circuit, a great free water park for the kids, and plenty of covered picnic areas and free gas barbecue grills. Stroll along the promenade or relax at one of the many cafes, restaurants, and bars while you gaze across the Coral Sea to Magnetic Island. For the more active, there are areas to in-line skate, cycle, walk, fish, or play half-court basketball. Four rocky headlands and a picturesque jetty adjacent to Strand Park provide good fishing spots, and two surf lifesaving clubs service the three swimming areas along the Strand. Cool off in the Olympic-size Tobruk Memorial Baths (A$5 adults, A$3 kids 2–12) or the seawater Rockpool or at the beach itself. During summer (Nov–Mar), three swimming enclosures operate to keep swimmers safe from marine stingers. If watersports are on your agenda, try jet-skiing, hire a canoe, or take to the latest in pedal skis. The state-of-the-art water park has waterfalls, water slides, and water cannons, plus a huge bucket of water that continually fills until it overturns and drenches laughing children.

Billabong Sanctuary ★★★ WILDLIFE VIEWING   You could easily spend 2 or 3 hours here, seeing Aussie wildlife in a natural setting and hand-feeding kangaroos and emus. You can also be photographed (starting at A$24) holding a koala, a (baby) crocodile, a python, or a wombat. Engaging interactive talks and shows run continuously starting at 9:15am; among the most popular are the saltwater-crocodile feeding at 1 and 3:15pm (for an extra A$99, you can also personally feed the croc from a large pole dangled over the fence). The sanctuary also has gas barbecues, a cafe, and a pool.

Bruce Hwy. (17km/11 miles S of Townsville). www.billabongsanctuary.com.au. Ⓒ **07/4778 8344.** A$38 adults, A$25 children 4–16, A$110 families of 5. Daily 9am–5pm. Closed Dec 25.

Museum of Tropical Queensland ★★ MUSEUM   If you're lucky enough to be here on the second Tuesday of the month, you'll have the chance to hear a museum expert give an hour-long lunchtime talk as part of the museum's "Discover More" lecture series. Subjects cover everything from underwater robotic research to frogs to maritime archaeology or the history of Townsville. With its curved roof, shaped like a ship under sail, this interesting museum holds the treasures salvaged from the wreck of the HMS *Pandora,* which sank in 1792 and lies 33m (108 ft.) underwater on the edge of the Great Barrier Reef. This is the highlight of the museum; the exhibit's centerpiece is a full-scale replica of a section of the ship's bow and its 17m-high (56-ft.) foremast, crafted by local shipwrights. The exhibition traces the ship's voyage and the retrieval of the sunken treasure—make sure you watch the film about the salvage. The museum has five other galleries, including a hands-on science center; a natural history display; one dedicated to north Queensland's indigenous heritage, with items from Torres Strait and the South Sea Islands; and stories about the settlement of north Queensland from people of different cultures. Another is devoted to touring exhibitions, which change every 3 months. Allow 2 to 3 hours.

70–102 Flinders St. (next to Reef HQ). www.mtq.qm.qld.gov.au. Ⓒ **07/4726 0600.** A$15 adults, A$8.80 children 4–16, A$38 families of 5. Daily 9:30am–5pm. Closed Good Friday, Anzac Day (Apr 25), and Dec 25–26.

Reef HQ Aquarium ★★★ AQUARIUM   Reef HQ is the education center for the Great Barrier Reef Marine Park Authority's headquarters and the largest living-coral-reef aquarium in the world. The highlight is walking through a 20m-long (66-ft.) transparent acrylic tunnel, gazing into a giant predator tank where sharks cruise silently. A replica of the wreck of the SS *Yongala* provides an eerie backdrop for blacktip and whitetip reef sharks, leopard sharks, and nurse sharks, sharing their 750,000-liter (195,000-gal.) home with stingrays, giant trevally, and a green turtle. Watching them feed is quite a spectacle. The tunnel also reveals the 2.5-million-liter (650,000-gal.) coral-reef exhibit, where hard and soft corals provide a home for thousands of fish, giant clams, sea cucumbers, sea stars, and other creatures. During the scuba show, the divers speak to you over an intercom while they swim with the sharks and feed the fish. Other highlights include a touch tank and a wild-sea-turtle rehabilitation center, plus interactive activities for children. Reef HQ is an easy walk from the city center.

2–68 Flinders St. www.reefhq.com.au. ℂ **07/4750 0800.** A$28 adults, A$14 children 5–16, A$42–A$70 families. Daily 9:30am–5pm. Closed Australia Day (Jan 26), Anzac Day (Apr 25), and Dec 25. All buses from the City Mall stop nearby.

Day Trips from Townsville to the Reef

Most boats visiting the Reef from Townsville are live-aboard vessels that make trips of 2 or more days, designed for serious divers. **Adrenalin Dive** (www.adrenalindive.com.au; ℂ **07/4724 0600**) operates day trips on which you can make introductory dives for A$80 for the first and A$120 for two; certified divers also dive for A$80, all gear included. The cruise costs A$249 for adults and A$199 for children 6 to 12. The price includes lunch, morning and afternoon tea, and snorkel gear. Cruises depart Townsville at 7am, with a pickup at Magnetic Island en route at 7:50am, on Tuesday, Thursday, Friday, and Sunday (and on Mon during high season, June–Sept). They also run day trips to the *Yongala* wreck on Wednesday and Saturday, in which you will do two dives on the *Yongala*. The cost is A$329, including all gear, and A$10 per dive for a guide, if you have logged fewer than 15 dives.

Day Trip from Townsville to Magnetic Island ★★

Magnetic Island—or just "Maggie"—is a delightful 51-sq.-km (20-sq.-mile) national-park island 20 minutes from Townsville by ferry. About 2,500 people live here, and it's popular with Aussies, who love the holiday atmosphere. Small settlements dot the coastline, offering a good range of restaurants and laid-back cafes. Most people come for the 20 or so pristine and uncrowded bays and white beaches, but hikers, botanists, and birders may want to explore the eucalyptus woods, patches of gully rainforest, and granite tors. The island got its name when Captain Cook thought its "magnetic" rocks were interfering with his compass readings. It is famous for koalas, easily spotted in roadside gum trees; ask a local to point you to the nearest colony. Rock wallabies are often seen in the early morning.

The island is not on the Great Barrier Reef, but surrounding waters are part of the Great Barrier Reef Marine Park. There is good reef snorkeling at Florence Bay on the southern edge; Arthur Bay on the northern edge; and Geoffrey Bay, where you can even reef-walk at low tide. (Wear sturdy shoes and do not walk directly on coral, to avoid damaging it.) First-time snorkelers will have an easy time of it in Maggie's weak currents and softly sloping beaches. Outside the stinger season (Oct–Apr), there is good swimming at any number of bays all around the island. Reef-free Alma Bay, with its shady lawns and playground, is a good choice for families; Rocky Bay is a small, secluded cove.

ESSENTIALS

ARRIVING   Sealink (www.sealinkqld.com.au; ℭ **07/4726 0800**) runs 19 round-trip ferry services a day from Townsville's Breakwater terminal on Sir Leslie Thiess Drive. Round-trip tickets are A$34 for adults, A$17 for children 5 to 14, and A$76 for families of five. The trip takes about 20 minutes.

VISITOR INFORMATION   There is no information center on Magnetic Island, but you can check **www.magneticinformer.com.au** online. Also, stop off at the **Townsville Bulletin Square Visitor Information Centre** (ℭ **1800/801 902** in Australia, or 07/4721 3660) before you cross to the island. It's open daily (Mon–Fri 9am–5pm, Sat–Sun 9am–1pm).

GETTING AROUND   You can take your car on the ferry, or rent a car on the island. For years, the classic way of getting around the island was in an open-sided minimoke (similar to a golf cart) from the many rental outfits on the island. Minimokes are unlikely to go much over 60kmph (36 mph). **Tropical Topless Car Rentals** (www.tropicaltopless.com; ℭ **07/4758 1111**) still rents them—and other vehicles—from around A$65 to A$80 a day. **Magnetic Island Bus Services** (www.sunbus.com.au; ℭ **07/4778 5130**) will get you anywhere on the island for A$3.70 adults and A$1.90 kids age 5 to 15 (or less, depending on where you want to go), or buy a daily ticket for A$7.20 adults and A$3.60 children.

EXPLORING MAGNETIC ISLAND

There is no end to the things you can do on Maggie—snorkeling, swimming in one of a dozen or more bays, catamaran sailing, waterskiing, parasailing, horseback riding on the beach, biking, tennis or golf, scuba diving, sea kayaking, sailing or cruising around the island, taking a Harley-Davidson tour, fishing, and more. Equipment for all these activities is for rent on the island.

One of the best, and most popular, of the island's 20km (13 miles) of hiking trails is the **Nelly Bay–Arcadia trail,** a one-way journey of 5km (3 miles) that takes 2½ hours. The first 45 minutes, starting in rainforest and climbing to a saddle between Nelly Bay and Horseshoe, are the most interesting. Another excellent walk is the 2km (1¼-mile) trail to the **Forts,** remnants of World War II defenses, which, not surprisingly, have great 360-degree sea views. The best koala spotting is on the track up to the Forts off Horseshoe Bay Road. Carry water when walking—some bays and hiking trails are not near shops.

If you feel like splurging, consider a jet-ski circumnavigation of the island with **Magnetic Jet Ski Tours** (www.facebook.com/MagneticJet; © **07/4778 5533**). The 3-hour circumnavigation tour on a two-seat jet ski costs A$395 per ski rental, and a 2-hour tour of the northern side of the island costs A$220 per ski. They'll kit you out with wetsuits, life jackets, and tinted goggles for the ride. Keep your eyes peeled for dolphins, dugongs (manatees), sea turtles, and humpback whales in season. Tours depart from "the Red Shed" on Pacific Drive, Horseshoe Bay. Minimum age is 6 years.

Bungalow Bay Koala Village (www.bungalowbay.com.au; © **07/4778 5577**), on Horseshoe Bay Road, Horseshoe Bay, is a backpacker hostel that has a wildlife sanctuary on its 6.5 hectares (16 acres). Tours of the koala park run at 10am, noon, and 2:30pm and take about 90 minutes. The first part is within the wildlife park, where you can wrap yourself in a python, pet a lizard, hold a small saltwater crocodile, and get up close with a koala, before heading off on a guided bush walk to explore nearby habitats of eucalyptus forest, wetlands, mangroves, or coastal dunes, and to learn about the history of the traditional owners, the Wulgurukaba people. Entry to the park costs A$30 adults, A$13 children 4 to 16, or A$80 for families of five. Koala-holding costs A$25 including a souvenir photo, with proceeds supporting Magnetic Island wildlife care groups.

THE WHITSUNDAYS ★★★

Airlie Beach: 640km (397 miles) S of Cairns; 1,146km (711 miles) N of Brisbane

A day's drive or a 1-hour flight south of Cairns brings you to the dazzling collection of 74 islands known as the Whitsundays. No more than 3 nautical miles (3.4km/2 miles) separate most of the islands, and altogether they represent countless bays, beaches, dazzling coral reefs, and fishing spots that make up one fabulous Great Barrier Reef playground. The Whitsundays share the same latitude as Rio de Janeiro and Hawaii, and the water is at least 72°F (22°C) year-round, the sun shines most of the year, and in winter you'll require only a light jacket at night.

Most of the islands consist of densely rainforested national parkland. The surrounding waters belong to the Great Barrier Reef Marine Park. But don't expect palm trees and coconuts—these islands are covered with dry-looking pine and eucalyptus forests full of dense undergrowth, and rocky coral coves far outnumber the few sandy beaches. Only a few islands have resorts, but all offer just about every activity you could ever want: snorkeling, scuba diving, sailing, reef fishing, water-skiing, jet-skiing, parasailing, sea kayaking, hiking, rides over the coral in semisubmersibles, fish feeding, putt-putting around in dinghies to secluded beaches, tennis, and more. Accommodations range from small, low-key wilderness retreats to midrange family havens to some of Australia's most luxurious resorts.

The village of **Airlie Beach** ★★ is the center of the action on the mainland. But the islands themselves are just as good a stepping stone to the outer Great

Barrier Reef as Cairns, and some people consider them better, because you don't have to make the 90-minute trip to the Reef before you hit coral. Just about any Whitsunday island has fringing reef around its shores, and there are good snorkeling reefs between the islands, a quick boat ride away from your island or mainland accommodations. The reef here is just as good as off Cairns, with many drop-offs and drift dives, a dazzling range of corals, and a rich array of marine life, including whales, mantas, shark, reef fish, morays, turtles, and pelagics. Visibility is usually around 15m to 23m (49–75 ft.).

A popular reef for both snorkeling and diving is **Blue Pearl Bay ★★** off Hayman Island, which has loads of corals and some gorgonian fans in its gullies, and heaps of reef fish, including Maori wrasse and sometimes manta rays. It's a good place to make an introductory dive, walking right in off the beach. A little island commonly called **Bali Hai Island ★★**, between Hayman and Hook islands, is a great place to be left to your own devices. You'll see soft-shelf and wall coral, tame Maori wrasse, octopus, turtles, reef shark, various kinds of rays including mantas, eagles, and cow-tails, plus loads of fish.

Note: In early 2017, the Whitsunday region took a direct hit from Cyclone Debbie, which caused extensive damage to some islands and to Airlie Beach. While much of this was quickly rectified, at press time the resorts on

Large grouper swimming with scuba divers in tropical reef near Hamilton Island.

Daydream (www.daydreamisland.com) and **Hayman** (www.intercontinental.com/HaymanIsland) islands were about to reopen. They should be in full swing by the time you get there.

Essentials

ARRIVING

BY PLANE   There are two air routes into the Whitsundays: **Great Barrier Reef Airport (HTI)** on Hamilton Island and **Whitsunday Coast Airport (PPP)** (www.whitsundaycoastairport.com.au) at Proserpine on the mainland. **Qantas** (www.qantas.com.au; ℂ **131 313** in Australia) flies direct to Hamilton Island from Cairns, Brisbane, and Sydney. **Virgin Australia** (www.virginaustralia.com; ℂ **136 789** in Australia) flies to Proserpine direct from Brisbane, with connections from other capitals, and direct from Brisbane, Melbourne, and Sydney to Hamilton Island. **Jetstar** (www.jetstar.com.au; ℂ **131 538** in Australia) flies from Brisbane to Proserpine, and from Melbourne to Hamilton Island. **TigerAir** (www.tigerair.com.au; ℂ **1300/174 266** in Australia or 07/3295 2104) flies into Whitsunday Coast Airport from Sydney. If you stay on an island, the resort may book your launch transfers automatically. These may appear on your airline ticket, in which case your luggage will be checked through to the island.

   Whitsunday Transit (www.whitsundaytransit.com.au; ℂ **07/4946 1800**) provides airport transfers from Proserpine to Airlie Beach for A$22 adults, A$12 children 4 to 14 one-way, or A$36 adults and A$20 children round-trip.

BY TRAIN   Several long-distance trains with **Queensland Rail** (www.queenslandrailtravel.com.au; ℂ **1300/131 722** in Australia) stop at Proserpine every week. The one-way fare from Brisbane on the *Spirit of Queensland* is A$289 for a premium economy seat. There is a bus link to Airlie Beach; book through Queensland Rail when booking the train.

BY BUS   **Greyhound Australia** (www.greyhound.com.au; ℂ **1300/473 946** in Australia) operates plentiful daily services to Airlie Beach from Brisbane (trip time: around 18 hr.) and Cairns (trip time: around 10 hr.). The fare is around A$260 from Brisbane, A$110 from Cairns.

BY CAR   The Bruce Highway leads south from Cairns or north from Brisbane to Proserpine, 26km (16 miles) inland from Airlie Beach. Take the Whitsunday turnoff to reach Airlie Beach and Shute Harbour, where most day-trip and charter boats depart. (Shute Harbor has several car-storage facilities if you're planning to go to the islands.) Allow a good 8 hours to drive from Cairns.

VISITOR INFORMATION

Contact **Tourism Whitsundays** (www.tourismwhitsundays.com.au; ℂ **07/4945 3967**) for information, or pick up brochures from the many private booking agents lining the main street of Airlie Beach. All stock a vast range of cruise, tour, and hotel information and make bookings free of charge. All have similar material, but because some represent certain boats exclusively, and because prices can vary a little from one to the next, it pays to shop around.

GETTING AROUND THE WHITSUNDAYS

BY BOAT   Airlie Beach has three different harbor areas: **Shute Harbour,** 10km (6.2 miles) east of Airlie Beach on Shute Harbour Road, where ferries, charter yachts, and water taxis depart; **Abell Point Marina,** where you'll find sailing yachts, luxury superyachts and some day tour operators, 15 minutes' walk west from Airlie Beach; and **Port of Airlie,** a marina complex that is also home to the **Cruise Whitsundays** (www.cruisewhitsundays.com.au; ✆ **07/4846 7000**) day-tour boats. Cruise Whitsundays operates transfer services between its maritime terminal at Port of Airlie, Hamilton Island Marina and Hamilton Island Airport, Whitsunday Coast Airport at Proserpine, Shute Harbour, and Daydream Island.

Island ferries and Great Barrier Reef cruises leave from the **Port of Airlie,** on the Cove Road, on the edge of Airlie Beach's shopping strip and an easy walk from most hotels in the town center. Some tour-boat operators and bareboat charters anchor at **Abell Point Marina,** a 15-minute walk west from Airlie Beach. Most tour-boat operators pick up guests free from Airlie Beach hotels and at some or all island resorts.

BY BUS   **Whitsunday Transit** (www.whitsundaytransit.com.au; ✆ **07/4946 1800**) meets all flights at Proserpine and provides door-to-door transfers to Proserpine, Airlie Beach, and Shute Harbour. It also runs buses regularly between Proserpine, Airlie Beach, and Shute Harbour.

BY CAR   **Avis** (✆ **07/4967 7188**) and **Hertz** (✆ **07/4946 4687**) have outlets in Airlie Beach and Proserpine Airport (telephone numbers serve both locations). **Budget** (✆ **07/4945 1024**) has an office at Proserpine Airport and **Europcar** (✆ **07/4946 4133**) has an office at Airlie Beach.

Where to Stay in the Whitsundays

The advantages of staying on the mainland include cheaper accommodations, a choice of restaurants, the freedom to visit a different island each day, and a bevy of activities such as jet skiing, kayaking, parasailing, catamaran sailing, and windsurfing.

But if you are here, it would be a shame not to spend at least a couple of days soaking up the island life. By staying on an island you get swimming, snorkeling, bushwalking, and a huge range of watersports, many of them free, right outside your door. You won't be isolated if you stay on an island, because most Great Barrier Reef cruise boats, sail-and-snorkel yacht excursions, Whitehaven Beach cruises, dive boats, fishing tour vessels, and so on stop at the island resorts every day or on a frequent basis. Be warned, however, that once you're "captive" on an island, you may be slugged with high food and drink prices. And although most island resorts offer nonmotorized watersports (such as windsurfing and sailing) free of charge, you will pay for activities that use fuel, such as parasailing, water-skiing, and dinghy rental.

AIRLIE BEACH

Coral Sea Resort ★★★   In Airlie Beach's best location, on the edge of Paradise Point, this resort is one of the best places to stay on the Whitsunday mainland. It suits everyone from honeymooners to families, and although it's relatively sprawling, the design is such that you can easily feel you're alone. The Coral Sea suites are divine, complete with a Jacuzzi and double hammock on the balcony. There are four styles of suites, plus apartments and family units. Bayview suites have a Jacuzzi inside. Coral Sea is done in a nice nautical theme throughout, with historic sailing images on the walls, lots of blue, and a scattering of yachting memorabilia and artifacts. It's a 3-minute walk along the waterfront to Airlie Beach village.

25 Oceanview Ave. www.coralsearesort.com. ✆ **1800/075 061** in Australia, or 07/4964 1300. 78 units. A$225–A$275 double; A$295–A$345 suite; A$310 family room; A$385 1-bedroom apt.; A$395 2-bedroom apt.; A$640 3-bedroom apt.; A$395–A$745 penthouse. Free parking. **Amenities:** Restaurant; bar; babysitting; bikes; exercise room; 25m (82-ft.) outdoor pool; room service; spa; watersports rental; free Wi-Fi.

Mantra Boathouse Apartments ★★   Right on the waterfront in the Port of Airlie development, which opened in 2015, these smart and spacious two- and three-bedroom apartments have everything you need. Large balconies open out to views over the marina and the Coral Sea. There is no restaurant, but downstairs in the Port of Airlie development are three dining options (at last count), and you are only a 5-minute walk from Airlie Beach town center. But you're also not far from nature; I awoke to a row of half a dozen sulphur-crested cockatoos lined up on my balcony rail!

33 Port Dr., Port of Airlie. www.mantra.com.au. ✆ **1300/987 604** in Australia, or 07/4841 4100. 56 units. A$319 2-bedroom apt. (sleeps 4); A$449 3-bedroom apt. (sleeps 6). Free secure parking. **Amenities:** Outdoor pool; tennis court; playground; free Wi-Fi.

ISLAND RESORTS

Palm Bay Resort ★★   Hammocks on the balcony of your private bungalow set the tone for pure relaxation. Palm Bay has no mobile phone reception and no Internet connection…go off the grid and revel in the peace and quiet. A 20-minute boat ride from Shute Harbour brings you to a curve of stony beach with a backdrop of lush bush. Take a kayak, hike the island's walking track, or relax by the pool. Rooms have no TVs, but there's one in a small lounge if you can't live without it. Self-catering is encouraged, with a communal, fully equipped cooking area between the pool and the restaurant. (Bungalows and suites come with kitchenettes with microwaves, sinks, and bar fridges.) A small store stocks nonperishables and basic foods like pastas and frozen meats and seafood, but you'll probably want to bring some supplies with you from the mainland. The restaurant has a limited menu for lunch and dinner, mostly pizza from the wood-fired oven.

Long Island (19km/12 miles SE of Airlie Beach). www.palmbayresort.com.au. ✆ **07/4777 7093.** 25 units. A$269–A$420 double. **Amenities:** Restaurant; bar; outdoor pool; spa; 2 tennis courts; watersports; no Wi-Fi.

Snorkeling on Hamilton Island.

Hamilton Island ★★ More a vacation village than a single resort, Hamilton has the widest range of activities, accommodations styles, and restaurants of any Great Barrier Reef island resort, and it's ideal for families. Accommodations options include extra-large rooms and suites in the high-rise hotel; high-rise one-bedroom apartments; Polynesian-style bungalows in tropical gardens (ask for one away from the road for real privacy); and glamorous rooms in the two-story, adults-only **Beach Club** (with a personal "host" to cater to your every whim, plus a restaurant, lounge, and pool for exclusive use of Beach Club guests); as well as one-, two-, three-, and four-bedroom apartments and villas, including villas at the waterfront Yacht Club. The best sea views are from the second-floor Beach Club rooms, from floors 5 to 18 of the **Reef View Hotel,** and from most apartments and villas. If your budget is huge, the poshest part of the resort is the ultraluxe **qualia,** an exclusive, adults-only retreat on the northern part of the island. It has 60 one-bedroom pavilions, each with a private swimming pool and a guest pavilion. There's a spa and two restaurants reserved just for qualia guests.

Most of the accommodations are set around a large freeform pool and swim-up bar and the curve of Catseye Beach. Nearby is a marina village with cafes, restaurants, shops, and a yacht club. Hamilton offers a huge range of watersports, fishing trips, cruises, speedboat rides, go-karts, quad bikes, a bowling alley, mini-golf, hiking trails, a wildlife sanctuary (you may have seen Oprah here, cuddling a koala), and an extensive daily activities program.

<table>
<tr><td colspan="2">The Secret of the Seasons</td></tr>
</table>

High season in the Whitsundays coincides with school vacations, which occur in mid-April, from late June to early July, from late September to early October, and in late December. The Aussie winter, June through August, is popular, too. You have to book months ahead to get high-season accommodations, but any other time you can indeed find some good deals: Specials on accommodations, sailing trips, day cruises, and diving excursions fairly leap off the blackboards outside the tour-booking agents in Airlie Beach.

There are no cars on the island, and because a steep hill splits the resort, the best way to get around is on the free bus service, which operates on two loops around the island from 7am to 11pm, or by rented golf buggy (A$59 for 2 hr.; A$87 for 24 hr.). The biggest drawback is that just about every activity costs extra, so you are constantly adding to your bill. To get away from the main resort area, hit the beach or the hiking trails—most of the 750-hectare (1,853-acre) island is virgin bushland.

Hamilton Island (16km/10 miles SE of Shute Harbour). www.hamiltonisland.com.au or www.qualia.com.au. © **137 333** in Australia, or 02/9007 0009 (Sydney reservations office), or 866/209 0891 toll-free or 424/206 5274 for North American inquiries. 880 units. A$410 Palm Bungalow; A$370–A$480 double; A$690–A$1,330 suite; A$720 Beach Club double; A$1,300–A$2,600 qualia; A$5,000 qualia house. **Amenities:** 12 restaurants, 7 bars; babysitting; child-care center for kids 6 weeks to 14 years (3 separate age groups); mini-golf and driving range; health club; 7 outdoor pools; room service; tennis courts; free Wi-Fi.

Where to Eat in the Whitsundays
AIRLIE BEACH
The Deck ★★ CONTEMPORARY   Stone and wood accents, lots of glass, and an open deck that overlooks Airlie Creek and the park beyond it makes this a lovely spot for breakfast, lunch, or dinner. Top that with friendly and helpful service and excellent food, and this makes a winning choice on Airlie Beach's main street. The interesting menu includes dishes like an Asian chicken salad, or grilled local reef fish with a red salad of beets, chickpeas, grapefruit, marinated goat's feta, and rocket (arugula). Steaks and seafood feature, or choose from the pizza menu (available 11am until late).

277 Shute Harbour Rd., Airlie Beach. © **07/4948 2721.** Main courses A$26–A$40. Daily 7am–late.

Northerlies Beach Bar & Grill ★★ CONTEMPORARY   Built around a nautical theme—with a real ship inside the bar—this is a great place for a night out. Looking out on palm trees and the Coral Sea, back to the twinkling lights of Airlie Beach after dark, it's a great place to be at sunset. A little bit out of town, Northerlies is worth the trip for its terrific atmosphere and is a popular spot for locals. The menu has everything from salads and burgers to expensive steaks, or a cold seafood platter for A$55. Sink your teeth into a rack of lamb with eggplant puree or pork tenderloin with mango laksa. The restaurant provides a free shuttle from Airlie Beach (and return) every 30 minutes from 11:30am to 10pm (pick it up at the Airlie Beach Town Centre car park). A taxi will cost around A$35 taxi ride, but ask the driver for a Cab Charge docket and A$10 will be put towards your restaurant bill when you pay.

116 Pringle Rd., Woodwark. www.northerlies.com.au. © **1800/682 277** in Australia. Main courses A$22–A$58. Fri–Tues 10am–11pm.

Whitsunday Sailing Club ★ CONTEMPORARY   This casual club is a popular hangout for locals, with one of the best views in the Whitsundays, overlooking Pioneer Bay and the islands. The menu includes light meals such as burgers or a Caesar salad; for something heartier go for steak topped with mushroom, pepper, or creamy garlic sauce, or fish 'n' chips. Great for drinks at sunset. Kids under 13 eat free on Thursday nights with every main meal over A$20, or choose from the A$10 kids' menu.

Airlie Point (enter from The Esplanade), Airlie Beach. www.whitsundaysailingclub.com. au. © **07/4946 6138.** Main courses A$18–A$37. Daily 11:30am–2:30pm and 5:30–8:30pm.

Exploring the Whitsundays

The little town of Airlie Beach, perched on the edge of the Coral Sea with views across Pioneer Bay and the Whitsunday Passage, is the focal point of activity on the Whitsunday mainland. Airlie Beach has a massive beachfront artificial lagoon, with sandy beaches and landscaped parkland, which solves the problem of where to swim in stinger season. The lagoon is the size of about six full-size Olympic swimming pools, set in 4 hectares (10 acres) of botanic gardens, with a children's pool, plenty of shade, barbecues, picnic shelters, toilets, showers, and parking. For a bird's-eye view of it all, head to the Lions Lookout.

Getting out on the water is the most important thing here. Countless opportunities are offered, with the focus firmly on sailing, snorkeling, and diving. Cruises and yachts depart from the Port of Airlie, or from Shute Harbour, a 10-minute drive south on Shute Harbour Road.

REEF CRUISES

Cruise Whitsundays (www.cruisewhitsundays.com.au; © **07/4946 4662**) makes daily trips to Hardy Reef in a high-speed, air-conditioned catamaran.

Safety in the Water	
Deadly **marine stingers** may frequent the shorelines of the Whitsundays from October through April. The best place to swim is in the beachfront Airlie Beach lagoon. The rivers in these parts are	home to dangerous **saltwater croco-diles** (which mostly live in fresh water, contrary to their name), so don't swim in streams, rivers, or water holes.

The boat has a bar, and a biologist gives a marine ecology talk en route. You anchor at the massive Reefworld pontoon, which was built to hold up to 600 people, and spend up to 3½ hours on the Reef. The day trip costs A$269 for adults, A$125 for children 4 to 14. Guided snorkel safaris cost A$59 extra for adults and A$35 for children. You can book dives on board for A$139 for first-time divers and A$109 for certified divers (A$59 for a second dive). Cruises depart at 8am from the Port of Airlie, picking up at Hamilton Island at 9am. Passengers from other islands take the ferry to Hamilton to board there.

A unique experience is Cruise Whitsundays' **ReefSleep**, during which you spend the night on the pontoon. You travel with the day-trippers, but when they leave at 3pm you will be with a maximum of nine people. This gives you a fabulous chance to snorkel at night when the coral is luminescent in the moonlight and nocturnal sea creatures get busy. The trip includes 2 full days on the Reef, all meals, and the chance to sleep on the upper deck under the stars in a swag (a type of outdoor sleeping bag). The cost is A$525 for a double swag or A$675 for a single. This is an experience only for those over 12 years old.

In and around the Whitsunday islands, you can visit many excellent dive sites close to shore. **Mantaray Charters** (www.mantaraycharters.com; ✆ **07/4948 1117**), based at Abell Point Marina, runs day tours to Whitehaven Beach and gives you the chance to dive near Hayman Island or Hook Island. Tours are limited to 36 passengers and leave at 8am, returning around 4:30pm. The cost is A$209 adults, A$107 kids age 4 to 12, and A$582 for a family of four. The cost includes lunch, snacks, and all equipment, whether you are diving or snorkeling. You'll pay A$100 for an introductory dive or A$80 if you're certified. Second dives cost A$60.

Heart Reef

The iconic image of the Great Barrier Reef is the stunning heart-shaped reef called—yes, **Heart Reef.** In my opinion, the best way to see this tiny reef's perfect shape is from the air, but since 2019 it has also been possible to spend the day at Heart Reef on a new "island" in a neighboring lagoon, a luxury A$2-million pontoon designed for just six people. The new "Heart Island" pontoon has been created by **Hamilton Island Air** (www.hamiltonislandair.com; ✆ **07/4969 9599**), to allow visitors an up-close look at this iconic reef. This is the first time water access has been given to Heart Reef, and at A$999 per person, it doesn't come cheap. A custom-designed glass-bottom boat takes you from the pontoon to circumnavigate Heart Reef, and there's also time for snorkeling in a nearby lagoon. The whole experience takes about 3 hours. There are many helicopter or seaplane options available for flying over Heart Reef for that perfect photo op (or, of course, if you are planning a mid-air proposal). A 1-hour seaplane flight over the Great Barrier Reef costs A$330 adults and A$290 children with **Air Whitsunday** (www.airwhitsunday.com. au; ✆ **07/4946 9111**), which offers a range of tours, including seaplane flights to a Reef pontoon to snorkel for a couple of hours.

OUTRIGGER sailing

For a different look at the Whitsunday Coast, take a 90-minute tour with **Whitsunday Sailing Outrigger** (www.whitsundaysailingoutrigger.com; ✆ **0402/473 059** mobile) to skim along the water aboard Steve and Michelle Lynes's lovely craft *Ohana*. With only four guests on board, this is a terrific, personal experience. Tours depart daily at 10am, 1pm, and 4pm, and cost from A$60 adults, A$50 children (age 7 and older), or A$170 for a family. A 2-hour tour to Pigeon Island, or a sunset champagne tour, costs from A$80 adults, A$65 children and A$225 family. Prices are slightly higher on weekends. Bookings are essential.

SAILING & SNORKELING TRIPS

A journey on one of the many yachts offering 3-day, 2-night sailing adventures is a great way to see the islands. You can learn to sail or get involved with sailing the boat as much or as little as you want, snorkel to your heart's content over one dazzling reef after another, beachcomb, explore national-park trails, stop at secluded bays, swim, sunbathe, and generally have a laidback good time. A few companies offer introductory and qualified scuba diving for an extra cost per dive. Most boats carry a maximum of 12 passengers, so the atmosphere is always friendly and fun. The food is generally good, the showers are usually hot, and you sleep in comfortable but small berths off the galley. Some have small private twin or double cabins.

Prices usually include all meals, Marine Park entrance fees, snorkel gear, and transfers to the departure point (Abell Point Marina or Shute Harbour). In the off-season, the boats compete fiercely for passengers; you'll see signboards on the main street in Airlie Beach advertising standby deals.

Prosail (www.prosail.com.au; ✆ **07/4946 4444**) runs sailing trips through the Great Barrier Reef Marine Park. All trips include sailing, snorkeling, scuba diving, and bushwalking, and you can sail on mega-yachts such as the *Condor, Broomstick,* and *Hammer.* A 2-day overnight trip costs A$349 per person.

These kinds of trips are a cheaper alternative to **"bareboating"** (skippering your own yacht)—which is a hugely popular thing to do, despite the cost. If you are confident about sailing yourself—and most yacht-charter companies in the islands will want one person on the boat to have a little experience— you do not need a license, and sailing is surprisingly easy in these uncrowded waters, where the channels are deep and the seas are protected from big swells by the Great Barrier Reef. The 74 islands are so close to one another that one is always in sight, and safe anchorages are everywhere. But for extra reassurance, the company may require you to take a skipper along at an extra cost of around A$400 per day (plus meals) if you want them to stay with you. Before departure, the company provides a thorough 2- to 3-hour briefing and easy-to-read maps marking channels, anchorage points, and the very few dangerous

Hitting the Sand at Whitehaven Beach

The 6km (3¾-mile) stretch of pure-white silica sand on **Whitehaven Beach** ★★ will leave you in rapture. The beach, on uninhabited Whitsunday Island, does not boast a lot of coral, but the swimming is good and the forested shore is beautiful. Take a book and chill out. Some sailboat day trips visit it, as do some motorized vessels. A half-day trip with **Cruise Whitsundays** (www.cruise whitsundays.com; © 07/4946 4662) costs from A$115 adults and A$45 children age 4 to 14 and gives you around 2 hours on the beach. You can travel in the morning (leaving the Port of Airlie at 7am) or in the afternoon (departing at noon), with pickups at Hamilton Island and Daydream Island on the way. Full-day trips combine Whitehaven Beach with other islands on some tours. **Air Whitsunday** (www.airwhitsunday.com. au; © 07/4946 9111) offers seaplane flights to Whitehaven Beach for A$310 adults or A$260 children, with a glass of bubbly when you land.

reefs. Your charter company will radio in once or twice a day to check that you're still afloat, and you can contact them anytime for advice.

You can buy your own provisions or have the charter company stock the boat at an extra cost of about A$30 per person per day. Most operators will load a windsurfer, fishing tackle, and scuba-diving equipment on request, for an extra fee if they are not standard.

In peak season, you may have to charter the boat for a week. At other times, most companies impose a minimum of 5 days, but many will rent for 3 nights if you ask, rather than let a vessel sit idle. In peak season (mid-Sept to mid-Oct, and Christmas to mid-Jan), expect to pay A$750 to A$985 per night for a standard four- to six-berth yacht, more if you want something luxurious. Rates in the off-season (mid-Jan to end of Mar), and even in one of the Whitsundays' busiest holiday times, June through August, will be anywhere from A$100 to A$200 less. If you are prepared to book within 14 days of when you want to sail, the deals can be even better; you should be able to find a boat that late in the off-season. You may be asked to post a credit card bond of up to A$2,000. Fuel and park fees are extra, and mooring fees apply if you want to stop at one of the island resorts overnight. A number of bareboat-charter companies offer **"sail-'n'-stay" packages** that combine a few days of sailing with a few days at an island resort.

Most bareboat charter companies will make complete holiday arrangements for you in the islands, including accommodations, transfers, tours, and sporting activities. The majority operate out of Airlie Beach, Hamilton Island, or both. Well-known operators include **Whitsunday Rent-A-Yacht** (www.rent ayacht.com.au; © **1800/075 000** in Australia, or 07/4946 9232); **Queensland Yacht Charters** (www.yachtcharters.com.au; © **1800/075 013** in Australia, or 07/4946 7400); and **Sunsail** (www.sunsail.com.au; © **1800/803 988** in Australia, or 02/8912 7040).

SOUTHERN GREAT BARRIER REEF REGION ★★

Off this stretch of the Queensland coast is the southernmost part of the Great Barrier Reef, where you will find the spectacular **Heron Island,** whose reefs are a source of enchantment for divers and snorkelers. Its waters boast 21 dive sites, and in summer, large turtles lumber ashore to nest on its beaches.

Off the small town of **Bundaberg** is another tiny coral cay, **Lady Elliot Island ★★**, a nesting site for tens of thousands of seabirds and home to a first-rate fringing reef. Bundaberg's major attraction is a mainland **loggerhead turtle rookery** that draws large crowds in summer.

Gladstone: Gateway to Heron Island

Gladstone: 550km (341 miles) N of Brisbane; 1,162km (720 miles) S of Cairns

The industrial port town of Gladstone is the departure point for beautiful Heron Island. Gladstone is on the coast 21km (13 miles) off the Bruce Highway. Most flights to Gladstone arrive in time to connect with the ferry to Heron Island, but if you need to stay overnight, a couple of good, centrally located options are **Mercure Gladstone** (www.accorhotels.com.au; ☎ **07/4979 8200**) and **Rydges Gladstone** (www.rydges.com; ☎ **07/4970 0000**).

ESSENTIALS
Arriving
BY PLANE Qantas (www.qantas.com.au; ☎ **131 313** in Australia) and **Virgin Australia** (www.virginaustalia.com.au; ☎ **136 789** in Australia) both have daily flights from Brisbane.

BY TRAIN Queensland Rail (www.queenslandrailtravel.com.au; ☎ **1800/872 467** in Queensland) operates trains to Gladstone from Brisbane and Cairns most days. The economy fare from Brisbane is A$119 on the high-speed **Tilt Train** (trip time: 6 hr.).

BY BUS Greyhound Australia (www.greyhound.com.au; ☎ **1300/473 946** in Australia) operates daily coaches to Gladstone on the Brisbane-Cairns run. The fare is around A$160 from Brisbane (trip time: 11½ hr.) and around A$230 from Cairns (trip time: 18½ hr.).

Getting Around
Avis (☎ **07/4978 2633**), **Budget** (☎ **07/4972 8488**), **Europcar** (☎ **07/4978 7787**), and **Hertz** (☎ **07/4978 6899**) have offices in Gladstone.

Visitor Information
The **Gladstone Visitor Information Centre** is in the ferry terminal at Gladstone Marina, 72 Bryan Jordan Dr. (www.gladstoneregion.info; ☎ **07/4972 9000**). It's open 8:30am to 4:30pm Monday through Friday and 9am to 1pm weekends and public holidays (closed Christmas Day).

Heron Island ★★★

72km (45 miles) NE of Gladstone

Heron Island is often referred to as "the jewel of the Reef." And rightly so. The difference between Heron and other islands is that once there, you are right on the Reef. Step off the beach and you enter magnificent fields of coral that seem to stretch for miles. And the myriad life forms that abound here are accessible to everyone through diving, snorkeling, or reef walks at low tide.

There has been a resort on Heron since 1932, and in 1943 the island became a national park. An experience of a lifetime is almost guaranteed at any time of year, particularly if you love turtles—Heron is a haven for giant green and loggerhead turtles. Resort guests gather on the beach from late November to February to watch female turtles lay eggs, and from February to mid-April to see the hatched babies scuttle down the sand to the water. Every night during the season, volunteer guides from the island's University of Queensland research station tag and measure the turtles before they return to the water. Only 1 in 5,000 hatchlings will live to return in about 50 years to lay its own eggs. Humpback whales also pass through from June through September.

Three days on Heron gives you plenty of time. The island is so small that you can walk around it at a leisurely pace in about half an hour. One of the first things to do is to take advantage of the organized activities that the resort offers several times a day, to give guests flexibility in planning their time. Book your activities at the resort information center. Snorkeling and reef walking are major occupations for visitors—if they're not diving, that is. The island is home to 21 of the world's most stunning dive sites.

Guided walks provide another way to explore the island. Walks include a visit to the island's research station. As for the reef walk, just borrow a pair of sand shoes, a balance pole, and a viewing bucket, and head off with a guide at low tide. The walk can take up to 90 minutes.

Heron is also home to colonies of mutton birds; be warned, they can be particularly noisy during the breeding and mating season, from November to January. They also create a fairly…shall I say…distinctive smell (you get used to it, but some people find it highly offensive). That's nature for you.

ARRIVING

A **170-seater launch** currently departs Gladstone Marina, Bryan Jordan Drive, at 9:30am, 5 days a week (no service on Tues or Thurs). Transfers cost A$69 each way for adults and A$32 for kids 2 to 12, including an airport transfer. Trip time is around 2 hours. Return transfers leave Heron Island at 12:45pm. Seaplane transfers can also be arranged for A$349 per person, and helicopter transfers are even more expensive.

WHERE TO STAY ON HERON ISLAND

Heron Island Resort ★★★ This is a lovely, low-key resort, with no day-trippers and a focus very much on the outdoors. The colors of the island's surrounding water and Reef are reflected in the interiors, and everything is

COAST VILLAGES: 1770 and agnes water

About 50km (31½ miles) from Gladstone, on the coast, are the lovely coastal hamlets of **Agnes Water** ★★ and **1770** ★ (so named by British explorer Captain James Cook the year he mapped the coastline of Australia). These tiny places are well worth the detour. Stop in at the **Agnes Water/1770 Visitor Information Centre**, 71 Springs Rd., Agnes Water (📞 **07/4902 1533**), to get the lowdown on things to do in the region. The info center is open Monday through Friday 9am to 5pm and weekends from 10am to 2pm; it's closed Christmas Day and Good Friday.

I highly recommend two tours in this area. The **1770 LARC! Tours** (www.1770larctours.com.au; 📞 **07/4974 9422**) will see you ride high on a bright pink amphibious craft that gives access to land and sea to explore the waterways and coast of 1770. Owner Neil Mergard and his team provide fascinating and entertaining commentary about the land and environment—you'll come away with a new appreciation of this part of Australia. One-hour afternoon tours cost A$40 adults, A$18 kids 5 to 16; a full-day tour costs A$160 adults, A$99 children.

Another way of getting out on the water is on a kayak tour with Simon and Janina of **1770 Liquid Adventures** (www.1770liquidadventures.com.au; 📞 **0428/956 630** mobile). A 2-hour tour costs A$50 per person; 2½-hour sunset tours cost A$55. You might spot dolphins, and you may also have the company of Bailey, their golden Labrador, who rides in the lead kayak.

light-filled and breezy. Heron's central complex is equal parts grand Queenslander home and laidback beach house, with bar and lounge areas open to ocean views and sunsets. Duplex-style Turtle rooms are designed for couples or families, or you can go for greater luxury in the Wistari or Point suites or the private Beach House (the only rooms with air-conditioning). Rooms are TV-free, but a lounge has TVs and public phones (only the four Point suites and the Beach House have private phones). The resort has no mobile phone coverage, but there are payphones and you can get Wi-Fi in the bar and lounge. The **Aqua Soul Spa** offers double treatment rooms and all the usual spa treatments and pampering.

Heron Island, off Gladstone. www.heronisland.com. 📞 **1800/875 343** in Australia, or 855/251 8261 in the U.S., or 07/4972 9055 (resort). 109 units. A$315 Turtle Room double or A$325 for families; A$380 Reef Room double or A$400 families; A$475–A$621 suites; A$653 Beach House. Rates include breakfast, dinner, and some activities. **Amenities:** Restaurant; bar; children's program (ages 7–12) during Australian school vacations; Jacuzzi; outdoor pool; spa; 2 lit tennis courts; limited watersports equipment rental.

Bundaberg ★: Gateway to Lady Elliot Island

384km (238 miles) N of Brisbane; 1,439km (892 miles) S of Cairns

The small sugar town of Bundaberg is the closest to the southernmost point of the Great Barrier Reef. If you visit the area between November and March, allow an evening to visit the **Mon Repos Turtle Centre** (p. 273). Divers may want to take in some of Australia's best shore diving right off Bundaberg's beaches. The southern reefs of the Great Barrier Reef are just as prolific, varied, and colorful as the reefs farther north off Cairns, with the added advantage that, because this part of the coast is less accessible, fewer snorkel and dive boats visit them.

There are two islands to visit in this area: **Lady Musgrave Island** (p. 275) and **Lady Elliot Island** (p. 275), both part of the Bunker Group, which are around 80km (50 miles) due north of Bundaberg. While the islands are due east of Gladstone and closer to that town, only live-aboard boats visit them from there.

ESSENTIALS

Arriving

BY PLANE Qantas (www.qantas.com.au; ✆ **131 313** in Australia) and **Virgin Australia** (www.virginaustralia.com.au; ✆ **136 789** in Australia) both fly from Brisbane daily. Flight time is about 55 minutes.

BY TRAIN Queensland Rail (www.queenslandrail.com.au; ✆ **1800/872 467** in Queensland) trains stop in Bundaberg every day en route between Brisbane and Cairns. The fare is A$89 from Brisbane in economy class or A$115 business class on the **Tilt Train;** the trip takes about 4½ hours.

BY BUS Greyhound Australia (www.greyhound.com.au; ✆ **1300/473 946** in Australia) stops here many times a day on runs between Brisbane and Cairns. The 8-hour trip from Brisbane costs around A$100.

BY CAR Bundaberg is on the Isis Highway, about 50km (31 miles) off the Bruce Highway from Gin Gin in the north and 53km (33 miles) off the Bruce Highway from just north of Childers in the south.

Getting Around

BY CAR Avis (✆ **07/4131 4533**), **Budget** (✆ **07/4155 0095**), **Europcar** (✆ **07/4151 4599**), **Hertz** (✆ **07/4154 1030**), and **Thrifty** (✆ **07/4151 6222**) all have offices in Bundaberg.

BY BUS Duffy's City Buses (www.duffysbuses.com.au; ✆ **1300/383 397** in Australia, or 07/4151 4226) operates the town bus service. There are no public buses on Sundays.

Visitor Information

The **Bundaberg Information Centre** (www.bundabergregion.org; ✆ **1300/722 099** in Australia, or 07/4153 8888), at 36 Avenue St., is open daily 9am to 5pm, public holidays 9am to 2pm. Closed Good Friday, Anzac Day (Apr 25), and Christmas Day.

WHERE TO STAY IN BUNDABERG

Zen Beach Retreat ★★★ Hosts Shane and Pascaline Emms have transformed an old beachfront motel into some of the best accommodations in the Bundaberg region. Four themed two-story villas sit behind the main building (no sea views, unfortunately), opening out onto a Balinese-style pavilion and the pool. The exotic and colorful Oriental villa is my favorite, with design touches from Morocco, Turkey, and the Middle East, but you might prefer the French villa, adorned with some of Pascaline's personal treasures. The Asian villa and a more subdued Executive suite round out the villa options. You can also book the main house, which has three bedrooms plus entertaining areas, as well as access to the expansive upstairs open-plan living area and gourmet kitchen.

54 Miller St., Bargara. www.zenbeachretreat.com. © **07/4154 7757.** 5 units. A$350–A$500 double; A$2,000–A$3,500 whole house (sleeps 6). Free parking. **Amenities:** Outdoor pool; spa; free Wi-Fi.

WHERE TO EAT IN BUNDABERG

Café 1928 ★ CAFE   Set in the leafy surrounds of the Bundaberg Botanic Gardens, this casual cafe is a nice spot for brunch or lunch. Apart from good coffee, it offers quite an extensive menu, everything from donuts, cakes, and sandwiches to salads, chicken parmigiana, and a range of burgers and pizzas. There's also an A$8 kids' menu.

Bundaberg Botanic Gardens, Young St. www.bundabergcafe.com.au. © **07/4153 1928.** Main courses A$8–A$18. Mon–Sat 9am–3pm (kitchen closes 2:30pm); Sun 9am–4pm; public holidays 10am–3pm.

EXPLORING BUNDABERG

By far the most popular attraction in Bundaberg is the annual turtle nesting season on Mon Repos Beach, about 14km (8¾ miles) from the city center. **Mon Repos Regional Park** is one of the two largest loggerhead-turtle rookeries in the South Pacific. The visitor center by the beach has a great display on the turtle life cycle and shows films at 7:30pm daily in summer. There is a strict booking system for turtle-watching tours, to help cope with the crowds. Access to the beach is by ticket only, and you must book your visit to Mon Repos during the turtle season. Tickets are sold through the **Bundaberg Information Centre** at 36 Avenue St. (© **1300/722 099** in Australia, or 07/4153 8888), or online at www.bundabergregion.org/turtles. The website has a lot of very useful information on how to get to the rookery and what to expect from your turtle-watching experience. Tours start at 7pm, but you may have to wait up to 2 hours or more, depending on when the turtles appear. Nesting happens around high tide; hatching usually occurs between 8pm and midnight. Take a sweater, as it can get quite cool.

The **Mon Repos Turtle Centre** (www.parks.des.qld.gov.au/parks/mon-repos; © **07/4159 1652**) at 141 Mon Repos Rd. is well signposted. During turtle-nesting season (Nov to late Mar), the park and information center are open daily 8am to 5pm (closed Christmas Eve, Christmas Day, and New Year's Eve). Public access to the beach is closed from 6pm to 6am, unless you are on a tour. Turtle-viewing tours run from 7pm until midnight daily (except for Dec 24, 25, and 31). From April to early November (when no turtles are around), the information center is open Monday to Friday (except public holidays) from 8am to 3:30pm, and the park is open 24 hours. Admission to the visitor center is free from April through November; but when the turtles start

nesting, you pay A$13 for adults, A$6.65 for children age 5 to 14, and A$31 for families of four, including your tour. It's the best value anywhere!

Lady Musgrave Island

Snorkelers and divers also head out from Bundaberg on a daily basis to pretty **Lady Musgrave Island** (www.ladymusgraveexperience.com.au; ☏ **07/4151 5225),** a vegetated 14-hectare (35-acre) national-park coral cay, 52 nautical miles off the coast. It is surrounded by a lagoon 8km (5 miles) in circumference, filled with hundreds of corals and some 1,200 of the 1,500 species of fish and other marine creatures found on the Great Barrier Reef.

Lady Elliot Island ★★

80km (50 miles) NE of Bundaberg

Reef walking, snorkeling, and diving are the main reasons people come to this 42-hectare (104-acre) coral cay, ringed by a wide, shallow lagoon filled with dazzling coral life. Divers will see a good range of marine life, including brilliantly colored fish, clams, sponges, urchins, and anemones. Green and loggerhead turtles nest on the beach November through March; whales pass by from June through September. You may snorkel and reef walk only during the 2 to 3 hours before and after high tide, so plan your day accordingly.

Lady Elliot is a sparse, grassy island rookery, not a sandy tropical paradise—it's so small you can walk across it in 15 minutes. Some find it too spartan; others relish chilling out in a beautiful, peaceful spot with reef all around. Just be prepared for the smell and constant noise of the birds.

ARRIVING

The 30-minute charter flight with **Seair Pacific** (www.seairpacific.com.au; ☏ **07/5599 4509**) from Bundaberg runs daily at 8:40am; it costs A$349 adults, A$220 kids 3 to 12, round-trip. You can make it a day trip by returning on the 4pm flight back to Bundaberg. (You can also do a day-trip flight from Brisbane—see p. 216.) Day trips include a welcome drink and orientation tour, glass-bottom-boat ride or guided snorkel tour, lunch, and use of the resort facilities (including towels, reef-walking shoes, sunscreen, and snorkel equipment). If you plan to stay longer than a day, book your flights with your accommodation, and remember there is a 10-kilogram (22-lb.) luggage limit.

WHERE TO STAY ON LADY ELLIOT ISLAND

Lady Elliot Island Eco Resort ★★★ Accommodations here are fairly basic, but visitors come for the Reef, not the room. The top-of-the-range rooms, the Island suites (the only rooms with air-conditioning), have one or two separate bedrooms and great sea views from the deck. Most Reef rooms sleep four and have decks with views through the trees to the sea. The cool, spacious safari-tent "eco-cabins" have four bunks, electric lighting, fans, and timber floors, but share toilets and showers. The limited facilities include a boutique, an education center, and a dive shop, which runs shore and boat

FACING PAGE: Turtle nesting at Mon Repos Regional Park.

dives and introductory dives, and rents equipment. Two "glamping" tents have private bathrooms. There are no TVs, radio, mobile phone reception, or phones in the rooms (but there is a public telephone). A program of mostly free activities includes glass-bottom-boat rides, table tennis, guided walks, and beach volleyball.

Great Barrier Reef, off Bundaberg, Runaway Bay. www.ladyelliot.com.au. ℭ **1800/072 200** in Australia, or 07/4156 4444. 43 units. A$398–A$450 eco-cabin double; A$636–A$738 double; A$764–A$804 glamping tent; A$830–A$880 suite. A$115–A$145 children 3–12 years; A$28 children under 3 (cot charge). 4-night minimum Christmas/New Year; 2-night minimum for suites. Rates include breakfast, dinner, and some guided tours. **Amenities:** Restaurant; bar; children's program (ages 5–12) during school holidays; saltwater pool; Wi-Fi hotspot available (in public areas) for a fee (from $5 for 3 days).

THE NORTHERN TERRITORY

Though there's no border between them, the Northern Territory is really two distinctly different regions. The "Top End" is a last frontier, a place of wild, rugged beauty and sometimes hardship, with its major center the capital, Darwin. The "Red Centre" is a landscape of endless horizons, vast red deserts, cloudless blue skies, and the Outback town of Alice Springs. At its heart lies the magnificent monolith Uluru (Ayers Rock), the main reason visitors are drawn to this arid land.

Darwin is a small, modern city, wealthy, tropical, and ever-changing. To the east, the wetlands of Kakadu National Park teem with crocodiles and birds; a third of the country's avian species are here. It's a wealth of experiences: You can visit an Aboriginal community, canoe along remote rivers, and soak in thermal pools.

Life in the Top End is different from life elsewhere in Australia. Locals relish its slightly lawless image, but in Darwin you'll also get a sense of a city on the move. Isolation, Wet season monsoons, crocs, and other dangers make 'em tough up here, but you don't have to do without the comforts you're used to.

The Red Centre is home to sprawling cattle ranches, ancient mountain ranges, palm trees that survived the Ice Age, cockatoos and kangaroos, ochre gorges, lush water holes, and desert tracks leading to heart-stopping landscapes. Aboriginal people have lived here for tens of thousands of years.

There's one important fact to get straight from the start: Alice Springs is a gateway to Uluru, but the two destinations are *not* side by side. Indeed, they are 462km (286 miles) apart. You can get to Uluru from Alice Springs and see it in a day, but in doing so you will miss much of the experience: Visiting Uluru is much more than just a quick photo op—it may well be the most meaningful and memorable part of your trip to Australia. You can also fly direct to Ayers Rock Airport, which takes its name from the European name given to Uluru by early explorers but is seldom used today.

One highway connects "The Alice" to Darwin; beyond that, a few roads and four-wheel-drive tracks make a lonely spider web across the Northern Territory. There are still many areas where non-Aborigines have never set foot.

Allow yourself a few days to experience all there is in both the Top End and the Centre—to do otherwise you deprive yourself of experiencing the essence of Australia.

TERRITORY ESSENTIALS

Visitor Information

Tourism NT has a great website (www.northernterritory.com) with special sections tailored for international travelers (choose your country). It details many hotels, tour operators, car-rental companies, and attractions, and offers information on local Aboriginal culture and Aboriginal tours. Tourism NT's **Territory Discoveries division** (www.territorydiscoveries.com; ℂ **1300/738 111**) offers package deals.

When to Go

The main factor to consider when visiting Darwin and Kakadu National Park is the difference between dry and wet seasons. The Dry (May–Oct) is the most popular time to go, with temperatures around 86°F (30°C) and sunny days. Many tours, hotels, and even campsites are booked a year in advance, so make sure you have reservations. In the Wet season (Nov–Apr), heat and humidity are extreme, and floodwaters may cover much of the Kakadu park, cutting off some attractions entirely. Some tour companies do not operate during the Wet, and park ranger talks, walks, and slide shows are not offered. The upside is that the crowds vanish, the brownish vegetation bursts into green, waterfalls swell from a trickle to a roar, and lightning storms are spectacular, especially in the hot "buildup" to the season in October and November. The landscape can change dramatically from one day to the next as floodwaters rise and fall, so be prepared for surprises—nice ones (such as giant flocks of geese) and unwelcome ones (such as blocked roads). Although it can pour down all day, it's more common for the rain to fall in late-afternoon storms and at night. Take it easy in the humidity, and make sure you are staying in air-conditioned accommodations.

For the Red Centre and Alice Springs, April, May, September, and October offer the best weather, with sunny days (coolish in May, hot in Oct). Winter (June–Aug) means mild temperatures with cold nights. Summer (Nov–Mar) is ferociously hot and best avoided. In summer, limit exertions to early morning and late afternoon, and choose air-conditioned accommodations. Rain is rare but can come at any time of year.

Driving Tips

The **Automobile Association of the Northern Territory,** 14 Knuckey St., Darwin, NT 0800 (www.aant.com.au; ℂ **08/8925 5901**), dispenses maps and advice and also offers emergency-breakdown service (ℂ **131 111**) to members of affiliated overseas automobile associations. It has no office in the Red

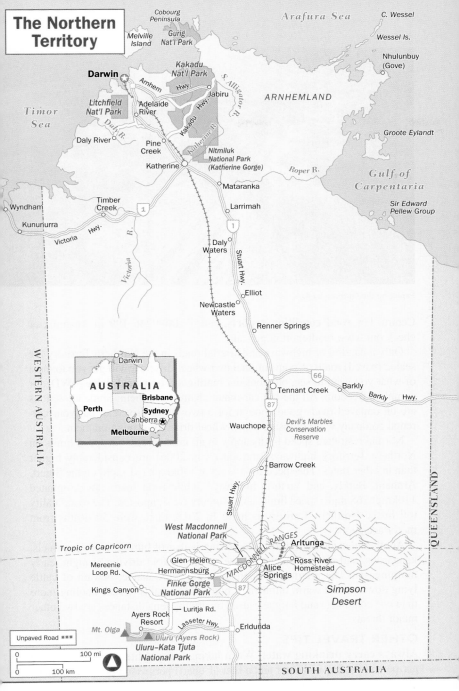

The Northern Territory

Arafura Sea

Cobourg Peninsula

Melville Island

Gurig Nat'l Park

C. Wessel

Wessel Is.

Nhulunbuy (Gove)

Darwin

Arnhem Hwy.

Kakadu Nat'l Park

Jabiru

S. Alligator R.

ARNHEMLAND

Litchfield Nat'l Park

Adelaide River

Daly R.

Kakadu Hwy.

Groote Eylandt

Timor Sea

Daly River

Pine Creek

Katherine R.

Katherine

Nitmiluk National Park (Katherine Gorge)

Roper R.

Gulf of Carpentaria

Mataranka

Sir Edward Pellew Group

Wyndham

Timber Creek

1

Larrimah

Kununurra

Victoria Hwy.

Victoria R.

1

Daly Waters

Stuart Hwy.

Elliot

Newcastle Waters

Renner Springs

AUSTRALIA

Darwin

Perth

Brisbane

Sydney

Canberra ★

Melbourne

66

Tennant Creek

Barkly

Barkly Hwy.

87

Wauchope

Devil's Marbles Conservation Reserve

WESTERN AUSTRALIA

Barrow Creek

Stuart Hwy.

QUEENSLAND

Tropic of Capricorn

West Macdonnell National Park

MACDONNELL RANGES

Arltunga

Glen Helen

Ross River Homestead

Mereenie Loop Rd.

Hermannsburg

Alice Springs

Kings Canyon

Finke Gorge National Park

87

Simpson Desert

Ayers Rock Resort

Luritja Rd.

Mt. Olga

Lasseter Hwy.

Erldunda

Uluru (Ayers Rock)
Uluru-Kata Tjuta National Park

SOUTH AUSTRALIA

Unpaved Road ▪▪▪

0   100 mi
0   100 km

Exploring the Outback by 4x4.

Centre. For **road condition reports,** call ✆ **1800/246 199** in Australia or check out www.roadreport.nt.gov.au.

Only a handful of highways and arterial roads in the Northern Territory are sealed (paved) roads. A conventional two-wheel-drive car will get you to most of what you want to see, but consider renting a **four-wheel-drive** (4WD) for complete freedom. All the big car-rental chains have them. Some attractions are on unpaved roads good enough for a two-wheel-drive car, but your car-rental company will not insure a two-wheel-drive for driving on them.

Normal restricted speed limits apply in all urban areas, but speed limits on Northern Territory highways (introduced in 2006) are considerably higher than in other states. The speed limit is set at 130kmph (81 mph) on the Stuart, Arnhem, Barkly, and Victoria highways, while rural roads are designated 110kmph (68 mph) speed limits unless otherwise signposted. The road fatality toll in the Northern Territory is high: In 2018, there were 50 deaths from motor accidents.

Another considerable risk while driving is that of hitting wildlife: camels, kangaroos, and other protected native species. Avoid driving at night, early morning, and late afternoon, when 'roos are more active; beware of cattle lying down on the warm bitumen at night. Road trains (trucks hauling more than one container) and fatigue caused by driving long distances are two other major threats.

OTHER TRAVEL TIPS

Always carry drinking water. When hiking, carry 4 liters (about a gallon) per person per day in winter and a liter (1 quart) per person per hour in summer. Wear a broad-brimmed hat, high-factor sunscreen, and insect repellant.

Bring warm clothing for chilly winter evenings. Make sure you have a full tank of gas before setting out and check distances between places you can fill up.

Package Tour Operators

Given the great distances between destinations in the Red Centre, you may want to consider opting for a package tour. Numerous coach, minicoach, and 4WD tour operators run tours that take in Alice Springs, Kings Canyon, and Uluru. These depart from Alice Springs or Uluru, offering accommodations ranging from spiffy resorts, comfortable motels, and basic cabins to shared bunkhouses, tents, or swags (sleeping bags) under the stars. Most pack the highlights into a 2- or 3-day trip, though leisurely trips of 6 days or more are available. Many offer one-way itineraries between Alice and the Rock (via Kings Canyon if you like), or vice versa, which will allow you to avoid backtracking.

Among the reputable companies are **AAT Kings** (www.aatkings.com; ✆ **1300/228 546** in Australia), which specializes in coach tours but also has 4WD camping itineraries, and **Intrepid** (www.intrepidtravel.com; ✆ **1300/339 501** in Australia), which conducts camping safaris (or if you prefer, hotel, motel, or lodge accommodations) in small groups for all ages. **Tailormade Tours** (www.tailormadetours.com.au; ✆ **08/8952 1731**) offers general tours as well as customized luxury charters. **Mulga's Adventures** (www.mulgas adventures.com.au; ✆ **1800/359 089** in Australia, or 08/8952 1545), operates a 3-day tour of the area, including Uluru and Kata-Tjuta (A$399).

DARWIN

1,489km (923 miles) N of Alice Springs

Australia's proximity to Asia is never clearer than when you are in Darwin. Named after the naturalist and biologist Charles Darwin (who visited Australia in 1836), the city is an exotic blend of frontier town, Asian village, and modern life. With a population of about 140,000, Darwin has had a turbulent history—and it shows. This city has battled just about everything that man and nature could throw at it. Most of its buildings date from the mid-1970s; Cyclone Tracy wiped out the city on Christmas Eve 1974. Despite all this destruction, some of Darwin's historic buildings—or at least parts of them—have survived, and you can see them around the city center.

The vibe here is relaxed and very casual. Don't bother bringing a jacket and tie; shorts and sandals will be acceptable most places—even the swankiest invitations stipulate "Territory Rig" dress, meaning long pants and a short-sleeved open-neck shirt for men.

Darwin is most commonly used as a gateway to **Kakadu National Park** (p. 296), and many Australians have never visited it—or at least not for long. And that's a shame, because it is an attractive and interesting place. Give yourself a day or two to wander the pleasant streets and park-lands, see the wildlife attractions, or shop for Aboriginal art and South

Sea pearls. An easy day trip is **Litchfield National Park ★★** (p. 293), one of the Territory's best-kept secrets, boasting waterfalls that you'd usually only see in vacation brochures.

Essentials

ARRIVING

BY PLANE   Qantas (www.qantas.com) serves **Darwin International Airport** (**DRW**; www.darwinairport.com.au) daily from Alice Springs, Adelaide, Brisbane, Cairns, Melbourne, Perth, Sydney, and Townsville, either direct or connecting through Alice Springs. **Virgin Australia** (www.virginaustralia.com) flies direct to Darwin from Sydney, Brisbane, Melbourne, Alice Springs, Adelaide, and Perth. **Tigerair** (www.tigerair.com.au; ℭ **1300/174 266** in Australia, or 07/3295 2104) flies from Brisbane.

From the Airport to the City Center

The **Darwin Airport Shuttle Service** (www.darwincityairportshuttleservice.com.au; ℭ **08/8947 3979**) meets every flight and delivers to any hotel between the airport and city for A$24 one-way or A$48 round-trip per person.

A **taxi** to the city is around A$35. For **car rentals, Avis** (www.avis.com.au; ℭ **08/8945 0662**), **Budget** (www.budget.com.au; ℭ **08/8945 2011**), **Europcar** (www.europcar.com.au; ℭ **08/8941 0300**), **Hertz** (www.hertz.com.au; ℭ **08/8945 0999**), or **Thrifty** (www.thrifty.com.au; ℭ **08/8924 2480**) have airport desks, as does **Redspot** (www.redspot.com.au; ℭ **08/8945 3909**).

BY BUS   **Greyhound Australia** (www.greyhound.com.au; ℭ **1300/473 946** in Australia) makes a daily coach run from Alice Springs. The trip takes around 22 hours, and the fare is A$292.

BY TRAIN   The Adelaide–Alice Springs–Darwin railway line is the Top End's only rail link. **Great Southern Railway**'s *Ghan* (www.greatsouthernrail.com.au; ℭ **1800/703 357** in Australia or 08/8213 4401) leaves Adelaide on Sunday at 12:15pm and Alice Springs on Monday at 6:15pm, arriving in Darwin at 5:30pm on Tuesday (with a stop each day for off-train excursions). The return trip leaves Darwin on Wednesday at 10am. The adult one-way fare starts at A$1,479 from Alice Springs or A$2,349 from Adelaide for a twin cabin; the fare is more for Platinum Class, which has cabins around twice the size of standard Gold Twin Cabins.

BY CAR   Darwin is at the end of the Stuart Highway. Allow at least 2 long days, 3 to be comfortable, to drive from Alice Springs. The nearest road from the east is the long and dull Barkly Highway, which connects with the Stuart Highway at Tennant Creek, 922km (572 miles) south. The nearest road from the west is Victoria Highway, which joins the Stuart Highway at Katherine, 314km (195 miles) to the south.

VISITOR INFORMATION

Tourism Top End runs the official visitor center at 6 Bennett St. (at Smith St.; www.tourismtopend.com.au; ℭ **1300/138 886** in Australia, or 08/8980 6000). They can make bookings and provide you with maps, national park notes, and

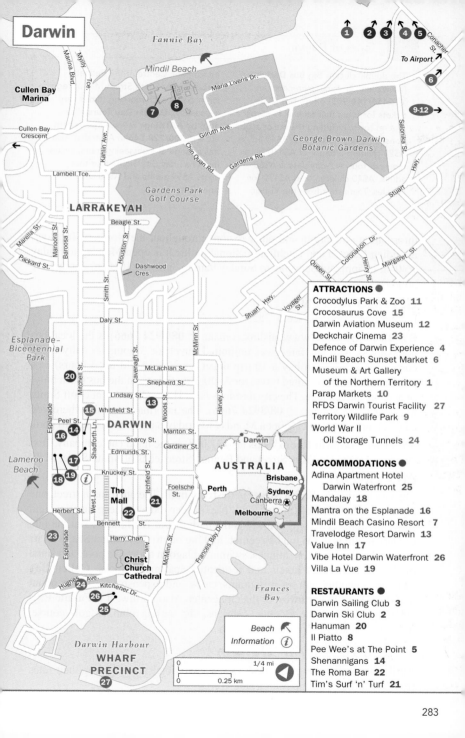

Darwin

Fannie Bay

Mindil Beach

Cullen Bay Marina

Cullen Bay Crescent

To Airport

Conacher St.

Salonika St.

Stuart Hwy.

Marina Blvd.

Myilly Tce.

Kahlin Ave.

Maria Liveris Dr.

Gilruth Ave.

Chin Quan Rd.

Gardens Rd.

George Brown Darwin Botanic Gardens

Lambell Tce.

Gardens Park Golf Course

LARRAKEYAH

Beagle St.

Houston St.

Marella St.

Manoora St.

Baroosa St.

Packard St.

Dashwood Cres.

Esplanade–Bicentennial Park

Daly St.

Smith St.

Cavenagh St.

Stuart Hwy.

Voyager St.

Queen St.

Coronation Dr.

Henry St.

Margaret St.

McLachlan St.

Shepherd St.

Lindsay St.

Whitfield St.

DARWIN

Mitchell St.

Peel St.

Esplanade

Lameroo Beach

Shadforth Ln.

Searcy St.

Manton St.

Edmunds St.

Gardiner St.

Woods St.

Harvey St.

McMinn St.

Knuckey St.

Foelsche St.

West La.

Litchford St.

The Mall

Herbert St.

Bennett St.

Harry Chan Ave.

Christ Church Cathedral

Hughes Ave.

Kitchener Dr.

Frances Bay Dr.

McMinn St.

Frances Bay

Darwin Harbour

WHARF PRECINCT

Beach 🏖
Information ℹ

0 ——— 1/4 mi
0 ——— 0.25 km

AUSTRALIA

Darwin

Perth

Brisbane

Sydney

Canberra

Melbourne

ATTRACTIONS ●
Crocodylus Park & Zoo **11**
Crocosaurus Cove **15**
Darwin Aviation Museum **12**
Deckchair Cinema **23**
Defence of Darwin Experience **4**
Mindil Beach Sunset Market **6**
Museum & Art Gallery
    of the Northern Territory **1**
Parap Markets **10**
RFDS Darwin Tourist Facility **27**
Territory Wildlife Park **9**
World War II
    Oil Storage Tunnels **24**

ACCOMMODATIONS ●
Adina Apartment Hotel
    Darwin Waterfront **25**
Mandalay **18**
Mantra on the Esplanade **16**
Mindil Beach Casino Resort **7**
Travelodge Resort Darwin **13**
Value Inn **17**
Vibe Hotel Darwin Waterfront **26**
Villa La Vue **19**

RESTAURANTS ●
Darwin Sailing Club **3**
Darwin Ski Club **2**
Hanuman **20**
Il Piatto **8**
Pee Wee's at The Point **5**
Shenannigans **14**
The Roma Bar **22**
Tim's Surf 'n' Turf **21**

information on Darwin and other regions throughout the Northern Territory, including Kakadu and Litchfield national parks. It is open Monday to Friday 8:30am to 5pm and Saturday to Sunday 9am to 3pm and 10am to 3pm public holidays.

GETTING AROUND

For car rental options, see p. 282.

BY BUS Buslink (www.buslink.com.au; 📞 **08/8924 7666**) is the local bus company. A A$3 bus fare gives unlimited travel for 3 hours. A daily ticket costs A$7, or you can buy a 10-trip ticket (each trip valid for 3 hours) or a weekly ticket for unlimited travel for A$20. Buy tickets on the bus (cash only) or at a bus interchange. The city terminus is on Harry Chan Avenue (off Smith St., near Civic Square; 📞 **08/8924 7666**). The information desk, where you can pick up a timetable, is open Monday to Friday 8am to noon and 1 to 4pm.

BY TAXI Darwin Radio Taxis (📞 **131 008**) is the main cab company. Taxi stands are at the Knuckey Street and Bennett Street ends of Smith Street Mall.

CITY LAYOUT

The city heart is the **Smith Street pedestrian mall.** The other main street, one street over, is **Mitchell Street,** with backpacker lodges, cheap eateries, and souvenir stores. Two streets away is the harborfront **Esplanade.** But the hub of Darwin life is the **Wharf Precinct,** looking out to the Arafura Sea, with its parklands, restaurants, boutiques, swimming lagoon and wave pool, and some of the city's swishest hotels and residential apartment blocks. **Cullen Bay Marina** is another hub for restaurants, cafes, and expensive boats; it's about a 25-minute walk northwest of the city center. Also northwest is **Fannie Bay,** where you'll find the Botanic Gardens, the sailing club, a golf course, museum and art gallery, and the casino.

Where to Stay in Darwin

April through October is the peak Dry season; hotels usually drop their rates from November through March (the Wet).

EXPENSIVE

Adina Apartment Hotel Darwin Waterfront ★★ This apartment hotel has a prime location overlooking the city's swimming lagoon and wave pool at Stokes Hill Wharf. From the top floor of the hotel, you can take a covered walkway right into the heart of the city, just minutes away. All one-bedroom apartments have balconies (studios do not), while all rooms have kitchens with microwaves. Apartments also have laundry facilities. Most apartments connect with a studio to make a two-bedroom apartment, if needed. There are also limited numbers of two-bedroom apartments.

7 Kitchener Dr. www.adinahotels.com. ✆ **1300/633 462** in Australia, or 08/8982 999. 121 units. A$169–A$203 studio double; A$199–A$254 1-bedroom apt; A$424–A$589 2-bedroom apt. Parking A$15. **Amenities:** Restaurant; bar; babysitting; exercise room; outdoor pool; room service; spa; free Wi-Fi.

Mantra on the Esplanade ★★ Right on the Esplanade overlooking Darwin Harbour and the Arafura Sea, and just a block from Smith Street Mall, this eight-floor apartment hotel is one of Darwin's most comfortable, elegant lodgings. Bright sofas and striking artwork in the lobby set a welcoming tone. Besides regular hotel rooms, two-thirds of the accommodations here are spacious contemporary-style one-, two-, and three-bedroom apartments with private balconies. Apartment kitchens feature granite countertops and

The Darwin waterfront is a popular spot for dining, shopping, and water sports.

stainless-steel appliances, including dishwashers, and all have laundry facilities. All rooms and apartments have city or harbor views.

88 The Esplanade (at Peel St.). www.mantra.com.au. ℗ **131 517** in Australia, or 08/8943 4333. 204 units. A$149–A$169 double; A$189–A$219 1-bedroom apt; A$199 2-bedroom apt; A$289 3-bedroom apt; A$479 penthouse. Parking A$15. **Amenities:** Restaurant; bar; concierge; executive-level rooms; Jacuzzi; outdoor pool; spa; free Wi-Fi.

Mindil Beach Casino Resort ★   Attached to Darwin's casino on Fannie Bay, this five-star complex resembles a tropical palace, with a private white-sand beach, infinity pool, and 12 hectares (30 acres) of gardens on Mindil Beach, next to the Botanic Gardens. The rooms are a cocktail of contemporary furniture and tropical elegance. All have balconies. It's worth paying a little extra for an ocean-facing room so you can watch Darwin's great Dry-season sunsets and spectacular Wet-season lightning storms. Superior rooms feature luxurious Japanese-inspired spa tubs and cool marble in the bathrooms. Full-length glass windows provide views over a private balcony terrace to lush tropical gardens and Mindil beach. "Resort rooms" have greater privacy, with views of the lagoon. A free shuttle runs four times a day to and from the city.

Gilruth Ave., The Gardens. www.mindilbeachcasinoresort.com.au. 152 units. A$259–A$309 double; A$339–A$509 suite. Free valet and self-parking. Bus: 4 or 6. **Amenities:** 5 restaurants; 7 bars; babysitting; exercise room; Jacuzzi; heated outdoor pool; room service; spa; sauna; free Wi-Fi.

MODERATE

Travelodge Resort Darwin ★   You're just a stone's throw from the city center at this modern hotel complex, where the tempting swimming pools and the **Treetops** restaurant, all shaded by the leaves of a sprawling strangler fig, have a castaway-island feel. Each room is a decent size and has a garden or pool view. As well as a range of hotel rooms, the complex has 32 self-contained one-bedroom town houses, a good option for families.

64 Cavenagh St. www.travelodge.com.au. ℗ **138 642** in Australia, or 08/8946 0111. 224 units. A$188–A$265 double; A$237–A$295 town house. Free off-street parking. **Amenities:** Restaurant; poolside cafe; 2 bars; babysitting; exercise room; 2 Jacuzzis; 2 outdoor pools; room service; free Wi-Fi.

Vibe Hotel Darwin Waterfront ★   This is a lovely casual place to stay and relax. The rooms are spacious and fresh, with a cheery white-and-aqua color scheme, but no balconies. Each has a small desk, and all have bathtubs as well as showers. Location is everything here, right in the heart of the waterfront precinct, within easy walking distance of the city center and major attractions. It's just 200m (660 ft.) from the wave pool and lagoon. The ground-level **Curve Restaurant & Bar** overlooks the parkland.

7 Kitchener Dr. www.vibehotels.com.au. ℗ **138 423** in Australia, 02/9356 5063 (Sydney reservations center), or 08/8982 9998. 121 units. A$299–A$349 double. Parking A$15. **Amenities:** Restaurant; bar; babysitting; exercise room; outdoor pool; room service; spa; free Wi-Fi.

If you're looking for a bit more space and privacy than a hotel room gives you, or perhaps are traveling as a family, a "home away from home" option is provided by **More Than a Room Darwin Accommodation** (www.morethanaroom.com.au; ℂ **08/8942 3012,** or 0418/616 888 mobile). The company has a portfolio of more than 20 properties, from one-bedroom waterfront apartments to luxurious villas. The stylish **Mandalay,** built in 1988 by Lord McAlpine, is on the Esplanade, close to the city center. It has three bedrooms, free Wi-Fi, a pool, barbecue area, off-street parking, and bikes for your use. Next door is **Villa La Vue,** which is equally spacious but has a different style. Rates range from around A$99 to A$695 per night.

INEXPENSIVE

Value Inn   The rooms at this neat little hotel in the Mitchell Street tourist precinct are tiny but tidy. Each room is just big enough to hold a queen-size and a single bed, a bar fridge, and a small writing table. The views aren't much, but you'll probably spend your time in the nearby cafes. Smith Street Mall and the Esplanade walking path are two blocks away. The hotel has a payphone (no phones in the rooms), cold drink and coffee vending machines, an iron on each floor, microwave ovens on the first and second floors, and a very small garden swimming pool off the parking lot. It's definitely 2.5-star and doesn't pretend to be otherwise.

50 Mitchell St. www.valueinn.com.au. ℂ **08/8981 4733.** 91 units. A$67 double. Free parking. **Amenities:** Bikes; outdoor pool; tennis courts; free Wi-Fi.

Where to Eat in Darwin

Cullen Bay Marina, a 25-minute walk or a short cab ride from town, is packed with trendy restaurants and cafes. If it's Thursday, don't even think about eating anywhere other than the **Mindil Beach Sunset Market ★★**. And on Saturday, head to the suburban **Parap Markets** for Asian goodies (see "Cheap Eats & More!" p. 288).

EXPENSIVE

Il Piatto ★★ ITALIAN   Classic Italian food in a beautiful airy restaurant—what could be better? Simple food very well done is the key to this place. As well as the pizza and pasta dishes, there are treats such as Northern Territory barramundi (fish) with cauliflower cream, vegetables, and crisp garlic wafers; or char-grilled butterflied chicken with grilled zucchini and a kipfler potato salad, with lemon sauce and salsa verde. Pizzas cost A$20 to A$26, and there's a design-your-own option too.

Skycity Darwin, Gilruth Ave., Mindil Beach. www.skycitydarwin.com.au/restaurants/il-piatto. ℂ **08/8943 8940.** Main courses A$26–A$61. Daily noon–2pm and 6–10pm.

Pee Wee's at the Point ★★ CONTEMPORARY   Surrounded on three sides by forest, this steel-and-glass venue affords views of Fannie Bay from

Cheap Eats & More!

If it's Thursday or Sunday, join the entire city and hundreds of other visitors at the **Mindil Beach Sunset Market** ★★ (www.mindil.com.au; ℂ **08/8981 3454**) to feast at the 60 terrific (and cheap—most dishes are less than A$10 a serving) Asian, Greek, Italian, African, Mexican, and Aussie food stalls. Listen to live music; wander among the 200 arts-and-crafts stalls; and mix and mingle with masseurs, tarot-card readers, and street performers as the sun sets into the sea. The action runs from 4 to 9pm from the last Thursday in April to the last Thursday in October (in the Dry). The beach is about a 20-minute walk or a A$10 cab ride from town, or take bus no. 14. Some hotels provide a shuttle bus, and there is free parking if you drive.

On Saturdays (8am–2pm), head to suburban **Parap Markets** ★, which transform a small street into a corner of Asia. The focus is on food, with a sprinkling of arts and crafts, and it's a favorite place for locals to have breakfast or brunch, choosing from the Southeast Asian soups, noodle dishes, and satays, washed down with fresh-squeezed tropical fruit drinks. The market stalls cover only about a block, on Parap Road in Parap (www.parapvillagemarkets.com. au; ℂ **08/8942 0805**, or 0438/882 373 mobile).

just about every table, inside, out on the deck, or down on the lawn. The food emphasizes fresh local produce and employs local ingredients as much as possible. An example: oven-baked saltwater barramundi crusted with macadamia nuts and lemon myrtle, with steamed greens and white bean puree. A tasting plate for two costs A$42. It's all complemented by an extensive wine list. Get here in time to watch the sunset.

Alec Fong Lim Dr., East Point Reserve (4km/2½ miles from town). www.peewees.com. au. ℂ **08/8981 6868**. Main courses A$41–A$55. Mon–Sat 4pm–late; Sun 3pm–late (Mar–Oct); Tues–Sat 4pm–late (Nov–Apr). Free parking.

Tim's Surf 'n' Turf ★ STEAK/SEAFOOD This Darwin favorite is housed in a classic elevated Darwin home that has been transformed into a modern restaurant. Diners can take a seat in the air-conditioned, open-plan dining and bar area, its walls hung with Top End Aboriginal artworks, or head outside to sit under shady trees and palms. Open for dinner only, the restaurant serves steaks, seafood platters, oysters, and vegetarian dishes, along with a range of salads, chicken, and pasta dishes. There's a kids' menu too, and children eat free Tuesday through Thursday before 6:30pm.

10 Litchfield St. www.timssurfandturf.com. ℂ **08/8981 1024**. Main courses A$20–A$55. Tues–Sun 5:30–9pm (Apr–Oct); Thurs–Sun 5:30–9pm (Nov–Mar).

MODERATE

Hanuman ★★ CONTEMPORARY ASIAN One of the most exotic places in Darwin to eat, Hanuman features "Nonya"-style cuisine, a fusion of Chinese- and Malaysian-style cooking. You can rely on dishes such as red duck curry with coconut, litchis, kaffir lime, Thai basil, and fresh pineapple;

or wok-tossed prawns in a coconut, wild ginger, and curry sauce. It also has a tandoori menu. A tasting plate for two (A$36) takes the agony out of choosing. This is a large restaurant, with seating for 90 diners inside and the same number outside. There's also a stylish cocktail bar. Service is prompt and friendly.

93 Mitchell St. (in the DoubleTree Hilton complex). www.hanuman.com.au. ℂ **08/8941 3500.** Main courses A$17–A$39. Daily noon–2:30pm and 6–10:30pm.

Shenannigan's ★ IRISH PUB FARE   Hearty pub grub—pork and sage sausages with mash and gravy, beef Guinness pie with mash and peas—along with a good smattering of local foods (croc bites, anyone?) is what you'll find at this convivial bar and restaurant. A friendly mix of solo travelers, families, seniors, and backpackers converge here. It also serves lighter fare, including vegetarian dishes, salads, wraps, and daily chef's specials.

69 Mitchell St. (at Peel St.). www.shenannigans.com.au. ℂ **08/8981 2100.** Main courses A$16–A$35. Daily 11:30am–5pm and 6–9:30pm.

INEXPENSIVE

The Roma Bar ★ CAFE   At this Darwin stalwart, you're likely to see media types rubbing shoulders with politicians, musicians, artists, and lobbyists. The coffee's good, and the food is tasty and well-priced. It's a great spot for breakfast, and the menu is slanted to an all-day breakfast, with omelets, banana pancakes, and avocado on sourdough. At lunch, burgers and sandwiches take over.

9 Cavenagh St. www.romabar.com.au. ℂ **08/8981 6729.** Main courses A$11–A$18. Mon–Fri 7am–3pm; Sat 8am–2pm; Sun 8am–1pm.

Exploring Darwin

Darwin's parks, harbor, and tropical clime make it lovely for strolling during the Dry. The **Esplanade** is nice for a pleasantly short and shady saunter, and the 42-hectare (104-acre) **George Brown Darwin Botanic Gardens** (ℂ **08/8999 4418**), on Gardens Road 2km (1¼ miles) from town, has paths through palms, orchids, every species of baobab in the world, and mangroves. Entry is free. The visitor center (daily 8am–4pm), near the Geranium Street entrance, has self-guiding maps to the Aboriginal plant-use trails.

Crocodylus Park & Zoo ★ ZOO   In addition to housing a small crocodile museum, this wildlife park, a 15-minute drive from town, holds croc-feeding sessions at 10am, noon, and 2pm and boat cruises to see large "salties" at 11am and 1pm. It doubles as Darwin's zoo, with exotic species including lions, Bengal tigers, leopards, meerkats, and monkeys on display.

815 McMillans Rd., Berrimah. www.crocodyluspark.com.au. ℂ **08/8922 4500.** A$40 adults, A$20 children 3–15, A$105 families. Daily 9am–5pm. Closed Dec 25.

Crocosaurus Cove ★ WILDLIFE VIEWING   Strong men have known to pale in the face of an attack by Chopper, a 790kg (1,742-lb.) crocodile with no front feet. At Crocosaurus Cove, the very brave can get into a plexiglass "cage" and be lowered into Chopper's enclosure, which also houses several huge crocs that have survived into their 70s and 80s, as well as large numbers of juveniles. These territorial beasts aren't usually happy with the intrusion—and the scratch marks on the 145mm (6-in.) thick walls of the cage tell the rest of the story. You spend about 15 minutes in the water. I confess: I have not done this and will not—not even in the interests of research! Less scary is the chance to swim in a pool next door to the younger crocs, with just a plexiglass wall between you and them. Crocosaurus Cove also has Australia's largest collection of reptiles, about 70 species, all from the Top End.

58 Mitchell St. www.crocosauruscove.com. © **08/8981 7522.** A$35 adults, A$23 children 4–15, A$77–A$132 families. Cage of Death A$170 for one person, A$260 for two. Daily 9am–6pm. Closed Dec 25.

Darwin Aviation Museum ★★★ MUSEUM   Even those who aren't military or aircraft buffs enjoy this excellent museum, about 10 minutes' drive from town. A B-52 bomber on loan from the United States is the prized exhibit, but the center also boasts a B-25 Mitchell bomber; Mirage and Sabre jet fighters; rare Japanese Zero fighter wreckage; funny, sad, and heartwarming (and heart-wrenching) displays on World War II and Vietnam; and displays about female aviators.

557 Stuart Hwy., Winnellie. www.darwinaviationmuseum.com.au. © **08/8947 2145.** A$15 adults, A$7 children 11 and under, A$35 families. Daily 9am–5pm. Closed Jan 1, Good Friday, Dec 25, and Dec 26.

Defence of Darwin Experience ★★ MUSEUM   Housed in a World War II gun command post, this small museum is another tribute to Darwin's wartime history. It has small but fine displays of photos, memorabilia, artillery, armored vehicles, weaponry old and new, and gun emplacements outside. Take time to watch the video of the 1942 and 1943 Japanese bombings.

5434 Alec Fong Lim Dr., East Point. www.defenceofdarwin.nt.gov.au © **08/8981 9702.** A$18 adults, A$8 children 5–15, A$40 families of 4. Daily 9:30am–5pm (May–Oct); 10am–3:30pm (Nov–Apr). Closed Jan 1, Good Friday, Dec 25, and Dec 26.

Museum and Art Gallery of the Northern Territory ★★★ MUSEUM   There's another attraction here for crocodile fans—the preserved body of **Sweetheart,** a 5m (16-ft.) man-eating saltwater croc captured

	Where Can I Swim?

Crocodiles and stingers render Darwin's beaches a no-swim zone year-round. The manmade lagoon at **Stokes Hill Wharf** solves the problem. Locals also sunbathe on Casuarina Beach and swim within view of the sea in **Lake Alexander** in East Point Reserve. About an hour's drive from the city, on the way to the Territory Wildlife Park, **Berry Springs Nature Park** has swimming holes with steps for easy access, and small waterfalls that create natural whirlpool action. They may be closed in the Wet season.

JOIN THE club

Two great places to catch Darwin's technicolor sunsets over a casual meal are the **Darwin Sailing Club** and the **Darwin Ski Club** (we're talking water-ski, of course). These are super-casual places to dine, with good food at good prices (mains around A$25–A$40). Ask a staff member to sign you in as a visitor, then grab a table, preferably outside.

The **Darwin Ski Club** (Conacher St., Fannie Bay, opposite the museum and art gallery; www.darwinskiclub.com.au; ℂ **08/8981 6630**) is a favorite for families, with its huge lawn and two saltwater pools. The outdoor Bali Bar is open from noon each day (except Good Friday and Christmas Day) and is a great place for a bistro meal (bucket of fresh prawns, anyone?). There's live music on Friday and Saturday nights.

The **Darwin Sailing Club** (Atkins Dr., Fannie Bay; www.dwnsail.com.au; ℂ **08/8981 1700**) waterfront bistro is open daily from noon to 2pm for lunch and 5:30 to 9pm for dinner (the bar stays open later), offering everything from laksa to burgers to a A$55 seafood platter (for one).

in Kakadu National Park. Beyond that, this museum and gallery is a great place to learn about Darwin's place in Australia's modern history. It has sections on Aboriginal, Southeast Asian, and Pacific art and culture, and a maritime gallery with a pearling lugger and other boats that have sailed into Darwin from Indonesia and other northern parts. A highlight is the Cyclone Tracy gallery, where you can stand in a small, dark room as the sound of the cyclone rages around you.

19 Conacher St., Bullocky Point. www.magnt.nt.gov.au. ℂ **08/8999 8364.** Admission free. Daily 10am–5pm. Closed Jan 1, Good Friday, Dec 25, and Dec 26.

RFDS Darwin Tourist Facility ★★★ MUSEUM   Despite its less-than-catchy name, this is one of the best attractions in Darwin—don't miss it. In a building shaped something like an old aircraft hangar, two attractions tell two different Darwin stories. One is that of the Royal Flying Doctor Service, founded in the Northern Territory in 1939 and affectionately known throughout Australia as the RFDS. The museum relates the experiences of the pilots, engineers, doctors and nurses, and patients of the RFDS. But it is the second story—the Bombing of Darwin on February 19, 1942—that will grip you. Darwin was bombed 64 times during World War II, and 12 ships were sunk in its harbor. As an Allied supply base, Darwin had many American airmen based here. The bombing of the harbor brought destruction to the city, and many of the experiences of that day are brought to life using holograms and virtual reality—making you feel that you are actually *there*! Another RFDS visitor center is in Alice Springs (p. 315).

45 Stokes Hill Rd., Stokes Hill Wharf. www.rfdsdarwin.com.au. ℂ **08/8983 5700.** A$28 adults, A$16 children 6–14, A$70 families of 5. Daily 9:30am–6pm, public holidays 10am–3pm. Last entry 1 hr. before closing. Closed Good Friday and Dec 25.

Territory Wildlife Park ★★ ZOO   Walk the many tracks, or take a free shuttle along bush trails to see native Northern Territory wildlife in re-created natural habitats, including monsoon rainforest boardwalks, lagoons with hides (shelters for watching birds), a walk-through aviary, a walk-through aquarium housing stingrays and sawfish, and a nocturnal house with marsupials such as the bilby. Bats, birds, spiders, crocs, frill-neck lizards, kangaroos, and other creatures also make their homes here (but not koalas, because they don't live in the Territory). A program of animal talks runs throughout the day. The best is the birds of prey show, at 11am (after which, for an extra A$10 per person— if you are 10 or older—you get to hold one of the raptors). Go first thing to see the animals at their liveliest, and allow 4 hours to see everything, plus 45 minutes traveling time.

Cox Peninsula Rd., Berry Springs, 45km (28 miles) S of Darwin. www.territorywild lifepark.com.au. © **08/8988 7200.** A$32 adults, A$16 children 5–16, A$55–A$87 families. Daily 9am–5pm. Closed Dec 25.

World War II Oil Storage Tunnels ★★ MUSEUM   Under the city's cliffs, this warren of empty World War II oil storage tunnels houses a collection of black-and-white photographs of the war in Darwin, each lit up in the dark. It's a simple but haunting attraction, offering an interesting window on yet another aspect of Darwin's war history. A gatekeeper has brochures, will answer questions, and sells history books.

Kitchener Dr., Wharf Precinct. www.ww2tunnelsdarwin.com.au. © **08/8985 6322.** A$8 adults, A$5 children 4–16. May–Sept daily 9am–4pm; Oct–Apr daily 9am–1pm. Closed December 7–25.

Shopping in Darwin

Darwin's best buys are Aboriginal art and crafts, pearls, opals, and diamonds. You will find many shops and galleries selling authentic Aboriginal artworks and artifacts at reasonable prices. To make a heavyweight investment in works by internationally sought-after artists, visit the Aboriginal-owned **Aboriginal Fine Arts Gallery,** on the second floor at 44 Mitchell St. (www.aaia.com.au; © **08/8981 1315**).

The world's best South Sea pearls are farmed in the Top End seas. Buy, or just drool in the window, at **Paspaley Pearls,** in the Charles Darwin Centre at 19 Smith St. (www.paspaleypearls.com; © **08/8930 4500**). If you fancy a pink

---

Cruising Darwin Harbour

If you have an evening free, get out on the harbor to see the sunset and the city lights. **Darwin Harbour Cruises** (www.darwinharbourcruises.com.au; © **08/8942 3131**) operates a sunset cruise aboard the 25m (82-ft.) catamaran *Charles Darwin*. Tickets cost A$58 per adult and A$35 for children 4 to 14; a three-course buffet dinner cruise is A$102 adults and A$68 children. Cruises leave from Stokes Hill Wharf at 6pm, returning around 8:30pm.

Deckchair Cinema

Lie back in a canvas deck chair under the stars at the **Deckchair Cinema** (www.deckchaircinema.com; ✆ **08/8981 0700**) to watch Aussie hits, foreign films, and cult classics. Located on the edge of Darwin Harbour, this Darwin institution is run by the Darwin Film Society. Take a picnic dinner and get there early to soak up the scene: the twinkling lights from boats anchored in the Arafura Sea and the fabulous sunsets. A kiosk sells wine, beer, soft drinks, and snacks, and there's a hot buffet every night (or you can bring your own food, but no alcohol). There are 250 deck chairs as well as about 150 straight-backed seats; cushions and even insect repellent are available if you need them. Entry is by a walkway from the Esplanade, or by car off Kitchener Drive (there's a parking lot). The box office and kiosk open at 6pm, and movies start at 7:30pm daily in the Dry (mid-Apr to mid-Nov), with double features on Friday, Saturday, and some Sundays. Tickets are A$16 adults, A$8 children 5 to 15, and A$35 for families of four; for double features, it's A$26 adults, A$13 children, and A$55 families.

diamond (the world's rarest) from the Argyle Diamond Mine in Kununurra, you can get them at **Creative Jewellers,** 32 Smith Street Mall (www.creative jewellers.com.au; ✆ **08/8941 1233**), an Argyle-appointed supplier that buys direct from the mine. It also stocks champagne diamonds, for which Argyle is renowned, and other Argyle diamonds, as well as opals and South Sea pearls.

Jokes about "snapping handbags" abound in croc country. For your own croc-skin fashion statement, head to **di Croco,** 27 Smith Street Mall (www.dicroco.com; ✆ **08/8941 4470**). You'll find bags, purses, wallets, belts, pens, and other accessories, all made from saltwater croc skins farmed locally.

Day Trip to Litchfield National Park ★★★

120km (74 miles) S of Darwin

An easy 90-minute drive south of Darwin is a miniature Garden of Eden full of forests, waterfalls, rocky sandstone escarpments, glorious swimming holes, and prehistoric cycads that look as if they belong on the set of *Jurassic Park*. Litchfield National Park is much smaller (a mere 146,000 hectares/360,620 acres) and much less famous than its big sister, Kakadu (p. 296), but it is no less stunning.

The park's main attractions are spring-fed swimming holes, like the magical plunge pool at **Florence Falls ★★★**, 29km (18 miles) from the forest. At Florence Falls, it's a 15-minute hike down stairs to the water, so the easily accessible pool at **Wangi Falls ★**, 49km (30 miles) from the eastern entrance, gets more crowds. (That's also a beautiful spot, surrounded by cliffs and forests with a lookout from the top.) More idyllic grottoes are 4km (2½ miles) from Florence Falls at **Buley Rockhole,** a series of tiered rock pools and waterfalls. You can't swim at **Tolmer Falls,** but during the Wet when they're flowing, take the boardwalk about 400m (1,312 ft.) to the lookout and see the

Buley Rockhole in Litchfield Park.

cascade against a backdrop of red cliffs. Roads to most swimming holes are paved, although a few are accessible only by four-wheel-drive.

A number of short **walking trails** run through the park, such as the half-hour Shady Creek Circuit from Florence Falls up to the parking lot.

Parts of the park are also home to thousands of 2m-high (6½-ft.) **"magnetic" termite mounds,** so called because they run north-south to escape the fierce midday heat. A display hut and a viewing point are 17km (11 miles) from the park's eastern entrance.

To get here from Darwin, head south for 86km (53 miles) on the Stuart Highway and follow the park turnoff on the right through the town of Batchelor for another 34km (21 miles). A number of day-trip tours run from Darwin. Crowds of locals can shatter the peace in Litchfield on weekends, especially in the Dry season, but the park is worth visiting, crowds or no crowds. Entry is free.

Tip: In the Wet (approximately Nov–Apr), some roads—usually the four-wheel-drive ones—may be closed, and the Wangi water hole may be off-limits due to turbulence and strong currents. Check with the **Parks & Wildlife Commission** (© **08/8999 4555**) before you leave Darwin during this time.

Day Trip to Nitmiluk National Park (Katherine Gorge) ★★★

In 1989, after a 10-year campaign, the indigenous Jawoyn people regained legal ownership of the land they had inhabited for tens of thousands of years before Europeans arrived, land that included the gorge formerly named

Katherine after the daughter of explorer John McDouall Stuart's sponsor, pastoralist James Chambers. The gorge now takes its name from *nitmiluk*, the Jawoyn word derived from the "nit-nit" sound of the cicadas you may hear. Nitmiluk Gorge is actually a series of 13 gorges, and cruising the Katherine River in an **open-sided boat** is the most popular way to appreciate its beauty. Most cruises ply only the first two or three, but you can go farther by canoe.

Nitmiluk Tours (www.nitmiluktours.com.au; © **1300/146 743** in Australia) operates all cruises. Most people take a 2-hour Aboriginal cultural cruise, available three times a day at 9 and 11am, and 2pm. The cost is A$92 for adults and A$46 for children 6 to 15. There is also a 4-hour cruise once daily, although you will probably be satisfied with 2 hours. They also run dawn cruises and sunset dinner cruises. Wear sturdy shoes; because each gorge is cut off from the next by rapids, all cruises involve some walking along the bank.

Cruising is nice, but in a **canoe** you can discover sandy banks and waterfalls and get up close to the gorge walls, the birds, and those crocs. (Don't worry—they're the freshwater kind and not typically regarded as dangerous to humans.) Rocks separate the gorges, so be prepared to carry your canoe quite often. You may even want to camp out on the banks overnight. A half-day canoe rental is A$70 for a single and A$81 double, with a A$50 cash deposit.

Canoeing at Katherine Gorge.

Canoeing the gorge is popular, so book canoes ahead, especially in the Dry season. (Canoe rentals are not available Dec–May.)

Some 100km (62 miles) of **hiking trails** crisscross Nitmiluk National Park, ranging in duration from a 1-hour walk to the lookout to a 5-day trek to Leliyn (Edith Falls; see below). Trails—through rocky terrain and forests, past water holes, and along the gorge—start from the Nitmiluk Visitor Centre, where you can pick up trail maps. Overnight walks require a permit, and a A$3.30 per-person camping permit, payable at the Nitmiluk Visitor Centre.

One of the nicest spots in the park is 42km (26 miles) north of Katherine, 20km (13 miles) off the Stuart Highway: **Leliyn ★** (also known as Edith Falls) is a wonderland of natural, croc-free swimming holes bordered by red cliffs, monsoonal forest, and pandanus palms. Among the bushwalks leading from Edith Falls is a 2.6km (1.5-mile) round-trip trail, which takes about 2 hours and incorporates a dip at the upper pool en route.

For a vaster perspective, it's also fascinating to get aerial views of the entire ravine-ridden Arnhem Plateau, which stretches uninhabited to the horizon. **Nitmiluk Scenic Flights** (www.nitmilluktours.com.au; © **08/8971 0877**) operates from a helipad near the Nitmiluk Gorge Visitor Centre and runs a range of scenic flights, starting from A$105 per person for a 10-minute flight over the first three gorges.

If you want to stay overnight, the lovely **Cicada Lodge** (www.cicadalodge. com.au; © **1300/146743** in Australia, or 08/8971 0877) is close to the park visitor center. Owned by the Jawoyn people, it is only 10 minutes' walk from the base of the first gorge on the Katherine River. The lodge has 18 rooms, an outdoor swimming pool with lounges and sun umbrellas, and a smart restaurant. There is also a **camping ground** with permanent tents (with beds, from A$120 per tent per night double) and camping sites (A$50 double powered; A$20 per person unpowered).

KAKADU NATIONAL PARK ★★★

257km (159 miles) E of Darwin

The ecological gem that is Kakadu National Park covers 1.7 million hectares (4.2 million acres), making this World Heritage area Australia's largest national park. You'll see only a fraction of it, but will remember it forever.

Cruising the lily-clad wetlands to spot crocodiles, plunging into exquisite natural swimming holes, hiking through spear grass and cycads, fishing for barramundi, soaring in a helicopter over torrential waterfalls during the Wet season, photographing thousands of birds flying over the eerie red-sandstone escarpment that juts 200m (650 ft.) above the floodplain, and admiring some of Australia's ancient Aboriginal rock-art sites—these are the activities that draw people to Kakadu. It is also one of the richest wildlife habitats in Australia, home to 275 species of birds and 75 species of reptiles. Wildlife viewing here is not quite as breathtaking as in an African game park, where herds roam the plains—even Australians get excited when they spot a kangaroo in the wild—but with patience, you may have some rewarding sightings.

Kakadu is a big place—about 200km (124 miles) long by 100km (62 miles) wide—so plan to spend at least a night. Day trips are available from Darwin, but it's too far and too big to see much in a day. It is best in the late Dry, around September and October, when crocs and birds gather around shrinking water holes. Note that facilities are limited: The only town of any size is Jabiru (population 1,100), a mining community where you can find banking facilities and a few shops.

Essentials

ARRIVING

Follow the Stuart Highway 34km (21 miles) south of Darwin, and turn left onto the Arnhem Highway to the park's northern entrance station. The trip takes 2½ to 3 hours. If you're coming from the south, turn off the Stuart Highway at Pine Creek onto the Kakadu Highway, and follow the Kakadu Highway for 79km (49 miles) to the park's southern entrance.

A big range of coach, minibus, and four-wheel-drive tours and camping safaris, usually lasting 1, 2, or 3 days, departs from Darwin daily. These are a good idea, because many of Kakadu's geological, ecological, and Aboriginal attractions come to life only with a guide. The best water holes, lookouts, and wildlife-viewing spots change dramatically from month to month, even from day to day.

Termite mounds, Kakadu National Park.

VISITOR INFORMATION

Before you arrive, you can find information on Kakadu and book tours at the **Tourism Top End** information center in Darwin. You can also contact the rangers at the park directly (© **08/8938 1120**).

Both the park entrances—the northern station on the Arnhem Highway used by visitors from Darwin and the southern station on the Kakadu Highway for visitors from Katherine—hand out free visitor guides with maps. In the Dry they also issue a timetable of free ranger-guided bushwalks, art-site talks, and slide shows taking place that week. Park entry costs A$40 adults, A$20 children 5 to 15, or A$100 families. Park permits can be purchased online (**www.parksaustralia.gov. au/kakadu**), or at the **Bowali Visitor Centre** (© **08/8938 1120**), on the Kakadu Highway, 5km (3 miles) from Jabiru, 100km (62 miles) from the northern entry

Kakadu's Heritage

The name Kakadu comes from Gagudju, the group of languages spoken by Aborigines in the northern part of the park, where they and their ancestors have lived for at least 50,000 years. Today, these traditional owners manage the park in conjunction with the Australian government. Their culture is on display at a cultural center and at rock painting sites.

station, and 131km (81 miles) from the southern entry station. Passes are also available through other outlets (check the website) and are valid for 7 days.

The Bowali Visitor Centre, an attractive, environmentally friendly Outback-style building, shows a program of 1-hour videos on the park's natural history and Aboriginal culture; it also has a library, displays, a gift shop, and a cafe. You may want to spend a good hour or so here, more to see a video. It is open daily from 8am to 5pm, except Christmas Day.

You can also book tours and get information at **Kakadu Tours and Travel,** Shop 6, Tasman Plaza, Jabiru (www.kakadutoursand travel.com.au; ✆ **08/8979 2548**).

GETTING AROUND

Most major attractions are accessible in a two-wheel-drive vehicle on sealed (paved) roads, but a four-wheel-drive vehicle allows you to get to more falls, water holes, and campsites. Car-rental companies will not permit you to take two-wheel-drive vehicles on unpaved roads. **Territory Thrifty** (www.thrifty. com.au/car-hire/jabiru; ✆ **08/8924 0000**) rents cars at the Mercure Kakadu Crocodile Hotel, Flinders Street, Jabiru, but must be prebooked; otherwise, rent a car in Darwin. If you rent a four-wheel-drive in the Wet season (Nov–Apr), always check floodwater levels on all roads at the **Bowali Visitor Centre** (✆ **08/8938 1120**). The Bowali Visitor Centre, many attractions such as Nourlangie and Yellow Water Billabong, and the towns of Jabiru and Cooinda usually stay above the floodwaters year-round.

Where to Stay & Eat Around Kakadu NP

Garnamarr Campground (named for the red-tailed black cockatoo commonly found in Kakadu) is near Jim Jim Falls and Twin Falls. It has sites for 200 people but doesn't accept reservations, so check at the **Bowali Visitor Centre** (✆ **08/8938 1120**) before driving there to see whether it is full. High season is April to late October or early November. The campground manager collects the fee of A$15 adults, A$7.50 children, and A$38 families (cash only). For details on other campgrounds, go to **www.parksaustralia.gov.au/ kakadu/stay/camping**.

Aurora Kakadu ★ This property's location—near the northern entrance to the park—might seem handy, but that makes it the farthest accommodation from such major attractions as Yellow Waters and Nourlangie (many tour operators do pick up here). However, the resort's green lawns and tropical gardens adorned with wandering peacocks and goannas and chattering native birds are a wonderfully restful haven from the harsh surroundings of Kakadu outside. A 3.6km (2-mile) nature trail winds from the hotel through monsoon forest and past a billabong. Don't yield to the temptation to dive into the lily-filled lagoon down the back—like every other waterway in Kakadu, it is home to saltwater crocs! But you can safely walk out on the fenced-off viewing platform for a close-up look at the wildlife. All rooms have a balcony or patio, and there are family rooms that sleep five.

Arnhem Hwy., South Alligator (41km/25 miles W of Bowali Visitor Centre). www.auro raresorts.com.au. *℃* **1800/818 845** in Australia, or 08/8979 0166. 138 units. A$195–A$238 double; A$204–A$215 family rooms. Free parking. **Amenities:** Restaurant; bar; Jacuzzi; shaded outdoor pool; shop; day/night tennis court; free Wi-Fi.

Bamurru Plains ★★★   There can be few experiences to beat waking up to the sight of buffalo roaming the green, lush floodplains of Kakadu in the Wet. This stylish luxury lodge on the edge of the Mary River floodplains, between the coast and the western boundary of Kakadu National Park, offers a rich array of wildlife encounters and an eco-friendly environment in which to base yourself. Your luxury tent has a timber floor, fine linens on the bed, and a high-pressure shower in the bathroom, but no phone, TV, or other distractions. Three tents have air-conditioning—at a price: To discourage the use of generator power, Bamurru Plains charges an extra A$120 for using the air-conditioning (it must be requested when booking). On three sides, the tents' walls are one-way screens that give stupendous views and total privacy. For the adventurous, a tree-house "sleep-out" called The Hide is available for two to four guests, a bit away from the main lodge, where you sleep on the floor surrounded by the sounds of the bush. I have only visited in the Wet, but other guests were repeat visitors, determined to see both seasons…a sure indication that their first visit—in the Dry—was memorable. Meals are served at the main lodge building around a communal table. Activities include guided walks, airboat safaris on the wetlands, river cruises, fishing, 4WD and quad bike safaris to view wildlife (*Bamurru* is the Aboriginal name for the magpie geese you will see in the thousands), and day tours to Kakadu or Arnhemland. *Tip:* The best way to get to Bamurru Plains is by light plane, a 30-minute flight from Darwin. If you drive to this working buffalo station, you will have to leave your car at the gate, and a staff member will pick you up for the 20-minute drive to the lodge. It is about a 3-hour drive from Darwin and 2½ hours from Jabiru.

Swim Creek Station, Harold Knowles Rd. (P.O. Box 1020), Humpty Doo. www.bamurru plains.com. *℃* **1300/790 561** in Australia, or 02/9571 6399. 10 units. A$2,504–A$2,792 double; A$627 children 17 and under sharing with adults; A$1,128 children sharing a separate room. Minimum 3-night stay. Rates include all meals, drinks, and activities. Closed Nov–Apr. **Amenities:** Restaurant; bar; swimming pool; no Wi-Fi.

Cooinda Lodge ★ These modest but pleasant accommodations are set among tropical gardens at the departure point for Yellow Water Billabong cruises. The simply furnished tile-floor bungalows are big, comfortable, and air-conditioned, and there are 22 family rooms that sleep up to four. The lodge is something of a town center, with a general store, gift shop, currency exchange, post office, fuel, camping sites, and other facilities. Eat at the rustic **Barra Bistro and Bar,** which serves an all-day snack menu, with live entertainment in the Dry season. Dining options can be limited between November and March in the Wet. Scenic flights take off from the lodge's airstrip, and the Warradjan Aboriginal Cultural Centre is a 15-minute walk.

Kakadu Hwy. (50km/31 miles S of Bowali Visitor Centre), Jabiru. www.accorhotels.com. *©* **08/8979 1500.** 48 units. A$329 double; A$379 family room (sleeps 4). **Amenities:** Restaurant; bar; outdoor pool; no Wi-Fi.

Mercure Kakadu Crocodile Hotel ★★ Some people think this hotel is kitsch; others declare it an architectural masterpiece. I like it. It was built to the specifications of its Aboriginal owners, the Gagudju people, in the form of their spirit ancestor, a giant crocodile called Ginga. The building's entrance is the "jaws," the two floors of rooms are in the "belly," the circular parking lot clusters are "eggs," and so on. From the ground, it's hard to see, but from the air, the shape is quite distinct. Love it or hate it, it is one of the best places to stay in Kakadu, a stylish modern hotel with basic but comfortable rooms. The lobby doubles as a gallery selling the works of local Aboriginal artists, and a trail leads to the Bowali Visitor Centre. A 9-hole golf course, tennis courts, and Olympic-size swimming pool are just a few blocks away.

1 Flinders St. (5km/3 miles E of Bowali Visitor Centre), Jabiru. www.accorhotels.com. *©* **1800/007 697** in Australia, or 08/8979 9000. 110 units. A$322–A$362 double; A$362 family room (sleeps 4). **Amenities:** Restaurant; 2 bars; babysitting; small outdoor pool; room service; free Wi-Fi.

Highlights En Route to Kakadu NP

En route to the park, stop in at the **Fogg Dam Conservation Reserve** (*©* **08/8988 8009**), 25km (16 miles) down the Arnhem Highway and 7km (4⅓ miles) off the highway. You'll get a close-up look at geese, finches, ibis, brolgas, and other wetland birds from lookouts over ponds of giant lilies, or by walking through monsoon forests to viewing "hides." There are two lookouts on the road and three walks, two that are 2.2km (1.5 miles) round-trip and one that is 3.6km (2.3 miles) round-trip. Entry is free. Crocs live here, so don't swim, and keep away from the water's edge.

Four kilometers (2½ miles) farther down the Arnhem Highway at Beatrice Hill, you can stop at the **Window on the Wetlands Visitor Centre** (*©* **08/8988 8188**), which offers views across the Adelaide River floodplain, as well as displays and touch-screen information on the wetlands' ecology. It's free and open daily from 8am to 5:30pm (except Christmas Day).

Just past Beatrice Hill on the highway at the Adelaide River Bridge—look for the statue of a grinning croc—**Adelaide River Queen Cruises**

NEVER smile AT A YOU-KNOW-WHAT!

The Aboriginal Gagudju people of the Top End have long worshiped a giant crocodile called Ginga, but the way white Australians go on about these reptilian relics of a primeval age, you'd think they worshiped them, too. There is scarcely a soul in the Northern Territory who will not regale you with his or her personal croc story, and each one will be more outrageous than the last.

Aussies may be good at pulling your leg with tall tales, but when they warn you not to swim in crocodile country, they're deadly serious. After all, crocodiles are good at pulling your leg, too—literally. Here are some tips:

- There are two kinds of crocodile in Australia: the highly dangerous and enormously powerful saltwater, or "estuarine," croc; and the "harmless" freshwater croc, which will attack only if threatened or accidentally stood on. **Note:** Saltwater crocs can and do swim in the ocean, but they live in fresh water.
- Don't swim in *any* waterway, swimming hole, or waterfall unless you have been specifically told it is safe. Take advice only from someone such as a recognized tour operator or a park ranger. You can never be sure where crocodiles lurk from year to year, because during every Wet season crocs head upriver to breed, and they spread out over a wide flooded area. As the floodwaters subside, they are trapped in whatever water they happen to be in at the time—so what was a safe swimming hole last Dry season might not be croc-free this year.
- Never stand on or walk along a riverbank, and stand well back when fishing. A 6m (20-ft.) croc can be 2½ centimeters (1 in.) beneath the surface of that muddy water yet remain invisible. It moves fast, so you won't see it until you're in its jaws.
- Make your campsite and clean your fish at least 25m (82 ft.) from the bank.

And if you do come face to face with a crocodile? There is little you can do. Just don't get into this situation in the first place!

(www.jumpingcrocodilecruises.com.au; ℂ **08/8988 8144**) runs the **jumping crocodiles cruise.** From the relative safety of a restored paddle steamer (or a smaller boat in the Wet), you can watch wild crocodiles leap out of the water for hunks of meat dangled over the edge by the boat crew—but don't lean out too far! It's an unabashed tourist trap, with a souvenir shop that sells all things croc, including crocodile toilet-seat covers. It may not be to my taste—or yours—but because crocs typically move fast only when they attack, it may be your only chance to witness their immense power and speed. The cruises depart at 9, 10, and 11am, and 1, 2, and 3pm March to October; check the website for details for other times of year. The cost is A$50 adults and A$30 for children 4 to 14 for all cruises. If you need transport, Adelaide River Transfers (www.adelaide rivertransfers.com; ℂ **0438/946 444** mobile) provides a return shuttle for A$105 adults and A$90 children 1 to 14 (including cruise fare).

Top Attractions in Kakadu National Park

WETLANDS CRUISES

One of Kakadu's most popular attractions is **Yellow Water Billabong,** 50km (31 miles) south of the Bowali Visitor Centre at Cooinda. It's rich with fresh-water mangroves, paperbark trees, pandanus palms, water lilies, and masses of birds gathering to drink—sea eagles, honking magpie geese, kites, china-blue kingfishers, and jaçanas (called "Jesus birds" because they seem to walk on water as they step across the lily pads). This is one of the best places in the park to spot saltwater crocs. Cruises in canopied boats with commentary depart near Cooinda Lodge six times a day starting at 6:45am in the Dry (Apr–Oct) and four times a day in the Wet (Nov–Mar). A 90-minute cruise is A$72 for adults and A$50 for children 4 to 15. A 2-hour cruise is A$90 for adults, A$62 for children (or A$99 adults and A$70 children for the early morning cruise, including breakfast). Book online (www.kakadutourism.com) or through **Cooinda Lodge (𝄐 08/8979 1500).**

Fair warning: In the Wet, when the Billabong floods and joins up with Jim Jim Creek and the South Alligator River, the bird life spreads far and wide over the park and the crocs head upriver to breed, so don't expect wildlife viewing to be spectacular.

Another worthwhile cruise is the Aboriginal-owned and -operated **Guluy-ambi Cultural Cruise** on the East Alligator River (www.kakaduculturaltours.com.au; 𝄐 **1800/525 238** in Australia). The East Alligator River forms the border between Kakadu and isolated Arnhemland. Unlike the Yellow Water cruise, which focuses on crocs, birds, and plants, this excursion teaches you about Aboriginal myths, bush tucker, and hunting techniques. The cruise lasts about 1 hour and 45 minutes, leaving at 9 and 11am, and 1 and 3pm daily May through November. It costs A$79 for adults, A$52 for children 4 to 14. Cruises are limited to 25 passengers, so book ahead.

ABORIGINAL ART & CULTURE

There are as many as 5,000 rock painting sites—some of them believed to be 50,000 years old—throughout the park, though for cultural reasons the indigenous owners make only a few accessible to visitors. The best are Nourlangie Rock and Ubirr Rock. Access to the sites is free (once you have your park permit, available from the Bowali Visitor Centre; see p. 297).

Nourlangie, 31km (19 miles) southeast of the Bowali Visitor Centre, features "X-ray"-style paintings of animals; a vivid, energetic striped Dreamtime figure of Namarrgon, the "Lightning Man"; and modern depictions of a white man in boots, a rifle, and a sailing ship. You'll also find rock paintings at **Nanguluwur,** on the other side of Nourlangie Rock. A 1.5km (1-mile) sign-posted trail winds past Nourlangie's paintings (short trails to the art sites shoot off it), and an easy 1.7km (1-mile) trail leads from the parking lot into Nanguluwur.

You'll find a variety of excellent sites at **Ubirr Rock,** which is more remote, around 43km (27 miles, or an hour's drive) from the Bowali Visitor

Saltwater croc in the Yellow Water Billabong waterway in the heart of Kakadu National Park.

Centre, and around 3km north of the Border Store at the East Alligator River. A 1km (.5-mile) signposted trail leads past the sites at Ubirr, and while you can see paintings at lower levels, it is worth the effort to hike to the top of the 250m (820-ft.) outlook for the additional art sites higher up, and for spectacular views of the floodplain. Unlike most sites in Kakadu, Ubirr is not open 24 hours—it opens at 8:30am April through November and at 2pm December through March, and closes at sunset year-round. Ubirr Rock can be cut off in the Wet, but the views of afternoon lightning storms from the top at that time are breathtaking.

Displays and videos about bush tucker, Dreamtime creation myths, and lifestyles of the Bininj Aborigines can be found at the **Warradjan Aboriginal Cultural Centre** at Cooinda (© **08/8979 0525**). At the direction of the Aboriginal owners, the center was built in the shape of a pig-nose turtle; its quality gift shop sells such items as didgeridoos, bark paintings by local artists, and baskets woven from pandanus fronds. The center is open daily from 9am to 5pm, and admission is free. A 1km-long (.5-mile) trail connects it to Cooinda Lodge (p. 300) and the Yellow Water Billabong (p. 302).

SCENIC FLIGHTS

Scenic flights over the floodplains and the rainforest-filled ravines of the escarpment are worth taking if the strain is not too great on your wallet. They're much more interesting in the Wet than in the Dry: The floodplains spread, and Jim Jim Falls and Twin Falls (see below) swell from their Dry season trickle to a flood. Viewing it from the air is also the best way to appreciate the clever crocodile shape of the Crocodile Hotel. **Kakadu Air Services** (www.kakaduair.com.au; ℂ **1800/089 113** in Australia, or 08/8941 9611) runs 30-minute fixed-wing flights from Jabiru for A$150 adults and A$120 children, as well as helicopter flights from A$245 per person for 20 minutes. **Airborne Solutions** (www.airbornesolutions.com.au; ℂ **1300/435 486** in Australia, or 08/8972 2345) runs a Kakadu helicopter day trip from Darwin for A$2,095 per person (minimum 2 people), in which you will cover nearly 700km (435 miles) and see places inaccessible to most people. The tour includes a lunch stop at Cooinda Lodge and isolated rock painting sites. It's expensive, but worth every cent in my book!

FISHING

Kakadu's wetlands are brimming with barramundi, and Territorians like nothing more than to hop in a tin dinghy barely big enough to resist a croc attack and go looking for them. **Kakadu Fishing Tours** (www.kakadufishingtours.com.au; ℂ **08/8979 2025**) takes you fishing in a 5.7m (19-ft.) sportfishing boat. Tours depart from Jabiru, 5km (3 miles) east of the Bowali Visitor Centre, and cost A$240 per person for 5½ hours from May to December, and A$380 per person for a full day (10½ hours) March to early May.

BUSHWALKING

Wide-ranging **bush and wetlands walking trails,** including many short walks and six half- to full-day treks, lead throughout the park. The Bowali Visitor Centre sells hiking-trail maps. Typical trails include a less than 1km

Nadab Lookout near Ubirr.

ABORIGINAL art AT INJALAK

If you are taking a tour to Arnhemland, make sure it goes to **Injalak Arts** (www.injalak.com; © **08/8979 0190**) at Gunbalanya (Oenpelli), a small Aboriginal township about 300km (186 miles) east of Darwin.

Injalak draws its inspiration from Injalak Hill, a site rich in rock paintings. Since it opened in 1989, the center has gained a reputation for producing fine indigenous contemporary art, carvings, and weavings. This is the place to buy them at their source and to meet the artists, some of whom are likely to be working on the veranda when you visit. Injalak is a nonprofit, community enterprise, and you can be sure that all artists are paid upfront in full for their work. Injalak is usually open Monday to Friday 8:30am to 5pm and Saturdays from 9am to 2pm, but it is advisable to check first.

Visitors to Injalak need a permit from the **Northern Land Council** (© **08/8920 5100** in Darwin, or 08/8938 3000 in Jabiru). It is only possible to drive to Gunbalanya in the Dry, May to November. Unless you have a 4WD, be sure to check road conditions with the NLC before setting out. You will need to drive across a flooded causeway on the East Alligator River, so check tide times. Between December and April, in the Wet, access is by air only. Permits are required whether driving or flying. The permit is to visit Injalak only—once you cross the East Alligator River you may not stop anywhere until you arrive at Injalak. It may sound difficult, but if you are fascinated by Aboriginal art and culture, you will find it very rewarding.

(less than .5-mile) amble through the Manngarre Monsoon Forest near Ubirr Rock; an easy 3.8km (2.5-mile) circular walk at the Iligadjar Wetlands near the Bowali Visitor Centre; and a tough 12km (7.5-mile) round-trip trek through rugged sandstone country at Nourlangie Rock.

One of the best wetlands walks is at **Mamukala wetlands,** 29km (18 miles) from Jabiru. Thousands of magpie geese feed here, especially in the late Dry season around October. An observation platform gives you a good view, and a sign explains the dramatic seasonal changes the wetlands undergo. Choose from a 1km (.5-mile) or 3km (1.8-mile) round-trip meander.

SWIMMING

In the eastern section of the park rises a massive red-sandstone escarpment that sets the stage for two waterfalls, **Jim Jim Falls** and **Twin Falls.** In the Dry, the volume of water may not be all that impressive, but the settings are magical. Both are accessible by four-wheel-drive only, and neither is open in the Wet.

A 1km (.5-mile) walk over rocks and through rainforest leads to a deep green plunge pool at **Jim Jim Falls,** 103km (64 miles) from the Bowali Visitor Centre. An almost perfectly circular 150m (492-ft.) cliff surrounds the water. Allow 2 hours to drive the final unpaved 60km (37 miles) off the highway. Because of floodwaters, Jim Jim Falls may not open until as late as June. At **Twin Falls,** the waterfalls descend into a natural pool edged by a sandy

Remember the idyllic pool that Paul Hogan and Linda Koslowski plunged into in *Crocodile Dundee*? That was **Gunlom Falls,** 170km (105 miles) south of the Bowali Visitor Centre. A climb to the top rewards you with great views of southern Kakadu. It is generally regarded as croc-free and safe for swimming. Access is by four-wheel-drive; it is cut off in the Wet.

beach, surrounded by bush and high cliffs. Note that you must swim or float the last 500m (1,640 ft.) to the base of the falls—and be warned that saltwater crocodiles have been found in this area.

Some people swim at spots that are generally regarded as croc-free, such as Jim Jim Falls; however, you do so at your own risk. Although rangers survey the swimming holes at the start of the season, and crocodiles are territorial creatures, no one can guarantee that a saltwater crocodile has not moved into a swimming hole. Ask at the Bowali Visitor Centre which pools are croc-free (it can change from year to year) before setting off. If you are unsure about a water hole's safety, the only place rangers recommend you swim is your hotel pool.

ALICE SPRINGS

462km (286 miles) NE of Uluru; 1,491km (924 miles) S of Darwin; 1,544km (957 miles) N of Adelaide; 2,954km (1,831 miles) NW of Sydney

"Alice" or "the Alice," as Australians fondly call it, is the unofficial capital of the Red Centre and a gateway to Uluru.

Many tourists visit Alice only to get to Uluru, but you might like to spend a few days here exploring its indigenous culture and outlying natural attractions. Home to about 29,800 people, it's a rambling, unsophisticated place that is the heart of the Aboriginal Arrernte people's country. Alice is a rich source of tours, shops, and galleries for those interested in Aboriginal culture, art, or souvenirs. However, parts of this region are also evidence that ancient Aboriginal civilization has not always meshed well with the 21st century, which has resulted in fractured riverbed communities plagued by alcohol and other social problems. And it is likely that you will see evidence of this on the streets.

No matter what direction you come from to get here, you will fly for hours over a vast, flat landscape. On arrival, you will see that in fact it is close to a low, dramatic range of rippling red mountains, the **MacDonnell Ranges.** Many visitors excitedly expect to see Uluru, but that marvel is about 462km (286 miles) down the road.

The red folds of the MacDonnell Ranges hide lovely gorges with shady picnic grounds. The area has an old gold-rush town to poke around in, quirky little museums, wildlife parks, a couple of cattle stations (ranches) that welcome visitors, hiking trails to put red dust on your boots, and one of the world's top 10 desert golf courses.

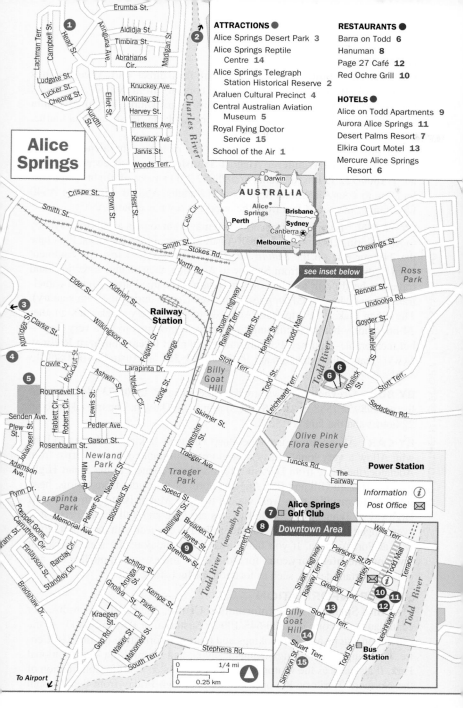

Alice Springs

AUSTRALIA

Darwin
Alice Springs
Perth
Brisbane
Sydney
Canberra
Melbourne

see inset below

Ross Park

Railway Station

Billy Goat Hill

Olive Pink Flora Reserve

Power Station

The Fairway

Information ⓘ
Post Office ✉

Newland Park

Traeger Park

Larapinta Park

Alice Springs Golf Club

Downtown Area

Billy Goat Hill

Bus Station

Todd River (normally dry)

0   1/4 mi
0   0.25 km

To Airport

Essentials

ARRIVING

BY PLANE **Qantas** (www.qantas.com) flies direct into **Alice Springs Airport** (**ASP;** www.alicespringsairport.com.au) from Sydney, Adelaide, Darwin, Perth, Melbourne, Brisbane, Cairns, and Uluru. **Virgin Australia** (www.virginaustralia.com) flies direct from Adelaide, Brisbane, Melbourne, and Darwin.

The airport is about 15km (9⅓ miles) out of town. The **airport shuttle** operated by **Alice Wanderer Airport Transfers** (www.alicewanderer.com. au; ✆ **1800/722 111** in Australia, or 08/8952 2111) meets all flights and transfers you to your Alice hotel door for A$17 adults, A$8.50 children, or A$40 for a family of four. A taxi from the airport to town is around A$35.

BY TRAIN If you are a train buff, you may want to plan a trip from Sydney to Alice Springs that takes in two of Australia's great train journeys. First take the 24-hour ride on the *Indian Pacific* (which travels across the continent from Sydney to Perth) from Sydney to Adelaide, then change direction (and trains) to head north to Alice on *The Ghan* (so named after Afghan camel-train drivers who carried supplies in the Red Centre during the 19th century). The *Ghan* makes the trip from Adelaide to Alice every week—it's another 24-hour ride—before continuing to Darwin. It promises to be a very long—but memorable—journey. For information, contact **Great Southern Railway** (www.greatsouthernrail.com.au; ✆ **1800/703 357** in Australia, or 08/8213 4401).

BY BUS **Greyhound** (www.greyhound.com.au; ✆ **1300/473 946** in Australia, or 08/8952 7888 in Alice Springs) runs from Darwin. The trip takes about 22 hours, and the fare is A$292.

BY CAR Alice Springs is on the Stuart Highway linking Adelaide and Darwin. Allow a very long 2 days or a more comfortable 3 days to drive from Adelaide, the same from Darwin. From Sydney, connect to the Stuart Highway via Broken Hill and Port Augusta north of Adelaide; from Cairns, head south to Townsville, then west via the town of Mount Isa to join the Stuart Highway at Tennant Creek. Both routes are long and dull. From Perth, it is even longer; drive across the Nullarbor Plain to connect with the Stuart Highway at Port Augusta. If you fancy a driving holiday of the area, check out **www.northernterritory.com** for advice on routes, accommodations, and other important details, such as locations of fuel stops.

VISITOR INFORMATION

The **Alice Springs Visitor Information Centre,** Todd Mall (www.discover centralaustralia.com; ✆ **1800/645 199** in Australia, or 08/8952 5800), is the official one-stop shop for bookings and touring information for the Red Centre, including Alice Springs, Kings Canyon, and Uluru–Kata Tjuta National Park. It also acts as the visitor center for the Parks & Wildlife Commission of the Northern Territory. It's open Monday through Friday from 8am to 6pm

Alice Springs was named after Alice Todd, wife of astronomer and engineer Charles Todd, who won the tender to construct the Overland Telegraph line. In 1871, surveyor William Mills was charged with finding a suitable location for a repeater station as part of the Overland Telegraph line and discovered a massive inland river system. He named it for his boss, Charles Todd—not knowing that the Todd River would almost always be dry. He found what he believed to be a natural spring in the river system and named it for Mrs. Todd. In fact, there was no spring, just a water hole left when the rest of the river had dried up. Alice Todd died in Adelaide in 1898, aged 52.

and weekends and public holidays (except Christmas Day, New Year's Day, and Good Friday) from 9:30am to 4pm.

GETTING AROUND ALICE SPRINGS

Virtually all tours pick you up at your hotel. If your itinerary traverses unpaved roads, as it may in outlying areas, you will need to rent a 4WD vehicle, because regular cars will not be insured on an unpaved surface. However, a regular car will get you to most attractions. **Budget,** 113 Todd Mall (www.budget.com.au; ✆ **08/8952 8899**); **Hertz,** 18 Kidman St. (www.hertz.com.au; ✆ **08/8953 6257**); and **Thrifty,** 71 Hartley St. (www.thrifty.com.au; ✆ **08/8952 9999**), all rent conventional and 4WD vehicles. **Avis** (www.avis.com.au; ✆ **08/8952 3694**) and **Europcar** (www.europcar.com.au; ✆ **08/8953 3799**) have desks at the airport, as do all the other companies.

Many rental outfits for motor homes (camper vans) have Alice offices. They include **Apollo Campers,** 40 Stuart Hwy. (www.apollocamper.com; ✆ **1800/777 779** in Australia or 08/8955 5305), and **Britz Campervan Rental,** corner of Stuart Highway and Power Street (www.britz.com; ✆ **1300/738 087** in Australia or 08/8952 8814). Renting a camper van can be significantly cheaper than staying in hotels and going on tours, but do the math first.

The best way to get around town without your own transport is aboard the **Alice Wanderer** bus (see "Organized Tours of Alice Springs," p. 315). **Public buses** (✆ **08/8924 7666**) run around town; the main bus stop is at the corner of Gregory Terrace and Railway Terrace. The A$3 fare gives you unlimited bus travel for 3 hours. A daily ticket costs A$7 and provides unlimited bus travel on that day. For A$20 you can buy a weekly ticket, valid for 7 days from the date of purchase, or a 10-trip flexi-trip ticket (each valid for 3 hours). Both A$20 tickets are electronic "tap-and-ride" cards. Tickets can be bought on the bus. There are no public bus services on Sundays or public holidays.

For a taxi, call **Alice Springs Taxis** (✆ **131 008**) or find one at the rank (stand) on the corner of Todd Street and Gregory Terrace. Taxi fares here are high.

9

THE NORTHERN TERRITORY

Alice Springs

The Henly-on-Todd Regatta of bottomless boats racing on the dry Todd River bed.

CITY LAYOUT

Todd Mall is the heart of town. Most shops, businesses, and restaurants are here or within a few blocks. Most hotels, the casino, the golf course, and many of the town's attractions are a few kilometers outside of town. The dry Todd River "flows" through the city east of Todd Mall.

Where to Stay in Alice Springs

Alice's hotel stock is not grand. Many properties have dated rooms and modest facilities; they're no match for the gleaming **Ayers Rock Resort** (p. 325). You may pay lower rates than those listed in the summer off-season (Dec–Mar) and even as late as June. Peak season typically runs from July through October or November.

If you've rented a camper van, the **Alice Springs Tourist Park,** Larapinta Drive, Alice Springs (www.alicespringstouristpark.com.au; ✆ **1300/823 404** in Australia, or 08/8952 2547), has powered sites costing A$40 a night. Cabins here cost between A$90 and A$175 per night, depending on the cabin and the season.

MODERATE/EXPENSIVE

Aurora Alice Springs ★★   This pleasant hotel is smack in the center of town. Rooms all have a fresh, contemporary decor. Executive rooms have a king-size bed and private balconies facing the Todd River; deluxe and standard rooms have either a double or queen bed and one single bed. Family rooms have a queen-size bed and two single beds. The small pool and Jacuzzi are tucked away in a corner, so this is not the place for chilling out poolside; stay here to be within walking distance of shops and restaurants. The hotel's **Red Ochre Grill** (p. 313) is recommended for gourmet "bush tucker" dining.

11 Leichhardt Terrace (backing onto Todd Mall). www.auroraresorts.com.au. ✆ **1800/089 644** in Australia, or 08/8950 6666. 109 units. A$148–A$228 double; A$158 family room. **Amenities:** Restaurant; barbecue in courtyard; airport shuttle; babysitting; Jacuzzi; small outdoor pool; room service; free Wi-Fi.

MODERATE

Alice on Todd Apartments ★★ Overlooking the Todd River, this contemporary complex has nice studios and one- and two-bedroom apartments. The one-bedroom "deluxe" apartments are a good option, particularly if you have kids. The apartments are very large, and some have two bathrooms. All but the studios have balconies, and some two-bedroom apartments have sofa beds. Each unit has a washing machine, and other amenities include free storage lockers. The hotel is a short stroll from town.

Strehlow St. and South Terrace. www.aliceontodd.com.au. ✆ **08/8953 8033**. 57 units. A$135 studio apt; A$165–A$180 1-bedroom apt; A$230–A$265 2-bedroom apt. Covered parking. **Amenities:** Babysitting; bikes; children's playground; Jacuzzi; pool; free Wi-Fi.

Desert Palms Resort ★★ This is one of the nicest places to stay in Alice. A large swimming pool with its own palm-studded island is the focal point at this complex of bright cabins, where privacy from your neighbors is ensured by trailing pink bougainvillea and palm trees. Don't be deterred by the prefab appearance; inside, the cabins are surprisingly large, well-kept, and inviting, with pine-pitched ceilings, kitchenettes, a tiny bathroom, and furnished front decks. Four rooms are suitable for travelers with disabilities. The pleasant staff at the front desk sells basic grocery and liquor supplies, and can also book tours. You are right next door to Lasseter's Casino (a debatable advantage) and the Alice Springs Golf Club.

74 Barrett Dr. www.desertpalms.com.au. ✆ **1800/678 037** in Australia, or 08/8952 5977. 80 units. A$150 double; A$185 family. **Amenities:** Pool; half-size tennis court; free Wi-Fi.

Mercure Alice Springs Resort ★★ This low-rise property, a 3-minute walk from town over the Todd River, underwent a A$2-million upgrade in mid-2017, with all new fittings in the standard bedrooms and bathrooms, along with the installation of artworks that reflect the history of the Alice Springs region in all rooms. Deluxe rooms have bathtubs and bathrobes, a

---

Behold the Bizarre

Alice Springs hosts a couple of bizarre events. The **Camel Cup** camel race (www.camelcup.com.au) takes place on the second Saturday in July. On the third Saturday in August, people from hundreds of miles around come out to cheer the **Henley-on-Todd Regatta** (www.henleyontodd.com.au), during which gaudily decorated, homemade bottomless "boats" race down the dry Todd River bed. Well, what else do you do on a river that rarely flows? See "Australia Calendar of Events" in chapter 2 (p. 36) for more details.

Incidents of violence and crime in Alice Springs, including attacks on tourists by groups of young people—fueled by alcohol and substance abuse—have made headlines in Australia in recent years. Much of the trouble is centered around the dry bed of the Todd River and Aboriginal "town camps." Visitors are advised not to wander the streets at night.

coffee machine, and a balcony or veranda overlooking the Todd River or the gardens. In summer, it's nice to repair to the pool under a couple of desert palms for a drink at the poolside bar. An outdoor amphitheatre is a hub for Aboriginal workshops and cultural sessions. It's also a 5-minute walk along the boardwalk to the Olive Pink Botanic Garden.

34 Stott Terrace. www.accorhotels.com. ✆ 08/8951 4545. 139 units. A$128–A$168 double. Amenities: Restaurant; 2 bars; free airport shuttle; babysitting; bikes; concierge; solar-heated outdoor pool; room service; free Wi-Fi.

MODERATE/INEXPENSIVE

Elkira Court Motel ★ The cheapest rooms in the heart of town—decent ones, that is—are at this clean, comfortable, unpretentious motel. You won't get better value. Rooms are basic, but all are air-conditioned. Deluxe rooms have kitchenettes, and some have king-size beds. Deluxe Spa rooms have two-person Jacuzzis. Ask for a room away from the road; the traffic is noisy during the day.

65 Bath St. www.elkiracourtmotel.com.au. ✆ **08/8952 1222.** 58 units. A$115–A$180 double. **Amenities:** Restaurant; airport shuttle; nearby golf course; Jacuzzi; outdoor pool; free Wi-Fi.

Where to Eat in Alice Springs

Barra on Todd ★★ CONTEMPORARY Part of the Mercure Alice Springs Resort, this restaurant serves up barramundi—of course—along with a variety of other dishes. Try your freshwater Barra with an almond and spinach crust, or your Australian blue-eye trevalla (a codlike fish) with a creamy mushroom risotto. If you're not a fan of fish, the menu offers a number of chicken, steak, lamb, and duck dishes. Barra on Todd does a **buffet breakfast** and has all-day (well, 11:30am–9pm) dining by the pool. It's popular for dinner, so book ahead.

In the Mercure Alice Springs Resort, 34 Stott Terrace. www.accorhotels.com. ✆ **08/8951 4545.** Main courses A$29–A$42. Daily 11:30am–5pm lunch; 6–9:30pm dinner.

Hanuman ★★★ CONTEMPORARY ASIAN This is one of the most exotic restaurants in Alice Springs. The cuisine is a fusion of Thai and Indian cooking, and the decor mixes Asian artifacts and moody lighting to atmospheric effect. You won't be disappointed by dishes such as red duck curry with coconut, lychees, kaffir lime, Thai basil, and fresh pineapple; or black pepper prawns with garlic, onion, and fresh curry leaf. The menu has plenty of vegetarian options too. There is another branch of Hanuman in Darwin (p. 288).

In the DoubleTree by Hilton, 82 Barrett Dr. www.hanuman.com.au. ✆ **08/8953 7188.** Main courses A$15–A$38. Daily noon–2:30pm and 6–10:30pm.

Page 27 Café ★★ CAFE   Tucked down a laneway, with tables outside and inside, this smart cafe is a great choice for breakfast or lunch. From beef burgers to quinoa bowls and fresh salads, the dishes are all interesting and healthy, and vegetarians and vegans will be happy, too. But that doesn't mean there aren't sweet treats too: homemade banana slice with whipped almond butter and honeycomb, or delicious vegan molasses spiced cookies, for example. And the coffee is excellent.

89 Todd Mall. www.facebook.com/Page27Cafe. ✆ **0420 003 874.** Main courses A$11–A$20. Tues–Fri 7am–2:30pm; Sat–Sun 7:30am–2:30pm.

Red Ochre Grill ★★ GOURMET BUSH TUCKER   The chef at this upscale restaurant fuses native Aussie ingredients with dishes from around the world. If you've never tried crocodile ribs (served with a mint pea and corn fritter) or chargrilled kangaroo filet with a red wine glaze, then this is your chance. Although it might seem a touristy formula, the food is delicious. Dine in the contemporary interior fronting Todd Mall or outside in the attractive courtyard. Reservations are recommended at dinner, when the menu offers the best "bush tucker" options.

Todd Mall. www.redochrealice.com.au. ✆ **08/8952 9614.** Main courses A$19–A$36. Daily 6:30–10am, noon–2:30pm, and 5–9pm (closed Dec 25).

Exploring Alice Springs

All the major attractions in Alice Springs are within easy reach of the city center.

Alice Springs Desert Park ★★★ WILDLIFE VIEWING   By means of an easy 1.6km (1-mile) trail through three reconstructed natural habitats, this impressive wildlife and flora park introduces you to 120 or so of the animal species that live in the desert around Alice but aren't spotted easily in the wild (including kangaroos you can walk among). Most of the creatures are small mammals (like the rare bilby), reptiles (cute thorny devil lizards), and birds. Don't miss the excellent **free-flying bird presentation** at 10am daily (also at 3:30pm Nov–Feb). For a different perspective, visit the park at night for a guided tour to see nocturnal species such as echidnas, bilbies, and mala. The 90-minute tour costs A$45 adults and A$29 children 5 to 15. It runs at 7:30pm Monday to Friday. A cafe is on premises. Allow 2 to 3 hours to visit the park. **Tailormade Tours** (www.tailormadetours.com.au; ✆ **08/8952 1731**) and **Alice Wanderer** (www.alicewanderer.com.au; ✆ **1800/722 111** in Australia, or 08/8952 2111) both offer transfers from accommodations several times a day in each direction.

Larapinta Dr., 6km (3¾ miles) W of Alice Springs. www.alicespringsdesertpark.com.au. ✆ **08/8951 8788.** A$32 adults, A$16 children 5–15, A$55–A$87 families. Daily 7:30am–6pm (last entry 4:30pm). Closed Dec 25.

Alice Springs Reptile Centre ★★ WILDLIFE VIEWING Kids love this place, where they can drape a python around their neck or have a bearded dragon (lizard) perch on their shoulder. Rex, the easygoing proprietor, helps you get the best photos and lets kids hand-feed bugs to the animals at feeding time. More than 50 species are on display, including the world's deadliest land snake (the taipan) and big goannas. Also here are brown snakes, death adders, and mulga, otherwise known as king brown snakes. Don't miss the saltwater croc exhibit, with underwater viewing. The best time to visit is between 11am and 3pm, when the reptiles are at their most active. There are talks at 11am and 1 and 3:30pm. Allow an hour or so.

9 Stuart Terrace (opposite the Royal Flying Doctor Service). www.reptilecentre.com.au. ℂ **08/8952 8900.** A$18 adults, A$10 children 4–16, A$46 families of 4. Daily 9:30am–5pm. Closed Jan 1 and Dec 25.

Alice Springs Telegraph Station Historical Reserve ★★ HISTORIC SITE This oasis marks the first European settlement of Alice Springs, which takes its name from the water hole nearby. Alice Springs began life here in 1872 as a telegraph repeater station, against a backdrop of red hills and sprawling gum trees. Arm yourself with the free map or join a free 45-minute tour at 9:30 and 11:30am, and 1:30 and 3:30pm (mornings only in summer). You can wander around the old stationmaster's residence; the telegraph office, with its Morse-code machine tap-tapping away; the shoeing yard, packed with blacksmithing equipment; and the stables, housing vintage buggies and saddlery. From the on-site computer, you can "telegraph" e-mail messages to your friends or be really old-fashioned and send mail through the Telegraph/Post Office, which will be stamped with a special franking stamp. It's a charming and much-underrated place. Allow an hour—more to walk one of the several hiking trails—or bring a picnic and stay longer. You are also likely to see kangaroos and rock wallabies. It has a gift shop and a kiosk where you can buy coffee and snacks. A pleasant way of getting there is to take the 4km (2½-mile) riverside pedestrian/bike track that starts in town near the corner of Wills Terrace and Undoolya Road.

Stuart Hwy., 4km (2½ miles) N of Alice Springs (past the School of the Air turnoff). www.alicespringstelegraphstation.com.au. ℂ **08/8952 3993.** Free admission to picnic grounds and trails; station A$15 adults, A$9.30 children 12–16, A$5.50 children 6–11, A$35 families of 4. Daily 9am–5pm (picnic grounds and trails 8am–9pm). Station closed Dec 25.

Araluen Cultural Precinct ★★ GALLERIES/MUSEUMS Take several hours to explore the many facets of this interesting complex of attractions. Impressive Aboriginal and contemporary Aussie art is on display at the **Araluen Arts Centre,** the town's performing-arts hub, which incorporates the **Araluen Art Collection,** focusing on works by Aboriginal artists from Central Australia from the early 1930s onwards, including Albert Namatjira and artists from the Papunya community in the early 1970s. Check out the "Honey Ant Dreaming" stained-glass window in the foyer. You can buy stylish crafts, and sometimes catch artists at work, in the **Central Craft** gallery. You may also want to amble among the fabulous outdoor sculptures, including the 15m (49-ft.) Yeperenye caterpillar, or among the gravestones in the cemetery next door, where "Afghani" camel herders (from what is now Pakistan) are buried facing Mecca. The **Museum of Central Australia** mostly shows local fossils, natural history displays, and meteorites, and the **Central Australian Aviation Museum** has a collection of old aircraft, radios, and wreckage that preserves the territory's aerial history. Located on the site of the 1939 Alice Springs "aerodrome," the museum includes the original hangar; among its highlights are a Beech 18 and a Wackett Trainer aircraft.

61 Larapinta Dr., at Memorial Ave., 2km (1¼ miles) W of Alice Springs. www.araluen artscentre.nt.gov.au. ✆ **08/8951 1122.** A$15 adults, A$10 children 5–16, A$40 families of 4. Daily 10am–4pm. Closed Good Friday and 2 weeks from Christmas Day.

Royal Flying Doctor Service Tourist Facility ★★ MUSEUM   Alice is a major base for this airborne medical service that treats people living and traveling in the vast Outback. The visitor center provides a great insight into the work the RFDS does. Guided tours run every half-hour from 9am (last tour at 4pm); allow another 30 minutes or so to browse the museum and listen to some of the recorded conversations between doctors and patients. You can explore a replica fuselage of a Pilatus PC12, test your hand at the throttle in a flight simulator, and "meet" the life-size hologram of RFDS founder Reverend John Flynn. It also has a cafe, gift shop, and art gallery.

8–10 Stuart Terrace (at end of Hartley St.). www.rfdsalicesprings.com.au. ✆ **08/8958 8411.** A$17 adults, A$10 children 6–15, A$52 families of 5. Mon–Sat 9am–5pm; Sun and public holidays 1–5pm. Closed Jan 1, Good Friday, Dec 25, and Dec 26.

School of the Air ★★★ BEHIND-THE-SCENES TOUR   Sitting in on school lessons may not be your idea of a vacation, but this school is different—it broadcasts by radio to a 1.3-million-sq.-km (502,000-sq.-mile) "schoolroom" of about 140 children on Outback stations. That area is as big as Germany, Great Britain, Ireland, New Zealand, and Japan combined—or twice the size of Texas. Visitors watch and listen in when classes are in session; outside class hours, you may hear taped classes. You can browse displays of the kids' artwork, photos, and video in the well-organized visitor center. Allow about an hour.

80 Head St. (2.5km/1½ miles NW from Alice Springs). www.assoa.nt.edu.au. ✆ **08/8951 6834.** A$12 adults, A$9 children 5–16, A$35–A$38 families. Mon–Sat 8:30am–4:30pm; Sun and public holidays 1:30–4:30pm. Closed Good Friday and usually Dec 21–Jan 5. Bus: nos. 100 or 101 (except Sun and public holidays).

Organized Tours of Alice Springs
AROUND TOWN & OUT IN THE DESERT
Alice Wanderer Centre Sightseeing (www.alicewanderer.com.au; ✆ **1800/722 111** in Australia, or 08/8952 2111) offers a large range of half- and full-day tours. It's well worth checking out its website to help you plan your time before you visit. The company also runs full- and half-day tours to

outlying areas, including to Palm Valley in the West MacDonnell Ranges (p. 317), costing A$155 for adults and A$116 for kids age 2 to 15.

Many Alice-based companies offer mini coach or 4WD day trips and extended tours of Alice and of outlying areas including the East and West Macs, Hermannsburg, and Finke Gorge National Park.

CAMEL SAFARIS

The camel's ability to get by without water was key to opening the arid inland parts of Australia to European settlement in the 1800s. With the advent of cars, the camels were released into the wild, and today more than 200,000 roam Central Australia. Australia even exports them to the Middle East! **Pyndan Camel Tracks** (www.cameltracks.com; ℂ **0416/170 164**) runs camel rides daily, with pickup from your hotel. A 1-hour tour, at noon, 2:30pm, or sunset, costs A$79 adults and A$39 for kids 14 and under (A$10 more at sunset). Kids 2 and under must ride with an adult. Make sure you wear comfortable, casual clothes, and sensible shoes—you are likely to get a bit dirty.

HOT-AIR BALLOON FLIGHTS

Dawn balloon flights above the desert are popular in Central Australia. (You do have to get up 90 min. before dawn, though.) **Outback Ballooning** (www. outbackballooning.com.au; ℂ **1800/809 790** in Australia, or 08/8952 8723) offers a 1-hour flight followed by a champagne breakfast in the bush for A$390 adults, A$318 for kids 6 to 16. A 30-minute breakfast flight costs A$295 adults, A$242 for children. Kids 5 and under are discouraged from participating because they cannot see over the basket. Don't make any other morning plans—you probably won't get back to your hotel until close to noon.

OUTBACK CYCLING

See Alice Springs and surrounds by pedal power on a tour with **Outback Cycling Tours** (www.outbackcycling.com; ℂ **08/8952 1541**). A half-day guided morning ride includes cycling along the dry bed of the Todd River. Cost is A$160 adults, A$40 children 7 to 12, and A$30 children 6 and under. More adventurous tours include a sunrise mountain bike ride into the bush surrounding the city, a sunset tour, and an overnight mountain bike ride into the West MacDonnell Ranges and camping under the stars.

Outdoor Activities

The **Alice Springs Golf Club,** 1km (.6 mile) from town on Cromwell Drive (www.alicespringsgolfclub.com.au; ℂ **08/8952 1921**), boasts a Thomson-Wolveridge course rated among the world's top desert courses by touring pros. The course is open from sunup to sundown. Nine holes cost A$27; 18 holes, A$48. Club rental is A$29, and a motorized cart, which many locals don't bother with, goes for A$35 for 18 holes. There's also a driving range (A$9 for a small bucket of balls). If lawn bowling is more your style, the golf club also has a bowling green (A$10 for a lane for 2 hr. for up to 8 people).

For those interested in a bit of bushwalking, the 223km (138-mile) **Larap-inta Trail** begins in Alice Springs and winds west through the picturesque semi-desert scenery of the **Tjoritja/West MacDonnell National Park.** For more details, see "Hiking the West MacDonnells," p. 319.

Shopping for Aboriginal Art

Alice Springs is one of the best places in Australia to buy Aboriginal art and crafts. You will find no shortage of paintings, didgeridoos, spears, clapping sticks, *coolamons* (dishes used by women to carry anything from water to babies), animal carvings, baskets, and jewelry, as well as books, CDs, and all kinds of merchandise printed with Aboriginal designs. Prices can soar for large canvases by world-renowned painters, but you'll also find plenty of smaller, more affordable works. Most galleries arrange shipment. Store hours can vary with the seasons and the crowds, so it pays to check ahead.

Mbantua Fine Art Gallery and Cultural Museum, 64 Todd Mall (www.mbantua.com.au; *C* **08/8952 5571**), is a highly respected and reliable source of authentic Aboriginal art, with a dazzling selection to choose from. The art comes from a harsh desert region called Utopia, home to several Aboriginal communities. Mbantua owner Tim Jennings began supplying locals with paints and canvas in the late 1980s during food deliveries to Utopia, first as sheriff, then as the general-store owner. Some of the 200 Utopia residents who paint have been recognized internationally, including Barbara Weir, Gloria Petyarre, the late Emily Kame Kngwarreye, and Minnie Pwerle. Jennings authenticates every piece of art; he and his team photograph the artist with the work and record the traditional meaning behind it. Works by established artists can be priced up to tens of thousands of dollars, but a much smaller investment can get you work by lesser-known but talented painters. Mbantua Gallery is a member of Art Trade, an organization that promotes the ethical trade of indigenous art. The gallery is open Monday to Friday 9am to 5pm, Saturday 9am to 3pm, and (May–Oct only) Sunday 10am to 2pm.

Papunya Tula Artists, 63 Todd Mall (www.papunyatula.com.au; *C* **08/8952 4731**), sells paintings on canvas and linen from Papunya, a settlement 240km (150 miles) northwest of Alice Springs, and work by other artists living in the Western Desert, as far as 700km (434 miles) from Alice Springs.

Day Trip to the MacDonnell Ranges ★★★

The key attraction of a day trip to the MacDonnell Ranges is unspoiled natural scenery and few crowds. Many Alice Springs companies run coach or 4WD tours—half- or full-day, sometimes overnight—to the West and East Macs; one of our favorites is **Alice Wanderer Centre Sightseeing** (www.alicewanderer.com.au; *C* **1800/722 111** in Australia, or 08/8952 2111).

ARRIVING

If you are not driving yourself, you can arrange to be dropped off by **Larap-inta Transfers** (www.larapintatransfers.com.au; *C* **1800/687 220** in Australia, or 08/8953 7057) at several stops in the Ranges. It costs A$100 per person (minimum of two) for the return trip to Simpson's Gap or Standley Chasm; A$170 to Ellery Creek, Serpentine Gorge, Ormiston Gorge, Glen Helen Gorge, or the ochre pits. The **Alice Wanderer** (see above) also does group tours.

THE WEST MACDONNELL RANGES

The 300km (186-mile) round-trip drive west from Alice Springs into **Tjoritja/ West MacDonnell National Park** ★★ (www.nt.gov.au/leisure/parks-reserves/find-a-park-to-visit/tjoritja-west-macdonnell-national-park) is a stark but picturesque expedition to a series of red gorges, semi-desert country, and the occasional peaceful swimming hole.

From Alice, take Larapinta Drive west for 18km (11 miles) to the 8km (5-mile) turnoff to **Simpson's Gap,** a water hole lined with ghost gums. Black-footed rock wallabies hop out on the cliffs in the late afternoon (so you may want to time a visit here on your way back to Alice). There are a couple of short trails here, including a .5km (.3-mile) Ghost Gum circuit and a 17km (11-mile) round-trip trail to Bond Gap. Swimming is not permitted. There is an information center/ranger station and free use of barbecues.

Twenty-three kilometers (14 miles) farther down Larapinta Road, 9km (5½ miles) down a turnoff, is **Standley Chasm** (www.standleychasm.com.au; ℂ **08/8956 7440**). This rock cleft is only a few meters wide but 80m (262 ft.) high, reached by a 10-minute creekside trail. Aim to be here at midday, when the walls glow orange in the overhead sun. A kiosk sells snacks and drinks. Admission is A$12 adults, A$7 children 5 to 14, and A$30 for a family of 4. The chasm is open daily from 8am to 5pm (last entry at 4:30pm; closed Christmas Day). This is a private reserve, owned by local Aboriginal people. Half-day indigenous tours are offered daily at 9am (bookings required) for A$85 adults and A$60 children.

Six kilometers (3¾ miles) past Standley Chasm, you can branch right onto Namatjira Drive or continue to Hermannsburg Historic Precinct (see below). If you take Namatjira Drive, you'll go 42km (26 miles) to picturesque **Ellery Creek Big Hole.** *Fair warning:* The spring-fed water is icy cold. A 3km (2-mile) walking trail explains the area's geological history.

Eleven kilometers (7 miles) farther along Namatjira Drive is **Serpentine Gorge,** where a trail leads up to a lookout for a lovely view of the ranges through the gorge walls. Another 12km (7½ miles) on are **ochre pits,** which Aboriginal people quarried for body paint and for decorating objects used in ceremonial performances. Twenty-six kilometers (16 miles) farther west, 8km (5 miles) from the main road, **Ormiston Gorge and Pound** (ℂ **08/8956 7799** for the ranger station/visitor center) is a good spot to picnic, swim in the wide, deep pool below red cliffs, and walk a choice of trails, such as the 30-minute Ghost Gum Lookout trail or the easy 7km (4⅓-mile) scenic loop (allow 3–4 hr.). The water is warm enough for swimming in the summer.

hiking THE WEST MACDONNELLS

The 223km (138-mile) Larapinta Trail winds west from Alice through some of the most unique and isolated country in the world: the **Tjoritja/West MacDonnell National Park** (p. 318). The hills, colors, birds, water holes, gorges, and the never-ending diversity of this trail will leave you spellbound by the beauty of Central Australia.

This long-distance walking track is divided into 12 sections, each a 1- to 2-day walk. Sections range from easy to hard. The shortest is 8km (5 miles), and they go up to 29km (18 miles). The trail begins at the old Alice Springs Telegraph Station and meanders through many gaps and sheltered gorges and climbs steeply over rugged ranges. Each section is accessible to vehicles (some by high-clearance 4WD only), so you can join or leave the trail at any of the trail heads.

Camping out under a sea of stars in the Outback is a highlight of the experience. Although they vary, most campsites offer picnic tables and hardened tent sites—all trail heads have a water supply, and some have free gas barbecues.

Tips: The Parks & Wildlife Commission of the Northern Territory strongly recommends any individual or group walking the Larapinta Trail to carry a satellite phone or a location device such as a PLB/EPIRBS or Spot Messenger. Don't attempt this walk in the height of summer unless you are very well prepared. **Warning:** Always carry drinking water. The trail may close in extremely hot summer periods.

Detailed track notes are at the Visitor Information Centre in Alice Springs and online at **www.nt.gov.au/leisure/recreation/bushwalking-hiking/larapinta-trail.** The website also lists companies that provide transfers to access points along the way, food drops, camping equipment, or fully guided and supported treks.

Farther on is **Glen Helen Gorge,** where the Finke River cuts through the ranges, with more gorge swimming, a walking trail, guided hikes, and helicopter flights. **Glen Helen Lodge** (www.glenhelenlodge.com.au; ℂ **1300/269 822** in Australia, or 08/8956 7208) has a restaurant and offers 4WD tours from A\$190 per person for a half-day and scenic helicopter flights from March through November (two-person minimum) from A\$89 per person.

HERMANNSBURG HISTORIC PRECINCT ★★   An alternative to visiting the West Mac gorges is to stay on Larapinta Drive all 128km (79 miles) from Alice Springs to the old **Lutheran Mission** at the **Hermannsburg Historic Precinct** (www.hermannsburg.com.au; ℂ **08/8956 7402**). Some maps show this route as an unpaved road, but it is paved. Settled by German missionaries in the 1870s, it's a cluster of 16 National Trust–listed farmhouse-style mission buildings and a historic cemetery. It has a museum, a gallery housing landscapes by Aboriginal artist Albert Namatjira, and tearooms serving light snacks and apple strudel from an old German recipe. The precinct is open daily 9am to 5pm; closed Good Friday and Christmas Day. Admission to the precinct is A\$12 for adults, free for children.

FINKE GORGE NATIONAL PARK ★★ Just west of Hermannsburg, turn south off Larapinta Drive to reach the 46,000-hectare (113,620-acre) **Finke Gorge National Park** (about a 2-hr. drive west of Alice Springs). You will need to have a four-wheel-drive vehicle or take a tour to explore this park; access along the last 16km (10 miles) of unpaved road, which follows the sandy bed of the Finke River, is limited to four-wheel-drive vehicles only. Heavy rains may cause this section of the road to be impassable. The park is most famous for **Palm Valley,** where groves of rare *Livistona mariae* cabbage palms have survived since Central Australia was a jungle millions of years ago. Four walking trails between 1.5km (1 mile) and 5km (3 miles) take you among the palms or up to a lookout over cliffs; one is a signposted trail exploring Aboriginal culture. For information, call the Visitor Information Centre in Alice Springs before you leave; there is no visitor center in the park.

THE EAST MACDONNELL RANGES ★★★

Not as many tourists tread the path on the Ross Highway into the East Macs, but if you do, you'll be rewarded with lush walking trails, fewer crowds, traces of Aboriginal history, and possibly even the sight of wild camels.

The first points of interest are **Emily Gap,** 10km (6 miles) southeast from Alice, and **Jessie Gap,** an additional 7km (4⅓ miles), a pretty picnic spot. You can cool off in the Emily Gap swimming hole if it has any water. Don't miss the *Caterpillar Dreaming* Aboriginal painting art on the wall, on your right as you walk through.

At **Corroboree Rock,** 37km (23 miles) farther along Hwy. 8, make a short climb up the outcrop, which was important to local Aborigines. The polished

ROAD trips TO THE EAST & WEST MACS

Facilities are scarce outside Alice, so bring food, drinking water, and a full gas tank. Leaded, unleaded, and diesel fuel are for sale at Glen Helen Resort and Hermannsburg. Wear walking shoes.

Many of the water holes dry up too much to be good for swimming—those at Ellery Creek (p. 318), Ormiston Gorge (p. 318), and Glen Helen (p. 319) are the most permanent. They can be intensely cold, so take only short dips to avoid cramping and hypothermia, don't swim alone, and be careful of underwater snags. Don't wear sunscreen, because it pollutes drinking water for native animals.

Two-wheel-drive rental cars will not be insured on unsealed (unpaved) roads, which includes the last few miles into Trephina Gorge Nature Park and the 11km (7-mile) road into N'Dhala Gorge Nature Park, both in the East Macs. If you are prepared to risk it, you can probably get into Trephina in a two-wheel-drive car, but you will definitely need a 4WD vehicle for N'Dhala and Arltunga. The West MacDonnell road is paved to Glen Helen Gorge; a few points of interest may require driving for short lengths on unpaved road. Before setting off, drop into the **Alice Springs Visitor Information Centre** (p. 308) for tips on road conditions and details on the free ranger talks, walks, and slideshows that take place in the West and East Macs from April through October. Entry to all sights, parks, and reserves (except Standley Chasm) is free.

Caterpillar Dreaming, Aboriginal painting at Emily Gap swimming hole.

rock "seat" high up in the hole means Aboriginal people used this rock for eons.

Twenty-two kilometers (14 miles) farther is the turnoff to **Trephina Gorge Nature Park,** an 18-sq.-km (7-sq.-mile) beauty spot with peaceful walking trails that can take from 45 minutes to 4½ hours. The last 5km (3 miles) of the road into the park are unpaved, but you can make it in a two-wheel-drive car.

N'Dhala Gorge Nature Park, 10km (6 miles) past Trephina Gorge Nature Park, houses an "open-air art gallery" of rock carvings, or petroglyphs, left by the Eastern Arrernte Aboriginal people. An interesting 1.5km (1-mile) sign-posted trail explains the Dreamtime meanings of a few of the 6,000 rock carvings, hundreds or thousands of years old, that are thought to be in this eerily quiet gorge. A 4WD vehicle is a must to traverse the 11km (7-mile) access road.

ULURU–KATA TJUTA NATIONAL PARK ★★★

462km (286 miles) SW of Alice Springs; 1,934km (1,199 miles) S of Darwin; 1,571km (974 miles) N of Adelaide; 2,841km (1,761 miles) NW of Sydney

Why travel so far to look at a large red rock? Because it will send a shiver up your spine. Because it may move you to tears. Because there is something indefinable and indescribable but definitely spiritual about this place. Up close, Uluru is more magnificent than you can imagine. It is immense and overwhelming and mysterious. Photographs never do it justice. There is what is described as a "spirit of place" here. It is unforgettable and irresistible (and you may well want to come back again, just for another look). It will not disappoint you. On my first visit—yes, I am one who will keep coming back—a stranger whispered to me: "Even when you are not looking at it, it is always just *there,* waiting to tap you on the shoulder." A rock with a presence.

"The Rock" has a circumference of 10.6km (6½ miles), and two-thirds of it is thought to be underground. In photos, it may look smooth and even, but the reality is much more interesting—dappled with holes and overhangs, with curtains of stone draping its sides, creating little coves that hide water holes and Aboriginal rock art. It also changes color from pink to a deep wine red depending on the angle and intensity of the sun. And if you are lucky enough to be visiting when it rains, you will see a sight like no other. Here, rain brings everyone outside to see the spectacle of the waterfalls created off the massive rock, which was formed by sediments laid down 600 to 700 million years ago in an inland sea and thrust up aboveground 348m (1,141 ft.) by geological forces.

In 1985, **Uluru–Kata Tjuta National Park** was returned to its Aboriginal owners, the Pitjantjatjara and Yankunytjatjara people, known as the Anangu, who manage the property jointly with the Australian government. A visit to Uluru isn't just about snapping a few photos and going home. There are many

The massive monolith known as Uluru.

It's a *loooong* day to visit Uluru in a day from Alice Springs by road. Many organized coach tours pack a lot—perhaps a Rock-base walk or climb, Kata Tjuta (the Olgas), the Uluru–Kata Tjuta Cultural Centre, and a champagne sunset at the Rock—into a busy trip that leaves Alice around 5:30 or 6am and gets you back late at night. You should consider a day trip only between May and September. At other times, it's too hot to do much from early morning to late afternoon.

ways of exploring it, and one of the best is to join Aboriginal people on guided walks. You can walk around the Rock, fly over it, ride a camel to it, circle it on a Harley-Davidson or a bicycle, trek through the nearby Olgas, and dine under the stars while you learn about them.

Just do yourself one favor: Plan to spend at least 2 days here, if not 3.

Isolation (and a lack of competition) makes such things as accommodations, meals, and transfers relatively expensive. A coach tour or 4WD camping safari is often the cheapest way to see the place (see "Package Tour Operators," p. 281).

Essentials

ARRIVING

BY PLANE **Qantas** (www.qantas.com) flies to **Ayers Rock (Connellan) Airport (AYQ)** direct from Alice Springs, Darwin, Adelaide, and Cairns. Flights from other airports go via Alice Springs. **Jetstar** (www.jetstar.com.au) flies from Sydney, Brisbane, and Melbourne. **Virgin Australia** (www.virgin australia.com) flies from Sydney.

The airport is 6km (3¾ miles) from Ayers Rock Resort. A free shuttle ferries all resort guests, including campers, to their door.

BY CAR Take the Stuart Highway south from Alice Springs 199km (123 miles), turn right onto the Lasseter Highway, and go 244km (151 miles) to Ayers Rock Resort. The Rock is 18km (11 miles) farther on. It is about a 4½-hour drive in total.

If you are renting a car in Alice Springs and want to drop it at Uluru and fly out from there, be prepared for a one-way penalty. Only Avis, Hertz, and Thrifty have Uluru depots (see "Getting Around," p. 324).

VISITOR INFORMATION

For online information before you arrive, check out the **Uluru–Kata Tjuta National Park** website, **www.parksaustralia.gov.au/uluru**. Another good source of online information is **Ayers Rock Resort** (www.ayersrockresort.com.au). The **visitor information center** in Alice Springs (p. 308) also can provide information before you head to Uluru.

One kilometer (.6 mile) from the base of the Rock, the **Uluru–Kata Tjuta Cultural Centre** (www.parksaustralia.gov.au/uluru/do/cultural-centre.html; ℭ **08/8956 1128**), owned and run by the Anangu, the Aboriginal owners of

Uluru, uses eye-catching wall displays, frescoes, interactive recordings, and videos to tell about Aboriginal Dreamtime myths and laws. It's worth spending some time here to understand a little about Aboriginal culture. A National Park desk has information on ranger-guided activities and animal, plant, and bird-watching checklists. The center also has a cafe, a souvenir shop, and two Aboriginal arts and crafts galleries. It's open daily 7am to 6pm.

> ### Cultural Etiquette
>
> The Anangu ask you not to photograph sacred sites or Aboriginal people without permission and to approach quietly and respectfully. Climbing Uluru is no longer allowed, by law (see p. 330).

You can book tours at the **tour desk** in every hotel at Ayers Rock Resort, or visit the **Tour & Information Centre** (✆ **08/8957 7324**) in the resort's Town Square. It's open daily 8am to 7pm.

PARK ENTRANCE FEES

Entry to the Uluru–Kata Tjuta National Park is A$25 per adult, A$13 children 5 to 15, or A$65 for a family; it's valid for 3 days. Some tours include this fee but others do not, so it pays to check. National Park tickets can be purchased from the National Park Entry Station or online. The park opens between 5 and 6:30am (depending on the time of year) and closes between 7:30 and 9pm.

GETTING AROUND

Ayers Rock Resort runs a **free shuttle** every 20 minutes or so around the resort complex from 10:30am to after midnight, but to get to the Rock or Kata Tjuta (the Olgas), you will need to take transfers, join a tour, or have your own wheels. The shuttle also meets all flights. There are no taxis at Yulara.

BY SHUTTLE   **Uluru Hop On Hop Off** (www.uluruhoponhopoff.com.au; ✆ **08/8956 2019**) provides a shuttle from Ayers Rock Resort to and from the Rock several times a day from before sunrise to sundown, and twice a day to Kata Tjuta. The basic round-trip fare is A$49 for adults and A$15 for kids 1 to 14. To Kata Tjuta, it costs A$95 adults and A$40 children. A 2-day pass that enables you to explore Uluru and Kata Tjuta costs A$160 adults and A$60 children; a 3-day pass costs A$210 adults and A$100 kids. A National Park entry pass, if you don't already have one, is A$25 extra.

BY CAR   If there are two of you, the easiest and cheapest way to get around is likely to be a rental car. All roads in the area are paved, so 4WD is unnecessary. Expect to pay around A$120 to A$140 per day for a medium-size car (rates drop a little in low season). Most car-rental companies give you unlimited kilometers on all vehicles but take the cost of your fuel into account because the round-trip from the resort to the Olgas is just over 100km (63 miles), and it's about 20km (13 miles) to the Rock and back. Rental periods of less than 3 days incur a one-way fee up to A$385. **Avis** (www.avis.com.au; ✆ **08/8956 2266**), **Hertz** (www.hertz.com.au; ✆ **08/8956 2244**), and **Thrifty** (www.thrifty.com.au; ✆ **08/8956 2030**) all rent regular cars and four-wheel-drives.

ORGANIZED TOURS

Several tour companies run a range of daily experiences: sunrise and sunset viewings, circumnavigations of the Rock by coach or on foot, guided walks at the Rock or the Olgas, camel rides, observatory evenings, visits to the Uluru–Kata Tjuta Cultural Centre, and innumerable combinations of all of these. Some offer "passes" containing the most popular activities. Virtually every company picks you up at your hotel. Among the most reputable are **AAT Kings** and **Tailormade Tours** (p. 281).

WHERE TO STAY & EAT NEAR ULURU

Ayers Rock Resort is not only in the township of Yulara—it *is* the township. Located about 30km (19 miles) from Uluru, outside the national park boundary, it is the only place to stay. It is an impressive contemporary complex, built to a high standard, efficiently run, and attractive—all things (along with its remoteness) that don't come cheaply. Because everyone either is a tourist, or lives and works here, it has a village atmosphere—with a supermarket, bank, post office, newsstand, medical center, beauty salon, gas station, and several gift, clothing, and souvenir shops.

You have a choice of seven places to stay, from luxury hotel rooms and apartments to campsites. No matter where you stay, even in the campground, you are free to use all the pools, restaurants, and other facilities of every hostelry, except the exclusive Sails in the Desert pool, which is reserved for Sails guests, and Longitude 131°.

You can book any of the accommodations through a **central reservations office** (www.ayersrockresort.com.au; © **1300/134 044** in Australia, or 02/8296 8010). High season is July through November. Book well ahead, and shop around for special deals on the Internet and with travel agencies. Ask about packages for 2- or 3-night stays—these rates will be considerably cheaper than the 1-night rate quoted below. All stays include a free indigenous activities program, including guided walks, dance shows, and access to the Mani Mani Indigenous Cultural Theatre.

In addition to the resort dining options, the small shopping center has the pleasant **Gecko's Café,** which offers gourmet pizzas, pastas, and burgers (as well as takeout); **Kulata Academy Cafe,** where the staff are part of an indigenous trainee program; and the **Ayers Wok Noodle Bar** (yes, really!). Several of the resort restaurants offer kids' menus.

Ayers Rock Campground ★

Instead of red dust, you get green lawns at this campground, which has barbecues, a playground, swimming pool, a small general store, clean communal bathrooms and kitchen, and an Internet kiosk. If camping's not your thing but you want to travel cheap, consider the modern two-bedroom cabins. They are a great value; each has air-conditioning, a

---

Water, Water...

Water taps are scarce and kiosks nonexistent in Uluru–Kata Tjuta National Park. Always carry plenty of your own drinking water when sightseeing.

TV, a kitchenette, dining furniture, a double bed, and four bunks (but no phone). All accommodation here is very popular, and prebooking is essential. Yulara Dr. www.ayersrockresort.com.au/accommodation/ayers-rock-campground. © **08/8957 7001.** 220 tent sites, 198 powered sites, 14 cabins with shared bathroom. A\$179–A\$185 cabin for up to 6; A\$39–A\$44 tent site; A\$48–A\$54 motor-home site. **Amenities:** Free airport shuttle; children's playground; outdoor pool.

Desert Gardens Hotel ★★   This is the only hotel in the resort complex that has views of Uluru (albeit rather distant ones) from some of the rooms. It is set amid wonderful ghost gum trees and the flowering native shrubs that give it its name. The accommodations are not as lavish as Sails in the Desert (below), but they're equally comfortable and were completely refurbished in 2016. The **Arnguli Grill** serves a la carte flame-grilled meals at dinner. Yulara Dr. www.ayersrockresort.com.au/accommodation/desert-gardens-hotel. © **08/8957 7714.** 218 units. A\$520–A\$650 double. **Amenities:** Restaurant, bar; free airport shuttle; outdoor pool; room service; free Wi-Fi.

Emu Walk Apartments ★★   Completely renovated and refurbished in 2015, these bright, contemporary apartments have full kitchens, separate bedrooms, and roomy living areas. The apartments sleep four or six people, so they're great for families or groups of friends. There's no restaurant or pool, but the Town Square cafes and supermarket are close, and you can cool off in the Desert Gardens Hotel pool. Daily maid service is included. Yulara Dr. www.ayersrockresort.com.au/accommodation/emu-walk-apartments. © **08/8957 7799.** 63 apts. A\$575 double 1-bedroom apt; A\$760 double 2-bedroom apt. **Amenities:** Free airport shuttle; free Wi-Fi.

Longitude 131° ★★★   When you wake in your luxury "tent" here, simply reach out from your king-size bed and press a button to raise the blinds on your window for a view unmatched anywhere in the world: Uluru as dawn strikes its ochre walls. Your bed, under a romantic, softly draped white canopy, is in one of 16 five-star eco-sensitive "tents" set among isolated sand dunes a mile or two from the main resort complex. Each room's decor combines tributes to the European explorers and pioneers of this region and fabulous indigenous art. There's a music system, but no TV (and who needs one?). The ultra-luxe **Dune Pavilion** is the only accommodation in Australia with views of both Uluru and Kata-Tjuta—and you pay more for the privilege. It also has a private plunge pool. The central area, the **Dune House,** has a restaurant with superb food, a 24-hour open bar, and a library. Settle in for some after-dinner chess or chat. For a special dining experience, book your place at **Table 131°,** where dinner is set up in style under the stars among gently rolling sand dunes. **Spa Kinara** is a cool escape where treatments are based on indigenous bush medicine and native beauty products. No children under 10. Yulara Dr. www.longitude131.com.au. © **08/8957 7131** (lodge), or 02/9918 4355 (bookings). 16 units. A\$3,000 double; A\$5,800 double Dune House. Rates include walking and bus tours, entry to the national park, meals, selected drinks. 2-night minimum. **Amenities:** Restaurant; bar; free airport shuttle; outdoor pool; free Wi-Fi.

9

THE NORTHERN TERRITORY | Uluru–Kata Tjuta National Park

FIELD OF light

The incredible Field of Light art installation, created by internationally acclaimed artist Bruce Munro, will run at Uluru until December 31, 2020. As darkness falls in the desert, a field of more than 50,000 stems of light, covering an area the size of seven football fields, comes to life. Thousands of visitors have walked through the pathways of light, aptly named **Tili Wiru Tjuta Nyakutjaku** or "looking at lots of beautiful lights" in local Pitjantjatja language, which was created in 2016. Entry passes cost from A$43 adults and A$30 children,

including transfers from all hotels. You can also take a camel ride or helicopter tour there or spend the whole evening. Field of Light is also packaged with the Sounds of Silence dinner (p. 328), at A$265 adults and A$133 children (10–15 years), including transfers from Ayers Rock Resort. Sunrise tours cost from A$75 adults and A$38 children age 2 to 15. Book through the **Ayers Rock Resort office** in Sydney (✆ **1300/134 044** in Australia, or 02/8296 8010) or online at www.ayersrockresort.com.au.

The Lost Camel Hotel ★   This boutique-style hotel has studio rooms, each with a king-size bed (that can separate into twins) and an open-plan bathroom. Refurbished in 2018, it's bright and fresh and a good choice for budget accommodation in a central location next to the Town Square. Rooms are compact, but you won't mind because there's plenty to do, including relax by the hotel swimming pool.

Yulara Dr. www.ayersrockresort.com.au/accommodation/the-lost-camel-hotel. ✆ **02/ 8296 8010.** 99 units. A$460 double. **Amenities:** Free airport shuttle; outdoor pool; free Wi-Fi.

Outback Pioneer Hotel & Lodge ★   An all-ages crowd congregates at this midrange collection of hotel rooms, budget rooms, shared bunkrooms, and dorms. Standard hotel rooms offer clean, simple accommodations with private bathrooms, a queen-size bed, and a single; these have TVs with pay movies, a fridge, a minibar, and a phone. Budget rooms have access to a common room with a TV, as well as a communal kitchen and laundry. Quad bunkrooms are coed and share bathrooms. The single-sex dorms sleep 20. Plenty of lounge chairs sit by the pool. The **Bough House Restaurant** offers buffet meals, or settle in at the **Outback Pioneer Bar,** where what seems like the entire resort gathers nightly. This barn with big tables, lots of beer, and live music is the place to join the throngs throwing a steak or sausage on the cook-it-yourself barbie (buy your meat at the bar).

Yulara Dr. www.ayersrockresort.com.au/accommodation. ✆ **08/8957 7605.** 125 units. A$390 double hotel room; A$280 budget room with bathroom; A$230 budget room without bathroom; A$184 budget quad room; A$46 bed in coed quad; A$38 dorm bed. **Amenities:** 2 restaurants; bar; free airport shuttle; outdoor pool; free Wi-Fi.

Sails in the Desert ★★★   This top-of-the-range hotel offers expensive, contemporary-style rooms with private balconies, many overlooking the pool,

DINNER IN THE desert

Why sit in a restaurant when you can eat outside and soak up the desert air? Ayers Rock Resort offers two fine-dining-under-the-stars experiences in the dunes outside the resort. The **Sounds of Silence** dinner is hugely popular (book well ahead, even up to 3 months ahead in peak season). In an outdoor clearing, you sip champagne and nibble canapés as the sun sets over the Rock to the strains of a didgeridoo. Then head to communal white-clothed, candlelit tables and a buffet meal that includes kangaroo, emu, crocodile, and barramundi. The food is not exceptional, but you're really here for the atmosphere. After dinner, the lanterns fade and you're left with stillness. For some city folk, it's the first time they have ever heard complete silence. Look up into the usually clear skies, and an astronomer will point out the constellations of the Southern Hemisphere. You can also look at the stars through telescopes. Sounds of Silence is held nightly, weather permitting, and costs A$225 adults and A$113 children, including transfers from Ayers Rock Resort. Surcharges apply for Christmas Day. A more intimate desert dinner is **Tali Wiru,** limited to only 20 people, where you can sit at a table for two or your own party of up to six people. This is a more upmarket experience, offering four courses, champagne, and waiter service. It costs A$375 per person, and runs April to mid-October only. Book through the **Ayers Rock Resort office** in Sydney (✆ **1300/134 044** in Australia, or 02/8296 8010) or online (www.ayersrockresort.com.au).

and some with Jacuzzis. You can't see the Rock from your room, but most guests are too busy sipping cocktails by the pool to care. The pool area is shaded by white shade "sails" and surrounded by sun lounges, and the lobby art gallery features artists in residence. **Ilkari** is a smart brasserie with a sumptuous buffet, with some dishes incorporating bush-tucker ingredients. The hotel's **Red Ochre Spa** is the only day spa at Yulara. It has four therapy rooms, with two rooms offering "dry" massage therapies and two "wet" rooms with tubs on the veranda.

Yulara Dr. www.ayersrockresort.com.au/accommodation/sails-in-the-desert. ✆ **08/8957 7888.** 228 units. A$680–A$810 double; A$1,100 suite. **Amenities:** Restaurant, 2 bars; free airport shuttle; heated outdoor pool; room service; 2 lighted tennis courts; free Wi-Fi.

Exploring Uluru

AT SUNRISE & SUNSET The peak time to catch the Rock's beauty is sunset, when oranges, peaches, pinks, reds, and then indigo and deep violet creep across its face. Some days it's fiery; on others, the colors are muted. A sunset-viewing car park is on the Rock's western side. Plenty of sunset and sunrise tours operate from the resort, and many throw in a glass of wine to toast the end of the day as you watch. At sunrise, the colors are less dramatic, but the bonus is seeing Uluru unveiled by the dawn to birdsong. It's an early

FACING PAGE: Tourists visiting the Uluru sacred mountain.

A SACRED rock

Climbing Uluru, a popular pastime for visitors to Uluru for more than 50 years, was banned under Australian law in September 2019. The move was a long time coming, but one that has been welcomed by the traditional owners, the Anangu ("the people," a term used by Aboriginal people from the Western Desert to refer to themselves), because of its deep spiritual significance to them.

In 1979 the Australian government recognized the traditional Aboriginal owners and created a national park to protect Uluru and Kata Tjuta. In 1983, the Anangu were granted ownership of the land, and the park was leased to the Australian National Parks and Wildlife Service for 99 years. Under that agreement, the climb would close permanently when climber numbers dropped below 20% of all visitors to Uluru, a time that came in 2019.

Climbing Uluru was against the wishes of the Anangu in part because they feel a duty to safeguard visitors in their land and experience great sorrow and a sense of responsibility when visitors are killed or injured. The 348m (1,142-ft.) hike up the face of "The Rock" is dangerously steep and rutted with ravines about 2.5m (8¼ ft.) deep; at least 35 people have died while climbing—either from heart attacks or falls—in the past 5 decades.

Visitors can still see the track marked by the feet of climbers over the years, a path that followed the trail the ancestral Dreamtime Mala (rufous hare-wallaby) men took when they first came to Uluru. But today there are many other ways to experience this mystical place, as outlined in this chapter.

start—most tours leave about 90 minutes before sunup. A typical sunrise tour is offered by **AAT Kings** (www.aatkings.com; ✆ **1300/228 546** in Australia). It includes morning tea and costs A$75 for adults, A$38 for children 2 to 15. AAT Kings offers several other tours around the area, so if large-group touring is what you want, check out its website.

BASE WALKS A paved road runs around the Rock. The easy 10.6km (6.5-mile) **Base Walk** circumnavigating Uluru takes about 2 hours (the best time is early morning), but allow extra time to linger around the water holes, caves, folds, and overhangs that make up its walls. A shorter walk is the easy 1km (.6-mile) round-trip trail from the **Mutitjulu** parking lot to the pretty water hole near the Rock's base, which has some rock art. The **Liru Track** is another easy trail; it runs 2km (1.2 miles) from the Cultural Centre to Uluru, where it links with the Base Walk.

Before setting off, it's a good idea to pick up the self-guided walking notes available from the **Cultural Centre** (see "Visitor Information," p. 323).

CYCLING Hire a bike to cycle the flat and easy paths around the base of the Rock. **Outback Cycling** (www.outbackcycling.com) has a trailer based at the Cultural Centre, where you can hire a basic bike (and a helmet) for a set 3-hour period in the morning or afternoon (times vary seasonally). The cost is A$50 adults, A$35 kids 6 to 10. Toddler seats to attach to your bike are A$20. This is a really fun and easy way to see the Rock.

FLYOVERS Several companies do scenic flights by light aircraft or helicopter over Uluru, Kata Tjuta (the Olgas), nearby Mount Conner, the vast white saltpan of Lake Amadeus, and as far as Kings Canyon. **Professional Helicopter Services** (www.phs.com.au; © **08/ 8956 2003**), for example, does a 15-minute flight over Uluru for A$150 per person, and a 25-minute flight, which includes Kata Tjuta, for A$245, among others. *Note:* Helicopters do not land on top of the Rock.

MOTORCYCLING Harley-Davidson tours are available as sunrise or sunset rides, laps of the Rock, and various other Uluru and Kata Tjuta tours with time for walks. A blast out to the Rock at sunset with **Uluru Motorcycle Tours** will set you back A$219; it includes a glass of champagne. The guide drives the bike, and you sit behind and hang on. Book through **Ayers Rock Resort** (www.ayersrockresort.com.au/experiences/detail/uluru-motorcycle-tours).

CAMEL RIDES Legend has it that a soul travels at the same pace as a camel; it's certainly a peaceful way to see the Rock. **Uluru Camel Tours** (www.ulurucameltours.com.au; © **08/8956 3333**) makes daily forays aboard

A camel-back tour is a peaceful way to see Uluru.

"ships of the desert" to view Uluru. Amble through red-sand dunes with great views of the Rock, dismount to watch the sun rise or sink over it, and ride back to the depot for billy tea and beer bread in the morning, or champagne in the evening. The 1-hour rides depart Ayers Rock Resort 1 hour before sunrise or 1½ hours before sunset and cost A$132 per person, including transfers from your hotel. All tours leave from the Camel Depot at the Ayers Rock Resort. Shorter rides are available.

Exploring Kata Tjuta ★★★

While it would be worth coming all the way to Central Australia just to see Uluru, a second unique natural wonder is just a 50km (31-mile) drive away. **Kata Tjuta,** or the Olgas, consists of 36 immense ochre rock domes rising from the desert, rivaling Uluru for spectacular beauty. Some visitors find it lovelier and more mysterious than Uluru. With its tallest dome 200m (656 ft.) higher than Uluru, Kata Tjuta ("many heads") figures more prominently in Aboriginal legend than Uluru.

English explorers first came upon this part of Australia's red heart in the 1870s. Ernest Giles named part of Kata Tjuta "Mount Olga" after the reigning Queen Olga of Wurttemberg, while William Gosse gave Uluru the name "Ayers Rock" after Sir Henry Ayers, the Chief Secretary of South Australia.

> ### Timing Your Trip
>
> Most tourists visit Uluru in the mornings and Kata Tjuta (the Olgas) in the afternoon. Reverse the order (do the Valley of the Winds walk in the morning and Uluru in the afternoon), and you'll likely find both spots a little more silent and spiritual.

Two walking trails wind among the domes: the 7.4km (4.6-mile) **Valley of the Winds ★★** walk, which is fairly challenging and takes 3 to 5 hours, and the easy 1-hour, 2.6km (1.6-mile) **Gorge** walk. The Valley of the Winds trail is the more rewarding in terms of scenery. Both have lookout points and shady stretches. The trail closes when temperatures hit 97°F (36°C).

PERTH

Western Australia's capital, Perth, may be one of the most remote large cities on earth, but it's a great place to visit. Alongside the broad Swan River and with the Indian Ocean on its western flank, it has a fabulous outdoor lifestyle with parks, rivers and beaches, a network of walking and biking trails, excellent food, and the beautiful historic port of Fremantle.

Western Australia is huge, more than three and a half times the size of Texas, but it has areas of true wilderness, some of the world's best beaches, spectacular spring wildflowers, great snorkeling and diving sites, magical places where the Outback meets the Indian Ocean, great wines, historic towns. But your visit is most likely to start in Perth, one of the world's most livable cities.

Perth is probably the most outdoorsy of all Aussie cities. The climate, Perth's brilliant setting along the Swan River and the Indian Ocean, and the abundance of parkland mean that it's almost obligatory to get outside and enjoy the sun and fresh air.

Perth has a wonderful Mediterranean climate that gives it more hours of sun than any other major city in Australia, from October through to April. This sunshine capital is also home to a thousand mining and exploration companies, which help bring a casual, can-do feel to the city.

All these elements give Perth a youthful and friendly, energetic vibrancy.

Stroll through the 400-hectare (1,000-acre) **Kings Park** in the middle of the city; visit art galleries and museums; eat at some of Australia's best restaurants; enjoy the riverside parks and gardens; catch a few waves at one of the beaches; stock up at the Aboriginal art and souvenir stores; or wander through the restored historic warehouses, museums, and working docks of bustling **Fremantle.**

More than most other Aussie capitals, Perth gives you good choices of day trips, covered in this chapter: Drop in on the Bene-dictine monks in the Spanish Renaissance monastery town of **New Norcia;** nip out to the **Swan Valley** vineyards; take the ferry to **Rottnest Island,** a small reef resort 19km (12 miles) offshore, to find a great snorkeling spot and see Australia's cutest marsupials; visit the weird landscape of the Pinnacles.

10

Perth's climate is fabulous for most of the year. Most visitors focus on the brilliant summer months of December through March, with lots of sun, sea, and sand, though the sea breezes can get strong. The winter months of June to August can be cold and rainy but still average 6 hours of sun a day, while April to May and September to November are often superb with mild, fine days.

ESSENTIALS

Arriving

BY PLANE

Perth Airport (**PER;** www.perthairport.com.au) is 12km (7½ miles) northeast of the city. The four main terminals are in two locations separated by about a 20-minute drive. Most international airlines use Terminal 1 (T1). **Qantas** (www.qantas.com.au; ☎ **131 313** in Australia) uses Terminal 4 (T4) for both its international and domestic services. Qantas's discount arm, **Jetstar** (www.jetstar.com.au; ☎ **131 538** in Australia) uses Terminal 3 (T3) for domestic services. **Virgin Australia**'s domestic services (www.virginaustralia.com.au; ☎ **136 789** in Australia) operate from both T1 and T2, which is also used by other domestic airlines (**Tigerair, Regional Express,** and **Alliance Airlines**). Confused? You're not alone; I can tell you from personal experience that you should check carefully to ensure you go to the right terminal when departing.

A **free transfer bus** operates 24 hours between the two terminal precincts, with bus stops right outside the terminal buildings. From 6am to midnight, buses leave T1 and T3/4 on the hour, and T2 at 10 minutes, 30 minutes, and 50 minutes past the hour. From midnight to 6am, they leave T1 every hour and half-hour, T2 at 25 and 55 minutes past the hour, and T3/4 at 15 and 45 minutes past the hour.

Look for the "Gold Coats" volunteers in bright gold jackets, who provide assistance and information. Luggage trolleys are free for international arrivals but cost A$4 (coins needed) curbside at all terminals and in domestic arrivals.

Airport Shuttle Perth (www.airportshuttleperth.net.au; ☎ **0420 244 802** mobile) runs door-to-door transfers from the airport to the city and Fremantle, but must be booked ahead. Prices are on a sliding scale depending on numbers in a group. Transfers to Perth cost A$24 one-way for one person, up to A$55 for four people, and A$99 for a group of 10. Fremantle transfers start at A$50 for one person, up to A$99 for eight, with prices higher between 10pm and 6am.

Public **bus** no. 380 runs to the city from T1 and T2, and bus no. 40 and 935 runs from T3 and T4. A **taxi** to the city costs about A$45, including a A$3 fee for picking up a taxi at the airport.

BY TRAIN

The 4-day, 3-night journey to Perth from Sydney, covering 4,352km (2,704 miles) via Broken Hill, Adelaide, and Kalgoorlie aboard the *Indian Pacific*, is operated by Great Southern Rail (www.journeybeyondrail.com.au; ☏ **1800/703 357** in Australia or 08/8213 4401) and is a great experience. It has the world's longest stretch of straight rail (over 483km/300 miles) along the Nullarbor Plain. The train runs twice a week (Sept–Nov and Jan–Mar, otherwise once a week) in each direction, and can carry your vehicle. The one-way fare ranges from A$3,799 per person in the spacious Platinum Service (in low season) to A$2,499 in a Gold Service twin cabin with meals and an en-suite bathroom, or A$2,239 in a Gold Service single cabin. Rail passes are available. The train leaves Sydney on Wednesday at 3pm, arriving in Perth on Saturday at 3pm. It leaves Perth at 10am on Sunday to head back to Sydney. There are connections from the *Overland* and *Ghan* trains. See "Getting There & Getting Around," in chapter 13, for full details.

Long-distance trains pull into the East Perth Terminal, West Parade, East Perth. A **taxi** to the city center costs about A$20, and there is an overpass from the terminal to the local train platforms for the city.

BY BUS

Greyhound Australia (www.greyhound.com.au; ☏ **1300/473 946** in Australia) does not service Perth or Western Australia's southwest region. You can get a Greyhound bus from Darwin to Broome, then hop on an **Integrity Coach Lines** (www.integritycoachlines.com.au; **08/92747464**) service from Broome to Perth, which operates twice a week, on Thursday and Saturday. But be warned: It's a *very* long haul. The bus leaves Broome at 8pm, travels through the night and all the next day, and arrives at 7am on the third day.

BY CAR

There are only two interstate routes—the 4,310km (2,694-mile) route from Darwin via Broome in the north, and the 2,708km (1,679-mile) odyssey from Adelaide across the Nullarbor Plain. Arm yourself with up-to-date details on sightseeing and the limited accommodations before setting off. See "Getting There & Getting Around," in chapter 13.

Visitor Information

The **Western Australian Visitor Centre,** 55 William St., Perth (www.wavisitorcentre.com.au; ☏ **1800/812 808** in Australia or 08/9483 1111), is open Monday to Friday 9am to 5pm and Saturday and Sunday from 9:30am to 4:30pm.

The **City of Perth's Information Kiosk** (www.visitperth.com.au; ☏ **08/9461 3333**), in the Murray Street Mall, near Forrest Place, is open Monday to Saturday 9:30am to 4:30pm (until 8pm Fri Sept–Apr) and public holidays, and Sunday 11am to 2:30pm. Volunteers provide free 90-minute orientation tours around the city from the kiosk, Monday to Saturday at 9:45am; on Monday, Wednesday, and Friday, there are 10:15am tours that focus more on the city's history, development, and public art. If you prefer, you can self-guide using maps available at the kiosk.

Another useful website is **www.perth.wa.gov.au**.

City Layout

The city center is 19km (12 miles) upriver from the Indian Ocean, on the north bank of a broad reach of the Swan River. Four long east–west avenues run between riverside parkland and the railway reserve. Designed as an oblong, the city grid runs four blocks north to south, but more than 30 blocks east to west. **St. Georges Terrace** (it becomes Adelaide Terrace at Victoria Ave.), known colloquially as "The Terrace," is the main thoroughfare and commercial and banking address, while **Hay Street** and **Murray Street** are the major retail avenues with pedestrian malls in the central blocks. All three, plus **Wellington Street** (which has Perth's suburban railway station on its northern side), are linked by the main north–south streets of Barrack and William, plus several shop-lined arcades.

Perth Neighborhoods in Brief

City Centre The central business district (CBD) is home to offices, shops, and department stores. It has a modest collection of 19th-century Heritage buildings, especially the convict-built Government House and Town Hall. A good introduction to Perth's charms is to take in the views from the pathway that skirts the river along Riverside Drive. Within walking distance is Kings Park & Botanic Garden ★★.

Northbridge Most of Perth's nightclubs, and a good many of its restaurants, bars, and cafes, are in this five-block precinct north of the railway line. It's within easy walking distance of the city center. The cultural hub is here too, with the Western Australian Museum, Art Gallery of Western Australia, State Library, the State Theatre Centre, and Perth Institute of Contemporary Arts.

Fremantle Not only is "Freo" a working port, it's also Perth's second city heart, and a favorite weekend spot to eat, drink, shop, and sail. A 1980s restoration of Victorian warehouses and hotels turned Freo into a marvelous example of a 19th-century seaport. Take the train 19km (12 miles) to Fremantle, at the mouth of the Swan River. See p. 358.

Subiaco This well-heeled inner suburb is on the other side of Kings Park. Take a stroll through "Subi's" village-like concoction of restaurants, cafes, markets, boutiques, pubs, and galleries. Most of the action is near the intersection of Hay Street and Rokeby

(pronounced *Rock*-er-bee) Road, with the Subiaco Hotel and Art Deco Regal Theatre on opposing corners. Take the train to Subiaco station.

Scarborough Beach This is one of Perth's prize beaches, 12km (7½ miles) northwest of the city center. The district is a little tatty, with an oversupply of cheap takeout-food outlets, but if you like sun, sand, and surf, this is the place to be. You will find bars, restaurants, and surf-gear rental stores here.

Cottesloe Beach This is another great beach, quieter and safer than Scarborough, with a protective rocky groyne to one side. The surrounding area is very pleasant with grassy slopes, good hotels, and cafes, and the entire suburb is defined by towering Norfolk pines.

Burswood/East Perth These two areas are on opposite sides of the Swan River just upstream of Perth city. Both are on land reclaimed from earlier industrial use, and show enlightened development with parkland, pathways, and artworks. Burswood has major entertainment complexes, a public golf course, and superb gardens. East Perth is mostly modern housing, parks, galleries, and restaurants, based around a river inlet with walkways.

Elizabeth Quay Redeveloped over recent years, this is a new hotspot for the city, with a swath of smart restaurants around the parkland and bobbing boats at Elizabeth Quay Jetty. It's close to the Perth Convention

& Exhibition Centre too, with bus and train transport hubs nearby.

Yagan Square Part of the Perth CityLink development, this 1.1ha (2.7 acres) space is always busy with commuters, diners, and visitors taking selfies. It has trees and green spaces, lots of public artworks, and is marked by a 45m (148-ft.) high digital tower. The square is named after Aboriginal leader Yagan, and there's a strong indigenous theme too.

Getting Around Perth

Transperth (www.transperth.wa.gov.au) runs Perth's buses, trains, and ferries. For route, bus stop, and timetable information, call ℭ **13 62 13** in Western Australia, or drop into the Transperth InfoCentres at the Perth Train Station, Perth Underground Station (Murray St. entrance), or Wellington Street or Elizabeth Quay bus stations. You can transfer between bus, ferry, and train services for up to 2 hours (Zones 1–4) or 3 hours (Zones 5–8). Travel costs A$3.20 in one zone, and A$4.90 in two, which gets you most places, including Fremantle, with discounts for kids aged 5 to 14.

SmartRider is an electronic ticketing system, which can save up to 20% off the cash fare, but it involves a basic A$10 cost plus a minimum A$10 travel component, so it's only of value if you plan to stay several days and use public transport a lot. To use SmartRider, you need to validate it by tagging on and off the machines onboard buses and ferries or at train station platforms.

Government House and landscaped gardens.

Take a Free Ride

A welcome freebie in Perth is the availability of free public transport within the city center and some nearby areas. You can travel on any free **CAT (Central Area Transit)** buses (see below) in the **Free Transit Zone (FTZ)** any hour, day or night. For free train travel in the FTZ, a **SmartRider** (see p. 337) must be used, but it's not economical for most visitors. The FTZ allows free travel to Kings Park, Northbridge, east to major sporting grounds, and anywhere within the city center. Signs mark the FTZ boundaries; just ask the driver if you're unsure.

A **DayRider** ticket can be purchased to allow 1 day of unlimited travel on the network after 9am on weekdays and all day on weekends and public holidays for A$13. A **FamilyRider** pass is valid for unlimited all-day travel anywhere on the network, for up to seven people, including two full fares, but only on weekends and public holidays, after 3pm on Fridays and after 6pm Monday to Thursday, or from 9am during school holidays, for A$13.

BY PUBLIC BUS

The **Perth Busport** is a cut above most Australian bus stations. Fully underground, it works almost like an airport, with buses leaving from 16 different "gates" for maximum efficiency. Clean and well organized, it's work popping down the escalators just for a look. There are three entrances, on King St., Queen St., or Yagan Square. The "departure lounge" that services all the gates has a service desk open weekdays 7am to 7pm, and in the afternoons only on weekends and public holidays. Most buses travel along St. Georges Terrace. You must hail the bus to ensure that it stops. Buy tickets from the driver. Buses run from about 5:30am until about 10:30 or 11:30pm, depending on the route.

The best way to get around town is on the free **CAT buses,** which run a continual loop of the city and Northbridge and to some other areas. They operate generally from between 6am and 7am weekdays, but start around 8:30am on Saturday and Sunday, with slightly less frequency. Transperth InfoCentres dispense free route maps.

The Red CAT runs east-west about every 5 minutes, Monday through Friday, and every 10 minutes weekends and public holidays. The last bus is 6:45pm Monday to Thursday, 8pm Friday, and 6pm weekends/holidays.

The Blue CAT runs north-south, between Northbridge and Barrack Street Jetty every 8 minutes Monday to Friday. The last service is at 6:52pm Monday through Thursday, but Friday it then runs every 15 minutes until 12:15am, and Saturday until 11:50pm. Last bus Sunday is 6:26pm.

The Yellow CAT runs between East Perth and West Perth every 8 minutes weekdays, and every 15 minutes weekends. Last bus is 6:38pm Monday to Thursday, 8pm Friday, and 6pm weekends.

BY SIGHTSEEING BUS

The bright red open-top **Perth Explorer** (www.perthexplorer.com.au; **08/9370 1000**) buses operate daily around Perth and King's Park. You can hop-on, hop-off for 1 or 2 days or stay on board and listen to the commentary for 2 hours (there's even a special commentary channel for kids). The tour takes in major sights including the Bell Tower, Elizabeth Quay, Perth Mint, the Art Gallery of Western Australia, city shopping malls, and more. The cost for 24 hours is A$40 adults, A$12 children 5 to 14 and A$95 for a family of 4, but it's not much more for 48 hours. Tours don't operate on Christmas Day, Australia Day (Jan 26), or Anzac Day (Apr 25).

BY FERRY

You can use ferries to visit South Perth and Perth Zoo. These run every 15 minutes daily from 6:30am until 9:30pm (or until 11:30pm Fri–Sat mid-Sept to June) between the Elizabeth Quay ferry terminal and Mends Street in South Perth. Buy tickets before you board from the vending machine on the wharf. The trip takes approximately 8 minutes. The **Little Ferry Company** (www. littleferryco.com.au; ✆ **0488 777 088** mobile phone), WA's only solar-powered ferry, operates from Elizabeth Quay to East Perth, including to Optus Stadium and The Camfield hotel (p. 347). It's a hop-on, hop-off service, running four times a day, at 10am and 4pm (bookings only), noon and 2pm. The round-trip takes about 2 hours and costs A$14 adults, A$12 children 4 to 14, or A$32 family of 4 for a single stop, or A$38 adults, A$32 children, and A$78 families for a day pass. The little ferry only takes 12 passengers, so it's wise to book.

Ferry leaving Elizabeth Quay Marina, with Perth skyscrapers in background.

You're allowed, even encouraged, to take your bicycle on Perth's suburban trains and ferries—at no extra charge. Just be sure to avoid the Monday-to-Friday peak services—toward the city from 7 to 9am, and away from the city between 4:30 and 6:30pm—and not have your bike at Perth, Perth Underground, or Elizabeth Quay stations during these times. You can also carry surfboards up to 2m (6.5 ft.) on trains, ferries, and bus route 990 (to Scarborough Beach) and up to 1.2m (3.9 ft.) on most buses.

BY TRAIN

Trains are fast and clean. They start at about 5:30am and run every 15 minutes or more often during the day, and every half-hour at night until midnight (about 2am Fri and Sat nights). All trains depart from Perth Station or the adjacent Perth Underground Station. Buy your ticket before you board, at the vending machines on the platform. There are five lines: north to Clarkson or Butler (called the Joondalup Line); northeast to Midland; southeast to Armadale; southwest to Fremantle; and south to the resort town of Mandurah.

BY TAXI

Perth's two biggest taxi companies are **Swan Taxis** (www.swantaxis.com.au; ℂ 13 13 30) and **Black & White Cabs** (www.blackandwhitecabs.com.au; ℂ 13 10 08). Ranks (stands) are at Perth Railway Station and at the Barrack Street end of Hay Street Mall. **Uber** also operates in Perth.

BY CAR

The major car-rental companies are **Avis** (ℂ 08/9232 7555), **Budget** (ℂ 08/9237 0022), **Europcar** (ℂ 08/9226 0026), **Hertz** (ℂ 08/9321 7777), and **Thrifty** (ℂ 08/9225 4466).

[FastFACTS] PERTH

ATMs/Banks Banks are open Monday through Thursday 9:30am to 4pm and until 5pm Friday, though some branches open Saturday mornings. ATMs are easy to find in the city center and most are available 24 hrs.

Business Hours General office hours are Monday to Friday 9am to 5pm. Most retail shops open 8am to 9pm Monday to Friday and 8am to 5pm Saturday.

They can also open on Sunday and holidays in Perth, Fremantle, Northbridge, and Subiaco. Note that not all stores open from 6pm onward.

Dentists LifeCare Dental (www.lifecaredental.com.au; ℂ 08/9221 2777, or 0411 960 492 mobile phone for emergencies) is on the Upper Walkway Level, Forrest Chase shopping complex, 419 Wellington St., opposite Perth Railway

Station. Open daily 8am to 8pm.

Doctors & Hospitals
Central City Medical Centre is on the Perth Railway Station concourse, 378 Wellington St. (www.ccmc.net.au; ℂ 08/9225 1188). It's open Monday to Friday 8am to 6pm, Saturday to Sunday 9am to 6pm. **Royal Perth Hospital,** in the city center, has a public emergency/casualty ward (ℂ 08/9224 2244). Enter from Victoria

Square, off the eastern end of Murray Street. **Travellers' Medical & Vaccination Centre,** in St Martins Arcade, 50 St Georges Terrace (www.traveldoctor.com.au; ☏ **08/6467 0900**), administers travel-related vaccinations and medications Monday to Friday 8:30am to 5pm.

Embassies & Consulates All foreign embassies are based in Canberra. The **United States Consulate-General** is at 16 St. Georges Terrace (☏ **08/6144 5100 1224**). The **Canadian Consulate** is at 267 St. Georges Terrace (☏ **08/9322 7930**). The **British Consulate** is at Level 12, 251 Adelaide Terrace (☏ **08/9224 4700**).

Emergencies Dial ☏ **000** for fire, ambulance, or police for emergencies only. This is a free call; no coins are needed from a public phone.

Mail & Postage The **General Post Office (GPO)** is at Perth Railway Station, 378 Wellington St. It's open Monday to Friday 9am to 5pm and Saturday 9am to 12:30pm. For the nearest post office, call ☏ **131 318** or find it online at www.auspost.com.au.

Newspapers & Magazines *The West Australian* newspaper is published 6 days a week, and *The Weekend West* on Saturdays. The Sunday paper is *The Sunday Times.* Another good source of news is **www.perthnow.com.au.**

Pharmacies Friendlies Chemist (☏ **08/9321 5391**), 849 Hay St., is open Monday through Thursday 7am to 6pm, until 7pm Friday, and Saturday 9am to 5pm.

Police In an emergency, dial ☏ **000.** Otherwise call

☏ **13 14 44** to be connected to the nearest station. **Perth Police Station,** corner of Fitzgerald and Roe streets, Northbridge, 60 Beaufort St. (☏ **08/9422 7111**), and **Fremantle Police Station,** 88 High St. (☏ **08/9430 1222**), are open 24 hours.

Safety Perth is safe, but steer clear of the back streets of Northbridge and the city center malls late at night even if you are not alone.

Time Zone Western Australian time (WS) is Greenwich Mean Time plus 8 hours. Standard time is 2 hours behind Sydney and Melbourne, but 3 hours behind October to March. Call ☏ **1194** for the exact local time.

Wi-Fi Perth has a widespread network of free Wi-Fi hot spots around the city center

WHERE TO STAY IN PERTH
EXPENSIVE

COMO The Treasury ★★★ Derelict for 20 years, this historic building is now one of Australia's top hotels. Built in the 1870s, it is the grandest building in Western Australia, and boasts the largest hotel rooms in Perth. Once the State Buildings, the hotel opened in 2015 and overlooks Cathedral Square. A stay here offers every luxury you could ask for: fresh fruit and wildflowers on the tables, bronzed mirrors, Italian crafted furniture, luxury linens. The bathrooms—some almost as big as the bedrooms—are positively decadent, with heated floors, bathtubs, and triple showers. Only 12 rooms have balconies, but all have windows that open. The **Wildflower** restaurant is very much a special-occasion place, with fabulous views overlooking the Stirling Gardens.

1 Cathedral Ave. www.comohotels.com/thetreasury. ☏ **08/6168 7888.** 48 units. A$387–A$811 double; A$897–A$1,441 suite. Valet parking A$50. **Amenities:** 2 restaurants; bar; concierge; gymnasium; 20m indoor heated pool; room service; spa; free Wi-Fi.

InterContinental Perth City Centre ★★★ Close to the high-end shopping and elegant architecture of the King Street Heritage precinct, this is a great location. Opened in late 2017, the hotel has all the amenities you'd expect from an InterContinental, but the standout feature is the beautiful collection of Western Australian art that adorns the walls, most of it specially created for the hotel. All rooms have gorgeous bathrooms with rainshowers; seven suites have bathtubs to luxuriate in.

815 Hay St. www.perth.intercontinental.com. ✆ **08/9486 5700.** 240 units. A$220–A$363 double; A$460–A$630 suite. Breakfast A$35. Parking A$35; valet parking A$65. Train: Perth Underground. **Amenities:** 3 restaurants; bar; concierge; room service; free Wi-Fi.

The Westin Perth ★★★ Opened in 2018, this is one of Perth's top hotels, with all the luxuries of the Westin brand. It's easy to spot from the street: Just look for the towering painting of a Western Australian girl on the side of the building—it's by one of Australia's top street artists, Rone. Beyond the lobby, a sprawling deck opens out onto Hibernian Place from the bar. Rooms are some of the largest in the city, and the best views are from those facing east. Little touches like the lavender balm on the bedside table and the roomy desks make the difference. On Wednesday mornings (7am!), guests can "run with the concierge," and it even has a fitness gear lending service (shoes, shirt, shorts) for A$5 a day.

480 Hay St. www.marriott.com. ✆ **08/6559 1888.** 368 units. A$245–A$345 double. Breakfast A$39. Valet parking A$55. Train: McIver. **Amenities:** 2 restaurants; bar; 24-hr gym; heated outdoor rooftop pool; spa; room service; free Wi-Fi.

MODERATE

Alex Hotel ★★ You may wonder if you've come in the wrong door when you walk into the Alex and find yourself behind the reception desk. The open plan and communal style of this smart hotel means some things aren't as you'd expect—and that there are no barriers to your welcome. There's certainly an immediate sense that this is a hotel with a difference. The ground-floor coffee shop is open to all, but the mezzanine is for guests only, with lounge spaces and a small library. Rooms are compact but more than adequate, some with king-size beds (and all with 100% cotton sheets). Windows that open, a rooftop terrace bar, and free bikes all add to the appeal. Opened in 2015, this hotel is a great choice for location and style.

50 James St., Northbridge. www.alexhotel.com.au. ✆ **08/6430 4000.** 74 units. A$160–A$255 double. Breakfast included. Parking nearby at the State Library. Train: Northbridge. **Amenities:** Restaurant; bar; bikes; room service; free Wi-Fi.

DoubleTree by Hilton ★★ Opened in early 2019, this smart new-build hotel is right in the heart of Northbridge's main street. You'll be welcomed with a warm chocolate chip cookie and a cool drink, setting the tone for great service. Rooms are spacious and comfortable, and it's just far enough from the bustle of the city center to be in a world of its own—but with all the benefits

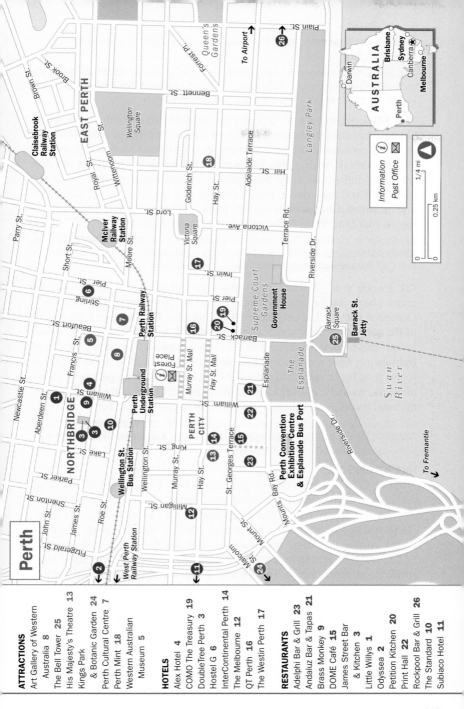

Perth

EAST PERTH

NORTHBRIDGE

PERTH CITY

To Airport ↑

To Fremantle ↓

Claisebrook Railway Station

McIver Railway Station

Perth Railway Station

Perth Underground Station

Wellington St. Bus Station

West Perth Railway Station

Forest Place

Queen's Gardens

Wellington Square

Langley Park

Supreme Court Gardens

Government House

The Esplanade

Barrack Square

Barrack St. Jetty

Swan River

Information (i)
Post Office ✉

AUSTRALIA

Darwin
Brisbane
Sydney ✪
Canberra ✪
Perth
Melbourne

0   1/4 mi
0   0.25 km

ATTRACTIONS
Art Gallery of Western
  Australia **8**
The Bell Tower **25**
His Majesty's Theatre **13**
Kings Park
  & Botanic Garden **24**
Perth Cultural Centre **7**
Perth Mint **18**
Western Australian
  Museum **5**

HOTELS
Alex Hotel **4**
COMO The Treasury **19**
DoubleTree Perth **3**
Hostel G **6**
InterContinental Perth **14**
The Melbourne **12**
QT Perth **16**
The Westin Perth **17**

RESTAURANTS
Adelphi Bar & Grill **23**
Andaluz Bar & Tapas **21**
Brass Monkey **9**
DOME Café **15**
James Street Bar
  & Kitchen **3**
Little Willys **1**
Odyssea **2**
Petition Kitchen **20**
Print Hall **22**
Rockpool Bar & Grill **26**
The Standard **10**
Subiaco Hotel **11**

343

of being just 5 minutes away. For panoramic views, ask for a room on the fifth floor or higher.

100 James St., Northbridge. www.doubletree3.hilton.com. ☎ **08/6148 2000.** 206 units. A$220–A$280 double. No parking. Train: Northbridge. **Amenities:** Restaurant; bar; concierge; exercise room; pool; room service; free Wi-Fi.

The Melbourne ★★★ Located on the West End of Perth, this gorgeous old hotel has been given new life. Part of the city streetscape since 1897, this grande dame now has all modern amenities. Every guest room is different, but all are luxurious, with quality linens and bathroom amenities, Bluetooth door entry, and full connectivity. Smartphones in each room are free for guests' use, and if you book direct, personally engraved luggage tags are waiting for you on arrival. Choose from heritage rooms or contemporary rooms, depending on your taste. Head to the rooftop bar for sunset cocktails.

33 Milligan St. (at Hay St.). www.melbournehotel.com.au. ☎ **08/9320 3333.** 73 units. A$145–A$181 double; A$199–A$281 suite. Valet parking A$39; self-parking A$18. Bus: Red CAT. **Amenities:** 4 restaurants; 2 bars; concierge; gym; free Wi-Fi.

QT Perth ★★ A wide-open lobby with lounge and bar to one side, tall cactus plants, and lots of circle motifs make this one of Perth's standout hotels. Opened in late 2018, it truly has a style of its own. The surprises keep coming in the guest rooms; for something different, ask for a "Carnaby's cockatoo" room—and hope the wallpaper won't keep you awake! Wooden floors, large bathtubs (in most rooms), and bold design schemes add to the mix. Deluxe rooms have better views and more light, but all rooms have opening windows, minibars, tea and coffee-making facilities, and soft black bathrobes. Upstairs, the hotel boasts Perth's highest, and possibly largest, rooftop bar.

133 Murray St. www.qthotelsandresorts.com/perth. ☎ **08/9225 8000.** 184 units. A$230–A$345 double. Valet parking A$40. Train: Perth. **Amenities:** Restaurant; 2 bars; 24-hr. gymnasium; room service; free Wi-Fi.

INEXPENSIVE

Hostel G ★ Perth's newest and largest hostel is a fresh, clean budget option. All rooms have en-suite bathrooms, and in addition to dorms there are doubles and family rooms that sleep four or six. An extra-large "G suite" sleeps six. Rooms offer under-bed storage, lockers, and USB ports. The communal spaces include a restaurant/bar, coworking spaces, half-size pool tables, and a theater-style space for movies and "G Talks" with local guest speakers on varied topics. There's also a communal kitchen if you want to self-cater. Live music or DJs play on Friday and Saturday nights.

80 Stirling St. www.hostelgperth.com. ☎ **0401 067 099** mobile phone. 296 beds. A$24–A$32 dorm bed; A$96–A$120 private room (sleeps 2–4); A$216 suite. No parking. Train: Perth. **Amenities:** Restaurant; bar; free Wi-Fi.

In Fremantle

Fremantle is so close to Perth that it's a great, quieter option when looking for a place to stay, offering some smart, affordable hotels.

MODERATE

Hougoumont Hotel ★★ Shipping containers have been used to create a modern and appealing hotel with a difference, just off Fremantle's main street. "Welcome aboard" is the personalized message on your bathroom mirror on arrival, and it's true that the rooms resemble ship's cabins, with timber-paneled walls. Each is cleverly designed to maximize space and equipped with Nespresso coffee machines, Rubra teas, and a minibar (personalized on request). State Rooms offer a little more space, but the whole place has a lovely minimalist feel to it. A happy hour from 5pm offers the chance to meet other guests over wine and cheese.

15 Bannister St. www.hougoumonthotel.com. © **08/6160 6800.** 37 units. A$147–A$294 double. Continental breakfast included. Parking A$25. **Amenities:** Restaurant (breakfast only); bar; concierge; room service; free bikes; free Wi-Fi.

INEXPENSIVE

Fremantle Prison YHA ★★ Housed in the former women's prison, this is a YHA with a difference. Built in the 1850s, the prison has UNESCO World Heritage status, and you can even sleep in a cell—but with all modern conveniences, of course! In addition to dorm rooms, some rooms have private bathrooms, and three self-contained cottages that sleep up to six are ideal for families. It has a games room, TV lounge, communal kitchen, and outdoor barbecue area.

6A The Terrace. www.yha.com.au. © **08/9433 4305.** 150 units. A$20–A$26 dorm bed; A$60–A$66 twin cell; A$82–A$88 double with bathroom; A$104–A$110 family room (sleeps 4); A$169–A$199 cottage (sleeps 6). Rates (except cottages) include continental breakfast. Train: Fremantle. **Amenities:** free Wi-Fi.

WHERE TO EAT IN PERTH

An array of upscale choices plus terrific ethnic spots make Perth's restaurant scene as sophisticated as Sydney's and Melbourne's—which is to say, excellent—though don't expect it to be cheaper! You'll find a great range in "restaurant city": Northbridge. In addition to the eateries listed below, many hotels have excellent restaurants, including the **Adelphi Grill** at the **Parmelia Hilton Perth** (www3.hilton.com; © **08/9215 2000**). The **Crown Casino** complex at Burswood has numerous restaurants, including the **Rockpool Bar & Grill** (www.rockpoolbarandgrill.com.au/perth; © **08/6252 1900**).

For an excellent introduction to the restaurant scene in Perth and farther afield in WA, check out *The West Australian Good Food Guide* at www.wagoodfoodguide.com.

There's been major growth in both the cafe culture and the availability of small bars (often with tapas-style menus), such as the sophisticated **Andaluz Bar & Tapas** (www.andaluzbar.com.au; © **08/9481 0092**), 21 Howard St., just off St. Georges Terrace. For excellent coffee and cake, inexpensive pasta, or a Turkish bread sandwich, you can't beat Perth's homegrown **DOME** chain of cafes. Look for the dark green logo, with its CBD outlet at Trinity Arcade overlooking St. Georges Terrace (www.domecoffees.com; ℭ **08/9226 0210**).

Note that Western Australian law bans smoking in enclosed public spaces, such as bars and restaurants. Some licensed premises have smoking zones in outdoor areas.

EXPENSIVE

Odyssea ★★★ CONTEMPORARY   With its beachfront setting, just 15 minutes' drive from the city center, this is a magic spot to dine. During the day, watch the waves roll in from the Indian Ocean; by night, get there in time for sunset beyond the palm trees. The menu is varied but has a seaside feel to it, notably the daily market fish and some prawn and salmon dishes. But it also offers other tastes of Australia, such as kangaroo. The chef's menu is A$69 per person for five courses, if you are too relaxed to make up your mind. There's a kids' menu, too.

187 Challenger Parade, City Beach. www.odysseacitybeach.com.au. ℭ **08/9385 7979.** Main courses A$22–A$49. Daily 7am–11pm (closed Dec 25). Bus: 82. Plentiful free parking.

Petition Kitchen ★★★ CONTEMPORARY   Industrial chic and an open kitchen make this a terrific choice for lunch or dinner. Solo diners, business meetings, groups of friends are all at ease under the soaring ceilings supported by brick walls. The food arrives on rustic stoneware plates, and might include a tasty risotto with cauliflower, hazelnuts, currants, and parmesan, or a veal and duck-leg ragu with braised shallots and native greens. It's a great spot to stop in for breakfast or lunch or Sunday brunch, and there's outdoor seating too.

State Buildings, St Georges Terrace (at Barrack St.). www.petitionperth.com/kitchen. ℭ **08/6168 7771.** Main courses A$18–A$40. Mon–Fri 7am–11pm; Sat–Sun 8am–11pm. Train: Perth or Elizabeth Quay. Bus: Red and Blue CAT.

MODERATE

James Street Bar + Kitchen ★ CONTEMPORARY   Walk in off the street and pick up the bar menu for a light meal and some people-watching, or head farther through to the main restaurant for a more formal setting. Although it's part of the new DoubleTree by Hilton hotel, it's not immediately obvious, given its stand-alone treatment. As well as some classic burgers and steaks, other taste-tempters include the braised beef cheek with celeriac and blueberries (highly popular) and an Asian-style salmon filet with coriander lime dressing. The bar menu is a limited version of the restaurant offerings.

100 James St. www.jamesstbarandkitchen.com. ℭ **08/6148 2000.** Main courses A$28–A$65. Mon–Fri 6am–late; Sat–Sun 6:30am–late. Train: Perth.

Print Hall ★ CONTEMPORARY   Housed in—and themed to reflect the world of newspapers—the Print Hall covers four levels, each with its own distinctive space and cuisine. **Small Print,** on the ground floor, is a cafe and bakery, perfect for a quick drop-in. The **Apple Daily,** named for Hong Kong's popular daily newspaper, has Asian street food, and **Gazette** is an elegant Italian restaurant with leather banquettes. Take the stairs, stopping to look at the newspapers that line the walls, to **Bob's Bar,** named for popular former

Australian Prime Minister Bob Hawke, one of Perth's favorite sons and once a frequent visitor. The rooftop terrace has great views.

Brookfield Place, 125 St. Georges Terrace. www.printhall.com.au. ☎ **08/6282 0000.** Main courses Gazette A$24–A$39, Apple Daily A$18–A$40, Small Print A$15–A$28. Hours vary; check the website for details. Train: Elizabeth Quay.

The Standard ★★ CONTEMPORARY   Walk into a buzzing bar that oozes cool, then head through to the garden courtyard or upstairs to the rooftop for dinner with city views. Timber tables, brick walls, potted trees, and fairy lights add to the atmosphere, and chatty, helpful waitstaff will offer tips about the menu. Share plates are best, and don't miss the duck with turmeric rolls or the rich swordfish curry with gnocci. Head out the back entrance to a laneway filled with street art.

28 Roe St., Northbridge. www.thestandardperth.com.au. ☎ **08/9228 1331.** Main courses A$17–A$38. Mon–Thurs 4pm–midnight; Fri–Sat noon–midnight; Sun noon–10pm. Train: Perth.

INEXPENSIVE

Little Willys ★ CAFE   This cozy little spot is ideal for breakfast, a snack, or just a quiet coffee. Open early, it's a favorite with locals, with a menu offering everything from basic bacon and eggs to brekkie burritos (available all day) to interesting dishes like raspberry porridge with rhubarb and banana. The lunch menu offers bagels and salads, a weekly frittata, and soup (in winter). Service is friendly and fast.

267 William St., Northbridge. ☎ **08/9228 8240.** Main courses A$12–A$15. Mon–Thurs 6am–3pm; Fri 6am–2:30pm; Sat–Sun 7am–noon. Train: Perth.

EXPLORING PERTH

Aquarium of Western Australia (AQWA) ★★★ AQUARIUM Step back in time aboard the Dutch sailing ship *Duyfken*, which explored the coast of Australia in the early 1600s. The *Duyfken* is the newest attraction at the aquarium, with 30-minute guided tours running daily from 10:30am to

Hillarys Boat Harbour, home to the Aquarium of Western Australia, is a popular destination.

2pm. There's lots to see and experience here, from exploring WA's various ocean ecosystems to taking a stroll in Australia's largest walk-through aquarium, where you are surrounded by sharks, stingrays, turtles, and hundreds of colorful fish. You can also come face to fin with leafy sea dragons, see some of the ocean's deadliest creatures, such as blue-ringed octopus and stonefish, or take a glass-bottom-boat ride. The touch pool is a great attraction for kids. Ocean Guides provide talks on marine creatures throughout the day. For A$195, you can **snorkel or dive with the sharks** (daily 12:45 and 2:45pm). Advance bookings essential. Allow half a day here.

Hillarys Boat Harbour, 91 Southside Dr., Hillarys. www.aqwa.com.au. ✆ **08/9447 7500.** A$30 adults, A$18 children 4–15, A$79 families of 4. Daily 10am–5pm (closed Dec 25). Duyfken tours (includes entry to aquarium): A$35 adults, A$23 children, A$99 families of 5.

Art Gallery of Western Australia ★★ GALLERY In 2020, this smartly laid-out and attractive gallery will celebrate 125 years since its foundation as the custodian of the State Art Collection, so expect some special events to mark the milestone. Outstanding among the international and Australian sections is the Aboriginal art collection, regarded as one of the finest in Australia. There are regular visiting exhibitions, with occasional blockbusters. Free 1-hour tours of a designated collection run Monday and Wednesday at 11am and 1pm and Thursday to Sunday at 1pm; check the website for details.

Cultural Centre, Roe St. and Beaufort St. (enter off the elevated walkway opposite Perth Railway Station), Northbridge. www.artgallery.wa.gov.au. ✆ **08/9492 6600** or 08/9492 6622 (24-hr. recorded info line). Free. Entry fee may apply to special exhibitions. Wed–Mon 10am–5pm. Closed Tues, Good Friday, Dec 25, and Apr 25 (Anzac Day). Train: Perth. Bus: Blue CAT.

The Bell Tower ★★★ LANDMARK   You may spot the Bell Tower from afar and wonder "what is that?!" This distinctive glass tower is the landmark at the end of Barrack Street and home to the **Swan Bells,** given to the people of Western Australia as part of Australia's Bicentennial celebrations in 1988. The tower includes 12 bells from London's St Martin-in-the-Fields, recast in the 16th century by Queen Elizabeth I. There are 18 bells in all, which are rung every Monday, Thursday, and Sunday from noon to 1pm (and on other occasions, if you are lucky to catch them). You can visit to just have a look at the displays about the history of the bells or take a tour that includes demonstrations with the bell-ringers—and you get to have a go at ringing them yourself! You can book a time for a tour or just turn up. Tours run Monday to Saturday at 10:30, 11, and 11:30am and 1:30, 2, and 2:30pm. The best time to visit is Monday or Thursday at 11:30am or 1pm, which allows you to do the tour, see the professional bell-ringers perform, and hear the Anzac Bell ring at noon for 1 minute. An observation deck has fabulous views of the city. Allow an hour.

Barrack Square, Riverside Dr. www.thebelltower.com.au. © **08/6210 0444.** A$9 adults, A$7 children 5–14, A$25 families. Tours: A$18 adults, A$9 children 5–14, A$44 families of 4. Daily 10am–4pm (closed Dec 25, Good Friday, and until noon on Apr 25).

Cohunu Koala Park ★★ WILDLIFE PARK   This is the only place in Western Australia where you can hold a koala. You can also hand-feed kangaroos, wallabies, and emus wandering in natural enclosures, see wombats and

Ronin the koala at the Cohunu Koala Park.

Cinema Under the Stars

For a truly magical experience, head to the **Sommerville Auditorium** (www.theatres.uwa.edu.au/venues/sommerville; ✆ **08/6488 1732**) at the University of Western Australia (UWA) for cinema under the stars. The big screen and seating (canvas deck chairs) are inside a "cathedral" (and that's what it feels like) of towering Norfolk pine trees, so it's like watching a movie in a forest. Take a picnic, or buy from one of the food trucks on-site. The cinema seats 1,000 people, as well as space for 200 on the grass, and on a warm evening it's a delightful place to be. Movie nights are usually run for special events such as the annual **Perth Festival** (see p. 36). Find the auditorium by heading to the campus entrance at 35 Stirling Hwy., Crawley.

dingoes, walk through an aviary housing native birds, and see wild water birds on the ponds. For A$4 you can ride a little train through the park's bushland setting. Caversham Wildlife Park in the Swan Valley (p. 369) has a larger range of native species but does not allow koala cuddling. It's about a 45-minute drive from the city, and hard to get here without a car.

Nettleton Rd., Byford (500m off the South West Hwy.). www.cohunu.com.au. ✆ **08/9526 2966**. A$15 adults, A$5 children 3–13. Koala holding A$30 (take your own photo/video). Daily 10am–4pm. Closed Dec 25. By car, take Riverside Dr. across Swan River onto Albany Hwy. to Armadale, then South West Hwy. for 5km (3 miles); turn left onto Nettleton Rd. for 500m (1,640 ft.).

His Majesty's Theatre ★★ THEATER   A lovely old Edwardian theater, opened in 1904, "The Maj" was rescued from demolition in 1979 and is run by the Perth Theatre Trust. It is Perth's major venue for the WA Ballet and Opera companies, cabaret performances (downstairs), and visiting theater productions, including many for the Perth International Arts Festival. Friends (volunteers) of His Majesty's are on hand Monday to Friday 10am to 4pm to provide information and tours of the auditorium (unless it's in use) and public areas (A$2 per person). Downstairs houses the **Museum of Performing Arts,** with an engrossing collection of costumes and other memorabilia. A modern cafe, **Barre,** is on the street level. **King Street,** just north of the theater, is a charming little thoroughfare with numerous restored buildings housing upmarket bistros, galleries, and fashion stores.

825 Hay St. (at King St.). ww.ptt.wa.gov.au/venues/his-majestys-theatre. ✆ **08/6212 9292**. A$2 Performing Arts Museum Mon–Fri 10am–4pm. Train: Perth. Bus: Red CAT.

Perth Cultural Centre ★★★ CULTURAL CENTER   Once a fairly unloved part of the city, this precinct is now a thriving hub of cultural activity. It encompasses many of the city's cultural performance spaces and really comes alive during festival times. Here you will find the **Art Gallery of Western Australian** (p. 348), the **State Library,** the **Western Australian**

FACING PAGE: The Bell Tower, in Barrick Square, is home to the Swan Bells.

Museum (p. 352), the **Perth Institute of Contemporary Arts (PICA),** small theaters, cafes, and some great public art. Look for the **Urban Orchard,** a colorful public garden where you can help yourself to fresh herbs or flowers. A children's playground is open daily 8am to 7pm.

Roe, Beaufort, Francis, and William sts., Northbridge. www.ptt.wa.gov.au/venues/perth-cultural-centre. Train: Perth. Bus: Blue CAT (stop 7 or 15).

Perth Mint ★★★ ICON   This lovely historic building—built in the 1890s to refine gold from the Kalgoorlie goldfields, and to mint currency—is one of the world's oldest mints operating from its original premises. It now produces commemorative coins for collectors around the world, and bullion is still traded here. Hourly guided tours allow visitors to see Australia's largest collection of nuggets, watch gold coins being minted, handle a 400-ounce gold bar, and engrave their own medallions. Tours start with a guided heritage walk and lead on to the molten-gold-pouring demonstration (hourly 10am–4pm daily). The shop sells gold coins and jewelry made from West Australian gold, diamonds, and pearls.

310 Hay St. (at Hill St.), East Perth. www.perthmint.com.au. Ⓒ **1300/366 520** in Australia or 08/9421 7376. A$19 adults, A$8 children 4–15, A$48 family of 4. Daily 9am–5pm. Closed Jan 1, Good Friday, Apr 25, and Dec 25–26. Bus: Red CAT.

Western Australian Museum ★★ MUSEUM   After undergoing a 4-year, A$428-million renovation and expansion, this museum is scheduled to reopen sometime in 2020 (check the website for updates). It will, by all accounts, be worth the wait. The completed museum will be four times larger than before, allowing more of its vast collection of treasures to be seen, including a full Blue Whale skeleton. The stunning new museum building will incorporate existing Heritage buildings including the Old Perth Gaol. Much of the detail had yet to be released as this book went to print, but the renovated museum will have four main galleries: Being Western Australian, Discovering Western Australia, Exploring the World, and Revealing the Museum (a behind-the-scenes experience).

Off James St. Mall, Perth Cultural Centre, Northbridge. www.museum.wa.gov.au. Ⓒ **1300/134 081** in Australia. Train: Perth. Bus: Blue CAT (Stop 8).

Yanchep National Park ★★★ MUSEUM   One of WA's oldest national parks, Yanchep is an excellent place to see Australian wildlife, including koalas and kangaroos. On Thursdays and Sundays, take a 45-minute Aboriginal

---

The Black Swan

It's the state emblem, and the Swan River was named after it, but sadly the black swan is rarely found here these days, because most of the swans' preferred habitat, the shallows, has been destroyed. **Lake Monger,** 3.5km (2 miles) northwest of the city, usually has hundreds by its shores, plus cormorants, native ducks, herons, coots, and swamp hens.

cultural tour, which includes didgeridoo playing. The park is 50km (32 miles) north of the city, set in glorious natural woodlands around a reed-fringed lake. You can follow a boardwalk through the koala enclosure, hire a rowboat, take a limestone cavern tour, and have a coffee and snack (or beer) at the tearooms or at the historic Tudor-style **Yanchep Inn** (www.yanchepinn.com.au; ✆ **08/9561 1001**). Kangaroos abound, and there are noisy Carnaby's black cockatoos; other birds include swans, pelicans, wrens, parrots, and kookaburras.

Off Wanneroo Rd., Yanchep. ✆ **08/9303 7759.** Entry fee A$13 per vehicle. Tours, including the Aboriginal Experience and caves tours, A$15 adults, A$7.50 children 6–15, A38 families of 4. Daily 9:15am–4:30pm. By car, take Wellington St. west and turn into Thomas St., which feeds into Wanneroo Rd. Follow this for about 45km (28 miles) to the park turnoff.

ORGANIZED TOURS

Harbor Cruises

Captain Cook Cruises (www.captaincookcruises.com.au; ✆ **08/9325 3341**) runs a wide assortment of cruises on the Swan River. There are regular departures downstream to Fremantle, with options to spend time in the harbor city and/or to take lunch before cruising back to Perth. Full-day cruises, with lunch, go upstream to historic homes and vineyards in the Swan Valley, operating daily from 9:45am to 5pm (from A$154 adults, A$106 children 4–12). A dinner cruise on the Swan operates Friday and Saturday, leaving at 7:30pm; the cost is A$128 adults, A$99 children.

From September through November, Perth's ocean waters are alive with humpback **whales** returning from the north with their calves. **Rottnest Fast Ferries** (www.rottnestfastferries.com.au/packages/whale-watching; ✆ **08/9246 1039**) operate 2-hour tours daily (except Tues and Thurs), with pickups from Perth hotels. Weekday prices are A$60 adults, A$30 children 4 to 12, A$20 children 2 to 3, A$5 under 2s, and A$150 for a family of 4. Weekend prices are about A$5 more.

Walking Tours

If you want to learn more about Perth's early history, book an excellent guided tour with **Two Feet and a Heartbeat,** based at the Perth Town Hall, on the corner of Hay and Barrack streets (www.twofeet.com.au; ✆ **1800/459 388** in Australia or 08/7007 0492). Most walks leave at 10am and 2pm, but some special evening tours are offered on request, such as a "Crimes of Perth" tour and a "World of Whisky" or cocktail tour. I recommend the Coffee, Culture and Art tour, which takes 2 hours and is a fabulous introduction to the city; do it on your first day if you can, because it will really help you get your bearings (and help you get over your jet lag). The tour costs A$45 per person.

Heli West (www.heliwest.com.au; ✆ **08/9499 7700**) offers a range of scenic helicopter flights: 30 minutes over the city or along the coastline to Fremantle and back for A$300 person. A trip to Rottnest Island for the day costs A$1,800 for one to four people. Prices are subject to change and availability.

Perth Luxury Tours (www.perthluxurytours.co; ℭ **1300/633 014** in Australia or 0405 136 930 mobile phone) is a specialist in small, private tours and offers carefully designed tour packages including experiences in Perth, Fremantle, the Swan Valley, and farther afield as well as private charter and transfers.

OUTDOOR ACTIVITIES

Hitting the Beach

Perth shares Sydney's good luck in having beaches in the metropolitan area—in an almost continuous line from Fremantle's Port Beach in the south to Quinns Rocks in the north. Mornings are often best, because the sea breeze can make the afternoons unpleasant in summer. Evenings and sunsets are lovely on quiet days (remember, Perth faces west over the Indian Ocean). Always swim between the red and yellow safety flags.

Bus no. 400 runs to Scarborough Beach every 15 minutes weekdays, half-hourly on Saturdays and hourly on Sundays, while 102 goes to Cottesloe Beach every 30 minutes. Bus no. 458 operates a summer timetable along the northern beaches from Scarborough to Hillarys, half-hourly on weekends and public holidays and hourly on weekdays, in both directions. Surfboards of 2m (6 ft., 7 in.) can be carried on the 400 and 458 provided they do not affect safety.

The three most popular beaches are Cottesloe, Scarborough, and Trigg.

o **Cottesloe** This pretty crescent, graced by the Edwardian-style Indiana Tea House, is Perth's most fashionable beach. It has grassed slopes overlooking the beach, safe swimming, and a small surf break. Some good cafes and hotels are nearby. Every March the beach is taken over by an eye-popping exhibition of **Sculpture by the Sea** (https://sculpturebythesea. com). Train: Cottesloe, and then walk several hundred meters (btw. a quarter- and a half-mile).

o **Scarborough** Scarborough's white sands stretch for miles. Swimming is generally safe, and surfers are always guaranteed a wave, although inexperienced swimmers should take a rain check when the surf is rough. The busy shopping precinct across the road means there's always somewhere to buy lunch and drinks.

o **Trigg** Surfers like Trigg best for its consistent swells, but it can have dangerous rips. Stay within the flags.

Parks & Gardens

Kings Park & Botanic Garden ★★ Overlooking both the city and Swan River, this 406-hectare (1,000-acre) hilltop jewel of parkland encompasses a botanical garden, numerous war memorials, and native bush. The main entry, along Fraser Avenue, is lined with magnificent lemon-scented gums, while each tree on the other roads is dedicated to a fallen soldier. The **State War Memorial** sits imposingly on a steep bluff above the river. You can

Cottlesloe Beach.

inspect Western Australian flora; experience the solitude of the bush; and bike, stroll, or drive an extensive network of roads and trails. A walk through the Botanic Garden highlights many of the state's plant species, including banksias and boabs, and leads to the **Federation Walkway,** a glass arched bridge that soars through the treetops. Visiting the spring **wildflower displays** (which peak Aug–Oct) is a highlight for many, with an excellent Wildflower Festival running through September. A range of maps and information is available online. An information center manned by volunteer guides is next to the stylish **Aspects of Kings Park** craft shop (p. 357).

Join one of the free guided walks leaving from the **Visitor Information Centre.** Walks depart daily at 10am, noon, and 2pm and take 1½ to 2 hours; or opt for one of the longer, 3-hour bushwalks from July to October. For an Aboriginal take on the park and the entire Perth region, don't miss out on experiencing one of the walks led by the traditional custodians of the park, the Wadjuk Nyoongar people. There are several, run by independent tour companies, so check the website for details.

Fraser Ave., off Kings Park Rd. www.bgpa.wa.gov.au. ✆ **08/9480 3634.** Free. Information Centre open daily 9:30am–4pm (closed Dec 25). Bus: 935 from St Georges Terrace, free from the city, stops at the Information Centre.

Biking

Perth's superb bike-track network stretches for miles along the Swan River, through Kings Park, around Fremantle, and all the way along the beaches. A great 9.5km (6-mile) track enables a complete loop around Perth Water, the broad expanse of river in front of the central business district.

WestCycle (www.westcycle.org.au; ✆ **08/6336 9688**) has information on bike routes in the city, as does **Trails WA** (www.trailswa.com.au).

Rental from **About Bike Hire** by the Swan River at Point Fraser Reserve (Causeway Carpark; www.aboutbikehire.com.au; ✆ **08/9221 2665**), about 2km (1¼ miles) from the city center (take bus 24 from St Georges Terrace), is A$10 for an hour or A$24 for a 24-hour day for adults, A$7 or A$22 for children under 12. The day rate, which drops the longer you have the bike, includes a helmet (required by law in Australia), lock, and pump. Electric bikes, road racers, tandems, and other specialized bikes can also be hired. It's open daily 9am to 5pm (8am–6pm weekends and daily in summer Nov to Apr).

Sailing

The tallest Tall Ship in Australia, the barquentine (three-masted) **SS *Leeuwin II*** (www.sailleeuwin.com; ✆ **08/9430 4105**), offers 3-hour sails from B Shed at Victoria Quay, Fremantle, when it is not on voyages around Western Australia. You'll get the chance to try your hand at sailing the way it used to be, even clambering up the rigging. The 3-hour sails cost A$110 adults or A$40 children 3 to 18, or A$245 for a family of 4. No experience is necessary. Check the website for details of sailing days and times.

Experienced sailors can sometimes find a spot on Wednesday afternoons and summer twilight events with members of the **Royal Perth Yacht Club,** Australia II Drive, Crawley (www.rpyc.com.au; ✆ **08/9389 1555**), if a place is available. It's not spinnaker sailing, so the action is at an easy pace. Dress standards apply.

Funcats Watersports (www.funcats.com.au; ✆ **0408 926 003** mobile phone) rents simple, small catamarans from the Coode St Jetty on the South Perth Foreshore. A Hobie Wave Cat costs A$55 for 1 hour or A$95 for 2 hours.

Scuba Diving & Snorkeling

Just 19km (12 miles) off Perth, Rottnest Island's corals, reef fish, wrecks, and limestone caverns, in 18-to-35m (59–115-ft.) visibility, are a gift from heaven to Perth divers and snorkelers. Contact **Perth Diving Academy** (www.perthdiving.com.au; ✆ **08/9344 7844;** see "Rottnest Island" in "Day Trips from Perth," p. 364), to rent gear and/or join a dive trip.

Surfing

You will find good surfing at many city beaches, Scarborough and Trigg in particular. See the "Hitting the Beaches" section, earlier in this chapter. Rottnest Island (see "Day Trips from Perth," below) also has a few breaks. **Surfing WA** (www.surfingwasurfschool.com.au; ✆ **08/9448 0004**) runs classes at Trigg Beach in Perth and around WA.

PERTH SHOPPING

Most major shops are downtown on the parallel **Hay Street** and **Murray Street malls,** and in the network of arcades running off them, such as the Plaza, City, Carillon, and Tudor-style **London Court** arcades. Off Murray Street Mall on Forrest Place is the **Forrest Chase shopping complex,** housing the Myer department store and boutiques on two levels. The other major department store, David Jones, opens on to both malls. Add to your collection of international designer brands on posh **King Street,** in the west end. **Watertown,** at the western edge of the city, is a large complex housing "factory outlets" of numerous retail chains.

If you want to avoid the chains, spend half a day in **Subiaco** ★ or "Subi," where Hay Street and Rokeby Road are lined with smart boutiques, galleries, and cafes.

For wonderful souvenirs, stop in to **Aspects of Kings Park,** behind the Visitor Centre in Kings Park (www.aspectsofkingspark.com.au; ✆ **08/9480 3900**), where you will find contemporary ceramic, textile, glass, and jewelry products.

Creative Native (www.creativenative.com.au; ✆ **0466 401 977** mobile phone), stocks Perth's widest range of Aboriginal arts and crafts and includes a gallery that sells original works by some renowned Aboriginal artists. You'll find it in the Murray Street Mall. The **Mossenson Galleries**, incorporating **Indigenart,** is at 115 Hay St., Subiaco (www.mossensongalleries.com.au; ✆ **08/9388 2899**), where you will fine works on canvas, paper, and bark, as well as artifacts, textiles, pottery, didgeridoos, boomerangs, and sculpture, by Aboriginal artists from all over Australia. In Fremantle, **Japingka Aboriginal Art** (www.japingkaaboriginalart.com; ✆ **08/9335 8265**) has a gallery at 47 High St. dedicated to encouraging and exhibiting Aboriginal Australian art, with all sales coming with a certificate of authenticity.

Western Australia is renowned for farming the world's best **South Sea pearls** off Broome, for Argyle **diamonds** mined in the Kimberley, and for being one of the world's biggest **gold** producers. **Kailis Jewellery,** 29 King St. (www.kailisjewellery.com.au; ✆ **08/9422 3888**), sells elegant South Sea pearls and gold jewelry. Another branch is located at the corner of Marine Terrace and Collie Street, Fremantle (✆ **08/9239 9330**). Some of Perth's other leading jewelers, where you can buy Argyle diamonds, Broome pearls, and opals set within locally designed WA gold jewelry, are **Linneys,** 37 Rokeby Rd., Subiaco (www.linneys.com.au; ✆ **08/9382 4077**), and **Costello's,** Shop

Perth shopping arcade London Court, built in 1937.

5–6, London Court (www.costellos.com.au; ✆ **08/9325 8588**). Linneys also has locations at 61 King St. and Crown Resort at Burswood. For opals to suit all budgets, head to the Perth outlet of **Quilpie Opals,** in the Mantra on Murray hotel, 305 Murray St. (www.quilpieopalsperth.com.au; ✆ **08/9321 8687**).

Most shops are open until 9pm weeknights in the city, Subiaco, and Fremantle.

DAY TRIPS FROM PERTH

Fremantle ★★★

19km (12 miles) S of Perth

The heritage port precinct of **Fremantle,** at the mouth of the Swan River, is probably best known outside Australia as the site of the 1987 America's Cup challenge, when Australia became the first country outside the USA to win the trophy in 132 years. Today, "Freo" is a bustling district of 150 National Trust heritage buildings, alfresco cafes, museums, galleries, pubs, markets, and shops in a masterfully preserved historical atmosphere. European influences are strong, thanks to the migrant fishermen, especially Italians, who made Fremantle their new home. It's still a working port, but many buildings are now part of the local Notre Dame University. Weekends are best, a wonderful hubbub of shoppers, coffee drinkers, tourists, and fishermen. Allow a full day to take in even half the sights, and don't forget to knock back a beer or two on the veranda of one of the gorgeous old pubs, or sip an espresso on the **Cappuccino Strip** (p. 360). There's something of a perpetual holiday atmosphere in this picturesque port city.

Public transport from Perth's city center is good, especially the train, making Fremantle a popular out-of-town base as an alternative to staying in the city.

ESSENTIALS

ARRIVING   Parking is plentiful, but driving can be frustrating in the maze of one-way streets. Most attractions are within walking distance (or accessible on the free CAT buses), so take the train to Fremantle and explore on foot. A nice way to get to Freo and see Perth's river suburbs is on the cruises that run a few times a day from Barrack Street Jetty (see p. 338).

VISITOR INFORMATION   The **Fremantle Visitor Centre** is in Town Hall, Kings Square (at High St.) (www.visitfremantle.com.au; ✆ **08/9431 7878**). It's open Monday through Friday 9am to 5pm, Saturday 9am to 4pm, Sunday and public holidays (except Good Friday and Christmas Day) 10am to 4pm.

GETTING AROUND   The free **Fremantle CAT** buses run on two loops; the Red Cat east to west between the Maritime Museum and Ord Street and the Blue Cat north to south between Fremantle train station and Douro Road. The **Red Cat** runs every 15 from 7:30am to 6:15pm Monday through Thursday (until 7:45pm Friday) and 10am to 6:15pm on weekends and public holidays. The Blue Cat runs at roughly the same times, but every 10 minutes. Buses don't run on Good Friday, Christmas Day, and December 26.

Fremantle street scene.

The Cappuccino Strip

Don't leave Freo without a "short black" (that's an espresso) or a "flat white" (coffee with milk) at one of the many alfresco cafes along South Terrace. On weekends, the street bursts at the seams with locals flocking to Italian-style eateries that serve good coffee and excellent focaccia, pasta, and pizza. **DOME** and **Gino's** are a couple to look for.

Fremantle Trams (www.fremantletrams.com; © **08/9473 0331**) runs hop-on, hop-off tours around the main sights. The tours, with a commentary, depart from Fremantle Town Hall five times a day (three in winter, May–Aug), starting at 10am, with the last tour leaving at 3:30pm (tours run at 11am, 12:25pm, and 2:10pm in winter). Tickets cost A\$30 adults, A\$5 children 5 to 14, and A\$65 for families of four. Combine the ticket with visits to the Fremantle Prison, Little Creatures brewery or Maritime Museum for discounts. The Friday-night Ghostly Tour includes a fish-and-chips dinner and a torchlight walking tour of Fremantle Prison. It runs from 6:45pm to 10:30pm and costs A\$85 adults and A\$65 children under 15. You must book for this.

EXPLORING FREMANTLE

You'll want to explore some of Freo's excellent museums and other attractions, but don't forget to stroll the streets and admire the 19th-century hotels and warehouses, many painted in rich, historically accurate colors. Take time to wander down to the docks—either **Victoria Quay** in the main harbor, where pleasure craft dodge between tugs and container ships, or **Fishing Boat Harbour,** off Mews Road, where the catches are brought in.

Join Michael Deller of **Fremantle Tours** (www.fremantletours.com.au; © **0418/885 445** mobile phone) for a walk around his hometown as he shares stories passed down through his family and lets you in on some of the city's hidden secrets and his personal favorite spots. You'll see fabulous street art and hear the stories behind each piece, find out more about the history of Fremantle, and get the scoop on the latest developments, and Michael will buy you a coffee along the way. It's fun and friendly (and may finish with a hug!). A 2-hour walking tour costs A\$30 per person. You can also do a bike tour (3 hr., A\$55 per person) or a tour that focuses on eating or drinking.

Freo's best **shopping** is for arts and crafts, from hand-blown glass to Aboriginal art to alpaca-wool clothing. Worth a look are the assorted arts, crafts, and souvenir stores on **High Street** west of the mall; and the **Fremantle Arts Centre** (see below). The **Fremantle Markets,** 74 South Terrace at Henderson Street (www.fremantlemarkets.com.au; © **08/9335 2515**), are the oldest and best markets in Perth. More than 150 stalls sell local and imported handicrafts, jewelry, clothing, and inexpensive food. They're open Friday 8am to 8pm and Saturday and Sunday 8am to 6pm.

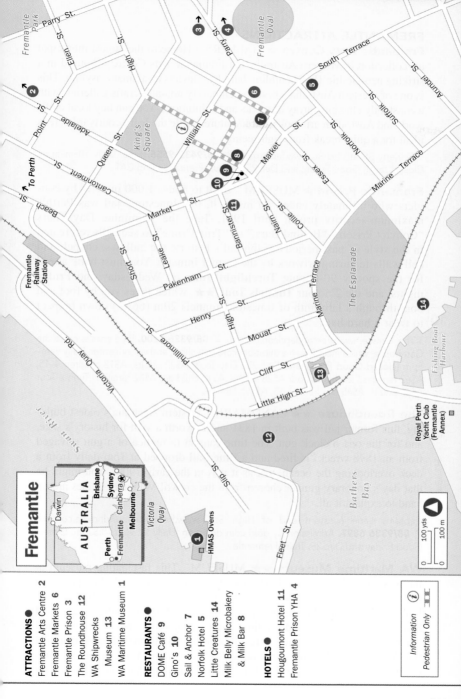

Fremantle

ATTRACTIONS ●
Fremantle Arts Centre **2**
Fremantle Markets **6**
Fremantle Prison **3**
The Roundhouse **12**
WA Shipwrecks
  Museum **13**
WA Maritime Museum **1**

RESTAURANTS ●
DOME Café **9**
Gino's **10**
Sail & Anchor **7**
Norfolk Hotel **5**
Little Creatures **14**
Milk Belly Microbakery
  & Milk Bar **8**

HOTELS ●
Hougoumont Hotel **11**
Fremantle Prison YHA **4**

Information (i)
Pedestrian Only

FREMANTLE ATTRACTIONS

Fremantle Arts Centre ★ GALLERY   Home to the largest municipal art collection in Western Australia, the Fremantle Arts Centre is housed in a striking neo-Gothic 1860s building built by convicts as a lunatic asylum. This is one of Western Australia's best contemporary arts-and-crafts galleries, with a constantly changing array of works and exhibitions. You can buy local craftwork and Australian art books and literature, while the leafy courtyard cafe is ideal for a quiet break from sightseeing.

1 Finnerty St. at Ord St. www.fac.org.au. © **08/9432 9555.** Free. Daily 10am–5pm. Closed Jan 1, Good Friday, and Dec 25–26. Bus: Fremantle Red CAT.

Fremantle Prison ★ MUSEUM   Built to house 1,000 inmates by convicts who ultimately ended up inside it, this limestone jail was Perth's maximum-security prison until 1991. Take the 75-minute Day Tours "Convict Prison," "Behind Bars," or "True Crime" to see cells re-created in the style of past periods of the jail's history, the gallows, chapel, and cell walls featuring artwork by the former inmates. You must book ahead for the spooky 90-minute **Torchlight Tour** on Wednesday and Friday nights, and the 2½ hour **Tunnels Tour** ★★, which takes you by foot and boat through a labyrinth of limestone tunnels 20m (66 ft.) down (expect to wear a hard hat).

1 The Terrace. www.fremantleprison.com.au. © **08/9336 9200.** Free admission to the Gatehouse, which includes an exhibition, cafe, gift shop, and visitor center. Daily 9am–5pm (closed Good Friday and Dec 25). Day Tours A$22 adults, A$12 children 4–15, A$62 families. Torchlight Tour A$28 adults, A$18 children, A$82 families. Tunnel Tour A$65 adults, A$45 children 12–15, A$195 families.

The Roundhouse ★★ LANDMARK   Western Australia's oldest building, this former jail was built in 1831 and is worth a visit for history's sake, and for the one o'clock gun. The time cannon (a replica of a gun salvaged from an 1878 wreck) is fired and a **time ball** dropped at 1pm daily from a deck overlooking the ocean, just as it was in the early 1900s. You might be that day's honorary gunner chosen from the crowd! Volunteer guides are on hand to explain it all.

Captains Lane (western end of High St.). www.fremantleroundhouse.com.au. © **08/9336 6897.** Admission by gold coin donation. Daily 10:30am–3:30pm. Closed Good Friday and Dec 25. Train: Fremantle.

WA Maritime Museum ★★ MUSEUM   This fascinating museum at the western end of Fremantle Harbour faces out through tall glass panels to the Indian Ocean—and focuses on WA's links to that ocean. The museum looks at Fremantle's history as a port, shipping in both the Indian Ocean and Swan River, signaling and piloting, sailing technology, naval defense, and Aboriginal maritime heritage. It features historic boats, including *Australia II* (the Aussie yacht that won the America's Cup in 1983). You can tour the submarine HMAS *Ovens* every half-hour from 10am to 3:30pm, but bookings are recommended. You can buy a ticket just for the sub, or a joint one for the museum and sub at a discount.

Victoria Quay Rd. ⓒ **1300/134 081** in Australia. www.museum.wa.gov.au/maritime. A$15 adults, free children 5–15, A$30 families of 4. Special gold coin admission 2nd Tues of each month. Submarine tour A$15 adults, A$7.50 children 5–15, A$40 family. Open daily 9:30am–5pm. Closed Good Friday, Dec 25–26, Jan 1, and until 1pm on Apr 25. Train: Fremantle. Bus: Fremantle Red CAT.

WA Shipwrecks Museum ★★ MUSEUM   The massive, and magnificent, remnant hulk of the Dutch ship *Batavia,* wrecked north of Perth in 1629, will stop you in your tracks when you enter this fascinating museum, located in a lovely old 1850s limestone building. The *Batavia*'s story is of survival and betrayal; most of the survivors of the wreck were massacred by a handful of mutineers. The mutiny and massacre have been the subject of films and an opera. The museum is world-renowned for its work in maritime archaeology and preservation, and you will love the displays of pieces of eight, cannons, and other deep-sea treasure recovered off the Western Australian coast. Displays date from the 1600s, when Dutch explorers became the first Europeans to encounter Australia.

Cliff St. www.museum.wa.gov.au/museums/shipwrecks. ⓒ **1300/134 081** in Australia. Free. Open daily 9:30am–5pm, Apr 25 from 1pm. Free tours daily 10:30am and 2:30pm (bookings essential). Closed Good Friday, Dec 25–26, and Jan 1. Train: Fremantle. Bus: Fremantle Blue CAT.

WHERE TO EAT IN FREMANTLE

Popular watering holes are the **Sail & Anchor,** 64 South Terrace (ⓒ **08/9431 1666**), and the **Norfolk,** 47 South Terrace at Norfolk Street (ⓒ **08/9335 5405**).

Little Creatures ★ PIZZA/PUB   Wood-fired pizzas, tapas-style dishes (think sticky lamb ribs or marinated octopus), hand-cut frites, and a buzzy atmosphere are what brings so many people here—be warned, it might be packed! Half of the huge tin sheds that house this eatery are also taken up by an award-winning microbrewery, so if beer if your drink, you're in the right place. It's all rather barn-like, with simple furnishings, an open kitchen, and an outdoor eating area by the harbor. The staff, known as "creatures," are friendly and efficient. You can also do a brewery tour for A$20 (including tastings) daily at noon, 1, 2, and 3pm.

40 Mews Rd., Fishing Boat Harbour. www.littlecreatures.com.au. ⓒ **08/6215 1000.** Main courses A$18–A$28; pizzas A$12–A$24. Mon–Fri 10am–11pm; Sat–Sun 9am–11pm; public holidays 11am–10pm.

Milk Belly Microbakery & Milk Bar ★★ CAFE   On a lane just off the main drag, this busy little bakery produces all manner of yummy treats, from donuts to toasted sandwiches to healthy salad wraps (made to order), as well as milkshakes and great coffee. It's perfect for grabbing something quick while you're out sightseeing. You might even find some gluten-free chocolate brownies or vegan-friendly cinnamon donuts, as the offerings change.

36 South Terrace. www.facebook.com/milkbelly. ⓒ **0403 736 930** mobile phone. Main courses A$6–A$10. Mon–Fri 7:30am–5pm; Sat 8:30am–5pm; Sun 8:30am–noon.

Rottnest Island: Meet the Quokkas ★★★

19km (12 miles) W of Perth

The delightful wildlife reserve of laidback and casual Rottnest Island, off the Perth coast, has been WA's favorite holiday island for a hundred years, in no small part because of its 63 beaches and 20 bays. It's surrounded by sheltering reefs, which ensure safe swimming and snorkeling in glorious, protected bays. Jewel-bright waters, warmed by a south-flowing current, harbor **coral outcrops** and 400 kinds of fish. The island is also home to more than 10,000 **quokkas,** cute little marsupials that live almost nowhere else in Australia. "Quokka selfies" are popular—if you can get close enough—spurred by a spate of celebrities (think tennis champion Roger Federer and actor Margot Robbie). But you are not supposed to feed the quokkas, so please restrain yourself even if they look at you expectantly. Quokkas are nocturnal, so the best time to see them is at night, but it's also likely you'll see a few here and there during the day. Try to spend a night here if you can.

The island is only 11km (7 miles) long and 4.5km (3 miles) across at its widest point, with two main areas of settlement. There are no private vehicles on the island, so getting about is restricted to walking and cycling, with a few buses taking visitors around the island or linking the settlements. Following mainland clashes between settlers and Aborigines, Rottnest was a "native prison" from 1839 until 1931. The main settlement now has WA's oldest, most intact precinct of heritage buildings and an Aboriginal cemetery. The island was a military base during World War II.

ESSENTIALS

ARRIVING   Rottnest Express (www.rottnestexpress.com.au; $\it{C}$ 1300/GO ROTTO [467 688] in Western Australia) operates trips from Perth's Elizabeth Quay (trip time: 1:45–2 hr.) and, more frequently, from Fremantle (about 30 min.). Round-trip same-day fares are A\$103 adults, A\$49 children 4 to 12, or A\$256 family of four from Perth, or A\$69 adults, A\$32 children, or A\$171 family from Fremantle. You'll pay about A\$6 extra if you return on a later date. Accommodations packages, bike hire, and various day trips (including Rottnest Express's Eco Adventure, cruising around the island bays and coves) are available.

Rottnest Air Taxi (www.rottnestairtaxi.com.au; $\it{C}$ **0421 389 831** mobile phone) provides transfers in four- or six-seater aircraft, about 12 minutes each way. A same-day round-trip in a four-seater costs from A\$430 for up to three passengers, and from A\$530 in a six-seater for up to five. **Kookaburra Air** (www.kookaburraair.com.au; $\it{C}$ **08/9417 2258**) also operates a range of tours to Rottnest. Both operate from Jandakot Airport, 20 minutes south of Perth.

VISITOR INFORMATION   The Rottnest Island Visitor Centre ($\it{C}$ **08/9372 9730**) is right at the head of the jetty when you arrive on the island. The center is run by the **Rottnest Island Authority** (www.rottnestisland.com; $\it{C}$ **08/9432 9111**), as is the entire island. It is open Monday to Thursday

7:30am to 5:30pm, Friday 7:30am to 7pm, and Saturday and Sunday 7:30am to 6pm.

GETTING AROUND   Ferries pull into the jetty in Thomson Bay, which has most of the facilities and hotels lining its shores. **Rottnest Island Pedal & Flipper** (*©* **08/9292 5105**) rents 1,300 bikes of every size, speed, and type, plus trailers and carriers (for surfboards, babies, etc.). A multispeed bike is A$30 for 24 hours (plus a A$50 refundable deposit), including a helmet (compulsory in Australia) and lock. The price reduces for subsequent days.

The air-conditioned **Island Explorer** bus does half-hourly circumnavigations in summer (hourly in winter), calling at 18 stops, including the best bays. You can get on and off as often as you like, with an all-day ticket costing A$20 for adults, A$15 for children 5 to 12, and A$50 for families of four. Weekend passes are also available. Buy tickets for this and the tours below at the visitor center, gift shop, main ticket booth, or on board.

A shuttle bus runs regularly between the main accommodation areas on the island, including Thomson Bay, Geordie Bay, Fay's and Longreach Bays, and on request to the airport and Kingstown Barracks. It costs A$3 per person.

Many first-time visitors take the 2-hour **Bayseeker Island Tour,** a good introduction to the bays and the island's cultural and natural history, which includes a stop to see the quokkas. It costs A$40 adults and A$24 kids 5 to 12. Tours depart from the Thomson Bay stop at 11:20am, 1:40, and 1:50pm daily.

EXPLORING ROTTNEST ISLAND

Most people come to Rottnest to swim, surf, snorkel, or dive. As soon as you arrive, rent a bike and your preferred aquatic gear, and pedal around the coast until you come to a beach you like. (Pack drinking water and food; only Settlement and Geordie Bay have shops.) The Basin, Little Parakeet Bay, Little Armstrong Bay, Little Salmon Bay, and Parker Point are good **snorkel** spots. There are two snorkel trails, with underwater information points, at Little Salmon and Parker Point. **Surfers** should try Cathedral Rocks or Strickland Bay.

Several companies conduct boat trips to some of the 100-plus dive sites around Rottnest, which feature reefs, limestone caverns, and the island's 14 shipwrecks. **Perth Diving Academy** (www.perthdiving.com.au; *©* **08/9344 1562**) has round-trip boat trips to Rottnest from Fremantle that include two dives and lunch for A$170. Trips run only on weekends and public holidays, leaving Fremantle at 8:30am and returning at around 3:30pm. The boat does not land on the island or stop at the jetty. Bookings and dive qualifications are essential, and equipment hire is extra. Trips are subject to the weather and minimum numbers. Snorkelers are also welcome, and pay A$85 per person, including lunch and morning and afternoon tea.

For history buffs, there are numerous heritage buildings, especially along the Thomson Bay foreshore, with WA's oldest and best-preserved **heritage precinct.** The Salt Store, Pilot's Boatshed, and numerous accommodation cottages date from the mid–19th century when the island was a prison.

The island became a major base during World War II, protecting the sea lane to Fremantle, and the Oliver Hill 9.2-inch guns are still in place. Guided 1-hour tours daily at 10am, 11am, noon, 1pm, and 2pm take visitors to see them as well as the battery tunnels. You can make your own way or take the small train that departs from the station near the Visitor Centre at 12:30, 1:30, and 2:30pm (the last trip is a train ride only—no tour). The return train ride plus the gun tour costs A$29 for adults, A$17 children 5 to 12, and A$62 families. Lower prices apply if you take only the train ride.

Volunteer guides run several free short walking tours (from 10 minutes to 1 hour). One is a historical tour around Thomson Bay, including the governor's residence, chapel, octagonal prison, and the small **museum** (© **08/9372 9703;** open daily 10am–3pm) Another heritage trail takes you to the memorial commemorating de Vlamingh, the Dutch explorer who named the island *Rottenest* ("Rat's Nest") in 1696 when he mistook quokkas for (very large) rats. There are also quokka walks, and the "Reefs, Wrecks, and Daring Sailors" tour, which includes a walk to Bathurst lighthouse.

WHERE TO STAY & EAT ON ROTTNEST ISLAND

Rottnest can be explored on a day trip from Perth or Fremantle, but to get the most out of it, you really need to stay overnight. The island has several accommodations options, but be warned that "Rotto" is hugely popular with Perth locals, so booking ahead is essential, especially during busy holiday times in summer and autumn.

The **Rottnest Island Authority** (© **08/9432 9111** for the accommodations booking service) runs most of the island's 300-plus holiday homes, villas, and cottages, and the campground. Don't expect anything grand: The Authority's units are all furnished and self-catering, with gas stoves and barbecues, but no air-conditioning and no televisions.

Both hotels (listed below) have good restaurants; otherwise, dining is available at the licensed **Aristos Waterfront Rottnest,** the **DOME Café,** and a couple of takeout joints. The newest arrival on the dining scene is the swish **Pinky's Beach Club** at Discovery Rottnest (see below).

Discovery Rottnest ★★ The island's first new accommodations in 30 years or so, this "glamping" village opened in early 2019, right on the beachfront at Pinky's Beach, just a short walk from the ferry wharf. Each tent has an en-suite bathroom (with flush toilets), comfortable beds, and a small deck at the front. **Pinky's Beach Club** is open for meals and is the best place to watch the sunset. It offers a range of dining and takeout options, as well as a poolside bar. There is direct beach access from the restaurant/lounge area. Boardwalks and paths link the tents, beach club, and pool area, and you're highly likely to see a few quokkas around.

Strue Rd. www.discoveryholidayparks.com.au/discovery-rottnest-island. © **08/8219 3009.** 83 units. A$255–A$308 double; A$287 family tent (sleeps 5). **Amenities:** Restaurant; bar; outdoor pool.

Hotel Rottnest ★★ Known to generations as the Quokka Arms, this 1864 building overlooking Thomson Bay began life as the state governor's summer residence and over the years has undergone major renovations and upgrades. The latest will add more than 60 new rooms to the island's accommodation stock by September 2020; call ahead to see if the renovations will be complete by the time you arrive. Meanwhile, the restaurant remains open and is a pleasant place to dine, offering local seafood, steaks, pizzas, and snacks.

1 Bedford Ave. www.hotelrottnest.com.au. © **08/9292 5011.** 80 units. Prices not available (check the website for updates). **Amenities:** Restaurant; 2 bars.

Karma Rottnest ★ This former colonial barracks (previously known as Rottnest Lodge) has been heavily modified to provide comfortable visitor accommodations, with units added at the rear, facing across salt lakes to the main Rottnest Lighthouse. The Lakeside Premium rooms have king-size beds, private balconies, and a spacious living area. The standard Lakeside rooms also have balconies, but with limited views. The remaining rooms are in the historic quarters.

Kitson St. www.karmarottnest.com.au. © **08/9292 5161.** 80 units. A$210–A$300 double. Rates include continental breakfast. **Amenities:** Restaurant; bar; small lagoon-style pool; limited room service; spa; free Wi-Fi.

The Swan Valley ★★

20km (13 miles) NE of Perth

The Swan Valley is only 25 minutes from the Perth city center (or less than 10 min. from the domestic airport), but has 30 or so wineries, a wildlife park, antiques shops, galleries, several restaurants, some of WA's early heritage architecture, and one of Australia's best golf resorts.

ESSENTIALS

ARRIVING Lord Street from the Perth city center becomes Guildford Road and takes you to the historic town of Guildford at the start of the Swan Valley.

VISITOR INFORMATION The **Swan Valley Visitor Centre** is in the historic old courthouse at the corner of Meadow and Swan streets, Guildford (www.swanvalley.com.au; © **08/9207 8899**), open daily 9am to 4pm. It provides helpful information and maps—including an excellent Food & Wine Trail map.

GETTING AROUND The best way of getting around the Swan Valley is with your own car, or to take a tour. Another option is the **Swan Valley Explorer** (www.goadams.com.au/swanvalley; © **1300/551 687** in Australia or 08/6270 6060), a hop-on, hop-off bus stopping at various attractions in the Swan Valley. It operates every 30 minutes Wednesday to Sunday, timed to meet trains from Perth at Guildford station. The cost is A$20 adults, A$15 children under 15, and A$50 family of 5.

EXPLORING THE SWAN VALLEY

A great way to experience this region is to follow the **Swan Valley Food and Wine Trail,** a scenic loop taking in some of Western Australia's finest wineries. The ones featured here are just a small sample of those you can visit along the way. In general, the tastings at most Swan Valley wineries are free, with some wineries charging a small fee for their premium offerings.

Don't miss **Mandoon Estate,** 10 Harris Rd., Caversham (www.mandoon estate.com.au; ℂ **08/6279 0500**), a beautiful boutique winery established in 2008 by the Erceg family on the historical Roe family property, which was first settled in the 1840s by the Swan River colony's first surveyor general, John Septimus Roe. Taste the Verdhelo, made from vines planted almost a century ago and available only at Mandoon, and stop off for lunch at the **Homestead** restaurant. It's very family-friendly, and the estate's new town-house-style accommodations, **The Colony,** with 32 rooms from A$200 per night, is perfect for a short getaway.

Most Swan wineries are small, family-run affairs. One exception is the multi-award-winning **Sandalford Wines,** 3210 W. Swan Rd., Caversham (www.sandalford.com; ℂ **08/9374 9374**), with daily 1-hour winery tours at noon for A$25 per person (bookings essential). A very popular tour is the "Winemaker Apprenticeship" Saturdays at noon. Besides the winery tour, you get to blend your own wine, which you can drink over a three-course lunch, all for A$145. The winery also has a pleasant restaurant (lunch noon–3pm) with a pretty vine-covered alfresco area. The cellar door is open 10am to 5pm daily except January 1, Good Friday, December 25 and 26, and the morning of April 25 (Anzac Day).

Western Australia's oldest and largest winery is **Houghton Wines** ★, Dale Road, Middle Swan (www.houghton-wines.com.au; ℂ **08/9274 9540**). The tasting room is light and airy, and there are lovely picnic grounds, where jacaranda trees blossom gloriously in November. The winery also has a café and a small museum of wine history. Hours are 10am to 5pm daily except Good Friday and Christmas Day.

The **Margaret River Chocolate Company** has an outlet at 5123 W. Swan Rd. (near the Reid Hwy.), West Swan (www.chocolatefactory.com.au/locations/swan-valley; ℂ **08/9250 1588**). It's open daily 9am to 5pm, except

---

A Side of Art with Your Meal

Taylor's Art and Coffee House, 510 Great Northern Hwy., Middle Swan (www.taylorscafe.com.au; ℂ **0447 441 223** mobile phone), is a quirky cafe that is simple yet appealing. The Taylor family has converted the old family home, with corrugated iron walls and polished floorboards, into part cafe and part gallery. The outside has a shady courtyard with a mix of tables, chairs, and sculptures, many made by co-owner Michael, who runs the cafe with his sister Caroline. The cafe is open 7:30am to 4pm Tuesday to Sunday (closed public holidays).

Feeding kangaroos in Caversham Wildlife Park.

Christmas Day. Another stop if you have a sweet tooth is **Mondo Nougat,** 640 Great Northern Hwy., Herne Hill (www.mondonougat.com.au; ✆ **08/9296 0111**), run by a migrant family following their southern Italian traditions. It's open Tuesday to Sunday 9:30am to 5pm.

Caversham Wildlife Park (www.cavershamwildlife.com.au; ✆ **08/9248 1984**) is a reserve of 4,300 hectares (10,621 acres) with a collection of 200 species of mostly Western Australian wildlife, the majority kept in natural surroundings. You can stroke koalas (but not hold them), feed kangaroos, pet a possum, meet a wombat, and watch the penguins being fed. There's also an interactive farmyard, which children love. It's at Whiteman Park, West Swan, and open daily 9am to 5:30pm (last entry 4:30pm), closed Christmas Day. Admission is A$30 for adults, A$14 children 3 to 14.

Antiques lovers should browse the strip of shops on James Street, Guildford (most shops are open daily), or visit **Woodbridge House,** a beautifully restored 1883 manor house on Ford Street, West Midland (www.nationaltrust.org.au/places/woodbridge; ✆ **08/9274 2432**). The house is open Thursday to Sunday from 1 to 4pm; closed July. Admission is A$8 adults, A$5 children 5 to 16, and A$20 families of four. The **Riverside at Woodbridge cafe** opens 9am to 4pm daily (except Wed) and 8:30am to 5pm weekends and public holidays.

WHERE TO EAT IN THE SWAN VALLEY

The Abbey at Chester's PIZZA/PUB FARE   This simple, almost rustic setting provides an alternative to wine, with a focus on Belgian beers to accompany the menu. Built in 1890 as a fruit shed by Sydney Chester, it also incorporates the Heafod Glen winery cellar door, and has lovely views past gum trees to open paddocks. The menu includes wood-fired pizzas, hearty dishes including lasagna, beef pie, or burgers, and Belgian waffles. There's also a kids' menu.

8691 West Swan Rd., Henley Brook. ✆ **08/9296 3444.** www.the-abbey.com.au. Main courses A$22–A$28. Mon 10am–4pm; Wed–Thurs 10am–4pm; Fri 10am–9pm; Sat 8:30am–9pm; Sun 8:30am–5pm. Closed Tues.

Lamont Winery Cellar Door ★ SEASONAL BAR MENU   The cellar-door kitchen serves food from a "small tastes" bar menu that features fresh seasonal produce. This could be a simple baguette or elegant dishes like lamb kofta with roast beetroot hummus, or duck parfait with caramelized onion jam and crostini. Sweet treats include orange and almond cupcakes, slices of cake (like a chocolate, caramel, and macadamia-nut slice), or assorted ice creams. Eat indoors or outside at the farm tables.

85 Bisdee Rd. (off Moore Rd.), Millendon, near Upper Swan. ✆ **08/9296 4485.** www. lamonts.com.au/dining/swan-valley. Main courses A$17–A$29. Thurs–Sun and public holidays 10am–5pm. Take the Great Northern Hwy. to Baskerville, near Upper Swan, take a right onto Haddrill Rd. for 1.6km (1 mile), turn right onto Moore Rd. for 1km (just over ½ mile), and make a right onto Bisdee Rd.

New Norcia: A Touch of Spain in Australia ★★

132km (82 miles) N of Perth

It's the last thing you expect to see in the Australian bush—a Benedictine monastery town, with elegant European architecture, a fine museum, and a large collection of Renaissance art—but New Norcia is no mirage. Australia's only monastic town (and still a working community) retains an aura of peace, quiet, and calm. The town was established in 1847 by Spanish Benedictine missionaries. Visitors can tour beautifully frescoed chapels, marvel at one of the finest religious art collections in Australia, attend prayers, or eat lunch (in silence) with the 11 monks who live here, and stock up on Abbey wines, Abbey Ale, or delicious New Norcia nut cake from the monastery's 120-year-old wood-fired oven.

ESSENTIALS

ARRIVING   New Norcia is an easy 2-hour drive from Perth. From down-town, take Lord Street, which becomes Guildford Road, to Midland, and fol-low the Great Northern Highway to New Norcia. Public bus N2 from Perth stops at the New Norcia roadhouse four times a week; contact **TransWA** (www.transwa.wa.gov.au; ✆ **1300/662 205**) for details. Several tour compa-nies also operate to New Norcia.

VISITOR INFORMATION   The **New Norcia Tourist Information Cen-tre** (www.newnorcia.wa.edu.au; ✆ **08/9654 8056**) is housed in the Museum and Art Gallery, open daily 9am to 4:30pm (except Dec 25–26).

EXPLORING NEW NORCIA

The intriguing 2-hour **tours** are a must. Tickets cost A$15 adults, A$13 chil-dren 5 to 13, and A$38 families of 4. Tours depart daily at 11am and 1:30pm,

A surreal LANDSCAPE

Thousands of limestone pillars, from a few inches to over 3m (10 ft.) high, rise up out of golden sand dunes. Some are just a small fragile tracery, others are tall, solid mushroom-headed giants, while the sharp, jagged versions could well be taken for fossilized dragon's teeth. From a distance, it looks like the remnants of a deserted city, with just a few desolate parts left standing. It's all best seen around dawn or dusk. These are **The Pinnacles**, a sight worth traveling the 162km (100 miles) north of Perth for (even as a day trip).

The Pinnacles (visitpinnaclescountry. com.au) are part of the **Nambung National Park,** and a one-way gravel loop road takes drivers past thousands of the pillars. There are numerous spots where you can park, get out and stroll around, even touch them; there are no fences here. Walk over the nearest sand ridge and you'll find yourself in a desert (and deserted) landscape with only pinnacles marching to the horizon for company.

At the entrance to the park, the **Pinnacles Desert Discovery Centre** (www. parks.dpaw.wa.gov.au/site/pinnacles-desert-discovery-centre; ✆ **08/9652 7913**), with adjacent toilets and walkways to the Pinnacles, provides information on the area's geology and bio-diversity. The park and surrounding area is incredibly rich in wildflowers that burst into blossom from August to October. The center opens 9:30am to 4:30pm daily, except Christmas Day, while access to the Pinnacles is open 24/7, with an entry fee of $13 per vehicle.

To get to The Pinnacles, take the Mitchell Freeway north from Perth's city center, then follow the signs to Yanchep and/or Lancelin, and finally take the Indian Ocean Drive. The drive to the Pinnacles should take about 2 hours. Several tour companies also bring visitors here from Perth.

and they allow time for you to attend prayers with the monks (see below) if you wish. Some tours are run using a golf buggy, depending on the size of the group (a blessing on hot days). The guide leads you around some of the town's 27 National Trust–classified buildings and gives insight into the monks' lifestyle. You also see the frescoes in the old monastery chapel and in St. Ildephonsus's and St. Gertrude's colleges.

The **Museum and Art Gallery** ★ is full of relics from the monks' past—old mechanical and musical instruments, artifacts from when New Norcia was an Aboriginal mission, gifts from the queen of Spain, and an astounding collection of paintings dating from the 1400s. Allow at least an hour. The Museum and Art Gallery are open daily 9am to 4:30pm (closed Dec 25–26). Admission is A$13 for adults, A$7.50 students 4 to 13, A$30 families. Combined tickets for entry and a tour are A$25 adults, A$15 children 5 to 13, and A$60 families of 4. Apart from joining the monks for prayers in the monastery chapel six times a day (noon and 2:30pm are the most convenient for day visitors), you can join them for Mass in the Holy Trinity Abbey Church Monday to Saturday at 7:30am or Sunday at 9am.

The Pinnacles Desert.

WHERE TO EAT & STAY IN NEW NORCIA

St. Benedict's rules of hospitality are paramount, which means that part of the monastery's 24-bed guesthouse is open to visitors (male and female), but it's really for those who are looking for a quiet, reflective place to stay and don't mind abiding by a few rules. There are eight twin-share rooms with private bathrooms, and six single rooms and one twin with shared bathrooms, as well as a cottage that sleeps six. The accommodation is spartan, and the cost is A$60 per person for bed and breakfast, or $100 per person for lodging and three meals a day. Contact the guesthouse (⌀ **08/9654 8002;** guesthouse@newnorcia.wa.edu.au) to book. For other visitors, the **New Norcia Hotel** (see below) and the **Salvado Roadhouse Café** (try the lemon and jam tarts), at the entrance to the town, are the best bets.

New Norcia Hotel It is said that when they thought a Spanish royal visit to New Norcia was imminent in 1926, the monks built this grandiose hotel fit for, well, a king. Sadly, the story is a myth, and the building was used for parents visiting their children boarding at the town's colleges. The grand central staircase, soaring pressed-metal ceilings, and imposing Iberian facade hint at its former splendor. The rooms are simple but comfortable, with no phone or television, and the only bathroom facilities are shared. Still, it's nice to eat a meal in the charmingly faded dining room and sit on the massive veranda upstairs. An exclusive beer, Abbey Ale, is available here.

Great Northern Hwy. www.newnorcia.wa.edu.au/hotel/accommodation. ⌀ **08/9654 8034.** 15 units. A$100 double/twin with shared facilities; A$80 single. Continental breakfast included. **Amenities:** Restaurant; bar; no Wi-Fi.

ADELAIDE

South Australia's capital, Adelaide, is big enough to offer variety and excitement without losing its country-town vibe. On its doorstep are the vineyards of the Barossa Valley, and Australia's longest river, the Murray, spills into the sea in the east of the state; to the west the spectacular cliffs of the Great Australian Bight follow the path of the longest, straightest road in the world across the Nullarbor Plain.

Adelaide (population 1.3 million) has always been a free-spirited, free-thinking type of place—the first to outlaw sexual and racial discrimination, the first to do away with capital punishment, the first to recognize Aboriginal land rights and legalize nude swimming, and the first state to give women the vote. Adelaide was the only capital to have been settled by free settlers, rather than convicts, and was totally self-sufficient, receiving no financial backing from the British government.

Australians who have never visited Adelaide tend to dismiss the city as little more than a large country town, but that is its greatest charm. Meticulously planned by surveyor-general Colonel William Light in 1837, the city is an elegant grid of broad streets surrounded by a green belt of parkland set beside the River Torrens, between the Adelaide Hills and the waters of Gulf St. Vincent. It's an easily navigable city, and everything is within walking distance.

Any season is a good time to visit Adelaide, though May through August can be chilly and January and February hot.

ESSENTIALS

Arriving

BY PLANE

Qantas (www.qantas.com.au; © 13 13 13 in Australia), **Virgin Australia** (www.virginaustralia.com; © 13 67 89 in Australia), and **Jetstar** (www.jetstar.com; © 13 15 38 in Australia) all fly from the other major state capitals into **Adelaide Airport** (**ADL;** www.adelaideairport.com.au). **Tiger Air** (www.tigerair.com.au; © 1300/174 266 in Australia) flies from Brisbane, Melbourne, and Sydney. If you're traveling to other parts of South Australia, **Regional Express** (REX; www.rex.com.au; © 13 17 13 in Australia) offers services to some regional centers.

Between the Airport and the City

The airport is 6km (4 miles) west of the city center. **Skylink Adelaide** (www.skylinkadelaide.com) provides information on public and private transport connections from the airport. Five dedicated airport bus lines from the airport to the city center operate as **JetExpress,** run by **Adelaide Metro** (www.adelaidemetro.com.au; ☎ **1300/311 108**). The Jet Express (J1X) line is the fastest and runs every 30 minutes on weekdays. **JetBus** links the airport to Glenelg, West Beach, and the North Eastern suburbs and operates daily from 4:30am to 11:35pm.

The **Airport City Shuttle** transports passengers door-to-door from the airport to Adelaide hotels and businesses (A$10 per person one-way; shuttle runs every half-hour 8am–9pm weekdays, 8am–6pm Sat, 8am–5pm Sun); no reservations required. Major **car-rental companies** (Avis, Budget, Hertz, and Thrifty) have desks in both the international and domestic terminals.

A **taxi** to the city from the airport will cost around A$20.

BY TRAIN

The **Keswick Interstate Rail Passenger Terminal,** 2km (1¼ miles) west of the city center, is Adelaide's main railway station. Three of Australia's great long-distance train journeys pass through Adelaide. **Great Southern Railways** (www.journeybeyondrail.com.au; ☎ **1800/703 357** in Australia or 08/8313 4401) operates the *Indian Pacific, The Ghan* and *The Overland.*

The *Indian Pacific* travels from Sydney to Adelaide (trip time: 28 hr.) every Wednesday at 3pm and from Perth to Adelaide (trip time: 36 hr.) on Sunday at 10am. One-way tickets from Sydney to Adelaide start from A$779 per person. From Perth to Adelaide, the one-way fare starts from A$1,589.

Another legendary train is *The Ghan,* which runs from Adelaide to Alice Springs and on to Darwin twice a week on Sunday and Wednesday at just after noon. Trip time from Alice Springs to Adelaide is 20 hours. From Alice Springs to Adelaide and vice versa, the one-way fare starts from A$1,319 per person. From Adelaide to Darwin, which is a 2-night trip, it costs from A$2,349 per person. Platinum Class offers luxury cabins twice the size of standard Gold cabins, with double beds, full en-suite bathrooms, and lots of extras thrown in. It costs from A$2,749 per person. Children ages 4 to 15 receive a 20% discount on tickets in Gold Service only.

The *Overland* operates three weekly trips from Adelaide to Melbourne (Mon and Fri at 7:45am) and Melbourne to Adelaide (Tues and Sat at 8:05am). Trip time is around 11 hours. From Melbourne to Adelaide, one-way ticket prices are A$269 per person in premium class, including all-inclusive dining, or A$164 per person in economy class. Because this is a daylight journey, no sleepers are provided, but you will get a comfortable semi-reclining seat that's much better than most airline seats.

BY BUS

Intercity coaches arrive and depart from the central bus station, 101 Franklin St. (☎ **08/8203 7532**), near the Central Markets in the city center. **Greyhound Australia** (www.greyhound.com.au; ☎ **1300/473 946** in Australia or 08/8212

Adelaide City Centre, viewed from the north side of Torrens River in Elder Park.

5066) runs a bus from Alice Springs that takes 20 hours and costs A$308, but not from Melbourne or Sydney. **Firefly Express** (www.fireflyexpress.com.au; ℂ **1300/730 740** in Australia or 03/8318 0318) runs a daily service from Melbourne to Adelaide, leaving at 7:30am or 8:15pm, costing A$60 and taking nearly 12 hours.

Another bus company, the **Nullarbor Traveller** (www.thetraveller.net.au; ℂ **08/8687 0455**), takes adventurous travelers from Adelaide to Perth (or the other way) on a 10-day camping tour across the Nullarbor Plain. The tour costs A$1,1695, including most meals. The company also runs adventure tours to other parts of South Australia, including the Eyre Peninsula and Flinders Ranges.

BY CAR

To drive from Sydney to Adelaide on the Hume and Sturt highways takes roughly 20 hours; from Melbourne it takes around 10 hours on the Great Ocean Road and Princes Highway; from Perth it takes 32 hours on the Great Eastern and Princes highways; and from Alice Springs it takes 15 hours on the remote Stuart Highway.

Visitor Information

The **Adelaide Visitor Information Centre,** James Place (off Rundle Mall; www.cityofadelaide.com.au/visitor; ℂ **1300/588 140** in Australia), has maps and travel advice, and makes hotel and tour bookings. It's open weekdays from 9am to 5pm, weekends from 10am to 4pm, and public holidays from 11am to 3pm (closed Christmas Day and Good Friday).

Another great source of information is **www.southaustralia.com.**

City Layout

The locals sometimes refer to Adelaide as "the 20-minute city," where nothing is more than 20 minutes from the next thing. **Victoria Square** is the geographical heart of the city, surrounded by grand government buildings, some of which have been reborn as elegant hotels. This is also where you'll find the **tram** that travels the short ride to the seaside suburb of **Glenelg,** with its famous long pier and white sandy beaches. On the western side of the square is the **Central Market,** Australia's oldest continuously operating produce market (since 1869), now home to the best range of international foods in Australia. Northwest of the city center is **Port Adelaide,** a seaport and the historic maritime heart of South Australia. It's home to some of the finest colonial buildings in the state, as well as good pubs and restaurants.

MAIN ARTERIES & STREETS   Bisecting the city from south to north is the main thoroughfare, **King William Street.** Streets running perpendicular to King William Street change their names on either side; Franklin Street, for example, changes into Flinders Street. Of these cross streets, the most interesting are the restaurant strips of **Gouger** and **Rundle streets,** the latter running into the pedestrian-only shopping precinct of Rundle Mall. Another is **Hindley Street,** with inexpensive restaurants and nightlife. On the banks of the

The Glenelg jetty at sunset.

Sunset at Rundle Mall, a popular shopping destination in South Australia.

River Torrens just north of the city center, you'll find the Riverbank Precinct, the home of the Festival Centre, the Convention Centre, and the SkyCity Adelaide Casino.

North Terrace is one of the four boundary streets that mark the edge of the city center and the beginning of the parkland belt that slopes down toward the River Torrens, where you'll find almost all of the city's major attractions and museums, most of which are free.

Follow King William Street north as it crosses the River Torrens and flows into sophisticated **North Adelaide,** an area crammed with Victorian and Edwardian architecture. The main avenues in North Adelaide, **O'Connell** and **Melbourne streets,** are lined with restaurants, cafes, and bistros that offer the tastes of a multicultural city.

Getting Around Adelaide
BY PUBLIC TRANSPORTATION
Adelaide Metro (www.adelaidemetro.com.au; ✆ **1300/311 108** in Australia) runs all bus and tram services throughout the city. If you plan to get around the city on public transportation, it's a good idea to purchase a Metrocard, which costs A\$5 (plus fares). A **Metrocard Visitor Pass** provides unlimited travel on all forms of transport for 3 consecutive days and costs A\$25. It can be recharged and used as a standard Metrocard after the first 3 days. Metrocards are available at most train stations, newsagents, and the **Adelaide Metro InfoCentre**s at Adelaide Railway Station or the WH Smith Express at Adelaide Airport.

BY PUBLIC BUS

Adelaide's public bus network covers two zones. The city center is in Zone 1. The single ticket fare in Zone 1 is A$3.70 from 9am to 3pm on weekdays and Sundays and A$5.60 most other times. Kids travel for around half-price. You can buy tickets on board. You can get timetable and destination information over the phone or in person from the **Adelaide Metro InfoCentre** at (www. adelaidemetro.com.au; ✆ **08/8210 1000**), on the corner of Currie and King William streets. It's open Monday to Friday from 8am to 6pm, Saturday 9am to 5pm, and Sunday from 11am to 4pm.

The free **City Connector bus** links most major tourist attractions and will also take you to North Adelaide. Look for bus numbers 99A and 99C in the inner city and 98A and 98C for North Adelaide. Buses run every 30 minutes on weekdays and 15 minutes on weekends, from early morning to 7:15pm, and 9:15pm on Fridays.

BY TRAM

A **free tram** operates between South Terrace and the Entertainment Centre, Botanic Gardens and Festival Plaza, as well as to the west end of North Terrace. The **Glenelg Tram** runs between the city center (Victoria Square and North Terrace) and the beachside suburb of Glenelg. The journey takes 29 minutes. The Glenelg Tram is free between the Brighton Rd. tram stop and Moseley Square.

BY BICYCLE

Adelaide's parks and riverbanks are very popular with cyclists. **Adelaide Free Bikes,** the city bikes scheme, allows you free bike hire (www.bikesa.asn.au; ✆ **08/8168 9999**) for use anywhere within the city limits. All you need is either your driver's license, proof of identity card, or passport. Your ID will be held as a deposit for the duration of the hire and will be returned to you when you return your city bike. You can get bikes from 14 locations around the city including **Bicycle SA** at 53 Carrington St. Check the website for other locations. If you want a bike for longer than a day, you can pay A$25 per day for overnight use (reducing the longer you keep it). Locks and helmets are provided free.

Every January, Adelaide is host to the **Tour Down Under** (www.tourdown under.com.au; ✆ **08/8463 4701**), which attracts some of the biggest names in world cycling. Keen cyclists can take part in special legs of the race and there are routes open to children and families too.

BY CAR

Major car-rental companies are **Avis,** 136 North Terrace (✆ **08/8114 3111**); **Budget,** 274 North Terrace (✆ **08/8418 7300**); **Europcar,** 142 North Terrace (✆ **08/8114 6350**); **Hertz,** 125 North Terrace (✆ **08/8231 2856**); and **Thrifty,** 28 Hindley St. (✆ **08/8410 8977**).

The **Royal Automobile Association of South Australia (RAA),** 41 Hindmarsh Sq. (www.raa.com.au; © **13 11 11** in South Australia for emergency breakdown service, or 08/8202 4600), has route maps and provides other touring information. Its shop is open Monday to Friday 8:30am to 5pm and Saturday 9am to 4pm.

BY TAXI

The major cab companies are **Yellow Cabs** (© **13 22 27** in South Australia), **Suburban Taxis** (© **13 10 08** in South Australia), and **Adelaide Independent Taxis** (© **13 22 11** in South Australia). **Access Taxis** (© **1300/360 940** in South Australia) offers wheelchair taxis.

[FastFACTS] ADELAIDE

ATMs/Banks Banks are open Monday to Thursday 9:30am to 4pm, until 5pm Friday. ATMs are easy to find in the city center and are open 24 hrs.

Business Hours Adelaide shops are generally open Monday to Thursday 9am to 5:30pm, Friday 9am to 9pm, Saturday 9am to 5pm, and Sunday 11am to 5pm.

Dentists **Adelaide Dentalcare** (© **08/8212 5976**), is centrally located at 45 Grenfell St., in the city center. The **Adelaide Dental Hospital** is on North Terrace and George St. (© **08/8222 8222**).

Doctors & Hospitals In an emergency, call **000** or go to the casualty department of the **Royal Adelaide Hospital,** Port Rd. (© **08/7074 0000**). **The Travellers' Medical & Vaccination Centre,** Suite 1, Ground Floor, 53-67 Hindmarsh Square (www.traveldoctor.com.au; © **08/8223 6225**), offers vaccinations and travel-related medicines.

The clinic is open Monday to Friday 9am to 5pm (7pm on Wed) and Saturday 9am to 1pm.

Embassies & Consulates The United States, Canada, Britain, and New Zealand have no representation in Adelaide; see chapter 4, "Sydney," for the nearest offices.

Emergencies Dial © **000** for fire, ambulance, or police help in an emergency. This is a free call from a private or public telephone. **Lifeline** (© **131 114**) is a 24-hour emotional crisis counseling service.

Mail & Postage The **General Post Office (GPO),** 141 King William St. (© **13 76 78** in Australia), is open Monday through Friday from 9am to 5pm (closed weekends).

Newspapers & Magazines *The Advertiser* (or "Tiser"; Mon–Sat) is Adelaide's daily newspaper. *The Sunday Mail* is the main Sunday newspaper. *Blaze,* South Australia's only magazine specifically for the

gay and lesbian community, is published fortnightly and can be picked up at some 400 outlets around Adelaide and South Australia.

Pharmacies (Chemist Shops) The **Midnight Pharmacy,** 192-198 Wakefield St. (© **08/8232 4445**), is open daily 9am to midnight.

Police Dial © **000** in an emergency, or © **131 444** for police headquarters. Police are stationed 24 hours a day at 176 Grenfell St. (© **08/7322 4800**).

Safety Adelaide is a safe city, though it's wise to avoid walking along the River Torrens and through side streets near Hindley Street after dark.

Wi-Fi Adelaide has plenty of public Wi-Fi, with hotspots throughout the city center and suburbs. If you need access to a computer, try the **State Library of South Australia,** corner of North Terrace and Kintore Ave. (www.slsa.sa.gov.au; © **08/8207 7250**).

WHERE TO STAY IN ADELAIDE

Expensive

InterContinental Adelaide ★★   The 20-story InterContinental is in the heart of the city and part of the complex that includes the Adelaide Festival Centre, the Casino, the Exhibition Hall, and the Convention Centre. The property overlooks the River Torrens and nearby parklands, offering great views from the higher floors. Rooms are a generous size, with marble bathrooms. All have a small work desk and a sofa. Executive rooms are larger still and have access to the Club Lounge. The **Riverside Restaurant** is popular for its A$25 lunch deal and high tea.

North Terrace, Adelaide, SA 5000. www.ihg.com. ℂ **08/8238 2400.** 367 units. A$222–A$327 double; A$343–A$827 suites. Valet parking A$45. Bus/tram: City Connector. **Amenities:** 2 restaurants; bar; concierge; health club; Jacuzzi; heated outdoor pool; room service; free Wi-Fi.

Mount Lofty House ★★   A 15-minute drive from the city center, in the Adelaide Hills (see p. 392), Mount Lofty House is one of South Australia's most historic and beautiful boutique hotels. Built in 1852 as the summer house of one of Adelaide's founders, Arthur Hardy, it has risen from the ashes of the 1983 Ash Wednesday bushfires—which left only the stone walls standing—to full restoration by new owners. In the style of a grand country house, the rooms are all beautifully decorated, with king-size four-poster beds. The best rooms overlook the Piccadilly Valley. If the weather is misty or wet—as it sometimes can be here—there's a cozy library with board games to play in front of the fire. Service standards are high, with little left to chance. Guests can take the free history tour of the house and garden at 5pm daily and join others for a pre-dinner drink in the atmospheric cellar at 7pm.

74 Mount Lofty Summit Rd., Crafers. www.mtloftyhouse.com.au. ℂ **08/8339 6777.** 33 units. A$399–A$579 double; A$639 suite. Free parking. **Amenities:** Restaurant; bar; golf course nearby; floodlit tennis court; outdoor pool; room service; sauna; spa; free Wi-Fi.

The Playford ★★★   With its sparkling chandeliers, marble columns, and gleaming brass, the Playford is all class. This gorgeous Art Nouveau hotel is elegant but welcoming. Each room is large, and all are slightly different but come with balconies and marble bathrooms, newly renovated in 2019. Level 1 rooms open onto a lovely courtyard, while other rooms overlook it. Windows are triple-glazed to keep out city traffic noise, ensuring a good night's sleep. There are also two loft suites, each with two bedrooms and two bathrooms.

120 North Terrace. www.theplayford.com.au. ℂ **08/8213 8888.** 182 units. A$175–A$245 double. **Amenities:** Restaurant; bar; indoor heated pool; Jacuzzi; gymnasium; free Wi-Fi.

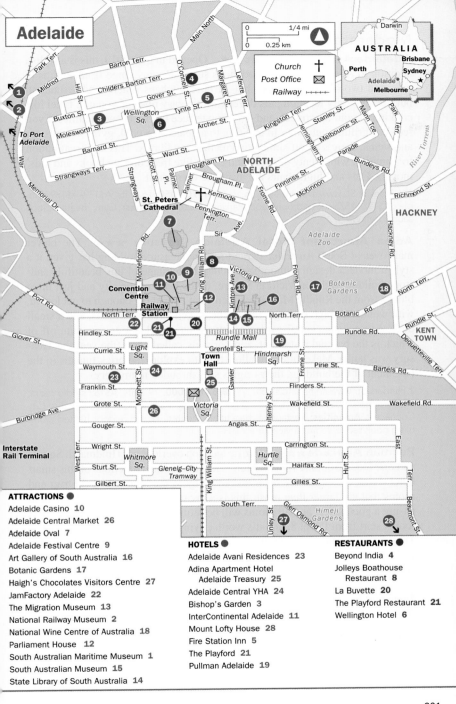

Adelaide

AUSTRALIA

Darwin
Perth
Brisbane
Sydney
Adelaide
Melbourne

Church ✝
Post Office ✉
Railway ┝━━━┥

To Port Adelaide

NORTH ADELAIDE

HACKNEY

St. Peters Cathedral

Convention Centre

Railway Station

Rundle Mall

Town Hall

KENT TOWN

Interstate Rail Terminal

ATTRACTIONS ●

Adelaide Casino 10
Adelaide Central Market 26
Adelaide Oval 7
Adelaide Festival Centre 9
Art Gallery of South Australia 16
Botanic Gardens 17
Haigh's Chocolates Visitors Centre 27
JamFactory Adelaide 22
The Migration Museum 13
National Railway Museum 2
National Wine Centre of Australia 18
Parliament House 12
South Australian Maritime Museum 1
South Australian Museum 15
State Library of South Australia 14

HOTELS ●

Adelaide Avani Residences 23
Adina Apartment Hotel
    Adelaide Treasury 25
Adelaide Central YHA 24
Bishop's Garden 3
InterContinental Adelaide 11
Mount Lofty House 28
Fire Station Inn 5
The Playford 21
Pullman Adelaide 19

RESTAURANTS ●

Beyond India 4
Jolleys Boathouse
    Restaurant 8
La Buvette 20
The Playford Restaurant 21
Wellington Hotel 6

381

Moderate

Adelaide Avani Residences ★★   Opened in mid-2019, this is a stylish addition to Adelaide's accommodations scene. Rooms range from studios to one- and two-bedroom suites—but all have kitchens. There's no restaurant, but the inner-city location puts dozens within easy reach if you don't feel like cooking in your apartment, and a rooftop terrace has barbecue facilities if you feel like grilling outdoors. In addition to a heated lap pool, gym, steam room and sauna, there's a golf simulator, cinema, and library. This is a great option for families, with plenty of space and extras like free coloring books and kids' movies. Cots and high chairs are available on request.

176 Franklin St. www.avanihotels.com. ✆ **08/8470 7050.** 76 units. A$139–A$179 double; A$195–A$259 2-bedroom apt. Parking A$20. **Amenities:** Gym; heated pool; sauna; free Wi-Fi.

Adina Apartment Hotel Adelaide Treasury ★★★   The clever makeover of South Australia's grand former Treasury building has given it a stylish modern design without sacrificing the heritage of this beautiful sandstone building right on Victoria Square, in the heart of the city and just three blocks from the Rundle Mall. Apartments are almost big enough to get lost in, with wonderful high ceilings, full kitchens, generous bathrooms, and a small desk. A gorgeous central garden courtyard has an elaborate fountain, off of which is the bar and restaurant, appropriately called **1860** (the year the Treasury was built). Make sure you allow time to explore the brick tunnels in the basement of the building, their origins still shrouded in mystery.

2 Flinders St. www.adinahotels.com. ✆ **08/8112 0000.** 79 units. A$169 studio room; A$199–A$259 1-bedroom apt; A$359 2-bedroom apt. Parking A$19 (nearby). Bus: City Connector. **Amenities:** Restaurant; bar; fitness center; Jacuzzi; indoor heated swimming pool; sauna; room service; free Wi-Fi.

Pullman Adelaide★★   A terrific location overlooking Hindmarsh Square and one block from the Rundle Mall is just one of the attractions of this smart hotel. From the expansive businesslike lobby to the brass and gold trim and rooms that are larger than most, this is a great choice. New beds throughout ensure a good sleep, and all rooms will be refurbished through 2020. The best rooms start from Level 8, and it's worth paying a little extra for better views. The large gym and excellent fitness facilities make this hotel a popular choice with sports organizations.

16 Hindmarsh Square. www.pullmanadelaide.com.au. ✆ **08/8206 8888.** 308 units. A$150–A$200 double; A$250–A$350 suite. Parking A$25 (nearby); valet parking A$45. **Amenities:** Restaurant; bar; concierge; gym; indoor heated pool; Jacuzzi; sauna; free Wi-Fi.

Inexpensive

Adelaide Central YHA ★★   This is a welcoming, clean, and well-run hostel with plenty of extras thrown in to ensure a pleasant stay. It's in a great inner-city location, right opposite leafy Light Square and a short walk from

Each of the 19 properties that are part of the **North Adelaide Heritage Group** (www.adelaideheritage.com; ☏ **08/8272 1355**) is interesting, but the standout is the elegant **Bishop's Garden** on Molesworth Street. Originally the house and gardens of Bishop Nutter Thomas, the fourth Anglican Bishop of Adelaide, it's full of gorgeous antiques and artwork collected by the current owners, Rodney and Regina Twiss. The Heritage Group also offers a suite in the old North Adelaide Fire Station; it comes complete with a full-size, bright red, very old fire engine and the original fireman's pole. All properties are within easy walking distance of the main attractions in the area. Rates range from A$250 to A$460 double.

some of the city's major attractions and the Rundle Mall. It has dorm rooms as well as private doubles and family rooms with en-suite bathrooms. Private rooms all have televisions and tea and coffee-making facilities, and some have small balconies. Free pancake breakfasts are provided daily, and 3 nights a week is A$5 pasta night—and it's not bad, either!

135 Waymouth St. www.yha.com.au. ☏ **08/8414 3010**. A$26–A$33 dorms; A$90 double with shared bathroom; A$108 en-suite double; A$115–A$129 family room (sleeps 5). Parking A$12. **Amenities:** Free Wi-Fi.

WHERE TO EAT IN ADELAIDE

With more than 600 restaurants, pubs, and cafes, Adelaide boasts more dining spots per capita than anywhere else in Australia. Many cluster in areas such as Rundle Street, Gouger Street, and North Adelaide—where you'll find almost every style of cuisine you can imagine. For cheap noodles, laksas, sushi, and cakes, head to Adelaide's popular **Central Market** (https://adelaidecentralmarket.com.au; ☏ **08/8203 7494**), behind the Hilton Adelaide between Gouger and Grote streets.

Glenelg has a host of nice cafes, including **Zest Café Gallery,** 2A Sussex St. (☏ **08/8295 3599**), which serves baguettes and bagels; **Café Blu,** 16 Holdfast Promenade (☏ **08/8350 3108**), next to the Glenelg Pier Hotel, which has good pizzas; and **The Greens Sandwich Bar & Café**, 47 Jetty Rd. (www.thegreenssandwichbarandcafe.com), in the main shopping strip, which does an all-day breakfast (until 3:30pm), bagels, and terrific sandwiches.

Expensive

Jolleys Boathouse Restaurant ★★ CONTEMPORARY Housed in an 1880s boathouse on the banks of the River Torrens with views of boats, ducks, and black swans, Jolleys is best suited for long lunches, as it closes early at night (8:30pm). It has a handful of outside tables, but if you miss out, the bright and airy interior, with its cream-colored tablecloths and directors' chairs, isn't too much of a letdown. Expect the likes of crispy-skin barramundi filet with celeriac puree, salsa verde, and Goolwa pipis (shell-fish), or chargrilled Scotch filet steak with roast potatoes, grain mustard, and horseradish butter.

1 Jolleys Lane. www.jolleysboathouse.com. © **08/8223 2891.** Main courses A$36–A$60. Sun–Fri noon–2pm; Mon–Sat 6–8:30pm.

The Playford Restaurant ★★★ CONTEMPORARY   French chef Kevin Martel brings his international experience to the Playford to create what's quite simply some of the best food I've tasted for ages. Start with something like free-range organic pork belly or pan-seared scallops, and allow yourself to be torn between the king salmon filet and charcoal-herbed lamb rump for a main course. Whatever you do, don't skip dessert. The pineapple and rum cake is divine, but if you're a chocolate lover you'll be in heaven. The restaurant also opens for breakfast.

120 North Terrace. www.theplayford.com.au. © **08/8213 8888.** Main courses A$34–A$39. Daily 6–10pm.

Moderate

Wellington Hotel ★★ PUB GRUB   The garden atrium restaurant at the back of this historic two-storied pub on Wellington Square has some of the best steaks in Adelaide. Take your pick from the pile of huge (450gm, or around 1 lb.) Coroong and Wagyu beef, and it's whisked away to be cooked just how you like it. There's also plenty of fresh seafood and Coffin Bay oysters from South Australia's Eyre Peninsula—which some people believe to be the best oysters on the planet. The wine list is predominately South Australian, and there are 20 beers on tap. The atmosphere is cheerful and friendly.

36 Wellington Sq., North Adelaide. www.wellingtonhotel.com.au. © **08/8267 1322.** Main courses A$17–A$32; steaks priced by weight A$38–A$50. Daily 9am–late (from 7:30am weekends and public holidays).

Inexpensive

Beyond India ★★ INDIAN   This busy eatery, Adelaide's favorite Indian diner, serves up a range of really, really good southern and northern Indian dishes with a modern twist. The long menu has plenty of the usual curries, but do yourself a favor and try the *lucknawi*—lamb shanks, slowly simmered in a

Top Food and Wine Tours	
Adelaide's Top Food and Wine Tours (www.topfoodandwinetours.com.au; © **08/8386 0888**) offers a range of food-based tours, including breakfast tours of the Central Market (p. 385).	These tours cost A$80 and start at 8am on Tuesday, Thursday, Friday, and Saturday; they last around 2 hours. Later tours depart at 9:30am and cost A$55.

double-glazed onion masala, one of the specialties of the house. Vegetarians will also find plenty to please them here.

170 O'Connell St., North Adelaide. www.beyondindia.net.au. *©* **08/8267 3820.** Main courses A$12–A$23. Daily noon–3pm and 5–10:30pm (till 11pm Fri and Sat).

La Buvette ★★ FRENCH   One of Adelaides's wonderful secret spots, this French wine bar is hidden down a tiny street. It serves a bar menu along with French and local wines, craft beers, and cocktails. Think charcuterie platters, terrines, and rillettes and fresh bread made daily by a local artisan baker. More substantial offerings include courgetti and Cantabrian anchovy tagliatelle pasta. Yes, there are escargots on the menu, and perhaps some crème brûlée for dessert.

27 Gresham St. www.labuvettedrinkery.com.au. *©* **08/8410 8170.** Main courses A$7–A$49. Tues–Thurs 4:30pm–10pm; Fri 4pm–midnight; Sat 4:30pm–midnight.

EXPLORING ADELAIDE

The best way to enjoy this pleasant, laidback city is to take things nice and easy. Walk beside the River Torrens, ride the tram to the beachside suburb of Glenelg, and spend the evenings sipping wine and sampling some of the country's best alfresco dining.

Adelaide Botanic Garden ★ GARDENS   Free daily guided walks of this green haven in the heart of the city are a great introduction to the gardens. Walks leave the information center at the Schomburgk Pavilion at 10:30am (except Good Friday and Christmas Day). Highlights include several grand avenues and arched walkways crowned in wisteria; the ornate 1877 glass **Palm House;** and the **Bicentennial Conservatory,** the largest single-span conservatory in the Southern Hemisphere, which houses tropical rainforest plants (and looks like a huge beetle from the air). The **Museum of Economic Botany,** the last purpose-built colonial museum in the world, is also here. The museum is open Wednesday to Sunday from 10am to 4pm.

North Terrace. www.botanicgardens.sa.gov.au. *©* **08/8222 9311.** Free. Mon–Fri 7:15am–sundown; Sat–Sun 9am–sundown.

Adelaide Central Market ★★★ FOOD MARKETS   Housed in a huge warehouse-like structure, Adelaide's Central Market, behind the Adelaide Hilton Hotel, is the largest produce market in the Southern Hemisphere. Established in 1869, it's still a great place to shop for vegetables, fruit, meat, fish, cheese, and the like, although the markets are worth popping into even if you're not looking for picnic fixings. It has more than 70 traders vying for your business, and as South Australia's most visited tourist attraction, it's always busy.

44-60 Gouger St. www.adelaidecentralmarket.com.au. *©* **08/8203 7494.** Free. Tues 7am–5:30pm; Wed–Thurs 9am–5:30pm; Fri 7am–9pm; Sat 7am–3pm. Closed public holidays. Bus: City Loop.

Most pubs are open from 11am to midnight. For all-age pubs, locals will point you toward the **Austral,** 205 Rundle St. (www.theaustral.com.au; ℂ **08/8223 4660**), which has good live music and hosts stand-up comedy during the Fringe Festival; the **Exeter,** 246 Rundle St. (www.theexeter.com.au; ℂ **08/8223 2623**); the **Lion,** at the corner of Melbourne and Jerningham streets (www.thelionhotel.com.au; ℂ **08/8367 0222**), with live entertainment every night; and the atmospheric **British Hotel,** 58 Finniss St. (www.britishhotel.com.au; ℂ **08/8267 2188**), in North Adelaide. **The Original Coopers Alehouse,** 316 Pulteney St., at Carrington Street (www.coopersalehouse.pub; ℂ **08/8223 6433**), is a popular pub for after-work drinks and the official home of South Australia's Coopers beer.

Adelaide's largest and most popular nightclub is **HQ**, at 149 Hindley Street (www.hqcomplex.com.au; ℂ **08/7123 2935**). The real action here starts in the huge main room from around 9pm Thursday to Saturday.

Right next to the Adelaide Hyatt, housed in a historic railway station, is the **Adelaide Casino** on North Terrace (www.adelaidecasino.com.au; ℂ **08/8212 2811**). The casino is open 24 hours a day, closing only on Christmas Day and Good Friday, and has four restaurants and three bars.

Adelaide Festival Centre ★ PERFORMING ARTS CENTER   The city's major concert hall, the Adelaide Festival Centre, encompasses four auditoriums: the 2,000-seat **Festival Theatre,** the 500-seat **Dunstan Playhouse,** the 350-seat **Space Centre,** and the grand old **Her Majesty's Theatre,** which will reopen in 2020 with 1,500 seats after a major redevelopment and upgrade. This is the place in Adelaide to see opera, ballet, drama, orchestral concerts, the Adelaide Symphony Orchestra, plays, and experimental drama. It's no wonder Adelaide is a UNESCO City of Music.

The complex also includes an outdoor amphitheater used for jazz, rock 'n' roll, and country-music concerts; an art gallery; a bistro; a champagne bar; and the Silver Jubilee Organ, the world's largest transportable concert-hall organ (built in Austria to commemorate Queen Elizabeth II's Silver Jubilee). King William Rd. www.adelaidefestivalcentre.com.au. ℂ **08/8216 8600** or 131 246 for the box office. Bus: City Loop.

Adelaide Oval ★★ SPORTS STADIUM   The Adelaide Oval may be the venue for international cricket matches during the summer, but it's also the site of one of the city's top adventures. **RoofClimb** (www.roofclimb.com.au; ℂ **08/8331 5222**) takes intrepid visitors to the top of the stadium for a bird's-eye view. Similar to bridge climbs, the experience takes 2 hours and costs A$109 adults and A$75 children 8 to 15. Twilight climbs cost A$119 adults, A$85 children; night climbs are A$124 per person. You can also take a guided tour of the stadium to see behind the scenes at the oval—widely regarded as

FACING PAGE: **Enjoying the shade of the Wisteria Arbor at the Adelaide Botanic Garden.**

Fruits and vegetables on display in Adelaide Central Market.

the most picturesque Test cricket ground in the world—and find out all you ever wanted to know about Australia's national game, and national hero, cricketing legend Sir Donald Bradman (who lived in Adelaide for most of his adult life). If you're a real cricket tragic, you'll also love the free **Bradman Collection Museum.** It's open daily 9am to 4pm (except public holidays and event days).

War Memorial Dr. and King William St. www.adelaideoval.com.au. ℂ **08/8211 1100.** Tours A\$25 adults, A\$15 children 5–15. Mon–Fri 8am–5:30pm; Sat–Sun 8am–4pm. Guided tours daily 10am, 11am, and 2pm (also at 1pm Sat and Sun).

Art Gallery of South Australia ★ GALLERY Adelaide's premier public art gallery has a good range of local and overseas works and a fine Asian ceramics collection. Of particular interest are Charles Hall's *Proclamation of South Australia 1836;* Nicholas Chevalier's painting of the departure of explorers Burke and Wills from Melbourne; several works by Australian painters Sidney Nolan, Albert Tucker, and Arthur Boyd; and some excellent contemporary art. For an introduction, take a free guided tour. Allow 1 to 2 hours.

North Terrace. www.agsa.sa.gov.au. ℂ **08/8207 7000.** Free. Daily 10am–5pm. Closed Dec 25. Guided tours daily 11am and 2pm. Bus: City Loop.

Haigh's Chocolates Visitors Centre ★ FACTORY If you have a sweet tooth—and perhaps have already tasted some Haigh's chocolate—head to Haigh's Chocolates Visitors Centre (a 5-min. drive from the city center) for free tastings, displays, and a peek into the chocolate production process.

Established in 1915, Haigh's is Australia's oldest chocolate manufacturer, and Adelaide locals swear it is the best-tasting chocolate anywhere. Free guided tours are run Monday and Saturday between 9am and 2:30pm and Tuesday to Friday 9am to 4pm, but you'll need to book and check the time. The factory is not fully operational on Saturday, so go midweek if you can.

154 Greenhill Rd., Parkside. www.haighschocolates.com.au. © **08/8372 7070.** Free. Mon–Fri 8:30am–5:30pm; Sat 9am–5pm. Closed public holidays. Bus: 197 from Victoria Sq.

JamFactory Adelaide ★ GALLERY/SHOPPING   This renowned creative arts center sells an excellent range of locally made ceramics, jewelry, glass, furniture, and metal items. You can also watch craftspeople at work here, including glassblowers. Meet the artists on free tours offered weekdays at 11am. There is also a changing exhibitions program. Another JamFactory is at Seppeltsfield in the Barossa Valley (p. 396).

19 Morphett St. www.jamfactory.com.au. © **08/8231 0005.** Free. Daily 10am–5pm. Closed Jan 1, Good Friday, and Dec 25–26. Bus: X1, C1. Tram: City Connector.

The Migration Museum ★★★ MUSEUM   This small museum dedicated to immigration and multiculturalism is fascinating. With touching personal displays, it tells the story of the waves of immigrants who have helped

Looking over the River Torrens to the Adelaide Oval.

shape this amalgamated society, from the boatloads of convicts who came in 1788 to the ethnic groups who have trickled in over the past 2 centuries.

82 Kintore Ave. www.migrationmuseum.com.au. ✆ **08/8207 7580.** Admission by donation. Mon–Fri 10am–5pm; Sat–Sun and public holidays 1–5pm. Closed Good Friday and Dec 25. Bus: any to North Terrace.

National Railway Museum ★ MUSEUM Train buffs will love this place. The former Port Adelaide railway yard is home to Australia's largest collection of locomotives and rolling stock. More than 100 are on display, including around 30 engines. Among the most impressive are the gigantic "Mountain" class engines, and "Tea and Sugar" trains that once ran between railway camps in the remote desert. Entrance includes a train ride, and on Sunday (Oct–Apr) a steam train operates on a coastal route between 11am and 4pm (A$8 adults, A$5 children 3–15, and A$20 families).

76 Lipson St., Port Adelaide. www.nrm.org.au. ✆ **08/8341 1690.** Admission A$12 adults, A$6 children 5–15, A$32 families of 5. Daily 10am–4:30pm. Closed Dec 25 and until noon on April 25. Train: Port Adelaide. Bus: 150.

The National Wine Centre of Australia ★★ WINE CENTER A great place to find out all about Australian wines, the National Wine Centre covers the diversity of the country's 65 wine regions. The **Tasting Gallery**'s wide range of wines and wine-tasting packages allow you to sample some of the rarest vintages. A restaurant and bar overlook the Wine Centre, which has its own vineyard. Take a 30-minute guided tour (A$15 adults, A$8 children) and learn to blend your own wine using a simulator—you may not be such a budding winemaker after all! Tours run Monday to Friday at 11am and 3pm.

Botanic Rd. (at Hackney Rd.). www.wineaustralia.com.au. ✆ **08/8313 7462.** Free. Daily 9am–6pm; public holidays 11am–5pm. Closed Jan 1, Good Friday, and Dec 25–26. Limited parking. Bus: CityLoop to Botanic Gardens.

South Australian Maritime Museum ★★★ MUSEUM Commemorating more than 150 years of maritime history, this museum is housed in an 1850s Bond Store, but also incorporates an 1863 lighthouse and three vessels moored alongside Wharf No. 1, a short walk away. The fully rigged replica of the 16m (52-ft.) ketch *Active II* is very impressive, and the three floors of exhibits showcase the best of the museum's collection of 20,000 objects. There are also re-creations of the ships' cabins in which immigrants sailed to Australia, and an interesting display about the pod of 30 dolphins who call the Port River home. Allow 1½ hours. Port Adelaide is approximately 30 minutes from the city center by bus.

126 Lipson St., Port Adelaide. www.maritimehistory.sa.gov.au. ✆ **08/8207 6255.** A$15 adults, A$6 children, A$35 family of 7. Daily 10am–5pm. Closed Good Friday and Dec 25. Bus: 151 or 153 from North Terrace opposite Parliament House to stop 40 (Port Adelaide). Train: Port Adelaide.

South Australian Museum ★★ MUSEUM The first thing you see when arriving at the museum is a sad-looking collection of stuffed native animals (including a few extinct marsupials, such as the Tasmanian tiger, and

World-class Festivals in Adelaide

Adelaide is home to Australia's largest performing arts festival, the **Adelaide Festival ★**, which showcases literary and visual arts as well as dance, opera, classical music, jazz, cabaret, and comedy. The festival also includes a Writers' Week and the **Adelaide Fringe Festival.** Visit **www.adelaidefestival.com.au**. It takes place over 3 weeks in March in even-numbered years.

In February or March, the 3-day **WOMADelaide Festival** of world music takes place. Crowds of 60,000 or more turn up to watch the performances of Australian and international artists. Visit **www.womadelaide.com.au**.

Miss Siam, an Indian elephant who lived and died in the Adelaide Zoo). Don't be put off; the star attraction of this interesting museum is the Australian Aboriginal Cultures Gallery. On display is an extensive collection of utensils, spears, tools, bush medicine, food samples, photographs, and the like. There's also a good collection of Papua New Guinea artifacts; and a fascinating gallery devoted to South Australia's most famous explorer, Antarctic expedition leader Douglas Mawson (the man on the Australian A$100 note). The museum offers free guided tours Monday to Friday at 11am and weekends and public holidays at 2 and 3pm.

North Terrace, btw. State Library and Art Gallery of South Australia. www.samuseum. sa.gov.au. ℂ **08/8207 7500.** Free. Daily 10am–5pm. Closed Good Friday and Dec 25, and until noon on April 25.

State Library of South Australia ★★ LIBRARY   A contemporary wing provides the entrance to the library, but what you really need to see here is the Mortlake Chamber. There are definite shades of Harry Potter's Hogwarts here, with soaring ceilings, two gallery walls lined with books, and study nooks complete with carved wooden chairs and desks. The ground level has interesting displays of aspects of Adelaide life and culture. Take a look at the Treasures Wall on Level 1 before crossing the walkway across to the Mortlake Chamber.

North Terrace (at Kintore Ave.). www.slsa.sa.gov.au. ℂ **08/8207 7250.** Free. Daily 10am–5pm (some areas such as the gallery stay open later). Closed public holidays.

ORGANIZED TOURS

BUS TOURS   **Gray Line** (www.grayline.com.au; ℂ **1300/858 687** in Australia) operates a half-day city sightseeing tour for A$67 adults and A$34 children. It operates from 9:15am to noon daily. A full day "Best of Adelaide" tour costs A$179 adults and A$132 children. Some tours incorporate a river cruise or visit to the Adelaide Oval (p. 387).

WALKING TOURS   Free walking tours are run by the **Adelaide Greeters** (www.cityofadelaide.com.au/adelaidegreeters; ℂ **08/8203 7203**) every day from 9am to 5pm. Tours generally last between 2 and 4 hours, and can be tailored to your interests, such as sports, architecture, arts, or other topics. It's a great way to orient yourself and learn about the city through a local's eyes. Book ahead—3 days if you can. The Adelaide Visitor Information Centre (p. 375) runs free 30-minute **First Steps** orientation tours every weekday (except public holidays) at 9:30am.

DAY TRIPS FROM ADELAIDE

The Adelaide Hills ★★★

15km (9 miles) SE of Adelaide

Just a 25-minute drive from Adelaide are the tree-lined slopes and pretty valleys, orchards, vineyards, winding roads, and historic townships of the Adelaide Hills. You might want to walk part of the **Heysen Trail** (see p. 394), browse the shops in Hahndorf, stop in Melba's Chocolate Factory in Woodside, or visit Cleland Wildlife Park. Otherwise, it's a nice outing just to hit the road and drive.

ESSENTIALS

ARRIVING The Adelaide Hills are 25 minutes from Adelaide by car on the South Eastern Freeway. **Adelaide Sightseeing** (www.adelaidesightseeing. com.au; ℂ **1300/769 762** in Australia) runs outings to the quaint but touristy town of Hahndorf (see below). An afternoon excursion to Hahndorf costs A$75 for adults and A$40 for children 3 to 14 (cheaper if booked online).

VISITOR INFORMATION Visitor information and bookings are available through the **Adelaide Hills Visitor Centre,** 68 Mount Barker Rd., Hahndorf (www.adelaidehills.org.au; ℂ **08/8393 7600**). It's open Monday through Friday from 9am to 5pm, weekends and public holidays 10am to 4pm (closed Christmas Day).

EXPLORING THE ADELAIDE HILLS

The historic German-style village of **Hahndorf** (pop. 2,670) is one of South Australia's most popular tourist destinations. Lutherans fleeing religious persecution in eastern Prussia founded the town, which is 29km (18 miles) southeast of Adelaide, in 1839. They brought their winemaking skills, foods, and architectural inheritance. Hahndorf still resembles a small German town and is included on the State Heritage List as a Historical German Settlement. The main street is packed with a range of craft shops, art galleries, and specialty shops, and can become quite crowded on weekends.

Visitors also come to the Adelaide Hills to visit the village of **Woodside** for **Melba's Chocolate Factory**, 22 Henry St. (www.melbaschocolates.com.au; ℂ **08/8389 7868**), where chocoholics will find a huge range of handmade treats—and you can watch them being made on historic machinery. Most likely though, you'll just want to gobble up as much as you can. Melba's is part of **Woodside Heritage Village,** a complex that includes the fantastic cheese maker **Woodside Cheese Wrights** (www.woodsidecheese.com.au; ℂ **08/8389 7877**). It's open daily from 11am to 4pm (closed Good Friday, Christmas Day and New Year's Day).

ADELAIDE HILLS ATTRACTIONS

National Motor Museum ★★★ MUSEUM   Even if you don't like cars, it's easy to spend a couple of hours in this museum, which is one of Adelaide's best. Not just for motor-heads, this museum examines the social influence of the motor car in Australia and has some great fun, interactive family exhibits, as well as one of the largest collections of cars, motorcycles, and commercial vehicles in the world, more than 300 vehicles dating from the turn of the century.

Shannon St., Birdwood. www.nationalmotormuseum.com.au. ✆ **08/8568 4000.** A$16 adults, A$6.50 children 5–15, A$35 family of 8. Daily 10am–5pm. Closed Dec 25.

Beerenberg Strawberry Farm ★ FARM   By now you've probably come across the cute little pots of delicious Beerenberg jams (jelly), favorites at hotel breakfast tables across Australia. Here you can taste (and buy) some of the extensive range of other jams, jellies, sauces, and pickles from this family-run farm. During strawberry season (Nov–Apr), you can grab a bucket from the shop and pick your own strawberries. You can't get much fresher than that!

Mount Barker Rd., Hahndorf. www.beerenberg.com.au. ✆ **08/8388 7272.** Admission to strawberry patch A$4 adults, free for children 12 and under. Daily (except Dec 25) 9am–5pm.

Main Street shop in the German-style village of Hahndorf.

Hiking the Heysen Trail

The **Heysen Trail** (www.heysentrail.com. au) is the longest dedicated walking trail in Australia, covering 1,200km (745 miles) through farmland, wine regions, and the arid South Australian Outback region of the Flinders Ranges. But you don't need to do the whole thing; sections of the trail can be accessed as short walks, loops, circuits, and bushwalks. Check the website for details.

The Cedars ★★★ HOUSE MUSEUM On the outskirts of Hahndorf, the homestead of famous Australian landscape painter Hans Heysen has virtually remained unchanged since the 1930s. It's furnished with original artifacts, family treasures, and paintings, including many portraits and still lifes. His studio is just as he left it, and inside the house is the studio of his daughter, Nora, a renowned artist in her own right, who died in 2003. Follow a walking trail around the 60-hectare (148-acre) property to the artist's favorite painting sites. You can tour the studios without a guide, but admission to the house is only by guided tour.

Heysen Rd., Hahndorf. www.hansheysen.com.au. *✆* **08/8388 7277.** Admission A$15 (free for children 14 and under) for full tour, A$10 for self-guided tour of studios and grounds. Tues–Sun and public holidays 10am–4:30pm. Guided tours at 11am, 1pm, and 3pm daily (except Mon). Closed Good Friday and Dec 25–26.

Cleland Wildlife Park ★ WILDLIFE PARK Almost at the top of Mount Lofty, this wildlife park is home to the usual Australian animals, including large red kangaroos. Visitors can meet at the Tasmanian devil enclosure at 2pm and join the animal-feed run by following a tractor around the park as it drops off food. Koala holding is allowed during photo sessions from 2 to 3pm daily (but not on very hot summer days); there's an additional session from 11am to noon on Sunday and public holidays. The privilege will cost A$31 per photo. The park also has a very good wetlands aviary. If you fancy exploring the park after dark, public guided nighttime walks cost A$51 adults and A$41 children.

365 Mount Lofty Summit Rd., Crafers. www.clelandwildlifepark.sa.gov.au. *✆* **08/8339 2444.** A$26 adults, A$12 children 4–15, A$61 families of 4. Daily 9:30am–5pm (last entry 4:30pm). Closed Dec 25.

WHERE TO EAT IN THE ADELAIDE HILLS

Hardy's Verandah Restaurant ★★★ CONTEMPORARY Choose from a "short story" or "full story" menu at this elegant restaurant in the historic Mount Lofty House. Whichever you choose, you'll be assured of quality dishes that look as good as they taste. The Wagyu beef brisket falls apart on your fork, and is teamed with riverine strip loin, scallop, and pearl onion; and the spiced lamb porterhouse with vegetatouille and raisin puree is also excellent. For dessert—if you can manage it—try the coconut sorbet with puffed rice and coriander curd, or dark chocolate with honeycomb wafer. Pace yourself; it's worth savoring every morsel.

1 Mawson Dr., Crafers. www.hardysverandahrestaurant.com.au. ℂ **08/8339 6777.** Short story: 2 courses A$79, 3 courses A$99, 4 courses A$119; Full story: 7 courses A$179 or A$120 with matching wines. Daily 6–10pm; Sat–Sun noon–2:30pm.

The Summit Cafe ★★ CAFE   Have lunch at this cafe atop Mount Lofty while enjoying the view back to Adelaide (weather permitting!). The menu offers daily specials of soup, pasta, and a curry, along with salads, burgers, fish-and-chips, pizza, and more interesting dishes such as lime and chili squid. It's fully licensed, so you can have a glass of wine too. It's also open for breakfast.

Mount Lofty Summit Rd., Crafers. www.mtloftysummit.com. ℂ **08/8339 2600.** Main courses A$15–A$34. Mon–Fri 9am–11:30am and noon–3:30pm; Sat–Sun 8:30am–11:30am and noon–3:30pm.

The Barossa Valley ★★

70km (43 miles) NE of Adelaide

More than a quarter of Australia's wines, and a disproportionate number of top labels, originate in the Barossa and Eden valleys—collectively known as **The Barossa.** The Barossa Valley is a snug collection of country towns surrounded by vineyards that is very easy to explore on a day trip from Adelaide. Distances between towns are small, and wineries are next door to one another, so you can visit a few in a very short time—just make sure you have a designated driver!

The Barossa has been famous for its rich, big-bodied Shiraz (Syrah) for many years, but the region's heritage of growing, curing, preserving, and cooking its own unique foods is less well known. The largely Lutheran settlers who came here 160 years ago have left not only a legacy of beautiful churches but a bounty of wonderful small meats, sausages, preserved fruits, cheeses, and delicious breads, all unique to the valley. Most restaurants and cafes pride themselves on serving as much local produce as possible. Tasting plates are served at many cellar doors.

Focal points of the area are **Tanunda,** the nearest town to the city, **Nuriootpa,** the center of the rural services industry; and **Angaston,** farthest from Adelaide. Expect nice architecture, crafts and antiques shops, and specialty food outlets.

The best times to visit the Barossa and other South Australian wine regions are in the spring (Sept–Oct), when it's not too hot and trees and shrubs are in flower, and in the fall (Apr–May), when leaves turn red. The main wine harvest is in late summer and early autumn (Feb–Apr). The least crowded time is winter (June–Aug).

ESSENTIALS

ARRIVING   If you have a car (by far the most flexible way to visit), take the scenic route from Adelaide. It takes about half an hour longer than the Main North Road through Gawler, but the trip is well worth it. Follow signs to

Birdwood, Springton, Mount Pleasant, and Angaston. Public buses run infrequently to the major centers from Adelaide. There are no buses between wineries.

Adelaide Sightseeing (www.adelaidesightseeing.com.au; ✆ **08/8413 6199**) offers a day trip from Adelaide, stopping off at four wineries. It costs A$129 for adults and A$60 for children (although they'll probably be bored), including lunch.

VISITOR INFORMATION The **Barossa Visitor Information Centre,** 66–68 Murray St., Tanunda, SA 5352 (www.barossa.com; ✆ **08/8563 0600**), is open Monday through Friday from 9am to 5pm and Saturday and Sunday from 10am to 4pm.

TOURING THE WINERIES

With some 75 wineries offering free cellar-door tastings, daily tours charting the winemaking process, or both, you won't be stuck for places to visit. All wineries are well signposted, and most are open every day. Below are just a few of my favorite places, but don't be shy about stopping whenever you come across a winery that takes your fancy. *A tip:* Try a sparkling red; it's the perfect red to drink in the hot Australian summer.

Jacobs Creek Visitor Centre ★ This large winery was established in 1847 and is the home of many award-winning wines, now sold worldwide. There are various activities on offer, but probably the most fun is learning how to blend wine. If you fancy creating your own wine—and taking home a personalized bottle—you can do so at 3pm and 4pm daily. The session takes about 45 minutes and you must be over 18 to take part; it costs A$65 per person. There's also a restaurant and plenty of wine tastings on offer.

2129 Barossa Valley Way, Rowland Flat. www.jacobscreek.com. ✆ **08/8521 3000.** Daily 10am–5pm. Closed Good Friday and Dec 25.

Penfolds ★ *Wine Spectator* magazine named Penfolds' iconic 1990 vintage Grange the "Best Red Wine in the World"—not bad considering Penfolds started when Dr. Christopher Rawson planted a few vines in 1844 to make wine for his patients. For A$150 you can take a tour of Penfolds that includes a taste of the legendary Grange (the 2015 vintage sells for A$900 a bottle). Tours are daily at 2pm, and bookings are essential, at least 24 hours ahead. The winery also has the largest oak barrel maturation cellars in the Southern Hemisphere.

30 Tanunda Rd., Nuriootpa. www.penfolds.com. ✆ **08/8568 8408.** Daily 9am–5pm, including public holidays (except Dec 25 and 26).

Seppeltsfield ★★ This National Trust–listed property was founded in 1857 by Joseph Seppelt, an immigrant from Silesia. The wine tour around the gardens and bluestone buildings is well worth doing. On a nearby slope, check out the family's Romanesque mausoleum, flanked by tall roadside palms, built during the 1930s recession to keep winery workers employed. The Heritage Tour runs daily at 11:30am and 3:30pm and costs A$15 (including

Vineyard in the Barossa Valley.

tastings); other tours cover everything from rare wines to barrel-making. All tours must be booked in advance.

3746 Seppeltsfield Rd., Seppeltsfield. www.seppeltsfield.com.au. ℂ **08/8568 6200.** Daily 10:30am–5pm. Tastings A$5; tours A$8–A$79 (including tastings).

Wolf Blass ★   This winery's Germanic-style black-label vintages have an excellent international reputation, while its cheaper yellow-label vintages have long been the toast of many an Australian dinner party. The **Wolf Blass Gallery & Museum** (www.wolfblassgm.com.au) is in the main street of Hahndorf, in the Adelaide Hills (p. 392) and worth a look.

97 Sturt Hwy., Nurioootpa. www.wolfblass.com. ℂ **08/8568 7311.** Daily 10am–4:30pm. Closed Dec 25.

Yalumba ★   This winery was built in 1849, making it the oldest family-owned winemaking business in Australia. It's also huge. The winery's **Signature Red Cabernet-Shiraz** ★ is among the best you'll ever taste. Several tours are offered, including an hour of tastings (A$35 per person) or a cooperage tour on weekdays at 9:50am, for A$40 per person, where you can see barrel-makers in action.

40 Eden Valley Rd., Angaston. www.yalumba.com.au. ℂ **08/8561 3309.** Daily 10am–5pm.

WHERE TO EAT IN THE BAROSSA VALLEY

The Barossa prides itself on its cuisine as well as its wine, so you'll find plenty of places of note to eat, many of them serving traditional German food. A hot spot for lunch or dinner is **Vintners Bar & Grill,** corner of Stockwell and Angaston roads, Angaston (www.vintners.com.au; ℂ **08/8564 2488**). Try the

AN overnight **VISIT**

If the lure of the wineries is so great that you think you'll need more than a day to explore—or you're simply looking for somewhere special to stay in the Barossa—the luxurious all-suite hotel **The Louise** (www.thelouise.com.au; ✆ **08/8562 2722**) is just the place. All of the 15 large, gorgeous rooms have great views over the valley and surrounding vineyards, best enjoyed from your own spacious gated courtyard and secluded rear terrace with a bottle of local wine. Inside, suites have wonderful bathtubs (with your own yellow rubber duck) as well as huge showers that also open out to reveal a private outdoor shower (some hardy guests don't care if it's cool out, so great is the lure). Some suites also have underfloor heating. The Louise's American owners, Jim and Helen Carreker, who fell in love with the region in 2005, have left nothing to chance, and it shows. The hotel has an outdoor infinity pool overlooking the surrounding vineyards, a sauna, gymnasium, and bikes for you to use free of charge. It's also home to one of the best restaurants in the Barossa Valley, **Appellation** (see below). Rooms have all amenities, including a minibar and free Wi-Fi, and cost from A$575 to A$1,780, including full breakfast. You'll find The Louise at the corner of Seppeltsfield and Stonewell roads, Marananga. Note that both hotel and restaurant are closed every July for maintenance and refurbishment.

Moroccan spiced kangaroo, with chickpea fritter, peas, and beets. Main courses cost A$36 to A$55, and it's open for lunch daily and Monday through Saturday for dinner. Another choice is **Salter's Kitchen** at Saltram Wines, Murray St., Angaston (www.saltramwines.com.au; ✆ **08/8561 0200**); local produce is the specialty, with dishes such as crumbed lamb cutlets, a chicken tarragon and truffle burger, or fried pork belly with cauliflower puree. Main courses are A$25 to A$31. It's open daily for lunch, except Christmas Day.

Perhaps the best German-style bakery in the valley is the **Lyndoch Bakery,** on the Barossa Valley Way, Lyndoch (www.lyndochbakery.com.au; ✆ **08/8524 4422**). One place not to miss **Maggie's Farm Shop** on Pheasant Farm Road, Nuriootpa (www.maggiebeer.com.au; ✆ **08/8562 4477**), the domain of celebrity foodie and chef Maggie Beer. You can have lunch at The Eatery (run by Maggie's daughter Elli) or sample some of the extensive range of Maggie Beer Foods, Barossa Farm Produce, and both Pheasant Farm and Beer Brothers wines, or just stock up on picnic fare. It's open daily (except major holidays) 10:30am to 5pm.

Appellation ★★★ CONTEMPORARY You may have to book up to a month in advance to get a table at Appellation, one of Barossa's best restaurants. Appellation is at The Louise luxury retreat (see above), and hotel guests are assured of a table if they reserve when booking their stay. Locals love this place too, for its fresh and innovative food, excellent wines, and relaxed atmosphere. Tables are nicely spaced, and you can opt for the multi-course set menus or make choices from the Selections Menu. A three-course menu might go like this: citrus cured salmon with horseradish, ice plant, and toasted brioche crumbs, followed by rolled porchetta with charred apple dust, pickled fennel, and a honey mustard dressing, with crushed kipfler potatoes, spring onion, and sour cream, finishing with a delectable rhubarb and pistachio sponge cake with baked vanilla custard. You won't be disappointed.

Corner Seppeltsfield and Stonewell rds., Maranaga. www.thelouise.com.au/dine. ⓒ **08/8562 2722.** 3-course set menu A$59; 5-course set menu (with wine pairings) A$200; 4 choices from the Selections Menu A$145. Wed–Sun 6:30pm–9:30pm. Closed during July.

The Fleurieu Peninsula ★★★

40km (25 miles) S of Adelaide

Practically on the outskirts of Adelaide, the Fleurieu Peninsula is one of South Australia's most popular holiday destinations, famous for its wine, gourmet produce, breathtakingly scenic coastline, and wildlife—expect to see plenty of kangaroos, sea lions, seals, dolphins, whales (the season is June–Oct), and Little Penguins, the world's smallest penguin species.

The heart of the wine-growing area is **McLaren Vale,** where olives and almond groves are scattered among the 50-plus vineyards, although you'll also find some very good wineries in and around **Currency Creek** and **Lang-horne Creek,** on the southeastern side of the peninsula. On Saturday

Port Noarlunga South beach, the Fleurieu Peninsula.

mornings, the tiny village of **Willunga,** just a few minutes' drive from McLaren Vale, comes alive with the weekly farmer's markets, where local growers and producers sell whatever they've picked or baked that morning. There are lots of fresh organic vegetables, boutique cheeses, homemade preserves, freshly baked sourdough breads, and delicious pies and pastries, as well as the famous local olive oil and almonds. On the second Saturday of the month, the stalls spill over into the Quarry markets across the road, where vendors sell bric-a-brac, secondhand books, and handmade jewelry and clothes.

Settled by Scottish immigrants in the 1830s, pretty **Stathalbyn** is a heritage town with 30 or so historic buildings. It's a popular place to shop for antiques and crafts, as is the equally quaint township of **Port Elliot. Victor Harbor** on the southern ocean side is the most popular seaside resort, with lots of family attractions, and a great place to go bushwalking (hiking), whale-watching, and surfing. The historic river port of **Goolwa** is at the mouth of the Murray River, Australia's longest river.

ESSENTIALS

ARRIVING   McLaren Vale is a 45-minute drive south from Adelaide via the Southern Expressway, or you can take the slower Main South Road.

GETTING AROUND   Adelaide Metro operates a public bus service from Adelaide and a public train service to Noarlunga (see www.adelaidemetro. com.au for details). **Premier Stateliner Coaches (© 08/8415 5555)** runs daily services to McLaren Vale for A$8.70 adults or A$4.35 children; and to Victor Harbor, Port Elliot, and Goolwa, all of which cost A$20 for adults and A$10 for children.

VISITOR INFORMATION   Visitor information and bookings are available through the **Victor Harbor Visitor Information Centre,** The Causeway, Victor Harbor, SA 5211 (https://encountervictorharbor.com.au; © **08/8552 5738**), and the **McLaren Vale & Fleurieu Visitor Centre,** Main Road, McLaren Vale, SA 5171 (www.visitonkaparinga.com; © **08/8323 9944**). Both centers are open daily. See also **www.southaustralia.com/FleurieuPeninsula.aspx**.

EXPLORING THE FLEURIEU PENINSULA

The Cockle Train ★★★ STEAM TRAIN   Take a ride along the oldest public railway line in Australia between the towns of Victor Harbor, Port Elliot, Middleton, and Goolwa aboard the historic, iconic Cockle Train. Built in 1887 to ferry goods from the last navigable port on the Murray River (Goolwa) to the seaports of Port Elliot and Victor Harbor, the 30-minute steam-train trip quickly became a popular trip for tourists as well, earning its rather quaint name from the large cockles that the sandy surf beaches of Goolwa are famous for. The train only runs on Wednesday and Sunday (daily during school holidays), so a good alternative if you've got bicycles with you is the 30km (19-mile) **Encounter Bikeway,** a dedicated bike path between the Bluff and Signal Point at Goolwa Wharf. The sealed path is suitable both for escorted toddlers on tricycles and those wanting a gentle, seaside cycle. (You can also walk a section of it.) Between June and October, look for southern right whales as you ride.

C **1300/655 991** in Australia. www.steamrangerheritagerailway.org. Return fares cost A$31 adults, A$16 children, A$76 families. Buy tickets at the station (Port Elliott only accepts cash). Runs most Sun and Wed but with varying timetables; to confirm train running times on the day, call either station

The d'Arenberg Cube ★★★ LANDMARK/WINERY

First, d'Arenberg is a winery, run since 1912 and now in the fourth generation of the Osborn family. But more than that, d'Arenberg is one of the most unusual wineries you may ever visit. The cellar door and restaurant here have been designed to look like a giant cube—sort of like a glass Rubik's Cube with all the sides open. Don't miss the **Alternate Realities Museum** on the ground floor, where the art installations will make your head spin. Through May 2020, an exhibition of 23 works by **Salvador Dali,** including bronze sculptures and graphic artworks, is on display. Entry to the exhibition is A$20 per person, including entry to the Cube.

58 Osborn Rd., McLaren Vale. www.darenberg.com.au. *C* **08/8329 4888.** Free to diners; A$10 per person (under 2s free). Daily 10am–5pm; restaurant open for lunch Thurs–Sun.

Encounter Coast Discovery Centre and Old Customs and Station Masters House ★★★ MUSEUM

Victor Harbor is on the shores of Encounter Bay, where in 1802, Englishman Matthew Flinders met the French explorer Nicholas Baudin while both were circumnavigating Australia. England and France were at war at the time, but despite this, the meeting between the two scientists was friendly and Flinders named the bay after the encounter. You can learn all about the meeting between English and French naval captains in this great museum, as well as plenty of local history. A great rainy day activity.

2 Flinders Parade, Victor Harbor. *C* **08/8552 5388.** Admission A$5 adults, A$3 children, A$13 families. Daily 1–4pm. Closed Good Friday and Dec 25.

Granite Island Recreation Park ★★★ NATURAL ATTRACTION

Take the country's only horse-drawn tram out to Granite Island, once a whaling station but now a lovely park linked to the township of Victor Harbor by a wooden causeway. It's home to a colony of 700 or so Little Penguins. The tramway is open daily 10am to 4pm, and a return trip costs A$10 for adults, A$7 for children, or A$28 for a family of four; but it's a nice walk out along the causeway, as you'll often see fur seals lazily drifting beneath the piers. If you want to see the penguins, you'll need to join one of the evening guided tours run by National Parks. Just remember, penguins have right of way!

Granite Island, Victor Harbor. www.graniteisland.com.au. *C* **08/8551 0777.** Penguin tours A$25; bookings essential. Tours run daily but departure times vary as sunset times and daylight saving times change. Telephone or check website for details.

Not your typical food and wine festival, which tends to be a more refined sip-and-taste affair, the annual **Sea and Vines Festival** in McLaren Vale is a rollicking celebration of food and wine that's more like a giant progressive party. Held over 3 days in early June, it has become one of the biggest of its type in South Australia, attracting upwards of 40,000 people each year. The valley's more than 26 wineries put up marquees, set out tables, bring in their favorite bands, and serve their wines matched up with local seafood cooked by local restaurants. To get the best out of the festival, get a copy of the program before you go and plan your day, because you'll need to book in advance. Tickets and more information are available at **www.seaandvines.com. au** or **moshtix.com.au**.

South Australian Whale Centre ★★★ MUSEUM Victor Harbor is one of the easiest places in South Australia to see southern right whales, who swim into the sheltered waters of Encounter Bay each winter to breed. They often come very close to shore along the coastline of the peninsula, and the town has a number of good vantage points from which to spot them. The South Australian Whale Centre keeps records of whale sightings, so call in to see where they are. The Centre also has an extensive collection of displays, murals, and videos, with lots of fun, hands-on activities for the kids.

2 Railway Terrace, Victor Harbor. www.sawhalecentre.com. ✆ **08/8551 0750.** A$9 adults, A$4.50 children 14 and under, A$24 families of 4. Daily 10:30am–5pm. Closed Dec 25.

WHERE TO EAT ON THE FLEURIEU PENINSULA

There's no shortage of great places to eat in the Fleurieu. For restaurants with million-dollar views, it's hard to top the cliff-top **Star of Greece Cafe ★★★** on the Esplanade, Port Willunga (www.starofgreece.com.au; ✆ **08/8557 7420**), or the **Flying Fish Cafe ★★★** on the water's edge of Horseshoe Bay, Port Elliot (www.flyingfishcafe.com.au; ✆ **08/8554 3504**). Both serve up fantastic fresh seafood. The Star of Greece is open Wednesday to Sunday noon to 3pm and Friday and Saturday for dinner from 6pm. Mains cost A$28 to A$35. The Flying Fish Cafe is open daily noon to 3pm, and 6pm to 8pm Friday and Saturday; mains cost A$29 to A$36. Or try the restaurants below, which have more of an emphasis on food than views.

Russell's Pizza ★ PIZZA This quirky pizzeria is housed in an eclectically decorated 1800 stone cottage. Don't expect your average pizza, though: Toppings include such delights as Turkish-style slow-cooked lamb or bleu cheese and walnut. It's only open on Friday and Saturday nights, so competition for tables can be fierce. Kids (4–12) eat for A$14 each and teens (12–17) for A$22.

13 High St., Willunga. www.russellspizza.com. ✆ **08/8556 2571.** 2 courses A$39; 3 courses A$44; pizza only A$26–A$29. Fri–Sat 6pm–late (and Thurs in Dec and Jan).

Salopian Inn ★★★ MODERN AUSTRALIAN This award-winning dining institution is housed in an 1850s slate-floored stone building. It offers superb seasonal, regional food in a relaxed country setting among the vines. If it's on the menu, try the cauliflower pakora, or the rabbit san choy bau for starters, or the pan-roasted snapper. An A$80 tasting menu introduces all the best dishes on the menu.

Corner of McMurtrie and McLaren Vale Main rds., McLaren Vale. www.salopian.com.au. ℗ **08/8323 8769.** Mains A$30–A$38. Lunch daily; dinner Thurs–Sat.

TASMANIA

A place of wild beauty colored by a tragic past, the Australian island of Tasmania stands separated from the rest of Australia by Bass Strait. For centuries, this island state has forged its own, not always smooth, path. While geographical isolation has preserved much of its unique wilderness, it has still had to contend with the worst efforts of man to spoil it at times.

Tasmanians have always been at the forefront of Australia's environmental movement, and some of Australia's fiercest battles over development have been waged in Tasmania. Among the issues Tasmania is grappling with right now are the possible extinction of Tasmanian devils due to a spreading facial-tumor disease (p. 420); reports that foxes have been introduced to this predator-free environment; and ongoing resistance against proposals for pulp mills that may hasten the destruction of forestlands. You will not, despite local legend, run into any Tasmanian tigers here—the last known one died in 1936 (despite more recent "sightings").

Tasmania's history has been a violent one. In the 19th century, the island was used as a dumping ground for convicts from Great Britain, often transported for petty crimes. The brutal system of control, still evident in the ruins at Port Arthur and elsewhere, spilled over into persecution of the native population. The last full-blooded Tasmanian Aborigine died in 1876, some 15 years after the last convict transportation.

Despite its dark history, Tasmania is a tranquil and largely unspoiled place to visit—more than 20% of it has been declared a World Heritage area, and nearly a third of the island is protected by national parks. The locals are friendly and hospitable—and have a reputation for producing some of Australia's best food. Remnants of the Aboriginal people who lived here for thousands of years are evident in rock paintings, engravings, and storytelling, as well as a pervasive aura of spirituality that still holds in places that modern civilization has not yet reached.

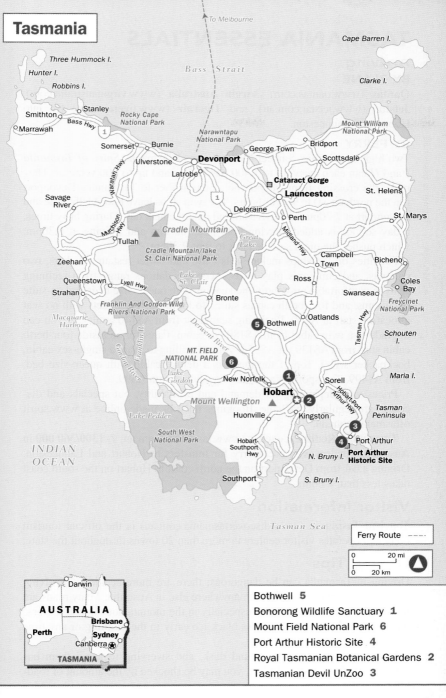

Tasmania

To Melbourne

Cape Barren I.

Three Hummock I.

Hunter I.

Bass Strait

Robbins I.

Clarke I.

Stanley

Smithton

Bass Hwy

Rocky Cape
National Park

Marrawah

Somerset

Burnie

Narawntapu
National Park

Mount William
National Park

Ulverstone

Devonport

George Town

Bridport

Latrobe

Scottsdale

Waratah Hwy

■ Cataract Gorge

St. Helens

Savage
River

Deloraine

Launceston

Murchison Hwy

Perth

St. Marys

Cradle Mountain

Great
Lake

Tullah

Cradle Mountain/lake
St. Clair National Park

Campbell
Town

Bicheno

Zeehan

Lake
St. Clair

Ross

Midland Hwy

Coles
Bay

Queenstown

Lyell Hwy

Swansea

Strahan

Bronte

Franklin And Gordon Wild
Rivers National Park

Freycinet
National Park

*Macquarie
Harbour*

Oatlands

Schouten
I.

5 Bothwell

Derwent River

6

MT. FIELD
NATIONAL PARK

Franklin River

Gordon River

Lake
Gordon

New Norfolk

1

Sorell

Maria I.

Hobart-Port Arthur Hwy

Hobart

Tasman Hwy

Tasman
Peninsula

Mount Wellington ▲

2

Lake Pedder

Huonville

Kingston

3 Port Arthur

South West
National Park

4

**Port Arthur
Historic Site**

INDIAN
OCEAN

Hobart-
Southport
Hwy

N. Bruny I.

Southport

S. Bruny I.

Tasman Sea

| Ferry Route | - - - - |

0 ———— 20 mi
0 ———— 20 km

Darwin

AUSTRALIA

Brisbane

Perth

Sydney

Canberra ⊛

TASMANIA

Bothwell **5**
Bonorong Wildlife Sanctuary **1**
Mount Field National Park **6**
Port Arthur Historic Site **4**
Royal Tasmanian Botanical Gardens **2**
Tasmanian Devil UnZoo **3**

TASMANIA ESSENTIALS

Arriving

BY PLANE

Qantas (www.qantas.com), **Virgin Australia** (www.virginaustralia.com), **Jetstar** (www.jetstar.com.au), and **Tigerair** (www.tigerair.com) fly into Hobart and Launceston.

BY FERRY

Two high-speed ships connect Melbourne and Tasmania. *Spirit of Tasmania I* and *II* can each carry up to 1,400 passengers and up to 500 vehicles. They make the crossing from Melbourne's Station Pier to Tasmania's Devonport (on the north coast) in 9 to 11 hours. The twin ships leave both Melbourne and Devonport at 7:30pm and arrive around 6am the next day. During busy times, a day service is added, leaving both ports at 9am and arriving at 6:30pm, which pushes the night service back to 9 or 9:30pm.

Facilities on the ships include a la carte and buffet restaurants, bars, two cinemas, and children's play areas. Accommodations range from reclining seats to comfortable air-conditioned cabins with queen-size beds and en-suite bathrooms, and four-berth cabins suited to families. Day tickets with no seat allocation start at A$69. Reclining seats cost from A$140 adults, or you can upgrade to a twin cabin from A$189 per cabin. Fares for an inside four-berth cabin start from A$139 (or A$35 if you are willing to share a single-sex cabin, backpacker style). Top of the range is a deluxe cabin with queen-size bed, from A$499. Transporting a standard car costs from A$99.

Prices vary depending on demand and availability, but specials and discounts are regularly available. Bookings must be made online at www.spirit oftasmania.com.au.

Tasmanian Redline Coaches (www.tasredline.com.au; ℂ **1300/360 000** in Australia) connect with each ferry for transfers to Hobart and Launceston. Driving a car from Devonport on the north coast to Hobart on the south coast takes less than 4 hours.

Visitor Information

Tourism Tasmania (www.discovertasmania.com.au) is the official tourism body and operates visitor centers in more than 20 towns throughout the state.

Driving Tips

Driving in Tasmania can be dangerous; there are more accidents involving tourists on Tasmania's roads than anywhere else in Australia. Many roads are narrow and bends can be tight, especially in the mountainous inland regions, where you may also come across black ice early in the morning or any time in winter.

Marsupials are common around dusk, and swerving to avoid them has caused countless crashes. In fact, you may be shocked by the amount of road-kill you will see here.

The Royal **Automobile Club of Tasmania** 179-191 Murray St., Hobart (www.ract.com.au; 🕿 **132 722** in Australia), offers emergency-breakdown service (🕿 **131 111**) to members of affiliated overseas automobile associations and dispenses maps and advice.

HOBART

281km (175 miles) S of Devonport; 200 km (124 miles) S of Launceston

Hobart (population 211,000), set on the Derwent River, is Tasmania's capital. Europeans settled in Hobart in 1804, a year after Tasmania's first colony was set up at Risdon (10km/6¼ miles up the Derwent), making it Australia's second-oldest city after Sydney.

The southernmost Australian state capital, Hobart is closer to the Antarctic coast than it is to Perth in Western Australia; navigators, whalers, and explorers have long regarded it as the gateway to the south. Hobart's main features are its wonderful harbor (the city's focal point) and the colonial cottages that line the narrow lanes of Battery Point.

Essentials

ARRIVING

BY PLANE **Qantas** (www.qantas.com.au) flies into **Hobart Airport** (www.hobartairport.com.au) from Melbourne and Sydney, and **Virgin Australia** (www.virginaustralia.com.au) flies to Hobart from Sydney, Melbourne, Brisbane, and Perth. **Tigerair** (www.tigerair.com) flies to Hobart from Melbourne.

The trip from the airport to the city center takes about 20 minutes and costs about A$50 by taxi. The **SkyBus** shuttle bus (www.skybus.com.au; 🕿 **1300/759 287** in Australia) meets all flights and delivers passengers to five stops in the city for A$20 one-way or A$37 round-trip for adults (up to four children travel free with an adult); a family of two adults and up to 4 children pays A$39 one-way or A$74 round-trip. Book online for cheaper fares.

Car- and camper-rental offices at the airport include **Avis** (www.avis.com.au; 🕿 **03/6248 5424**), **Budget** (www.budget.com.au; 🕿 **03/6248 5333**), **Europcar** (www.europcar.com.au; 🕿 **03/6248 5849**), **Hertz** (www.hertz.com.au; 🕿 **03/6335 1111**), and **Thrifty** (www.thrifty.com.au; 🕿 **03/6248 5695**). You might find better bargains at some of the local rental companies such as **Redspot** (www.redspot.com.au; 🕿 **03/6248 4043**).

VISITOR INFORMATION

The city of Hobart's **Tasmanian Travel and Information Centre,** at 20 Davey St. (www.hobarttravelcentre.com.au; 🕿 **03/6238 4222**), can arrange travel passes, ferry and bus tickets, car rentals, cruises, and accommodations. It is open daily 9am to 5pm (closed Christmas Day).

CITY LAYOUT

Hobart straddles the Derwent River on the south coast of Tasmania. The open ocean is about 50km (31 miles) down the river, though the Derwent empties into Storm Bay just 20km (12 miles) downstream.

Along the waterfront, the popular areas of Salamanca Place and nearby Battery Point overlook **Sullivan's Cove,** home to hundreds of yachts. The row of sandstone warehouses that dominates **Salamanca Place** dates to the city's heyday as a whaling base in the 1830s. Behind Princes Wharf, **Battery Point** is the city's historic district, which in colonial times was the home of sailors, fishermen, whalers, coopers, merchants, shipwrights, and master mariners. The **central business district** is on the west side of the water, with the main thoroughfares—Campbell, Argyle, Elizabeth, Murray, and Harrington streets—sloping down to the busy harbor.

The Tasman Bridge and regular passenger ferries cross the Derwent River. Set back from and overlooking the city is 1,270m-tall (4,166-ft.) **Mount Wellington/Kunanyi,** a popular day-trip destination.

GETTING AROUND

Central Hobart is very small, and most of the attractions are in easy walking distance. **Metro Tasmania** (www.metrotas.com.au; ✆ **132 201** in Australia) operates public buses throughout the city and suburbs. The buses operate on an electronic Green Card system, or you can just buy a ticket on board. Single tickets cost from A\$3.50, and the most you'll pay is A\$7.20.

For a taxi, call **Yellow Cabs** (✆ **131 924** in Australia) or **Taxis Combined** (✆ **133 227** in Australia).

Where to Stay in Hobart

EXPENSIVE

The Henry Jones Art Hotel ★★★   One of Australia's most unique and interesting hotels, the Henry Jones takes its name from one of Hobart's most successful pioneering entrepreneurs. Henry Jones's name, and that of his IXL brand of jam, is still on the factory building that became Australia's first dedicated art hotel. The walls of this luxurious hotel are hung with more than 400 works, in changing exhibitions, often by young, emerging Tasmanian artists, many from the Tasmanian School of Arts next door. Guest rooms are works of art in themselves, reflecting Australia's early trade with China and India in an eclectic mix of modern and historic. Sandstone walls abut ultra-modern glass and stainless steel bathrooms. (All but standard rooms have double spa tubs.) Every room has a view, either of the harbor or the hotel's magnificent glass atrium. I've stayed here several times, and so far my favorite is the spacious Art Installation Suite, which has a small balcony.

25 Hunter St. www.thehenryjones.com. ✆ **03/6210 7700.** 56 units. A\$280–A\$490 double; A\$760–A\$1,020 suite. Free parking. **Amenities:** Restaurant; bar; room service; free Wi-Fi.

The Islington ★★★   This luxury boutique hotel, just 10 minutes' walk from the city center, may make you feel as if you are staying in someone's home. Someone wealthy. The Islington is lavishly but tastefully decorated with fine artworks and antiques, its contemporary extension (with soaring glass walls and ceilings, and views of Mount Wellington) blending beautifully

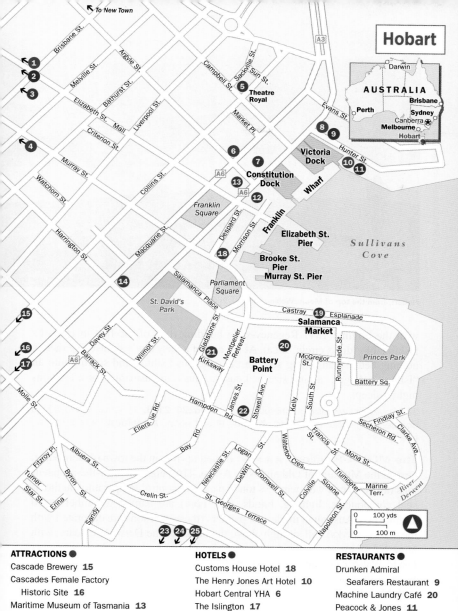

Hobart

AUSTRALIA

Darwin
Perth
Brisbane
Sydney
Canberra
Melbourne
Hobart

To New Town

Brisbane St.
Melville St.
Argyle St.
Bathurst St.
Campbell St.
Sackville St.
Sun St.
Elizabeth St. Mall
Liverpool St.
Market Pl.
Theatre Royal 5
Evans St.
8
9
Criterion St.
6
Hunter St.
Victoria Dock
10
11
Murray St.
Collins St.
7
A6
13
Constitution Dock
A6
12
Wharf
Watchorn St.
Franklin Square
Despard St.
Morrison St.
Franklin
Elizabeth St. Pier
Harrington St.
Macquarie St.
18
Brooke St. Pier
Murray St. Pier
Sullivans Cove
14
Salamanca Place
Parliament Square
St. David's Park
Castray Esplanade
19
Salamanca Market
15
Davey St.
Wilmot St.
Gladstone St.
Montpelier Retreat
21
Kirksway
20
McGregor St.
Runnymede St.
Princes Park
16
Barrack St.
A6
Battery Point
Kelly St.
South St.
Battery Sq.
17
Molle St.
James St.
Stowell Ave.
22
Hampden Rd.
Francis St.
Findlay St.
Secheron Rd.
Clarke Ave.
Ellers lie Rd.
Bay Rd.
Logan
Newcastle St.
DeWitt
Cromwell St.
Waterloo Cres.
Colville
Sloane
Mona St.
Trumpeter
Marine Terr.
River Derwent
Fitzroy Pl.
Albuera St.
Turner
Byron St.
Star St.
Erina
Sandy
Crelin St.
St. Georges Terrace
Napoleon St.
23 24 25

0   100 yds
0   100 m

Hobart, from the top of Mount Wellington

with the original 1847 Regency-style building (one of the first in Hobart's fashionable "dress circle" area). At the end of a busy day's sightseeing there's nothing better than a long soak in the generous bathtub and sinking into an "Islington Angel," a king-size bed custom-made in Tasmania, for a fabulous night's sleep.

321 Davey St. www.islingtonhotel.com. © **03/6220 2123.** 11 units. A$495–A$630 double. Rates include breakfast. No kids 14 and under. **Amenities:** Restaurant; bar; free Wi-Fi.

The MONA Pavilions ★★★ Located upriver in the town of Berriedale, next to the Museum of Old and New Art (p. 416), eight state-of-the-art pavilions (all equipped with wireless touch panels to control temperature, audiovisual components, lighting, blinds, and more) are named for either noted architects or Australian modernist painters (these pavilions are decorated with the artists' works). All sit high above the banks of the Derwent Estuary, with large balconies overlooking the water. Antiquities and artworks from owner David Walsh's private collection are included in the decor of each pavilion. Each of the one- or two-bedroom pavilions also has a private cellar stocked with Moorilla wines and Moo Brew beer from the estate. Guests can arrive by private boat or on the fast catamaran from Hobart. A MONA bus from Brooke Street Pier costs A$22 per person (kids 3 and under free) for either one-way or round-trip. MONA is about 15 minutes' drive from the city center, but the river is an even more appealing way to get there.

655 Main Rd., Berriedale. www.mona.net.au/stay/mona-pavilions. © **03/6277 9900.** 8 units. A$750–A$1,200 double. Rates include breakfast. Bus: 510, 520, 521, 522, or X20. **Amenities:** Restaurant; bar; gym; heated indoor pool; room service; sauna; free Wi-Fi.

Zero Davey ★   With a great waterfront location, and fresh, contemporary studios and apartments, Zero Davey is a good choice for those who want a bit of space. The three-bedroom Zero Penthouse, with its pink, orange, and red decor, will fulfill those rock-star fantasies; the Davey Penthouse has harbor views, and some studios have balconies and Jacuzzis. All are very functional as well as being bright, fun, and a little bit funky.

15 Hunter St. www.zerodavey.com.au. ☎ **1300/733 422** in Australia, or 03/6270 1444. 31 units. A$280 studio double; A$340–A$600 apt. **Amenities:** Restaurant; exercise room; sauna; free Wi-Fi.

MODERATE

Customs House Hotel ★★   You won't find a better value than the rooms above this historic sandstone pub overlooking the waterfront. Built in 1846, the Heritage-listed property offers large, clean, and comfortable colonial-style rooms, seven of which look across at the water and some of which have been newly refurbished. Other rooms look across Parliament House and its gardens, and the rest are toward the back of the hotel with no views to speak of. Downstairs, the restaurant and public bar overlook the water. Live music plays downstairs (Wed–Sat nights). A "quad saver" room sleeps five (a queen bed and three singles). Rooms above the bar are cheaper, but noisier, especially during the summer period, when the Sydney Hobart Yacht Race comes to town. But you can't beat the location for being central to all the action.

1 Murray St. www.customshousehotel.com. ☎ **03/6234 6645.** 22 units. A$140–A$260 double. Rates include breakfast. **Amenities:** Restaurant; bar; free Wi-Fi.

The Lodge on Elizabeth ★   The convict-built Lodge on Elizabeth is among the oldest buildings in Tasmania, completed in 1829 and now listed by the National Trust. Originally a gentleman's residence (including, at one time, a Tasmanian premier), it later became the first private boys' school in Tasmania. It's well situated, just a 12-minute walk from Salamanca Place, and is surrounded by restaurants. All rooms are decorated with antiques; many are quite romantic, with four-poster beds and some with Jacuzzis. Complimentary drinks are served in the communal living room in the evening. The Convict Cottage is a cute, self-contained spa cottage, just for two, on the grounds.

249 Elizabeth St. www.thelodge.com.au. ☎ **03/6231 3830.** 13 units. A$175–A$200 double; A$235–A$250 Convict Cottage (2-night minimum). Rates include breakfast. No children 13 and under. **Amenities:** Bar; free Wi-Fi.

Macquarie Manor ★★   As soon as you walk into this classic colonial-style manor, you'll know you want to stay. Macquarie Manor was built in 1875 as a surgeon's operating office and residence. Extra rooms were added in 1950. Thick carpets and double-glazed windows keep the place very quiet, even though it's on the main road, two blocks from the central bus terminal. Rooms, which vary enormously and include singles, are comfortable and elegantly furnished. One is suitable for people with disabilities. Check out the delightful dining room and the drawing room, complete with old couches and a grand piano.

172 Macquarie St. www.macmanor.com.au. ℂ **03/6224 4999.** 16 units. A$148–A$178 double; A$148–A$208 suite. Parking A$20. **Amenities:** Free Wi-Fi.

Salamanca Inn ★★ Conveniently located on the edge of the central business district and toward the waterfront near Battery Point, Salamanca Inn features modern and pleasant suites and apartments, all of which benefitted from a multimillion-dollar refurbishment in 2015. Rooms have queen- or king-size beds, leather couches, Tasmanian oak and leather furniture, galley-style kitchens, and spacious living areas. The pricier suites are a bit plusher and have personal computers as well as iPhone/iPod docking stations. The rooftop has a heated indoor pool.

10 Gladstone St. www.salamancainn.com.au. ℂ **1800/030 944** in Australia, or 03/6223 3300. 60 units. A$269–A$322 double; A$360–A$431 suite. Bus: 54B. **Amenities:** Restaurant; bar; babysitting; Jacuzzi; indoor pool; room service; free Wi-Fi.

Wrest Point ★ This Hobart landmark, built in 1973, launched Australia's annual A$2-billion casino industry. Beside the Derwent River, 3km (almost 2 miles) from the city center, the casino-hotel complex looks out across the harbor and the city and up to nearby Mount Wellington. All rooms feature Tasmanian oak furniture and plush carpets, and more expensive units have exceptional views. Rooms were refurbished in 2018, giving them a fresh, contemporary look. While it may be a little out of the city center (though it's certainly a walkable distance from downtown), the views make it a worth-while choice. The hotel's signature restaurant, the **Point Revolving Restaurant,** is another city icon. It's open for dinner from 6:30 to 10:30pm Tuesday to Sunday, on Fridays for lunch from noon, and for high tea from 2:30 to 4:30pm Wednesday to Sunday.

410 Sandy Bay Rd., Sandy Bay. www.wrestpoint.com.au. ℂ **03/6111 4628.** 197 units. A$179–A$359 double; A$389–A$409 suite. Bus: 54 or 55 from Franklin Square, Macquarie St., to stop 15. **Amenities:** 5 restaurants; 4 bars; babysitting; concierge; 9-hole putting course; health club; indoor pool; room service; tennis court; free Wi-Fi.

INEXPENSIVE

Hobart Central YHA ★ With a great location just two blocks from the waterfront and close to both the city center and Salamanca precinct, this is a great value-for-money location. Rooms are clean, comfortable, and basic. Double rooms (some with en-suite bathrooms) and family rooms are available, along with dorms, and there is a small, plainly furnished lounge area, as well as a laundry and small kitchen.

9 Argyle St. www.yha.org.au. ℂ **03/6231 2660.** 22 units. A$104–A$132 double; A$24–A$44 dorms; A$149–A$164 family room (sleeps 4). **Amenities:** Bar; free Wi-Fi.

Where to Eat in Hobart

Tasmania is known for its fresh seafood, including oysters, crab, crayfish, salmon, and trout. Although the seafood here was once cheap, in recent years prices have crept up to match or even surpass those on the mainland. Generally, the food in Tasmania is of very good quality.

EXPENSIVE

The Source ★★★ TASMANIAN/AUSTRALIAN   As you climb the stairs to this amazing restaurant, your eyes will be drawn to the painting from which it takes its name: *The Source,* by Australian artist John Olsen, is a stunning 6m-tall (20-ft.) work set into the ceiling directly above the central staircase. It will take your breath away. So too will the entire experience of dining here, which promises delivery "with a MONA twist" (the restaurant is part of the Museum of Old and New Art; see p. 416). The menu changes daily, but be assured that seasonal and local produce (with an eye toward "food miles") is important here. Offerings might include dishes such as ocean trout with borlotti beans, mussels, and kimchi, or pork belly with almond-and-raisin mole, green apples, tamarind, and cauliflower. Huge windows afford stunning views of the Derwent River.

Moorilla Estate, 655 Main Rd., Berriedale. www.mona.net.au/eat-drink/the-source-restaurant. © **03/6277 9904.** Main courses A$32–A$40. Wed–Mon 7:30–10am and noon–3pm; Fri–Sat 6pm–late. Free parking. Bus: 510, 520, 521, 522, or X20. A MONA bus operates from Brooke Street Pier and costs A$22 per person (kids 3 and under free) for either one-way or round-trip.

MODERATE

Drunken Admiral Seafarers Restaurant ★ SEAFOOD   The Drunken Admiral, on the waterfront, is an extremely popular spot with tourists and can get raucous on busy evenings. The main attraction to start the meal is the famous seafood chowder, brimming with anything that was on sale at the docks that morning. The seafood platter for two (A$79.50 per person; minimum 2) is a huge plate of squid, oysters, fish, mussels, and prawns. But the menu has plenty of simpler dishes, too. Try the crunchy fried prawns or the steamed mussels in a tomato, garlic, and white wine sauce.

17–19 Hunter St. www.drunkenadmiral.com.au. © **03/6234 1903.** Main courses A$30–A$45. Daily 6–10:30pm.

Peacock & Jones ★★ CONTEMPORARY   A fireplace in the atrium of the Henry Jones factory building might lure you in to this smart and buzzing addition to the Hobart dining scene, but it's the cozy atmosphere and fine food inside that will keep you here. The open kitchen produces unique combinations, with a focus on local produce. Start with a scallop pudding with chicken liver parfait or a charcuterie selection, then move on to heartier fare such as Tasmanian steaks with smoked tongue and dauphine potatoes.

33 Hunter St. www.peacockandjones.com.au. © **1800/375 692.** Snacks A$11–A$25; main courses A$36–A$39. Daily 6–9pm.

Peppermint Bay Hotel ★★ CONTEMPORARY   You'd be hard pressed to find a lovelier setting for lunch. A 150-year-old oak tree dominates the gardens, and the relaxed **Terrace Bar** has water's-edge views of Bruny

Island and the D'Entrecasteaux Channel. The menu includes Tasmanian oysters, lamb, and fish dishes, and always offers something interesting, such as homemade pasta with calamari, smoked chili, and sea herbs. For something special, try the slow-cooked lamb shoulder (A$78 for two). **Peppermint Bay Cruises** (🕾 **1300/137 919** in Australia) runs scenic cruises, priced from A$118 adults and A$88 children under 12, which include lunch here at Peppermint Bay.

3435 Channel Hwy., Woodbridge (35km/22 miles S from Hobart). www.peppermintbay. com.au. 🕾 **03/6267 4088.** Main courses A$14–A$29. Daily noon–3pm; Thurs–Sat 5:30–8:30pm.

INEXPENSIVE

Machine Laundry Cafe ★★ CAFE   Here's a colorful and cute retro-style cafe that's popular with all demographics. There are bright tables and chairs outside on Salamanca Square if you prefer, or a cozy interior that is separated by the line of washing machines in the Laundromat next to a large window. Yes, wash your clothes while you eat! Great for breakfast or brunch, with offerings such as scrambled eggs in roti, eggs Benedict, or ricotta hotcakes.

12 Salamanca Square. 🕾 **03/6224 9922.** Main courses A$15–A$20. Mon–Sat 7:30am–5pm; Sun 8:30am–5pm.

Exploring Hobart

Simply strolling around the harbor and popping into the shops at **Salamanca Place** can keep you nicely occupied, but don't miss the lovely colonial stone cottages of **Battery Point.** This area got its name from a battery of guns set up on the promontory in 1818 to defend the town against potential invaders (particularly the French). Today, you'll find tearooms, antiques shops, restaurants, and atmospheric pubs interspersed among grand dwellings.

Bonorong Wildlife Sanctuary ★★★ WILDLIFE VIEWING   Tasmanian devils and wallabies are the main attractions at Bonorong (it means "native companion"). Most of the animals have been rescued after injury; owner Greg Irons is passionate about saving and conserving indigenous creatures. You'll also find snakes, koalas, echidnas, kangaroos, and wombats here. Everyone gets a free bag of kangaroo food on entry. Koala cuddling isn't

---

Hello, Sailor!

The annual **Sydney Hobart Yacht Race,** which launches from Sydney Harbour on December 26, fills Hobart's Constitution Dock Marina and harbor area close to overflowing with spectators and partygoers when the yachts finally turn up in Tasmania. This world-class sailing event takes anywhere from 2 to 4 days, making it very handy for sailors and fans to stay on in Hobart to celebrate New Year's Eve.

Conveniently, food and wine lovers can also indulge themselves after the race at the **Taste of Tasmania** festival, which starts on December 28.

For magnificent views over Hobart and across a fair-size chunk of Tasmania, drive inland to the Pinnacle lookout on top of **kunanyi/Mount Wellington** (www.wellingtonpark.org.au), about a 40-minute drive from the city center. Take a warm coat; the wind in this alpine area can really bite. An extensive network of walking trails offers good hiking. You can order a copy of the Wellington Park Recreation Map, as well as other day-walk maps, for A$12 online from **Tasmap** (www.tasmap.tas.gov.au). The website also has other free maps for download, including street maps of Hobart and Launceston.

allowed in Tasmania, but you may get to stroke one. Tour times are 11:30am, and 2 and 3:30pm daily, with a special Tasmanian devil tour at 10am. Night tours (A$160 adults, A$85 children 3–15) allow you to see the animals when they are most active, and are highly recommended. Feeding Frenzy tours (A$160 adults, A$85 children) and 10-minute Animal Encounters (with devils, sugar gliders, wombats, echidnas, possums, or tawny frogmouths; A$25 per person) are also on offer. Private tours are available but cost more.

593 Briggs Rd., Brighton (25 min. N of Hobart on Rte. 1). www.bonorong.com.au. ℰ **03/6268 1184.** A$30 adults, A$16 children 3–15, A$85 families of 4. Daily 9am–5pm.

Cascade Brewery ★ FACTORY TOUR   Cascade Premium is one of Australia's most popular beers. To see how this heady amber nectar is produced, head to Australia's oldest brewery and tag along on a 90-minute tour, which includes a stroll through the grand old **Woodstock Gardens** behind the factory. Wear flat shoes and long trousers for all tours. Tours include tastings for participants age 18 and over.

140 Cascade Rd., South Hobart. www.cascadebreweryco.com.au. ℰ **03/6212 7801.** Tours A$30 adults, A$25 seniors, A$15 ages 16–18. No children 15 and under. Tours daily at 11am, 12:30, 1, 2:15, 2:30, 3:35, 5, and 6pm. Closed Dec 25 and Good Friday. Reservations required. Bus: 446 or 449 (stop 18).

Cascades Female Factory Historic Site ★ HISTORIC SITE   Unless you are really into convict history, you may wish to save yourself for Port Arthur (p. 420). All that is left here are the stone walls of this prison and a memorial garden, but recent improvements to the interpretation of the site—including the stories of 57 women incarcerated here—help tell its important history. The "factory" prison, where women worked at spinning, washing, and sewing, operated from 1828 to 1856, housing up to 1,200 women and children. After it ceased operation as a female factory, the institution continued as a jail until 1877. Taking a guided tour ensures you get the most from your visit. Another interesting option is a dramatized tour that tells the personal stories of prisoners. "Her Story" is a 45-minute dramatized tour performed by two actors daily at noon, and "The Proud and The Punished" is a one-woman show performed Tuesday to Friday at 2:30pm. Each costs A$25 adults, A$15 children, or A$70 families.

16 Degraves St., South Hobart. www.femalefactory.org.au. © **1800/139 478.** A$8 adults, A$5 children 7–17, A$20 families of 8. Tours A$18 adults, A$12 children, A$45 families. Daily 9:30am–4pm. Tours daily 10 and 11am, and 1, 2, and 3pm. Closed Dec 25. Bus: 446, 447, or 449 from Franklin Square (stop 13).

Maritime Museum of Tasmania ★★★ MUSEUM   Renowned as one of the best of its type in Australia, this museum explores the influence of the sea on the lives of Tasmanians and the island's strong maritime heritage. It has displays about Aboriginal watercraft, early European explorers and whalers, and how ships helped develop Tasmanian industries. Collections include ship models, artifacts, paintings, boat builder's tools, historic dinghies, and navigation instruments. There's also a section on shipwrecks. Free 1-hour talks are held on the first Tuesday of each month (except Jan) at noon.

16 Argyle St. (at Davey St.). www.maritimetas.org. © **03/6234 1427.** A$10 adults, A$5 children 13–18, free for children 12 and under, A$20 for families. Daily 9am–5pm. Closed Dec 25.

Mawson's Hut Replica Museum ★★ MUSEUM   Designed to raise funds for the conservation and maintenance of the originals, these wooden huts on the Hobart waterfront, just opposite Mawson Place, are exact replicas of the shelter afforded to the explorer Douglas Mawson and his expedition team from 1912 to 1914. One of Hobart's newest attractions, the huts are fast becoming one of the city's most popular. Inside are tributes to the men and 50 huskie dogs that traveled with them to the frozen south.

Corner Argyle and Morrison sts. www.mawsons-huts-replica.org.au. © **03/6231 1518,** or 1300/551 422. A$15 adults, A$4 kids 15 and under, A$35 families. Oct–Apr daily 9am–6pm; May–Sept daily 10am–5pm. Closed Good Friday, Apr 25, and Dec 25.

Museum of Old and New Art (MONA) ★★★ MUSEUM   Australia's largest privately owned art gallery promises to "shock and offend." Owner David Walsh wants his art museum to be daring and provocative—and so it is. More often, however, it delights and amazes. This museum of old and new art challenges, informs, and entertains, with a collection that ranges from antiquities from Egypt, Greece, Italy, Africa, and Mesoamerica to contemporary art, including Australian modernism and contemporary Australian, British, European, and American art. For the sensitive (or those bringing children with them), the museum provides a map showing how to avoid works that are sexually explicit or "potentially confronting." The museum is part of Walsh's Moorilla Estate, also home to a winery, a microbrewery, a restaurant (**The Source** ★★★; p. 413), and stunning accommodations (**The MONA Pavilions** ★★★; p. 410). It's almost worth going to Tasmania just for this.

655 Main Rd., Berriedale. www.mona.net.au. © **03/6277 9900.** A$28 adults, free for kids 17 and under. Wed–Mon 10am–6pm; daily (same hours) in Jan. Closed Dec 25. Bus: 510, 520, 521, 522, or X20. A MONA bus from Brooke Street Pier costs A$22 per person (kids 3 and under free) for either one-way or round-trip.

The Museum of Old and New Art (MONA) is located in the Moorilla Winery.

Narryna Heritage Museum ★ HISTORIC HOME   One of the houses worth looking into at Battery Point is Narryna, which depicts the life of upper-class pioneers. Built by Captain Andrew Haig in 1837 to 1840, it was later the home of several Hobart businessmen and -women, lawyers, politicians, and bankers.

103 Hampden Rd. www.tmag.tas.gov.au. ✆ **03/6234 2791.** A$10 adults, A$8 students, A$4 children 5 and under. Tues–Sat 10am–4:30pm (closes 12:30–1pm Tues–Fri); closed Sun–Mon. Closed Jan 1, Good Friday, Hobart Show Day (late Oct), Dec 25–26, and any other Tasmanian public holidays.

Royal Tasmanian Botanical Gardens ★ GARDENS   Established in 1818, these gardens are known for their English-style plant and tree layouts—including a great conifer collection—a superb Japanese garden, and seasonal blooming plants. A restaurant serves lunch and teas. A walk here from the city center, partly along a pleasant country lane known as Soldier's Walk, takes around 40 minutes, or you can use the cycle track or arrive by ferry. You can get maps of the gardens at each entrance; visitor guides and self-guided tour brochures are available at the Visitor Centre, which is near the entrance on Lower Domain Road.

Queens Domain, near Government House. www.rtbg.tas.gov.au. ✆ **03/6166 0451.** Free. Oct–Apr daily 8am–6:30pm; May–Sept daily 8am–5pm.

Salamanca Market ★★ OPEN-AIR MARKET   If you are in Hobart on a Saturday, don't miss this—it's one of the best markets in Australia. Some 300 stalls offer everything from fruit and vegetables to crafts made from

Hobart's famed Salamanca Market offers everything from produce to crafts.

pottery, glass, and native woods. Salamanca Place also has plenty of crafts shops that are worth exploring, though the prices sometimes reflect the fashionable area.

Salamanca Place. www.salamanca.com.au. Sat 8am–3pm.

Tasmanian Museum & Art Gallery ★ MUSEUM   Come here to find out more about Tasmania's Aboriginal heritage, its history since settlement, and the island's wildlife. This wonderful museum has undergone a major redevelopment—with more to come—to open up new areas and transform it, while still telling Tasmania's story. Traveling exhibitions are mounted from time to time, but always on display are colonial-era paintings, including an impressive collection of works by Australian Impressionist Tom Roberts and several convict artists. The pride of the collection is the historically significant *The Conciliation,* by Benjamin Duterreau. You can also find out about the fate of the Tasmanian tiger and see archival film of this lost treasure. Free 40-minute guided tours are run Wednesday to Sunday at 11am, 1 and 1:30pm. One-hour theatrical tours called "Settlement Secrets" run through the museum buildings at 11:30am and 2pm Wednesday to Friday and cost A$20 adults, A$15 children 15 and under, or A$60 families of six (visit **www.antipodean entertainment.com.au** for details and bookings).

Dunn Place (via Macquarie and Davey sts.). www.tmag.tas.gov.au. ℂ **03/6165 7000.** Free. Daily 10am–4pm (closed Mon Apr–Dec 24 except public holidays). Closed Good Friday, Apr 25, and Dec 25.

Theatre Royal ★ THEATER   Built in 1837, this 747-seat venue is the oldest theater in Australia. It's known for its excellent acoustics and classical Victorian decor, and is the centerpiece of a A$96-million performing-arts development taking place around it. At press time, the redevelopment was expected to be completed by late 2019. As Hobart's major stage venue, the theater will be upgraded and a modern extension added. Until the theater reopens, shows continue to run at other venues in Hobart, with the box office operating from the Tasmanian Museum & Art Gallery, Dunn Place (see p. 418).

29 Campbell St. www.theatreroyal.com.au. © **03/6146 3300** (box office daily 9am–4pm).

Organized Tours
WALKING TOURS

Hobart Historic Tours (www.hobarthistorictours.com.au; © **03/6234 5550**) runs fascinating 90-minute walking tours of Hobart. The Historic Walk departs from outside the **Tasmanian Travel and Information Centre** (p. 407) at 2pm Wednesday to Sunday. The Old Hobart Pub Tour (not recommended for children), departing at 5pm on Thursday, Friday, and Saturday, takes you to two waterfront pubs and will enthrall you with stories of alcohol-fueled shenanigans. Tours cost A$33 per person. A 3-hour Grand Hobart Walk costs A$50 per person and runs Wednesday to Sunday at 2pm.

CRUISES

Bruny Island Cruises (www.brunycruises.com.au; © **03/6293 1465**) offers a range of tours including a full-day jaunt from Hobart to Bruny Island, leaving Franklin Wharf at 8am and returning around 5:30pm daily. A bus and ferry deliver you to Bruny Island, where (after morning tea) you take a 3-hour boat trip along the coastline to a seal colony and a memorable (but sometimes wet) foray onto the wild Southern Ocean—warm, shower-proof coats are provided. On returning, lunch includes much-needed hot soup to warm you up, before you get back on the bus for the trip back to Hobart. It's a pleasant day out, although considering the hours spent, serious wildlife fans might be disappointed. The trip costs A$225 adults, A$165 children ages 3 to 16.

BUS TOURS

Gray Line (www.grayline.com.au; © **1300/858 687** in Australia) offers a range of sightseeing tours of Hobart and Mount Wellington by coach. A 3-hour tour costs A$55 for adults, A$28 for kids. Gray Line also runs tours to other Tasmanian destinations including Russell Falls, Bruny Island, Port Arthur, Cradle Mountain, Richmond, and the Bay of Fires.

To get to the top of Mount Wellington, jump aboard the hop-on, hop-off **Mt Wellington Explorer Bus** (www.mtwellingtonexplorer.com.au). An all-day bus pass includes a 2-hour loop tour with the option to hop on and off along the way at five stops. The tour allows a 30-minute stop to enjoy the views from the summit, and costs A$35 adults, A$25 children 6 to 16. Another option is to buy a one-way ticket for A$25 adults and A$15 children, and walk back down, which takes around 3 hours.

TASMANIAN DEVIL disaster

Tasmania's unique carnivorous mammal, the handsomely sleek Tasmanian devil, is much more interesting than his namesake, the manic character from Bugs Bunny cartoons. Whereas dingoes wiped out the devil's cousin on the Australian mainland, the dogs never crossed Bass Strait, and so Tasmania's devils flourished, becoming one of the island's iconic mascots. But now, the Tasmanian devil population is in desperate trouble.

Since 1996, the animals have been afflicted by a deadly cancer known as Devil Facial Tumour Disease (DFTD). This malady has decimated the wild population—in some areas by an estimated 90%—and the disease is spreading rapidly. It's believed that around half of the state's approximately 150,000 Tasmanian devils have already died, and some scientists fear that it may soon wipe out the wild population entirely. Healthy specimens are being captured and relocated in an urgent campaign to try to preserve the species from extinction.

There are several places where you can see captive Tasmanian devils and learn more about this one-of-a-kind animal. About 88km (55 miles) from Hobart, on the Port Arthur Highway, Taranna, is the **Tasmanian Devil UnZoo** (www.tasmaniandevilunzoo.com.au; *℃* **1800/641 641** in Australia), which is currently working to breed devils with genes that could make them resistant to the disease. The park is open daily from 9am to 5pm (except Christmas Day). Devil feeding is at 10 and 11am, and 12:15, 1:30, 3, and 5pm (4:30pm May–Sept) daily. Entry is A$36 adults, A$20 children 4 to 16, and A$89 for a family of six.

Another great place to see devils near Hobart is the **Bonorong Wildlife Sanctuary** (p. 414).

For more information on devil conservation efforts, visit **www.tassiedevil. com.au**.

DAY TRIPS FROM HOBART

Port Arthur ★★★

96 km (60 miles) southeast of Hobart

Port Arthur, on the Tasman Peninsula, is an incredibly picturesque yet haunting place. Set on one of Australia's prettiest harbors, it shelters the remains of Tasmania's largest penal colony. It's the state's number-one tourist destination, and you really should plan to spend at least a day here.

From 1830 to 1877, Port Arthur was one of the harshest institutions of its type anywhere in the world. It was built to house the most notorious prisoners transported from Great Britain, many of whom had escaped from lesser institutions elsewhere in Australia. Nearly 13,000 convicts found their way here, and some 2,000 died while incarcerated.

A strip of land called Eaglehawk Neck connects Port Arthur to the rest of Tasmania. Guards and dogs kept watch over this narrow path, while the authorities perpetuated rumors that the waters around the peninsula were shark-infested. Only a few convicts ever managed to escape, and most of them

FACING PAGE: Cute but fierce, Tasmanian Devils are an endangered species found only in Tasmania.

either eventually perished in the bush or were tracked down and hanged. As you pass through Eaglehawk Neck, look out for the blowhole and other weird coastal formations, including Tasman's Arch, Devil's Kitchen, and the Tessellated Pavement.

The **Port Arthur Historic Site** ★★ (www.portarthur.org.au; ℂ **1800/659 101** in Australia, or 03/6251 2310) is large and scattered, with around 30 19th-century buildings. You can tour the remains of the church, the guard tower, a prison, and several other buildings. Don't miss the fascinating museum in the old lunatic asylum, which has a scale model of the prison complex, as well as leg irons and chains. The main feature of the visitor center is an interesting **Interpretive Gallery,** which takes visitors through the process of sentencing in England to transportation to Van Diemen's Land (Tasmania's original name). The gallery contains a courtroom, a section of a transport ship's hull, a blacksmith's shop, a lunatic asylum, and more.

Port Arthur's tragic history did not finish at the end of the convict era. In 1996, the Port Arthur Historic Site became the scene of one of Australia's worst mass murders, when a lone gunman killed 35 people and injured dozens more, including tourists and staff. The devastating events of that day led to new gun-control laws for Australia that are among the strictest in the world. The gunman was sentenced to life imprisonment with no eligibility for parole. Many of the staff at Port Arthur lost friends, colleagues, and family members,

Until 1877, the asylum of Historic Site Port Arthur was a penal colony for prisoners.

A DAY TRIP TO bothwell

A charming little town an hour's drive north of Hobart (take Highway 1 and then A5), **Bothwell** ★★ sits on the picturesque Clyde River at the foothills of the central Tasmanian highlands. The town was settled by Scottish colonists in 1822, with convict labor building many of the sandstone establishments still lining the streets today.

Bothwell's major claim to fame is as the home of **Ratho,** Australia's oldest golf course (www.rathofarm.com; ✆ **03/6259 5553**), which was also established in 1822, as soon as the Scottish settlers arrived. **Ratho Farm,** on which the 18-hole course sits, is also home to new luxury accommodations in the form of 16 converted convict cottages and stables, priced from A$175 double. Ratho is a public course, and greens fees are only A$25 for 9 holes or A$40 for 18 holes.

After a round of golf, drop in to the **Australasian Golf Museum** (www.ausgolfmuseum.com; ✆ **03/6259 4033**), which doubles as the local information center, on Market Place. It's open daily 10am to 4pm September to May and 11am to 3pm June to August. While you're there, pick up a brochure that gives you a self-guided tour of Bothwell's many historic buildings.

Another spot worth ducking into is the historic **Castle Hotel** (www.facebook.com/CastleHotelBothwell; ✆ **03/6259 5502**) in Bothwell's main street. The sandstone pub, built in 1829, is one of Australia's oldest, and like much of the town, is Heritage-listed. There are three guest rooms upstairs, but the action is mostly in the bar, where locals gather to swap tales of trout fishing.

and they still find it difficult and painful to talk about that tragic day. Visitors are requested not to question their guide about these events, but instead to read the plaque at the Memorial Garden.

The site is open daily from 9am to dusk; buildings are open 10am to 5pm. (On Christmas Day, the site closes at 3pm.) Admission is A$40 adults, A$18 children 4 to 17, and A$102 for families of two adults and up to six children. The admission price includes a guided walking tour and a boat cruise around the harbor.

Passes that combine different experiences and tours are also available. You can get off the harbor cruise for a 45-minute guided walk on the **Isle of the Dead,** where 1,769 convicts and 180 free settlers were buried, mostly in mass graves with no headstones, or at **Point Puer,** which was once home to 800 boys shipped to Tasmania for a "better life" or for petty crimes. The tour costs an extra A$29 adults, A$19 kids, and A$77 families. Lantern-lit **Ghost Tours** of Port Arthur leave nightly at 6 and 8pm and cost A$27 adults, A$15 kids, or A$75 families. Reservations are essential. Tours last about 90 minutes. Various other passes and tours are available; check the website.

Port Arthur Historic Site is a 90-minute drive from Hobart. Take the Tasman Highway (A3) past the airport to Sorell, then turn south on the Arthur Highway (A9) and continue until you reach Port Arthur. The Historic Site is well signposted along the way.

Mount Field National Park ★★

80 km (50 miles) northwest of Hobart

Mount Field National Park is one of the prettiest landscapes in Tasmania. It was proclaimed a national park in 1916 to protect a plateau dominated by dolerite-capped mountains (**Mount Field West** is the highest point at 1,417m/4,647 ft.) and dramatic glaciated valleys (some of the lakes and tarns were formed as much as 30,000 years ago). Since 2013, it has been included as part of the Tasmanian Wilderness World Heritage Area.

The most mountainous regions support alpine moorlands of cushion plants, pineapple and sword grass, waratahs, and giant pandani. You can get a look at these various ecosystems on a 16km (10-mile) drive from the park entrance to Lake Dobson. Note that this drive is along an unpaved and often badly rutted road, which is not suitable for conventional vehicles in winter or after heavy rains. As you follow the drive, you'll notice that wallabies, wombats, bandicoots, Tasmanian devils, and quolls are prolific, as is the birdlife: You may spot such bird species as black cockatoos, green rosellas, honeyeaters, currawongs, wedge-tailed eagles, and lyrebirds.

Many walking trails run through the park, including one to the spectacular 45m-high (148-ft.) **Russell Falls,** near the park's entrance. The walk to the falls along a paved, wheelchair-accessible track takes 15 minutes and passes

Hiker in Mount Field National Park.

The historic Ross Post Office.

ferns and forests, with some of Tasmania's tallest trees, swamp gums that stand up to 85m (279 ft.) high.

Mount Field National Park is just over an hour's drive from Hobart via the town of New Norfolk. From Hobart, take the Brooker Highway (A10) northwest to New Norfolk. After New Norfolk, you can follow the road on either side of the Derwent River (the A10 or B62) until you reach Westerway. From there, it is a short drive to the clearly marked entrance to Mount Field National Park. There is an entrance fee of A$12 per person or A$24 per car (up to eight people).

The park's visitor center (www.parks.tas.gov.au; © **03/6288 1149**) on Lake Dobson Road has a cafe and information on walks. It's open daily from 8:30am to 5pm between November and April and 9am to 4pm in winter.

LAUNCESTON

198km (123 miles) N of Hobart; 92 km (57 miles) SE of Devonport

Tasmania's second-largest city is Australia's third oldest, after Sydney and Hobart. Situated at the head of the Tamar River, 50km (31 miles) inland from the state's north coast, and surrounded by delightful undulating farmland, Launceston is crammed with elegant Victorian and Georgian architecture and plenty of remnants of convict days. Launceston (pop. 86,000) is one of Australia's most beautiful cities, with delightful parks and churches. It's also the gateway to the wineries of the Tamar Valley, the highlands and alpine lakes of the north, and the stunning beaches to the east.

Essentials

ARRIVING

BY PLANE **Qantas** (www.qantas.com) flies to Launceston from Melbourne, and **Jetstar** (www.jetstar.com.au) flies from Sydney and Brisbane. **Virgin Australia** (www.virginaustralia.com.au) flies from Adelaide, Perth, Melbourne, Brisbane, and Sydney. The **Launceston Airport** (www.launcestonairport.com.au) is approximately 15km (9 miles) south of Launceston.

The **Airporter Shuttle** (✆ **1300/385 522** in Australia, or 0488/200 700 mobile) meets all flights and runs between Launceston city hotels and the airport for A$15 one-way. **Taxis** from the airport run A$35 to A$38 one-way.

Avis (www.avis.com.au; ✆ **136 333** in Australia), **Budget** (www.budget.com.au; ✆ **03/6391 8566**), **Europcar** (www.europcar.com.au; ✆ **03/6391 9161**), **Hertz** (www.hertz.com.au; ✆ **1300/030 222**), **Thrifty** (www.thrifty.com.au; ✆ **03/6391 8105**), and **Redspot** (www.redspot.com.au; ✆ **03/6391 9060**) all have airport car-rental desks.

BY BUS Tasmania's **Redline Coaches** (www.tasredline.com.au; ✆ **1300/360 000** in Australia) departs Hobart for Launceston several times daily (trip time: around 3 hr.). The one-way fare is A$42. If you're arriving on the ferry from Melbourne, Launceston is around 1½ hours from Devonport, and the bus ride will cost A$25.

BY CAR Driving from Hobart to Launceston takes just over 2 hours on Hwy. 1.

VISITOR INFORMATION

The **Launceston Visitor Information Centre** is located in the historic GPO building, 68–72 Cameron St. (www.northerntasmania.com.au; ✆ **1800/651 827** in Australia); it's open Monday through Friday from 9am to 5pm, and Saturday, Sunday, and public holidays from 9am to 1pm. Closed Good Friday and Christmas Day.

CITY LAYOUT

The main pedestrian shopping mall, **Brisbane Street,** along with St. John and Charles streets on either side, forms the heart of the central area. The Victorian-Italianate Town Hall is two blocks north on **Civic Square,** opposite the redbrick post-office building dating from 1889. The **Tamar River** slips quietly past the city's northern edge and is crossed at two points by **Charles Bridge** and **Tamar Street. City Park,** to the northeast of the central business district, is a nice place for a stroll.

GETTING AROUND

BY BUS **Metro Tasmania** (www.metrotas.com.au; ✆ **132 201** in Australia) operates public buses throughout the city and suburbs. The buses operate on an electronic Green Card system, or you can just buy a ticket on board. Single tickets cost from A$3.50, and the most you'll pay is A$7.20. The free **Tiger Bus**—painted with the distinctive black stripes of the extinct Tasmanian

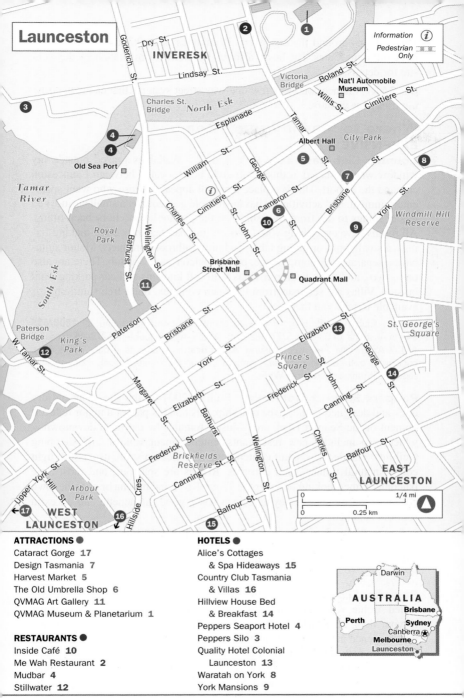

Launceston

INVERESK

Dry St.

Goderich St.

Lindsay St.

Charles St. Bridge

North Esk

Esplanade

Victoria Bridge

Boland St.

Willis St.

Nat'l Automobile Museum

Cimitiere St.

Tamar St.

Albert Hall

City Park

William St.

George St.

Cimitiere St.

St. John St.

Cameron St.

Brisbane St.

York St.

Windmill Hill Reserve

Charles St.

Old Sea Port

Tamar River

Royal Park

Bathurst St.

Wellington St.

Brisbane Street Mall

Quadrant Mall

South Esk

Paterson St.

Brisbane St.

Elizabeth St.

St. George's Square

Paterson Bridge

King's Park

York St.

Prince's Square

George St.

W. Tamar St.

Margaret St.

Elizabeth St.

Bathurst St.

St. John St.

Frederick St.

Canning St.

Charles St.

Balfour St.

EAST LAUNCESTON

Upper York St.

Hill St.

Arbour Park

Hillside Cres.

Frederick St.

Brickfields Reserve St.

Canning St.

Balfour St.

WEST LAUNCESTON

0 — 1/4 mi
0 — 0.25 km

Information ⓘ
Pedestrian Only

ATTRACTIONS ●
Cataract Gorge **17**
Design Tasmania **7**
Harvest Market **5**
The Old Umbrella Shop **6**
QVMAG Art Gallery **11**
QVMAG Museum & Planetarium **1**

RESTAURANTS ●
Inside Café **10**
Me Wah Restaurant **2**
Mudbar **4**
Stillwater **12**

HOTELS ●
Alice's Cottages
& Spa Hideaways **15**
Country Club Tasmania
& Villas **16**
Hillview House Bed
& Breakfast **14**
Peppers Seaport Hotel **4**
Peppers Silo **3**
Quality Hotel Colonial
Launceston **13**
Waratah on York **8**
York Mansions **9**

AUSTRALIA

Darwin
Perth
Brisbane
Sydney
Canberra
Melbourne
Launceston

Tiger—loops around the city every 30 minutes from 9:30am to 3:50pm on three different routes. The bus is also run by Metro Tasmania; check the website for details.

BY CAR   Launceston has a few one-way street systems that can make driving tricky for visitors.

Where to Stay in Launceston
EXPENSIVE

Country Club Tasmania & Villas ★   Wallabies grazed outside my window when I stayed at this resort-style hotel located between Launceston city and the airport. This is a place that will appeal to those who want space, entertainment, and activities. It has an 18-hole golf course, a small casino, and lots of things to do, from fly-fishing on the private lake to horseback riding. All rooms have everything you'd expect: minibar, tea and coffee-making fixings, a small work or dining table, and nice bathroom products. Manor suites have a separate bedroom, lounge, private balcony, and spa tub. There are also one-, two-, and three-bedroom villas with full kitchens and car parking right outside. Villas are set apart from the main complex, but a free shuttle bus is available to take you there.

Country Club Ave., Prospect Vale. www.countryclubtasmania.com.au. ✆ **1800/635 344** in Australia, or 03/6335 5777. 182 units. A$159–A$219 double; A$278–A$309 suite; A$159–A$359 villa. Free valet parking. **Amenities:** 5 restaurants; 4 bars; babysitting; concierge; golf course; exercise room; Jacuzzi; indoor heated pool; room service; sauna; 2 lit tennis courts; free Wi-Fi.

Peppers Seaport Hotel ★★   Built in 2004 on the site of an old dry dock and designed in the shape of a ship, this hotel is part of a major redevelopment of the Seaport Dock area—just 5 minutes by car from downtown—which also includes new restaurants, entertainment venues, and shopping facilities. The decor is smart contemporary nautical in style, using soft, light colors, natural timbers, and chromes. Rooms are spacious, and most have balconies either looking out over the Tamar River and marina or over the town center to the mountains beyond. Each has a good kitchenette and an extra fold-out sofa bed.

28 Seaport Blvd. www.peppers.com.au/seaport. ✆ **1300/987 600** in Australia, 07/5665 4426 (central reservations), or 03/6345 3333 (hotel). 60 units. A$229–A$259 double; A$274–A$339 suite. Parking A$10. **Amenities:** Restaurant; bar; babysitting; concierge; room service; free Wi-Fi.

Peppers Silo ★★   You'll be greeted at reception by a black Labrador called Archie, who is available for walks and may later bring your newspaper to your door. And that's not the only notable thing about this terrific hotel, which opened in mid-2018. One of Tasmania's—and maybe Australia's—most innovative new hotels, it is built in and between four former grain silos, massive circular structures that have been transformed into a nine-level hotel. Rooms have views of the Tamar River and Cataract Gorge. Adjacent to the

THE heritage HIGHWAY

The **Heritage Highway** links Launceston in the north with Hobart in the south, cutting through the middle of Tasmania. By the 1820s, several garrison towns had been built between the two towns, and by the middle of the 19th century convict labor had produced what was considered to be the finest highway of its time in Australia. Today, many of the towns along the road retain magnificent examples of Georgian and Victorian architecture. It takes about 2 hours to drive between Launceston and Hobart on this route (also known as the A1, or the Midland Highway), but you could easily spend a couple of days exploring.

Picturesque **Ross** (121km/75 miles north of Hobart or 78km/48 miles south of Launceston) is one of Tasmania's best-preserved historic villages. Ross was established in 1812 on a strategically important crossing point on the Macquarie River. **Ross Bridge,** the third oldest in Australia, was built in 1836. The bridge is decorated with Celtic symbols, animals, and faces of notable people of the time. It is lit up at night, and there are good views of it from the river's north bank. The town's **main crossroads** is the site of four historic buildings, humorously known as "Temptation" (the Man-o'-Ross Hotel), "Salvation" (the Catholic church), "Recreation" (the town hall), and "Damnation" (the old jail). The **Tasmanian Wool Centre,** 48 Church St., details the growth of the region and the wool industry since settlement. It also houses the **Ross Visitor Information Centre** (www.visitross.com.au; ✆ **03/6381 5466**); both are open from 9:30am to 5pm Monday through Friday, and 10am to 5pm Saturday and Sunday. If you are so charmed you want to stay overnight, try the historic **Colonial Cottages of Ross** (www.rossaccommodation.com.au; ✆ **03/6381 5354**) on Church Street.

silos, the North Tower is a contemporary addition with more rooms and suites (some with private balconies) furnished with natural tones and interesting artwork reflecting the hotel construction project. It's a 10-minute walk to the city center. The hotel also has a helipad and offers scenic aerial tours (see p. 430).

89-91 Lindsay St. www.peppers.com.au/silo. ✆ **1300/987 600** in Australia, 07/5665 4426 (central reservations), or 03/6700 0600 (hotel). 108 units. A$244–A$334 double; A$314–A$544 suite. Parking A$10. **Amenities:** Restaurant; bar; babysitting; gymnasium; room service; spa; free Wi-Fi.

Quamby Estate ★★ This gorgeous historic house, built in 1848, is about a 20-minute drive from Launceston. Rooms are large and beautifully appointed, with massive bathtubs (some are spa tubs). Each room is different from the others, with original art, antique furniture, and gleaming hardwood floors. Some rooms have doors opening onto the wraparound veranda. Some of the layout is a little odd, but that just adds to the historic feel. Bikes are available for exploring, or you can hit the golf course (watch out for Sir Richard Branson, he holds the No.1 membership here!).

1145 Westwood Rd., Hagley. www.quambyestate.com.au. ✆ **03/6392 2135.** 10 units. A$169–A$349 double. Breakfast A$25. Free parking. Free airport shuttle. **Amenities:** Restaurant; babysitting; CD, DVD, and book library; 9-hole golf course; tennis court; free Wi-Fi.

York Mansions ★★★ Within the walls of the National Trust–classified York Mansions, built in 1840, are five spacious two-bedroom apartments and one three-bedroom apartment, each with its own distinct character. The Lodge apartment is fashioned after a gentleman's drawing room, complete with rich leather sofa, antiques, and an extensive collection of historical books. The light and airy Duchess and Countess apartments are more feminine. Each apartment has its own kitchen, dining room, living room, bedrooms, bathroom, and laundry. There's also a delightful cottage garden with a massive Heritage-listed oak tree—just the spot for sundowners.

9–11 York St. www.yorkmansions.com.au. ℂ **03/6334 2933.** 6 units. A$170–A$250 double. Free parking. **Amenities:** Free Wi-Fi.

MODERATE

Alice's Cottages & Spa Hideaways ★★ Tucked down a romantic lane and known collectively as the Shambles, these themed cottages are designed to bring out the romantic in you. Four of the six cottages, each of which sleeps only two, are named for the places the "colonials" came from: England, Wales, Ireland, and Scotland. The other two are the Camelot and Boudoir "spa hideaways." Four-poster beds, soft drapes, roaring log fires…you get the picture.

121–129 Balfour St. www.alicescottages.com.au. ℂ **0498/525 716** mobile. 6 units. A$200–A$210 double. Rates include breakfast basket for two. Free parking. **Amenities:** Free Wi-Fi.

Quality Hotel Colonial Launceston ★ Those who are looking for tried-and-true above-standard motel lodging will feel at home at the Colonial, a place that combines old-world ambience with modern facilities. Beautiful gardens surround the property; rooms are fairly standard but they are large, with attractive furnishings. There are also family rooms and apartments. The clientele tends to be mostly corporate.

31 Elizabeth St. www.coloniallaunceston.com.au. ℂ **03/6331 6588.** 70 units. A$180–A$350 double; A$290 family room; A$295–A$500 apartments. Free parking. **Amenities:** Restaurant; exercise room; room service; free Wi-Fi.

Waratah on York ★ This Victorian mansion was built in 1862 for Alexander Webster, an ironmonger who was mayor of Launceston in the 1860s and 1870s. Some original features—pressed brass ceiling roses and a staircase with a cast-iron balustrade—remain, while others have been faithfully re-created. Six rooms come with a Jacuzzi, one with a balcony, and another with a sunroom. All have high ceilings and ornate (but nonfunctioning) fireplaces. The executive rooms have four-poster beds and sweeping views of the Tamar River, and there is a three-bedroom apartment.

12 York St. www.waratahonyork.com.au. ✆ **03/6331 2081.** 10 units. A$200–A$300 double. Rates include breakfast. Free parking. **Amenities:** Bar; free Wi-Fi.

INEXPENSIVE

Hillview House Bed & Breakfast ★ The rooms at this restored farmhouse are cozy and quite comfortable. Each comes with a double or queen bed and a shower. The family room has an extra single bed; it's the nicest unit and has the best views. The hotel overlooks the city (the hill is a bit steep to walk up), and the large veranda and colonial dining room have extensive views over the city and the Tamar River. No children age 4 and under.

193 George St. www.hillviewhouse.net.au. ✆ **03/6331 7388.** 9 units. A$139–A$149 double; A$165 family room (sleeps 3). Rates include breakfast. Free parking. **Amenities:** Free Wi-Fi.

Where to Eat in Launceston

Inside Cafe ★ CAFE Set in an 1880s warehouse, this open and airy cafe shares its space with a homewares shop. It's a great spot for breakfast—your eggs might come with truffle mushrooms or smashed avocado—and the lunch menu is equally tasty, with offerings such as duck salad, halloumi and sweetcorn fritters, or crab tacos. There's a kids' menu too.

10–14 Patterson St. www.insidecafe.com.au. ✆ **03/6331 7348.** Main courses A$14–A$24. Mon–Fri 7:30am–4pm; Sat 8am–3:30pm.

Me Wah Restaurant ★★★ CHINESE The name of this restaurant means "exquisite setting," and exquisite food is what you'll find here. Old-style courtesy and service, coupled with wonderful flavors, will have you coming back for more. The Peking duck is divine, and a host of Cantonese dishes will leave you drooling, including the Greenlip abalone found off the shores of Tasmania's King and Flinders islands. It's expensive, but the elegant Chinese décor and wonderful service make it memorable and worthwhile.

39-41 Invermay Rd. www.mewah.com.au/launceston. ✆ **03/6331 1308.** Main courses A$28–A$45. Tues–Sun 11:30am–2:30pm and 5–9:30pm (10:30pm Fri–Sat). Closed Mon.

Mudbar ★★ CONTEMPORARY One of Launceston's best restaurants, Mudbar has a lovely setting overlooking the marina and river. Locals flock here, helped along by excellent staff and a terrific relaxed vibe. Take a table in the dining area or grab a bar table or couch in the lounge area. The menu has an Asian twist to it, with dishes like soy-roasted duckling with Thai basil or Chinese slow-braised lamb chili, and there's also grass-fed local beef on the char grill. A vegetarian menu is available.

28 Seaport Blvd. www.mudbar.com.au. ✆ **03/6334 5066.** Main courses A$29–A$30; dinner fixed price menus A$60 for 2 courses, A$78 for 3 courses. Daily noon–3pm; dinner seatings at 6pm and 8pm; breakfast 8am–11am Sat–Sun.

Stillwater ★★ CONTEMPORARY   This fabulous and popular eatery is located inside an old mill beside the Tamar River. Come for a good breakfast, a casual lunch at one of the tables outside overlooking the river, or an atmospheric dinner. Menus change seasonally and sometimes at short notice, but the food is always fascinating, with all sorts of delicacies on offer. Maybe something like Tasmanian eye filet rolled in sea salt and served with Sicilian olive and yuzu tapenade, with a dessert of pine tree leaf–infused parfait with strawberries or green apple panna cotta. Small plates might include whiskey-cured Tasmanian salmon with dill and honey vinaigrette, salmon pearls, and puffed wild rice. The wine cellar brings up a good selection of Tasmanian wines. If you just can't decide, go for the five-course tasting menu at A$125 (A$195 with matching wines). Reservations recommended.

2 Bridge Rd. (at Paterson St.). www.stillwater.net.au. 𝒞 **03/6331 4153.** Main courses A$21–A$65. Daily from 8am for breakfast and noon for lunch; Tues–Sat 6–10pm. Closed Good Friday and Dec 25.

Exploring Launceston

Cataract Gorge ★★ NATURAL WONDER   Created by violent earthquakes that rattled Tasmania some 40 million years ago, this natural attraction is a must-see. It's a wonderfully scenic area, and you can walk there along the riverbank from the city in about 15 minutes. The South Esk River flows through the gorge and collects in a small lake called the Basin, traversed by a striking suspension bridge and the longest single-span **chairlift** in the world (308m/1,010 ft.). The chairlift operates daily from 9am to 4:30pm (later in summer) and costs A$16 for adults and A$10 for children 15 and under, round-trip. A funicular **cable car** also runs to higher parts of the gorge. The hike to the **Duck Reach Power Station,** now an interpretive center, takes about 45 minutes. Other walks in the area are shorter and easier. The **Gorge Restaurant** (𝒞 **03/6331 3330;** closed Mon) and the cafe next door are open daily from 9am, with glorious views from the outdoor tables.

Cataract Gorge Reserve, Basin Rd. www.launcestoncataractgorge.com.au. 𝒞 **03/6331 5915** (chairlift office). Free admission.

Design Tasmania ★ MUSEUM   Inspiring and innovative contemporary design is the focus here, from the building itself—a light-filled structure added on to a Heritage-listed church hall—to its contents. The permanent display is the Tasmanian Wood Design Collection, but you will also find changing exhibitions of ceramics, textiles, works on paper, and mixed media.

Cruise the Tamar	
Tamar River Cruises (www.tamarrivercruises.com.au; 𝒞 **03/6334 9900**) offers regular 50-minute cruises to Cataract Gorge up the Tamar River from Home	Point Wharf in Launceston. The cost is A$33 adults, A$15 children 5 to 17, and A$80 for families of four. Longer cruises are also available.

Alexandra Suspension Bridge at Cataract Gorge's First Basin.

The museum hosts a new exhibition every month, from the industrial to the aesthetic. There's a shop as well.

City Park, Brisbane St. (at Tamar St.). www.designtasmania.com.au. ☏ **03/6331 5506.** Free admission. Mon–Fri 9:30am–5:30pm; Sat–Sun 10am–4pm.

The Old Umbrella Shop ★ HISTORIC SITE   Built in the 1860s, this unique shop is the last genuine period store in Tasmania. Run by three generations of the umbrella-making Shott family since the turn of the 20th century until a few years ago, it is now operated by the National Trust. Umbrellas spanning the last 100 years are on display, and modern "brollies" and souvenirs are for sale.

60 George St. www.nationaltrust.org.au/places/old-umbrella-shop. ☏ **03/6331 9248.** Free admission. Mon–Fri 9am–5pm; Sat 9am–noon. Closed Jan 1, Good Friday, and Dec 25–26.

The Queen Victoria Museum & Art Gallery ★★ MUSEUM   This museum, opened in honor of Queen Victoria's Golden Jubilee in 1891, is in two parts: the art gallery on Wellington Street, Royal Park, in the heart of Launceston, and the other in the inner suburb of Inveresk, just a few minutes' drive away (or catch the Tiger Bus). The Inveresk complex, a smart redevelopment of old rail yards, is home to the Launceston Planetarium and focuses on science, which kids will find fun. Free tours are run on Sundays, at the art gallery at 11am and the museum at 1pm.

2 Invermay Rd., Inveresk, and 2 Wellington St., Royal Park. www.qvmag.tas.gov.au. ☏ **03/6323 3777.** Free admission. Planetarium admission A$7 adults, A$5 children, A$18 families of 4 (no children 4 and under). Daily 10am–4pm (5pm in Jan). Closed Good Friday and Dec 25. Planetarium closed Sun–Mon and public holidays; show times Tues–Fri 1 and 3pm, Sat 2 and 3pm.

Harvest Markets

Launceston's community farmer's market runs every Saturday morning. This is where you can see (and buy) produce exclusively grown in Tasmania. The **Harvest Market** (www.harvetmarket.org.au) is held in the Cimitiere Street car park from 8:30am to 12:30pm.

Woolmers Estate ★★ HISTORIC HOME   The grand estate of pioneer Thomas Archer is an extraordinary time capsule. It is inscribed on the World Heritage List of Australian Convict Sites. Once the most powerful family in Tasmania's north, the Archers settled at this homestead near Longford, about 25km (16 miles) from Launceston, in 1817. The six generations who lived here until 1994 have left an unrivaled legacy in the almost-untouched Woolmers Estate. There are 20 buildings, from the grand mansion to the servants' quarters, shearing sheds, a blacksmith's shop, and seven free settler's cottages. (You can stay in some of them, for A$150 per night.) Entry to the homestead is by guided tour only, or you can take a self-guided tour of the gardens and outbuildings. A restaurant serves Devonshire teas, lunches, and snacks. Take time to smell the roses next door at the **National Rose Garden of Australia** (free entry), where more than 2 hectares (5 acres) are planted with around 4,000 bushes.

658 Woolmers Lane, Longford. www.woolmers.com.au. © **03/6391 2230.** Entry to grounds A$16 adults, A$7 children, A$35 family; guided tour A$22 adults, A$9 children 15 and under. Daily 9:30am–4pm. Closed Good Friday, Apr 25 until 1pm, and Dec 25. House tours at 10 and 11:15am, and 12:30, 2, and 3:30pm daily; convict tours Wed at 10:15 and 11:30am and 1pm.

PLANNING YOUR TRIP TO AUSTRALIA

A little preparation is essential before you start your journey to Australia, especially if you plan to do any special-interest activities, such as diving the Great Barrier Reef or visiting the Aboriginal landmarks in the Red Centre. This chapter provides a variety of planning tools, including information on how to get there and on-the-ground resources.

ARRIVING

By Plane

Australia is a very long haul from just about anywhere except New Zealand. Sydney is a nearly 15-hour nonstop flight from Los Angeles, and even longer if you come via Honolulu, Hawaii. If you're flying from the East Coast of the United States, add 5½ hours. If you're coming from the U.S. via Auckland, add transit time in New Zealand plus 3 hours for the Auckland-Sydney leg.

If you are coming from the United Kingdom, brace yourself for a flight of 12 hours, more or less, from London to Asia, followed possibly by a long day in transit, because flights to Australia have a habit of arriving in Asia early in the morning and then not departing until around midnight, after which you still have an 8- to 9-hour flight to Australia.

Sydney (SYD), Cairns (CNS), Melbourne (MEL), Perth (PER) and Brisbane (BNE) are all international gateways. Sydney is the major entry point into Australia, but you may also fly through another airport first, depending on where you're departing from. Major airlines flying to Australia from North America are **Qantas** (www.qantas.com.au), **Virgin Australia** (www.virginaustralia.com.au), **Air Canada** (www.aircanada.com), **American Airlines** (www.americanairlines.com.au), **Delta** (www.delta.com), **Hawaiian Airlines** (www.hawaiianairlines.com.au), and **United** (www.united.com). **Qantas** has direct London-Sydney and London-Perth nonstop routes; several other airlines connect the U.K. with Australia but make one or two stops en route, traveling either east or west.

Singapore-based low-cost carrier **Scoot** (www.flyscoot.com; ☎ **808/206 7487** in the U.S., or **02/9009 0860** in Australia) flies to Sydney, Perth, Melbourne, and Queensland's Gold Coast.

By Cruise Ship

Sydney Harbour is Australia's main port for cruise ships and the only port in Australia with two dedicated cruise-passenger terminals—the Overseas Passenger Terminal at Circular Quay (in the heart of the city, close to major tourist attractions) and the White Bay Cruise Terminal in the suburb of Rozelle, about 5km (3 miles) from the city center. Melbourne and Brisbane are also major cruise ports, and some cruises also stop off at Adelaide, Darwin, Hobart, and Perth. Cruise lines offer hundreds of itineraries that include Australia; most also include New Zealand and the South Pacific. Major cruise companies to check out include **Carnival Cruises** (www.carnival.com.au), **Cunard** (www.cunardline.com.au), **Holland America** (www.hollandamerica.com), **P&O Cruises** (www.pocruises.com.au), **Princess Cruises** (www.princess.com), **Royal Caribbean** (www.royalcaribbean.com), **Seabourn Cruises** (www.seabourn.com), and **Silversea Cruises** (www.silversea.com).

GETTING AROUND
By Plane

Australia is a big country with a small population to support its air routes, so airfares may be higher than you are used to paying. Don't assume there is a direct flight to your chosen destination, or that there is a flight every hour or even every day.

Most domestic air travel is operated by **Qantas** (www.qantas.com.au; ☎ **800/227-4500** in the U.S. and Canada, 131 313 in Australia, 0800/964 432 in the U.K., 0800/808 767 in New Zealand), **Virgin Australia** (www.virginaustralia.com; ☎ **1855/253-8021** in the U.S., 136 789 or 07/3295 2296 in Australia, 0800/051 1281 in the U.K., 0800/670 000 in New Zealand), or Qantas-owned **Jetstar** (www.jetstar.com.au; ☎ **1866/397-8170** in the U.S., 131 538 or 03/9645 5999 in Australia, 0800/800 995 in New Zealand).

Between them, Virgin Australia and Qantas and its subsidiaries, QantasLink and Jetstar, service every capital city, as well as most major regional towns on the east coast. **Regional Express** (www.rex.com.au; ☎ **131 713** in Australia) serves some regional ports in New South Wales, Victoria, South Australia, Tasmania, and Queensland.

Note that Melbourne has two airports: the main international and domestic terminals at Tullamarine, and Avalon Airport, about 50km (31 miles) from the city, which is used by some Jetstar flights. Make sure you check which one your flight will leave from before you book. Similarly, if you are changing planes in Perth, be aware that the international and domestic terminals are a

FACING PAGE: Melbourne's Flinders Street Station and a City Circle tram.

considerable distance from one another; you cannot walk between them and will need to allow time for transfers.

Competition is hot and the airline industry constantly changing, so it's possible that all airlines will have changed their route networks by the time you read this.

DISCOUNTED FARES FOR INTERNATIONAL TRAVELERS

Qantas offers international travelers discounts off the full fares that Australians pay for domestic flights bought within Australia. To qualify, quote your passport number and international ticket number when reserving. Don't assume the fare for international travelers is the best deal, though—the latest deal in the market that day (or even better, perhaps, a package deal with accommodations thrown in) may be cheaper still.

AIR PASSES

If you are visiting from the U.S. and plan on visiting more than one city, purchasing a **Qantas Explorer pass** is much cheaper than buying regular fares. The pass is for economy-class travel only and must be purchased along with your Qantas or American Airlines fare from the U.S. to Australia. Prices vary according to which "zone" you are traveling to, and there are more than 30 Australian destinations to choose from, but the deals will get you to all major destinations covered in this book.

By Car

Australia's roads sometimes leave a bit to be desired. The taxes of 24 million people get spread pretty thin when it comes to maintaining roads across a continent. Some "highways" are two-lane affairs with the occasional rut and pothole, often no outside line markings, and sometimes no shoulders to speak of. You will strike these if you plan to drive in the Red Centre.

If you plan long-distance driving, get a road map (see "Maps," p. 441, for sources) that distinguishes between paved and unpaved roads.

You can use your current driver's license or an international driver's permit in every state of Australia. By law, you must carry your license with you when driving. The minimum driving age is 16 or 17, depending on which state you visit, but some car-rental companies require you to be 21, or sometimes 26, if you want to rent a four-wheel-drive (4WD) vehicle.

CAR RENTALS

Think twice about renting a car in tourist hot spots such as Cairns. In these areas most tour operators pick you up and drop you back at your hotel door, so having a car may not be worth the expense.

The "big four" car-rental companies—**Avis** (www.avis.com.au), **Budget** (www.budget.com.au), **Hertz** (www.hertz.com.au), and **Thrifty** (www.thrifty.com.au)—all have networks across Australia. Other major car-rental companies are **Europcar** (www.europcar.com.au), which has the third largest fleet in Australia, and **Red Spot Car Rentals** (www.redspot.com.au), which has depots in all state capital cities as well as other major centers such as Cairns, Townsville, and Rockhampton.

A small sedan for zipping around a city will cost about A$45 to A$80 a day. A feistier vehicle with enough grunt to get you from state to state will cost around A$70 to A$100 a day. Rentals of a week or longer usually reduce the price by A$5 a day or so.

A regular car will get you to most places in this book, except for some parts of the Red Centre, where you will need a 4WD vehicle. All the major car-rental companies rent them. Four-wheel-drives are more expensive than a regular car, but you can get them for as little as A$75 per day if you shop around (cheaper for rentals of a week or longer).

The rates quoted here are only a guide. Many smaller local companies— and the big guys, too—offer competitive specials, especially in tourist areas with distinct off-seasons. Advance purchase rates, usually 7 to 21 days ahead, can offer significant savings.

If you are concerned about reducing your carbon emissions, consider hiring a hybrid car. In Australia, the major car-hire companies have the hybrid Toyota Prius available. Ask when making your bookings.

INSURANCE

Insurance for loss of or damage to the car and third-party property insurance are usually included, but read the agreement carefully because the fine print contains information the front-desk staff may not tell you. For example, damage to the car body may be covered, but not damage to the windshield or tires, or damage caused by water or driving too close to a bushfire.

The deductible, known as **"excess"** in Australia, on insurance may be as high as A$2,000 for regular cars and up to A$5,500 on 4WDs and motor homes. You can reduce it, or avoid it altogether, by paying a premium of between about A$20 to A$50 per day on a car or four-wheel-drive, and around A$25 to A$50 per day on a motor home. The amount of the excess reduction premium depends on the vehicle type and the extent of reduction you choose. Your rental company may bundle personal accident insurance and baggage insurance into this premium. And again, check the conditions; some excess reduction payments do not reduce excesses on single-vehicle accidents, for example.

Insurance Alert

Different car-rental companies have very different rules and restrictions, so make sure you check each one's coverage. Damage to a rental car caused by an animal (hitting a kangaroo, for instance) may not be covered by your car-rental company's insurance policies. Some will not cover animal damage incurred at night, for example. The same applies to the rules about driving on unpaved roads, of which Australia has many. Avis and Budget say you may only drive on roads "properly formed and constructed as a sealed, metalled, or gravel road," while the others limit you largely to sealed roads. Check the fine print.

ONE-WAY RENTALS

Australia's long distances often make one-way rentals a necessity, for which car-rental companies can charge a hefty penalty amounting to hundreds of dollars. A one-way fee usually applies to motor-home rentals, too—usually around A$260 to A$360. An extra A$650 remote-location fee can apply for Outback areas such as Alice Springs. And there are minimum rental periods of between 7 and 21 days.

MOTOR HOMES

Motor homes (Aussies call them camper vans) are popular in Australia. Generally smaller than the RVs in the United States, they come in two- to six-berth versions and usually have everything you need, such as a minifridge and/or freezer (icebox in the smaller versions), microwave, gas stove, cooking and cleaning utensils, linens, and touring information, including maps and campground guides. All have showers and toilets, except some two-berthers.

Most of these camper vans have air-conditioned driver's cabins, but note that not all have air-conditioned living quarters, which is more or less a necessity to have in most parts of the country from November through March. Ask to make sure that the vehicle you're renting is fully air-conditioned if you're traveling this time of year. Four-wheel-drive campers are available, but while they offer an advantage in traversing wilderness roads, they tend to be small, and some lack hot water, toilet, and shower, not to mention air-conditioning.

Australia's biggest national motor-home-rental companies are **Apollo Motorhome Holidays** (www.apollocamper.com; ℂ **1800/777 779** in Australia, or 07/3265 9200), **Britz Campervan Rentals** (www.britz.com; ℂ **1800/331 454** in Australia, or 800/2008 0801 from outside Australia), and **Maui** (www.maui-rentals.com; ℂ **800/2008 0801** from anywhere in the world, or 1800/827 821 within Australia, or 02/9316 9071).

Rates vary with the seasons and your choice of vehicle. May and June are the slowest months; December and January are the busiest. It's sometimes possible to get better rates by booking in your home country before departure. Renting for longer than 3 weeks knocks a few dollars off the daily rate. Most companies will require a minimum 4- or 5-day rental. Give the company your itinerary before booking, because some routes may need the company's permission. Note that the minimum driver age for renting motor homes is usually 21.

Most local councils take a dim view of "free camping," the practice of pulling over by the roadside to camp for the night. Instead, in most places you will have to stay in a campground—and pay for it.

ON THE ROAD

GAS Prices go up and down, but at press time you were looking at around A$1.40 a liter (about ¼ gal.) for unleaded petrol in Sydney, and slightly more in the Outback. Most rental cars take unleaded gas, and motor homes run on diesel.

DRIVING RULES Australians drive on the left, which means you give way to the right. Left turns on a red light are not permitted unless a sign says so.

Roundabouts (traffic circles) are common at intersections; approach these slowly enough to stop if you have to, and give way to all traffic on the roundabout. Flash your indicator (turn signal) as you leave the roundabout (even if you're going straight, because technically that's a left turn).

The maximum permitted blood alcohol level when driving is .05%, which equals approximately two 200-milliliter (6.6-oz.) drinks in the first hour for men, one for women, and one drink per hour for both sexes after that. The police set up random breath-testing units (RBTs) in cunningly disguised and unlikely places all the time, so getting caught is easy. You will face a court appearance if you do.

The speed limit is 50kmph (31 mph) or 60kmph (37 mph) in urban areas, 100kmph (62 mph) in most country areas, and sometimes 110kmph (68 mph) on freeways. In the Northern Territory, the speed limit is set at 130kmph (81 mph) on the Stuart, Arnhem, Barkly, and Victoria highways, while rural roads are designated 110kmph (68 mph) unless otherwise signposted. *Be warned:* The Territory has a high death toll. Speed-limit signs show black numbers circled in red on a white background.

Drivers and passengers, including taxi passengers, must wear a seatbelt at all times when the vehicle is moving forward, if the car is equipped with a belt. Young children are required to sit in the rear seat in a child-safety seat or harness; car-rental companies will rent these to you, but be sure to request them in advance. Tell the taxi company you have a child when you book a cab so that it can send a car with the right restraints.

MAPS The maps published by the state automobile clubs listed below in "Auto Clubs" will likely be free if you are a member of an affiliated auto club in your home country. None will mail them to you overseas; pick them up on arrival. Remember to bring your auto-club membership card to qualify for discounts or free maps.

Two of the biggest map publishers in Australia are **HEMA Maps** (www. hemamaps.com) and **UBD Gregory's** (www.hardiegrant.com/au/travel). Both publish an extensive range of national (including road atlases), state, regional, and city maps. HEMA has a strong list of regional maps, while UBD Gregory's produces a complete range of street directories by city, region, or state. HEMA produces 4WD and motorbike road atlases and many regional 4WD maps—good if you plan to go off the trails. Many of its maps are also available as smartphone apps.

TOLL ROADS Electronic "beeper" or e-tags are used on all major Australian toll roads, including Melbourne's City Link motorways, Brisbane's tunnels and Logan and Gateway motorways, the Sydney Harbour Bridge and tunnel, and all of Sydney's major tunnels and motorways. The tag is a small device attached to the vehicle's front windshield, which transmits signals to toll points on the road. This deducts the toll amount from your toll account.

Wildlife on the Roads

It's a sad fact, but kangaroos are a road hazard. Avoid driving in country areas between dusk and dawn, when 'roos are most active. If you hit one, always stop and check its pouch for live joeys (baby kangaroos), because females usually have one in the pouch. Wrap the joey tightly in a towel or old sweater, don't feed or over-handle it, and take it to a vet in the nearest town or call one of the following wildlife care groups: **Wildlife Information & Rescue Service (WIRES)** in New South Wales (℗ **1300/094 737**); **Wildlife Victoria** (℗ **03/8400 7300**); **Wildcare Australia** in Queensland (℗ **07/5527 2444**) or Western Australia (℗ **08/9474 9055**); or **Wildcare NT** in Darwin (℗ **08/8988 6121** or 0408 885 341 mobile phone. In South Australia,

Fauna Rescue SA (℗ **08/8289 0896**) has a 24-hour hotline. In Tasmania, **Bonorong Wildlife Sanctuary** (℗ **03/ 6268 1184**) has the state's only 24-hour wildlife rescue service. Most vets will treat native wildlife for free.

Some highways run through unfenced stations (ranches), where sheep and cattle pose a threat. Cattle like to rest on the warm bitumen road at night, so put your lights on high to spot them. If an animal does loom up, slow down—but never swerve, or you may roll. If you have to, hit it. Tell farmers within 24 hours if you have hit their livestock.

Some car-rental companies will not insure for animal damage to the car, which should give you an inkling of how common an occurrence this is.

The same e-tag can be used on all Australian toll roads. While some toll roads still have physical collection points where you can pay the toll, others—such as Melbourne's freeways—don't. If you are likely to need an e-tag, your car-rental company can arrange one for you.

ROAD SIGNS   Australians navigate by road name, not road number. The easiest way to get where you're going is to familiarize yourself with the major towns along your route and follow the signs toward them.

AUTO CLUBS   Every state and territory in Australia has its own auto club. Your auto association back home probably has a reciprocal agreement with Australian clubs, which may entitle you to free maps, accommodations guides, and roadside assistance. Don't forget to bring your membership card.

Even if you're not a member, the clubs are a good source of advice on local traffic regulations, touring advice, road conditions, traveling in remote areas, and any other motoring questions you may have. The clubs sell maps, accommodations guides, and camping guides to nonmembers at reasonable prices. They even share a website: **www.aaa.asn.au**.

ROAD CONDITIONS & SAFETY

Here are some common motoring dangers and ways to avoid them:

FATIGUE   Fatigue is a killer on Australia's roads. The rule is to take a 20-minute break every 2 hours, even if you don't feel tired. In some states, "driver reviver" stations operate on major roads during holiday periods. Serving free tea, coffee, and cookies, they are often found at roadside picnic areas with restrooms.

ROAD TRAINS Road trains consist of as many as three big truck carriages (tractor-trailers) linked together to make a "train" up to 54m (177 ft.) long. If you're in front of one, give the driver plenty of warning when you brake, because the trains need a lot of distance to slow down. Allow at least 1 clear kilometer (.6 miles) before you pass one, but don't expect the driver to make it easy—"truckies" are notorious for their lack of concern for motorists.

UNPAVED ROADS Many country roads are unsealed (unpaved). They are usually bone-dry, which makes them more slippery than they look, so travel at a moderate speed—35kmph (22 mph) is not too cautious, and anything over 60kmph (37 mph) is dangerous. That said, when you are on a heavily corrugated or rutted road (which many are), you may need to keep to a higher speed (60kmph/37 mph) just to stay on top of them. Don't overcorrect if you veer to one side. Keep well behind any vehicles, because the dust they throw up can block your vision.

FLOODS Floods are common north of Cairns from November or December through March or April (the "Wet" season). Never cross a flooded road unless you are sure of its depth. Crocodiles may be in the water, so do not wade in to test it! Fast-flowing water is dangerous, even if it's very shallow. When in doubt, stay where you are and wait for the water to drop; most flash floods subside in 24 hours. Check the road conditions ahead at least once a day in the Wet season.

RUNNING OUT OF GAS Gas stations (also called "roadhouses" in rural areas) can be few and far between in the Outback, so fill up at every opportunity.

TIPS FOR FOUR-WHEEL DRIVERS Always keep to the four-wheel-drive track. Going off-road causes soil erosion, a significant environmental problem in Australia. Leave gates as you found them. Obtain permission from

---

What If Your Vehicle Breaks Down?

Warning: If you break down or get lost, **never leave your vehicle.** Many a motorist—often an Aussie who should have known better—has died wandering off on a crazy quest for help or water, knowing full well that neither is to be found for maybe hundreds of miles. Most people who get lost do so in Outback spots; if that happens to you, conserve your body moisture by doing as little as possible and staying in the shade of your car.

The **emergency breakdown assistance** telephone number for every Australian auto club is 🕐 **131 111** from anywhere in Australia. It is billed as a local call. If you are not a member of an auto club at home that has a reciprocal agreement with the Australian clubs, you'll have to join the Australian club on the spot before the club will tow or repair your car. This usually costs around A$80, not a big price to pay when you're stranded—although in the Outback, the charge may be considerably higher. Most car-rental companies also have emergency assistance numbers.

the owners before venturing onto private station (ranch) roads. On an extended trip or in remote areas, carry 5 liters (1⅓ gal.) of drinking water per person per day (dehydration occurs fast in the Australian heat); enough food to last 3 or 4 days more than you think you will need; a first-aid kit; spare fuel; a jack and two spare tires; spare fan belts, radiator hoses, and air-conditioner hoses; a tow rope; and a good map that marks all gas stations. In seriously remote areas outside the scope of this book, carry a high-frequency and a CB radio (a mobile phone may not work in the Outback). Advise a friend, your hotel manager, the local tourist bureau, or a police station of your route and your expected time of return or arrival at your destination.

By Train

Australia's trains are clean, comfortable, and safe, and for the most part service standards and facilities are perfectly adequate. The rail network in Australia links Perth to Adelaide and on to Melbourne, and north to Sydney, Brisbane, and Cairns. There's also a line into the interior from Adelaide to Alice Springs and Darwin. Trains generally cost more than buses but are still reasonably priced.

Most long-distance trains have sleepers with big windows, air-conditioning, electric outlets, wardrobes, sinks, and fresh sheets and blankets. First-class sleepers have en-suite bathrooms, and fares often include meals. Second-class sleepers use shared shower facilities, and meals are not included. Some second-class sleepers are private cabins; on other trains, you share with strangers. Single cabins are usually of broom-closet dimensions but surprisingly comfy, with their own toilet and basin. The onboard food ranges from mediocre to pretty good. Note that smoking is banned on all Australian rail networks.

Different entities manage Australia's rail routes. They include the government-owned **Queensland Rail** (www.queenslandrailtravel.com.au; ℭ **1300/131 722** in Australia, or 07/3606 6630), which handles rail within that state, and **NSW TrainLink** (www.transportnsw.info/regional; ℭ **132 232** in Australia or 02/4907 7502), which manages travel within New South Wales and from Sydney south to Melbourne and north to Brisbane. **Great Southern Rail** (www.greatsouthernrail.com.au; ℭ **1800/703 357** in Australia, or 08/8213 4401) has a range of fabulous Outback train journeys, including *The Ghan* (p. 374), which links Adelaide, Alice Springs, and Darwin, *The Indian Pacific* (p. 374), which travels between Sydney and Perth, and *The Overland,* between Melbourne and Adelaide.

Queensland Rail operates the high-speed *Spirit of Queensland* five times a week on the Brisbane-Cairns route with business-class-style seating and "rail-beds" (similar to business-class lie-flat airline beds). The trip takes around 24 hours. The **Tilt Train** runs between Brisbane and the coastal towns of Bundaberg and Rockhampton. All Queensland and New South Wales long-distance trains stop at most towns en route, so they're useful for exploring the eastern states.

RAIL PASSES   NSW TrainLink's **Discovery Pass** gives you unlimited economy-class trips anywhere on its network, including to Melbourne and Brisbane, for up to 6 months. A 14-day pass costs A$232, a 1-month pass A$275, a 3-month pass A$298, and a 6-month pass A$420.

The **Queensland Explorer** pass offers unlimited economy seat travel for 1 or 2 months across the Queensland Rail network, from Cairns in the north to Brisbane in the south, and in the Queensland Outback. It costs A$299 for 1 month or A$389 for 2 months. If you only fancy the coast, the **Queensland Coastal Pass** allows travel between Brisbane and Cairns for A$209 for 1 month, A$289 for 2 months. *Note:* These passes are only available to international travelers.

By Bus

Bus travel in Australia is as comfortable as it can be, given the nature of long-distance coach travel. Terminals are centrally located and well lit, the buses—called "coaches" Down Under—are clean and air-conditioned, you sit in leather adjustable seats, with USB chargers and free Wi-Fi, and drivers are polite and sometimes even point out places of interest along the way. Buses are all nonsmoking, and some have restrooms. The country's extensive bus network will take you almost everywhere.

Australia has one national coach operator: **Greyhound Australia** (www.greyhound.com.au; ✆ **1300/473 946** in Australia, or 07/3155 1550; no relation to Greyhound in the U.S.). In addition to point-to-point services, Greyhound Australia offers a limited range of tours at popular locations on its networks, including Uluru in the Northern Territory and the Whitsunday islands in Queensland.

Fares and some passes are considerably cheaper for students, backpacker cardholders, and Hostelling International/YHA members.

BUS PASSES   Bus passes are a great value. Note that during school vacation periods, which are always busy, booking as much as a week ahead is smart. Greyhound Australia's **Whimit Passes** let you travel any route, in any direction. There are seven passes to choose from: 15, 30, 60, 90, 120, or 365 days. You'll pay A$329 for 15 days, and A$1,699 for the whole year. **Hop-on, hop-off Passes** are valid for 90 days and link most of the popular destinations: from Sydney, Brisbane, or Melbourne to Cairns; Melbourne or Sydney to Brisbane. Travel from Melbourne to Cairns costs A$579.

[FastFACTS] AUSTRALIA

ATMs/Banks   The easiest and best way to get cash away from home is from an **ATM (automated teller machine),** sometimes referred to as a "cash machine" or "cashpoint."

The **Cirrus** (www.mastercard.com) and **PLUS** (www.visa.com) networks span the globe. Be sure you know your daily withdrawal limit before you depart.

Note that Australian ATMs use a four-digit code, so check with your bank and make sure you change yours before you leave. *Note:* Some banks impose a fee every time you use a card at another bank's ATM, and that fee can be higher for international transactions (A$5 or more). In addition, the bank from which you withdraw cash may charge its own fee. For international withdrawal fees, ask your bank.

Customs The duty-free allowance in Australia is A$900 or, for those 17 and under, A$450. Anyone 18 and over can bring in up to 25 cigarettes or 25 grams of cigars or other tobacco products, 2.25 liters (41 fluid oz.) of alcohol, and "dutiable goods" to the value of A$900 (A$450 if you are 17 or under). "Dutiable goods" are luxury items such as perfume, watches, jewelry, furs, plus gifts of any kind. Keep this in mind if you intend to bring presents for family and friends in Australia; gifts given to you also count toward the dutiable limit.

Personal goods that you're taking with you are usually exempt from duty, but if you are returning with valuable goods that you already own, file form B263. Customs officers do not collect duty—less than A$50—as long as you declared the goods in the first place.

For more information, contact the **Australian Border Force** (✆ **131 881** in Australia), or check out **www.abf.gov.au**.

You need not declare cash in any currency, and other currency instruments, such as traveler's checks, under a value of A$10,000.

Australia is a signatory to the **Convention on**

International Trade in Endangered Species (CITES), which restricts or bans the import of products made from protected wildlife. Banned items include ivory, tortoise (marine turtle) shell, rhinoceros, or tiger products, and sturgeon caviar. Bear this in mind if you stop in other countries en route to Australia, where souvenirs made from items like these may be sold. Australian authorities may seize these items.

Because Australia is an island, it is free of many agricultural and livestock diseases. To keep it that way, *strict* **quarantine** applies to importing plants, animals, and their products, including food. "Sniffer" dogs at airports detect these products (as well as drugs). Some items may be confiscated, and others may be held over for you to take with you when you leave the country. Heavy fines apply to breaches of the laws. Amnesty trash bins are available before you reach the immigration counters in airport arrivals halls for items such as fruit. Don't be alarmed if, just before landing, the flight attendants spray the aircraft cabin (with products approved by the World Health Organization) to kill potentially disease-bearing insects. For more information on what is and is not allowed, contact the nearest Australian embassy or consulate, or Australia's **Department of Agriculture and Water Resources** (www.agriculture.gov.au/travelling; ✆ **1800/900 090**

in Australia or 03/8318 6700).

For information on what you're allowed to bring home, contact one of the following agencies:

U.S. Citizens: U.S. Customs & Border Protection (CBP), 1300 Pennsylvania Ave. NW, Washington, DC 20229 (www.cbp.gov; ✆ **877/CBP-5511** [227-5511]).

Canadian Citizens: Canada Border Services Agency, Ottawa, Ontario, K1A 0L8 (www.cbsa-asfc.gc.ca; ✆ **800/461 9999**).

U.K. Citizens: Check with HM Revenue & Customs (www.gov.uk/duty-free-goods).

New Zealand Citizens: The Customhouse, 1 Hinemoa St., Harbour Quays, Wellington, 6011 (www.customs.govt.nz; ✆ **09/927-8036,** or 0800/428-786 in New Zealand).

Doctors & Hospitals Doctors are listed under "M," for "Medical Practitioners," in the Yellow Pages in Australia, and most large towns and cities have 24-hour clinics. Your hotel may be able to help you find a local doctor. Failing that, go to the local emergency room. See "Fast Facts" in other chapters of this book for local details.

Drinking Laws Hours vary from pub to pub, but most are open daily from 10am or noon to 10pm or midnight. The minimum drinking age is 18.

Random breath tests to catch drunk drivers are common, and drunk-driving laws are strictly enforced. Getting caught drunk behind the wheel will mean a court appearance, not just a fine. The maximum permitted blood-alcohol level is .05%.

Alcohol is sold in liquor stores, in the "bottle shops" attached to every pub, and in some states in supermarkets.

Electricity The current is 240 volts AC, 50 hertz. Sockets take two or three flat, not rounded, prongs. Bring a connection kit of the right power and phone adapters, a spare phone cord, and a spare Ethernet network cable—or find out whether your hotel supplies them to guests. North Americans and Europeans will need to buy a converter before they leave home. (Don't wait until you get to Australia, because Australian stores are likely to stock only converters for Aussie appliances to fit American and European outlets.) Some large hotels have 110V outlets for electric shavers (or dual voltage), and some will lend converters, but don't count on it in smaller, less expensive hotels, motels, or B&Bs. **Note:** Power does not start automatically when you plug in an appliance; you need to flick the switch beside the socket to the "on" position.

Embassies & Consulates Most diplomatic posts are in Canberra.

United States: United States Embassy, 21 Moonah Place, Yarralumla, Canberra, ACT 2600 (http://au.usembassy.gov; *℃* **02/6214 5600**), the United States Consulate General, 553 St Kilda Rd., Melbourne (*℃* **03/9526 5900**); the United States Consulate General in Sydney, Level 10, 19-29 Martin Place (*℃* **1300/139 399**); or the United States Consulate General in Perth, 16 St George's Terrace (*℃* **08/6144 5100**.

Canada: High Commission of Canada, Commonwealth Avenue, Yarralumla, Canberra, ACT 2600 (www.canadainternational.gc.ca/australia-australie; *℃* **02/6270 4000**).

Ireland: Consulate General of Ireland, Level 26, 1 Market St., Sydney, NSW 2000 (www.irishconsulatesydney.net; *℃* **02/9264 9635**).

New Zealand: New Zealand High Commission, 140 Commonwealth Ave., Yarralumla, Canberra, ACT 2600 (www.mfat.govt.nz; *℃* **02/6270 4211**).

United Kingdom: British High Commission, Commonwealth Avenue, Yarralumla, Canberra, ACT 2600 (www.gov.uk/world/australia; *℃* **02/6270 6666**).

Emergencies Dial *℃* **000** anywhere in Australia for police, ambulance, or the fire department. This is a free call from public and private telephones and needs no coins. The TTY emergency number is *℃* **106.**

Family Travel Australians travel widely with their own kids, so facilities for families, including family passes to attractions, are common.

Many hotels offer connecting units or "family rooms." Ask when booking. Most Australian hotels will arrange babysitting when given a day's notice.

Many Australian resorts have "kids' clubs" with extensive programs designed for children 11 and under and, in some cases, teenagers. Other resorts have "kids stay, eat, and play free" offers, particularly during holiday periods.

A great accommodations option for families is Australia's huge stock of holiday apartments (with or without daily maid service). Often less expensive than a hotel room, they offer a living room, a kitchen, a bathroom or two, and the privacy of a separate bedroom for adults.

International airlines and domestic airlines in Australia charge 75% of the adult fare for kids 11 and under. Most charge 10% for infants under 2 years not occupying a seat. Australian transport companies, attractions, and tour operators typically charge half-price for kids under 12 or 14 years.

Don't forget that children entering Australia on their parent's passport still need their own visa.

Resources for Family Travel: Two terrific Australian travel magazines are devoted to traveling with children. *Holidays with Kids* (www.holidayswithkids.com.au) and *Out & About*

Family Travel

With Kids (www.outand aboutwithkids.com.au) both have comprehensive websites listing great options for family travel in Australia. **Family Travel Forum** is also a good resource; see **www. myfamilytravels.com** for destinations, ideas, and more.

Health   No vaccinations are needed to enter Australia unless you have been in a yellow fever danger zone—that is, South America or Africa—in the 6 days prior to entering.

Australian pharmacists may only fill prescriptions written by Australian doctors, so carry enough medication with you for your trip. Doctors are listed under "M," for "Medical Practitioners," in the Yellow Pages, and most large towns and cities have 24-hour clinics. Failing that, go to the local hospital emergency room.

Generally, you don't have to worry much about health issues on a trip to Australia. Hygiene standards are high, hospitals are modern, and doctors and dentists are well qualified. Because of the continent's size, however, you can sometimes be a long way from a hospital or a doctor. Remote areas are served by the Royal Flying Doctor Service. But it may be advisable to purchase standard medical travel insurance.

Insurance   Standard medical and travel insurance is advisable for travel to Australia. Divers should also ensure that they have the appropriate insurance. For

information on traveler's insurance, trip cancellation insurance, and medical insurance while traveling, please visit www.frommers. com/tips.

Internet Access   Most hotels throughout Australia offer dataports for laptop modems, high-speed Internet access, and free Wi-Fi. Check the list of hotel amenities in each hotel listing to see what kind of Internet service your hotel offers, and at what cost.

Most **youth hostels** and **public libraries** have Internet access. Avoid **hotel business centers** unless you're willing to pay exorbitant rates. Cybercafes (called **Internet cafes** in Australia) are found almost everywhere.

Most major cities also have free Wi-Fi hubs that you can hook into in public places. Most major airports have **Internet kiosks** that provide basic Web access for a per-minute fee that's usually higher than cyber-cafe prices.

Legal Aid   If you find yourself in trouble with the long arm of the law while visiting Australia, the first thing you should do is contact your country's embassy or nearest consulate in Australia. See contact details for Canberra diplomatic posts under "Embassies & Consulates" above. Embassies or consulates with posts in state capitals are listed in "Fast Facts" in chapters 4, 5, and 6.

The U.S. Embassy considers an "emergency" to be either your arrest or the

loss of your passport. If arrested in Australia, you will have to go through the Australian legal process for being charged, prosecuted, possibly convicted and sentenced, and for any appeals process. U.S. consular officers (and those of other countries) provide a wide variety of services to citizens arrested abroad and to their families. These may include providing a list of local attorneys, providing info about judicial procedures, and notifying your family and/or friends, if you wish. However, they cannot demand your release, represent you at your trial, give you legal advice, or pay your fees or fines.

LGBTQI Travelers   Sydney is one of the most gay-friendly cities in the world, and across most of Australia the gay community has a high profile and lots of support services. Same-sex marriage was legalized in Australia in 2017.

There are plenty of gay and lesbian bars, and most Saturday nights see a privately operated gay dance party taking place in an inner-city warehouse somewhere. The cafes and pubs of Oxford Street in Darlinghurst, a short cab ride or long stroll from Sydney's downtown area, are the liveliest gay spots in that city. The annual **Sydney Gay & Lesbian Mardi Gras,** culminating in a huge street parade and party in late February or early March, is a high point on the city's calendar. In Melbourne, gay

KNOW BEFORE YOU GO: health hazards

Tropical Illnesses Some parts of tropical far-north Queensland have sporadic outbreaks of the mosquito-borne dengue fever. The areas affected include Cairns, Port Douglas, and Townsville. But as dengue-fever mosquitoes breed in urban environments, tourist activities in north Queensland such as reef and rainforest trips carry a modest risk as well. The risk can be minimized by staying in screened or air-conditioned accommodations, using insect repellent at all times, and wearing long, loose, light-colored clothing that covers arms and legs.

Bugs, Bites & Other Wildlife Concerns Snake and spider bites may not be as common as the hair-raising stories you will hear would suggest, but it pays to be wary. Your other concerns should be marine life, including jellyfish and saltwater crocodiles. For more information and background on the fauna of Australia, and how to avoid dangerous encounters with them, see p. 30.

Sun/Elements Australians have the world's highest death rate from skin cancer because of the country's intense sunlight. Limit your exposure to the sun, especially during the first few days of your trip, and from 11am to 3pm in summer and 10am to 2pm in winter.

Remember that UV rays reflected off walls, water, and the ground can burn you even when you're not in direct sunlight. Use a broad-spectrum sunscreen with a high protection factor (SPF 30 or higher). Wear a broad-brimmed hat that covers the back of your neck, ears, and face (a baseball cap won't do it), and a long-sleeved shirt.

Remember that children need more protection than adults do. Don't even think about traveling without sunglasses, or you'll spend your entire vacation squinting against Australia's "diamond light."

Extreme Weather Exposure Cyclones sometimes affect tropical areas, such as Queensland's coastal regions, from about Gladstone north, during January and February. Serious damage is normally rare.

pride is celebrated in early February at the **Midsumma Festival**.

In rural areas of Australia, you may still encounter a little conservative resistance to gays and lesbians, but Australians everywhere are generally open-minded. Noosa, on Queensland's Sunshine Coast, is a favored destination for gay revelers after Mardi Gras, and a couple of resorts in north Queensland cater to gay and lesbian travelers. One of the best known is **Turtle Cove Beach Resort** (www. turtlecove.com;

𝓒 **1300/727 979** in Australia, or 07/4059 1800), located on a private beach between Cairns and Port Douglas.

LGBTQI Resources: A service you may find useful is **Twenty10** (incorporating the Gay & Lesbian Counselling Service of NSW), which runs a national hotline (*𝓒* **1800/184 527** in Australia) from 3pm to midnight daily. Its website, **www. twenty10.org.au**, has lots of useful information. In Sydney, the **Albion Street Centre** (www.thealbion centre.org.au; *𝓒* **1800/451**

600 in Australia, or 02/9332 9600) is a clinic and information service for gay men's health. In Melbourne, the **Victoria Pride Centre**, due to open in 2020, is a hub for LGBTI groups and communities, based at St Kilda. Check the website, www. pridecentre.org.au, for more details about the opening date. **The International Gay and Lesbian Travel Association (IGLTA;** www. iglta.org; *𝓒* **954/630-1637** in the U.S.) offers an online directory of gay- and lesbian-friendly travel businesses and tour operators.

13

PLANNING YOUR TRIP TO AUSTRALIA

LGBTQI Travelers

Visit Gay Australia (www. galta.com.au) has listings of businesses in each state.

Mail & Postage A postcard or letter (up to 50g/1.7 oz. in weight) will cost A$2.10 to send from Australia to New Zealand, or A$3 from Australia to the U.S., Canada, or U.K. Mail will take up to 8 business days to reach North America or Europe from Australia.

A parcel of up to 500g (1.1lb.) will cost A$17 to send to the United States by airmail.

Mobile Phones The three letters that define much of the world's wireless capabilities are **GSM** (Global System for Mobile Communications), a big, seamless network that makes for easy cross-border cellphone use throughout Europe and dozens of other countries worldwide.

In the U.S., T-Mobile and AT&T Wireless use this quasi-universal system; in Canada, Microcell and some Rogers customers are GSM; and all Europeans and most Australians use GSM.

GSM phones function with a removable plastic SIM card, encoded with your phone number and account information. If your cellphone is on a GSM system, and you have a world-capable multiband phone, you can make and receive calls around much of the globe.

Just call your wireless operator and ask for "international roaming" to be activated on your account.

But be sure to check the cost of "data roaming" on smartphones, because the cost can be astronomical, and you do not want a nasty (and I mean *really* nasty!) surprise on your return home when you get the bill. Unless you turn off your data roaming, it will activate automatically.

For many, **renting** a phone is a good idea. While you can rent a phone from any number of overseas sites, including kiosks at airports and at car-rental agencies, we suggest renting the phone before you leave home. North Americans can rent one before leaving home from **RoadPost** (www. roadpost.com; ℂ **888/290-1616,** or 416/253-4539) or **InTouch U.S.A.** (www. intouchglobal.com; **800/872 7626**). InTouch will also give free advice on whether your existing phone will work overseas; simply call ℂ **703/222-7161** between 9am and 4pm EST, or go to **http:// intouchglobal.com/travel. htm**.

In Australia—reputed to have one of the world's highest per-capita rates of ownership of "mobile" telephones, as they are known here—the cell network is digital, not analog. Calls to or from a mobile telephone are generally more expensive than calls to or from a land line. The price varies depending on the telephone company, the time of day, the distance between caller and recipient, and the telephone's pricing plan.

Buying a prepaid phone can be economically attractive. Once you arrive in Australia, stop by a local cellphone shop and get the cheapest package; you'll probably pay less than A$100 for a phone and a starter calling card with a significant amount of free credit.

In Australia, the mobile phone company **Vodafone** (www.vodafone.com.au; ℂ **1300/650 410** in Australia, or +61/426 320 000) has outlets at Brisbane international airport and at both international and domestic terminals in Sydney selling SIMs, handsets, and mobile broadband. **Optus** (www. optus.com.au; ℂ **1300/727 414** in Australia) has stores at Sydney and Melbourne airports.

Charges vary depending on the kind of phone and coverage you want, but some of the benefits include one low call rate throughout Australia, free incoming calls, international direct-dialing access, text messaging, and voicemail. Alternatively, you should be able to rent a mobile phone or SIM card for your existing mobile phone to stay in touch while you're traveling.

Money & Costs The Australian dollar is divided into A100¢. Coins are A5¢, A10¢, A20¢, and A50¢ pieces (silver) and A$1 and A$2 pieces (gold).

Bank notes come in denominations of A$5, A$10, A$20, A$50, and A$100.

THE VALUE OF THE AUSTRALIAN DOLLAR VS. OTHER POPULAR CURRENCIES

Aus$	US$	€	Can$	NZ$	UK£
1	0.71	0.63	0.95	1.05	0.54

Note that Australian prices often end in a variant of A1¢ and A2¢ (for example, A78¢ or A$2.71), a relic from the days before 1-cent and 2-cent pieces were phased out. In these cases, prices are rounded to the nearest A5¢—so A77¢ rounds down to A75¢, and A78¢ rounds up to A80¢.

Frommer's lists exact prices in the local currency. However, exchange rates always fluctuate, so before departing consult a currency exchange website such as **www.oanda.com/currency/converter** to check up-to-the-minute rates.

You should consider changing a small amount of money into Australian currency before you leave (though don't expect the exchange rate to be ideal), so that you can avoid long lines at airport ATMs or exchange desks. You can exchange money at your local American Express or Thomas Cook office or your bank.

If you're using a **credit card,** note that Visa and MasterCard are universally accepted in Australia; American Express and Diners Club are less common; and Discover is not used. Always carry a little cash, especially in Outback regions.

Beware of hidden credit-card **fees** while traveling.

Check with your credit- or debit-card issuer to see what fees, if any, will be charged for overseas transactions. Fees can amount to 3% or more of the purchase price. Check with your bank before your departure to avoid any surprise charges on your credit card statement.

For help with currency conversions, tip calculations, and more, download Frommer's convenient **Travel Tools app** for your mobile device. Go to www.frommers.com/go/mobile and click on the Travel Tools icon.

Newspapers & Magazines The national daily newspaper is *The Australian,* which publishes an expanded edition with a color magazine on Saturday. All capital cities also have their own daily papers. Newspapers and magazines can be bought at a wide range of retail outlets including newsagents, supermarkets, gas stations, and convenience stores.

Packing Tips Dressing in layers (and packing layers) is the best way of kitting yourself out for Australia.

Depending on where you are going in Australia—and the season—you will need different gear. For example, if you are visiting

Queensland or central Australia in the summer, pack only light clothing (but always throw in a little something warm just in case). But if you're heading for Victoria in winter you'll need full cold-weather outfits.

Wherever and whenever you go, take a light rain jacket: Summer in the tropics can often be quite wet!

Most restaurants in Australia accept "smart casual" dress; in the cities, you will need proper shoes (no flip-flops) and often (for men) a shirt with a collar to dine in most places.

For more helpful information on packing for your trip, download Frommer's convenient Travel Tools app. Go to **www.frommers.com/go/mobile** and click on the Travel Tools icon.

Police Dial © **000** anywhere in Australia. This is a free call from public and private telephones and requires no coins.

Safety Travelers to Australia should follow the same precautions against petty theft and potential identity theft as they would at home or in any other country. Violent crime is, of course, not uncommon, but you are not likely to become a target in the normal course of your travels.

Driving probably poses one of the greatest safety risks to visitors to Australia. Australians drive on the left, something that North American and European visitors often have difficulty remembering. Drivers and passengers, including taxi passengers, must wear a seatbelt at all times, by law.

Senior Travel Seniors—often called "pensioners" in Australia—from other countries don't always qualify for the discounted entry prices to tours, attractions, and events that Australian seniors enjoy, but it's always worth asking. Inquire about discounts when booking hotels, flights, and train or bus tickets. The best ID to bring is something that shows your date of birth or that marks you as an "official" senior, such as a membership card from AARP.

Senior Resources: Many reliable agencies and organizations target the 50-plus market. **Road Scholar** (www.roadscholar.org; ☎ **800/454-5768** in the U.S.) arranges worldwide study programs—including to Australia—for those ages 55 and over.

Smoking Smoking is banned in most indoor public places throughout the country, including government buildings, museums, cinemas, theaters, restaurants, and airports (and on all aircraft).

In Queensland, you are not allowed to smoke on a patrolled beach or near children's playgrounds; in Victoria, you may find that some

pubs have outdoor (or rooftop) smoking areas. Laws vary from state to state, so the safest thing is to ask before you light up.

Student Travel Australia has agreements with many countries, including the U.S., Canada, and the U.K., that give students between 18 and 30 years old the right to apply for a "working holiday" visa to stay in Australia for up to 12 months. You must apply for your visa outside of Australia, show evidence of your student or recent graduate status, and hold a return ticket as well as sufficient funds for the first part of your stay. For more information, check the website **www.homeaffairs.gov.au**.

Check out the **ISIC Association** (www.isic.org) website for comprehensive travel-services information and details on how to get an **International Student Identity Card (ISIC),** which qualifies students for substantial savings on rail passes, plane tickets, entrance fees, and more. It also provides students with basic health and life insurance and a 24-hour helpline. The card is valid for a maximum of 16 months. You can apply for the card online or in person at your university or a host of other outlets (check the website). If you're no longer a student but are still under 31, you can get an **International Youth Travel Card (IYTC),** which entitles you to some discounts.

Travel CUTS (www.travel-cuts.com; ☎ **800/667-2887**) offers similar services for Canadians and U.S. residents. Irish students may prefer to turn to **USIT** (www.usit.ie; ☎ **01/602-1906**), an Ireland-based specialist in student, youth, and independent travel.

Taxes Australia applies a 10% **Goods and Services Tax (GST)** on most products and services. Your international airline tickets to Australia are not taxed, nor are domestic airline tickets for travel within Australia *if you bought them outside Australia.* If you buy Australian airline tickets once you arrive in Australia, you will pay GST on them.

There are other exceptions. Items bought in duty-free stores will not be charged GST. Nor will items you export—such as an Aboriginal painting that you buy in a gallery in Alice Springs and have shipped straight to your home outside Australia. Basic groceries are not GST-taxed, although restaurant meals are.

Other taxes include a "reef tax," officially dubbed the **Environmental Management Charge,** of A$7 per day (or A$3.50 for a half-day) for every person over the age of 4 every time he or she enters the Great Barrier Reef Marine Park on a commercial tour. This charge goes toward park upkeep, and is sometimes (but not always) included in the ticket price.

GETTING YOUR GST refund

Through the **Tourist Refund Scheme** (TRS), Australians and international visitors can claim a refund of the 10% Goods and Services Tax (and of a 14.5% wine tax called the Wine Equalisation Tax, or WET) paid on a purchase of more than A$300 from a single outlet, within the last 60 days before you leave. More than one item may be included in that A$300. For example, you can claim the GST you paid on 10 T-shirts, each worth A$30, as long as they were bought from a single store. Do this as you leave by presenting your receipt or "tax invoice" to the Australian Customs Service's TRS booths, in the International Terminal departure areas at most airports.

Items must be taken as carry-on baggage, because you must show them to Customs. You can use the goods before you leave Australia and still claim the refund, but you cannot claim a refund on things you have consumed (say, perfume or food). You cannot claim a refund on alcohol other than wine.

Claims at airports are available up to 30 minutes before your flight's scheduled departure.

You can also claim a refund if you leave Australia as a cruise passenger from Sydney, Melbourne, Brisbane, Cairns, Darwin, Hobart, or Fremantle (Perth). Claims at seaports should be made no later than 1 hour before the scheduled departure time of the ship. If your cruise departs from elsewhere in Australia, or if you are flying out from an airport other than Sydney, Melbourne, Brisbane, Adelaide, Cairns, Perth, Darwin, or the Gold Coast, telephone the **Department of Home Affairs** (📞 **1300/555 043** in Australia, or 02/6245 5499) to see if you can still claim the refund.

Most airlines and an increasing number of tour operators, such as cruise companies and long-distance trains, also impose a "fuel surcharge" to help them combat rising fuel costs. This is usually added to the price of your ticket.

Time Australian Eastern Standard Time (EST, or sometimes AEST) covers Queensland, New South Wales, the Australian Capital Territory, Victoria, and Tasmania. Central Standard Time (CST) is used in the Northern Territory and South Australia, and Western Standard Time (WST) in Western Australia. When it's noon in New South Wales, the ACT, Victoria, Queensland, and Tasmania, it's 11:30am in South Australia and the Northern Territory and 10am in Western Australia. All states except Queensland, the Northern Territory, and Western Australia observe daylight saving time, usually from the first Sunday in October to the first Sunday in April. The east coast of Australia is Greenwich Mean Time (GMT) plus 10 hours. When it is noon on the east coast, it is 2am in London (the same day) and 6pm in Los Angeles and 9pm in New York (the day before), except during daylight saving, so allow for that in your calculations. New Zealand is 2 hours ahead of the east coast of Australia, except during daylight saving,

when it is 3 hours ahead of Queensland.

Tipping Tipping is not expected in Australia, but it is always appreciated. It is usual to tip around 10% or round up to the nearest A$10 for a substantial meal in a family restaurant.

Some passengers round up to the nearest dollar in a taxicab, but it's quite okay to insist on every bit of change back. Tipping bellboys and porters is sometimes done, but no one tips bar staff, barbers, or hairdressers.

Toilets Public toilets are easy to find—and free—in most Australian cities and towns. If you are driving, most towns have "restrooms" on the main street (although the cleanliness may vary wildly).

In some remote areas, public toilets are "composting," meaning there is no flush, just a drop into a pit beneath you.

If you really want to plan ahead, consult the **National Public Toilet Map** (www.toiletmap.gov.au) or download the app on your phone.

Travelers with Disabilities   Most disabilities shouldn't stop anyone from traveling to Australia. There are more options and resources than ever before. Most hotels, major stores, attractions, and public restrooms in Australia have wheelchair access. Many smaller lodges and even B&Bs are starting to cater to guests with disabilities, and some diving companies cater to scuba divers with disabilities. National parks make an effort to include wheelchair-friendly pathways. Taxi companies in bigger cities can usually supply a cab equipped for wheelchairs. TTY facilities are still limited largely to government services. A good Australian website for accessible travel is **www. cangoeverywhere.com.au**, which has listings for

accommodations, restaurants, and tourist attractions. **Travel Without Limits** is Australia's first disability-specific travel magazine with lots of good advice, tips, and reviews and is also available online at **www. travelwithspecialneeds. com.au**.

Visa & Entry Requirements   Along with a current passport valid for the duration of your stay, the Australian government requires a visa from visitors of every nation, except New Zealand, to be issued before you arrive. If you are a short-term visitor, the process is easy and can be done online in a few minutes using the Australian government's **Electronic Travel Authority** (**ETA;** www.eta.homeaffairs.gov. au). This is an electronic visa that takes the place of a stamp in your passport. Tourists from the U.S. and Canada should apply for a **Visitor ETA.** The visa itself is free, though there is a A$20 service charge (payable by credit card) for getting it online, and allows unlimited visits to Australia of up to 3 months each, within a 1-year period. You can apply for an ETA

yourself, or have your travel agent or airline do it when you book your plane ticket. (This service may incur an additional fee from the airline or travel agent.) European and U.K. passport holders should apply through **www.immi.home affairs.gov.au/visas**. You can also apply for the visa at Australian embassies, high commissions, and consulates. Children traveling on their parent's passport must have their own ETA.

In the United States, Canada, the United Kingdom, Ireland, and many other countries, most agents and airlines are ETA-compatible. If you are someone other than a tourist or a business traveler—for example, a student studying in Australia; a businessperson staying longer than 3 months; a long-term resident; an athlete going for a competition; a member of the media on assignment; a performer; or a member of a social group or cultural exchange, you will need to apply for a more specific non-ETA visa. Application fees for other kinds of visas vary. Check the website for details.

Index

Restaurants

Photo Credits

p. i, © Tooykrub / Shutterstock.com; p. iii, © Martin Valigursky; p. 4, © Debra James / Shutterstock.com; p. 5, © VarnaK; p. 6, © dinozzaver / Shutterstock.com; p. 7, © Visual Collective; p. 8, © Meghan Lamb; p. 9, © amophoto_au / Shutterstock.com; p. 10, © Courtesy of Longitude 131; p. 12, © Lepidlizard; p. 15, © EcoPrint / Shutterstock.com; p. 18, © Taras Vyshnya / Shutterstock.com; p. 23, © fritz16 / Shutterstock.com; p. 26, © Janelle Lugge; p. 30, © Mikulas P; p. 35, © Taras Vyshnya; p. 37, © PomInOz / Shutterstock.com; p. 40, © paulmichaelNZ; p. 41, © CoolR / Shutterstock.com; p. 45, © Invisiblesane / Shutterstock.com; p. 46, © fritz16 / Shutterstock.com; p. 47, © Maurizio De Mattei / Shutterstock.com; p. 49, © Marc Witte; p. 50, © Johnny Jet; p. 51, © Alan Samuel; p. 52, © Brian Gratwicke; p. 54, © Michele Piemonte / Shutterstock.com; p. 53, © ChameleonsEye; p. 56, © Meghan Lamb; p. 61, © byvalet / Shutterstock.com; p. 63, © PomInOz / Shutterstock.com; p. 70, © tourpics_net; p. 84, © Courtesy of OTTO/ Nikki To; p. 88, © f11photo; p. 89, © Jean-Philippe Menard / Shutterstock.com; p. 91, © Benny Marty / Shutterstock.com; p. 97, © Dan Breckwoldt / Shutterstock.com; p. 102, © Yunsun_Kim; p. 104, © CoolR / Shutterstock.com; p. 107, © wolffpower; p. 112, © PomInOz; p. 116, © Chadwick Clark; p. 118, © ChameleonsEye / Shutterstock.com; p. 127, © LittlePanda29 / Shutterstock.com; p. 128, © Sukhvinder Saggu / Shutterstock.com; p. 125, © Loralya / Shutterstock.com; p. 129, © ChameleonsEye / Shutterstock.com; p. 130, © ChameleonsEye / Shutterstock.com; p. 131, © katacarix / Shutterstock.com; p. 132, © ChameleonsEye / Shutterstock.com; p. 133, © Elle Deep-Loumanis / Shutterstock.com; p. 135, © ChameleonsEye / Shutterstock.com; p. 136, © ChameleonsEye / Shutterstock.com; p. 139, © Aleksandar Todorovic; p. 162, © ChameleonsEye / Shutterstock.com; p. 164, © Hanafi Latif / Shutterstock.com; p. 167, © MagSpace / Shutterstock.com; p. 168, © beefung / Shutterstock.com; p. 169, © TK Kurikawa / Shutterstock.com; p. 171, © Jesse33 / Shutterstock.com; p. 173, © Sunflowerey / Shutterstock.com; p. 176, © ChameleonsEye / Shutterstock.com; p. 177, © zulkamalober; p. 189, © fritz16 / Shutterstock.com; p. 196, © Alizada Studios / Shutterstock.com; p. 198, © Gordon Bell / Shutterstock.com; p. 199, © ChameleonsEye / Shutterstock.com; p. 205, © EQRoy / Shutterstock.com; p. 208, © Alan Bilsborough / Shutterstock.com; p. 210, © ChameleonsEye / Shutterstock.com; p. 211, © Martin Valigursky / Shutterstock.com; p. 213, © simoncritchel; p. 214, © David Bostock / Shutterstock.com; p. 218, © John Carnemolla; p. 222, © SISTROMATIC studio; p. 235, © Jack Foto Focus / Shutterstock.com; p. 238, © Angelina Pilarinos; p. 241, © ChameleonsEye / Shutterstock.com; p. 249, © electra; p. 259, © Ian Scott; p. 263, © Tomas Sykora; p. 274, © Amacphoto7 / Shutterstock.com; p. 280, © ronnybas; p. 285, © Daniela Constantinescu / Shutterstock.com; p. 294, © fritz16 / Shutterstock.com; p. 295, © John Carnemolla; p. 297, © Piotr Gatlik; p. 303, © GTS Productions; p. 304, © Martin Helgemeir; p. 310, © Lauren Cameo / Shutterstock.com; p. 321, © mark higgins / Shutterstock.com; p. 322, © augsonsawaang / Shutterstock.com; p. 329, © Gimas / Shutterstock.com; p. 331, © wargunner / Shutterstock.com; p. 337, © anastas_styles; p. 339, © Benny Marty / Shutterstock.com; p. 348, © bmphotographer; p. 350, © Benny Marty / Shutterstock.com; p. 349, © Ed G; p. 355, © Gordon Bell; p. 358, © f11photo / Shutterstock.com; p. 359, © jamesteohart / Shutterstock.com; p. 369, © Benny Marty; p. 372, © Julian W; p. 375, © amophoto_au / Shutterstock.com; p. 376, © amophoto_au; p. 377, © amophoto_au / Shutterstock.com; p. 386, © Sharon Wills / Shutterstock.com; p. 388, © amophoto_au / Shutterstock.com; p. 389, © Fotoaray; p. 393, © amophoto_au / Shutterstock.com; p. 397, © kwest; p. 399, © Mariangela Cruz; p. 410, © gnoparus / Shutterstock.com; p. 417, © Cyrus_2000 / Shutterstock.com; p. 418, © TK Kurikawa / Shutterstock.com; p. 421, © Kummeleon / Shutterstock.com; p. 422, © Benny Marty / Shutterstock.com; p. 424, © Pixelheld; p. 425, © FiledIMAGE; p. 433, © Ikonya; p. 437, © fritz16.